The Signs of Language Revisited

■ ■ ■

An Anthology to Honor
Ursula Bellugi and Edward Klima

The Signs of Language Revisited

■ ■ ■

An Anthology to Honor Ursula Bellugi and Edward Klima

Edited by

Karen Emmorey
The Salk Institute for Biological Studies

and

Harlan Lane
Northeastern University

LAWRENCE ERLBAUM ASSOCIATES, PUBLISHERS
2000   Mahwah, New Jersey   London

Lawrence Erlbaum Associates, Inc., Publishers
10 Industrial Avenue
Mahwah, NJ 07430

Cover design by Kathryn Houghtaling Lacey

Library of Congress Cataloging-in-Publication Data

The signs of language revisited : an anthology to honor Ursula Bellugi and
Edward Klima / edited by Karen Emmorey, Harlan Lane
    p.   cm.
   Includes bibliographical references and index.
   ISBN 0-8058-3246-7
   1. Sign language. 2. American Sign Language. I. Emmorey, Karen.
II. Lane, Harlan L. III. Bellugi, Ursula, 1930–   .
HV2474.S573 2000
419.21—dc21   99-041589

Contents

Preface

Few disciplines can trace their body of knowledge and techniques, and the ranks of their practitioners, so extensively to the efforts of one pair of scholars as can signed language research. The two scholars, for whom this volume is published in tribute by their students and collaborators, are Ursula Bellugi and Edward Klima at The Salk Institute for Biological Studies.

Bellugi and Klima's pioneering work, which gave rise to further investigation by scholars worldwide, was in fields as diverse as signed language morphology and syntax, discourse structure, and art forms; memory; neuroscience; language acquisition; and spatial cognition. Their first paper together, titled "Language in Another Mode," appeared in 1974. Two of their books were particularly acclaimed and influential: *The Signs of Language* (Harvard University Press, 1979) and *What the Hands Reveal About the Brain* (MIT Press, 1987; with Howard Poizner). One of their most recent publications—for their active program of research continues apace—is "Neural Organization of Language: Evidence From Sign Language Aphasia" (with Greg Hickok), published in the journal *Trends in Cognitive Sciences*.

Bellugi and Klima's intellectual contribution has extended well beyond signed language studies into adjacent disciplines. Because signed languages are indeed language in another mode (visual–manual rather than aural–oral), the facts uncovered about their structure and function probe the more general conceptions (invariably rooted in spoken language) that guide those disciplines. Consider the example of neuroscience: Bellugi and Klima's finding that aphasias of sign language—like those of spoken language—are associated with left-hemisphere lesions indicates that hemispheric dominance for language is rooted in something as abstract as grammatical structure and not in mechanisms of speech production and perception as was widely believed. Within the fields of psychology and linguistics, Bellugi and Klima illustrated how the study of signed languages can provide critical insights into the nature of human cognition and language. They were the first to pose many significant questions in this domain: Does the visual modality (and conversely, the auditory modality) affect the nature of grammatical systems? How do children learn a visual-gestural language and what does this tell us about the nature of human language acquisition? What cognitive processes are involved in the comprehension of visual as opposed to auditory language? Researchers are still pondering these questions, which is a testament to their depth and importance.

Students of the culture that uses American Sign Language (ASL), known as the Deaf-World, are aware of the way in which a single Deaf educator, Laurent Clerc, ended up profoundly influencing educational practices and ASL throughout the United States, through a ramifying process in which he taught Deaf pupils and hearing superintendents, and they created schools and taught more in turn, and *their* pupils created further schools and taught others, and so on. So, too, Bellugi and Klima have trained numerous scholars in their laboratories who went on, not only to make contributions of their own but in many cases also to train students in turn, who went on. . . . The sweep of their influence is actually constructed of many small personal epiphanies; in the following, Harlan recounts his own: In 1973, I was visiting professor of linguistics at the University of California, San Diego. Ursie greeted me warmly on arrival (we had both been students of Roger Brown's at Harvard) and asked me if I would like "to play" with her across the road at The Salk Institute. As it turned out, "play" captured the sheer delight of discovery and intellectual engagement that sparked across the roundtable at which we gathered daily, but it did not capture the fierce and focused commitment and long hours, and it was much too playful a word to bespeak the astonishing discovery—especially to the student of speech perception that I was—that language could be conducted by hand and by eye, and indeed was so conducted by Deaf communities all over the world. This seemed to me to open an entire new avenue to exploring language structure and use; I leapt aboard.

As for Karen, she recounts a similar epiphany several years later: I arrived at The Salk Institute at the end of 1987 with a fresh PhD in linguistics from UCLA, knowing very little about sign language. Vicki Fromkin (my thesis advisor and a contributor to this volume) had introduced me to Ursie and Ed. From the early days in the 1970s to now, the lab has always been a hubbub of exciting ideas and questions. From the famous roundtable discussions, I was astonished to realize how much we can learn about the nature of human language and cognition by investigating signed languages and that there was so much to discover! Like Harlan, I leapt aboard.

The impact of Bellugi and Klima's research on the Deaf liberation movement in the United States and abroad has been enormous, albeit largely indirect. Their scholarly work has been the bedrock on which other scholars have constructed the field of Deaf studies, political analyses of the Deaf struggle, and proposals for reform. To cite one instance, much of what has been contributed in the area of Deaf empowerment has followed simply and ineluctably from the evidence provided by Bellugi and Klima along with their students for the status of ASL and other signed languages as autonomous natural languages. Without that evidence, the logic of much of the Deaf agenda collapses; with it, everything is possible. Take the example of "BiBi" (bilingual and bicultural education of Deaf children)—the sole promising proposal on the table for the reform of Deaf education. Without the evidence that ASL is an autonomous natural language, BiBi makes no sense. With that evidence, it is the leading sensible proposal. As Bellugi and Klima's initial findings appeared in the 1970s, growing numbers of Deaf leaders, some of them trained in their laboratory, carried the word to the American Deaf-World, particularly through workshops and word of hand: Our precious language is fully legitimate and autonomous; it has the dignity of English. We are, then, a language minority; our idioms are in fact our language; our "ways" are seen to be our culture. Bellugi and Klima teamed up with the Communication Skills Program [*sic*] of the National Association of the Deaf to create linguistically informed materials to teach ASL and linguistically informed Deaf teachers to do the job.

If we contrast Deaf studies today with their standing some three decades ago when Bellugi and Klima began their research, we find that Deaf culture and language are surely better understood and documented and more widely appreciated. There is growing formal recognition of ASL in the United States (more high schools and universities find it fulfills the second language requirement) and of signed languages around the world (e.g., the European Commission has urged its member states to protect and encourage their national signed languages). There are more linguistic and sociolinguistic studies of ASL and other signed languages. More on the acquisition of ASL and other signed languages as native languages. More dictionaries of signed languages and more textbooks and videotapes for learning those languages. More about the profession of interpreting and the ethics and skills involved. More about Deaf peoples' gifts in perception and cognition and more about how their brains process information. More publications about and schools implementing bilingual-bicultural education of Deaf children. More works of ASL poetry and narrative. We are witnessing the development of Deaf Studies programs in schools and colleges and the growth of the field as a professional specialization. And many more developments that are indirectly rather than directly related to advances in understanding signed language. For example, there are many more studies of the history of Deaf cultures here and abroad. More political analyses of the struggle of Deaf cultures for autonomy. More about minorities in the Deaf-World. Numerous books about the experiences of Codas (hearing children of Deaf adults). More about ministry to Deaf people and more on culturally informed counseling and mental health services. There is more attention to winning fundamental human rights for Deaf people around the world.

All this progress is in substantial part the fruit of Bellugi and Klima's scholarly contributions. Their impact extends beyond the United States because scholars and Deaf leaders in other lands took their cue from the early developments in America. France is an illustration. In the 1970s, American Deaf and hearing scholars, equipped with the new findings and perspectives arising from Bellugi and Klima's research, gave a series of lectures in France, established classes there to teach *la Langue des Signes Française* (LSF), and taught a series of summer institutes at Gallaudet University for French scholars, parents, and Deaf leaders. On their return to France, one group of participants began to investigate LSF, compile an LSF dictionary, and offer classes in LSF. Other graduates of the summer institutes launched a nationwide association that created bilingual classes for Deaf children, ran workshops at which Deaf Americans disseminated the findings of Bellugi and Klima (among other things), and created regional groups engaged in applied research and development related to LSF.

When the early American Deaf leader, Thomas Brown, proposed in the mid-19th century that the mutes of America should raise a monument in tribute to Thomas Gallaudet and Laurent Clerc, "the flame of love ran like a prairie fire through the hearts of the whole deaf-mute band," a journalist reported, "scattered though they were through various parts of the country." Similarly, when we suggested a Festschrift as a monument to Ursula Bellugi and Edward Klima, their students and collaborators warmly embraced the plan, scattered though they are throughout the world. That embrace is easy to understand, considering their impact, which this preface has sketched and which this book more fully documents.

—Harlan Lane
—Karen Emmorey

Contributors

Adele Abrahamsen
Department of Psychology
Washington University

C. Tane Akamatsu
Toronto District School Board
Ontario, Canada

Robbin M. Battison
Canadian Embassy
Stockholm, Sweden

Jeffrey G. Bettger
Department of Special Education
San Francisco State University

Penny Boyes Braem
Center for Sign Language Research
Basel, Switzerland

Bernard Bragg
Actor/Writer/Director

Thüring Bräm
Lucerne Conservatory
Lucerne, Switzerland

Diane Brentari
Department of Audiology and Speech
  Sciences
Purdue University

David P. Corina
Department of Psychology
University of Washington

Antonio R. Damasio
Department of Neurology
University of Iowa College of
  Medicine

Hanna Damasio
Department of Neurology
University of Iowa College of
  Medicine

Karen Emmorey
Laboratory for Cognitive
  Neuroscience
The Salk Institute for Biological
  Studies

Lou Fant
Interpreter Training Program
Seattle Central Community College

Susan D. Fischer
Applied Language and Cognition
  Research
National Technical Institute for the
  Deaf

Mary French
Aurora Technologies

Nancy Frishberg
New Media Centers

Victoria A. Fromkin
Department of Linguistics
University of California, Los Angeles

Vicki L. Hanson
IBM Research Division
Thomas Watson Research Center

Judy Kegl
Center for Molecular and Behavioral
  Neurosciences
Rutgers University and University of
  Southern Maine

Graeme Kennedy
Deaf Studies Research Unit
Victoria University of Wellington
Wellington, New Zealand

Marlon Kuntze
School of Education
Stanford University

Mary Lanaville
CSC Interpreters, Inc.

Harlan Lane
Department of Psychology
Northeastern University

Scott K. Liddell
Department of Linguistics
Gallaudet University

Diane Lillo-Martin
Department of Linguistics
University of Connecticut and Haskins
  Laboratories

Ruth C. Loew
Educational Testing Service

David McKee
Deaf Studies Research Unit
Victoria University of Wellington
Wellington, New Zealand

Richard P. Meier
Departments of Linguistics and
  Psychology
University of Texas at Austin

Elissa L. Newport
Department of Psychology
University of Rochester

Carol A. Padden
Department of Communications
University of California, San Diego

Laura Ann Petitto
Department of Psychology
McGill University and Montreal
  Neurological Institute
Canada

Richard C. Pillard
Department of Psychiatry
Boston University School of Medicine

Elena Pizzuto
Institute of Psychology
National Research Council
Rome, Italy

Howard Poizner
Center for Molecular and Behavioral
  Neurosciences
Rutgers University

Judy Reilly
Department of Psychology
San Diego State University

Patricia Siple
Department of Psychology
Wayne State University

Ted Supalla
Department of Linguistics
University of Rochester

Martha E. Tyrone
Center for Molecular and Behavioral
  Neurosciences
Rutgers University

Virginia Volterra
Institute of Psychology
National Research Council
Rome, Italy

Ronnie B. Wilbur
Department of Audiology and Speech
  Sciences
Purdue University

Margaret Wilson
Department of Psychology
North Dakota State University

James Woodward
Ratchasuda College
Mahidol University at Salaya,
  Thailand

I

Reminiscences

1

Two Memorable Meals
With Ursula and Ed

Lou Fant
Seattle Central Community College

The National Theatre of the Deaf (NTD) was but 2 years old, so it must have been in 1969. It was about 2:00 in the afternoon, and I was in the New York office of the NTD when I received the call. The secretary said that a Doctor Bellugi wanted to talk to me. We got calls from all kinds of people wanting to know about the NTD, so I assumed this was one of those calls. Instead, a woman invited me to lunch with her and her husband at the faculty dining room at Rockefeller University. I assumed they were interested in having the NTD perform somewhere, and we desperately needed bookings, so I deigned to meet with them. One must make all kinds of sacrifices in the name of Art, I silently thought.

After they introduced themselves—I still had not clearly gotten her name or her husband's—we sat down to lunch and the first words out of her mouth, as I recall, were, "So, what do you think of Stokoe's work?"

This question did not sound as if they were interested in booking the NTD. What had I gotten myself into, I wondered? I had left the faculty of Gallaudet College only 2 years before and at that time, the faculty was hotly divided on the value of Stokoe's work. I had not yet decided what I believed about it. In fact, it took me about three more years before I understood what a masterful thing he had done, and here she was asking for an immediate personal assessment of his work.

I have no idea what I said, but it must not have put them off too much because we talked for 2 or 3 hours. They asked me all kinds of questions,

3

and I shudder to think what I must have said. In spite of having known Bill Stokoe personally, having read his work, and having incorporated some of his ideas into the first text I published on American Sign Language (ASL), I had not yet awakened to the fact that ASL was a language. I had signed ASL since infancy, but I had never thought of it as a language, it was just a way to communicate with deaf people.

Ursula and Ed informed me that they were returning to The Salk Institute soon. When I told them that I was moving to Los Angeles the following year, they invited me to visit them at Salk, which I did several times. I spent many wonderful hours videotaping and answering questions about why I signed things this or that way. Ursula could ask the darndest questions, which is why she is such a brilliant researcher.

On one of my visits, Ursula invited me to her house for dinner to meet a young man. She seemed very keen that he know more about deaf people, ASL, and Deaf culture and thought that perhaps I could help. I cannot recall whether he was visiting her personally at Salk, or was a guest lecturer at the University. At dinner, I tried to relate the saga of how the Abbé Sicard escaped death several times during the Reign of Terror in Paris. He seemed quite interested and at a later date, he sent me a copy of Sicard's escapades, in French. I thanked them for the opportunity to have met Harlan Lane early in his career.

My encounter with Ed and Ursula at Rockefeller University and later at Salk was the beginning of my education concerning the status of ASL as a language. Their probing was sufficient to cause me to conclude that if such distinguished people as these thought Stokoe's work was brilliant and that ASL was truly a language, then maybe I ought to take a second, closer look.

I reflect on my acquaintance with Ursula and Ed with much appreciation of what their lives have meant for me. Had it not been for them, I wonder how long it would have taken me, if not forever, to understand and appreciate what Bill Stokoe did. I will go so far as to say that they are primarily responsible for the deep affection that I feel for Bill. Had it not been for them, it might have been years, if not forever, before I got to know Harlan, one of the most brilliant minds to come to our field this century. I do not know the details of how Ed and Ursula became attracted to our field, I only know that it was a wondrous day when they did. Had it not been for them, I might have floundered along for years before recognizing what ASL truly is. My love for ASL, for the beauty of its construction and execution, had its origin with my encounters with these two wonderful people.

2

American Sign Language Linguistics 1970–1980: Memoir of a Renaissance

Robbin M. Battison
Canadian Embassy, Stockholm, Sweden

For those who work intimately with sign languages or Deaf culture, it is self-evident that sign languages are autonomous languages with their own linguistic principles. But this has not always been the case: The development of this idea owes much to the seminal contributions of Ursula Bellugi-Klima and Edward Klima, as well as to those they inspired and guided through the years.

This is a memoir focused on the period 1970–1980, because those are the only "sign research years" I can legitimately remember. It was in 1970 that I joined the Bellugi-Klima group (BKG) as a research assistant, and it was in 1980 that I left the field of sign language (SL) linguistics.[1] Because this is a memoir, and not a proper history, I make no apologies for its anecdotal nature nor the paucity of references—in fact, I don't discuss signs at all.

Central to this tale is what others thought about sign languages and what we linguists thought was worth investigating at the time. SL

---

[1]All right, I've tapped other people's memories of the 1970s too, principally those of Dennis Cokely, Penny Boyes-Braem, Nancy Frishberg, Joe McLaughlin, and François Grosjean. I remain responsible for any false memories we might have created while reconstructing the past, and any sweeping generalizations are of course my own. As for other decades, forget it. I believe it was the folk singer Judy Collins who said: "If you can remember the 60s, then you weren't really there."

researchers today might not be aware of how little we knew when we started, or how little understanding or support was forthcoming from the educational establishment, or how blunt our analytical tools were.

The background to this period includes a dismal analysis by the speech and hearing establishment, which held a steady hand on deaf education. A 1950 textbook, reprinted as late as 1975, proclaimed that "The language of gesture is devoid of prepositions, conjunctions, and abstract words. . . . Abstract verbs are replaced by specific concepts that permit the essential meaning to be communicated" (Eisenson & Boase, 1975). Another textbook published closer to the period in question was equally bizarre: "It is generally agreed [!] that sign language is bound to the concrete and is rather limited with respect to abstraction, humor, and subtleties such as figures of speech which enrich expression" (Davis & Silverman, 1970). These pronouncements were made without any scientific evidence whatsoever, which makes us shudder at both the audacity of their authors and the gullibility of those who believed them. The implications for Deaf education are also depressingly clear.

Against this background, there were three significant contemporary trends that would shape the research on American Sign Language (ASL) that the BKG conducted—trends stemming from philosophy, demography, and technology.

The philosophical trend was due to Noam Chomsky of the Massachusetts Institute of Technology (MIT) and the so-called Chomskian revolution of the late 1960s, which led to a set of paradigm-busting theories that were loosely referred to as TG, or transformational-generative grammar. This led to the following changes in linguistic theory and practice:

1. Linguistic competence and linguistic performance were distinguished, allowing the use of both intuitions and utterances as evidence for theory building. Linguists could shift focus to the mental nature of language. This was analogous to examining how a computer's central processing unit works and putting the computer peripherals aside. Speech (the physical phenomenon) was thus separate from language per se. Language competence was something more abstract than language performance.

2. Linguistic research, although still based on fieldwork, was guided by a heuristic construct: the "ideal speaker-listener in a homogenous speech community." Native speakers of a language were the norm. Monolingualism was assumed and bilingualism was hardly ever mentioned.

3. The search was on for the "psychological reality" or mental counterparts of linguistic constructs. In other words, the validity of linguistic

models was not based on pure formalism but also required the model to explain something about how the mind worked. This dovetailed with another emerging field, cognitive psychology.

These theoretical changes in turn supported the emerging linguistic focus on sign languages. If language competence is like a central processing unit, then the actual physical nature of the inputs and outputs may be able to be factored out in some way. In other words, what does it matter to the core linguistic competence if inputs are acoustic strings or visual displays and outputs are spoken words or gestures? Does it matter? This became a central question for SL researchers in the 1970s.

This new and exciting way of doing linguistics coincided with a demographic trend, as recounted by Frederick Newmeyer (1980) in his history of linguistic theory in America:

> In the mid and late 1960s, American universities underwent the greatest expansion in history. New linguistics departments sprung up in a dozen locations and some existing ones literally quadrupled in size. The reputation of Chomsky's theory had grown to the point where, by and large, transformationalists were sought to fill the new positions. In fact, linguistics grew at a much greater rate than almost any other field—a testament to the intellectual appeal of the theory. (p. 20)

In fact, the Linguistics Department at University of California, San Diego (UCSD) had a heavy influx of "Easterners" from Harvard and MIT in the late 1960s, including Paul Chapin, Sandy Schane, Edward Klima, and Yuki Kuroda. This resulted in a "bicoastal zeitgeist" that bound these universities' researchers together in practice, as when Harlan Lane filled a visiting professorship at UCSD in the early 1970s.

UCSD hired Ed Klima, and Ursula Bellugi established herself at The Salk Institute for Biological Studies, a few hundred yards down the street. This institute, founded and headed by Jonas Salk of polio vaccine fame, is of course primarily a biological research center. Bellugi's initial sponsor there was the late Dr. Jacob Bronowski, a distinguished mathematician who was refocusing his work on the history of science and the humanities. Moreover, as the Institute is perched on a cliff with a magnificent unobstructed view of the Pacific Ocean, it lent itself to making unobstructed intellectual forays into the mental nature of language.

The third major trend shaping the ASL research of the BKG was technological: the emergence of new consumer electronic equipment that made recording of gestural data practical, affordable, and accessible.

Video cameras and tape recorders made it possible to record gestural data and use it in ways undreamed of only a few years previously, when researchers depended on still photography and film. Of course, video back then was pretty primitive, as we shall show.

ASL RESEARCH AND NATIVE SIGNERS

Homogeneous monolingual signing communities don't exist. About 90% of Deaf people are born to hearing, nonsigning parents, grow up in restrictive linguistic environments, and emerge as adults into bilingual and multilingual signing and speaking language situations. There is no monolingual community of Deaf signers on some remote Atlantis, waiting to be discovered. The near exceptions prove the rule: Frishberg (1986) managed to do some fieldwork in a Ghanaian village with about 15% deaf people and widespread signing, and Groce (1985) researched the once-extensive bilingual signing communities of Martha's Vineyard, an island off the coast of Massachusetts.

Ursula Bellugi's early research on ASL, studying how Deaf children acquire ASL from their Deaf parents, can be viewed as a logical extension of her work with Roger Brown on patterns of child language acquisition in English. It was natural that her early focus was more about language acquisition than about adult linguistic competence. But there was another advantage to starting with Deaf children: This was the closest one could come to studying monolingual native speakers of this uncharted language.

Bellugi's early program of research on child language included two children from two different families in different California cities. Each child participated in a monthly videotaped "informant session," with home visits alternating with visits to The Salk Institute. In those early days, Bonnie Gough was our Deaf research assistant and primary source of information on ASL and Deaf culture. Her daughter, Darlene Scates, was a professional interpreter who assisted in these elicitation sessions. The roles we research assistants played in the beginning were general factotum, cameraman, recording engineer, and driver, as well as the most demanding job of all—transcriber of tapes.[2]

---

[2]How challenging these simple roles were can best be illustrated by the fact that I did get lost in the desert while driving home from an informant session. Also, when accompanying Ursie and Ed to Paris for a conference and research session in 1971, I managed to record videotapes that could not be shown on any known U.S. system. Plus, I mixed up the still pictures of French signs with the vacation pictures from my Parisian girlfriend's camera. Neither Ursie nor Claudine has ever forgiven me.

Our camera equipment was simple, having fewer buttons than modern telephones and thus offering fewer chances to do something stupid. The taping equipment consisted of an ever-increasing phalanx of Sony video recorders, which, as I recall, required changing tape reels every half hour. This required rewinding and threading the tape, cuing it up with the help of a ridiculously clumsy tape counter (with an apparent accuracy of +/– 6 seconds), and of course labeling it—all the while taking copious notes on the signing session. Today's electronic marvels, with videocasettes, digital frame counters and precision electronic editing, existed on drawing boards or in unreliable prototype versions.

Transcription was a chore, especially because the signing expertise in the group naturally took years to develop adequately. But even here, the theoretical work depended heavily on progress made in linguistic description. We transcribed ASL conversations at first by glossing: finding a roughly equivalent English word to match the apparent meaning of the sign. Soon we found ourselves richly hyphenating our glosses to try to capture all the morphological and semantic nuances.

We sometimes used an adapted "Stokoe notation," and even tried a kind of 8-track notation that looked like a musical score, seeking to capture more and more of the physical details of signing in our efforts to separate the important from the unimportant parts of the linguistic signal. Don Newkirk of the BKG created a system allowing signs to be transcribed using an ordinary typewriter.

THE THRILL OF IT ALL

Working with Ed and Ursie was both challenging and thrilling during those early exploratory years. We were numerous students, associates, assistants, visiting researchers, and visiting poets who got together every Friday afternoon for a formal discussion of whatever topic was at hand, but the real interaction took place everywhere and anywhere. A suggestion or question one day would turn into a working paper within a few weeks. Someone would notice a single sign that would cause us to open (or close) a line of inquiry. New discoveries came almost daily. We felt we were really developing the tools to answer the question, "How does ASL work?"

Work was carried out on a broad front simultaneously: lexicography, "phonology," "phonetics," morphology, psycholinguistics, syntax, semantics, poetics, folklore, and neurolinguistics. We fed each other (sometimes literally), consulted each other, and worked out individual areas of expertise.

Bellugi and Klima encouraged the group's exploratory work in developing binary feature analyses for ASL phonetics and phonology, partly as a way to improve the basic lexical descriptions, but also to pave the way for many later phonological investigations.

Another member of the group, the late Frank Allen Paul, made unique contributions to ASL descriptions by developing special techniques for transferring video frame shots of signers to line drawings that captured crucial spatial and temporal information. Parts of his illustration style have since been adopted by others, both in the United States and abroad.

I chose to work on ASL phonology because it seemed to me that work on the sublexical level was essential to moving forward in other areas. But refining impulses came from others in the group. Ed wondered out loud one day in 1971, "I wonder if there are any signing aphasics?" thus sidetracking me into working with one in 1972 and another in 1975 (Kimura, Battison, & Lubert, 1976). But it was my fellow student Richard Lacy who turned me in the direction of working with morpheme structure constraints, while we were standing on a hill in 1973 overlooking Stanford University and he was trying to talk me down from preconference jitters. And it was my friends and informants Ella Mae Lentz and Carol Padden who so overwhelmed me with data in 1975 that I decided that my whole dissertation would pivot on lexical borrowing in ASL (Battison, 1978). ASL linguistics works better in groups.

GETTING THE WORD OUT

Sharing the results of our work with Deaf people and practitioners in Deaf education or interpreting was another matter. The more technical we became, the harder it became for nonspecialists to understand what we were up to. And Ursula, for one, resisted getting involved with educational controversies or policy issues at all; she seemed to feel more comfortable with science. Although practitioners did not always wait for researchers to deliver the goods, we did have memorable meetings with individuals who were able to turn linguistic findings into changes in educational content or policy.

Lou Fant was fascinated to find that linguists actually had terms that corresponded to something he had been dealing with for years, namely, the difference between translation and transliteration (this distinction was adopted by the Registry of Interpreters of the Deaf, the U.S. interpreters' organization, in 1979). The late T.J. O'Rourke was able to turn the

National Symposia on Sign Language Research and Teaching (NSSLRT) into forums for both researchers and practitioners. But I remember having to go head-to-head in public at the first NSSLRT in 1977 with a well-known special educator who insisted that ASL was not a language. During the second NSSLRT, I recall being sharply questioned for stating that a hearing student's goal in learning SL should be "to learn to sign like a Deaf person." What was self-evident to a linguist was still controversial to a larger professional public! (If it's not self-evident to you, try replacing "SL" and "Deaf" with the word "French" and the word "sign" with "speak.")

In the background of the 1970s lurked the pseudolinguists, who had created signing systems that aped the morphology and syntax of English. Imagine my surprise when I found myself trapped in a Holiday Inn in Iowa for a weekend seminar with 30 young teachers of the Deaf, all of them hearing, all of them chatting away in some variety of signed English that no one but they could understand. It vexed the spirit sorely.

In 1975, Harlan Lane and I were actively seeking funds to establish a new training program for "communication specialists with the Deaf," which I suppose now would be called "sign resource specialists." We met with an influential woman on the U.S. Senate staff, who listened politely to our pitch over lunch and then wondered why we hadn't first consulted with "her expert on Deafness," an otorhinolaryngologist in California. Of course we received no funds back then, but I've heard that a similar proposal was recently funded. Times change.

But the 1970s did undeniably represent a renaissance for ASL, nearly a century after the infamous 1880 Milan Congress on the education of the Deaf, which tried to bury SL once and for all. It is interesting to note the number of firsts in the following chronology of the 1970s as well as the interplay of practical and research-related milestones. This table is based on that provided by Dennis Cokely and Charlotte Baker (from Baker & Battison, 1980, p. xv–xx).

1970 • Ursula Bellugi (The Salk Institute for Biological Studies) and Edward Klima (Linguistics, UCSD) establish ASL research group.
   • National Theater of the Deaf is established.
1971 • William Stokoe establishes Linguistics Research Lab at Gallaudet College, independent of other academic departments.
1972 • First SL journal—William Stokoe begins publishing *Sign Language Studies.*
   • First book on teaching ASL, "Ameslan" by Lou Fant.

1973   • First PhD dissertation on ASL. Author: James Woodward.
       • First play involving attitudes toward ASL ("Sign Me Alice"
         by Gil Eastman).
1974   • First SL Conference held at Gallaudet College.
       • First International Symposium on SL takes place at the Amer-
         ican Anthropological Society conference in Mexico City.
1975   • First Deafness and Mental Health Conference, Chicago.
1976   • First PhD dissertation on ASL produced by the BKG. Author:
         Nancy Frishberg.
1977   • First National Symposium on Sign Language Research and
         Teaching (NSSLRT), Chicago.
1978   • NSSLRT II in San Diego, "Bilingual and Bicultural Educa-
         tion."
       • First conference on ASL poetry, University of Indiana at
         South Bend.
1979   • First survey book on ASL linguistics: Klima and Bellugi pub-
         lish *The Signs of Language.*
       • First (freestanding) International SL Symposium, Stockholm.
       • First NATO Advanced Study Institute "Language & Cogni-
         tion" devoted to SL linguistics, in Copenhagen.
1980   • First multidisciplinary international conference on SL,
         "Signed and Spoken Language: Biological Constraints on
         Linguistic Form," Dahlem Conference, Berlin.
       • NSSLRT III in Boston.
       • First ASL books for teachers and students based on linguistic
         analyses—Baker and Cokely produce the "Green Books."
       • First ASL festschrift, in honor of William Stokoe, by Baker
         and Battison.

CROSSING THE POND

ASL linguistics took a little different turn than European sign linguistics
did, partly owing to the general trends outlined in Newmeyer's (1980) history, but also because many European SL research groups had different
starting points, different goals, and different methods—as well as different
social, political, and economic contexts.

In most of Western Europe, social and educational services, including
anything to do with the Deaf, were delivered by centralized government
agencies. Many SL researchers in Europe seem to have concentrated more

on education and service delivery—whether using SL was beneficial, which kind of SL, combined with what, and so forth—rather than on descriptive or theoretical issues.

The practical consequence was that the vital linguistic role of native signers—whether hearing or Deaf—was apparently not as salient from the beginning in European SL linguistics. Valid data might come from any signer, and the backgrounds of the signers were not always documented in the literature of the 1970s. In addition, data during this period were often collected in classrooms with peer-to-peer or student–teacher signing (because of the educational focus) rather than free-ranging home and family settings with deaf intergenerational signing.

Some theoretical underpinnings were also slower to take root in parts of Europe. A BKG researcher who relocated to Europe in the early 1970s noted a lack of enthusiasm then for new TG theories. At the end of a meeting with a linguistics professor, the professor leaned forward and asked her earnestly, "Before you go, tell me something. Do all Americans really take Chomsky seriously?" In any case, she noted that "sign language research in her country couldn't ride in on any Chomsky coattails."

In addition to differences in SL linguistics on the two sides of the Atlantic, there were also barriers to free communication. The late 1960s and early 1970s were a time of student revolts, reform, and quasi-reform of European universities, dominated by a general political shift to the left. Due to the U.S. role in the later stages of the Vietnam War, many European academics found it fashionable to spurn anything American, regardless of its scientific or political merits. As one visiting ASL researcher said to me of her year in Europe a decade later, in the late 1980s, "I got tired of fighting the Vietnam War every time I was invited to a dinner party. And I was part of the war resistance in the U.S.!"

Some of this anti-American sentiment may have been exacerbated by the "not-invented-here" syndrome or by envy, as U.S. language research labs of the time were often better equipped than their European counterparts (due to the expansions already mentioned). For example, my colleague at Northeastern University (NU), François Grosjean (now at the University of Neuchâtel), regularly hosted European psycholinguistic researchers who wanted to use our lab facilities at NU in the summer to run experiments.

These points and others may have led to the conflicts that surfaced at the 1979 NATO Advanced Study Institute on Language and Cognition in Copenhagen. This event was organized by Harlan Lane, François Grosjean, and me and attracted about 110 SL scholars from around the world.

One of the European participants—who missed the whole point of this scientific symposium and of much of the work that was presented—opened his presentation by condemning the gathering as "an insult to Deaf people," apparently because it didn't touch sufficiently on socially relevant issues such as language policy in the classroom.

Resistance to certain empirical methods also occurred. When ASL linguistics had apparently advanced further in phonology and phonetics than any other SL studied to date, several groups, the BKG and Harlan Lane's lab at NU among them (with Howard Poizner in the forefront), experimented with instrumental phonetic methods, modeled on instrumental studies of speech. These groups tried everything to measure sign movements exactly; using two or three cameras at different angles; attaching points of light to hands that were filmed in darkness; taping accelerometers borrowed from a space engineering lab to signers' hands (these devices were hard to calibrate); and adapting instrumentation used in physical therapy (like elgonometers).

When this work on instrumental phonetics was introduced at the conference in Copenhagen in 1979, several Europeans publicly ridiculed the whole idea. Attaching lights and wires and gadgets to signers' bodies to gain insights into the structure of sign languages was viewed as somehow "unnatural" and a "violation of personal integrity." Twelve years later, one of the researchers who had rejected the approach asked me how to set up a program for instrumental phonetics. The idea had somehow become attractive, or at least unavoidable.

In the age of communication over the Internet and via CD-ROMs, it is apparent that precise instrumental recordings of sign behavior may teach us how to electronically code sign languages in new interactive media and telecommunications, in which optimizing temporal and spatial resolution buys precious bandwidth and transmission time. Success here depends on knowledge of signs down to the last digit.

OF APES AND MEN

As The Salk Institute is a biological institute, replete with white lab coats, it wasn't uncommon for visitors in the early 1970s to ask us, "Where do you keep the chimps that you're teaching sign language?" This was slightly annoying but easily corrected.

More annoying were encounters with scientists who were working with apes and signs. My first encounter was at an international conference, when I saw one of them trying to discreetly sign to another "What time is it?" while they were sitting next to each other on a discussion panel. As the addressee couldn't understand this simple signed question, they had to resort to speech to communicate. So much for involving yourself in the object of study!

My second contact came during a site visit, when I was a member of a reviewing team convened by a federal granting agency. During a tour of the site, two of us reviewers witnessed an ape making an indiscriminate, isolated gesture that touched his head. Our host researcher immediately pronounced this gesture to be the sign for "comb" but demonstrated it using a very different gesture. We helpfully pointed out this "pronunciation difference," but our point was hotly contested. Needless to say, any credibility this researcher had for gathering empirical data on gestures was considerably weakened in our eyes.

The third contact with signing apes came in reviewing the proposals for two different ape signing studies, again at a granting agency's request. I found a remarkable indifference to data transcription. What the apes were actually doing with their hands was apparently uninteresting, as the observers merely wrote down the English equivalents of what they thought the apes were trying to convey. If sign language researchers working with Deaf people had used a similar methodology, a great Sign Renaissance might never have occurred. This was all the more reason to appreciate the emphasis that Bellugi and Klima placed on careful recording and transcription.

A PERSONAL CLOSING

Those who use and work with ASL today owe a debt of thanks to the Bellugi-Klimas for helping to grow a new generation of researchers. We know that future generations will thank them as well.

REFERENCES

Baker, C., & Cokely, D. (1980). *American Sign Language: A teacher's resource text on grammar and culture.* Silver Spring, MD: T. J. Publishers.

Baker, C., & Battison, R. (Eds.). (1980) *Sign language and the deaf community—Essays in honor of William C. Stokoe.* Silver Spring, MD: National Association of the Deaf.

Battison, R. (1978). *Lexical borrowing in American Sign Language.* Silver Spring, MD: Linstok Press.

Davis, H., & Silverman, S. R. (1970) *Hearing and deafness.* New York: Holt, Rinehart & Winston.

Eastman, G. (1974). *Sign me Alice: A play in sign language.* Washington, DC: Gallaudet College.

Eisenson, J., & Boase, P. (1975). *Basic speech* (3rd ed.). New York: Macmillan.

Fant, L. (1972). *Ameslan.* Silver Spring, MD: National Association of the Deaf.

Frishberg, N. (1976). *Some aspects of the historical development of signs in ASL.* Unpublished doctoral dissertation, University of California, San Diego.

Frishberg, N. (1986). *Ghanaian Sign Language.* In J. van Cleve (Ed.), *The encyclopedia of deafness and deaf people* (Vol. 3, pp. 78–79). New York: McGraw-Hill.

Groce, N. E. (1985). *Everyone here spoke sign language.* Cambridge, MA: Harvard University Press.

Kimura, D., Battison, R., & Lubert, B. (1976). *Impairment of nonlinguistic hand movements in a deaf aphasic. Brain and Language, 3,* 566–571.

Klima, E., & Bellugi, U. (1979). *The signs of language.* Cambridge, MA: Harvard University Press.

Newmeyer, F. (1980). *Linguistic theory in America.* New York: Academic Press.

Woodward, J. (1973). *Implicational lects on the deaf diglossic continuum.* Unpublished doctoral dissertation, Georgetown University.

3

A Fish Story for Ursula and Other Remembrances

Bernard Bragg

My friendship with Ursula Bellugi began in 1969, a couple of years after the National Theatre of the Deaf (NTD) was established. I was deeply involved in exploring a new way of illuminating the language of signs for theater use. For lack of a better word to describe it, I coined "Sign-Mime." Some of my writings on this subject were included in the grant application, submitted to the U.S. Department of Health, Education, and Welfare, to found the NTD. I think it was about the same time that Dr. Bellugi was in the process of establishing her research laboratory at The Salk Institute. Her aim was to analyze the sign language from a linguistic point of view, whereas mine was to bring it to stage as an art form. She gave the language a new name—American Sign Language (ASL). The difference between Sign-Mime and ASL lies in the fact that the former focuses on adapting English dialogue and poetry into sign whereas the latter represents the communicative mode of the Deaf community.

After attending the performance of the NTD in San Diego, Dr. Bellugi invited me to visit her research lab at The Salk Institute. We had a lengthy discussion on the nature of sign language, and, much to our mutual surprise, we found that each of us saw it quite differently. She perceived it as a pure language unto itself with its own unique grammar and syntax, completely devoid of English; whereas I had long since understood it to be a language of signs strongly influenced by English, or rather, blended with it. Such language was later labeled Pidgin Sign English. Our different perceptions resulted in a continuing dialogue for many years. It took me quite a while before I was convinced that ASL can and does stand on its own, but I have always maintained my own conviction that as one becomes older and more literate, his or her use of ASL gradually reflects many English borrowings. Dr. Bellugi admitted to me years later that English does influence ASL greatly.

We understand each other well. She is a scientist focusing on the nature of sign language as used by deaf parents with their deaf children. She has studied it objectively. I am a native user of the language. My use of ASL has been greatly influenced by older deaf people, both deaf teachers and hearing teachers at school and college, my deaf parents and relatives, and their deaf friends.

Because of our longtime friendship and my frequent visits to her lab, I was inspired to write articles, letters to the editor, even a book, depicting how I see the language of Deaf people and their use of it. Indeed, their use of the language varies greatly. In brief, there are four basic categories of the language, namely (a) Traditional ASL (pure), (b) Modern ASL (creole), (c) Englished ASL (blended with English borrowings), & (d) Rarefied ASL (theatricalized). On the whole, I see ASL as the generic term for these varieties of the language, as used by the Deaf community.

In one of my visits to her research lab, Ursula had me translate Shakespeare's famous love poem into ASL, or, in my own terms—Sign-Mime. The poem was recorded in its entirety on videotape, and with this videotape played back, I went on to describe why I translated it the way I did— sign by sign, phrase by phrase, expression by expression. Frankly, I did not know what she was going to do with the videotape. I asked, but she simply looked at me with a smile. It was not until several years later— when, much to my astonishment and delight, I found her thorough analysis of my Shakespearean translation in her first published book—that I finally understood the reason behind this probing. In it, she included tracings of my signs, with emphasis on the harmonious flow of hand movement, as I sign-mimed the poem for her. I did it intuitively, but she saw it scientifically. We complemented each other, indeed.

Oftentimes, I shared with her my observations and discoveries from my world travels of how Deaf people communicate among themselves or with other Deaf persons from other countries. She has always been very interested and encourages me to make comparisons from my own perspective.

What excited us the most was that there are a great number of universals in our sign languages. In my workshop during The Deaf Way Congress at Gallaudet University in 1989, I set up an experiment using five pairs of Deaf foreigners and studied how in each pair, one member described to his partner what he had previously seen on a videotaped clip, which showed the action of two clandestine lovers in trouble. Low and behold, we caught a great number of similarities in their different sign languages, namely, eye movement, hand placement, emotional expression through nonmanuals, gestures, and body language. Despite the diversity of the sign languages and cultures, the universals, as discovered from this videotaped experiment, tell us pretty much about why Deaf peoples of the world find it so very easy to make known their thoughts or ideas to each other and how they are able to quickly grasp meaning in their conversations. I mailed this videotape to Dr. Bellugi along with the following story as an example: I once rode in an elevator with a Deaf foreigner whom I met by chance, but when I arrived at the eleventh floor, I already knew his entire life story.

Dr. Bellugi is one of the very few linguists who have shown genuine respect for my own perspective, whether they agree with it or not. She asked me many times to give lectures to various professionals at The Salk Institute and, without fail, videotaped my talks either at the roundtable or in the lecture room. Again, she is one of the very few who analyzed ASL and wrote books about it without going out to proselytize how we should use it. I am proud of my part in her work and value her influence on my life, my thinking, and my understanding of what ASL is all about.

In closing, I would like to share with you one of her favorite stories, which she invariably related while introducing me to her audiences at The Salk Institute. Here it is: In one of the videotaping sessions with me, she asked me to tell a particular story without any facial expression whatever. I argued that it was not sensible or practical to do so. She looked at me with a smile and asked if I didn't realize that it was only for the purpose of research and that "You ain't no actor for nothing." She challenged me, indeed. Emboldened, I went on and told the story as best as I could without a single facial expression. To my shock, I did use one slight expression (or should I say it simply crept into my face?), so I had to do it all over again from the top of the story. I did it very laboriously, but I tried to make it look as if I were doing it effortlessly. With straight face all the way, I described how I went out fishing in a rowboat with a friend, which included telling one another wild jokes, laughing hysterically, picking up worms squeamishly from a can, catching a huge fish excitedly, struggling to get it into the boat, hitting it repeatedly with a paddle but instead accidentally hitting my thumb, and suffering the throbbing pain. Actually, I succeeded in telling the whole story without a hint of facial expression. Everyone in the audience was floored in fits of laughter. Finally, when they quieted down, Dr. Bellugi came up to me to congratulate me, but I bowled over, covering my face with my hands. She was alarmed, and asked me what was the matter. I looked up and signed with a full expression of agony on my face: "Ouch, my face hurts!"

II

Historical and Comparative Analyses of Sign Languages

4

Sign Languages and Sign Language Families in Thailand and Viet Nam

James Woodward
Ratchasuda College
Mahidol University at Salaya, Thailand

I have a long-standing interest in the history of sign languages and the historical relations of sign languages. Part of this interest stems from my own training in sociolinguistic variation and change, and part stems from contact with Ursula Bellugi and other researchers working with her. Specifically, Ursula Bellugi's early comparative sign language research work (see Klima & Bellugi, 1979), as well as Nancy Frishberg's (1975, 1976) seminal work on historical change in American Sign Language (ASL), played extremely important roles in some of my early efforts to apply general historical-comparative linguistic techniques to sign language research. One such work, "Historical Bases of American Sign Language" (Woodward, 1978), focused on the historical relations of French Sign Language and ASL. Since that time, I have applied historical-comparative linguistic techniques to a number of other sets of sign language varieties: sign language varieties in India (Vasishta, Woodward, & Wilson, 1978); in Costa Rica (Woodward, 1991, 1992); in India, Pakistan, and Nepal (Woodward, 1993b); in Hong Kong and Shanghai (Woodward, 1993a); in Thailand (Woodward, 1996, 1997a); and in Viet Nam (Woodward, 1997b).

This chapter is intended to add to previous research on the relations of Asian sign language varieties by comparing sign languages in Thailand with sign languages in Viet Nam. To determine the possible linguistic relations of sign language varieties in Thailand and in Viet Nam, this chapter (a) describes the sources of comparative data for sign language varieties in Thailand and in Viet Nam, (b) summarizes the findings of previous comparative lexical research on sign language varieties in Thailand, (c) summarizes the findings of previous comparative lexical research on sign language varieties in Viet Nam, (d) compares for cognates in basic vocabulary between each distinct sign language in Thailand with each distinct sign language in Viet Nam, (e) discusses the results of the analysis, and (f) concludes with implications for future research.

SOURCES OF DATA

This section discusses the type of linguistic data collected and the background of the Deaf consultants from whom the data were collected.

The Type of Linguistic Data Collected

The amount of data available on the language varieties determines the historical-comparative technique that should be used to analyze the data.

Standard books on historical linguistics (e.g., Crowley, 1992; Lehmann 1992) point out that lexicostatistics is often used for determining relationships across unwritten languages that are underdescribed or undescribed and for which there are relatively limited amounts of data available. As Crowley (1992) stated, "There is a . . . technique for subgrouping languages that is often used with languages for which there are relatively limited amounts of data available, and that is lexicostatistics" (p. 168). Lexicostatistics has been especially useful in the classification of 959 distinct, underdescribed Austronesian spoken languages and 250 distinct, underdescribed Australian spoken languages (Lehmann, 1992).

Given the facts that (a) all seven sign language varieties examined in this chapter are unwritten, (b) six out of the seven language varieties are underdescribed, and (c) there is limited data on six out of the seven languages, lexicostatistics was chosen as the appropriate historical-linguistic technique for analysis.

The reason why lexicostatistics is such an appropriate technique for underdescribed languages is that as Crowley (1992) pointed out:

> Lexicostatistics is a technique that allows us to determine the degree of relationship between two languages, simply by comparing the (core or basic) vocabularies of the languages and determining the degree of similarity between them. . . .[C]ore vocabulary includes items such as pronouns, numerals, body parts, geographical features, basic actions, and basic states." (pp. 168–169)

According to standard lexicostatistical guidelines for subgroupings (Crowley, 1992; Gudschinsky, 1956; Lehmann, 1992), dialects of the same language should have an 81% to 100% rate of cognates, and languages belonging to the same language family should have a 36% to 81% rate of cognates.

To compare basic vocabulary, Crowley (1992) stated that "most lexico-statisticians tend to operate with 200-word lists. The most popular list of this length is known as the *Swadesh list,* which is named after the linguist Morris Swadesh, who drew it up" (pp. 170–171).

Whereas it is common to use the original 200-word Swadesh list to compare for cognates in basic vocabulary across spoken languages, it is not generally desirable to use the same list for sign language research. Use of the original 200-word Swadesh list in sign language research may result in slight overestimation of the relation of closely related sign languages, moderate overestimation of the relation of loosely related sign languages, and great overestimation of the relation of historically unrelated sign languages (Woodward, 1993a).

These overestimations occur because the original 200-word Swadesh list contains many items, such as body parts and pronouns, which are represented indexically (i.e., simply by pointing) in many sign languages. The comparison of such indexic signs results in a number of false potential cognates.

To avoid these problems of overestimation, a special vocabulary list (Table 4.1) has been used for comparisons of sign language varieties within Thailand and Viet Nam.

The list in Table 4.1 is a modification of the 200-word Swadesh list that removes typically indexic signs and has proven useful in earlier comparisons of sign languages (Woodward, 1978, 1991, 1992, 1993a, 1993b).

The Background of the Deaf Consultants

Sign translations of the basic vocabulary list in Table 4.1 were collected from fluent Deaf signers in four signing communities in Thailand and from three signing communities in Viet Nam.

The four signing communities in Thailand include (a) the Ban Khor signing community, (b) the Original Chiangmai signing community, (c) the Original Bangkok signing community, and (d) the Modern Thai signing community.

The Ban Khor signing community refers to a small community of signers living in certain rice farming villages in the district of Ban Khor in Nakornpanom province in Northeastern Thailand. From this community, signs were obtained from 9 female signers and 5 male signers ranging in age from 13 years to more than 60 years of age. Signs were elicited in Ban Khor in 1996.

The Original Chiangmai signing community refers to the community of signers in Chiangmai before 1951 and to certain signers older than 45 still

TABLE 4.1

Special Modified Swadesh Vocabulary List for Sign Languages

1. all	26. grass	51. other	76. warm
2. animal	27. green	52. person	77. water
3. bad	28. heavy	53. play	78. wet
4. because	29. how	54. rain	79. what
5. bird	30. hunt	55. red	80. when
6. black	31. husband	56. correct	81. where
7. blood	32. ice	57. river	82. white
8. child	33. if	58. rope	83. who
9. count	34. kill	59. salt	84. wide
10. day	35. laugh	60. sea	85. wife
11. die	36. leaf	61. sharp	86. wind
12. dirty	37. lie	62. short	87. with
13. dog	38. live	63. sing	88. woman
14. dry	39. long	64. sit	89. wood
15. dull	40. louse	65. smooth	90. worm
16. dust	41. man	66. snake	91. year
17. earth	42. meat	67. snow	92. yellow
18. egg	43. mother	68. stand	93. full
19. grease	44. mountain	69. star	94. moon
20. father	45. name	70. stone	95. brother
21. feather	46. narrow	71. sun	96. cat
22. fire	47. new	72. tail	97. dance
23. fish	48. night	73. thin	98. pig
24. flower	49. not	74. tree	99. sister
25. good	50. old	75. vomit	100. work

living in the urban Chiangmai area in Northern Thailand. Signs were obtained from 1 male signer in his late forties from this community. Signs were elicited in Chiangmai in 1996.

The Original Bangkok signing community refers to the community of signers living in the urban Bangkok area before 1951 and to certain signers older than 45 still living in the urban Bangkok area. From this community, signs were obtained from 1 male signer in his late fifties and 1 female signer in her late forties. Signs were elicited in Bangkok in 1996.

The Modern Thai signing community refers to the majority of signers younger than 40 living in the urban areas of Thailand. From this community, signs were obtained from a total of 8 signers younger than forty: 2 males and 2 females from Bangkok and 2 males and 2 females from Nakornpanom City in Northeastern Thailand. Signs were elicited in Bangkok and Nakornpanom City in 1996.

The three signing communities in Viet Nam include (a) the Ho Chi Minh City signing community, (b) the Ha Noi signing community, and (c) the Hai Phong signing community.

The Ho Chi Minh signing community refers to the community of signers living in the Ho Chi Minh City Metropolitan Area of Southern Viet Nam. Signs were obtained from 2 female signers in their early twenties from this community. Signs were elicited at a conference in Ha Noi in 1997.

The Ha Noi signing community refers to the community of signers living in the Ha Noi Metropolitan Area in Northern Viet Nam. Signs were obtained from 1 male signer in his twenties from this community. Signs were elicited in Ha Noi in 1997.

The Hai Phong signing community refers to the community of signers living in the Hai Phong Metropolitan Area of Northern Viet Nam. From this community, signs were obtained from 2 female signers in their late twenties and 1 male signer is his early twenties. Signs were elicited at a conference in Ha Noi in 1996.

PREVIOUS RESEARCH ON SIGN LANGUAGES IN THAILAND

Previous research (Woodward, 1996, 1997a) compared for cognates in basic vocabulary across the four signing communities in Thailand: (a) the Ban Khor signing community, (b) the Original Chiangmai signing community, (c) the Original Bangkok signing community, and (d) the Modern

TABLE 4.2
Summary Results of Previous Cognate Comparisons of Thai Sign Language Varieties

	Ban Khor SL (%)	Original Chiangmai SL (%)	Original Bangkok SL (%)	Modern Thai SL (%)
Ban Khor SL	X	34	33	24
Original Chiangmai SL		X	65	29
Original Bangkok SL			X	26
Modern Thai SL				X

Note: SL = sign language.

TABLE 4.3
Summary Results of Previous Cognate Comparisons of Sign Language Varieties in Viet Nam

	Ho Chi Minh City SL (%)	Ha Noi SL (%)	Hai Phong SL (%)
Ho Chi Mihn City SL	X	58	54
Ha Noi SL		X	54
Hai Phong SL			X

Note: SL = sign language.

Thai signing community. Table 4.2 shows a summary of the results of the cognate comparisons of the sign language varieties used in these four communities.

Following standard lexicostatistical guidelines for subgroupings[1] (Crowley, 1992; Lehmann, 1992), these four sign language varieties were classified as four separate languages that belong to three separate language families. Fig. 4.1 illustrates this classification with a traditional family tree diagram.

PREVIOUS RESEARCH ON SIGN LANGUAGES IN VIET NAM

Previous research (Woodward, 1997b) compared for cognates in basic vocabulary across the three signing communities in Viet Nam: (a) the Ho Chi Minh City signing community, (b) the Ha Noi signing community, and (c) the Hai Phong signing community.

Table 4.3 shows a summary of the results of the cognate comparisons of the sign language varieties used in these three communities.

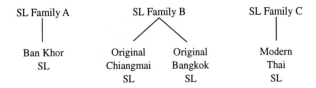

FIG. 4.1. Sign Languages in Thailand Classified by Traditional Language Family Trees.

FIG. 4.2. Sign Languages in Viet Nam Classified by a Traditional Language Family Tree.

Following standard lexicostatistical guidelines for subgroupings[1] (Crowley, 1992; Lehmann, 1992), these three sign language varieties should be classified as three separate languages that belong to the same language family. Fig. 4.2 illustrates this classification with a traditional family tree diagram.

COMPARISON OF BASIC VOCABULARY IN SIGN LANGUAGES IN VIET NAM WITH BASIC VOCABULARY IN SIGN LANGUAGES IN THAILAND

To determine the possible relationships of sign languages in Viet Nam with sign languages in Thailand, we compare for cognates in basic vocabulary from each of sign languages in Viet Nam with basic vocabulary from each of the sign languages from the three sign language families in Thailand.

Tables 4.4 to 4.15 (in the Appendix at the end of this chapter) show detailed comparisons of individual pairs of sign languages. In each of these tables, possible cognates are shown in **bold** print; missing data are

---

[1]According to standard lexicostatistical guidelines for sub-groupings (Crowley, 1992; Gudschinsky, 1956; Lehmann, 1992), dialects of the same language should have an 81% to 100% rate of cognates, and languages belonging to the same language family should have a 36% to 81% rate of cognates. These percentages are based on the results of historical linguistic studies in 13 languages for which there are written records going back more than 1,000 years (Crowley, 1992) and are considered the standard measuring tool for lexicostatistical studies.

TABLE 4.4
Summary Results of Cognate Comparisons of Sign Languages
in Viet Nam With Sign Languages in Thailand

	Ho Chi Minh City SL (%)	Ha Noi SL (%)	Hai Phong SL (%)
Ban Khor SL	~~18~~	~~19~~	~~26~~
Original Chiangmai SL	~~23~~	~~33~~	46
Original Bangkok SL	~~25~~	~~31~~	48
Modern Thai SL	39	45	40

Note: SL = sign language.

shown ~~struck out~~; and noncognates are shown in straight print. All fractions in percentages are rounded to the next highest whole number.

Table 4.16 shows such a summary of the findings in Table 4.4 through Table 4.15. Percentages lower than 36% are ~~struck out~~, because language varieties with less than 36% cognates should be classified as belonging to different language families.

We can summarize the language family relations in Table 4.16 as follows:

1. The seven sign languages in Thailand and in Viet Nam can be classified into three language families.
2. The first language family includes Ban Khor Sign Language. Ban Khor Sign Language is the only known member of this sign language family.
3. The second language family includes Original Chiangmai Sign Language, Original Bangkok Sign Language, and Hai Phong Sign Language.
4. The third language family includes Modern Thai Sign Language, Ha Noi Sign Language, Ho Chi Minh Sign Language, and Hai Phong Sign Language.

DISCUSSION

The composition of the second family and the composition of the third language family are a bit surprising, particularly in regard to the lexicostatistical classifications of Modern Thai Sign Language and of Hai Phong Sign Language.

Specifically, we need to answer the following three questions:

1. How can the lexicostatistical classification of Modern Thai Sign Language in a separate language family from original sign languages in Thailand be explained?
2. How can the lexicostatistical classification of Modern Thai Sign Language in the same language family with sign languages used in Viet Nam be explained?
3. How can the lexicostatistical classification of Hai Phong Sign Language as a member of two separate language families be explained?

The answer to Question 1 lies in the different histories of sign languages in Thailand. Research on Modern Thai Sign Language (Woodward, 1996) has shown that the introduction of vocabulary from ASL into schools for the Deaf in Thailand has resulted in a 52% rate of cognates between basic vocabulary in Modern Thai Sign Language and ASL.

Given the great amount of foreign contact and borrowing that has influenced Modern Thai Sign Language's development and use and the lack of such contact and borrowing in other sign languages in Thailand, there should be little doubt why Modern Thai Sign Language is not closely related to any other sign language in Thailand and why it belongs to a separate language family from any other sign language in Thailand.

The answer to Question 2 can be found by examining external factors that have influenced the history of Modern Thai Sign Language and sign languages in Viet Nam. The relation of Modern Thai Sign Language to sign languages in Viet Nam is in fact not a result of direct contact but of indirect contact. Ha Noi Sign Language, Ho Chi Minh Sign Language, and Hai Phong Sign Language all show very strong influences from French Sign Language, which was introduced into schools for the Deaf in Viet Nam. French Sign Language and ASL have a 61% rate of cognates in basic vocabulary and therefore belong to the same language family (Woodward, 1978). Thus, the influence of ASL on Modern Thai Sign Language and the influence of French Sign Language on Ha Noi Sign Language, Ho Chi Minh Sign Language, and Hai Phong Sign Language result in a large number of shared cognates between Modern Thai Sign Language and sign languages in Viet Nam.

We can now turn to the final issue of why Hai Phong Sign Language appears to belong to two separate sign language families. Ha Noi Sign Language, Ho Chi Minh Sign Language, and Hai Phong Sign Language have all three been influenced by French Sign Language. However, Hai Phong signers, perhaps because of their relative isolation from Ha Noi and

Ho Chi Minh City, have managed to preserve more original Southeast Asian signs than the other signers in Ha Noi and Ho Chi Minh City.

Even when Hai Phong has borrowed a French sign for a vocabulary item, Hai Phong signers sometimes keep the original Southeast Asian sign along with the French sign. This has resulted in pairs of cognates for a number of words. One sign in the cognate pair is cognate with original sign languages in Thailand and one with French Sign Language. Examples of this can be found in signs for WIFE, HUSBAND, and PIG, among others. Because of these pairs, Hai Phong Sign Language shows strong similarities to Southeast Asian sign languages that *have not* been influenced by French Sign Language or ASL (Original Chiangmai Sign Language and Original Bangkok Sign Language) and also shows strong similarities to Southeast Asian sign languages that *have* been influenced by French Sign Language or ASL (Ha Noi Sign Language, Ho Chi Minh Sign Language, and Modern Thai Sign Language).

When we put all of these facts together, an interesting picture of linguistic relations emerges. This picture is graphically represented in Fig. 4.3.

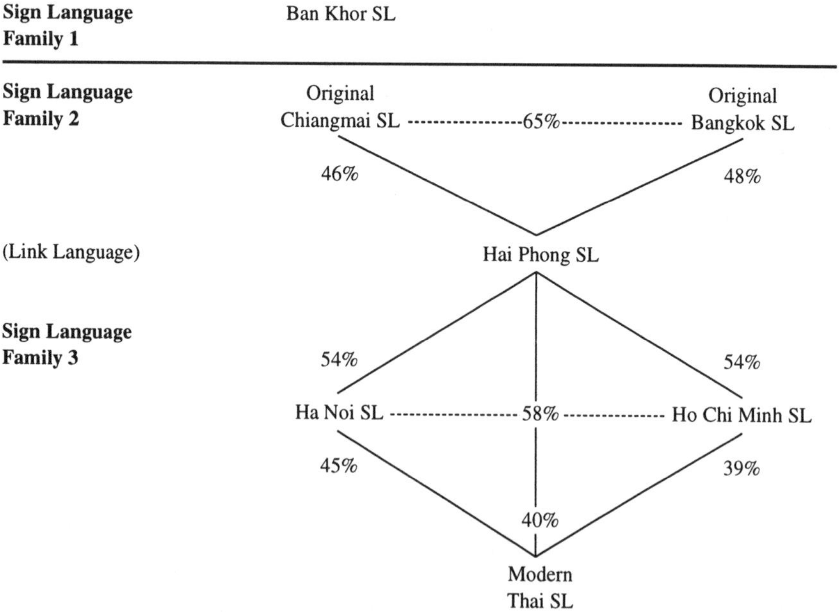

Sign Language Family 1   Ban Khor SL

Sign Language Family 2   Original Chiangmai SL ----------------65%------------------ Original Bangkok SL

46%   48%

(Link Language)   Hai Phong SL

Sign Language Family 3   54%   54%

Ha Noi SL ------------------ 58% ---------------- Ho Chi Minh SL

45%   39%

40%

Modern Thai SL

FIG. 4.3.   Linguistic Relations Between Sign Languages in Thailand and Viet Nam.

The first family is an indigenous sign language family in Thailand that includes Ban Khor Sign Language. Ban Khor Sign Language developed in a small village with a large proportion of Deaf people. Thus, Ban Khor Sign Language developed in isolation from other sign languages in Southeast Asia. There may be other related indigenous sign languages in other small villages with large Deaf populations in the same general region in Northeast Thailand. For example, the villages of Pla Bag and Bang Na, which are relatively close to Ban Khor, also appear to have larger Deaf populations than expected, and Pla Bag and Bang Na may have sign language varieties related to Ban Khor Sign Language. There may also be other indigenous sign language families in Thailand and in Viet Nam.

The second sign language family includes original Southeast Asian sign languages that developed in contact with other sign languages in Southeast Asia but with no contact (or extremely limited contact) with Western sign languages. This sign language family includes Original Chiangmai Sign Language and Original Bangkok Sign Language. Hai Phong Sign Language is still linked to this family. Other related original sign languages may have existed in urban areas in Thailand and Viet Nam. For example, it is likely that there were original sign languages in the Northeastern and Southern parts of Thailand. It is also likely that there was an Original Ha Noi Sign Language and an Original Saigon (Ho Chi Minh City) Sign Language before French Sign Language had an impact on sign languages in Viet Nam. Some of these original sign languages may still exist among older signers. Some probably have already died out.

The third sign language family includes "modern" sign languages that are mixtures, probably creolizations, of original sign languages with French Sign Language, ASL, or both. Modern sign languages have already replaced original sign languages among younger signers in Thailand and in Viet Nam. Within 50 years, it is highly likely that all original sign languages in Thailand and Viet Nam will be extinct, dying out with the users who still remember them.

IMPLICATIONS FOR FUTURE RESEARCH

In conclusion, although we have gained some knowledge about the relations of sign language varieties in Thailand and Viet Nam, there are still many gaps in our knowledge. For example, we still do not know the following:

- How many original sign languages and how many indigenous sign languages exist or have existed in Thailand or in Viet Nam, not to mention in other countries in Southeast Asia
- How many language families these original sign languages and indigenous sign languages belonged to
- What intercountry and intracountry relations exist among original sign languages in Southeast Asia
- How many "link languages," like Hai Phong Sign Language, may still exist in Southeast Asia
- What the future of endangered original and endangered indigenous sign languages in Southeast Asia may be.

What is needed at this point is a large-scale, in-depth sociolinguistic study of sign languages in Southeast Asia. This sociolinguistic study must look at a large number of Deaf linguistic informants who have competence in one or more sign languages in Southeast Asia. These Deaf people must be selected from various stratified age groups and various regions of Southeast Asia, and they should represent various Deaf social identities in Southeast Asia. This research needs to include original, indigenous, and modern sign languages and needs to focus primarily on sign languages that are most endangered and on link languages. Link languages, which preserve older forms and still link certain sign languages in modern sign language families with certain sign languages in original sign language families, provide important clues about the history of sign languages in Southeast Asia.

At this point, it is likely that the great majority of users of original sign languages in most countries in Southeast Asia are around 50 years old. If the documentation of these original sign languages is not completed in one generation, it is quite likely that they will be lost to linguistic study forever, because there are currently no records of these sign languages.

If original sign languages in Southeast Asia die out before they can be properly documented and described, Deaf people in Southeast Asia will lose a valuable part of their history, all Southeast Asian people will lose a valuable part of their national or regional heritage, and the rest of us will lose one of the important keys to understanding the history of sign languages in Southeast Asia.

ACKNOWLEDGMENTS

Research on which this chapter is based was supported in part by the Research Department at Ratchasuda College; by an internal Mahidol University Grant, "A Study of the Bangkok Metropolitan Variety of Thai Sign Language"; by an external grant from the Thai Government, "A Study of the Grammar of Thai Sign Language and of Thai Deaf Culture"; by a grant from Ratchasuda Foundation, "A Pilot Study of Sign Language Varieties in Ban Khor, Nakornpanom"; and by Sign Language Research, Inc. Parts of this chapter were presented at the 1997 Annual Meeting of the American Anthropological Association, Washington, D.C., in section 4-025, Ethnically Deaf: Identity, Culture, and the Making of Sign Language Communities, organized by Karen J. Nakamura and Lelila Monaghan. I would like to thank Angela M. Nonaka for her comments and criticisms on an earlier draft of this chapter.

REFERENCES

Crowley, T. (1992). *An introduction to historical linguistics.* Oxford, UK: Oxford University Press.
Frishberg, N. (1975). Arbitrariness and iconicity: Historical change in American Sign Language. *Language, 51,* 676–710.
Frishberg, N. (1976). *Some aspects of the historical development of signs in American Sign Language.* Unpublished doctoral dissertation, University of California, San Diego.
Gudschinsky, S. (1956). The ABCs of lexicostatistics (glottochronology). *Word, 12,* 175–210.
Klima, E., & Bellugi, U. (1979). *The signs of language.* Cambridge, MA: Harvard University Press.
Lehmann, W. (1992). *Historical linguistics: An introduction.* New York: Routledge.
Vasishta, M., Woodward, J., & Wilson, K. (1978). Sign language in India: Regional variation within the Deaf population. *Indian Journal of Applied Linguistics, IV*(2), 66–74.
Woodward, J. (1978). Historical bases of American Sign Language. In P. Siple (Ed.), *Understanding language through sign language research* (pp. 333–348). New York: Academic Press.
Woodward, J. (1991). Sign language varieties in Costa Rica. *Sign Language Studies, 73,* 329–346.
Woodward, J. (1992). Historical bases of New Costa Rican Sign Language. *Revista de Filología y Lingüística de la Universidad de Costa Rica, 18*(1), 127–132.
Woodward, J. (1993a). Lexical evidence for the existence of South Asian and East Asian sign language families. *Journal of Asian Pacific Communication, 4*(2), 91–106.
Woodward, J. (1993b). The relationship of sign language varieties in India, Pakistan, and Nepal. *Sign Language Studies, 78,* 15–22.
Woodward, J. (1996). Modern Standard Thai Sign Language, influence from ASL, and its relationship to original sign language varieties in Thailand. *Sign Language Studies, 92,* 227–252.
Woodward, J. (1977a). *A Preliminary examination of Ban Khor Sign Language.* Unpublished manuscript, Research Department, Ratchasuda College, Mahidol University at Salaya.
Woodward, J. (1997b, February). *Sign language varieties in Viet Nam.* Paper presented at the First Australasian Deaf Studies Conference, National Institute of Deaf Studies, La Trobe University, Melbourne, Australia.

APPENDIX

TABLE 4.4
Ho Chi Minh City SL/Ban Khor SL: 18% Possible Cognates (17/97)

1. all	26. grass	51. other	**76. warm**
2. animal	27. green	52. person	77. water
3. bad	28. heavy	53. play	**78. wet**
4. because	29. how	54. rain	79. what
5. bird	30. hunt	**55. red**	80. when
6. black	31. husband	56. correct	81. where
7. blood	32. ice	57. river	82. white
8. child	33. if	58. rope	83. who
9. count	34. kill	**59. salt**	**84. wide**
10. day	35. laugh	60. sea	85. wife
11. die	36. leaf	61. sharp	86. wind
12. dirty	37. lie	62. short	87. with
13. dog	38. live	**63. sing**	88. woman
14. dry	39. long	**64. sit**	89. wood
15. dull	40. louse	~~65. smooth~~	~~90. worm~~
16. dust	41. man	66. snake	91. year
17. earth	42. meat	67. snow	92. yellow
18. egg	43. mother	68. stand	93. full
~~19. grease~~	**44. mountain**	69. star	94. moon
20. father	45. name	70. stone	95. brother
21. feather	46. narrow	71. sun	96. cat
22. fire	47. new	72. tail	97. dance
23. fish	48. night	73. thin	98. pig
24. flower	**49. not**	74. tree	99. sister
25. good	50. old	**75. vomit**	100. work

Note: SL = sign language.

TABLE 4.5
Ha Noi SL/Ban Khor SL: 19% Possible Cognates (18/97)

1. all	26. grass	51. other	**76. warm**
2. animal	27. green	52. person	77. water
3. bad	28. heavy	53. play	78. wet
4. because	29. how	54. rain	79. what
5. bird	30. hunt	**55. red**	80. when
6. black	31. husband	56. correct	81. where
7. blood	32. ice	57. river	82. white
8. child	33. if	58. rope	83. who
9. count	34. kill	**59. salt**	**84. wide**
10. day	35. laugh	60. sea	85. wife
11. die	36. leaf	61. sharp	86. wind
12. dirty	37. lie	62. short	87. with
13. dog	38. live	**63. sing**	88. woman
14. dry	39. long	**64. sit**	89. wood
15. dull	40. louse	~~65. smooth~~	~~90. worm~~
16. dust	41. man	66. snake	91. year
17. earth	42. meat	67. snow	92. yellow
18. egg	43. mother	**68. stand**	93. full
~~19. grease~~	**44. mountain**	69. star	94. moon
20. father	45. name	70. stone	95. brother
21. feather	**46. narrow**	71. sun	96. cat
22. fire	47. new	72. tail	97. dance
23. fish	48. night	73. thin	98. pig
24. flower	**49. not**	74. tree	99. sister
25. good	50. old	**75. vomit**	100. work

Note: SL = sign language.

TABLE 4.6
Hai Phong SL/Ban Khor SL: 26% Possible Cognates (25/97)

1. all	26. grass	51. other	**76. warm**
2. animal	27. green	52. person	77. water
3. bad	28. heavy	53. play	**78. wet**
4. because	29. how	**54. rain**	79. what
5. bird	30. hunt	**55. red**	80. when
6. black	31. husband	56. correct	81. where
7. blood	32. ice	57. river	82. white
8. child	33. if	58. rope	83. who
9. count	**34. kill**	**59. salt**	**84. wide**
10. day	35. laugh	60. sea	85. wife
11. die	**36. leaf**	61. sharp	86. wind
12. dirty	37. lie	62. short	87. with
13. dog	38. live	**63. sing**	88. woman
14. dry	39. long	**64. sit**	89. wood
15. dull	40. louse	~~65. smooth~~	~~90. worm~~
16. dust	41. man	66. snake	91. year
17. earth	42. meat	67. snow	92. yellow
18. egg	43. mother	68. stand	93. full
~~19. grease~~	**44. mountain**	**69. star**	**94. moon**
20. father	45. name	70. stone	95. brother
21. feather	**46. narrow**	71. sun	96. cat
22. fire	47. new	72. tail	97. dance
23. fish	48. night	73. thin	98. pig
24. flower	**49. not**	74. tree	99. sister
25. good	50. old	**75. vomit**	100. work

Note: SL = sign language.

TABLE 4.7
Ho Chi Minh City SL/Original Chiangmai SL: 23% Possible Cognates (22/97)

1. all	26. grass	**51. other**	76. warm
2. animal	27. green	**52. person**	77. water
3. bad	28. heavy	53. play	**78. wet**
4. because	29. how	54. rain	79. what
5. bird	30. hunt	**55. red**	80. when
6. black	31. husband	56. correct	81. where
7. blood	32. ice	57. river	82. white
8. child	33. if	58. rope	83. who
9. count	34. kill	**59. salt**	**84. wide**
10. day	35. laugh	60. sea	85. wife
11. die	36. leaf	61. sharp	86. wind
12. dirty	37. lie	**62. short**	87. with
13. dog	38. live	63. sing	88. woman
14. dry	39. long	**64. sit**	89. wood
15. dull	40. louse	65. ~~smooth~~	90. ~~worm~~
16. dust	41. man	66. snake	91. year
17. earth	42. meat	67. snow	92. yellow
18. egg	43. mother	68. stand	93. full
19. ~~grease~~	**44. mountain**	69. star	94. moon
20. father	45. name	70. stone	**95. brother**
21. feather	46. narrow	71. sun	96. cat
22. fire	47. new	72. tail	**97. dance**
23. fish	**48. night**	73. thin	98. pig
24. flower	**49. not**	**74. tree**	**99. sister**
25. good	50. old	**75. vomit**	100. work

Note: SL = sign language.

TABLE 4.8
Ha Noi SL/Original Chiangmai SL: 33% Possible Cognates (32/97)

1. all	26. grass	51. other	76. warm
2. animal	27. green	**52. person**	77. water
3. bad	28. heavy	53. play	78. wet
4. because	29. how	54. rain	79. what
5. bird	**30. hunt**	**55. red**	80. when
6. black	31. husband	56. correct	81. where
7. blood	32. ice	57. river	**82. white**
8. child	33. if	**58. rope**	83. who
9. count	34. kill	**59. salt**	**84. wide**
10. day	35. laugh	60. sea	85. wife
11. die	36. leaf	61. sharp	86. wind
12. dirty	37. lie	**62. short**	**87. with***
13. dog	38. live	63. sing	88. woman
14. dry	**39. long**	**64. sit**	89. wood
15. dull	40. louse	~~65. smooth~~	~~90. worm~~
16. dust	41. man	66. snake	91. year
17. earth	42. meat	67. snow	92. yellow
18. egg	43. mother	**68. stand**	93. full
~~19. grease~~	**44. mountain**	69. star	94. moon
20. father	45. name	**70. stone****	**95. brother**
21. feather	**46. narrow**	71. sun	96. cat
22. fire	47. new	**72. tail**	**97. dance**
23. fish	**48. night**	73. thin	98. pig
24. flower	**49. not**	**74. tree**	**99. sister**
25. good	50. old	**75. vomit**	100. work

Note: SL = sign language.
*Original Chiangmai SL has 2 signs; one is cognate with Ha Noi SL.
**Ha Noi SL has a compound sign; one part is cognate with Original Chiangmai SL.

TABLE 4.9
Hai Phong SL/Original Chiangmai SL: 46% Possible Cognates (44/97)

1. all	26. grass	**51. other****	76. warm
2. animal	27. green	**52. person**	77. water
3. bad	28. heavy	53. play	**78. wet**
4. because	29. how	**54. rain**	79. what
5. bird	**30. hunt**	**55. red**	**80. when**
6. black	**31. husband****	56. correct	81. where
7. blood	32. ice	**57. river**	82. white
8. child	33. if	**58. rope**	83. who
9. count	34. kill	**59. salt**	**84. wide**
10. day	35. laugh	60. sea	**85. wife****
11. die***	**36. leaf**	61. sharp	86. wind
12. dirty	**37. lie****	**62. short**	**87. with***
13. dog	**38. live**	63. sing	88. woman
14. dry	39. long	**64. sit**	89. wood
15. dull	**40. louse**	~~65. smooth~~	~~90. worm~~
16. dust	41. man	66. snake	**91. year**
17. earth	42. meat	67. snow	92. yellow
18. egg	43. mother	68. stand	93. full
~~19. grease~~	**44. mountain**	**69. star**	94. moon
20. father	45. name	70. stone	**95. brother**
21. feather	**46. narrow**	71. sun	96. cat
22. fire	47. new	72. tail	**97. dance**
23. fish	48. night	73. thin	**98. pig****
24. flower	**49. not**	**74. tree**	**99. sister**
25. good	**50. old**	**75. vomit**	100. work

Note: SL = sign language.
*Original Chiangmai SL has 2 signs; one is cognate with Hai Phong SL.
**Hai Phong SL has two signs; one is cognate with Original Chiangmai SL.
***Hai Phong SL has a compound sign; one part is cognate with Original Chiangmai SL.

TABLE 4.10
Ho Chi Minh City SL/Original Bangkok SL: 25% Possible Cognates (24/97)

1. all	26. grass	**51. other**	76. warm
2. animal	27. green	52. person	**77. water**
3. bad	28. heavy	53. play	**78. wet**
4. because	29. how	54. rain	79. what
5. bird	30. hunt	**55. red**	80. when
6. black	31. husband	56. correct	81. where
7. blood	32. ice	57. river	82. white
8. child	33. if	58. rope	83. who
9. count	34. kill	**59. salt**	**84. wide**
10. day	35. laugh	60. sea	85. wife
11. die	36. leaf	61. sharp	86. wind
12. dirty	37. lie	**62. short**	87. with
13. dog	38. live	63. sing	88. woman
14. dry	39. long	**64. sit**	89. wood
15. dull	40. louse	~~65. smooth~~	~~90. worm~~
16. dust	41. man	66. snake	91. year
17. earth	42. meat	67. snow	92. yellow
18. egg	43. mother	68. stand	93. full
~~19. grease~~	**44. mountain**	69. star	94. moon
20. father	45. name	70. stone	**95. brother**
21. feather	46. narrow	71. sun	**96. cat**
22. fire	47. new	72. tail	**97. dance**
23. fish	**48. night**	73. thin	98. pig
24. flower	**49. not**	74. tree	**99. sister**
25. good	50. old	**75. vomit**	**100. work**

Note: SL = sign language.

TABLE 4.11
Ha Noi SL/Original Bangkok SL: 31% Possible Cognates (30/97)

1. all	26. grass	51. other	76. warm
2. animal	27. green	52. person	**77. water**
3. bad	28. heavy	53. play	78. wet
4. because	29. how	54. rain	79. what
5. bird	**30. hunt**	**55. red**	80. when
6. black	31. husband	56. correct	81. where
7. blood	32. ice	57. river	82. white
8. child	33. if	**58. rope**	83. who
9. count	34. kill	**59. salt**	**84. wide**
10. day	35. laugh	60. sea	85. wife
11. die	36. leaf	61. sharp	86. wind
12. dirty	37. lie	**62. short**	**87. with**
13. dog	38. live	63. sing	88. woman
14. dry	39. long	**64. sit**	89. wood
15. dull	40. louse	~~65. smooth~~	~~90. worm~~
16. dust	41. man	66. snake	91. year
17. earth	42. meat	67. snow	92. yellow
18. egg	43. mother	**68. stand**	93. full
~~19. grease~~	**44. mountain**	69. star	94. moon
20. father	45. name	70. stone	**95. brother**
21. feather	**46. narrow**	71. sun	96. cat
22. fire	47. new	72. tail	**97. dance**
23. fish	**48. night**	73. thin	98. pig
24. flower	**49. not**	74. tree	**99. sister**
25. good	50. old	**75. vomit**	**100. work**

Note: SL = sign language.

TABLE 4.12
Hai Phong SL/Original Bangkok SL: 48% Possible Cognates (46/97)

1. all	26. grass	**51. other***	76. warm
2. animal	27. green	52. person	**77. water**
3. bad	28. heavy	53. play	**78. wet**
4. because	29. how	**54. rain**	79. what
5. bird	**30. hunt**	**55. red**	**80. when**
6. black	**31. husband***	56. correct	81. where
7. blood	32. ice	57. river	82. white
8. child	33. if	**58. rope**	83. who
9. count	**34. kill**	**59. salt**	**84. wide**
10. day	35. laugh	60. sea	**85. wife***
11. die**	**36. leaf**	61. sharp	**86. wind**
12. dirty	**37. lie***	**62. short**	87. with
13. dog	38. live	63. sing	**88. woman****
14. dry	**39. long***	**64. sit**	89. wood
15. dull	**40. louse**	65. smooth	90. worm
16. dust	**41. man***	66. snake	**91. year**
17. earth	42. meat	67. snow	92. yellow
18. egg	43. mother	68. stand	93. full
19. grease	**44. mountain**	**69. star**	**94. moon**
20. father	45. name	70. stone	**95. brother**
21. feather	**46. narrow**	71. sun	**96. cat**
22. fire	47. new	72. tail	**97. dance**
23. fish	48. night	73. thin	**98. pig***
24. flower	**49. not**	74. tree	**99. sister**
25. good	50. old	**75. vomit**	**100. work**

Note: SL = sign language.

*Hai Phong SL has two signs; one is cognate with Original Bangkok SL.

**Hai Phong SL has a compound sign; one part is cognate with Original Bangkok SL.

TABLE 4.13
Ho Chi Minh City SL/Modern Thai SL: 39% Possible Cognates (37/97)

1. all	26. grass	51. other	**76. warm***
2. animal	27. green	52. person	77. water
3. bad	**28. heavy**	53. play	78. wet
4. because	**29. how**	54. rain	79. what
5. bird	**30. hunt**	**55. red**	80. when
6. black	**31. husband**	56. correct	81. where
7. blood	32. ice	**57. river**	82. white
8. child	33. if	58. rope	83. who
9. count	34. kill	**59. salt**	**84. wide**
10. day	35. laugh	60. sea	**85. wife**
11. die	36. leaf	61. sharp	**86. wind**
12. dirty	37. lie	**62. short**	**87. with**
13. dog	**38. live**	**63. sing**	88. woman
14. dry	39. long	64. sit	**89. wood**
15. dull	40. louse	~~65. smooth~~	~~90. worm~~
16. dust	41. man	66. snake	**91. year**
17. earth	**42. meat**	67. snow	92. yellow
18. egg	43. mother	**68. stand**	**93. full**
~~19. grease~~	**44. mountain**	69. star	94. moon
20. father	**45. name**	70. stone	**95. brother**
21. feather	46. narrow	71. sun	96. cat
22. fire	47. new	72. tail	97. dance
23. fish	48. night	**73. thin***	**98. pig**
24. flower	**49. not**	74. tree	**99. sister**
25. good	50. old	**75. vomit**	100. work

Note: SL = sign language.
*Modern Thai SL has two signs; one is cognate with Ho Chi Minh City SL.

TABLE 4.14
Ha Noi SL/Modern Thai SL: 45% Possible Cognates (43/97)

1. all	26. grass	**51. other**	**76. warm***
2. animal	27. green	52. person	77. water
3. bad	**28. heavy**	53. play	78. wet
4. because	**29. how**	54. rain	79. what
5. bird	30. hunt	**55. red**	80. when
6. black	**31. husband**	56. correct	81. where
7. blood	32. ice	**57. river**	**82. white**
8. child	33. if	**58. rope**	83. who
9. count	34. kill	**59. salt**	**84. wide**
10. day	**35. laugh**	**60. sea**	**85. wife**
11. die	36. leaf	61. sharp	**86. wind**
12. dirty	37. lie	**62. short**	87. with
13. dog	38. live	**63. sing**	88. woman
14. dry	39. long	64. sit	**89. wood**
15. dull	40. louse	~~65. smooth~~	~~90. worm~~
16. dust	41. man	66. snake	**91. year**
17. earth	**42. meat**	**67. snow**	92. yellow
18. egg	43. mother	68. stand	**93. full**
~~19. grease~~	**44. mountain**	69. star	94. moon
20. father	**45. name**	70. stone	**95. brother**
21. feather	**46. narrow**	71. sun	96. cat
22. fire	47. new	72. tail	97. dance
23. fish	48. night	**73. thin***	**98. pig**
24. flower	**49. not**	74. tree	**99. sister**
25. good	50. old	**75. vomit**	**100. work****

Note: SL = sign language.
*Modern Thai SL has two signs; one is cognate with Ha Noi SL.
**Ha Noi SL has a compound sign; one part is cognate with Modern Thai SL.

TABLE 4.15
Hai Phong SL/Modern Thai SL: 40% Possible Cognates (38/97)

1. all	26. grass	**51. other****	**76. warm***
2. animal	27. green	52. person	77. water
3. bad	**28. heavy**	53. play	78. wet
4. because	29. how	**54. rain**	79. what
5. bird	30. hunt	**55. red**	80. when
6. black	**31. husband****	56. correct	81. where
7. blood	32. ice	57. river	82. white
8. child	33. if	**58. rope**	83. who
9. count	34. kill	**59. salt**	**84. wide**
10. day	**35. laugh**	60. sea	**85. wife****
11. die	**36. leaf**	61. sharp	86. wind
12. dirty	**37. lie****	**62. short**	87. with
13. dog	38. live	**63. sing**	88. woman
14. dry	**39. long****	64. sit	89. wood
15. dull	40. louse	~~65. smooth~~	~~90. worm~~
16. dust	**41. man****	66. snake	91. year
17. earth	42. meat	67. snow	92. yellow
18. egg	43. mother	68. stand	93. full
~~19. grease~~	**44. mountain**	**69. star**	94. moon
20. father	**45. name**	70. stone	**95. brother**
21. feather	**46. narrow**	71. sun	96. cat
22. fire	47. new	72. tail	97. dance
23. fish	**48. night**	**73. thin***	**98. pig****
24. flower	**49. not**	74. tree	**99. sister**
25. good	50. old	**75. vomit**	100. work

Note: SL = sign language.
*Modern Thai SL has two signs; one is cognate with Hai Phong SL.
**Hai Phong SL has two signs; one is cognate with Modern Thai SL.

5

Lexical Comparison of Signs From American, Australian, British, and New Zealand Sign Languages

David McKee
Graeme Kennedy
Deaf Studies Research Unit
Victoria University of Wellington

New Zealand Sign Language (NZSL) has its roots in British Sign Language (BSL), brought to New Zealand by successive Deaf immigrants from the United Kingdom from the mid-19th century (Collins-Ahlgren, 1989). Australian Sign Language (Auslan) has similar colonial origins. There is no record of indigenous sign languages in New Zealand before European contact, although we may assume that wherever there were communities of Deaf people, sign languages would have evolved.

From 1880, it was government educational policy in New Zealand for Deaf children to be taught to speak and lipread in special schools for the Deaf. Signing and fingerspelling were not permitted and no teachers employed in the schools were deaf themselves. A version of signed English, the Australasian[1] Total Communication System (Jeanes & Reynolds, 1982) was introduced to New Zealand from Australia by the New Zealand Department of Education in 1979 and was used with some Deaf children until the early 1990s. However, in the intervening century, NZSL had evolved unofficially in the residential deaf schools, and in adult Deaf

---

[1]*Australasian* is the term used to refer collectively to New Zealand and Australia.

communities from the sign language transmitted by Deaf immigrants from the United Kingdom, from New Zealand children sent to Australian Deaf schools around the turn of the century, and from the influence of at least one private teacher of the Deaf who used BSL (Collins-Ahlgren, 1989). Thus, despite official educational policy, NZSL continued to have a life of its own as an unrecognized or discouraged form of manual communication with low status, even though it was the usual means of communication among the Deaf. Only since the mid 1980s in New Zealand has NZSL been accorded status as the natural and preferred language of most Deaf people.

According to anecdotal evidence of Deaf travellers and migrants, Auslan, BSL, and NZSL are mutually intelligible, although significant differences in vocabulary and style have been noted (Collins-Ahlgren, 1989; Deuchar, 1984; Kyle & Woll, 1985; Woll, 1991). For example, the extent to which fingerspelling is used, degree of "mouthing," and the rate of signing are features that appear to differ among the three language communities. American Sign Language (ASL) and BSL are considered to be mutually unintelligible although, of course, they are both used in countries where English is the main spoken language (Deuchar, 1984). It has been recorded that Deaf people used indigenous sign languages in North America before Laurent Clerc, a Deaf, French schoolteacher, was brought to America by Thomas Gallaudet to start the first public school for Deaf children. Groce (1985) noted that BSL may have reached North America during colonial times. This may account for the creolization process by which American indigenous sign languages, French Sign Language, and BSL developed into the current ASL (Woodward, 1978).

Comparison of BSL and ASL at the levels of phonology and grammar has revealed both similarities and differences (Deuchar, 1984). Deuchar considered that the structures of these two sign languages differ because of their developmental histories. Examination of the contemporary lexicons of American, Australian, British, and New Zealand sign languages enables us to compare some of their linguistic characteristics and to show how they vary.

In comparative studies of other sign languages, Woodward (1978, 1991, 1993, 1996) employed the methodology of lexicostatistics to determine the possible historical relations of language varieties through comparison of cognates in basic vocabulary (Gudschinsky, 1956). As Crowley (1992) and Lehmann (1992) pointed out, lexicostatistics is best used for determining relations across unwritten languages, and this method has been used to examine the relation between sign language varieties in countries such as Japan, Thailand, and Costa Rica, although there are some problems with using this technique (Osugi, Supalla, & Webb, 1998; Woodward, 1991).

COMPARISON OF 100 CORE CONCEPTS (MODIFIED SWADESH LIST)

This study is an initial attempt to establish how closely NZSL is related to the lexicon of ASL, Auslan, and BSL. Two techniques were used to compare the lexicons of ASL, Auslan, BSL, and NZSL. First, a list of 100 common core concepts in human languages from a set devised by Swadesh (1955), and modified by Woodward (1978) for sign language research, was used to compare systematically the ways in which these concepts are realized in ASL, Auslan, BSL, and NZSL. Woodward's modified list excluded items such as pronouns and body parts, which are represented indexically (i.e., by pointing). The list of concepts is shown in Appendix A.

The method of comparison was as follows: For a given concept, say *bad*, the bilingual (Sign-to-English) dictionaries and CD-ROMs of ASL (Sternberg, 1981), Auslan (Johnston, 1989, 1998), BSL (Brien, 1992), and NZSL (Kennedy, Arnold, Dugdale, Fahey, & Moskovitz, 1997) were consulted to see whether there was an entry for the concept. For any two of the four sign languages, the signs for a concept could be identical, completely different, or related but different. In this third category of related-but-different signs, the basis of difference could be in any one of the parameters of handshape, location, movement, or orientation of the palm. These parameters are phonemic in sign languages. Nonmanual differences such as facial characteristics of signs were not included in the comparison. However, where signs use the nondominant hand as the base hand or where a sign is part of a compound sign, these differences were noted in the analysis.

First, the signs in the three historically related sign languages (Auslan, BSL, and NZSL) for the 100 concepts were compared with each of the other languages (McKee & Kennedy, 1999). In all three sign languages, 64 signs were identical. However, when we added ASL to the comparison, the number of identical signs dropped dramatically down to 19 signs across the four languages.

TABLE 5.1
Basis of Difference in Related Signs in the Pairs of Four Languages

Auslan–BSL		Auslan–NZSL		BSL–NZSL	
movement	3	movement	2	movement	3
handshape	6	handshape	3	handshape	4
location	0	location	0	location	0
orientation	1	orientation	2	orientation	1
compound	0	compound	0	compound	0
two-handed	1	two-handed	1	two-handed	1
different base	1	different base	3	different base	1
ASL–Auslan		ASL–NZSL		ASL–BSL	
movement	1	movement	1	movement	1
handshape	3	handshape	0	handshape	1
location	0	location	0	location	0
orientation	1	orientation	0	orientation	3
compound	0	compound	0	compound	0
two-handed	1	two-handed	0	two-handed	1
different base	3	different base	2	different base	1

Note: BSL = British Sign Language; NZSL = New Zealand Sign Language; ASL = American Sign Language.

Appendix B shows the 64 concepts from the Swadesh list for which the signs were found to be identical in the three languages (Auslan, BSL and NZSL), and Appendix C shows the 19 concepts from the Swadesh list for which the signs were found to be identical in all four languages (ASL, Auslan, BSL, and NZSL).

A further 30 related-but-different signs were analyzed in terms of which parameter (handshape, location, movement, or orientation) was different between any two of the sign languages. An extra category, "other" was included for signs that differed in ways other than according to the four main parameters. For instance, the Auslan sign for *bug* required a base hand for the dominant hand to move on, whereas the NZSL sign for *bug* did not require a base hand.

Appendix D shows a list of the related-but-different signs in each pair of the four languages, and also shows which parameters account for the differences. These are summarized in Table 5.1, which shows that handshape and direction of movement are the main basis for differences between the related signs in the four sign languages.

Appendix E shows a list of those signs that are completely different for each pair of the four sign languages: Auslan–BSL (7 signs), Auslan–NZSL (12 signs), BSL–NZSL (14 signs), ASL–NZSL (73 signs), ASL–BSL (64 signs), and ASL–Auslan (65 signs).

TABLE 5.2
Analysis of Concepts From the Swadesh List Found in Pairs of Sign Languages (in percentage)

	NZSL-Auslan	NZSL-BSL	Auslan-BSL
Identical	77	69	77
Related	10	10	10
Different	12	14	7
Not found	1	7	6
	ASL-Auslan	ASL-BSL	ASL-NZSL
Identical	24	25	23
Related	8	6	3
Different	66	64	72
Not found	2	5	2

Note: NZSL = New Zealand Sign Language; BSL = British Sign Language; ASL = American Sign Language.

Table 5.2 shows the proportions of the signs that were identical, completely different, or related-but-different among the three languages. The item "Not found" means that signs were not found in one or both of the dictionaries.

The proportions of the Swadesh concepts that are realized with identical signs in pairs of the three historically linked languages (Auslan, BSL, and NZSL) range from 69% to 77%. However, when we included ASL in this comparison, the proportions of Swadesh concepts that have identical signs in pairs of languages changed greatly, indicating that ASL is much less mutually intelligible with any of the other three sign languages. The reason for the higher degree of commonality between Auslan and BSL is possibly due to historical patterns. That is, early Australian schools for the Deaf had Deaf teachers using BSL and have had a stronger tradition of sign language use than in New Zealand, where signing was completely proscribed in formal education until comparatively recently.

If we combine identical signs with related-but-different signs that differ only in one parameter (handshape, location, movement, or orientation of the palm), there is a higher degree of commonality among the languages, as shown in Table 5.3.

According to the lexicostatistical model (Crowley, 1992), if two or more languages share between 36% and 81% of their core vocabularies, they are considered to be languages of a family. If languages share more than 81% of their core vocabularies, they are considered to be dialects of a language. The lexicostatistical classification of languages is as follows:

Level of Subgrouping	*Cognate Percentage in Core Vocabularies*
Dialects of a language	81%–100%
Languages of a family	36%–81%
Families of a stock	12%–36%

It was anticipated that there would probably be a high degree of stability of the signs in the Swadesh list for three historically linked languages (Auslan, BSL, and NZSL) because these signs are mostly of high frequency. ASL is shown to be a separate language according to these criteria. However, because the Swadesh list contains only high-frequency concepts, it could provide a misleading picture of the degree of similarity between the signs used in the different linguistic communities.

Further, in using the lexicostatistical method, the authors were aware that it is by no means uncontroversial. Dixon (1997, p. 36) argued that it is not legitimate to assume that there is a distinction between a so-called core vocabulary that behaves differently from noncore vocabulary; or that the lexicon of all languages is replaced at a constant rate; or even that genetic relations can be derived from lexical studies alone. In the present study, the method was used not to model the process of language change but to provide baseline data on the extent to which the four languages shared their lexicons.

COMPARISON OF RANDOMLY SELECTED SIGNS

Because the use of a core vocabulary for comparing the lexical similarity of sign languages is not unproblematical, and because it seemed possible that it might overestimate the amount of similarity between the sign languages under investigation here, it was therefore decided to use a second

TABLE 5.3
Percentages of Swadesh List Signs That Are Cognate (Both Identical and Related Signs)

	BSL	*Auslan*	*NZSL*	*ASL*
BSL	—	87	79	31
Auslan	87	—	87	32
NZSL	79	87	—	26
ASL	31	32	26	—

Note: BSL = British Sign Language; NZSL = New Zealand Sign Language; ASL = American Sign Language.

method of comparison. Two hundred signs were randomly selected from A Dictionary of New Zealand Sign Language (Kennedy et al., 1997) and compared with the signs for corresponding concepts in ASL, Auslan, and BSL. In this comparison, NZSL signs were compared with the other three languages, but BSL, Auslan, and ASL were not compared with each other.

The method of random selection was simply to select the sign located in the top left-hand corner of every seventh page of A Dictionary of New Zealand Sign Language for the first 100 signs and then select the second 100 signs by locating each sign in the bottom right-hand corner of every seventh page of A Dictionary of New Zealand Sign Language. If that sign had already been included in the Swadesh inventory or there was no gloss for that sign in the dictionaries of ASL, BSL, or Auslan, then the next adjacent sign was selected. English glosses for these 200 randomly selected signs are given in Appendix F.

We attempted to match the gloss of each NZSL sign with similar glosses of ASL, Auslan, and BSL by referring to the dictionaries and CD-ROMs of these sign languages. Where there were several signs with similar glosses, we looked at each gloss to determine whether that sign was identical or related to the corresponding NZSL sign. If there was one different parameter between two corresponding signs, we listed them as "related-but-different." If two signs differed in more than one parameter, they were rated as "different." The results of the analysis are contained in Appendix G for NZSL–Auslan, Appendix H for NZSL–BSL, and Appendix I for NZSL–ASL.

Table 5.4 shows a summary of the comparison of the randomly selected NZSL signs with ASL, BSL, and Auslan, and Table 5.5 shows the percentages of cognates (both identical and related) between NZSL and the three sign languages.

When compared with the Swadesh inventory of core concepts in Appendices A and B, it can be seen that for randomly selected concepts,

TABLE 5.4
Analysis of Randomly Selected NZSL Signs That Are Cognate With ASL, Auslan, and BSL

NZSL	ASL		Auslan		BSL	
Identical	35	17.5%	90	45.0%	78	39.0%
Related	32	16.0%	41	20.5%	47	23.5%
Different	133	66.5%	69	34.5%	75	37.5%

Note: NZSL = New Zealand Sign Language; ASL = American Sign Language; BSL = British Sign Language.

TABLE 5.5

Percentages of Randomly Selected NZSL Signs (Identical And Related Signs)
That Are Cognate With the Three Sign Languages (ASL, Auslan, And BSL)

	BSL	Auslan	ASL
NZSL	62.5	65.5	33.5

Note: NZSL = New Zealand Sign Language; BSL = British Sign Language; ASL = American Sign
Language.

TABLE 5.6

Basis of Difference in Signs Related to NZSL From ASL, Auslan, and BSL (Number of Instances)

ASL		Auslan		BSL	
Handshape	13	Handshape	15	Handshape	23
Movement	5	Movement	10	Movement	10
Location	1	Location	2	Location	2
Orientation	5	Orientation	5	Orientation	5
Compound	4	Compound	4	Compound	3
Two-handed	3	Two-handed	4	Two-handed	1
Different base	1	Different base	1	Different base	3

Note: NZSL = New Zealand Sign Language; BSL = British Sign Language; ASL = American Sign
Language.

the rate of commonality with Auslan and BSL drops dramatically from the
range of 69%–77% to 39%–45% for identical signs and from the range of
79%–87% to 62.5%–65.5% for a combination of both identical and
related signs. For ASL, the rate of commonality is far less than for the first
three languages. The rate of commonality with NZSL signs is only 17.5%
if only identical signs are included, or 33.5% if both identical and related
signs are included.

A slightly higher rate of commonality between NZSL and Auslan than
between NZSL and BSL is probably due to the geographical proximity of
New Zealand and Australia and to the introduction of Australasian Signed
English into New Zealand schools for the deaf in 1979. The Australasian
signs have been used by teachers and children up to the early 1990s and
many young Deaf people have incorporated some of these Signed English
signs into their NZSL.

Appendices J through L show which parameters account for the differences in each pair of the four languages. The basis of the differences is
summarized in Table 5.6, which shows only those signs we have termed
related-but-different where there were partial differences among the signs
for the randomly selected concepts. The analysis shows that where a sign

is related-but-different in any two of the sign languages, the basis of the difference is most likely to be handshape, followed by direction of movement, with the other parameters about equally represented.

From our list of 200 randomly selected signs from NZSL, there are 62 identical signs across three languages—Auslan, BSL, and NZSL (Appendix M) but only 27 identical signs across all four languages including ASL (Appendix N). Some of the signs that are identical across three or four of the sign language varieties we examined are high frequency concepts (e.g., *we*, *hello*, *speak*). Others are less frequent (e.g., *card*, *nausea*, *parallel*). It is not clear, therefore, whether there is a particular factor that determines or influences identicalness for the signs for particular concepts across several varieties. Our analysis has enabled us to draw certain tentative conclusions about the extent to which the four sign languages share signs in common.

DISCUSSION

When we compare how certain core concepts (as identified by Swadesh) are expressed in the three British-based sign language varieties, it is clear that between 79% and 87% of the concepts have identical or related signs to express those concepts, depending on which pairs of sign languages are compared. It seems that NZSL and BSL have drifted further apart than NZSL and Auslan or BSL and Auslan.

However, when we include ASL in the comparison, between 26% and 32% of the concepts can be shown to have identical or related signs in ASL and the other three sign languages. ASL is more distant from NZSL than from Auslan and BSL, although lexical borrowing from ASL into NZSL (and probably into Auslan and BSL) that has occurred over the last decade has possibly made the strength of the relation even stronger than it would have been in a slightly earlier historical period.

If we move away from core concepts, a comparison of how 200 randomly selected concepts are expressed shows that only between 39% and 62.5% of the signs of NZSL are identical or similar to the BSL signs made for the same concepts. NZSL and Auslan share between 45% and 65.5% of signs, depending on whether we include only identical signs or both identical and similar signs. Thus, the two daughter languages, NZSL and Auslan, are closer to each other than NZSL is to BSL. However, only between 17.5% and 33.5% of the signs of NZSL are identical or similar to the ASL signs. Auslan and BSL signs are similarly distant from ASL.

On the basis of this study, it seems that when sign languages diverge, the drift to what have become related-but-different signs can be based on handshape, movement, orientation of the palm, or on other factors such as whether the sign is made with one or two hands. Changes in handshape are the most frequent way in which signs differ. Changes in the location and orientation are comparatively rare.

Whereas the distance between ASL and the other languages clearly shows that ASL has different origins, it is not easy to decide whether NZSL can claim the status of a separate language or whether it is, like Auslan, a dialect of BSL. As we noted, on lexicostatistical grounds (Crowley, 1992), 36% to 81% commonality of signs in two languages suggests that the languages belong to the same family. Above 81%, they are dialects of the same language. It is clear, therefore, that the evidence relating to Swadesh's core concepts summarized in Table 5.3 shows that the three varieties—Auslan, BSL, and NZSL—are dialects of the same language. On grounds of mutual intelligibility, the anecdotal evidence from the Deaf community also supports this position. However, using the randomly selected NZSL signs as the basis for comparison, the three sign languages are shown to have less in common. On the evidence of the analysis of randomly selected NZSL signs, we are obliged to suggest that the speech varieties share between 62.5% and 66% of their lexicon and that some significant divergence has occurred within the family of languages.

ASL has less mutual intelligibility with any of the other three sign languages than they do with each other. This is consistent with the fact that ASL is a separate language from Auslan, BSL, and NZSL. Further research is needed to determine why particular concepts have common signs across all four sign languages, whether universal classifiers are involved, and how the languages compare syntactically, before a definite answer can be given to the question of how close ASL, Auslan, BSL, and NZSL are to each other.

Establishing the degree of similarity between NZSL, BSL, and Auslan has implications for the use of sign language in professional services and the education of Deaf people in New Zealand. For example, New Zealand continues to have a shortage of sign language interpreters and other professionals specializing in working with Deaf people. Over the past few years, an increasing number of interpreters have been recruited from the United Kingdom and Australia with the assumption that fluency in BSL or Auslan is completely transferable to interpreting in the New Zealand Deaf community. Sign language teaching and the provision of educational resources for Deaf children are other areas where lexical borrowing from

Auslan and BSL has at times occurred. More accurate information about the degree of difference or transferability between the three language communities can contribute to a more informed context for such decisions, by giving a more accurate picture about the actual extent of overlap between the sign language varieties.

REFERENCES

Brien, D. (Ed.). (1992). *Dictionary of British Sign Language/English.* London: Faber & Faber

Collins-Ahlgren, M. (1989). *Aspects of New Zealand Sign Language.* Unpublished doctoral dissertation, Victoria University of Wellington, New Zealand.

Crowley, T. (1992). *An introduction to historical linguistics.* Oxford, UK: Oxford University Press.

Deuchar, M. (1984). *British Sign Language.* London: Routledge & Kegan Paul.

Dixon, R. M. W. (1997). *The rise and fall of languages.* Cambridge, UK: Cambridge University Press.

Groce, N. G. (1985). *Everyone here spoke sign language: Hereditary deafness on Martha's Vineyard.* Cambridge, MA: Harvard University Press.

Gudschinsky, S. (1956). The ABCs of lexicostatistics (glottochronology). *Word, 12:* 175–210.

Jeanes, R. C., & Reynolds, B. E. (Eds.). (1982). *Dictionary of Australasian signs for communication with the deaf.* Melbourne: Victorian School for Deaf Children.

Johnston, T. (1989). *Auslan dictionary: A dictionary of the sign language of the Australian deaf community.* Maryborough, Victoria: Australian Print Group.

Johnston, T. (Ed.). (1998). *Signs of Australia on CD-ROM: A dictionary of Auslan.* Sydney, Australia: Royal Institute for Deaf and Blind Children.

Kennedy, G., Arnold, R., Dugdale, P., Fahey, S., & Moskovitz, D. (Eds.). (1997). *A dictionary of New Zealand Sign Language.* Auckland: Auckland University Press with Bridget Williams Books.

Kyle, J. G., & Woll, B. (1985). *Sign language: The study of deaf people and their language.* Cambridge, UK: Cambridge University Press.

Lehmann, W. P. (1992). *Historical linguistics: An introduction.* New York: Routledge.

McKee, D., & Kennedy G. (1999). *Lexical comparison of signs from Auslan, British Sign Language, and New Zealand Sign Language.* In G. Kennedy (Ed.), *New Zealand Sign Language: Distribution, origins, reference* (pp. 59–74). Deaf Studies Research Unit, Occasional Publication No. 2, Victoria University of Wellington.

Osugi, Y., Supalla, T., & Webb, R. (1998). *The use of word lists to identify distinctive gestural systems on Amami Island.* Unpublished manuscript, University of Rochester, Sign Language Research Center.

Sternberg, M. L. A. (1981). *American Sign Language: A comprehensive dictionary.* New York: Harper & Row.

Swadesh, M. (1955). Toward greater accuracy in lexicostatistic dating. *International Journal of American Linguistics, 21,* 121–137.

Woll, B. (1991). Historical and comparative aspects of British Sign Language. In S. Gregory & G. M. Hartley (Eds.), *Constructing deafness* (pp. 188–191). London: Printer Publishers.

Woodward, J. (1978). Historical bases of American Sign Language. In P. Siple (Ed.), *Understanding language through sign language research* (pp. 333–348). New York: Academic Press.

Woodward, J. (1991). Sign language varieties in Costa Rica. *Sign Language Studies, 73,* 329–346.

Woodward, J. (1993). The relationship of sign language varieties in India, Pakistan, and Nepal. *Sign Language Studies, 78,* 15–22.

Woodward, J. (1996). Modern Standard Thai Sign Language: Influence from American Sign Language and its relationship to original Thai Sign Language varieties. *Sign Language Studies, 92,* 227–252.

APPENDIX A
SWADESH VOCABULARY LIST MODIFIED
FOR COMPARISON OF SIGN LANGUAGES

ALL	NAME
ANIMAL	NARROW
BAD	NEW
BECAUSE	NIGHT
BIRD	NOT
BLACK	OLD
BLOOD	OTHER
BORING	PERSON
BROTHER	PIG
BUG	PLAY
CAT	RAIN
CHILD	RED
CORRECT	RIVER
COUNT	SALT
DANCE	SEA
DAY	SHARP
DIE	SHORT (TIME)
DIRTY	SING
DOG	SISTER
DRY	SIT
DUST	SMOOTH
EARTH	SNAKE
EGG	SNOW
FATHER	STAND
FEATHER	STAR
FIRE	STONE
FISH	STRING
FLOWER	SUN
FULL	TAIL
GOOD	THIN
GRASS	TREE
GREASE	VOMIT
GREEN	WARM
HEAVY	WATER
HOW	WET
HUSBAND	WHAT
ICE	WHEN
IF	WHERE
KILL	WHITE
LAUGH	WHO
LEAF	WIDE
LIE	WIFE
LIVE	WIND
LONG	WITH
LOOK FOR	WOMAN
MAN	WOOD
MEAT	WORK
MOON	WORM
MOTHER	YEAR
MOUNTAIN	YELLOW

APPENDIX B
SIXTY-FOUR CONCEPTS FROM THE SWADESH LIST THAT HAVE IDENTICAL SIGNS ACROSS THREE SIGN LANGUAGES (AUSLAN, BSL, AND NZSL)

ALL	FATHER	NAME	SING
ANIMAL	FISH	NARROW	SISTER
BAD	FULL	NEW	SNAKE
BIRD	GOOD	NIGHT	STAND
BLACK	GREEN	NOT	SUN
BORING	HEAVY	OLD	WET
BROTHER	HUSBAND	OTHER	WHAT
CAT	ICE	PERSON	WHEN
CHILD	LAUGH	PIG	WHERE
DANCE	LIE	PLAY	WHO
DAY	LONG	RAIN	WIDE
DIE	MAN	RED	WIFE
DIRTY	MEAT	RIGHT	WIND
DOG	MOON	SALT	WORK
DRY	MOTHER	SEA	WORM
EARTH	MOUNTAIN	SHORT (TIME)	YEAR

APPENDIX C
NINETEEN CONCEPTS FROM THE SWADESH LIST THAT HAVE IDENTICAL SIGNS ACROSS FOUR SIGN LANGUAGES (ASL, AUSLAN, BSL, AND NZSL)

BAD	FISH	RAIN	WATER
BIRD	GOOD	RED	WET
CAT	HEAVY	SNAKE	WHERE
CHILD	ICE	STAND	WIDE
DOG	NARROW	SUN	

APPENDIX D
CONCEPTS FROM THE SWADESH LIST THAT HAVE RELATED-BUT-DIFFERENT SIGNS IN PAIRS OF LANGUAGES, WITH THE BASIS OF DIFFERENCE

Auslan & BSL	Dez (Handshape)	Tab (Location)	Sig (Movement)	Ori (Orientation)	Other
EGG			■		
GRASS			■		Different weak hand
LOOK FOR	■				Two-handed in BSL
KILL			■		
LIVE	■				
RIVER	■				
SIT	■				
TAIL	■				
THIN				■	
WOOD	■				

Auslan & NZSL	Dez (Handshape)	Tab (Location)	Sig (Movement)	Ori (Orientation)	Other
BUG					Auslan uses base hand
COUNT			■		
FIRE				■	
FLOWER					Two-handed in Auslan
GRASS			■		Different weak hand
LIVE	■				
STAR	■				
TREE					Auslan uses base hand
WITH	■				
WOMAN				■	

BSL & NZSL	Dez (Handshape)	Tab (Location)	Sig (Movement)	Ori (Orientation)	Other
BUG					BSL uses base hand
COUNT			■		
EGG	■				
FIRE				■	
FLOWER			■		
LOOK FOR	■				Two-handed in BSL
KILL	■				
SMOOTH			■		
SNOW	■				
WATER					Sign for *drink*

ASL & Auslan	Dez (Handshape)	Tab (Location)	Sig (Movement)	Ori (Orientation)	Other
DANCE					Different weak hand
FIRE				■	Different weak hand
FLOWER	■				
NEW			■		
SEA					ASL compound & two-handed
SIT	■				
WOOD	■				
WORM					Different weak hand

ASL & NZSL	Dez (Handshape)	Tab (Location)	Sig (Movement)	Ori (Orientation)	Other
DANCE					Different weak hand
SEA			■		
WORM					Different weak hand

ASL & BSL	Dez (Handshape)	Tab (Location)	Sig (Movement)	Ori (Orientation)	Other
BLOOD				■	
DANCE				■	Different weak hand
FIRE				■	
NEW			■		
RIVER	■				
SEA					ASL compound & two-handed

APPENDIX E
CONCEPTS FROM THE SWADESH LIST
WHICH HAVE DIFFERENT SIGNS IN PAIRS
OF SIGN LANGUAGES

Auslan–BSL

HOW
LEAF
STAR
WARM
WHITE
WOMAN
YELLOW

Auslan–NZSL

EGG
GREASE
IF
LEAF
RIVER
SHARP
SNOW
STONE
TAIL
THIN
VOMIT
WOOD

BSL–NZSL

BECAUSE
BLOOD
GRASS
HOW
RIVER
SHARP
STAR
STONE
THIN
WARM
WHITE
WOMAN
WOOD
YELLOW

ASL–NZSL

ALL	IF	SISTER
ANIMAL	KILL	SIT
BECAUSE	LAUGH	SMOOTH
BLACK	LEAF	SNOW
BLOOD	LIE	STAR
BORING	LIVE	STONE
BROTHER	LONG	STRING
BUG	LOOK FOR	TAIL
COUNT	MAN	THIN
DAY	MEAT	VOMIT
DIE	MOON	WARM
DIRTY	MOTHER	WHAT
DRY	MOUNTAIN	WHEN
DUST	NAME	WHITE
EARTH	NIGHT	WHO
EGG	OLD	WIFE
FAT/GREASE	OTHER	WIND
FATHER	PERSON	WITH
FEATHER	PIG	WOMAN
FLOWER	PLAY	WOOD
FULL	SALT	WORK
GRASS	SEA	YEAR
GREEN	SHARP	YELLOW
HOW	SHORT(TIME)	
HUSBAND	SING	

ASL–BSL

ALL	HUSBAND	SISTER
ANIMAL	KILL	SIT
BECAUSE	LEAF	SMOOTH
BLACK	LIE	STAR
BROTHER	LIVE	STONE
BUG	LOOK FOR	STRING
CORRECT	MAN	TAIL
COUNT	MEAT	THIN
DAY	MOON	VOMIT
DIE	MOTHER	WARM
DIRTY	MOUNTAIN	WHAT
DRY	NAME	WHEN
DULL/BORING	NIGHT	WHITE
EARTH	OLD	WHO
EGG	OTHER	WIFE
FAT/GREASE	PERSON	WIND
FATHER	PIG	WOMAN
FLOWER	PLAY	WORK
FULL	SALT	YEAR
GRASS	SHARP	YELLOW
GREEN	SHORT(TIME)	
HOW	SING	

ASL–Auslan

ALL	HOW	SALT
ANIMAL	HUSBAND	SHARP
BECAUSE	IF	SHORT(TIME)
BLACK	KILL	SING
BLOOD	LAUGH	SISTER
BORING	LEAF	SMOOTH
BROTHER	LIE	STRING
BUG	LIVE	TAIL
COUNT	LOOK FOR	VOMIT
DAY	MAN	WARM
DIE	MEAT	WATER
DIRTY	MOON	WHAT
DRY	MOTHER	WHEN
DUST	MOUNTAIN	WHITE
EARTH	NAME	WHO
EGG	NIGHT	WIFE
FAT/GREASE	OLD	WITH
FATHER	OTHER	WOMAN
FEATHER	PERSON	WORK
FULL	PIG	YEAR
GRASS	PLAY	YELLOW
GREEN	RIGHT	

APPENDIX F
200 RANDOMLY SELECTED NZSL SIGNS
FOR COMPARISON WITH ASL,
AUSLAN, AND BSL

ABSENT	DEBATE	ITALY	SELL
ACCEPT	DELICIOUS	JOB	SHALLOW
ADVANCE	DEPRESSED	JOKE	SHARE
AGE	DESIRE	KEEN	SLOW DOWN
AIR	DIVE	KISS	SMALL
ALWAYS	DOUBTFUL	LATER	SMELL
AMERICA	DREAM	LEADER	SOIL
ANGRY	DRESS	LEISURE	SOUR
APPEAR	DROUGHT	LETTER	SOW
APPOINTMENT	DUCK	LIFT	SPADE
APRON	EMPTY	LIPREAD	SPEAK
ARRIVE	EQUAL	MAXIMUM	SPECIAL
ATTITUDE	EVERY	MEAN	SQUASH
AUSTRALIA	EXCHANGE	MEDICINE	STILL
BACK	EXCITED	MEET	STRONG
BAG	EXPECT	MISSING	STUDENT
BALD	FACE	MIX	SUIT
BALL	FAITH	MONTH	SUNDAY
BANK	FAMILY	MORNING	SUPPOSED TO
BAPTIZE	FAMOUS	MOST	SUSPECT
BAWL	FAST	NAUSEA	TAKE AN OATH
BEARD	FIGURE OUT	NERVOUS	TEAR
BECAUSE	FISH	NERVOUS	TEDDYBEAR
BEE	FLAT	NICE	THEMSELVES
BEFORE	FLOUR	NUN	TICKET
BIG	FOOL	NURSE	TIME
BLUE	FORCE	OBSERVE	TOILET
BONE	FORGET	OPEN	TOOTHACHE
BORN	FRIEND	ORANGE	TOOTHBRUSH
BOSS	GLORY	OTHER	TOUCH
BRAIN	GOODBYE	OVERTAKE	TREASURER
BRANCH	GRANDMOTHER	PARALLEL	UNCLE
BRAVE	GRATEFUL	PERHAPS	USUAL
BROOM	HALLELUJAH	POSSIBLE	VIDEOCAMERA
BUSY	HAPPY	PROMISE	VIDEOTAPE
CARD	HARD	PROTECT	VIP
CHECK OFF	HEAR	PROTEST	WALL
CHIPS	HEARTBEAT	PROTESTANT	WASHING MACHINE
CLEVER	HELL	PUNISH	WE
CLIMB	HELLO	QUEEN	WEAK
COLLAPSE	HERE	RECEPTIONIST	WHAT A PITY
COLLISION	HOSPITAL	RECORD	WORD
COME	HOUSE	REFRIGERATOR	WORSE
CONFERENCE	HOW MUCH	RELAX	WRESTLING
CONFUSED	HUNDRED	REPETITIVE	
COPY	IGNORE	ROAD	
CORNFLAKES	INDEPENDENT	RUDE	
COW	INDIA	SALT	
CRAWL	INFLUENCE	SAME	
CUPBOARD	INFORMATION	SAUSAGE	
CUT	INVOLVE	SAVE	
DART	ISRAEL	SCHOOL	

APPENDIX G
COMPARISON OF RANDOMLY SELECTED NZSL SIGNS WITH AUSLAN

Identical (90)

ABSENT	DELICIOUS	INDIA	OVERTAKE	SOUR
ACCEPT	DRESS	JOKE	PARALLEL	SPADE
ALWAYS	DROUGHT	KISS	POSSIBLE	SPEAK
ARRIVE	EVERY	LEISURE	PROMISE	SPECIAL
AUSTRALIA	EXCITED	LIPREAD	PROTEST	SQUASH
BAG	FACE	MEAN	PUNISH	STRONG
BAWL	FAMILY	MEET	QUEEN	SUNDAY
BEARD	FAST	MISSING	RECEPTIONIST	TAKE AN OATH
BIG	FISH	MIX	RECORD	TEAR
BLUE	FLAT	MONTH	REFRIGERATOR	TICKET
BRAIN	FORGET	MOST	REPETITIVE	TIME
CARD	FRIEND	NAUSEA	SAME	TOILET
CHIPS	HEAR	NERVOUS	SAVE	TOOTHBRUSH
COME	HELL	NUN	SCHOOL	TOUCH
COPY	HELLO	NURSE	SHALLOW	UNCLE
CUPBOARD	HERE	OPEN	SHARE	WALL
CUT	HOUSE	ORANGE	SMALL	WE
DEBATE	HUNDRED	OTHER	SOIL	WORSE

Related (41)

AGE	COLLAPSE	GRATEFUL	SELL
AIR	COLLISION	HAPPY	SUIT
APRON	COW	HARD	SUSPECT
BACK	DART	IGNORE	THEMSELVES
BALD	DESIRE	INDEPENDENT	VIDEOCAMERA
BANK	DOUBTFUL	INVOLVE	VIDEOTAPE
BAPTIZE	DREAM	ITALY	WASHING
BEFORE	DUCK	LATER	MACHINE
BOSS	EXCHANGE	NERVOUS	WHAT A PITY
BROOM	FAITH	NICE	
CLIMB	FOOL	SAUSAGE	

Different (69)

ADVANCE	CORNFLAKES	INFLUENCE	SALT
AMERICA	CRAWL	INFORMATION	SLOW DOWN
ANGRY	DEPRESSED	ISRAEL	SMELL
APPEAR	DIVE	JOB	SOW
APPOINTMENT	EMPTY	KEEN	STILL
ATTITUDE	EQUAL	LEADER	STUDENT
BALL	EXPECT	LETTER	SUPPOSED TO
BECAUSE	FAMOUS	LIFT	TEDDYBEAR
BEE	FIGURE OUT	MAXIMUM	TOOTHACHE
BONE	FLOUR	MEDICINE	TREASURER
BORN	FORCE	MORNING	USUAL
BRANCH	GLORY	OBSERVE	VIP
BRAVE	GOODBYE	PERHAPS	WEAK
BUSY	GRANDMOTHER	PROTECT	WORD
CHECK OFF	HALLELUJAH	PROTESTANT	WRESTLING
CLEVER	HEARTBEAT	RELAX	
CONFERENCE	HOSPITAL	ROAD	
CONFUSED	HOW MUCH	RUDE	

APPENDIX H
COMPARISON OF RANDOMLY SELECTED
NZSL SIGNS WITH BSL

Identical (80)

ARRIVE	DEBATE	MONTH	SHALLOW
BAG	DEPRESSED	MOST	SHARE
ABSENT	DRESS	NAUSEA	SLOW DOWN
ACCEPT	EXCITED	NERVOUS	SMALL
AGE	FACE	NICE	SPADE
BALL	FISH	NUN	SPEAK
BANK	FLAT	ORANGE	SPECIAL
BAPTIZE	FOOL	PARALLEL	SQUASH
BAWL	FORGET	POSSIBLE	STRONG
BEARD	FRIEND	PROTEST	SUIT
BIG	HARD	PROTESTANT	SUNDAY
BLUE	HEAR	PUNISH	TAKE AN OATH
BOSS	HELLO	QUEEN	TICKET
BRAIN	HERE	RECEPTIONIST	TOILET
CARD	KISS	RECORD	TOOTHBRUSH
CHECK OFF	LATER	REFRIGERATOR	WE
COME	LEISURE	RELAX	WHAT A PITY
COPY	LIPREAD	REPETITIVE	WORSE
CUT	MISSING	SAME	
DART	MIX	SAVE	

Related (47)

AIR	DESIRE	HOUSE	OVERTAKE
APPEAR	DOUBTFUL	HUNDRED	SAUSAGE
APRON	DREAM	IGNORE	SOIL
ATTITUDE	DROUGHT	INDEPENDENT	SUSPECT
BACK	DUCK	INDIA	TEAR
BEFORE	EQUAL	INFLUENCE	TIME
BROOM	FAMILY	INVOLVE	TOOTHACHE
CLIMB	FAST	LETTER	TOUCH
COLLAPSE	GOODBYE	MEET	VIDEOCAMERA
COLLISION	GRATEFUL	NERVOUS	VIDEOTAPE
COW	HEARTBEAT	OPEN	WALL
CRAWL	HOSPITAL	OTHER	

Different (75)

ADVANCE	FORCE	CORNFLAKES	MEAN
ALWAYS	HAPPY	CUPBOARD	MORNING
APPOINTMENT	HOW MUCH	DELICIOUS	PERHAPS
AUSTRALIA	INFORMATION	DIVE	PROMISE
BALD	LEADER	EMPTY	ROAD
BECAUSE	MEDICINE	EXPECT	RUDE
BONE	NURSE	FAITH	SALT
BORN	OBSERVE	FIGURE OUT	SCHOOL
BRANCH	PROTECT	GLORY	SELL
BRAVE	SOUR	GRANDMOTHER	SMELL
BUSY	SOW	HALLELUJAH	STUDENT
CHIPS	STILL	HELL	SUPPOSED TO
CLEVER	USUAL	ISRAEL	TEDDYBEAR
CONFERENCE	WEAK	ITALY	THEMSELVES
CONFUSED	WORD	JOB	TREASURER
EVERY	WRESTLING	JOKE	UNCLE
EXCHANGE	AMERICA	KEEN	VIP
FAMOUS	ANGRY	LIFT	WASHING
FLOUR	BEE	MAXIMUM	MACHINE

APPENDIX I
COMPARISON OF RANDOMLY SELECTED
NZSL SIGNS WITH ASL

Identical (35)

ACCEPT	DART	LIPREAD	SOIL
BAG	DIVE	MIX	SPADE
BAWL	FACE	NAUSEA	SPEAK
BEARD	FISH	NERVOUS	SQUASH
CARD	FLAT	NUN	STRONG
CHECK OFF	HEAR	ORANGE	VIDEOCAMERA
CLIMB	HELLO	PARALLEL	VIDEOTAPE
COME	HOUSE	SAME	WE
CUT	KISS	SMALL	

Related (32)

AIR	DOUBTFUL	INFLUENCE	SHARE
ARRIVE	DRESS	INVOLVE	SMELL
BACK	DUCK	JOB	TEAR
BIG	EQUAL	LEISURE	TOOTHBRUSH
BRAIN	FAMILY	LETTER	WASHING
BROOM	GOODBYE	NERVOUS	MACHINE
COLLISION	GRATEFUL	OVERTAKE	
COPY	HEARTBEAT	SAUSAGE	
CRAWL	INDIA	SHALLOW	

70

Different (133)

ABSENT	RECORD	INFORMATION	SAVE
ADVANCE	CUPBOARD	ISRAEL	SCHOOL
AGE	PERHAPS	ITALY	SELL
ALWAYS	DEBATE	JOKES	SLOW DOWN
AMERICA	DELICIOUS	KEEN	SOUR
ANGRY	DEPRESSED	LATER	SOW
APPEAR	DREAM	LEADER	SPECIAL
APPOINTMENT	DROUGHT	LIFT	STILL
APRON	EMPTY	MAXIMUM	STUDENT
ATTITUDE	EVERY	MEAN	SUIT
AUSTRALIA	EXCHANGE	MEDICINE	SUNDAY
BALD	EXCITED	MEET	SUPPOSED TO
BALL	EXPECT	MISSING	SUSPECT
BANK	FAITH	MONTH	TAKE AN OATH
BAPTIZE	FAMOUS	MORNING	TEDDYBEAR
BECAUSE	FAST	MOST	THEMSELVES
BEE	FIGURE OUT	NICE	TICKET
BEFORE	FLOUR	NURSE	TIME
BLUE	FOOL	OBSERVE	TOILET
BONE	FORCE	OPEN	TOOTHACHE
BORN	FORGET	OTHER	TOUCH
BOSS	FRIEND	POSSIBLE	TREASURER
BRANCH	GLORY	PROMISE	UNCLE
BRAVE	GRANDMOTHER	PROTECT	USUAL
BUSY	HALLELUJAH	PROTEST	VIP
REFRIGERATOR	HAPPY	PROTESTANT	WALL
CHIPS	HARD	PUNISH	WHAT A PITY
CLEVER	HELL	QUEEN	WEAK
COLLAPSE	HERE	RECEPTIONIST	WORD
CONFERENCE	HOSPITAL	RELAX	WORSE
CONFUSED	HOW MUCH	REPETITIVE	WRESTLING
CORNFLAKES	HUNDRED	ROAD	
COW	IGNORE	RUDE	
DESIRE	INDEPENDENT	SALT	

BASIS OF DIFFERENCE BETWEEN NZSL AND AUSLAN SIGNS THAT ARE RELATED BUT DIFFERENT

Sign	H.S.	Loc	Mov	Ori	Other
AGE			■		
AIR			■		
APRON	■				
BACK		■			
BALD	■				
BANK	■				Auslan base hand different
BAPTIZE	■				
BEFORE	■				
BOSS	■				
BROOM				■	
CLIMB	■				
COLLAPSE		■			
COLLISON	■				
COW	■				
DART	■				
DESIRE			■		
DOUBTFUL					NZSL compound
DREAM	■				
DUCK	■				
EXCHANGE			■		
FAITH	■				
FOOL			■		
GRATEFUL					NZSL compound
HAPPY					Auslan two-handed
HARD			■		
IGNORE				■	
INDEPENDENT					Auslan compound 'self'
INVOLVE			■		
ITALY					NZSL compound
LATER					Auslan uses base hand
NERVOUS				■	
NICE			■		NZSL gloss-'lovely'
SAUSAGE	■				
SELL				■	
SUIT					Auslan one-handed
SUSPECT	■				
THEMSELVES	■				
VIDEOCAMERA				■	Auslan uses base hand
VIDEOTAPE				■	
WASHING MACHINE					Auslan two-handed
WHAT A PITY					Auslan two-handed

APPENDIX K
BASIS OF DIFFERENCE BETWEEN NZSL AND BSL SIGNS THAT ARE RELATED BUT DIFFERENT

Sign	H.S.	Loc	Mov	Ori	Other
AIR					two-handed in BSL
APPEAR			■		
APRON	■				
ATTITUDE	■				
BACK		■			
BEFORE	■				
BROOM				■	
CLIMB	■				
COLLAPSE				■	
COLLISON	■				
COW	■				
CRAWL	■				
DESIRE			■		
DOUBTFUL					NZSL compound
DRAW/EVEN			■		
DREAM	■				
DROUGHT			■		
DUCK	■				
FAMILY			■		
FAST			■		
GOODBYE			■		
GRATEFUL					NZSL compound
HEARTBEAT	■				
HOSPITAL	■				
HOUSE	■				
HUNDRED	■				
IGNORE				■	
INDEPENDENT			■		
INDIA	■				
INFLUENCE					Base hand (NZSL both hands symmetrical)
INVOLVE			■		
LETTER					BSL compound
MEET	■				
NERVOUS			■		
OPEN		■			
OTHER	■				
OVERTAKE	■				
SAUSAGE	■				
SOIL			■		
SUSPECT	■				
TEAR	■				
TIME	■				
TOOTHACHE	■				
TOUCH					BSL uses base hand
VIDEOCAMERA			■		BSL two-handed
VIDEOTAPE	■				Different base hand
WALL			■		

APPENDIX L
BASIS OF DIFFERENCE BETWEEN NZSL AND ASL SIGNS THAT ARE RELATED BUT DIFFERENT

Sign	H.S.	Loc	Mov	Ori	Other
AIR					ASL two-handed
ARRIVE				■	
BACK		■			
BIG	■				
BRAIN	■				
BROOM				■	
COLLISON	■				
COPY					ASL two-handed
CRAWL	■				
DOUBTFUL	■				NZSL compound
DRAW/EVEN			■		
DRESS				■	
DUCK	■				
FAMILY	■				
GOODBYE			■		
GRATEFUL					NZSL two-handed
HEARTBEAT	■				
INDIA	■				
INFLUENCE					Different base hand
INVOLVE			■		
JOB				■	
LEISURE			■		
LETTER					ASL compound
NERVOUS				■	
OVERTAKE	■				
SAUSAGE			■		
SHALLOW					ASL compound
SHARE			■		
SMELL	■				
TEAR	■				
TOOTHBRUSH	■				
WASHING MACHINE					ASL two-handed

APPENDIX M
IDENTICAL SIGNS ACROSS THREE SIGN LANGUAGES (AUSLAN, BSL AND NZSL)

ABSENT
ACCEPT
ARRIVE
BAG
BEARD
BEG
BLUE
BRAIN
CARD
COME
COPY
CRY
CUT
DEBATE
DRESS
EXCITED
FACE
FISH
FLAT
FORGET
FRIEND

HEAR
HELLO
HERE
KISS
LEISURE
LIPREAD
MISSING
MIX
MONTH
MOST
NAUSEA
NERVOUS
NERVOUS
NUN
ORANGE
PARALLEL
POSSIBLE
PROTEST
PUNISH
QUEEN
RECEPTIONIST

RECORD
REFRIGERATOR
REPETITIVE
SAME
SAVE
SHALLOW
SHARE
SMALL
SPADE
SPEAK
SPECIAL
SQUASH
STRONG
SUNDAY
TAKE AN OATH
TICKET
TOILET
TOOTHBRUSH
WE
WORSE

APPENDIX N
IDENTICAL SIGNS ACROSS FOUR SIGN LANGUAGES
(ASL, AUSLAN, BSL, AND NZSL)

ACCEPT

BAG

BEARD

CARD

COME

CRY

CUT

FACE

FISH

FLAT

HEAR

HELLO

KISS

LIPREAD

MIX

NAUSEA

NERVOUS

NUN

ORANGE

PARALLEL

SAME

SMALL

SPADE

SPEAK

SQUASH

STRONG

WE

6

Origins of the American Deaf-World: Assimilating and Differentiating Societies and Their Relation to Genetic Patterning

Harlan Lane
Northeastern University

Richard C. Pillard
Boston University School of Medicine

Mary French
Aurora Technologies

The Deaf-World in the United States has major roots in a triangle of New England Deaf communities that flourished early in the past century: Henniker, New Hampshire; Martha's Vineyard, Massachusetts; and Sandy River Valley, Maine. The social fabric of these communities differed, a reflection of language and marriage practices that were underpinned, we hypothesize, by differences in genetic patterning. To evaluate that hypothesis, this chapter uses local records and newspapers, genealogies, the silent press, Edward Fay's (1898) census of Deaf marriages, and Alexander Graham Bell's (1888) notebooks to illuminate the Henniker Deaf community for the first time, and it builds on prior work concerning the Vineyard community.

HENNIKER, NEW HAMPSHIRE

The first great American Deaf leader was Thomas Brown (1804–1886), who was born in Henniker, New Hampshire, 13 years before the American Asylum for the Deaf and Dumb opened in Hartford, Connecticut, and who died in Henniker 6 years after the Congress of Milan. Our story begins with his.

Thomas Brown's grandfather, also named Thomas, lived in Stow, Massachusetts, with his wife, eight daughters, and a son, Nahum—the first, as far as anyone knew, Deaf-mute in the family (see Fig. 6.1[1]). The senior Thomas Brown was the grandson of Jabez Brown, who emigrated from England and settled in Concord, Massachusetts. Jabez's son, Joseph, moved to Stow, where his son, Thomas Brown Sr., was born and raised, took up the trade of blacksmith and, in 1763, married Persis Gibson.

In 1785, Thomas Brown Sr. fled Stow with his family to Henniker, a virtual wilderness some hundred miles away. At the time of the Revolution, the colonial states printed their own money, "fiat money," not backed by coin. Too much of this money was printed and Thomas's money lost its value. According to his son, Nahum, he once took a bushel of fiat money and dumped it into a grain bin in the attic (Thwing, 1868). Increasingly, lenders wanted repayment in British gold, pounds, or other hard currency. It seems that Thomas had contracted a hard currency debt that he was unable to pay with rapidly depreciating colonial currency. Fearing debtor's prison, he set out for Henniker where his wife's family, former residents of Stow, had moved.

On arriving, Thomas made a clearing and built a log cabin, which stood for nearly a century and came to be known as the Brown House. Then, according to one account, he sent word to Nahum (it is not clear how he would have told his 13-year-old Deaf son to do this) to hitch two yoke of oxen to a sled, load the furniture and food, bundle his mother and sisters atop the load and, armed with a goad, prod the oxen 100 miles through the snow to Henniker (Thwing, 1868). According to another account, Nahum preceded his father to Henniker and was living with his uncle; it was his father, Thomas, who brought the family (Braddock, 1975; Cogswell, 1880/1973).

---

[1]The primary sources for the pedigrees of which the figures are excerpts were Banks (1966); Gordon (1892); Cogswell (1880/1973); Mayhew (1991); E. A. Fay's census of Deaf marriages (Fay, 1898); the data forms for Fay's census in the Gallaudet University Archives; and the records of the New England Historic Genealogical Society. The pedigrees are incomplete and may contain inaccuracies, as conflicting information is occasionally found in these sources.

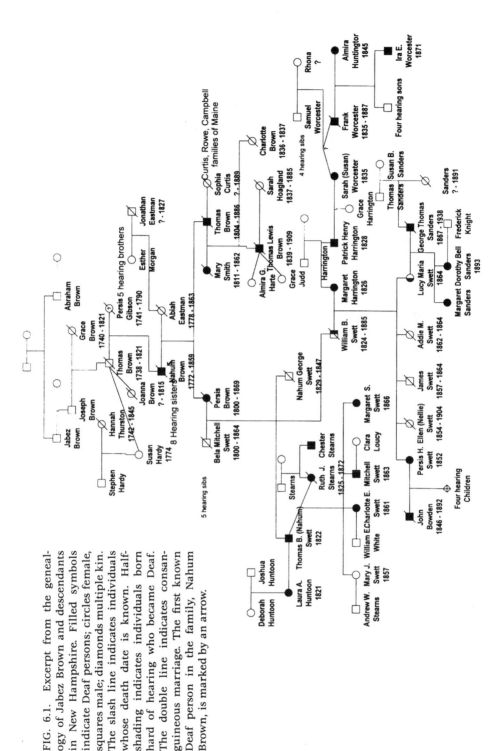

FIG. 6.1. Excerpt from the genealogy of Jabez Brown and descendants in New Hampshire. Filled symbols indicate Deaf persons; circles female, squares male; diamonds multiple kin. The slash line indicates individuals whose death date is known. Half-shading indicates individuals born hard of hearing who became Deaf. The double line indicates consanguineous marriage. The first known Deaf person in the family, Nahum Brown, is marked by an arrow.

The contemporaries of Thomas Brown Sr. described him as smart, energetic, and fond of books; he held minor elected posts in later years. His eight daughters—tall, blue-eyed, and good looking—were said to be brilliant, witty, and well educated; most became teachers. Neighbors and relatives had a harder time judging Nahum's intellect because he was Deaf; he was called plucky, skillful as an axeman and hunter, a model farmer, and a first-rate teamster of oxen and horses. Of course, no one thought of his becoming a teacher or even of his going to school.

Curiously, the first deed of land to the Browns that is recorded was 100 acres to Nahum, who was only 17 at the time. Perhaps his father could not afford to buy land some 4 years after moving to Henniker, and it was Nahum's mother's family that bought the land and gave it as a gift to Nahum, endeavoring to provide for their Deaf grandchild. The elder Thomas Brown died when he was 82—old enough to outlive two of his three wives; to attend the marriage of his son Nahum to Abiah Eastman, a hearing woman of the town; to witness the birth of their daughter, Persis, in 1800 and their son, Thomas, in 1804, both Deaf; and to hear tell of the opening of the first school for the Deaf—in Hartford, in 1817. His grandson Thomas would enroll there 5 years later.

As a young man in Henniker, Nahum did not wear shoes; to chop wood, he stood on warm planks in the doorway of his family cabin. The many chores he performed as the sole male child with eight sisters prepared him for a life of responsibility and hard labor. According to son Thomas, he worked hard from dawn to dusk and was known as a good parent and neighbor (Brown, 1860). He never learned to read or write. He communicated in pantomime or "natural sign." His wife served as his interpreter and aided him in such activities as buying and selling cattle. Like his father, Nahum had a long life, dying at age 88. He raised his two Deaf children, Persis and Thomas, and saw them marry and raise his five grandchildren, three of them Deaf. The following generation brought nine great grandchildren, five of them Deaf. In an era when deafness was most often attributed to maternal fright (Groce, 1983), Nahum and his family must surely have been puzzled. Nahum saw his son Thomas become educated, among the first Deaf-mutes in the nation to do so, and emerge as a preeminent Deaf leader, beginning at mid century. Five years before Nahum's death, a group of Thomas's Deaf friends gathered in the Brown household to draft a constitution for the first enduring Deaf organization in America, the New England Gallaudet Association of Deaf Mutes. Nahum's sight had begun to fail. He suffered severe headaches and became blind first on one side, then the other. "During his helpless and blind situation," son

Thomas related, "he would sign for [us] to come and see what he wanted. With his arms moving slowly, he understood the movement of our hands" (Brown, 1860, p. 12; Swett, 1859). Just before his death, he signaled for his wife to come near; with her hands on him, he passed peacefully away.

When Thomas Brown was 18—a slender, powerful man with a large head, gray eyes, and a facial tic from a childhood encounter with an ox—he enrolled at the American Asylum. The town of Henniker annually voted funds to assist Thomas in paying his educational expenses, until the state legislature undertook to pay for Deaf-mute pupils from New Hampshire (Brown, 1888). Thomas and his sister Persis, 4 years older, were both considered bright—Thomas was "shrewd, wild but not vicious"—and both could no doubt have attended the school, but Persis was bound by a marriage contract to a hearing carpenter from Henniker, Bela Mitchell Swett, and was not free to go (Childs, 1861). Thomas studied under the founders of American Deaf education, the Deaf Frenchman Laurent Clerc and the hearing American Thomas Gallaudet, and under an intellectual leader of the profession, Harvey Peet, who would later direct the New York school for the Deaf (Lane, 1984). Thomas, we are told, was an excellent student; at the completion of his 5-year course, he agreed to stay on for 2 years as monitor and carpentry instructor. However, at the end of that period, 25 years old, he declined to become a teacher at the Ohio school for the Deaf and returned instead to Henniker to help his parents work their 123 acres. (After the death of his father and a protracted family wrangle over the settlement of Thomas Sr.'s estate on his third wife, Nahum had sold his house and land in what later became the center of town and had moved to a farm in West Henniker in 1825, while his son Thomas was away at school in Hartford.)

In view of Thomas's tireless efforts in later years to organize Deaf people, to honor their leaders past and present, and to promote their interests, one wonders to what extent and in what ways his years at the American Asylum developed his early consciousness of Deaf people as a distinct social group. The Central Society of the Deaf in Paris, with its annual banquets honoring Deaf language, history, and leaders, began shortly after Thomas left school, so he could not have learned about it while he was a pupil of Clerc's, although no doubt he learned of it subsequently for it was clear to American educators of the Deaf that their methods derived from the French, and transatlantic visits were made in both directions. Perhaps the sense of Deaf people as a distinct group was in the very air at the American Asylum in the 1820s. After all, a single language was emerging that connected Deaf people despite wide differences among them in region, family circumstances, isolation, and former methods of communication; with it, a sense of we-who-use-this-language might naturally have emerged. Indeed, the first initiative for creating a Deaf state was organized by a group of seniors at the American Asylum just 2 years after Thomas left (Chamberlain, 1858). It was, however, short-lived.

One of the scattered enclaves of Deaf people that were gathered and to some extent amalgamated by the schooling of their number at the American Asylum was the Deaf community of Martha's Vineyard; it was indeed the largest single source of pupils at the Asylum for several years. While at school, Thomas met Mary Smith, whose family came from the Vineyard, where Deaf people—especially in some remote communities "up island," such as Tisbury and Chilmark—were quite common. Three years after his return to his father's farm in Henniker, Thomas made the journey to the coast, where he took a boat for the Vineyard, 6 miles off the Massachusetts shore, and then traveled a day on horseback to arrive at the village of Chilmark, where he and Mary were married (April 1, 1832) in the presence of her many Deaf and hearing relatives and friends.

CHILMARK, MASSACHUSETTS

Mary Smith's mother, Sally Cottle, was hearing (see Fig. 6.2); she was the daughter of Silas Cottle (hearing) and Jerusha Tilton (Deaf). Jerusha's mother and father (Mary's great grandparents) were cousins and descendants of Governor Thomas Mayhew, who bought Martha's Vineyard in 1640 from the two patentees under royal charter then disputing ownership of the island. Jerusha's father, a Tilton, also traced his island ancestry back to one Samuel Tilton, who had come to the Vineyard in 1673. Because the Tiltons early intermarried with the Skiffes, Mary was also descended from James Skiffe who, in 1699, purchased land on the Vineyard, settled in Tisbury, and sold the remaining tracts there to friends. Jerusha's maternal great grandmother was James Skiffe's daughter.

Mary's father, Mayhew Smith, was hearing, but her paternal grandfather, Elijah Smith, was Deaf and married a hearing woman; he was descended from the island's first Smith, John Smith, who arrived in 1653 (see Fig. 6.3). Mary had eight hearing siblings and an older Deaf sister, Sally, who also attended the American Asylum. Sally married a hearing cousin, Hariph Mayhew, who had seven Deaf siblings and three hearing. Mary's brother, Capt. Austin Smith, married Levinia Poole (she was hearing and also descended from Samuel Tilton); they had two hearing chil-

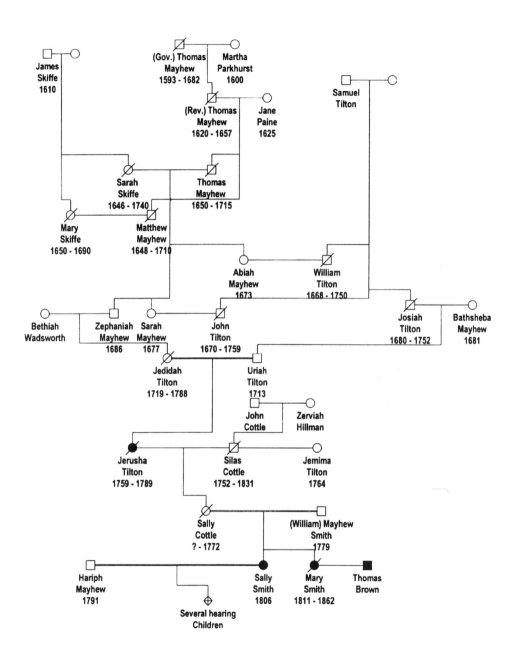

FIG. 6.2. Excerpt from the Mayhew-Tilton-Skiffe-Lambert pedigrees as they relate to Mary Brown's maternal ascendants on Martha's Vineyard. Symbols are as in Fig. 6.1. Mary Smith, the wife of Thomas Brown, is marked by an arrow.

FIG. 6.3.   Excerpt from the Mayhew-Tilton-Skiffe-Lambert pedigrees as they relate to Mary Brown's paternal ascendants on Martha's Vineyard. Symbols are as in Fig. 6.1.

84

dren and two Deaf. One of their Deaf children, Freeman, married a Deaf cousin—Deidama West. (There is no record of the other three children marrying.) Deidama had three Deaf siblings and four hearing. Deidama's parents (mother, Deaf; father, hearing) were distant cousins, both descended from Gov. Thomas Mayhew, and her father was descended from the first recorded Deaf person on the island, Jonathan Lambert, a carpenter, who arrived from Barnstable in 1694.

In her work on the Vineyard Deaf, Groce (1985) identified 72 Deaf individuals of whom 63 could trace their ancestry to James Skiffe, 32 to Samuel Tilton, and 9 to Benjamin Lambert. Most of the island Deaf had all three of these colonists in their pedigrees. Remarkably, Groce found that all three families were linked before they arrived on the Vineyard. In 1634, a minister named Lothrop and some 200 members of his congregation and their servants, all from parishes in an area in the English county of Kent known as the Weald, arrived in Boston harbor. They made their way to Scituate, where half the population was from the Weald, then to Barnstable on Cape Cod. In 1670, several of these families moved to the Vineyard when James Skiffe, who was from Kent, sold land in Tisbury. In the ensuing decades, more of these families, Tiltons, Lamberts and others, moved across Vineyard Sound, settling in the Chilmark area (Banks, 1966). Because of the very early appearance of Deaf people on the island, and because all the known Deaf Vineyarders cannot be traced to a common Vineyard ancestor, Groce concluded that the island's Deaf heritage, and thus Mary Smith's, originated in the Weald and arrived on the island with the colonizing families.

The colonizers were drawn to the Vineyard by availability of farmland, the long growing season, the surrounding sea that abounded in lobster and fishes, and the numerous ponds, where game birds were to be found, along with fish and shellfish of vast variety. The sandy soil was adapted to sheep raising. The Indians were friendly and taught the islanders how to catch whales—nearly every family on the Vineyard had a member aboard a whaler by the time of Thomas's wedding there (Freeman, 1807/1976; Mayhew, 1956; Poole, 1976). In 1700, there were 400 people on the Vineyard; the population stopped growing about 1800 at some 3,000. Not surprisingly for this relatively isolated community whose ancestors were from the same parishes, most people married someone to whom they were already related and who was from their own village on the island (Groce 1980). A symptom of this practice was the proliferation of the same family names: an 1850 census counted 132 Mayhews and 87 Tiltons in Tisbury and Chilmark (Groce, 1985). In 1807, 32 names comprised three fourths of the island population (Groce, 1981).

Mary Smith's marriage to a man from off-island was thus an anomaly, one brought about by the opening of the American Asylum and the desire of families on the Vineyard to see their Deaf children educated. The number of Deaf people gradually rose, peaking around the time of Thomas's marriage at 45. Groce (1985) estimated that, later in the 19th century, 1 in every 155 people on the Vineyard was born Deaf (0.7%), whereas in the nation at large, the figure was closer to 1 in 2,730 (0.04%). An 1830 census found 12 Deaf people in Chilmark; no doubt Mary Smith was one of them. The town's population was 694; hence, 1.7% of the town was Deaf, whereas only 0.01% of the population in the neighboring islands was Deaf (Burnet, 1835; Deaf and Dumb, 1895).

The marriage of Thomas Brown and Mary Smith was anomalous in a second sense: Unlike the practice on the mainland, most Deaf people on the island married hearing people. On the mainland, about 80% of Deaf people married Deaf; on the Vineyard, the figure only rose to 35% after the opening of the American Asylum (Groce, 1985). The high rate of mixed marriages on the Vineyard was probably a reflection of, and contributor to, a broader feature of life there—the blending of Deaf and hearing lives. Like Mary Smith (and her Deaf grandmother, Jerusha), most children born Deaf on the Vineyard (65% vs. 20% on the mainland) had both parents hearing, as well as many hearing siblings, the more so as birth rates were high on the island (Groce, 1980). Another reflection of, and contributor to, this blending was the widespread use of a sign language among both Deaf and hearing people (no doubt with varying degrees of fluency [Bahan, personal communication, 1998]). The language may originally have been British Sign Language brought over by the colonizers: When Martha's Vineyard signs elicited from elderly hearing residents in 1977 were presented to a British Deaf signer, he identified 40% of the signs as British Sign Language cognates. (An ASL informant found 22% overlap [Bahan & Poole-Nash, 1995]). There have been 12 generations since Jonathan Lambert settled on the Vineyard, so there has been a lot of time for Martha's Vineyard sign language to diverge from its origins, the more so as most Deaf children, like Mary Smith, were sent to the American Asylum, where they encountered other sign language practices and most, unlike Mary, returned to the island.

Bahan and Poole-Nash (1995) made the case that Deaf people on the Vineyard were thoroughly assimilated and, as with Deaf people in the Mayan community studied by Johnson (1994), they valued their village more than they valued the company of other Deaf people: "Being Deaf itself is irrelevant, as Deaf people have access to everyone in the village" (Bahan & Poole-Nash, 1995, p. 19). In accord with this "village-first" value in assimilative societies, the Mayan villagers, according to Johnson (1994), tended to identify first with their family, then with the village, and then with Mayan society. When Johnson gave a party for all the Deaf people in the village and their families, he learned that it was the first event in the village that singled out Deaf people. Similarly, Groce (1980) related that on the Vineyard, "all these [Deaf] people were included in all aspects of daily life from their earliest childhood. . . . One of the most striking aspects of this research is the fact that rather than being remembered as a group, every one of the Deaf islanders who is remembered is remembered as a unique individual" (p. 95).

Mary Smith would find her life quite changed when she took up residence on the mainland in the intensely Deaf Brown family, far from her hearing family, and numerous relatives and friends on the island. She decided to take with her some remembrances of her island home—a whalebone, some beautiful big seashells, and shark teeth with scrimshaw sailor carvings on them (Colby, 1961). Then Mary and Thomas began the trek to Henniker. Their descendants would have the combined Deaf heritage of the Vineyard, some 6 generations deep, and of the Henniker Deaf enclave, merely a generation old at that time.

HENNIKER, NEW HAMPSHIRE

Thomas and Mary settled on his parents' farm; his father was 60, his mother 66, and strong hands were sorely needed. More than that, Thomas brought to the task many natural gifts. He was a good horseman. He drove his own oxen and won prizes at the county fairs in Concord, New Hampshire, for drawing a load with a large boulder, weighing more than a ton, the allotted distance. He won awards for plowing and for his colts, and Mary drew a premium of $2 for a nice lot of cheese she had prepared (Anon, 1869a). He raised cattle and poultry, and grew fruit, wheat and hay. Thomas divided the large farm into lots of pasturage, tillage, orchard, woodland, and so forth, and each lot had a name. Those that have come down to us were figures in Deaf education such as Gallaudet, Clerc, and Peet (Chamberlain, 1886). He kept his accounts carefully. He was frugal, practical, methodical (Anon., 1861; Brown, 1888). Sometimes it was very hard: There were years of early and severe frosts that killed the crops;

there were seasons extremely dry, when small fruit withered and fell from the trees and clouds of grasshoppers settled on the fields, devouring everything (Cogswell, 1880/1973).

The close-knit family and Deaf community made it bearable, even rewarding. In addition to his father, Nahum, and sister, Persis, there were Persis's and Bela's two Deaf sons, Thomas B. Swett (called Nahum in honor of his grandfather), born the year Thomas went off to school, and William B. Swett, 2 years older. In 1837, Thomas B. Swett went to the American Asylum and Mary gave birth to a hearing daughter, Charlotte, but illness took the infant's life within a year. Then, 2 years later, William Swett went off to school and Mary gave birth to a Deaf son, Thomas Lewis Brown. On return from Hartford, the Swett boys took Deaf wives. William married Margaret Harrington, a Deaf woman from Ireland whose Deaf brother had also married into a large Deaf family. William had a colorful career as an explorer, showman, mechanic, writer, and artist, before settling down. They had three hearing children, two of whom died quite young, and two Deaf daughters who married Deaf men. William's brother, Thomas Swett, and his wife Ruth Stearns had three Deaf children and one hearing (Fig. 6.1).

Joseph Livingstone, a Deaf carpenter who owned the blind and sash company where William B. worked, lived with the Swetts. Sometimes Deaf workmen would live on the Brown farm: Joel Lovejoy, one of the Deaf Lovejoys from Concord, New Hampshire, and Josiah Smith, with Deaf relatives in Hillsboro, are two examples. There was also a Deaf couple nearby, named the Goves, who were close friends. (Abigail Clark Gove was from two towns away, New Boston, where there was the Deaf Smith clan, good friends of the Browns.) So it was quite a little community that worked and celebrated together and prayed together at the interpreted services in the Congregational Church (Colby, 1961). However, the Deaf community extended beyond Henniker and into contiguous towns. Thomas Brown socialized with Thomas Head and his family in Hooksett and George Kent and others in Amherst (both two towns away from Henniker); Mrs. Head was from a large Deaf family in nearby Francestown, one town away from Henniker (Anon., 1869b, 1874; Turner, 1880). In his notebooks devoted to genealogical studies of the Deaf, Alexander Graham Bell (1888) listed all the Deaf persons in New Hampshire according to the Seventh Census of the Deaf and Dumb, conducted in 1880. Including only towns that are contiguous to Henniker, or at one remove, we find an additional 13 Deaf residents, for a total of 27, including Henniker itself.

A different gauge of the size of the Deaf community in and around Henniker may be had from the 1887 publication of cumulative enroll- ments at the American Asylum since its opening in 1817. There were 6 children enrolling from Henniker and an additional 38 from townships contiguous or at one remove, for a total of 44. Both the census and enroll- ment measures are in one respect underestimates of the Henniker Deaf enclave, as participants could certainly live more than two towns away and, indeed, with the coming of the railroads, could live a considerable distance away. On the other hand, presumably not all Deaf people within easy reach of Henniker chose to participate in its social life.

As mid-century approached, an idea germinated in Thomas's mind that would prove epochal: the largest gathering of Deaf people to be assembled anywhere, any time, in history. Brown proposed that the mutes of America should gather to show their gratitude to Thomas Gallaudet (who had retired from the American Asylum in 1830) and Laurent Clerc (who, at 65, was still teaching). Later events would reveal that Brown likely had a political agenda that went beyond gratitude and sought to counteract the inherent diaspora of Deaf people by gatherings that could also serve as a basis for improving the lot of his class. When Brown, no doubt leveraging off his standing in the New Hampshire Deaf commu- nity, suggested a tribute to Gallaudet and Clerc, and asked for contribu- tions, "the flame of love ran like a prairie fire through the hearts of the whole Deaf-mute band, scattered though they were through various parts of the country" and $600 was soon raised (Rae, 1851, p. 42). A total of 200 Deaf people, some from as far away as Virginia, and 200 pupils of the American Asylum gathered in Hartford for the ceremony in which beautifully engraved silver pitchers were presented to the founders of American Deaf education. Significantly, the engraving was rich in sym- bolism from Deaf history: On one side of the pitcher, Gallaudet and Clerc are shown leaving France; the ship is at hand and beyond the waves can be seen their future school. On the other side, there is a schoolroom with Deaf pupils. On the front is a bust of Clerc's teacher, the Abbé Sicard, and around the neck, the arms of the New England states (Syle, 1887). For the presentation, there was a procession in Hartford's Center Church, in the presence of the Governor of Connecticut, and then Brown, tower- ing above the celebrants, his red beard streaked with gray, gave the wel- coming address, the first of several orations in sign. In their replies, Gallaudet and Clerc reviewed the progress of Deaf education from France to the United States. At an evening gathering, there were toasts, addresses, and resolutions, and many Deaf participants stayed on through the weekend to enjoy a service interpreted into sign language.

As it turned out, the tribute in Hartford in 1850 was the forerunner of conventions and associations of the Deaf in the United States. The following year, Thomas Gallaudet died; at the funeral, Clerc announced that Thomas Brown and others would form a society of the Deaf and frame a constitution, to raise funds for a Gallaudet monument. A convention was held for the purpose in Montpelier, Vermont, in 1853, with Deaf participants from that state as well as from Massachusetts and New Hampshire; many used free passes provided by the railroads. Brown reported on successful fundraising for the monument and urged the formation of a permanent society "for the intellectual, social and moral improvement of Deaf-mutes" (Convention of Deaf-Mutes, 1853, p.4). A committee under Thomas Brown was appointed to organize such a society. Accordingly, less than a year later, on January 4, 1854, Deaf representatives from each of the New England states gathered at the Brown household in Henniker for a week to frame a constitution for the New England Gallaudet Association (NEGA). From the resolutions of thanks for hospitality, it appears that some representatives were lodged in the Brown home, others at the Swetts, still others at the Goves. The constitution drafted envisioned the publication of a newspaper by and for Deaf-mutes, the *Gallaudet Guide and Deaf-Mute Companion*. Thomas Brown was chosen president of the new organization, which was scheduled to convene at the same time as the Gallaudet monument unveiling, in Hartford in September of that year.

In the fall, Deaf-mutes from "all parts of the union" gathered at Hartford for the unveiling of the Gallaudet monument. Among other Deaf orators, whose sign was interpreted for hearing members of the audience, Thomas Brown gave a speech reviewing the history of Deaf education. The design of the monument was by Deaf artist Albert Newsam, and the panels were by Deaf sculptor John Carlin. Indeed, "the whole monument was to be the exclusive product of Deaf-mute enterprise" (Rae, 1854, p. 19). As planned, the "Henniker Constitution" was read out and adopted and officers were elected with Thomas Brown president. Thus was the first formal organization of and for Deaf people created in America (Chamberlain, 1854).

The second biennial meeting of NEGA took place in Concord, New Hampshire, in 1856 (Chamberlain, 1857). A listing of the members that appeared shortly thereafter showed 44 from Massachusetts (including 4 Mayhews and 3 Tiltons from Chilmark); New Hampshire, 34 (mostly from towns close to Henniker); Connecticut, 30; Vermont, 19; Maine, 11; Rhode Island, 7; Illinois, 1; and Louisiana, 1. It was at this meeting that the eminent Deaf minister and teacher, Job Turner, dubbed Thomas Brown "the mute Cincinnatus of Americans," because he was so ready to drop his plow and come to the aid of his fellow mutes. The honorific, Mute Cincinnatus, stuck.

The construction of the Deaf as a distinct class had clearly emerged. It was not too great a step to imagine an enclave of Deaf people much larger than that to be found in the vicinity of Henniker or, for that matter, at the American Asylum. The idea of a Deaf commonwealth, debated at length at the 1858 meeting of the NEGA, responded to the yearnings of many (Chamberlain, 1858). The following convention was held in 1860 at the American Asylum, with some 300 attending (Anon, 1860; Chamberlain, 1860). Brown gave the presidential oration and Laurent Clerc took the assembly to historic sites in Deaf history, such as the house in which he met the little Deaf girl Alice Cogswell who had inspired efforts to found American Deaf education. In the evening, there was the conventional Deaf banquet with its toasts, orations, and resolutions. It was in 1860 that Thomas's friend and collaborator, William Chamberlain, began publishing monthly the organ of the NEGA, the *Gallaudet Guide and Deaf-Mute Companion,* one of the earliest periodicals in America printed exclusively for Deaf readers. The publication contained news of Deaf meetings, marriages, illnesses, and deaths; discussions of Deaf issues such as education and of broader social issues such as slavery and religion. (Prior to the NEGA's own publication, the proceedings of their conventions and their communications were judged sufficiently important to be carried in the *American Annals of the Deaf,* and all members of the NEGA received a subscription to the *Annals* on joining.)

Just at this time when his network of Deaf friends and associates was the strongest yet, Thomas, age 56, suffered a series of personal losses. The year before, he had lost his father, Nahum, age 87, who gradually became blind and helpless. Then, 2 years later, his wife Mary died at age 61 after an excruciating, year-long illness. Some months later death took his mother, Abiah, age 85. Then Bela Swett, and Bela's grandchildren Addie and James, died. Bela's son, Thomas's nephew, William B. Swett, deeply depressed at the loss of his children to diphtheria, left to pursue the life of an adventurer and guide in the White Mountains. Thomas's son, Thomas Lewis Brown, age 20, graduated from the American Asylum and accepted a position as teacher in the Deaf and Dumb Asylum at Flint, Michigan. It was not uncommon in that era for a widower to remarry; Thomas's

thoughts turned to the scion of one of the large Deaf families in Southern
Maine, Sophia Curtiss.

SANDY RIVER VALLEY, MAINE

In the period after the American Revolution, several of the families on
Martha's Vineyard—among them Tiltons, Smiths, Mayhews, and Wests—
decided to migrate to southeastern Maine. They had had enough of the
despotic rule of Governor Thomas Mayhew. Then, too, the extensive land
required for sheep raising was becoming scarce with the growing population. The war had crippled the whaling industry, which was increasingly
centered in the South Pacific. And Massachusetts offered free land in the
province of Maine (Poole, 1976).

The first settlers from the Vineyard went to the Sandy River Valley,
abundantly forested with all sorts of game and streams that teemed with
fishes such as trout and salmon. Other Vineyarders soon followed, creating
the towns of New Vineyard, New Sharon, New Gloucester, and 27 others.
Intermarriage among the Vineyard families continued on the mainland,
although some of the settlers gave up and returned to the island, and still
others married into unrelated Deaf families on the mainland. A total of 27
Deaf pupils who gave one of these 30 towns as their residence enrolled at
the American Asylum between its opening and 1887. This includes large
Deaf families such as the Rowes and Campbells in New Gloucester, Maine,
and the Lovejoys in Sidney. There were, however, significant numbers of
Deaf people in nearby townships—for example, the Sebec branch of the
Lovejoys; the Jacks and Jellisons, in Monroe; the Browns, Jellisons, and
Staples in Belfast; and the Berrys in Chesterville. The Lovejoy-Jellison-
Berry family of Southeastern Maine has the distinction of being one of
only two early American Deaf families in the Northeast with three or more
consecutive generations of Deaf people (with the first born before 1800);
the Brown-Swett-Sanders family of central New Hampshire was the other
(Jones, 1996). Sophia Curtiss's family was apparently from Leeds, Maine
(two townships away from New Sharon, three from Sidney), but moved to
New Gloucester; she and her parents were hearing, but she had four Deaf
and two hearing siblings, who intermarried with Deaf Rowes and Campbells. Perhaps Thomas met Sophia through her brother George, who overlapped with him at the American Asylum. The wedding notice in the
National Deaf-Mute Gazette (successor to the *Guide*) reveals both Brown's

stature and the need to explain his mixed marriage: "Mr. Brown is too well known to need any notice at our hands. His wife is a hearing lady whose relationship to and constant intercourse with mutes enables her to use their language" (Anon, 1867). Thomas and Sophia were married in Yarmouth, Maine, in November of 1864 and then took up residence in Henniker.

HENNIKER, NEW HAMPSHIRE

Thomas continued his life as a farmer—and Deaf leader. In 1866, the NEGA met in Hartford to coincide with the 50th anniversary celebration of the American Asylum. Some 500 people heard Brown give the presidential address, in which he announced that, after 12 years of service, he would resign in favor of his vice-president (Chamberlain, 1867). Two years later, the *Deaf-Mute's Friend* (successor to the *Gazette*) published a letter from Thomas Brown proposing a national convention of Deaf-mutes. According to an eminent Deaf teacher and journalist who endorsed the suggestion in the following issue, Brown had first made this proposal "to the convention in Syracuse in 1865"—no doubt the meeting of the Empire State Association of Deaf-Mutes (Brown, 1869). In the same year, 1869, Thomas's sister, Persis, died, as did Laurent Clerc (Chamberlain, 1869b). Thomas, 65 years old, won awards at the state fair and cattle show. His son, Thomas Lewis, came home from Michigan to host a large birthday party for his father. Just as the *Gazette* reassured its readers that Brown's new wife knew sign language, so the *Friend* explained to its readers that one of the storytellers at the birthday party "although a hearing man is a very good sign-maker" (Swett, 1869, p. 123). In 1874, Brown took on the presidency of the Clerc Monument Association (Brown, 1888) and 4 years later, he founded the Granite State Deaf-Mute Mission and was elected president (Tillinghast, 1878). William B. Swett followed in his uncle's footsteps in promoting Deaf welfare: He published (with William Chamberlain) the *Deaf-Mute's Friend*; he was a director of the Deaf-Mute Library Association; he was business manager of the Boston Deaf-Mute Mission; and he founded a school of industrial arts for Deaf adults, which shortly added an educational program for Deaf children; it continues today as the Beverly School for the Deaf (Swett, 1874). Thomas Brown was a trustee of the school in its early years (Brown, 1888). In 1880, the first national convention of the Deaf in America was convened just as Brown had proposed—except for the venue: It was held in Cincinnati, not Hartford, and Brown, 76 years old, could not attend. He did, however, attend the meeting in New York in 1884 and then traveled to the Vineyard with his son Thomas Lewis to visit friends of his late wife (Brown, 1884).

Thomas Brown died March 23, 1886.

ASSIMILATIVE AND DIFFERENTIATING SOCIETIES

The story of Thomas Brown and the emergence of the first American organizations of and for Deaf people that he led can be seen as the story of emerging class consciousness, which surfaced clearly in the mid-19th century. The formation of the numerous societies of Deaf people over which he presided; the explicit goals of the first enduring organization, the NEGA, which he founded: "We, Deaf-mutes, desirous of forming a society in order to promote the intellectual, social, moral, temporal and spiritual welfare *of our mute community . . .*" [italics added]; the ritual-like rehearsal at meetings of the great events in Deaf history; the raising of monuments to important figures—all these testify that Brown and his associates saw the Deaf as a distinct group with a language and way of life that should be fostered: "That these conventions tend to keep alive the feelings of brotherhood and friendship among the mutes at large cannot be disputed," wrote William Chamberlain (Chamberlain, 1869a). Consequently, he supported the gatherings of "the children of silence." In the silent press, Brown was referred to as the "patriarch of the silent tribe" (David, 1879) and his eulogist stated that Brown was always ready to do his share "for any plan which promised to promote the welfare of his class" (Brown, 1888). ("Class" here clearly refers to the "tribe," i.e. the Deaf-World, and it is in this sense that we use the term in this chapter.)

In stark contrast, the accounts available to us of the lives led by Deaf and hearing people in Tisbury and Chilmark during the same era are marked by an apparent absence of events and structures that would set Deaf people apart from hearing people. These accounts do not reveal any leader, any organization, any gathering place, any banquet or other ceremony, any monuments—indeed anything at all that suggests that Deaf people on the Vineyard had class consciousness. Now that we have made this bald claim, something contrary may well come to light, but it seems unlikely that the difference in degree will be eliminated by future discoveries.

The pedigrees that we have constructed (of which excerpts appear in

Figs. 6.1–6.3), although they are currently incomplete, have led us to the hypothesis that a difference in the genetic basis of the Deaf societies in the two locations is responsible for the difference in the emergence of class consciousness. Other possible explanations come to mind, foremost among them, perhaps, differences between the two locations in language and marriage practices. We argue later, after presenting the genetic hypothesis, that those differences are, like class consciousness, heavily influenced by the genetic difference.

The hereditary difference between hearing and Deaf people can be traced to any of numerous genes, most often acting singly. As a result, the occurrence of Deaf and hearing people in the family tends to follow the "laws of heredity" first spelled out by Austrian botanist Gregor Mendel in mid-19th century (but not widely recognized until the end of the century). Mendel identified two main patterns of genetic transmission, called dominant and recessive.

The Brown family of Henniker exemplifies the dominant pattern of inheritance (or transmission). To the best of our knowledge, none of the 23 ascendants of Nahum Brown that we ascertained was Deaf, but Nahum and some of his descendants in every generation were Deaf, indicating that the genetic difference in this family began with Nahum. If the pattern of genetic transmission was dominant in Nahum's family, then on average, half of his children would inherit that genetic difference and be born Deaf, whereas the other half should be born hearing. This is, within a small margin of statistical sampling, just what happened. About half of Nahum's descendants were Deaf: 12 out of 21. All Deaf members of the family had a Deaf parent (except Nahum, of course), and all Deaf members who married had at least one Deaf child.

The Mayhew, Tilton, Lambert, and Skiffe families of Martha's Vineyard (Figs. 6.2 and 6.3), who intermarried extensively both before and after arriving on the island, exemplify the recessive pattern of inheritance. In this pattern, many people in the family will possess the critical gene and yet not be Deaf themselves (hence the term *recessive*). If both parents have that gene, then one quarter of their children will be Deaf, but if only one parent has it, none of their children will be Deaf, unlike dominant transmission. Many Deaf children will not have Deaf parents (because their parents must be carrying the gene but may not be Deaf themselves). The odds of both parents having exactly the same recessive gene are much greater if they are related to one another. Intermarriage among relatives is most likely in a community that is isolated—on an island, say. This was indeed the picture on Martha's Vineyard. Many Deaf children on the Vineyard had no Deaf parents, and many Deaf parents, provided they married hearing people, had no Deaf children (cf. Figs. 6.2 and 6.3). Consequently, far fewer than half the descendants of any progenitor are Deaf; there are many more hearing people in the families of Deaf people.

In dominant transmission such as we believe occurred in Henniker then, there are likely to be Deaf children in every generation: Each Deaf person receives a Deaf heritage and may pass it along; each generation of his or her parents and grandparents, children and grandchildren will likely contain Deaf individuals. Marriage between relatives is not necessary for such generational depth to occur. In recessive transmission such as we believe occurred on the Vineyard, on the other hand, a Deaf person may have cousins, uncles and aunts, grandparents, or more distant relatives who are Deaf, but it is less likely among the immediate family when compared with dominant transmission. That Deaf person may readily have hearing parents, hearing children, or both; generational depth is less likely, and marriage among relatives is characteristically required for any Deaf family members to occur at all. In such a setting, the Deaf person may feel a part of a rather extended family that includes hearing people, because he or she is related to so many people in the community. But that Deaf person may not feel like a crucial link in the chain of Deaf heritage from the past down to the future.

A clear result of the difference in genetic patterning in the two communities is that the Henniker community necessarily had many fewer hearing people as an integral part of the family structure compared to the Chilmark community. The numerous hearing children of Deaf parents (Codas) in Chilmark would be likely to acquire sign language as a native language; they and their Deaf siblings would thus form a critical mass within the family for sign language use. The Deaf children of hearing parents would learn the language from their parents, if they knew it, or, if not, from Deaf peers, elders, and Codas, and they would seek to use it with their own parents and hearing siblings. Numerous hearing relatives in the community might also be motivated to master the sign language, at least to some extent, to communicate with their Deaf relatives. Thus, the difference between Henniker and Chilmark in the spread of sign language into the hearing environment may be traceable, in part, to the difference between them in genetic patterning.

The incidence of mixed hearing and Deaf marriages on the Vineyard seems to have been more than triple that on the mainland, as cited earlier. This difference may be attributable, at least in part, to the more widespread use of the sign language among hearing people, as a common language greatly facilitates meeting one's life partner in the first place and then developing a deep interest in and affection for that person.

Finally, we hypothesize that the differences in language use and marriage practice, which are underpinned in part by the differences in genetic patterning, mediate in turn differences in class consciousness. What we are suggesting is that it takes a "them" for an "us" to develop, and the blending of hearing and Deaf lives on the Vineyard, because of shared family life and language (underpinned by genetics), discouraged the construction of hearing people as "them." Conversely, many members of the Henniker Deaf enclave had Deaf parents, Deaf grandparents, and Deaf great grandparents, and the boundary with the surrounding hearing community was relatively sharply demarcated. That said, other factors may also have fostered Chilmark blending, such as a sense of isolation on a remote island and an awareness of shared ancestry.

Recent findings concerning the Deaf and hearing residents of a village in Bali help to evaluate the notion that Deaf genetic patterning, marriage and language practices, and class consciousness are related. Of the 2185 people in this village, 2.2% are Deaf (Winata et al., 1995). Following Branson, Miller & Marsaja (1996), we will refer to the village as Desa Kolok ("Deaf Village"—not its official name). The genetic patterning in Desa Kolok is recessive as on the Vineyard and, as on the Vineyard, marriages between hearing and Deaf people are completely acceptable. There are 16 families in Desa Kolok with 2 hearing parents and at least 1 Deaf child, so it is clear that there is more blending of hearing and Deaf lives in the nuclear family than in Henniker where there were no families with hearing parents and Deaf children. However, the blending may not be as great as on the Vineyard, since the 20 families with a Deaf parent (or two) had 75% Deaf children.

Beyond the blending of hearing and Deaf lives within the nuclear family in Desa Kolok, there are cultural and social forces that ensure widespread contact between Deaf and hearing people. Of particular note, Balinese villages are kin based and Deaf people grow up in house yards shared with their hearing relatives. Thus, with respect to the mixing of hearing and Deaf lives, the extended family of the Desa Kolok house yard may be more like Vineyard families than Henniker families. Perhaps for this reason, the use of a sign language in Desa Kolok is nearly universal and Deaf people are integrated in many facets of social life including groups organized for work and for some religious practices. Moreover, hearing attitudes toward the Deaf, many of whom are relatives, are generally positive (Hinnant,1998, 1999; Branson, Miller & Marsaja, 1996).

Thus, the evidence from Desa Kolok suggests that the mixing of hearing and Deaf people in the family determines their mixing in community life, as we hypothesize was the case on the Vineyard.

It is not clear to us whether Deaf people in Desa Kolok lack class (i.e., group) consciousness, as we hypothesize was the case on the Vineyard. On the one hand, certain activities in Desa Kolok are associated with Deaf villagers who also have specific roles with regard to certain festivals, which might engender such group consciousness. Moreover, being Deaf restricts one's prospects outside the village and participation in some skilled labor and in musical events (Hinnant, personal communication). On the other hand, the Deaf villagers interact freely and equally with other villagersî (Branson, Miller & Marsaja, 1996, p. 42). Perhaps the mixed evidence for group consciousness is a reflection of an intermediate status for Desa Kolok between Henniker and the Vineyard with regard to the blending of hearing and Deaf lives.

ACKNOWLEDGMENTS

We are grateful to the following for their assistance: Kathleen Arnos, Genetics Program, Department of Biology, Gallaudet University; Ben Bahan, Department of Deaf Studies, Gallaudet University; Jan Branson, National Institute for Deaf Studies and Sign Language Research; Nora Groce, School of Public Health, Yale University; Ulf Hedberg, Gallaudet University Archives; John Hinnant, Department of Religious Studies, Michigan State University; Carole Mair, Librarian, Michigan School for the Deaf; New England Historic Genealogical Society; Don Miller, Department of Anthropology and Sociology, Monash University; Michael Olsen, Gallaudet University Archives; Joan Poole-Nash, Newton, MA; Volta Bureau, Alexander Graham Bell Association.

REFERENCES

Anon. (1860) Fourth Convention of the New England Gallaudet Association of Deaf-Mutes. *American Annals of the Deaf and Dumb, 12* (4), 236–243.
Anon. (1861). *Gallaudet Guide and Deaf Mute's Companion, 2*(4), 14.
Anon. (1867). [T. Brown marries Sophia Sumner née Curtiss]. *National Deaf-Mute Gazette, 1*(1),16.
Anon. (1869a). [Annual fair]. *Deaf-Mute's Friend, 1* (11), 344.
Anon. (1869b). Letter from New Hampshire. *Deaf-Mute's Friend, 1*(1), 26–27.
Anon. (1874). A festival of Deaf-mutes. *Literary Budget, 1*(1), 3.

Bahan, B., & Poole-Nash, J. (1995, April). *The signing community on Martha's Vineyard.* Unpublished address to the Conference on Deaf Studies IV, Haverhill, MA.

Banks, C. E. (1966). *The history of Martha's Vineyard, Dukes County, Massachusetts in three volumes.* Edgartown, MA: Dukes County Historical Society.

Bell, A. G. (1888). *Unpublished notebooks.* Washington, DC: Volta Bureau.

Braddock, G. C. (1975). *Notable Deaf persons.* Washington, DC: Gallaudet College Alumni Association.

Branson, J., Miller. D., & Marsaja. G. (1996). Everyone here speaks sign language, too: A Deaf village in Bali, Indonesia. In C. Lucas (Ed.), *Multicultural aspects of sociolinguistics in Deaf communities* (pp. 39–57). Washington, DC: Gallaudet University Press.

Brown, T. (1860). [Sketch of Nahum Brown]. *Gallaudet Guide and Deaf-Mute's Companion, 1*(3), 12.

Brown, T. (1869). [signed T. B.] Letter. *Deaf-Mute's Friend, 1*(6), 188–190.

Brown, T. (1884, March 6). [Address by Thomas Brown at his 80th birthday]. *Hillsboro Messenger.*

Brown, T. L. (1888). *In memoriam: A tribute to the memory of Thomas Brown.* Flint, MI: School for the Deaf.

Burnet, J. R. (1835). *Tales of the Deaf and Dumb.* Newark, NJ: Olds.

Chamberlain, W. M. (1854). Constitution of the New England Gallaudet Association of Deaf-Mutes. *American Annals of the Deaf, 6,* 64–68.

Chamberlain, W. M. (1857). Proceedings of the Convention of the New England Gallaudet Association of Deaf-Mutes. *American Annals of the Deaf, 9,* 65–87.

Chamberlain, W. M. (1858). Proceedings of the Third Convention of the New England Gallaudet Association of Deaf-Mutes. *American Annals of the Deaf, 10,* 205–219.

Chamberlain, W. M. (1860). Proceedings of the Fourth Convention of the New England Gallaudet Association of Deaf-Mutes. *Gallaudet Guide and Deaf-Mutes' Companion, 1*(10), 1–2.

Chamberlain, W. M. (1867). Celebration of the fiftieth anniversary. *National Deaf-Mute Gazette, 1*(1), 1–4.

Chamberlain, W. M. (1869a). [Concerning a national convention]. *Deaf-Mute's Friend, 1*(8), 241–242.

Chamberlain,W. M. (1869b). Obituary of Laurent Clerc. *Deaf-Mute's Friend, 1,* 216–217.

Chamberlain, W. M. (1886). Thomas Brown. *American Annals of the Deaf, 31,* 204–210.

Childs, S. (1861). [Sketch of Nahum and Thomas Brown]. *Gallaudet Guide and Deaf-Mutes' Companion, 2*(4), 14–15.

Cogswell, L. W. (1973). *History of the town of Henniker.* Somersworth, NH: New Hampshire Publishing Co. (Original work published 1880.)

Colby, R.E. (1961). *On the Thomas Brown place.* Unpublished manuscript, Henniker Historical Society.

Convention of Deaf-Mutes. (1853). *Monument to Thomas H. Gallaudet. Proceedings. 23–24 February 1853.* Montpelier, VT: Walton.

David, J. O. (1879, January 10). From New Hampshire: An interesting letter from Mr. David. *Michigan Deaf-Mute Mirror,* p. 2.

Deaf and Dumb of Squibnocket. (1895). *Deaf-Mutes' Journal, 24*(5), 1.

Fay, E. A. (1898) *Marriages of the Deaf in America.* Washington, DC: Volta Bureau.

Freeman, J. (1976). Dukes County 1807. *Dukes County Intelligencer, 12*(4), 1–51. (Original work published in 1807.)

Gordon, J.C. (1892). *Education of Deaf Children. Evidence of E.M. Gallaudet and A.G. Bell presented to the Royal Commission of the United Kingdom on the Condition of the Blind, the Deaf and the Dumb.* Washington, DC: Volta Bureau.

Groce, N. (1980). Everyone here spoke sign language. *Natural History, 89,* 12–15.

Groce, N. (1981). The island's hereditary deaf: A lesson in human understanding. *Dukes County Intelligencer, 22,* 83–95.

Groce, N. (1983). *Hereditary deafness on the island of Martha's Vineyard: An ethnohistory of a genetic disorder.* Unpublished doctoral dissertation, Brown University, Providence, RI.

Groce, N. (1985). *Everyone here spoke sign language.* Cambridge, MA: Harvard University Press.

Hinnant, J. (1999). Adaptation to dearness in a Balinese community. In B. Keetz & C. Berlin (Eds.), *Hearing loss and genetics.* San Diego, CA: Singular Publishing Group.

Hinnant, J. (1998, October). *Music to their eyes. Deaf life and performance in a Balinese village.* Address at the National Institutes of Health, Bethesda, MD.

Johnson, R. E. (1994). Sign language and the concept of deafness in a traditional Yucatec Mayan village. In C. Erting, R. E. Johnson, D. L. Smith, & B. D. Snider (Eds.), *The Deaf way: Perspectives from the International Conference on Deaf Culture* (pp. 103–109). Washington, DC: Gallaudet University Press.

Jones, T. W. (1996). America's first multi-generation deaf families (A genealogical perspective). *Deaf American Monographs, 46,* 49–54.

Lane, H. (1984). *When the mind hears: A history of the deaf.* New York: Random House.

Mayhew, C. M. (1991). *Vital records of Chilmark, Massachusetts to the year 1850. With additional Chilmark Births, Marriages and Deaths.* Bowie, MD: Heritage Books.

Mayhew, E. R. (1956). *Martha's Vineyard: A short history and guide.* Edgartown, MA: Dukes County Historical Society.

Poole, D. C. (1976). *A new Vineyard.* Edgartown, MA: Dukes County Historical Society.

Rae, L. (1851). Presentation of silver plate to Messrs. Gallaudet and Clerc. *American Annals of the Deaf, 3,* 41–64.

Rae, L. (1854). Ceremonies at the completion of the Gallaudet Monument. *American Annals of the Deaf, 7,* 19–54.

Swett, W. B. (1859). Obituary of Nahum Brown. *American Annals of the Deaf and Dumb, 11*(4), 237–240.

Swett, W. B. (1869). A birthday party. *Deaf Mutes' Friend, 1*(4), 123.

Swett, W. B. (1874). *Adventures of a Deaf-Mute.* Boston: Deaf-Mute Mission.

Syle, H. W. (1887). *Biographical Sketch of Thomas Hopkins Gallaudet.* Philadelphia: Cullingworth.

Thwing, E. P. (1868, April). White Mountain memories. *National Deaf Mute Gazette, 16,* pp. 8–9.

Tillinghast, J. T. (1878, November 29). Gathering of mutes at Amherst, New Hampshire. *Michigan Deaf-Mute Mirror, 4,* p. 3.

Turner, J. (1880). Biographical sketch of Thomas Brown. *Deaf-Mutes' Journal, 9*(43), 2.

Winata, S., Arhya, I., Moeljopawiro, S., Hinnant, J., Liang, Y., & Friedman, T. (1995). Congenital non-syndromal autosomal recessive deafness in Bengkala, an isolated Balinese village. *Journal of Medical Genetics, 32*(5), 336–343.

III

Language in the
Visual-Spatial Modality

7

Sign Language Research at the Millennium

Elissa L. Newport
Ted Supalla
University of Rochester

Ursula Bellugi and Ed Klima hold a remarkable position in the field of sign language research, and also therefore in the broader field of the cognitive sciences. Within the field of sign language research, they established one of the two research groups that founded the field, and during the formative years of the field they were responsible both for producing most of the findings on sign language structure and acquisition and for training almost everyone who subsequently entered the field. It is therefore hard to overestimate the debt our field owes to them. Even more significant, however, is the fact that they framed the central questions of the field in such a way that this relatively small subarea has had an enormous impact on and importance to the entire enterprise of cognitive science and cognitive neuroscience. Their questions have always been the big ones: Are sign languages structured and acquired in the same ways as spoken languages, or are there important differences? Is language therefore a faculty specially developed and evolved in the auditory mode, or is there independence of language from modality? What does this tell us about the nature of language and about the nature of the cognitive and neural mechanisms that produce it? Because they have always framed their questions in this way, those of us who have worked with them and have entered the field through working in their lab have also thought about these same "big questions." The result of continually keeping their eye (eyes?) on this perspective has meant that only 25 or 30 years of research by two profoundly thoughtful investigators and their students and collaborators have entirely changed the way the field of cognitive science thinks about language. Jerry Kagan recently asked one of us, in casual conversation, what the 10 most important findings in the field were. Only one came to mind: the findings of the last two decades on signed languages. We have been extremely fortunate to participate in the field during this period of time and to work with Ursula and Ed during important parts of it.

For the last Theoretical Issues in Sign Language Research (TISLR) conference in Montreal, Lissa was invited to give an address looking back and forward to the next millennium, asking what sign language research has found thus far and what our field needs to discover in our future work. This invitation prompted us to discuss together, at great length, what we thought about these issues. What we discovered, in part, was how much our answers to these questions were framed by Ursula and Ed in our earliest years in the field. In tribute to them, this chapter is an attempt to answer these same large questions with our own perspective on what research in the field of sign language structure, processing, and acquisition has suggested thus far.

THE PRE-SIGN LANGUAGE ERA

When we were graduate students (in the 1970s) and each first introduced to the field of psycholinguistics, the prevailing view was clear: Language was thought to have an essential and unique relation to the auditory–vocal mode. Table 7.1 lists a number of important lines of evidence supporting this view, each of which, at that time, looked quite empirically strong, and which together formed a coherent picture of the language faculty.

TABLE 7.1
Our Concept of Language in the 1960s and Early 1970s

- Speech is special: Categorical perception only for speech
- Linguistic universals apply only to spoken languages
- Specialized neural mechanisms for spoken language
- Language is qualitatively different from all nonlinguistic behavior (even including signed language, written language, gesture)

One line of evidence supporting this view came from the work on categorical perception, suggesting that there was a special "speech mode" for processing auditory linguistic material (Liberman, 1970). Research in this line of work showed that continua of speech stimuli, synthesized with continuously varying acoustic dimensions such as voice onset time or second formant frequency, were not perceived as continuously distinct; rather, such stimuli were perceived in phonetic categories, within which listeners were unable to distinguish further acoustic variation. Categorical perception was believed to be a mode of perception restricted to speech; in the earliest studies, even auditory stimuli very similar to speech, but not perceived as linguistic (e.g., inverted speech or the 50-millisecond "chirps" spliced out of the onset of speech stimuli), were not perceived categorically.

A second line of work concerned the discovery of linguistic universals and the accompanying claim that these universals were restricted to spoken languages. Greenberg (1963) and Chomsky (1965), among others, began to note in the middle 1960s that a wide variety of unrelated spoken languages shared a surprising number of structural properties or fell into a small number of distinct structural types. Although some of Stokoe's (1960) work on ASL phonology had already appeared at that time, most of the research on ASL had not yet begun, and none had yet impacted the linguistic community's view of language. An extremely interesting statement of the view of language held at that time appeared in an article published in *Cognition* by Osherson and Wasow (1976). In that article, Osherson and Wasow argued for specialized innate constraints or mechanisms underlying human spoken language abilities, using as their strongest claim the evidence that even apparently close systems, sharing many or all of the same communicative functions with spoken language, do not share either categorical perception or linguistic universals. Their two examples were writing systems and sign languages.

Similarly, all the available literature on neural mechanisms underlying language suggested that speech was special here as well. Neurological damage to specific areas of the left hemisphere could result in the loss of language without any accompanying loss of other motor or cognitive skills. By the Geschwind model (1972), these regions subdivided into linguistic components such as comprehension (relatively posterior) and production (relatively anterior).

Thus in many ways—structural as well as neural—language was thought to contrast with nonlinguistic behavior (e.g., gesture), and even with closely related behavior such as written language and sign language. If correct, this view was extremely interesting and theoretically powerful.

One would think, after all, that the structural properties and computational mechanisms involved in a behavioral domain would derive fairly directly from the computational functions this behavioral domain entailed. Converging lines of evidence to the contrary thus demanded a quite different way of thinking about the nature of language. The alternative that seemed obvious at the time was that a special set of mechanisms must have evolved for handling human language that were, for reasons of evolutionary history, inextricably linked to the auditory–vocal channels in which most human language use occurs.

We must emphasize, particularly to an audience of sign language researchers, that this is not at its core a view derived from a prejudiced or politically inappropriate view of sign languages. It could have been true— indeed, to some degree, could still be true—that a faculty for handling spoken language would be separate and distinct from one called into play for handling signed language, without denying that signed languages are legitimate, complex, and full human languages. It could have been that the universal principles of spoken languages are different from those of signed languages. But at the beginning of this era of research, it wasn't even clear that humans could develop a complex communicative system without the mouth and the ear.

THE FIRST PHASE OF SIGN LANGUAGE RESEARCH: DISCOVERIES ABOUT ASL

As already noted, Stokoe's earliest work on American Sign Language (ASL) preceded much of the research cited above. But research on ASL began in earnest during the 1970s, and began to impact the linguistic community in a major way at a Linguistic Society of America (LSA) meeting in 1973–1974. We ourselves were not yet at The Salk Institute (we both arrived there in 1974, Ted as Ursula's first graduate student and Lissa as a new Assistant Professor at UCSD); but the generation of students and collaborators who preceded us in working with Ursie and Ed—Harlan Lane, Susan Fischer, Nancy Frishberg, Robbin Battison, Pat Siple, and many others—were performing truly groundbreaking, landmark work on the structure and acquisition of ASL. We have been told by members of the audience at the 1973–1974 LSA meeting that the presentations of the lab at this meeting, reporting on the phonological structure of ASL and its path of historical change into a contrastive phonological system, received a standing ovation.

The research of the next 15 years not only brought us an understanding of ASL; it also changed the way the field viewed human language. In virtually every regard, and in many extremely surprising ways, ASL has turned out to be organized and acquired like other languages. This in turn has meant that language cannot be uniquely linked to the ear and mouth but must instead arise from mechanisms independent of those modalities.

Table 7.2 lists a number of findings and interpretations that resulted from this new field of research on ASL. The central findings came from an understanding of the linguistic structure of ASL, much of the work performed or begun by Ursula, Ed, and their collaborators and students (Klima, Bellugi et al., 1979). These linguistic analyses of ASL revealed that it is a language with a quite different type of structure than that of English, but one that is found among spoken languages (e.g., it shares certain typological similarities with Navajo). Word structure in ASL is quite complex, particularly in verbs. Typical verbs are marked morphologically for agreement in person and number with both subject and object, and for temporal aspect and other grammatical features common to verbs in other languages (Fischer, 1973; Padden, 1988). Verbs of motion are particularly complex, with stems involving morphemes for path, manner of motion, orientation, and classifier morphemes marking the semantic category or size and shape of both the moving object and a secondary object with respect to which the movement path occurs (T. Supalla, 1982). As is common in spoken languages with complex morphology, word order in ASL is relatively free, with an unmarked SVO order but a number of order-changing syntactic structures commonly used (e.g., topicalization of the object, subject, or VP). Moved constituents are obligatorily marked by grammaticized facial expressions, which are produced throughout the signing of the words of that constituent (Liddell, 1980). When verbs are marked for agreement and/or when discussing subjects and objects that have already been mentioned, the subject and object NPs may be omitted from the sen-

TABLE 7.2

Our Concept of Language Deriving From Research on ASL

- Language is special, no difference between spoken and signed language
- Linguistic universals apply to all languages
- Acquisition and processing universals apply to all languages (if input early)
- Same neural mechanisms apply to all languages (if input early)
- Language is qualitatively different from nonlinguistic behavior (now including only written language, gesture)

tence—that is, the language permits null arguments (Lillo-Martin, 1991). In short, the grammatical properties of ASL are unlike those of English but are quite familiar to students of other languages of the world. This body of findings thus suggests that principles of word and sentence structure are, at least to some degree, common to both signed and spoken languages and are not inherently connected to the auditory–vocal mode.

Studies of the online processing of ASL by fluent adult signers, of the representation of ASL in the brain, and of the acquisition of ASL by native-speaking Deaf children also show many similarities with the principles of processing, neurological organization, and acquisition of spoken languages of the world. For example, ASL is acquired on approximately the same timetable as spoken languages with similar typology. Acquisition begins with manual babbling appearing at around 10 months or earlier (Petitto & Marentette, 1991); first signs appear at about 1 year of age; two-sign sentences appear during the second year; and each of these stages show structural characteristics like those of other languages (Meier & Newport, 1990; Newport & Meier, 1985). Adult signers process ASL using the same types of parsing strategies as those used in the processing of spoken languages (Emmorey, 1991), and, like speakers of auditory–vocal languages, represent ASL in the left hemisphere of the brain (Neville, 1995; Poizner, Klima, & Bellugi, 1987).

One highly unusual feature of signing communities is that native users are so rare; 95% or more of Deaf signers are first exposed to their language beyond infancy and sometimes not until late childhood or even adulthood. This has therefore presented to researchers the opportunity to study of the effects of age of exposure on the mastery of a primary language. A number of such studies have shown that there is a substantial effect of age on the acquisition of ASL: native and early ASL learners show much more fluency, consistency, and complexity in the grammatical structures of the language, and more extensive and rapid processing abilities, than those who have acquired ASL later in life (Emmorey, 1991; Mayberry & Fischer, 1989; Newport, 1990). These effects persist even after as much as 50 years of daily use of ASL as a primary language (Newport, 1990). Together with the work of Lenneberg (1967) and Curtiss (1977) and also comparable effects of age of exposure on the acquisition of English as a second language in hearing foreigners (Johnson & Newport, 1989), these results provide important evidence of a critical, or sensitive, period for the acquisition of language.

All of these findings on ASL suggest that the cognitive abilities supporting language and its acquisition in humans are not restricted or specialized to speech but rather permit the development of signed as well as spoken languages. However, it is important to note that this striking similarity between signed and spoken languages arises predominantly from studying *one* sign language. As sign language researchers have begun to study other sign languages, some new and old questions reappear.

RECENT FINDINGS IN SIGN LANGUAGE RESEARCH: QUESTIONS ABOUT SIGN LANGUAGE TYPOLOGY, VARIATION, AND EMERGENCE

As we have begun to move beyond the study of a single sign language and examine other sign languages of the world, an unexpected first impression appears. For those of us accustomed to the sometimes wild differences among unrelated spoken languages, distinct signed languages look much less wildly different. Unrelated sign languages are certainly mutually unintelligible, as has been noted by many investigators, and vary greatly in their lexicons and basic word orders. But a long dinner among Deaf users of different sign languages will, after a while, permit surprisingly complex interchanges in a rapidly developed pidgin, and World Federation of the Deaf meetings are regularly and successfully conducted in such a pidgin (T. Supalla & Webb, 1995). Moreover, cross-linguistic research on sign languages does not yet include any languages that are radically different in typology from ASL. In short, whereas each sign language looks like some spoken language of the world, different sign languages thus far look unexpectedly like each other. Is this a mistaken impression from too early and too small a sample of cross-linguistic research? Is it the result of studying only young languages, which have also been claimed to look surprisingly like one another in the auditory–vocal mode? Or is it something important and revealing about the true nature of modality and language? Only further research can untangle these questions.

Table 7.3 lists a number of recent lines of research suggesting that there may be some important differences between signed and spoken languages that we have not yet fully understood. One of these lines of work concerns the acquisition of SEE2 (Signing Exact English), a sign system that has not developed naturally but was devised by adults for educational purposes. Sam Supalla (1986, 1989, 1991) showed that the closed-class morphology of SEE2 is not readily acquired by deaf children, even when this is the only communicative system to which they are exposed, and even

TABLE 7.3
More Recent Findings on Sign Languages: Unanswered Questions

- SEE2
- Cross-linguistic comparison of signed languages
- International Sign as a pidgin
- Home sign
- Nonlinguistic gesture
- Neural mechanisms

when they are exposed to it from relatively early in life. He suggested that this learning problem arises because SEE2 was devised with a type of morphology that is entirely commonplace in English and other spoken languages—consisting of multiple, phonologically different syllables in sequence—but that is quite unnatural for the visual–gestural mode. This may not in fact be the only structural problem in SEE2: There are a number of other linguistic oddities of SEE2 (e.g., not distinguishing phonologically between open-class [typically strong] and closed-class [typically weak] elements), which may be unnatural for both spoken and signed languages. It is therefore possible that many formal problems, not special to sign languages and their modality, make SEE2 difficult to learn. But S. Supalla's work raises the important possibility that there are natural differences between spoken and signed languages in the types of morphological and phonological structure that most readily develop.

A second set of findings that accords with S. Supalla's suggestion are the early results of cross-linguistic comparisons among sign languages that have arisen naturally in different parts of the world. Our own analysis of case marking and verb agreement in 15 different sign languages (T. Supalla & Webb, 1995; T. Supalla, 1997) shows a number of differences between these languages in the types of morphological devices they use. At the same time, however, there are also striking similarities among the languages, with all using locations and movement through space in common ways to mark grammatical agreement with subject and object. Investigators have also noted classifier structures in verbs of motion in many sign languages. Presumably because of such similarities among unrelated sign languages, speakers of mutually unintelligible sign languages are able to develop a signed pidgin (called International Sign) that retains these morphological structures and that is thus unexpectedly more complex than spoken pidgins (T. Supalla & Webb, 1995; Webb & T. Supalla, 1994).

In short, from what little we know thus far about sign languages of the world, it is possible that sign languages show more typological similarity to one another, at least in their morphological structure, than do an equivalent range of spoken languages.[1] Why might this be true? T. Supalla & Webb (1995) have suggested several possibilities. One important possibility is that we have not yet studied enough sign languages, and that the typological differences we find between spoken Navajo and Chinese also await us in signed languages that no one has yet analyzed. A second possibility is that the sign languages studied thus far are all quite young, with communities of Deaf signers only recently formed by forces such as public education. Young languages, spoken as well as signed, have been argued to share more structural properties with one another than is common among unrelated languages (Bickerton, 1981; Fischer, 1978). Sign languages may thus diverge from one another more as they develop longer histories. A third possibility, however, is that the visual–gestural modality may produce more uniformity of structure and typology than does the auditory–vocal modality.

In the auditory–vocal mode, there is a large distance between the non-linguistic resources from which languages develop and the linguistic systems that eventually result. This is certainly not absolute: A number of interesting and important suggestions have been made about perceptual and motor constraints on spoken language structure. For example, we now know that the phonetic categories of languages arise from auditory perceptual categories that predate the phonetic contrasts both developmentally and evolutionarily. Nonetheless, compared with gesture, the auditory–vocal modes seem strikingly arbitrary, even empty. No isolated child has yet been discovered who has babbled an invented auditory language to her mother; no hearing participants, brought into the lab and asked to make sounds to one another, will quickly produce even the beginnings of Russian or Tagalog. This gap is filled, for well-developed languages, with a very wide array of relatively arbitrary systems of grammaticization, with some languages relying predominantly on linear order and others more heavily utilizing tone or contrasting segments for expressing the same functions. Infants are remarkable in the auditory–vocal mode for their

---

[1]There is, however, no reason from available evidence to believe that there is special similarity among sign languages in their syntactic structure: Basic word order, for example, varies in the same way as in spoken languages.

ability to rapidly learn the widely differing patterns to which they are exposed (Saffran, Aslin, & Newport, 1996).

In contrast, in the visual–gestural mode, there appears to be a great deal more structure in nonlinguistic behavior, and also, perhaps, more uniform tendencies across sign languages to grammaticize these nonlinguistic resources in very similar ways. Deaf children raised in hearing families, without exposure to a sign language, will nonetheless develop a surprisingly rich "home sign" system (Goldin-Meadow & Mylander, 1990, 1998; Coppola, Senghas, Newport, & Supalla, 1997). Hearing adults, brought into the lab for a brief experiment and asked to gesture, do not produce well-structured or complex grammatical systems, but they do produce remarkable beginning use of the devices that appear in well-developed sign languages (Dufour, 1992; Singleton, Morford, & Goldin-Meadow, 1993). Even nonlinguistic gesture, produced by hearing people while speaking, has recently been shown to have more structure than previously believed. Webb (1996) studied hearing speakers ranging from a talk show host to a philosophy professor. She found that each has a recurring "lexicon" of gestures, many shared across speakers and some composed of smaller gesture parts (e.g., a recurring circle to convey repeated action, or a gesture to the head to accompany talk of mental states) that resemble some of the much more well-developed components of sign languages.

These seeds of structure in the visual–gestural mode—our human tendencies to use motion and space in particular ways to express conceptual and grammatical contrasts—may thus tend to propel sign languages more commonly toward one or a few of the several ways in which linguistic systems may be formed. On this view, each individual sign language is fully comparable, in complexity and typology, to spoken languages, each falling well within the expected range of linguistic structure; but the range of variation across distinct sign languages may be different, and more focused on particular types of organizational structure, than that for spoken languages. If this is correct—and, we reiterate, it may well be quite incorrect and based prematurely on too little cross-linguistic research—the relation between spoken and signed languages may be somewhat different than our field had initially anticipated. Universals of signed and spoken languages may neither be precisely the same as one another nor entirely different; rather, modality (along with other cognitive constraints that shape languages) may affect which of the available ways to build a linguistic system is utilized, and therefore where there is and is not cross-linguistic variation.

A clearer answer to these questions awaits a myriad of new lines of research: more cross-linguistic studies of distinct sign languages, particularly those that have long histories but little contact with the Western sign languages already somewhat well studied; more analysis of how new languages emerge; more research on historical change in signed as well as spoken languages. We are enormously grateful to Ursula Bellugi and Ed Klima, who have not only forged the beginnings of this road and have provided the field with an understanding of the importance of sign language research to the cognitive sciences, but who have also pointed the way for all the rest of us.

ACKNOWLEDGMENTS

We are grateful to our collaborators and students for their important contributions to the work we review in this chapter, to Harlan Lane for his comments on this chapter, and especially to Ursula Bellugi and Ed Klima for introducing us to the field and to each other. This work was supported in part by NIH grant DC00167.

REFERENCES

Bickerton, D. (1981). *Roots of language*. Ann Arbor, MI: Karoma Publishers.

Chomsky, N. (1965). *Aspects of the theory of syntax*. Cambridge, MA: MIT Press.

Coppola, M., Senghas, A., Newport, E., & Supalla, T. (1997). *The emergence of grammar: Evidence from family-based sign systems in Nicaragua*. Paper presented at the Boston University Conference on Language Development, Boston, MA.

Curtiss, S. (1977). *Genie: A psycholinguistic study of a modern-day "wild child."* New York: Academic Press.

Dufour, R. (1992). *The use of gesture for communicative purposes: Can gestures become grammaticized?* Unpublished doctoral dissertation, University of Illinois.

Emmorey, K. (1991). Repetition priming with aspect and agreement morphology in American Sign Language. *Journal of Psycholinguistic Research, 20*, 365–388.

Fischer, S. (1973). Two processes of reduplication in American Sign Language. *Foundations of Language, 9*, 469–480.

Fischer, S. (1978) Sign language and creoles. In P. Siple (Ed.), *Understanding language through sign language research* (pp. 309–331). New York: Academic Press.

Geschwind, N. (1972). Language and the brain. *Scientific American, 226*, 76–83.

Goldin-Meadow, S., & Mylander, C. (1990). Beyond the input given: The child's role in the acquisition of language. *Language, 66*, 323–355.

Goldin-Meadow, S., & Mylander, C. (1998, January 15). Spontaneous sign systems created by deaf children in two cultures. *Nature, 391*, 279–281.

Greenberg, J. (Ed.). (1963). *Universals of language*. Cambridge, MA: MIT Press.

Johnson, J. S., & Newport, E. L. (1989). Critical period effects in second language learning: The influence of maturational state on the acquisition of English as a second language. *Cognitive Psychology, 21*, 60–99.

Klima, E., and Bellugi, U., with Battison, R., Boyes-Braem, P., Fischer, S., Frishberg, N., Lane, H., Lentz, E., Newkirk, D., Newport, E., Pederson, C., & Siple, P. (1979). *The signs of language.* Cambridge, MA: Harvard University Press.

Lenneberg, E. (1967). *Biological foundations of language.* New York: Wiley.

Liberman, A. M. (1970). The grammars of speech and language. *Cognitive Psychology 1,* 301–323.

Liddell, S. (1980). *American Sign Language syntax.* The Hague, Netherlands: Mouton.

Lillo-Martin, D. (1991). *Universal grammar and American Sign Language.* Dordrecht, Netherlands: Kluwer.

Mayberry, R., & Fischer, S. D. (1989). Looking through phonological shape to lexical meaning: The bottleneck of non-native sign language processing. *Memory and Cognition, 17,* 740–754.

Meier, R. P., & Newport, E. L. (1990). Out of the hands of babes: On a possible sign advantage in language acquisition. *Language, 66,* 1–23.

Neville, H. (1995). Developmental specificity in neurocognitive development in humans. In M. Gazzaniga (Ed.), *The cognitive neurosciences* (pp. 219–231). Cambridge MA: MIT Press.

Newport, E. L. (1990). Maturational constraints on language learning. *Cognitive Science, 14,* 11–28.

Newport, E. L., & Meier, R. P. (1985) The acquisition of American Sign Language. In D. I. Slobin (Ed.), *The cross-linguistic study of language acquisition* (pp. 881–938). Vol. 1. Mahwah, NJ: Lawrence Erlbaum Associates.

Osherson, D., & Wasow, T. (1976). Task-specificity and species-specificity in the study of language: A methodological note. *Cognition 4,* 203–214.

Padden, C. (1988). *Interaction of morphology and syntax in ASL.* New York: Garland.

Petitto, L., & Marentette, P. (1991). Babbling in the manual mode: Evidence for the ontogeny of language. *Science, 251,* 1493–1496.

Poizner, H., Klima, E. S., & Bellugi, U. (1987). *What the hands reveal about the brain.* Cambridge MA: MIT Press.

Saffran, J. R., Aslin, R. N., & Newport, E. L. (1996). Statistical learning by 8-month old infants. *Science, 274,* 1926–1928.

Singleton, J., Morford, J., & Goldin-Meadow, S. (1993). Once is not enough: Standards of wellformedness in manual communication created over three different timespans. *Language, 69,* 683–715.

Stokoe, W. C., Jr. (1960). Sign language structure: An outline of the visual communication systems of the American deaf. *Studies in Linguistics,* Occasional Papers 8.

Supalla, S. (1986). *Manually Coded English: The modality question in signed language development.* Unpublished master's thesis, University of Illinois.

Supalla, S. (1989). *Segmentation of Manually Coded English: Problems in the mapping of English in the visual/gestural mode.* Doctoral dissertation, University of Illinois.

Supalla, S. (1991). Manually Coded English: The modality question in signed language development. In P. Siple & S.Fischer (Eds.), *Theoretical issues in sign language research* (pp. 85–109). Vol. 2: Psychology. Chicago: University of Chicago Press.

Supalla, T. (1982). *Structure and acquisition of verbs of motion in American Sign Language.* Unpublished doctoral dissertation, University of California, San Diego.

Supalla, T. (1997). *An implicational hierarchy in verb agreement in American Sign Language.* Department of Linguistics, University of Rochester.

Supalla, T., & Webb, R. (1995). The grammar of International Sign: A new look at pidgin languages. In K. Emmorey & J. Reilly (Eds.), *Language, gesture, and space* (pp. 333–352). Mahwah, NJ: Lawrence Erlbaum Associates.

Webb, R. (1996). Linguistic properties of metaphoric gestures. Unpublished doctoral dissertation, Department of Linguistics, University of Rochester, NY.

Webb, R., & Supalla, T. (1994). Negation in International Sign. In I. Ahlgren, B. Bergman, & M. Brennan (eds.), *Perspectives on sign language structure: Proceedings of the Fifth International Symposium on Sign Language Research* (pp. 173–185). Hamburg, Germany: Signum.

8

Attentional Resources and Working Memory: A New Framework for the Study of the Impact of Deafness on Cognition[1]

Patricia Siple
Wayne State University

When the psycholinguistic study of American Sign Language (ASL) was in its infancy, I, as a graduate student at the University of California at San Diego, was invited by Ursula Bellugi to come to The Salk Institute for a discussion about short-term memory and sign language processing. That initial meeting resulted in a collaboration with Ursula Bellugi and Ed Klima that lasted more than 2 years. During that time, I became convinced that the study of sign language processing had important implications for the development of theories of language processing and the application of those theories to the education of Deaf children. This chapter takes a new look at issues related to my first work in sign language research—issues involved in the comparison of the early stages of processing of signed and spoken language.

---

[1]A version of this chapter was presented at the Impact of Deafness on Cognition Conference held in San Diego, CA, in April 1998.

INTRODUCTION TO THE ISSUES

Suppose that the following event were to happen while you were on an elevator in an office building on a university campus:

> The elevator stops and two coworkers get on the elevator together. As they enter the elevator, they are in the middle of a conversation about a mutual friend and one says, "I like Joe, but, you know, he can't walk and chew gum at the same time." They both laugh.

With no additional information you would conclude that the two coworkers don't think that Joe is very smart. Why? Because in some cases, we interpret the ability to do two different things at the same time as a sign of enhanced cognitive ability.

Consider a second scenario:

> You are at a family gathering and the uncle of a young child tells the child to pat his head and rub his belly at the same time. The child tries and tries but fails each time. Everyone who has witnessed this event laughs.

Would you conclude that the uncle is pointing out that the child is not very smart? I don't think so. Instead, you would conclude that the uncle is having some fun with the child because he is not old enough to know that it is nearly impossible to do these two particular things at the same time.

Now consider a final scenario:

> You are sitting at home eating breakfast and looking out the window. You see a neighbor boy on his bicycle delivering newspapers. As he rides down the street, he reaches back, grabs a newspaper out of his pouch, and throws it so that it lands just in front of your front door. You smile, remembering when he was much younger and just learning to ride a bicycle.

Do you smile because you conclude that the neighbor boy has superior intellectual ability? No, you smile because you know how many weeks it took him to be able to ride his bicycle without falling. You also know that, since that time, he has ridden his bicycle many hours per week. Even then, when he first started delivering papers, he had difficulty getting them where they needed to go. You smile because you are aware that, in some cases, we are able to carry out complex activities at the same time only after a great deal of practice.

These three scenarios illustrate that there are some things that we can easily do at the same time, other things that we can do at the same time only after a great deal of practice, and still others that we have great difficulty doing at the same time no matter how much we practice. The study of the ability, or lack of ability, to do two or more things at the same time, or carry out two or more cognitive processes at the same time, is the study of attention. I argue that understanding how deafness affects attention and related cognitive processes as we engage in cognitive activities is crucial to understanding the impact of deafness on cognition. Yet, the study of attention per se has all but been ignored by researchers investigating the relation between cognition and deafness.

In the remainder of this chapter, I argue that an understanding of attention and its relation to working memory in Deaf individuals and when language is signed is important for an understanding of language and cognitive processing in general and for the Deaf population in particular. To set the stage, I first provide some background on theories of attention and working memory (originally called *short-term memory*) and suggest that attention may have been ignored by researchers because older views of attention did not make interesting predictions about the influence of deafness on cognition. Next, I examine contemporary theories that provide a new framework for studying attention and working memory. Once this groundwork is laid, I consider some examples of studies that examine attention, working memory, and deafness within the new framework. Finally, I discuss implications of our new understanding of attentional capacity, attentional limitations, and working memory as we now understand these cognitive characteristics, for the study of the impact of deafness on cognition.

THEORIES OF ATTENTION AND
SHORT-TERM MEMORY: A BRIEF HISTORY

The first modern theory of attention was described in 1958 by Donald Broadbent, and it is this view that was predominant when researchers began to investigate the impact of deafness on cognition from an information-processing perspective as a part of what has been called the cognitive revolution. A diagram of Broadbent's conception of the human information-processing system is shown in Fig. 8.1. In Broadbent's theory, several types of environmental information are processed simultaneously by the various sensory systems and the encoded information is represented

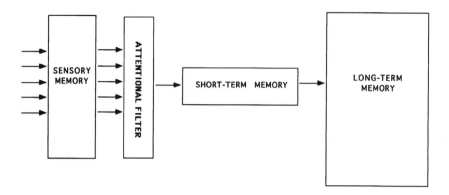

FIG. 8.1.   Schematic diagram of Broadbent's (1958) theory of attention.

briefly in "channels" of the sensory systems. Broadbent described attention as a "bottleneck" or filter, with the attention mechanism selecting
only one of the many channels of information for further processing.
Because input from the perceptual system to the cognitive system is
reduced to a single channel at any one time, processing is limited by the
speed of transmission of information on the selected channel and the
speed with which attention can be switched to a different channel. Information on the selected channel is passed on to short-term memory, where
it can be integrated with information in long-term memory and responses
can be made.

The short-term memory system proposed by Atkinson and Shiffrin
(1968, 1971) was consistent with Broadbent's (1958) view of attention. In
Atkinson and Shiffrin's model (recently called the "modal model" by
Baddeley, 1986), information from the channel selected by the attention
mechanism enters short-term memory—a limited capacity, temporary
storage of information—and remains there until it decays or is replaced by
new information. Control processes operating on information in short-
term memory make long-term memory storage and response initiation
possible. One important control process—rehearsal—provides for recir-
culation of information in short-term memory, but the system's small
capacity limits the amount of information that can be maintained at any
one time. Processing in the information-processing system described by
Broadbent (1958) and Atkinson and Shiffrin (1968, 1971) is parallel up to
the attentional filter, but serial thereafter.

Within this kind of processing system, deafness reduces the number of
channels of information available for selection and may change the types

of information present on the remaining channels. What needs to be studied, then, is the impact of deafness on the types of information present on the sensory channels and the ways that later memory systems maintain and use this information. Thus, many early studies of deafness and language processing concentrated on the codes used by Deaf individuals to maintain language information in short-term memory (e.g., Bellugi, Klima, & Siple, 1975; Conrad, 1979; Locke & Locke, 1971) Because deafness had no predicted effect on the attentional system itself in Broadbent's theory, there was no reason to pursue studies of attention, per se, in Deaf people.

Many developments have occurred within the field of attention since Broadbent first proposed his theory, but these developments have been slow to make their way into research involving deafness. Broadbent characterized the attention mechanism as a structural filter that occurs early in the processing of information derived from the sensory systems. Newer theories of attention differ from Broadbent's theory both in the characterization of the attention mechanism and in the location of the point in processing where attention is thought to influence ongoing cognitive activity.

In Broadbent's formulation, a filter occurring early in processing limits the processing of incoming information. In the 1970s several theorists proposed a new resource, characterization of attention (e.g., Kahneman, 1973; Norman & Bobrow, 1975; Shiffrin & Schneider, 1977).[2] In these newer theories, attentional limitations are viewed, at least in part, as limitations of the attentional resources or processing "energy" available rather than as limitations imposed by a structural filter. According to these views, the attention mechanism allocates attentional resources to tasks based on an assessment of the ongoing needs of the cognitive system. Two or more types of information can be processed or two or more types of cognitive activity can take place, as long as they, together, do not make demands on the attention system that exceed the amount of capacity or resources available.

Characterizing attention as allocation of resources brought a new way to address an ongoing conflict in the attention literature. Shortly after Broadbent proposed his theory, conflicting evidence about the location of attentional limitations on processing resulted in a theoretical debate about whether the attentional filter occurred "early" or "late" in the processing of information. Within a resource allocation framework, however, the

---

[2]Of course, not all theorists agree with a resource characterization of attention. Pashler (1990), for example, retained a position much like Broadbent's original position.

location of processing limitations is determined by which processes require attentional resources rather than by the location of a structural filter. Theoretically, attentional limitations can be early or late, depending on whether specific operations at different points in processing require attentional resources.

To know whether two tasks can be performed at the same time, one needs to ask whether a particular attention-demanding process in one task interferes with an attention-demanding process in the second task. Researchers quickly developed dual-task methodologies to measure the interference of performance of one task or process on the performance of another task or process. Results from dual task studies have indicated that some processes do not interfere with other processes and, therefore, do not require attention. Processes that do not require attention have been described as automatic processes, whereas those that do require attention are described as attentional or control processes (Shiffrin & Schneider, 1977). In some cases, control processes can become automatic, but only after a great deal of practice. A skilled typist, for example, often initiates the typing of groups of letters by a single attention-demanding process, whereas the less skilled typist uses attentional resources to initiate typing each individual letter.

Dual-task studies were also carried out in what had traditionally been the domain of short-term memory. Some of these studies demonstrated patterns described as selective interference. In general, it was shown that one task selectively interferes with another task to the extent that the two tasks include the same or similar processes. For example, a task involving visual-spatial rehearsal processes interferes with another task involving visual-spatial rehearsal processes but not with a task involving auditory rehearsal processes (Brooks, 1968). The flip side of interference is, of course, enhancement. If tasks involving the same or similar processes can be restructured so that they do not draw on these processes at the same time, overall processing will be enhanced.

Developments related to resource theory and studies demonstrating selective interference and enhancement led new theorizing in two directions. Theorists attributing interference effects to the sharing of attentional resources proposed theories of attention that included multiple pools of attentional resources. Multiple resource theories (e.g., Navon & Gopher, 1979; Wickens, 1984) include several independent subsystems of attention, each with its own limited pool of attentional resources. These theories may also include a general subsystem of attention that controls the flow of information to and from the other subsystems. Other theorists, working in the domain of what had come to be called working memory, proposed multiple component models of working memory (Baddeley, 1986; Baddeley & Hitch, 1974; Schneider & Detweiler, 1987). These theories include separate components for visual, auditory, and perhaps other domains of information. A general attention, or controlling and scheduling, mechanism is also included in these theories. According to these working memory theories, interference between tasks occurs when processes related to the same working memory component are required at the same time.

These two types of theories, multiple resource theories of attention and multiple component theories of working memory, account for many of the same results in much the same way. Whether specific dual-task interference results are attributed to competition for attentional resources, competition for working memory processes, or both, appears to depend on the scope attributed to each system. Pashler (1990), maintaining a Broadbent-like position on attention, for example, argued that certain types of interference lie outside the domain of attention and are attributable to factors affecting short-term memory. Conceptualization of the human processing system as constrained in a variety of specific ways producing interference that can be attributed to attention or memory components of the system over the course of processing provides a new framework for the study of the impact of deafness on cognition.

I began this discussion with three scenarios. We can now see how contemporary theories of attention or working memory can bring these three situations together and account for our general intuitions about them. Both children and adults have difficulty patting their heads and rubbing their bellies at the same time because these two activities require the same pool of limited attentional resources or the same working memory processes. The neighbor boy who begins to deliver newspapers from his bicycle initially suffers from the same kind of problem. Riding a bicycle and throwing newspapers include tasks that depend on the same pools of attentional resources or the same working memory processes, creating interference that decreases performance. With a great deal of practice, however, some of the sequences of processes become automatic, reducing processing interference. Interference was most likely further reduced by restructuring the two tasks so that processes demanding the same resources or processes were sequenced in such a way as to allow time sharing. These two types of changes occurring over time made it possible to carry out the two complex activities at the same time. Finally, there appear to be individual differences in our ability to automate processes and integrate and control attentional resources and working memory processes. A person who cannot walk and chew gum at the same time would be at the disadvantageous end of a distribution of these abilities.

What effects might deafness have on attention and working memory given these new views? From the scenarios we have considered, we see that it is important to determine several things. We need to know which processes interfere with each other and which do not; which processes can become automatic and which cannot; and, for specific tasks, which processes can be rearranged or restructured to enhance processing. Only then can we predict which activities we can learn to perform together without effort and which will present problems. This understanding is especially true for language activities because the processing system must carry out several different activities at the same time to communicate through language. Deafness changes the nature and types of processing necessary to carry out certain language activities. How do theses changes affect the ability of the attention and working memory systems to carry out language processes? Keeping this question in mind, we now consider a multiple resource theory of attention and a multiple component theory of working memory in detail.

MULTIPLE RESOURCE AND MULTIPLE COMPONENT THEORIES

The multiple resource theory of Wickens (1980, 1984), which has gained prominence in applied human factors settings, exemplifies the multiple resource view of attention. A diagram of Wickens's theory is shown in Fig. 8.2. In Wickens's theory, for distinct pools of attentional resources operate at different stages of processing, different input modalities, different types of memory codes, and different response modalities. Thus, determining whether one task interferes with another at any point requires a complex analysis of the processes involved in each task to determine whether processes from the different tasks make demands on the same pool of attentional resources at the same time. This theory can account for a wide array of data from situations that involve carrying out two activities at the same time. Before turning to implications of this theory for the study of the impact of deafness on cognition, we describe Wickens's theory in greater detail.

Multiple resource theory essentially unites Broadbent's concept of processing channels with the later concept of attentional resources. Wickens argued that there are different channels or types of information at different

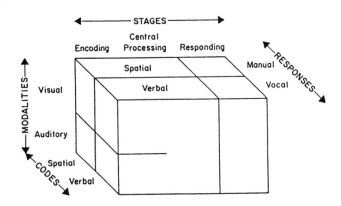

FIG. 8.2. Multiple resource model of attention proposed by Wickens (1984).

stages of processing. Early in processing, we take in sensory information from different sensory channels. Wickens considered visual and auditory sensory input modalities as channels, although there are, of course, others. Selected information from the different modalities is then transformed or recoded into internal processing codes. Wickens considered spatial and verbal codes, although there may be others. Processing operations are carried out on coded representations until the new information is stored in memory or until a decision is made to produce a particular response. Wickens considered voice and manual response modalities. He left it to future research to determine exactly how many independent subsystems of attention with independent pools of resources exist at the different stages of processing.

Although the data are far from in, research has produced examples of independence, interference, and enhancement of processes at different stages of processing. At the earliest stages of processing, attention limits the amount of information that can be encoded and selected for further processing. Encoding and selection of information from different perceptual modalities appears to draw on different pools of attentional resources, whereas selection of similar information within the same modality appears to draw on the same pool of resources. Treisman & Davies (1973), for example, found greater interference between two monitoring tasks when they were presented in the same modality (visual or auditory) than when they were in different modalities. Similarly, Allport, Antonis, and Reynolds (1972) found that shadowing (repeating prose passages) had little effect on recognition memory for pictures but reduced recognition memory for auditorily presented words to chance level.

Attention also limits the amount of similar information that can be encoded and selected from a particular perceptual modality. In the visual system, for example, visual attention is typically allocated to a location in the visual field. In most cases, attention moves with the fovea, or point of focus, but this need not be the case. Attention can be allocated to different locations in the visual field without moving the eyes (Posner, 1978). Attempts to process information from two or more visual locations reduces the efficiency of processing from any one area; that is, interference occurs (Kiefer & Siple, 1987; Posner, Snyder, & Davidson, 1980). Studies like these led Johnson and Dark (1986) to conclude that spatial attention is best characterized as an attentional spotlight. It may be possible to direct the "beam" of the spotlight over a somewhat larger area or to split the beam over nonadjacent areas visual field (e.g., Egly & Homa, 1984), but this results in a loss of processing efficiency.

Deafness increases the likelihood that more and different types of simultaneously available information will need to be processed through the visual modality. In many cases, this information will occur in different places in the visual field. Interference, or reduced processing, is expected when the amount and nature of visual information to be processed exceeds the limits of visual attention. With experience and practice, it should be possible to automate some processing of often-experienced visual information. Working out the factors that influence the automatization of processing of specific types of visual information should be an important challenge to researchers investigating the impact of deafness on cognition.

Material selected for further processing is maintained in internal memory codes. We turn now to a multiple component theory of working memory proposed by Baddeley (Baddeley, 1986; Baddeley & Hitch, 1974), because he has provided a more comprehensive description of this part of the processing system. Baddeley's working memory model consists of three components: a central executive, a phonological loop, and a visuo-spatial sketchpad, shown schematically in Fig. 8.3. The central executive regulates the flow of information into and out of the other two component systems through allocation of a general pool of attentional resources. The phonological loop functions to encode speech and nonspeech language inputs into speech-based phonological codes so that they can be temporarily maintained through articulatory rehearsal. The phonological loop itself has two components: a phonological short-term store and an articulatory rehearsal mechanism, as shown in Fig. 8.3. This system, with its own specialized processes or resources, plays an important role in several spoken language activities, including vocabulary acquisition and the development

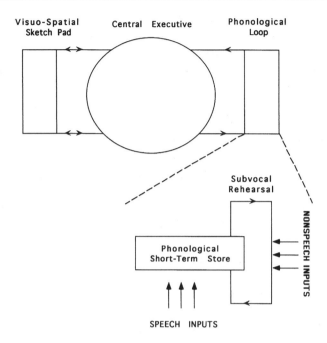

FIG. 8.3. Schematic diagram of the working memory model of Baddeley and Hitch (1974) and a more detailed diagram of the phonological loop (Baddeley, 1986). From *Working Memory and Language* (p. 8), by S. E. Gathercole and A. D. Baddeley, 1993, Hove, United Kingdom: Psychology Press Ltd. Copyright © 1993 by Psychology Press Ltd. Reprinted with permission.

of reading skills (Gathercole & Baddeley, 1993). Finally, the visuo-spatial sketchpad is specialized for encoding and maintaining visual and spatial information and for generating images from verbal material. It, too, has specialized processes or resources. Because the phonological loop and visuo-spatial sketchpad possess independent processes or resources, there is little or no interference between processing operations carried out within the two separate subsystems.

Working within Baddeley's working memory framework, Wilson and Emmorey (1997) examined how signed language is processed in working memory by native signers. Deaf signers use a sign-based temporary memory code similar to that used by hearing individuals to hold speech in working memory (e.g., Bellugi, et al., 1975). Summarizing research analogous to that described by Baddeley, Wilson and Emmorey (1997) concluded that this sign-based information is held and maintained in a subsystem of working memory similar to Baddeley's phonological loop. Like the phonological loop, the sign loop consists of two components: a short-term store that holds sign-based phonological representations of signs and a rehearsal mechanism based on sign articulation.

The functions of these two components appear to be similar as well. Sign stimuli are immediately represented in the short-term store. The rehearsal mechanism both refreshes this store and adds new information that has been translated from other formats to a sign-based code for storage in the short-term store. Some differences between the sign loop and phonological loop were noted by Wilson and Emmorey (1997). In addition to the difference in form of representation, the speech-based phonological loop and the sign-based phonological loop appear to rehearse serial-order information differently.

Wilson and Emmorey (1997) provided a detailed description of the sign phonological loop. We do not know, however, how this subsystem fits within the overall structure of working memory. Some Deaf children show evidence of the use of speech-based working memory codes and speech-based articulatory rehearsal (e.g., Conrad, 1979). Is it possible to have both a speech phonological loop and a sign phonological loop or is there a single phonological loop that is involved in the processing of linguistic stimuli? If there is only one phonological loop, must the processing of sign-based codes compete with the processing of speech-based codes for limited phonological loop resources? Answers to these questions are important for understanding signed and spoken language processing, signed and spoken vocabulary acquisition, and the development of reading skills in Deaf children.

Response selection, initiation, and production occur late in processing. Results of several studies indicate that dual-task interference occurs when responses involve the same modality but is reduced or eliminated when different responses (e.g., vocal and manual) are required. For example, performance on a task involving manual tracking of a visual target is reduced when a concurrent task requires a manual choice response to a tone but not when the response to the tone is vocal (McLeod, 1977). In our example, our paperboy has difficulty throwing a newspaper while steering his bicycle (two responses involving the same response modality) until he has automated or restructured many elements of the two tasks. Pashler (1990) argued that some response-related interference effects can be accounted for with a single-channel response-selection bottleneck theory. By this single-channel account, our paperboy would still have difficulty carrying out the two tasks until aspects of his two tasks become either automated or restructured to permit time sampling and attention switching.

Processes or resources used in response selection and production are generally separate from resources involved in earlier processing. Studies of event-related brain potentials (ERPs) have demonstrated that the size of a specific component of the ERP is influenced by the amount of information in a visual display but is not influenced by requiring manual responses or by the frequency of those responses (Israel, Chesney, Wickens, & Donchin, 1980; Israel, Wickens, Chesney, & Donchin, 1980). This dissociation of early and late processes may not occur for linguistic tasks, however, as there is a closer relation between perception and production of language stimuli (Liberman & Mattingly, 1985). Thus, perception and production of linguistic materials may share resources and specialized processes, and, therefore, interfere with each other.

Selecting and producing action responses is particularly important in language production. In some instances, the same output system is used to convey different types of information or levels of linguistic information. Such multifunctionality appears to be a pervasive characteristic of signed language. In ASL, for example, facial expression conveys both affective (Meadow-Orlans, MacTurk, Prezioso, Erting, & Day, 1987; Reilly, McIntire, & Seago, 1992) and linguistic information (Baker & Cokely, 1980; Baker & Padden, 1978; Liddell, 1978; Reilly, McIntire, & Bellugi, 1990). Interference is expected when a signer is learning to convey different messages or parts of a message using the same output modality. With experience and practice, however, it should be possible to automate some elements and restructure others to carry out complex language interaction. The "reconstruction" stage suggested by Reilly (chap. 22, this volume), during which children acquiring ASL work out the timing between manual and nonmanual signals, may reflect these kinds of changes. As with encoding, it is important to work out the factors that influence automatization and restructuring in response selection and production.

IMPLICATIONS FOR THE STUDY
OF COGNITION AND DEAFNESS

This new framework for the study of attention and working memory has important implications for the study of the impact of deafness on cognition. A Deaf person depends on the visual input channel for more information and for more types of information than does a hearing person. The nature of the internal codes generated and the types of processes carried out on these internal codes may differ. Finally, the modality of response may differ for a Deaf person. These differences are particularly important for language processing, whether the input is spoken, written, signed, or some combination of these forms of language. We consider, by example, one area of language research—face-to-face communication—because this is an area where the influence of attentional and working memory limitations may be dramatic.

In face-to-face communication, three types of information are conveyed simultaneously (Kendon, 1967; Rutter, 1984). The linguistic message itself is one. In addition to the information conveyed linguistically, culturally specific strategies are used by communication partners to regulate and maintain the flow of information. These strategies include procedures for getting a partner's attention and initiating interaction, negotiating smooth turn taking, monitoring one's partner during a turn, and terminating a turn or an interaction. The third type of information conveyed during communication is emotional information that may or may not be related to the linguistic message.

A hearing person communicating in spoken language uses different sensory channels to convey different kinds of information. The primary cues used to get a potential listener's attention occur in the auditory channel. In addition, the message is received through the auditory channel in spoken language communication. The visual channel is used in a complementary way to convey paralinguistic information, including turn taking and other cues that serve to maintain and regulate interaction, as well as emotional content (Argyle & Cook, 1976; Goodwin, 1979, 1981; Kendon, 1967; Rutter, 1984).

For a Deaf person, reception of both signed and spoken language depends heavily on information received visually. For signed language, the visual channel is used, to some extent, for all of the functions carried out on both the auditory and visual channels for a hearing person using a spoken language. The visual channel is used for both attention getting and conveying the message. Once visual attention is achieved, the signer also uses visual cues to monitor, maintain, and regulate conversation (Baker, 1977; Baker & Padden, 1978; Wilbur & Petitto, 1983). Emotional content is conveyed visually as well.

Oral language communication also relies more heavily on visual information for a Deaf person. As with signed language, the need to establish visual attention before beginning a conversation is important for oral communication. Reception of oral language depends on visually "reading" speech cues on the speaker's face and mouth, even when a hearing aid is used. Cues for the regulation and maintenance of conversation and information about emotional content are also present on the visual channel.

Greater reliance on the visual channel for more types of information opens up the possibility of greater competition for attentional processing resources. I am not suggesting that deafness necessarily makes cognitive processing more difficult or inefficient. It should be clear by now that there is a great deal of redundancy and complexity built into the system to permit us to carry out more than one activity at the same time. In addition, there are mechanisms to help turn inefficient processing into efficient processing. Some processes may forever interfere with each other. Many others, however, can be made compatible. Some processes and processing sequences can become automatic with practice. In other cases, tasks may be restructured such that different tasks do not draw on the same resources or processes at the same time. Depending on the nature of the specific attention or processing mechanism, processing may be restructured in one of two ways: by efficient time-sampling and attention-switching strategies (Pashler, 1990) or by efficient time sharing of resources (Wickens, 1984).

Because both of these mechanisms for reducing interference and freeing up resources—automaticity and restructuring—require time to practice the tasks or to carry out restructuring activities, it seems reasonable to suggest that attention and working-memory limitations will have their greatest impact early in the acquisition or learning of specific language activities. Application of the new framework to studies of situations in which multiple, competing tasks are involved requires analysis and comparison of the time course of processing for each of the tasks. The task analyses should include information about processes that may always interfere, processing that can be automated to some degree, and situations in which restructuring can be carried out to reduce the competition for specific processes or resources.

There are several types of face-to-face communication environments that lend themselves to this kind of analysis. Simultaneous communication is an important one. To what extent do limitations of visual attention at input affect one's ability to take in visual information about both speech and sign components of the message? Is this potential limitation damaging, or can it be gotten around by learning and practice? Maxwell and Bernstein (1985) suggested that there is a synergy between the signed and spoken components of simultaneous communication. Is it possible that, with practice, the two parts of the message come to enhance each other? Duncan (1984) suggested that attention is at least in part object based. That is, when attention is allocated to an object, its features become available without the allocation of additional resources. With experience, the face and hands of the signer may come to be automatically processed as part of the same "object," reducing the demands of simultaneous communication on visual attention. Additionally, restructuring may occur such that some Deaf individuals may learn to recode the visual speech information in simultaneous communication into an articulatory code. The processing of simultaneous communication could then be restructured such that the speech part of the message uses a separate pool of resources, different working memory components, or both.

Native acquisition of ASL provides another important communication environment. Because more types of visual information are present simultaneously when language is signed, the demands on the visual attention system are greater than when language processing can be shared by the auditory and visual channels. These greater demands for visual attentional resources may change the course of the acquisition of language and communication, although, I suspect, not its final outcome. That is, adult signers communicate successfully, but the development of this ability may differ from the course of development described for the acquisition of spoken language by hearing children.

In a recent study of language acquisition by a set of monolingual twins acquiring ASL and a set of hearing, bilingual twins acquiring ASL and spoken English, we found that initiation of signed interactions by the twins was delayed relative to initiation of spoken English interactions by the bilingual-bimodal twins (Siple, Richmond-Welty, Howe, Berwanger, & Jasper, 1994). Other aspects of language development, including the emergence of language, the rate of vocabulary acquisition, and the development of language-specific gaze strategies for maintaining and regulating conversation, occurred within the same time frame for these children as that reported for hearing children acquiring a spoken language (Richmond-Welty & Siple, 1999; Siple & Akamatsu, 1991; Siple, Akamatsu, & Loew, 1990). Objects are an important topic of conversation at the time that children learn to initiate language interaction; and, when children of this age talk about objects, they are typically looking at them. Signed communication requires that visual attention also be directed to the communication partner. We believe that these increased demands on visual attention are at least in part responsible for our finding that signed initiation of interaction is delayed for these children.

SUMMARY AND CONCLUSIONS

Since the beginning of the cognitive revolution in the late 1950s, most of the work on the impact of deafness on cognition has focused on static structural components of cognition. Few studies have addressed the dynamic components of cognition represented by contemporary views of attention and working memory. At the beginning of the cognitive revolution, the attention mechanism was viewed as a structural filter that selected one of a large number of perceptual channels of information for further processing. Short-term memory was described as a buffer that provided temporary storage of information. Four decades of research have resulted in more complex and more dynamic views of attention and working memory.

Contemporary theories of attention and working memory offer a new framework for the study of the impact of deafness on cognition. In this new framework, different components of the human processing system regulate and schedule processing, encode perceptual information, maintain domain-specific information, and prepare and initiate responses. Attention in this system is characterized by many as limited by the amount of available processing capacity or "energy" rather than as a single-channel bottleneck. Cognitive processing is limited by competition for limited attentional resources and by competition for specialized processes or resources available to components of the system. Limitations can often be overcome, however, through automatization of a process or series of processes through practice or through a restructuring of the task or tasks to avoid interference. This new framework provides a mechanism for explaining many somewhat contradictory results in research on deafness, provides a way of capturing the locus of processing differences that may be associated with deafness, and holds the promise of providing new ways to think about the nature of the interaction of deafness, cognition and language processing.

Much has been made of cognitive deficits in Deaf children; yet Deaf adults, in general, are quite successful in their lives. How can this be? From the perspective discussed here, the so-called deficits may be reflections of attentional and memory-processing limitations produced by a greater reliance on visual information for carrying out cognitive activities. With time, many of these processing limitations may be overcome through automatization of some processing activities and restructuring of others to allow time sharing of processes and resources. It seems that not all Deaf people take the same path, however. In most data sets, there is more variance or heterogeneity in Deaf groups than in hearing groups. The multiple resource–component framework may provide a way to capture differences in processing strategies. When processing limitations do occur, localizing the source of processing limitations provides the first step toward developing interventions that will surmount them.

When visual cues serve functions for Deaf people that auditory cues serve for hearing people, differences between visual attention and auditory attention can change the complexity and nature of processing necessary to carry out those cognitive functions. The few studies that have examined the role of visual attention in Deaf versus hearing people and in signed versus spoken language have led to important new understandings of the cognitive activities under study. These studies have only begun to explore the issues involved, however. There is a need for comprehensive studies of the role of attention and working memory in both signed and spoken interactions with and among Deaf people. Results of these studies will have important implications for both basic and applied research. Understanding the multifunctional uses of different subsystems of attention and working memory in language interaction by Deaf people will inform basic psycholinguistic research and theory. This understanding will also provide a foundation for intervention, particularly in the domain of language. For example, different and increased use of gaze and visual attention in signed language must be taught to second-language learners whose first language is spoken (e.g., hearing parents of Deaf children, interpreters, and teachers) if successful signed communication is to be achieved. Similarly, differences in the use of visual attention in oral and simultaneous communication with Deaf people must be taught to hearing teachers and parents. Finally, including information about differences in the use of visual attention and working memory in communication in bilingual-bicultural educational programs may be important for their success.

REFERENCES

Allport, D. A., Antonis, B., & Reynolds, P. (1972). On the division of attention: A disproof of the single channel hypothesis. *Quarterly Journal of Experimental Psychology, 24,* 225–235.

Argyle, M., & Cook, M. (1976). Gaze and mutual gaze. Cambridge, UK: Cambridge University Press.

Atkinson, R. C., & Shiffrin, R. M. (1968). Human memory: A proposed system and its control processes. In K. W. Spence & J. T. Spence (Eds.), *The psychology of learning and motivation: Advances in research and theory* (Vol. 2, pp. 89–195). New York: Academic Press.

Atkinson, R. C., & Shiffrin, R. M. (1971). The control of short-term memory. *Scientific American, 225,* 82–90.

Baddeley, A. D. (1986). *Working memory.* New York: Oxford University Press.

Baddeley, A. D., & Hitch, G. J. (1974). Working memory. In G. Bower (Ed.), *The psychology of learning and motivation* (Vol. 8, pp. 47–90). New York: Academic Press.

Baker, C. (1977). Regulators and turn-taking in American Sign Language. In L. A. Friedman (Ed.), *On the other hand: New perspectives on American Sign Language* (pp. 215–236). New York: Academic Press.

Baker, C., & Cokely, D. (1980). *American Sign Language: A teacher's research text on grammar and culture.* Silver Spring, MD: T. J. Publishers.

Baker, C., & Padden, C. A. (1978). Focusing on the nonmanual components of American Sign Language. In P. Siple (Ed.), *Understanding language through sign language research* (pp. 27–58). New York: Academic Press.

Bellugi, U., Klima, E. S., & Siple, P. (1975). Remembering in signs. *Cognition, 3,* 93–125.

Broadbent, D. E. (1958). *Perception and communication.* London: Pergamon.

Brooks, L. R. (1968). Spatial and verbal components of the act of recall. *Canadian Journal of Psychology, 22,* 349–368.

Conrad, R. (1979). *The deaf school child.* London: Harper & Row.

Duncan, J. (1984). Selective attention and the organization of visual information. *Journal of Experimental Psychology: General, 4,* 501–517.

Egly, R., & Homa, D. (1984). Sensitization of the visual field. *Journal of Experimental Psychology: Human Perception and Performance, 10,* 778–793.

Gathercole, S. E., & Baddeley, A. D. (1993). *Working memory and language.* Hove, UK: Lawrence Erlbaum Associates.

Goodwin, C. (1979). The interactive construction of a sentence in natural conversation. In G. Psathas (Ed.), *Everyday language: Studies in ethnomethodology* (pp. 97–121). New York: Irvington.

Goodwin, C. (1981). *Conversational organization: Interaction between speakers and hearers.* New York: Academic Press.

Israel, J. B., Chesney, G. L., Wickens, C. D., & Donchin, E. (1980). P300 and tracking difficulty: Evidence for multiple resources in dual-task performance. *Psychophysiology, 17,* 259–273.

Israel, J. B., Wickens, C. D., Chesney, G. L., & Donchin, E. (1980). The event-related brain potential as an index of display-monitoring workload. *Human Factors, 22,* 211–224.

Johnson, W. A., & Dark, V. J. (1986). Selective attention. *Annual Review of Psychology, 37,* 43–75.

Kahneman, D. (1973). *Attention and effort.* Englewood Cliffs, NJ: Prentice-Hall.

Kendon, A. (1967). Some functions of gaze direction in social interaction. *Acta Psychologica, 26,* 1–27.

Kiefer, R. J., & Siple, P. (1987). Spatial constraints on the voluntary control of attention across visual space. *Canadian Journal of Psychology, 41,* 474–489.

Liberman, A. M., & Mattingly, I. G. (1985). The motor theory of speech perception revisited. *Cognition, 21,* 1–36.

Liddell, S. (1978). Nonmanual signals and relative clauses in American Sign Language. In P. Siple (Ed.), *Understanding language through sign language research* (pp. 59–90). New York: Academic Press.

Locke, J. L., & Locke, V. (1971). Deaf children's phonetic, visual and dactylic coding in a grapheme recall task. *Journal of Experimental Psychology, 89,* 142–146.

Maxwell, M., & Bernstein, M. (1985). The synergy of sign and speech in simultaneous communication. *Applied Psycholinguistics, 6,* 63–82.

McLeod, P. D. (1977). A dual-task response modality effect: Support for multiprocessor models of attention. *Quarterly Journal of Experimental Psychology, 29,* 651–667.

Meadow-Orlans, K., MacTurk, R., Prezioso, C., Erting, C., & Day, P. (1987, April). *Interactions of deaf and hearing mothers with three- and six-month old infants.* Paper presented at the Meeting of the Society for Research in Child Development, Baltimore, MD.

Navon, D., & Gopher, D. (1979). On the economy of the human information processing system. *Psychological Review, 86,* 214–255.

Norman, D. A., & Bobrow, D. G. (1975). On data-limited and resource-limited processes. *Cognitive Psychology, 7,* 44–64.

Pashler, H. (1990). Do response modality effects support multiprocessor models of divided attention? *Journal of Experimental Psychology: Human Perception and Performance, 16,* 826–842.

Posner, M. I. (1978). *Chronometric explorations of mind.* Mahwah, NJ: Lawrence Erlbaum Associates.

Posner, M. I., Snyder, C. R. R., & Davidson, B. J. (1980). Attention and the detection of signals. *Journal of Experimental Psychology: General, 109,* 160–174.

Reilly, J. S., McIntire, M. L., & Bellugi, U. (1990). Faces: The relationship of language and affect. In V. Volterra & C. Erting (Eds.), *From gesture to language in deaf and hearing children* (pp. 128–141). New York: Springer-Verlag.

Reilly, J. S., McIntire, M. L., & Seago, H. (1992). Affective prosody in American Sign Language. *Sign Language Studies, 75,* 113–128.

Richmond-Welty, E. D., & Siple, P. (1999). Differentiating the use of gaze in bilingual-bimodal language acquisition: A comparison of two sets of twins with deaf parents. *Journal of Child Language, 26,* 321–338.

Rutter, D. R. (1984). *Looking and seeing: The role of visual communication in social science.* Chichester, UK: John Wiley & Sons.

Schneider, W., & Detweiler, M. (1987). A connectionist/control architecture for working memory. In G. H. Bower (Ed.), *The psychology of learning and motivation: Advances in research and theory* (Vol. 21, pp. 54–119). New York: Academic Press.

Shiffrin, R. M., & Schneider, W. (1977). Controlled and automatic human information processing: II. Perceptual learning, automatic attention, and a general theory. *Psychological Review, 84,* 127–190.

Siple, P., & Akamatsu, C. T. (1991). Emergence of American Sign Language in a set of fraternal twins. In P. Siple & S. D. Fischer (Eds.), *Theoretical issues in sign language research: Psychology* (pp. 25–40). Chicago: University of Chicago Press.

Siple, P., Akamatsu, C. T., & Loew, R. C. (1990). Acquisition of American Sign Language by fraternal twins: A case study. *International Journal of Sign Linguistics, 1,* 3–13.

Siple, P., Richmond-Welty, E. D., Howe, J. N., Berwanger, P., & Jasper, J. E. (1994, January). Gaze, joint attention and interaction in twins with deaf parents. Paper presented at the Boston University Conference on Language Development and the Annual Meeting of the Linguistics Society of America, Boston, MA.

Treisman, A. M., & Davies, A. (1973). Divided attention to ear and eye. In S. Kornblum (Ed.), *Attention and performance IV* (pp. 101–117). London: Academic Press.

Wickens, C. D. (1980). The structure of attentional resources. In R. S. Nickerson (Ed.), *Attention and performance VIII* (pp. 239–257). Mahwah, NJ: Lawrence Erlbaum Associates.

Wickens, C. D. (1984). Processing resources in attention. In R. Parasuraman & R. Davies (Eds.), *Varieties of attention* (pp. 63–102). New York: Academic Press.

Wilbur, R. B., & Petitto, L. A. (1983). Discourse structure in American Sign Language conversations (or, How to know a conversation when you see one). *Discourse Processes, 6,* 225–241.

Wilson, M., & Emmorey, K. (1997). Working memory for sign language: A window into the architecture of the working memory system. *Journal of Deaf Studies and Deaf Education, 2,* 121–130.

9

When Does Modality Matter? Evidence From ASL on the Nature of Working Memory

Margaret Wilson
North Dakota State University

Karen Emmorey
The Salk Institute for Biological Studies

The Signs of Language included a chapter titled "Remembering Without Words: Manual Memory," which was written with Patricia Siple and presented some of the very first studies examining Deaf people's memory for American Sign Language (ASL) signs. Previously, memory research focused on how deaf people remembered English and rarely considered the possibility that they might code information for memory using sign language. Klima and Bellugi and their colleagues discovered that there were several parallels between memory for words and memory for signs. For example, Bellugi, Klima, and Siple (1974) found evidence for a *primacy effect* (initial list items are recalled well) and a *recency effect* (the last few items on a list are recalled well) for lists of ASL signs. The primacy effect is argued to be due to the fact that items early in a list get more rehearsal, and finding such an effect for sign language provided some initial evidence for a rehearsal process for signs. The recency effect has been argued to be due to "echoic" memory or to a "precategorical acoustic store" that retains just-heard words prior to active rehearsal (Crowder & Morton, 1969). And yet Bellugi et al. (1974) had observed a recency effect for lists of ASL signs that could not be due to acoustic memory. Shand and Klima (1981) went on to present evidence that the recency effect and the associated suffix effect[1] do not arise from an acoustic sensory store, rather they argued that these effects are related to memory for a primary linguistic code, which can be either acoustic (speech) or visual (sign). Thus, not only did the early work of Klima and Bellugi begin to reveal the structure of working memory for sign language, their work also provided important insight into the nature of working memory for spoken language.

Another important finding described in the "Remembering without words" chapter was that signers exhibited poorer recall for lists of formationally similar signs (e.g., NAME, SOCKS, EGG, MONTH) than for lists of random (unrelated) signs. This result is parallel to results found with speakers; that is, lists of similarly sounding words (e.g., *mad, man, cat, cad*) yield poorer memory performance compared to lists of phonologically dissimilar words (e.g., *pit, cow, day, bar* [Conrad & Hull, 1964]). This pattern of memory performance is referred to as the *phonological similarity effect* and has been used to argue that information is coded in working memory in some type of phonological (or articulatory) code, rather than in a semantic code. The fact that Klima and Bellugi found an analog to the phonological similarity effect for ASL provided evidence for the phonological status of formational aspects of signs (e.g., handshape, place of articulation) and provided support for the hypothesis that information is stored in a sign-based form for ASL working memory.

MODALITY INDEPENDENT PROCESSES
IN LINGUISTIC WORKING MEMORY

Building on and inspired by these early results, we initiated a series of studies examining the precise nature of working memory for sign language (Wilson and Emmorey, 1997a, 1997b, 1998a, 1998b, in press). For hearing participants, linguistic working memory has been argued to consist of a phonological store with an articulatory process that refreshes information within the store (e.g., Baddeley, 1986). Evidence for this architecture derives from several effects and their interactions. Both the phonological similarity effect and the *articulatory suppression effect* provide evidence for a speech-based code in memory for hearing participants. The articulatory suppression effect refers to the finding that when partici-

---

[1]The suffix effect refers to the finding that when an additional not to be remembered item (a "suffix") is presented at the end of a list, the recency advantage is reduced or eliminated for auditorily presented items.

pants are asked to produce irrelevant mouth movements, for example, saying "ba, ba, ba" during presentation of a list of words to be remembered, overall performance declines. The decrement in memory performance suggests that some type of articulatory rehearsal is involved.

Crucially, articulatory suppression and the phonological similarity effect interact in different ways, depending on how stimuli are presented. When English words are presented auditorily, the phonological similarity effect is not affected by articulatory suppression. However, when stimuli are presented visually as print or pictures, then the phonological similarity effect is eliminated under articulatory suppression (Murray, 1968). This pattern indicates that an articulatory mechanism is required to translate visual materials into a phonological code and that the phonological similarity effect is a product of the phonological store to which spoken materials have direct access. In contrast, the *word-length effect* (lists of long words yield poorer memory performance than lists of short words) is abolished under suppression (Baddeley, Lewis, & Vallar, 1984). This result suggests that the word-length effect arises from the articulatory rehearsal processes itself, unlike the phonological similarity effect, which is tied to the phonological storage buffer.

We examined each of the aforementioned effects in ASL using an immediate serial recall task. First, we replicated the Klima and Bellugi (1979) study: Deaf signers exhibited poorer recall for lists of phonologically similar signs (signs with the same handshape; e.g., BOOK, BROOM, SOAP, BREAD) than dissimilar signs (signs with varied handshapes; e.g., EARTH, EGG, KEY, SOCKS). In addition, we found that producing meaningless movements of the hands during presentation yielded poorer memory performance, suggesting an articulatory rehearsal mechanism. Crucially, this suppression effect did not interact with the phonological similarity effect, indicating that the two effects are independent, arising from separate components of working memory (Wilson & Emmorey, 1997a).

We next examined these effects for stimuli that had to be recoded to be stored in a sign-based form. Deaf signers were presented with nameable pictures and asked for the ASL sign for each picture at the time of recall. The results paralleled those with hearing participants. That is, we found an ASL phonological similarity effect when there was no hand motion during encoding, but the effect disappeared under suppression. Thus, an articulatory process is required to translate materials into an ASL code for working memory. When this process is removed through competing movements of the hands, evidence for sign-based memory disappears. This pattern of results supports a working-memory system for sign language that includes a phonological buffer and an articulatory rehearsal loop.

Further evidence for this architecture stems from the finding of a sign-length effect, parallel to the word-length effect (Wilson & Emmorey, 1998b). We found that deaf participants exhibited poorer memory for lists of long signs (e.g., PIANO, BICYCLE, CROSS, LANGUAGE) compared to lists of matched short signs (e.g., TYPEWRITER, MILK, CHURCH, LICENSE). Long signs contained circular or path movements whereas short signs involved short repeated movements. Unlike the ASL phonological similarity effect, the sign-length effect was eliminated under articulatory suppression, suggesting that the length effect is a direct consequence of the articulatory rehearsal process, which is unavailable under suppression. The phonological similarity effect appears to arise directly from a sign-based phonological store, and it is only eliminated when materials cannot be recoded into a phonological form (i.e., when picture stimuli are presented during manual suppression).

The fact that a phonological loop exists for a visual–spatial language suggests that the architecture of working memory is not fixed, but responds flexibly to experience with either visual or auditory linguistic information during development. We suggest that the phonological loop should be conceived of as a configuration of mechanisms that arise in response to appropriate linguistic input—regardless of the modality of that input.

MODALITY DEPENDENT PROCESSES
IN WORKING MEMORY

However, working memory for sign and for speech may not be completely parallel. Specifically, working memory for ASL may involve a type of spatial coding that is unavailable for spoken language. We were led to this hypothesis when we noticed that during serial recall, some of our deaf participants spontaneously responded by signing each item at a separate spatial location. This response pattern suggests that introducing a spatial component into the memory representation may assist performance, and that certain participants spontaneously discovered a strategy of coding in this manner.

To investigate this hypothesis, we presented deaf participants with a serial-recall task comparing memory for signs with a *moveable location* (neutral space signs such as MILK, LIBRARY, BATHROOM, ONE-DOLLAR) to signs with a *fixed body location* (body-anchored signs were all produced at the chin, e.g., BAR, LEMON, TWINS, CANDY). We hypothesized that deaf participants would be able to use spatial coding only for the signs with moveable locations because only these signs could be mentally "rehearsed" in diverse locations.

Our results supported this hypothesis: Signs with a neutral space location were remembered more accurately than signs with a body-anchored location (Wilson & Emmorey, in press). In addition, several participants were observed to spontaneously articulate the neutral space signs in a sequence of distinct locations. These results demonstrate that spatial coding can be used as a memory device over and above mere repetition of the to-be-remembered material. Furthermore, we found that when signs were presented at distinct locations on the videoscreen (e.g., in one of four quadrants), serial recall was not improved compared to central presentation. This finding indicates that when the spatial coding is nonlinguistic (i.e., the locations on the videoscreen are not part of ASL phonology), signers do not take advantage of spatial coding for recall. Because the spatial coding used by ASL signers is unavailable to speech-based working memory, these findings suggest that language modality can alter the structure of working memory.

Further support for the hypothesis that ASL working memory involves some type of spatial coding for serial order is found in a study conducted in collaboration with Ed Klima. Wilson, Bettger, Niculae, and Klima (1997) examined deaf and hearing children's ability to recall lists of digits (signed or spoken) in either forward or backward order. Many studies have shown that recalling a list of auditory words in reverse order is more difficult than recalling a list in the order presented, suggesting a unidirectional form of coding, much as time is unidirectional. However, spatial coding does not entail a necessary directionality. Thus, if sign-based working memory can capture serial order in a spatial form rather than a temporal form, then there may be little difference between backward and forward recall. This is exactly the result observed by Wilson et al. (1997). Deaf children performed equally well on forward and backward recall of signed numbers, exhibiting essentially no cost for the requirement to reverse the order of stimulus input. In contrast, hearing children were substantially worse on backward than forward recall—the standard finding for spoken-language materials. These data suggest that sign-based rehearsal mechanisms are not entirely parallel to speech-based mechanisms in working memory.

Thus far, we have been primarily concerned with the "rehearsal" aspect of ASL working memory—effects based generally on articulatory processes. Although the actual articulators differ for signed and spoken languages, the motoric systems available for rehearsal have similar properties. For example, both are hierarchical, rule governed, exhibit coarticulation effects, and involve rapid changes in articulator configuration. However, unlike the motoric output system, there are radical differences in the perceptual input systems to working memory for sign and speech. Vision and audition have grossly different processing capabilities and constraints. They differ in what kind of information they capture and also in how they code that information in terms of spatial and temporal characteristics, as we noted earlier. Further, the two modalities may differ in their ability to filter out unattended information. Thus, it is possible that those aspects of the working memory system that are directly dependent on perceptual processing will fail to show parallel structure between spoken language and sign language.

We investigated this possibility by looking for an *irrelevant sign effect* parallel to the *irrelevant speech effect* (Wilson & Emmorey, 1998a). This effect refers to reduced memory performance when participants are presented with meaningless speech or other structured auditory input irrelevant to the memory task (e.g., Baddeley, 1986; Jones & Macken, 1993). We investigated whether memory for signs would be disrupted by presentation of meaningless "signs" or other structured visual input. The question here is whether there is a single amodal input store for working memory (as proposed by Jones, Beaman, & Macken, 1996) or whether the input store is modality specific and sensitive only to disruption within the relevant modality.

To investigate this question, we presented deaf and hearing participants with an immediate serial-recall task. Deaf participants were presented with ASL signs on videotape, and hearing participants were presented with printed English words (glosses of the ASL signs), also on videotape. We tested two types of irrelevant visual material for both groups. The first consisted of pseudosigns, which are phonologically possible but nonoccurring ASL signs, and the second consisted of moving nonnameable jagged shapes (Atteneave figures). The irrelevant visual material was presented during a retention interval (after participants had seen the to-be-remembered list of words or signs but before they responded). For the baseline condition, participants watched a uniform grey screen alternating with dark grey during the retention interval.

Our results indicated that irrelevant material only disrupted memory for deaf participants viewing signs and not for hearing people reading English words. Hearing participants may have automatically translated the printed words into phonological or quasi-auditory form within working memory (perhaps for the purposes of rehearsal). Once in this recast form, they were not vulnerable to disruption from incoming visual material. In contrast, when deaf signers were required to watch either pseudosigns or moving shapes while trying to retain a list of ASL signs, they performed quite poorly compared to the baseline grey-field condition. This finding suggests some type of visual coding of ASL signs within working memory. In addition, this pattern of results argues against amodal representations in working memory. However, the memory disruption from irrelevant input is not specific to the modality of the stimulus itself (both hearing and deaf participants were presented with visual materials) but to the modality of the primary expressive form of the language whose phonological code is used for memory maintenance.

FUTURE DIRECTIONS

As Klima and Bellugi first demonstrated, sign language provides a unique window into the nature of representations that can be maintained in working memory and into the factors that shape the system itself. One of our future goals is to uncover the nature of the spatial coding used to encode serial order in sign-based working memory. For example, is the coding articulatory (and thus eliminated by manual suppression) or is it associated with the phonological store (and thus unaffected by suppression)? We are also exploring the possible role of motoric rehearsal for nonlinguistic visual–spatial memory. For example, does sign language expertise provide a strategy for rehearsing nonlinguistic visual stimuli that is unavailable to nonsigners? Answers to these questions will help us to understand the impact of language modality on the structure of linguistic and nonlinguistic visual–spatial working memory.

REFERENCES

Baddeley, A. (1986). *Working memory.* Oxford, UK: Oxford University Press.

Baddeley, A. D., Lewis, V. J., & Vallar, G. (1984). Exploring the articulatory loop. *Quarterly Journal of Experimental Psychology, 36,* 233–252.

Bellugi, U., Klima, E. S., & Siple, P. (1974). Remembering in signs. *Cognition, 3,* 93–125.

Conrad, R., & Hull, A. (1964). Information, acoustic confusion and memory span. *British Journal of Psychology, 55,* 429–432.

Crowder, R. G., & Morton, J. (1969). Precategorical acoustic storage (PAS). *Perception & Psychophysics, 5,* 365–373.

Jones, D. M., Beaman, P., & Macken, W. J. (1996). The object-oriented episodic record model. In S. Gathercole (Ed.), *Models of short-term memory.* (pp. 209–237). Hove, UK: Psychology Press.

Jones, D. M., & Macken, W. J. (1993). Irrelevant tones produce an irrelevant speech effect: Implications for phonological coding in working memory. *Journal of Experimental Psychology: Learning, Memory, and Cognition, 19*(2), 369–381.

Klima, E. S., & Bellugi, U. (1979). *The signs of language.* Cambridge, MA: Harvard University Press.

Murray, D. (1968). Articulation and acoustic confusability in short-term memory. *Journal of Experimental Psychology, 78,* 679–684.

Shand, M. A., & Klima, E. S. (1981). Nonauditory suffix effects in congenitally deaf signers of American Sign Language. *Journal of Experimental Psychology: Human Learning and Memory, 7,* 464–474.

Wilson, M., Bettger, J. G., Niculae, I., & Klima, E. S. (1997). Modality of language shapes working memory: Evidence from digit span and spatial span in ASL signers. *Journal of Deaf Studies and Deaf Education, 2,* 150–160.

Wilson, M., & Emmorey, K. (1997a). A visual-spatial "phonological loop" in working memory: Evidence from American Sign Language. *Memory and Cognition, 25*(3), 313–320.

Wilson, M., & Emmorey, K. (1997b). Working memory for sign language: A window into the architecture of working memory. *Journal of Deaf Studies and Deaf Education, 2*(3), 123–132.

Wilson, M., & Emmorey, K. (1998a). *An "irrelevant sign effect" in working memory for sign language.* Manuscript under review.

Wilson, M., & Emmorey, K. (1998b). A "word length effect" for sign language: Further evidence on the role of language in structuring working memory. *Memory and Cognition, 26*(3), 584–590.

Wilson, M., & Emmorey, K. (In press). *Functional consequences of modality: Spatial coding in working memory for signs.* In V. Dively, M. Metzger, S. Taub, & A. M. Baer (Eds.), Sixth Conference on Theoretical Issues in Sign Language Research. Washington, DC: Gallaudet University Press.

10

A Pilot Study of the Expressive Gestures Used by Classical Orchestra Conductors

Penny Boyes Braem
*Center for Sign Language Research,
Basel, Switzerland*

Thüring Bräm
*Lucerne Conservatory,
Lucerne, Switzerland*

A Personal Note About Ursie, Ed, and Music

Our first contact with Ursula Bellugi and Ed Klima came in the early 1970s when I (Penny) began my Ph.D. studies at Berkeley, with the intention of writing a dissertation on sign language. My advisor, Dan Slobin, recommended that I make contact with his old Harvard classmate, Ursie, who was just setting up a lab for sign language studies at the Salk Institute. The result for me was an exciting period of research with Ursie's team at Salk. Thüring was studying in the music department at Berkeley at the time and in his trips down to San Diego was included in the parties and dinners that Ursie and Ed would somehow find the energy to put on after working at least 14 hours straight on linguistics. We discovered that all four of us shared an interest in music, from different points of view (being a conductor, being related to a conductor, having been a dancer, etc.). Thüring and I have finally managed, after 25 years, to find a project on

143

which a sign language researcher and a classical music conductor could work together—namely, the hand gestures of conductors. We both are particularly happy that our joint effort can be included in a book for Ursie and Ed, in fond memory of the many spirited hours we spent with them, with conversations that roamed freely between the worlds of sight and sound.

INTRODUCTION

The purpose of this study is to extend the traditional analysis of the gestures that the orchestral conductor makes with the dominant hand, to those "expressive" gestures that are usually made with the nondominant hand. Our research questions are the following: Is there a repertoire of "expressive" gestures? If so, how do they compare with the hand gestures that accompany speech and with the more highly coded sign languages of the Deaf? Are conducting gestures systematized in any way beyond the organizing, structuring patterns of the classical orchestral conductor?

The music historian, Harvey Sachs (1993), in *Reflections on Toscanini,* recounted an anecdote that directly concerns these topics. The incident occurred during a performance of *Pictures at an Exhibition* by the Vienna Philharmonic orchestra in Budapest. Toscanini, who always conducted from memory, began to conduct the wrong episode. The principal bassoonist of the orchestra recounted the following:

> *Not one musician started to play!* It was ghost-like, a little like a nightmare: Toscanini conducted in the air, and not one sound occurred! Toscanini, for a tenth of a second, was flabbergasted and stony-faced: how come nobody plays? But in another tenth of a second he realized that instead of *Tuileries* he had conducted the beginning of *Bydlo*, which was very different in dynamic character. And with an almost indiscernible nod, he gave the right dynamic sign for the beginning of *Tuileries*, and then the orchestra, most harmoniously, as if nothing had happened, started to play. Afterwards he said: 'This is the greatest compliment an orchestra can pay me: I make a mistake, and the orchestra at once realizes I am wrong.' Why? Because his *Zeichengebung*, his gesture for communication and conducting, is so unmistakable in its one possible meaning that you cannot take it as meaning anything else. . . . (From Sachs, 1993, p. 148)

There are two relevant observations in this incident: First, there was a gestural communication from the conductor that was so clear that a hundred players reacted "correctly." Second, there is something, in addition to the organizational signs that operate as a communicative entity, whether it be an "indiscernible nod" or the "stony-face," that in a tenth of a second can give an unambiguous signal.

The conductor George Szell described Toscanini's technique as "deceptively simple":

> Toscanini . . . made a distinction between the responsibilities of the right and left arms. His right arm generally moved in broad, clear, compelling strokes, not merely beating time but drawing the musicians into the music and helping them to progress through it, persuading them to bring it to life; it activated and shaped the music. His left hand was responsible for the fine tuning: from a position directly in front of him, where it was invisible to much of the audience, it cautioned and exhorted. (Sachs, 1993, p. 150)

THE TRADITIONAL DESCRIPTION OF THE CONDUCTING GESTURES OF THE DOMINANT HAND

Equally important to what is shown by the conductor is what is not shown. The conductor does not indicate all the important elements of the music that can be found in the printed score: the pitches and the rhythmic values. The dominant hand indicates the organization (the beginnings and ends), the tempo, and the rhythmic raster, or tact. The nondominant hand shows special dynamics, sound colors, uniquely occurring events, entrances, and articulation. Naturally, all of these parameters influence each other and whether they are signaled by the dominant or the nondominant hand is more of a general tendency than a firm rule. However, most books on conducting describe a general division of labor between the hands, an asymmetry of movements and functions that is one of the difficult techniques that students of conducting must master.

This view is also found in one of the most authoritative treatments of conducting, *The Grammar of Conducting* by Max Rudolf (1994). A conductor himself, Rudolf was also the musical director of the Metropolitan Opera in New York in the 1940s and thus was in constant contact with other conductors such as Toscanini, Walter, and Szell. Rudolf treated the basic patterns of the right hand (the neutral 2 pattern, the staccato, and the legato beats) and the organizational "details" shown by the left hand. The musically most impressive interpretations are, of course, not solely due to these learnable techniques but are dependent on a thorough knowledge of the piece's structure and musical intent. Given that the conductor has this background knowledge, the dominant hand gestures are generally used to "direct the musical traffic." Examples for this directing function of the right hand are shown in the fundamental beating patterns represented in Fig. 10.1.

In books on conducting and in conducting courses, the use of the non-dominant hand has usually been mentioned in a more general way, giving the impression that it is up to the individual conductor to develop gestures that will show other aspects of the music, such as sound texture, fore-grounding of instrumental voices, density, atmosphere, and expression. Exactly how the nondominant hand (together with the facial and body expression and eye gaze) actually manages to communicate all these aspects of the conductor's message has never, to our knowledge, been studied in detail.

ANALYSES OF THE CONDUCTING
GESTURES OF THE NONDOMINANT HAND

Theoretical Bases

In this pilot study of the gestures of the nondominant hand of the conductor, the theoretical starting point is not historical or technical but is based

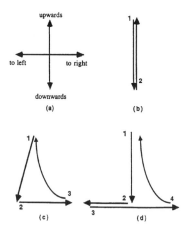

FIG. 10.1.   Dominant hand (from the conductor's perspective): (a) traditional division of the conducting space, showing the temporal organization of the music; (b) 2 beats; (c) 3 beats; (d) 4 beats.

instead on the componential analysis of the signs of Deaf sign languages as well as of gestures that hearing people use to accompany speech. These gestural components are then considered from the point of view of cognitive linguistic theories, which postulate the metaphoric underpinnings of much of human conceptualization.

The Componential Analysis of Hearing Gestures and Deaf Signs

Linguists who have studied the visual-corporal sign languages used by Deaf persons have found that the signs in these language are not global, nonanalyzable units but instead are composed of several distinct parameters, some of which are manual and others nonmanual (cf. for example Stokoe et al., 1965; Klima & Bellugi, 1979; Boyes Braem, 1995). The manual parameters that have been found to be important for this form of language include the location of the hand, its handshape and orientation, as well as its movement. The significant nonmanual parameters include the facial expression, position, and movements of the head and trunk and direction of eye gaze. Within these parameters, there are limited sets of subcomponents used in the individual sign languages. For example, of the many handshapes the human is physically capable of making, only a limited number are used linguistically in any one sign language.

In a subset of signs (productive or polymorphemic verbs with classifier handshapes), the handshapes can convey distinct meanings, depending on how they are combined with the other parameters and the context of the message. For example, the concept of "grasping an object" can be denoted by some of these verbs, in which the category of object being grasped is indicated by a specific handshape (cf. Fig. 10.2).

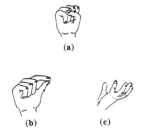

FIG. 10.2. "Grasp" handshapes for different kinds of objects; (a) for heavy objects (e.g. a suitcase); (b) for small, light, thin objects (a thread); (c) for fairly large, roundish objects (a ball, a pipe).

In other combinations of the parameters, the handshapes shown in Fig. 10.2 can convey other, nongrasping, meanings. The fist handshape in Fig. 10.2a, for example, when combined with a repeated linear movement, can mean "pounding" or "beating." The "pincer" handshape in Fig. 10.2b, if combined with repeated short, sharp, downward movements, could mean "pecking." In other words, the handshapes themselves are not tied to any one meaning but are polysemous, capable of conveying several meanings, depending on the context of the other parameters.

Calbris (1990) found this same polysemy in her study of the gestures that hearing French people use with speech, as did Boyes Braem (1998) for the interpretation of signs from Italian Sign Language by nonsigning hearing persons from several European countries.

The Metaphoric Basis of Conceptual Thinking

Although speech-accompanying gestures are polysemous, this does not mean that any one handshape can be substituted for another. One would not use a "fist" handshape, for example, to accompany a meaning that had to do with "small, fine detail," "precision," and so forth.

Polysemous gestures are thus constrained by a more basic system that, we propose, is that which several cognitive linguists have argued structures most of our conceptual thinking and spoken language (Johnson, 1987; Lakoff & Johnson, 1980; Lakoff & Turner, 1989; Sweetser, 1990).

According to Lakoff and Johnson (1980), much if not all thinking and communication about abstract concepts is made possible through the use of metonymic and metaphoric structures. Of particular relevance to this study of conducting gestures are their comments on the concepts humans have of "object," "substance," and "container":

> We experience ourselves as entities, separate from the rest of the world—as containers with an inside and an outside. We also experience things external to us as entities—often also as containers with insides and outsides. We experience ourselves as being made up of substances—e.g., flesh and bone—and external objects as being made of various kinds of substances—wood, stone, metal, etc. We experience many things through sight and touch, as having distinct boundaries, and, when things have no distinct boundaries, we often project boundaries upon them—conceptualizing them as entities and often as containers (for example, forests, clearings, clouds, etc.). (p. 58)

Several researchers have proposed that this kind of metaphoric–metonymic thinking not only underlies spoken languages but also Deaf sign languages and speech-accompanying gestures used by hearing persons (cf. e.g., Boyes Braem, 1981; Brennan, 1990; Taub, 1997; Wilcox, 1993 for sign language research; Boyes Braem, 1998; Kendon, 1995 for studies of hearing persons' gestures.)

Here, we argue that this kind of basic metaphoric thinking is also the basis for the communicative gestures that conductors make with their nondominant hand. The gestural space of the conductor is like a small stage, on which the actors are the conductor's hands, body, face, and eye gaze, all of which play out specific aspects of the musical score through the indication of basic metaphors. The size of this stage is about the same as that of the "signing space" of Deaf sign language, ranging vertically from the top of the head to the waist, and horizontally, an arm's length to either side and to the front. The effective conductor typically does not move his whole body much, as this would make it difficult for the musicians who are also concentrating on their scores to quickly focus on the conductor standing in front of them.

The conductor's stage is often a metaphorical container in which there are objects that one can manipulate: hold ("tenuto"), "pick-up," "drop," "push-away," "pull towards oneself," "touch," "stroke," "scratch," and so forth. The orchestra is the primary public for this gestural theater. It understands the gestural message and translates the underlying metaphors into sounds for the audience, a process of translating a theater for the eye (Greek *theaomai* = to see) into one for the ear.[1] Essential for this transfer of the musical message from the printed score to the musicians' musical thinking is a conceptual system of essentially body-based metaphors.

METHODOLOGY AND GENERAL FINDINGS

The data for this study are based on the analyses of the videotaped gestures of a variety of different conductors. This chapter deals only with manual gestures, although it is clear that facial and body expressions as well as eye gaze are also very important in the conductor's communication. The nondominant hand gestures used by these conductors were notated according to their subcomponents as well as their musical meaning.

---

[1]For the use of metaphors in theater, see Rozik (1992).

The compositional analyses of the gestures was done by the coauthor Boyes Braem, who is a sign language researcher; the interpretation of the musical intent of the gesture was made by the coauthor Bräm, who is himself a classical orchestra conductor and a teacher of conducting. For the illustrations, Bräm has also reproduced examples of all the gestures discussed.

Compared to the relatively large number of different handshapes that are phonological components of sign languages, the number of handshapes regularly used by conductors seems to be quite limited (cf. Fig. 10.3). In this respect, conducting gestures are similar to gestures used to accompany speech. The limited set of handshapes includes those found in most sign languages of the world, and those that are used first by young Deaf children learning sign languages. It is quite probably the fact that this is a basic, limited set of handshapes which makes the conducting gestures so easily interpretable by musicians in orchestras around the world, even when they are confronted by a conductor who has never directed them before and might be from a different culture. Most of these handshapes are also sufficiently different from each other that they can be easily distinguished. This is important, because in large orchestra formations, many musicians are seated at some distance from the conducting podium. As the dominant hand of most conductors of classical music is usually grasping a baton and beating the musical structure, most of the gestures for indicating "expression" are one handed.

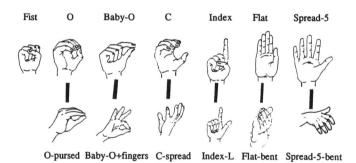

FIG. 10.3.   The limited set of handshapes used by the conductor in non-dominant hand gestures.

A REPERTOIRE OF NONDOMINANT
HAND GESTURES

The gestures that were used repeatedly by the conductors in this data seem to be based on the kinds of metaphoric associations that have been found in studies of the lexicon of sign languages and in speech-accompanying gestures used by hearing persons.

They can be grouped into the following categories, according to the source domain of the metaphor on which they are based:

  (a) manipulating objects
  (b) showing the path or form of an object
  (c) indicating direction
  (d) portraying an object
  (e) indicating a body part
  (f) holophrastic interjections

(a) Manipulating Objects = Sound Quality, Structure, Articulation, Musical Development, Psychological Motivation

A great many conducting gestures fall into the category of manipulation of objects. These are gestures that represent a grasping of an object, a touching, holding, or letting go of an object, hitting or chopping, painting, playing something.

"Pulling out an object"
   In this gesture, a rounded "pincer" handshape moves in a straight line from a musician toward the conductor, who is metaphorically pulling a sound, like a thread, out from the musicians' mouth. The pincer handshape (see Fig. 10.4a) indicates that a thin sound is desired and is typically used for flute sounds and vocalists. For the drawing out of a fuller sound (e.g., from a brass instrument), all the components of the gesture remain the same (location, movement, orientation of the hand), but a full cupped grasp handshape would be used instead of the pincer handshape (Fig. 10.4b).
"Taking out of view"
   Another common left-hand gesture used by many conductors is based on the metaphor of "taking something away from the visual

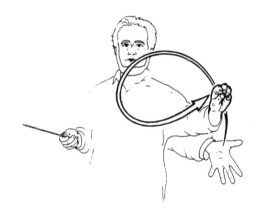

FIG. 10.4. "Pulling out an object": (a) thin sound and (b) a full sound.

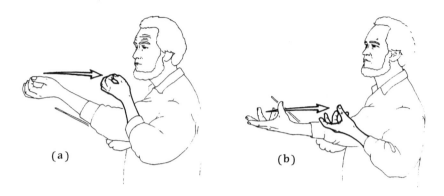

FIG. 10.5. "Taking out of view" = stop playing!

FIG. 10.6. "Gathering objects" = homogenous sound quality.

field" (see Fig. 10.5). In this case, what is being metaphorically taken away is all the sound. The gesture is used at the end of the piece or section to indicate "stop the production of sound." For this purpose, an open hand closes to a closed grasp hand and can be combined with a movement toward the conductor or with a movement to "off-stage," which can be in a direction out of the conducting space (i.e., below the waist, to the side, even to behind the back). Which of these movements are used seems to be up to the personal preference of the individual conductor, many of whom seem to have their trademark "taking out of view" gesture. The manner of the closing of the hand into the grasp handshape can indicate more precisely how the music should end: an abrupt cut-off with a fast movement; a slowly dying sound if the fingers close successively while the hand moves out of sight.

Several other types gestures have been observed in the data that involve the handling of an object are described briefly next:

"Gathering objects," or individual sounds, in order to elicit a homogenous sound quality or an increasingly focused one (Fig. 10.6);

"Supporting an object" to sustain a solid sound quality (Fig. 10.7);

"Hitting a hard object," which, depending on the type of movement with which it is combined, is used for a hard and precise or heavy sound quality (Fig. 10.8a). If the orientation of the hand is turned, the association becomes more specifically one of "hacking, as in hacking wood" and is used for different grades of staccato (Fig. 10.8b). If a less hard attack is desired, the handshape component of this gesture can be changed to that of an open flat hand, palm oriented downward.

"Pushing an object," which pushes the sound away (out in front, upward or downward) to where in the beat the point of playing—the attack—begins, as well as how strong the attack should be (Fig. 10.9).

"Touching a surface," which, depending on the type of movement and the handshape can indicate, for example, a smooth, homogeneous sound with the full flat handshape (Fig. 10.10) or a scratchy sound (claw handshape).

"Feeling a substance" such as moving the hand through flour, honey, water, kneading bread dough, squeezing clay, and so forth, to elicit

FIG. 10.7. "Supporting an object" = sustained sound.

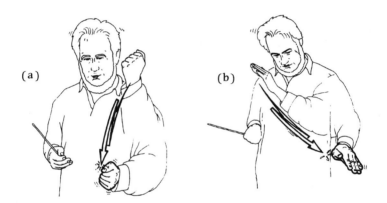

(a)

(b)

FIG. 10.8. "Hitting an object" = (a) hard or (b) hacking sound quality.

FIG. 10.9. "Pushing an object" = point and strength of attack.

FIG. 10.10. "Touching a surface" = sound quality (e.g., homogeneous sound quality).

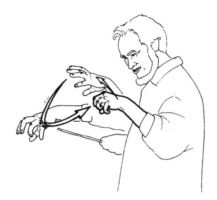

FIG. 10.11. "Feeling a substance" = sound quality (e.g., thick, dense).

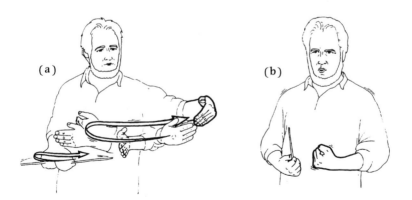

FIG. 10.12. "Playing an instrument" = play out your instrument (a) strings or (b) brass.

specific sound qualities such as "feather light," "sticky," "thick,"
and "fur-like" (Fig. 10.11).

"Playing an instrument" mimics the hand and body motions as well as
facial expressions typically used by players of particular instruments (bowing for strings, beating for timpani, showing an embou-
chure for winds, strumming strings for harp, rippling a keyboard,
etc.) to encourage the musicians to thoroughly savor and "play out"
this passage on their instrument (Fig. 10.12a and 10.12b).

"Drawing or painting," in which an open, flat hand is held downward,
and moves like a brush between two locations to "smooth together
the surfaces" (Fig. 10.13a); a pincer handshape, as if holding a
small brush or pen, when combined with repeated, short jabbing
movements, marks important points in the musical passage, which
often are turning points in the musical development (Fig. 10.13b).

(b) Showing the Path or Form
of an Object = Structure

Some gestures are indicators of musical paths in that they show where a
musical development begins and in which direction it develops. These
paths can be the development of the content or motive of the music, or be
a purely "geographical" indication of the movement of the playing of the
motive first by one musical group, then another. The significant components here are the locations where the gesture begins (for geographical
indications, the group of musicians who play the beginning of the development), and the location where it ends (the group that continues the
development). The handshape can be a traditional deictic index finger or a
flat whole hand handshape with digits together or separated, or even a
lightly cupped handshape. The manner of movement as the hand moves
from group to group can be varied to indicate more details of the development: slow, brisk, abrupt change, and so forth (Fig. 10.14).

The general structure of a musical "form" is indicated either by an
index finger alone to stress the sound "line," or by a full, flat hand in an
arcing movement to indicate a fuller structure, usually a combination of
harmony and "grain" (Fig. 10.15).

(c) Vertical Direction = Dynamics

Vertical levels within the conducting space can indicate the dynamics of
the music: high level = more = louder; low level = less = softer. These lev-

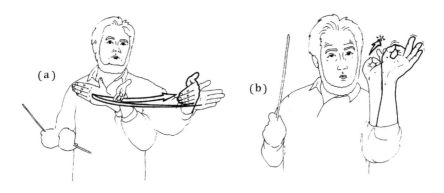

FIG. 10.13. "Drawing, painting" = (a) connected musical sequence; (b) important points, pivots in musical passage.

FIG. 10.14. "Path" = movement of musical material between instruments.

FIG. 10.15. "Form" = harmony and "grain" of a musical motive.

els are indicated by a gesture with an open flat hand, moving upward or downward, palm held horizontally (Fig. 10.16a, and 10.16b). An accompanying lateral spreading or closing of the digits can augment the "louder" or "softer" effect. (An analogous opening = louder and closing = softer metaphor can be indicated by the arms moving horizontally apart or together.)

(d) Portraying an Object = Sound Quality

A gesture in which a closed hand, palm oriented up, opens into a spread-5 handshape is used for a particular timbre of the sound, a light, radiating quality (Fig. 10.17). In many sign languages, this opening gesture is the metaphoric base of signs associated with "radiating" objects (streams of water, rays of light, etc.). In the conducting gesture, the metaphor is "radiating sound." If the movement component of the hand is changed, from moving upward to moving out toward the orchestra, and is combined with a sharp, emphatic opening of the digits, the gesture means "louder and more brilliant."

(e) Indicating a Body Part = Intensity, Focusing, Intonation

Gestures that involve pointing to particular parts of the body can metonymically refer to functions of that body part or, in further derivation, to metaphoric meanings associated with it in particular cultures:

Heart/Solar plexus: In pointing to these parts of the body, the
    conductor is indicating that at this passage of the music, there
    should be an emotional intensity, or (in the case of the solar plexus),
    that a "concentrated/centered" quality of playing is desired.
    (Fig. 10.18a).
Ear: When a conductor points to, touches, or grabs his ear, he is
    making an association with the ear's biological function, which is
    hearing, and thereby indicating to the musicians, "Listen!"
    Specifically, this gesture is used when the conductor wants the
    musicians to pay closer attention to or correct their intonation
    (Fig. 10.18b).
Lips: The indication of the lips can have at least two different
    meanings:

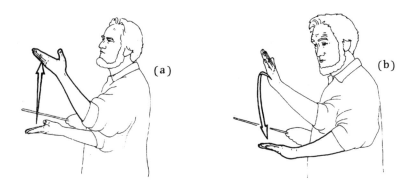

FIG. 10.16.   (a) Upward = louder; (b) downward = softer.

FIG. 10.17.   "Rays" = sound quality (radiating, bright timbre).

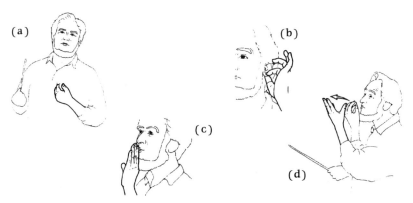

FIG. 10.18.   Body parts = sound quality (a) heart/solar plexus = play with emotion/concentrated; (b) ear = correct intonation; (c) lips = softer or more sensuous; (d) nose = light "perfumed" sound.

—The widely conventionalized meaning of "shh, keep quiet" is used by the conductor to indicate "play softer!" (Fig. 10.18c).

—If a "pursed" handshape is used as in Fig 10-8(d) and the hand is brought close to the lips, the association is that of something that tastes good. The gesture is used by the conductor when a "sensuous" sound quality is wished.

Nose: The indication of the nose by conductors is interesting, in that— unlike the largely negative associations that the nose has in gestures used by speakers ("stinks," "odious," "snotty," "snobby" and so forth), the association for an orchestra is generally that of a positive sensuous quality. The flat O handshape is used, often together with a slight intake of breath, to indicate that a lightly "perfumed" sound is desired (Fig. 10.18d).

(f) "Holophrastic Interjections" = Tempo, Structure, Motivation

Another kind of category of conducting gestures is based on more cultur- ally encoded gestures used by speakers for "holophrastic interjections," such as exhortations to the addressee to "go on, continue," or "be careful."[2] The following are examples of this kind of gesture in the conducting data:

- A gesture meaning "keep moving!" in which the most important component is a repeated forward circling movement of the hand. If tempo of repetitions is increased, it means "move faster" (Fig. 10.19).
- The vertically extended index finger, which in many cultures means "pay attention!" is usually used by the conductor as a preparation for something new or important that is coming up in the music (Fig. 10.20)
- The "offering" gesture seems to have a psychological function of encouraging the musicians to whom it is directed to "take this

---

[2]We are grateful to Isabelle Poggi for her suggestion of the term "interjections" for this category of conducting gestures. She defines interjections as the only case in spoken language of a "holophrastic signal." A holophrastic signal "cannot be separated into subsignals without completely losing its mean- ing—[it] conveys all the meaning of a Communicative Act, i.e. both its performative and its proposi- tional content" (Poggi, 1998, pp. 8–9). An example of a holophrastic gesture in the Italian culture is one that has an open, flat handshape, palm down, fingers forward, combined with an up-and-down movement. The meaning of this gestures is "come here" and includes the predicate (to come), the argu- ments (hearer should come to speaker), and the performative (a command). (See also Poggi, 1987.)

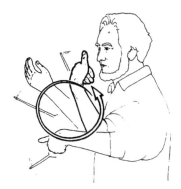

FIG. 10.19.　"Keep moving!" = "continue playing as you are."

FIG. 10.20.　"Pay attention" = "important change is coming up."

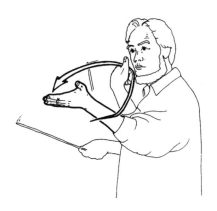

FIG. 10.21.　"Offering" = "take it, it's your turn."

passage," in the sense, "it's your turn, carry it on" (Fig. 10.21). The form of this gesture is the flat hand held with palm facing upward, the fingertips pointed forward, sometimes simply held or combined with a slight movement toward the orchestra. Important to this gesture is the simultaneous eye contact, raised eyebrows, and positive facial expression. This "offering" gesture is similar to one of the first gestures that young children use in their prelinguistic communications. Kendon (personal communication, Berlin, April 1998) suggested that in its derived sense ("it's your turn"), it is used by speakers as a kind of conversational regulator, which is also how it seems to function in the context of the orchestra.

- The "pursed" handshape, with palm oriented upward (Fig. 10.22) is, according to Kendon (1995), used in some European cultures by speakers to focus on some aspect of the accompanying speech. Some conductors use this gesture in an analogous way to indicate a focus on some aspect of a musical passage.
- Another more culturally encoded gesture used by some conductors is similar to the "cut-off," or "finish" gesture used by umpires in sport matches. This is a two-handed gesture, in which the open flat hands, palms down, are initially crossed over each other in front of the torso, then the arms move rapidly out to the side. The conductor uses this gesture for indicating abrupt endings to musical passages.

Different gestures are often produced successively, to give a series of instructions; for example, a "moving through a thick substance" gesture followed by a "radiating burst" gesture, finishing with a "supporting/sustaining" gesture.

DISCUSSION

The gestures described here are a representative but certainly not exhaustive list of the repertoire of gestures used by conductors. Further analyses from a wider variety of conductors would undoubtedly add gestures to the

FIG. 10.22.   Pursed handshape = focused element.

list. However, the added gestures would probably involve one of the limited set of handshapes. Furthermore, they would probably fall into one of the major categories discussed in the previous section. This is because most conducting gestures are based on metaphoric–metonymic connections between aspects of the music and physical experiences that human beings have with objects in everyday life. Some of these experiences have to do with handling objects (grasping, letting go, supporting, touching, etc.) whereas others have to do with biological functions of the body (smelling, hearing), and still others have to do with describing visible forms (drawing lines, painting surfaces). Or the conducting gesture would be borrowed from a culturally encoded gesture used by speakers as a "holophrastic interjection."

Factors Influencing Range and Choice of Gestures Used

Perhaps because many of the expressive gestures of conductors have so much in common with other aspects of human experience and communication, they can function effectively—with no accompanying verbal explanation—with musicians from a wide variety of cultures. There very probably are, however, some differences between cultures as to which gestures from the repertoire are preferred. European-trained conductors seem to use many of the "handling" gestures in which aspects of the music are metaphorically conceptualized as concrete objects or lines to represent musical paths and turning points. Instead of the line, some Japanese-trained conductors prefer gestures that indicate the turning points as dots in a pattern. Seiji Osawa, for example, is known among conducting students as having a "painterly" style. For many Europeans, Bernstein has a typical "American" style. Even for conductors from the same culture, there are clearly different styles of conducting, a different selection of the gestures in the repertoire described earlier, and a difference in the frequency of use of nondominant hand gestures. These stylistic differences are influenced by several different factors in the communication situation: the musical setting, the nature of the audiences, the style of the work, and the personality of the conductor.

The Musical Setting. The conducting style can vary, depending on whether the situation is a concert, rehearsal, radio, or TV recording. For example, the gesture of grasping the ear to indicate that intonation should be corrected is used during a rehearsal but usually not during a concert. The acoustic environment is also influential—different styles of conducting will be used depending on the room size, its resonance, if the concert is outdoors, and so forth.

The Style of the Work.   Very important is the style of the music: The works of Bach, Mozart, Bruckner, Johann Strauss, Webern, Berlioz, or Lutoslawski all require a selection of different gestures from the repertoire.

The Audiences.   A conductor has two audiences: the orchestra and the listening public. For the orchestra, not only are the size and nature of the musical ensemble important, but also how well the conductor and the orchestra know each other. If the two know each other very well, the conductor can be much more economical with gestures than would be the case with doing a first concert with an orchestra. In the older films of the first generation of European conductors (e.g., Richard Strauss), a more limited set of gestures seems to be used as compared to many modern conductors. Although there could be many reasons for this, one certainly is that in that time, a conductor did not jet around the world, conducting a different orchestra every week, but stayed in one place and gave regular weekly concerts with one orchestra. The musicians of these orchestras perhaps did not need additional indications through gestures, as they knew their permanent and long-time chief conductor and his styles of interpretation very well.

Another audience factor is whether the ensemble is professional or amateur. When conducting an amateur chorus, many more creative, "improvised" gestures are needed than when standing in front of a professional chorus, with whom the same effect can be elicited with a small smile.

The public as audience is a factor, depending on the personality of the conductor. The early conductors did not constantly conduct in front of film and television cameras and so perhaps did not feel the temptation to conduct for the audience as well as for the musicians. Some conductors seem to conduct more for the public than for the orchestra, using gestures that are correspondingly dramatic when viewed from behind.

The Personality and Culture of the Conductor.   This brings us to another important factor—the personality and cultural background of the conductor. Conductors have different images of themselves and of their functions as a conductor. The different personality types we observed include the following: Organizer, Interpreter of the Score, Animator, Hypnotist, Trainer, Buddy, Self-Realizer, and Showman. The strong contrast between the styles of Leonard Bernstein and Sergiu Celibidache, for example, is probably due in large part to their basically different personality types.[3] The New Yorker—Bernstein—is a Showman type, using many expressive gestures in his conducting. A videotape of his rehearsals of "Romeo and Juliet" with a student orchestra, during which he often stops the music to explain some aspect of the story to the musicians, provides good evidence that the gestures he uses in conducting are similar in quantity and quality to those he uses to accompany his speech. The Rumanian—Celibidache—on the other hand, was a Hypnotist type, who relied more on the power of his eye gaze than on his gestures. The gestures he did use, both in his conducting and in videotaped conversations, although quantitatively fewer, do fall into the categories proposed here.

How effectively the individual conductor uses the nondominant hand gestures described here depends also on how well he has, somehow, learned them. The more control the conductor has over this repertoire of gestures for specific musical purposes, the more likely the gestures will be used spontaneously and appropriately to model the sound and bring out its many meanings. The effective use of these gestures for conducting does seem to be something that has to be learned, as indicated by the sometimes awkward, often inappropriate and distracting gestures of young conducting students. Perhaps the "repertoire" of nondominant hand gestures, with their underlying metaphoric associations between experiences in the physical and in the musical worlds, could be dealt with more systematically in the curriculum of conducting courses.

CONCLUDING REMARKS

The expressive gestures of orchestral conductors, like signs of Deaf sign languages and speech-accompanying gestures, seem to be composed of a limited set of subcomponents that can be associated with several different kinds of meanings. I. Poggi (personal communication, Berlin, April 1998) suggested that these conducting gestures might be best classified as "descriptives which are used as directives."

Unlike sign language, the conducting gestures are polysemous entities

---

[3]These observations are from the following videotapes: Bernstein—"Taktschlagen kann jeder" (Rehearsals and performance of Berlioz's "Romeo and Juliet," Schleswig-Holstein Music Festival); and Celibidache conducts Bruckner (Symphony No. 6 in A Major), Munich Philharmonic, Recorded at the Müncher Philharmonie am Gasteig, November 26–30, 1991. Sony Classical Production, 1992.

whose exact meaning is only clear when set in a specific context. At one level, the meanings of these gestures are accessible through metaphoric–metonymic association with actions that the body can make, or with body parts, or, like conventionalized gestures ("emblems"), have more specifically encoded cultural meanings. At this level of interpretation, these gestures might be termed "iconic" in the sense that a broad range of persons would be able to associate an appropriate general meaning to them (e.g., "grasping something," "raising something up," etc.). However, the special derived meaning of these gestures ("tenuto," "staccato," "marcatissimo," "stress the sound line") is only interpretable to persons who know the second target domain of these gestural metaphors, the playing of classical orchestral music.

Grosjean (1998) made a comparison between improvisation in music and the creative production of new sentences in everyday language use. In contrast, the performance of classical orchestral music is to a large extent bound to the interpretation of works that have been notated in a fixed written form. In this context, the expressive gestures of the conductor become even more important, as they allow the addition of individual interpretation and spontaneous, even surprising, elements to the preprogrammed structure of the musical work.

ACKNOWLEDGMENTS

The authors are grateful for helpful comments on this study given by orchestral musicians at the workshop on conducting gestures at the Third International Congress for Improvisation in Lucerne, Switzerland (October, 1996) as well as by participants at the International Symposium "The Semantics and Pragmatics of Everyday Gestures" held in Berlin in April, 1998. An earlier form of this chapter was published in German (Bräm & Boyes Braem, 1998). All illustrations of conducting gestures were drawn by Katja Tissi, based on videotaped demonstrations done by T. Bräm.

REFERENCES

Boyes Braem, P. (1981). *Significant features of the handshape in American Sign Language.* Unpublished doctoral dissertation, University of California, Berkeley.

Boyes Braem, P. (1995). *Eine Einführung in die Gebärdensprache und ihre Erforschung* (3. Ed.) [An introduction to sign language and its research, third edition]. Hamburg, Germany: Signum.

Boyes Braem, P. (1998a). Kulturell bestimmte oder freie Gesten? Die Wahrnehmung von Gesten durch Mitglieder unterschiedlicher (hörender und gehörloser) Kulturen [The interpretation of gestures by hearing and deaf members of different European cultures]. In W. Fähndrich (Ed.), *Improvisation III.* Winterthur, Switzerland: Amadeus. (An English version of this study has been submitted for publication under the title: The Interpretation of Gestures by hearing and deaf members of different European cultures: A metonymic model for assigning meaning to gestures.)

Boyes Braem, P. (1998b). Kulturell bestimmte oder freie Gesten? Die Wahrnehmung von Gesten durch Mitglieder unterschiedlicher (hörender und gehörloser) Kulturen [The interpretation of gestures by hearing and deaf members of different European cultures]. In W. Fähndrich (Ed.), *Improvisation III* (pp. 192–219). Winterthur, Switzerland: Amadeus.

Bräm, Th., & Boyes Braem, P. (1998). Der Versuch einer Klassifizierung der Ausdrucksgesten des Dirigenten [An attempt to classify the expressive gestures of orchestral conductors]. In W. Fähndrich (Ed.), *Improvisation III* (pp. 220–248). Winterthur, Switzerland: Amadeus.

Brennan, M. (1990). *Word formation in British Sign Language.* Stockholm: University of Stockholm Press.

Calbris, G. (1990). *The semiotics of French gestures.* Bloomington: Indiana University Press.

Grosjean, F. (1998). *Language: From set patterns to free patterning.* In W. Fähndrich (Ed.), *Improvisation III* (pp. 71–84). Winterthur, Switzerland: Amadeus.

Johnson, M. (1987). *The body in the mind.* Chicago: University of Chicago Press.

Kendon, A. (1995). Gestures as illocutionary and discourse structure markers in Southern Italian conversation. *Journal of Pragmatics, 23,* 247–279.

Klima, E., & Bellugi, U. (1979). *The signs of language.* Cambridge: Harvard University Press.

Lakoff, G., & Johnson, M. (1980). *Metaphors we live by.* Chicago: University of Chicago Press.

Lakoff, G., & Turner, M. (1989). *More than cool reason.* Chicago: University of Chicago Press.

Poggi, I. (Ed.). (1987). *Le parole nella testa. Guida a un' educazione linguistica cognitivista* [The words in the head. Guide to a cognitive linguistic education]. Bologna, Italy: Il Mulino.

Poggi, I. (1998, April). *The Italian gestionary. Lexical gestures of Italian hearing people.* Presentation at the symposium, "The Semantics and Pragmatics of Everyday Gestures," Technical University of Berlin and Free University of Berlin, Germany.

Rozik, E. (1992). *Metaphorical handshapes in the theater.* Tel Aviv: Assoph.

Rudolf, M. (1994). *The grammar of conducting: A comprehensive guide to baton technique and interpretation* (3rd ed.). New York: Schirmer.

Sachs, H. (1993). *Reflections on Toscanini.* Rocklin, CA: Prima.

Stokoe, W., Casterline, D., & Croneberg, C. (1965). *A dictionary of American Sign Language on linguistic principles.* Washington, DC: Gallaudet College Press.

Sweetser, E. (1990). *From etymology to pragmatics.* Cambridge, UK: Cambridge University Press.

Taub, S. (1997). *Language in the body: Iconicity and metaphor in American Sign Language.* Unpublished doctoral dissertation, University of California, Berkeley.

Wilcox, P. (Forthcoming). *Metaphorical mapping metaphors in American Sign Language.* Washington, DC: Gallaudet College Press.

11

An Interpreter Creates
the Space

Nancy Frishberg
New Media Centers, San Francisco

This study relates an interpreting experiment in which a speaker—the author—retold a childhood experience about a particular outdoor space. The speaker used spoken words, pausing, and rhythmic structure—but no manual gestures. The interpreter's challenge was to portray the physical space using signing space. Analysis of this interpreting sample illustrates that a skilled interpreter can be vague, that the interpretation is dependent on the speaker's meaning being revealed through speech time, and that the interpreter's processing time can extend over the interpretation, reaching resolution much later.

Sign language interpreting is a complex cognitive and linguistic task. We hold interpreters to an ideal of performance that may be unachievable. Let me make a few of those idealizations explicit.

The Idealization

- The interpreter has the same knowledge as the speaker, available while creating the interpretation.
- The interpreter's signing choices are much like the speaker's would be if the speaker were using sign language directly and skillfully.
- The interpreter can choose to lay out the space as he or she wishes.

From the example of a single 3-minute English-to-American Sign Language (ASL) interpretation executed by an acknowledged expert, we begin to adjust to more realistic expectations.

The Realities

- The interpreter is much like any other listener, making sense of the discourse as it is expressed through time.
- The interpreter's signing choices are those of a listener's construction, rather than those of the speaker who knows where the rest of the narrative will lead.
- The spatial arrangement of signs in an interpreted narrative depends on the speaker's meanings as revealed successively through speech time and understood by the working interpreter.
- The spatial arrangement of signs in a skillful interpretation is also constrained by the conditions (phonological dominance relations, discourse structures) that signers generating their own messages follow.

Of course, greater background knowledge of the topic, familiarity with the speaker's perspective and speech habits, awareness of the audience's prior experience with the topic and speaker, and preparation for a specific assignment can privilege the interpreter, moving the interpretation toward the idealization.

A few published studies on interpreting between spoken and signed language have examined actual samples of interpreting events (Cokely, Roy, Zimmer, and J. Davis, inter alia). Much of this work has concentrated on phenomena generally characterized as sociolinguistic (languages in contact, comparisons of discourse structures, turn taking, and regulators). In this study, I describe the circumstances of an interpreting experiment undertaken in 1972 and analyzed only recently. Here is the detailed examination of how an interpreter, using signing space, recreates the physical space described by the speaker. The interpreter remains vague about the specifics of the space until he arrives at a satisfactory solution using the clues revealed in the spoken source message.

THE SCENE IN 1970

In Fall 1970, I was a first-year graduate student in linguistics at the University of California at San Diego. My graduate assistantship, as that of my officemate Richard Lacy, paid me for teaching the reading and grammar part of the Beginning Russian language courses. Native speakers—graduate students in other departments—taught speaking and listening. On the first Friday of that first term, Rick (a second-year student) invited me to Salk, "Do you want to go to The Salk Institute this afternoon—it's the seminar on child language acquisition of sign language?" Hey! Sure, why not? I already knew the manual alphabet in fingerspelling and remembered about a dozen signs from my junior high school days; my best friend in those years had deaf grandparents. I had met Ed Klima at the orientation for new graduate students, now I would meet Ursula Bellugi.[1]

My recollection of the first year at Salk is learning sign language, its structure, meanings, and production. Only a few months earlier, Ursula Bellugi had been awarded a National Science Foundation grant to study child language acquisition in a language none of the investigators knew. She had made contact with Darlene Scates and her mother, Bonnie Gough. Bonnie became our deaf consultant, teaching all of us sign and transcribing endless videotapes. Darlene began her professional career as an interpreter then.

Evolving Friday Seminars

Friday afternoons were seminar time. The first few months of Fall 1970 through Spring 1971, we prepared sentences for Bonnie to translate from English. If she signed HAVE SEVERAL WAY "There are several ways [to translate into signs]" we had hit pay dirt, linguistically. We tortured her with English ambiguities in our quest for distinct translations into sign for the several meanings.

Bonnie also gave basic lessons during the weekdays to some of us grad students, in which she pressed the issue of which English senses needed to be distinguished in sign. Her primary method, used also for her adult education night classes, was to introduce vocabulary lists from a single

---

[1]I use the familiar "sign," "sign language," and "signing" even though at most points the discussion concerns only ASL. I have not made a strong contrast between culturally and audiologically deaf individuals and thus used only the lower case form "deaf" with the intent that it stand for either sense.

semantic or structural domain (school, family, adjectives). In (semi-)private tutorials, she also let us each produce sign narratives about meaningful events in our own lives, which she would repeat in fluent signing, modeling good syntax, appropriate vocabulary choices, and clarity of diction, while letting us check that the ideas had indeed been communicated.

Meanwhile, Friday seminars changed their flavor. Ursula encouraged and invited a delightful variety of visitors to stop by and make a presentation to the research team, in a generally less formal atmosphere than most academic presentations. (How could you be formal in a room chock-a-block with children's toys and child-sized stools for seats? Who wouldn't relax after seeing the lab director's desk hidden behind brightly colored, pivoting panels, overlooking the cliffs, gliders, and the Pacific Ocean?)

In June 1972, Lou Fant visited the Bellugi Lab at The Salk Institute—perhaps for the first time—from California State University at Northridge (CSUN), where he taught sign language and interpreting. Certainly he and Ursula were acquainted from her visits to CSUN, where she conducted psycholinguistic experiments with the deaf and hearing graduate students. That same year, Lou Fant was certified as an interpreter in the first group to be tested under the Registry of Interpreters for the Deaf. He was also one of the pioneers in making sign language an academic course by writing language instruction textbooks. He comes from a family with many deaf members, although he is hearing.

Collecting Data

On this occasion, Ursula invited all of us[2] in as she and Lou experimented with techniques for him to "play with the language." This was her usual phrase, open-ended and quite unscientific in tone, fishing for intriguing language behavior from people, some of whom didn't believe their gestures constituted language. Lou held signing in the highest regard and could make many subtle and sophisticated distinctions among styles

---

[2]My best reconstruction of who was in the studio when we videotaped this segment includes those who are visible on the videotape (Ursula Bellugi, Lou Fant, and me) and those who are audible. Lou's eyes move among several people in the group present, which would have included Bonnie Gough and Steve Turner (during a summer internship from Gallaudet), two deaf people. I don't recall whether Ed Klima was present. There were probably another half dozen (hearing) people present, which may have included Battison, Abrahamsen, Fischer, Newkirk, Siple, or Lacy. Ursula Bellugi walked in front of the camera several times, just before the actual videotaping began, in a signature gesture, as if to say "pay no attention to the camera, even though it's pointing at you and someone is focusing now. You see, it's so unimportant that I can pass in front of the lens and we don't even care."

appropriate to the stage, the classroom, the courthouse, and the play-ground. On that occasion, he offered to show us the difference between transliterating and interpreting. I volunteered to provide the spoken language stimulus. Lou transliterated my first anecdote; then I told another anecdote and Lou interpreted.[3] In this discussion, I only look at the initial 3 minutes of the interpretation piece.

Spontaneous Speech Stimuli

I chose the events to use as the narrative anecdotes. In the first case (transliterating), the topic was the academic party a group of us had attended the night before. The group included several of the people who were present in the room, as well as several other people not present and perhaps unknown to those present. Lou was at a disadvantage, as I recall. He had not been present on the previous night, had just met most of us. I remember feeling concerned that he had less information than he needed. What I didn't know was how well informed he was, and thus how much experience could fill in for particulars. In the second case (interpreting), I spoke of how I had gotten a black eye at age 9 while playing with a sled; Lou didn't know any more or less about the situation than anyone else in the room (see Fig. 11.1).

Two Experimental Conditions

My own understanding of the terms *transliterate* and *interpret* in June 1972 corresponded to a set of stereotypes I had been exposed to through local interpreter organization workshops, as well as from the visitors to our lab and whatever I might have read about interpreting by then.[4] The basic definitions of the terms might not be very different from today: *Transliterate* means render a spoken message into a variety of signing more closely tied to English, and *interpret* means to render the speech into a more (real deaf) sign version—what William Stokoe called American

---

[3]Later, he performed some rehearsed material (making a "radio" out of yowling cats at his deaf grandma's house), in signs only. Ursula asked that he do it a second time using signs and speech simultaneously. These four short pieces were part of the afternoon session captured on helical scan 1/2-inch reel-to-reel videotape. I returned to Salk several years later and harvested these four pieces (transliteration, interpretation, and two versions of the radio story) onto VHS cassette.

[4]My first experience of interpreter training with a larger scope came later that summer, when the RID held its national convention in Long Beach, California.

FIG. 11.1.   Nancy Frishberg and Louie J. Fant at Salk Institute, June 1972.

Sign Language, and Lou abbreviated to Ameslan.[5] The stereotyping I refer to is revealed by my subject matter: a childhood reminiscence for the ASL translation and the reporting of a recent academic meeting for the English-influenced variety.

At that time, many training materials for interpreters were audiotapes of children's stories, chosen perhaps because the speech rates were slower on those tapes than on recordings of college-level business, psychology, or engineering lectures. The students of interpreting were presumably able to

---

[5]When we asked people "what do you call this?" in sign, it looks like (forward or backward) circling forearms, index fingers extended. In English, it came out "deaf sign," "real deaf sign," "the sign language," or "sign." Stokoe named the variety used in the U.S. ASL and Lou Fant shortened it, not to initials but to something pronounceable: AmeSLan (am'-e-slan). The amazing part is that some deaf and some hearing people managed to misunderstand Ameslan as a separate entity from either "(deaf) sign" or ASL.

At the Salk lab we used American Sign Language and ASL (pronounced as three letter names: [e:-es-el]) as the standard terms: we were looking for academic acceptance of linguistic study, and therefore needed a set of terms on analogy with the terms for spoken language. Today the struggle for academic acceptance is most often about the legitimacy of ASL for language study; see most recently the *Chronicle of Higher Education* from June 4, 1998 (Davis, L.), and the subsequent exchange of letters to the editor, published in the print version on July 24, 1998, although available to subscribers in online colloquy much earlier (Russell, Ervin).

keep up, to focus more on translations issues other than speech rate. Perhaps there was also the sense that children's stories were simpler (in choices of words, structures, and meanings) and therefore more suitable in the initial steps of preparing interpreters. Children's stories had the advantage over college-style lectures that they involved distinct characters, in addition to a narrator, and thus lent themselves to role playing. One of the negative consequences of using this sort of material is that some students (and even some trainers of interpreters) assumed that only childlike ideas and rudimentary grammar could be expressed well in ASL.

On this occasion, I consciously inhibited my manual gestures while speaking to avoid influencing the interpreter's translation. (Even without manual gestures from the speaker, laughter and other face or body gestures may still have been visible.) I was seated on Lou's right, holding the microphone. Lou preferred to stand, facing an audience of 5 to 10 hearing and deaf adults, all seated but the camera operator (another graduate student). The camera captured only him. I made a mental note at the time to look at how he represented the places I was describing. Had I given him the right cues to know where the house was, how the driveway was situated relative to the street and the house, how we used the wheeled Flexiflyer sled on the sidewalk?

THE TASK

An interpreter has several tasks in this situation:

- Accurately describe the space and portray how objects move in the space and how the events unfold through time.
- Keep track of how many participants there are and evaluate their relative importance to know how and when to refer to them as the story develops.
- Convey the speaker's mood or attitude about the events (both at the time of the events and at the time of the telling).
- Keep up with the speaker's rapid speech rate (about 190 wpm) employing appropriate processing time (also called lag time or décalage).
- Track the "hand–voice" lag time to hit key junctures (transitions, punchlines, and the like) in the narrative at roughly the same time as the speaker.

Lou Fant has urged interpreters, "Your interpretation should be so good that the audience believes it's really your own story." This point of view advocates that the interpreter assume the role of each speaker, rather than report what the speaker says. It is a perspective that each interpreting event has an audience, invites the interpreter to be an actor, and contrasts with the view that each interpretation is an interaction (Roy, 1992).[6] It also reminds the interpreter to take the perspective of whomever is speaking or portrayed and represent that person faithfully (Frishberg, 1990; Stewart et al. 1998).[7]

The remainder of this discussion focuses only on the first task mentioned, portrayal of space through the time of speaking, and even that in a sketchy way. A generation after it was recorded, examining these few minutes of the videotaped interpretation, I learned that this expert interpreter chose several different ways to portray the space as the story unfolded, committing to the specific relations in space only as the speaker's intent became evident. The interpreter cannot portray the speaker immediately because the interpreter doesn't know the speaker's mind, and does not have prior context. For source language material unfamiliar to the interpreter, the audience gets to watch the interpreter construct meaning. In this case where the meaning involves description of space and action within space, we see construction of the space. The interpreter acts initially more like the ideal audience member (attentive, constructing meaning) than like Lou's own idealization of the interpreter as speaker's foil.

Description

The interpreter's challenge is to portray the physical space just well enough to tell the speaker's story.

The initial portion of the reminiscence, lasting just under 3 minutes, describes two children (one of them the speaker) using a sled (with

---

[6]Lou worked as an actor for many years in Los Angeles, on stage, in movies and TV, and in work unrelated to sign language. Many of us remember him as the Ace Hardware guy from the 1980s. Some of his many contributions to the ASL literature repertoire are still available: a member of the National Theater of the Deaf in "My Third Eye" in the late 1960s; his versions of Old Testament stories for Joyce Films in the mid-1970s; as one of the Sign Media ensemble "Four for You" retelling Aesop's fables and other fairy tales for children; his voice renditions of several Sign Enhancers videos; and probably several more commercially available videotapes I'm forgetting.

[7]A second principle, modeled and verbalized for me by Donna Panko, another expert interpreter, is equally useful. Donna's encouraging reminder, when a novice puzzled over what to do about those speakers who seem to talk too fast, was "They always have to take a breath." For truly spontaneous speech (in contrast to reading a document aloud), the speaker will likewise often take a metaphoric breath by making an aside or otherwise increasing processing time.

wheels) in a particular outdoor space, the driveway of a neighbor's house. (The remainder of the anecdote recounts speaker's injury, recovery, and return to school.) For convenience of reference, the source text (see Appendix) has been segmented and the Segments labeled A through H. The terms *left* and *right* refer to the interpreter's perspective, rather than the viewer's perspective.

Segment A names the characters (the speaker and her childhood friend, Judy) [00:25:16]. Segment B offers the first hint of the physical space, that Judy lived "on a big hill." The interpreter places the hill and its houses to his right [00:54:17–00:58:08], using both eye gaze and positioning of the ASL nominals (HILL, HOUSE, HOUSES). The remainder of this segment recounts the borrowing of a sled with wheels from a neighbor. The position of the neighbor's house relative to the hill is offered in speech as "down the hill," which the interpreter renders as toward the lower right limit of his ordinary signing space.

In Segment C, we first learn that the driveway of the house in question has an unusual shape. The interpreter defines the driveway on a path between himself and his audience, with a dip in the middle. While the speaker uses the term "U-shaped," the interpreter concentrates on the extent of the driveway from higher to lower elevation (at the position of the house) and back to higher again, using forward and backward movement of a flat, palm-down hand as well as a tracing gesture with both hands, depicting the left–right boundary of the driveway. These two aspects of the physical shape (a 180° turn in the horizontal plane and the change of elevation) are not integrated. The interpreter looks at the audience members during the description of the driveway and then back to his space. At the point when the interpreter completes the description of the driveway [1:36:06], the speaker is well into the next segment.

In Segment D, the interpreter starts the ride "swinging down the hill" with the rider's motion shown from the interpreter toward the audience. The interpreter shows the rider lying down (using a V-classifier for prone body on the B-hand sled surface), switches to the Classifier for holding the handles, keeps the left (nondominant) hand in the Handle classifier while making the flat right (dominant) hand depict the downward path of the sled, shows the rider turning the handle (both hands) briefly toward the right, again holds the Handle on the left hand while showing the upward path of the sled with eyes and dominant hand. The speaker gives no clue whether the driveway and thus the ride required a left or right turn. The interpreter indicates a right turn [1:41:00] with the manual portion of the signal but does not commit fully with eye gaze, still moving the uphill leg of this first journey from signer to audience [1:42:00] with strong upward movement, as shown in Fig. 11.2. Of interest here is the interpreter's strong use of a side-to-side body rocking motion to indicate the excitement and turbulence of the ride, taking a cue from the speaker's phrase "swinging down . . . " and from vocal speed and pitch changes but without a strong portrayal of the turn in mid-ride, which will prove the key to the incident.

In Segment E, the speaker describes the second ride following the same path, but the interpreter changes his strategy slightly. The signs portray the rider lying down on the sled, taking off downhill from the upper left part of the space. When the Handles are grasped, the body banks to the left. The B-hand classifier portrays the sled's path downward. Now the eyes engage with the righthand Handles classifier turn at "Turned the handle at the bottom" [2:08:08], again the dominant hand representing the neutral vehicle (B-hand) in its curving rightward path. The eyes and hands both indicate a change of direction for the completion of this second journey, moving again in the signer-to-audience direction, for "steered her way back up" [2:08:24]. It's noteworthy that the eye gaze is not completely organized yet, as Fig. 11.3 indicates, slightly overshooting the usual signing space at the bottom, exaggerating the curve, and indicating slightly the upward path on the second leg. The two aspects of motion (downward and upward, with the full turn) are represented but not smoothly integrated yet.

In Segment F, the interpreter has a chance to describe the entryway to the house, the lowest point of the driveway, as a static tableau with plants on either side of the door. The speaker's internal dilemma, presuming she can't steer the sled, is offered with inward focused gaze [2:36:18, 2:37:18], shown in Fig. 11.4. The interpreter's shows the speaker's internal monologue, portraying the turn as a righthand turn.

In Segment H, the internal monologue is repeated, this time as rehearsal for the actual ride [3:01:25], still with a strong righthand turn (Fig. 11.5). The shouts of the bystanders to turn the handle [3:07:03, 3:07:09] are interpreted with only a strong righthand turn (Fig. 11.6); the urgency represented by the interpreter's facial gestures, including closed eyes. Failure to steer again shows a righthand turn, this time addressed to the audience, as befits the speaker's report of the fact to the audience (Fig. 11.7).

Finally, the speaker reveals that her eye was injured just above the eyebrow. The interpreter shows the right eye, as would be correct for the space he constructed where the sled moves from the left side to the right side of the driveway. The speaker mentions that it is was an injury to the left eye. The interpreter lets it stand uncorrected; there is no consequence in the remainder of the narrative.

"turned the handle"
[1:41:00]

"swinging back up"
[1:42:05]

FIG. 11.2.   First ride down the driveway: "turned the handle" [1:14:00],
"swinging back up" [1:42:05].

"rode down again"
[2:07:21]

"Turned the handle at the bottom"
[2:08:08]

FIG. 11.3. Second ride down the driveway: "rode down again" [2:07:21], "Turned the handle at the bottom" [2:08:08], "steered her way back up" [2:08:24].

"steered her way back up"
[2:08:24]

FIG. 11.3.   (Continued.)

ISSUES

We have learned more about how spatial dimensions of ASL are used in both monolingual language interaction and interpreted interactions in the years since this interpretation was recorded. Much of this work was undertaken either at The Salk Institute or within its influence.

Space for Spatial Language

In recent years, Emmorey and her colleagues in The Salk Institute laboratory have looked analytically at the encoding of linguistic, geometric, and locational information using spatial mechanisms of ASL. Some strategies inherent in the visual–spatial modality of a sign language that uses two articulators are thus not available to English speakers (Emmorey & Casey, 1995), including (a) phonological dominance relations between the hands and discourse backgrounding constraints both bias signers toward a choice of ground object; (b) verbs with Handle morphemes function primarily to express (actual or potential) movements, rather than describing the manner of holding.

[2:36:18]

"couldn't turn the handle"
[2:37:18]

FIG. 11.4. Internal monologue; "couldn't turn the handle" [2:36:18], [2:37:18].

"how to turn the handle"

[3:01:25]

FIG. 11.5.   Practice steering; "how to turn the handle" [3:01:25].

[3:07:03]

FIG. 11.6.   Shouting of the bystanders; "Turn it! TURN IT!" [3:07:03], [3:07:09].

[3:10:18]

"I didn't turn it."

FIG. 11.7. Speaker's report; "I didn't turn it" [3:10:10], [3:10:18].

In her keynote address to the Sixth International Conference on Theoretical Issues in Sign Language Research, Emmorey (1998) reviewed evidence that signers discuss objects in space with viewers differently from the ways that English speakers do. Indeed, signers behave differently when the objects and participants are all physically copresent than when the objects are remote from the signer and from the viewer. Signers have the option to refer to objects in the shared (actual) space when objects, addressee, and signer are all physically present. In the remote condition, where English speakers nearly universally adopt the viewer's point of view to communicate about objects at a distance, signers choose nearly equally the signer's point of view and the viewer's point of view. (In this condition, the third option of shared space is found, but only rarely.) When does an interpreter behave like the speaker whose message he is sending and when like the viewer who is receiving the message? To what extent are the answers to these questions under the conscious choice of the interpreter and to what extent dictated by the languages or messages being processed?

Space for Interpreting

Marina McIntire (1993, p. 61) asked "what strategies successful interpreters use to shift an essentially linear message (source language: spoken English) to an essentially three-dimensional message (target language: signs)?" She claimed that using space skillfully, linguistically, is advantageous to the deaf viewer's understanding; is inherently more efficient physically, providing protection for the interpreter (from injuries provoked by nonspatial gestural production); and demonstrates that the interpreter has taken time to understand the speaker's message (creating the interval between utterance of source language and production of target language rendition). McIntire identified seven mechanisms in a signed message (a nonexhaustive list) that add to the spatial quality of the signal:

a) eye gaze away from neutral or from eye contact with the viewer
b) directional verbs
c) pronouns and pointing
d) signs made out of normal sign space (other than directional verbs)
e) body shift (including head and shoulder movements)
f) classifiers
g) base hand counters

McIntire also cited linguistic structures (again a nonexhaustive list) that may trigger use of these spatial mechanisms. Notice that few if any of these items refer to the translation task:

A) introduction of nominals
B) remention of nominals
C) listing
D) plurals
E) time sequences
F) character shifts
G) locatives and prepositional phrases
H) coincidental use of a directional verb equivalent
I) anecdotes, especially those involving spatial interaction of animates
J) description of physical layout of setting
K) intonation giving cues about focus

McIntire's analysis extends insightfully to more complex discourse in which the spatial cues of signing are imposed on nonspatial relations among the entities in a spoken message. In the present study, we are concerned primarily with literal relations in space.

Analysis

Analysis of this interpreting sample illustrates that a skilled interpreter can be vague, that the interpretation is dependent on the speaker's meaning being revealed through speech time, and that the interpreter's processing time can extend over the interpretation, finding resolution much later.

This chapter opened with idealizations about interpreters and their tasks contrasted with the realities of the work. To encapsulate: Ideally, an interpreter has the same knowledge as the speaker, expressing meanings known to him before the interpreting commences. More often, the reality is that an interpreter has the perspective of the listener, constructing the meaning while producing the translation.

The interpreter in this instance exploits strategies inherent in ASL. In this narrative, the shape of the driveway, the sled's path down one arm of the driveway and back up the other, and the contrast of the sled's abrupt stop at the bottom of the driveway (see Fig. 11.8) easily lend themselves to spatial representation (McIntire's A, B, F, G, J). In addition the speaker retells (I) an anecdote involving spatial interaction, with strong (K) intonational information. This expert interpreter commits to a spatial arrange-

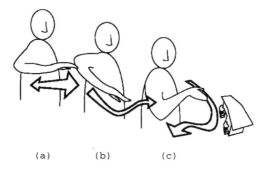

(a)   (b)   (c)

FIG. 11.8.   The interpreter's successive construction of the sled's path on the driveway, from (a) straight line to (b) with a dip in elevation to (c) moving down the left leg with a strong righthand curve and back up to street level.

ment only enough to be accurate for the information he has at the time. Initially the driveway is a straight line, next gains variation in elevation, and only later incorporating a sharp U-shaped curve. As he knows more he shows more. He uses the Handle morpheme to express motion, continues to articulate it on the non-dominant hand while showing the sled's path with his dominant, both in segments D. and E.[8] This is visible in Fig. 11.2 and Fig. 11.3. (By contrast, we would expect the speaker, signing her own story, to introduce a closer approximation of the shape of the driveway right from the first mention, emphasizing both the change in elevation and the shape.)

Ella Mae Lentz in her unpublished address to the NSSLRT in Boston (1980) described metaphoric use of lefthand and righthand space. In her analysis, the left (nondominant) side is where action arrives from; it moves toward the right (dominant) side for presentation or resolution. Positive or prominent characters are positioned on the right relative to weak or negative characters.[9] Lentz's suggestions dovetail with my own work (1985), from which we know that dominance reversals of hand pref-

---

[8]This technique of switching between two views is often described using camera metaphors (long shot vs. close-up) by signing actors.

[9]Emilie Young and Chuck Clanton have given a day-long tutorial on application of animation techniques and film craft to the audience of computer software designers. Independent of any reference to sign language or linguistics, they note the role of the left-right axis of composition in film: The eye scans from left to right. Characters or plot sequences are introduced from the left side of the screen, sent off the screen toward the viewer's right-hand side. I would claim then that some of the leftside–rightside contrasts are more generally available in the culture than purely dictated by linguistic criteria.

erence allow for parenthetical remarks, backgrounded information and nonessential characters to be positioned on the nondominant side of space, potentially using the nondominant hand in a brief interlude as dominant. The interpreter here starts with the sled's path in neutral space, but made by the right hand in Segment D. In Segment E, he takes advantage of the viewer's implicit knowledge of the sort of metaphoric use of left and right space, to have the sled enter from the left, move into "center stage" toward the right. The phonologically unmarked form of "turn the handle" for a righthanded signer would be toward the right, leading into the prominent side of the space.

At the end of three minutes, Lou Fant created a representation of the physical space in which the narrative took place . . . but, his interpretation is mirror image from events in the world. The action in the original incident proceeded from the righthand leg of the driveway to the left, with a strong left-hand turn (Fig. 11.9). The speaker never made this clear, and the interpreter was free to choose either direction of the turn. In fact, by the spatial nature of ASL, the interpreter was forced to choose a direction. His skill was demonstrated by his ability to continue to interpret while working out how the space might be arranged. His strategy in Segment D of using rocking body motion rather than a strong classifier or other manual sign to indicate change of direction affords him longer processing time, in fact into the next segment. The speaker's first mention of the dilemma of steering occurs at [1:39:00], but the interpreter avoids committing to one direction of turning the handles or the other until the internal monologue at [2:36:20]. That is, both because of his own choices and the speaker's meanderings, the interpreter gained nearly a full minute of processing time by remaining noncommittal. And, of course, during that minute, more information arrived to either define the layout of the space more clearly or eliminate possible arrangements of the landscape and objects.[10]

Unexamined Questions

Many questions about the nature of skilled interpreting—best practices—are implied by the idealizations, task list, and description of the interpreting event. We have left for another occasion the more thorough discussion

---

[10]I make no claim that this was a conscious decision to be vague or delay the specifying of the space, rather that the interpreter's task was to make sense of what little information the speaker provided. The interpreter found a successful solution to the puzzle of what physical space the speaker was describing. That solution fits the unmarked values for ASL phonology and discourse.

FIG. 11.9.   The speaker's recollection of the sled's path on the driveway, the mirror image of Fig. 11.8(c).

of how eye gaze helps organize the space, how the interpreter manipulates the voice–hand lag, and what other linguistic and paralinguistic aspects make this a satisfying interpretation. Consider in addition these questions:

- How do we teach interpreters how and when to be vague in the target language? What are the cues from the input message that warn of the need to be vague? What are the techniques in the target language that permit such noncommitment?
- What is the range of lag time that a skillful interpreter can take advantage of? How much of lag time is under conscious control and to what extent can it be trained? What is the relation between both speed and structure of the source message to the lag time and minimization of error in outputs?
- How have the conventions of transliterating and interpreting changed over the past 25 years? How stable is an individual's performance within one or the other variety? Do viewers share the judgment of which category a particular translation belongs in with the producer? With one another?
- Does the target audience (deaf signing individuals for this example) agree among itself about which ways translations succeed or miss the mark? Do those judgments agree with the interpreter?

A CLOSING WORD

Let me close then by acknowledging my several debts to the Salk laboratory: for opening a world of ideas that continues to stimulate my imagination; for allowing me to meet Lou Fant, whose interpretations always leave me in awe; to Ed Klima for his careful and caring rigor; and to Ursula Bellugi for modeling voracious curiosity. I treasure my experiences with them all.

ACKNOWLEDGMENTS

My thanks to the staff of the Television Center at De Anza College and Academic Technology Lab at Stanford University for their help in digitizing the video and preparing images to support this chapter. I acknowledge especially Ruth Williams, formerly of the ATL, for her coaching and illustrations used in Figs. 11.8 and 11.9. Thanks also to readers of a draft version of this chapter for useful feedback.

APPENDIX: FLEXIFLYER TRANSCRIPT

Following is the transcript of the spoken version of the Flexiflyer narrative.

Boldface indicates words and phrases that all refer to the same physical space and the actions therein: the hill; the house with a U-shaped driveway opening onto the hill; the house, at the bend of the U, set below street level with its large redwood planters flanking the front doors.

Italicized segments summarize portions of the transcript that have been elided for the purposes of this discussion.

Numbers in square brackets refer to the approximate time at which the sign translation appears for the underscored target word or phrase. Many of the phrases highlighted in this way appear as Figures in the body of the article. The time is calculated from a 3-minute digitized excerpt of the VHS videocassette copy of the original half-inch reel-to-reel tape. [00:00:00] represents [minutes:seconds:frames]. The video segments are available at http://www.fishbird.com.

A.
When I was nine years old [00:25:16], . . .
[introduction of speaker's friend Judy and how the girls played together]

B.
She lived on a **big hill**. There were a **bunch of houses on the hill** . . .
[description of borrowing the Flexiflyer]

C.
We went up the hill to these other people's house. It had a very steep **driveway**. **It went down** on one part and **got to the house** at the bottom

and **went up** at the other part, sort of like a **U-shape**. **It went down and back up**.

D.

And so she got on the Flexiflyer, lay down on it, and she **went swinging down the hill and**—[1:36:06]—**and <u>turned the handle</u>** [1:41:00] **at the bottom, and <u>swinging back up</u>** [1:42:05] **and she got all the way to the top at the other end of the driveway**. It was very exciting and I was just scared to death.

E.

So—uh, she brought it back around to the **beginning of the driveway** again, and said "Now you try it." And I said, "No, no, that's okay. You go ahead. I'm having a real scary time just watching." So she got on and rode **down again** [2:07:21]. **<u>Turned the handle at the bottom</u>** [2:08:08] and **<u>steered her way back up</u>** [2:08:24] **to the other end** of the driveway. She was having a great time. She was sure I should try it. I was sure I shouldn't try it.

F.

At the **bottom of the driveway** was the door of the house, see, **and they had 2 big wooden planters**. They, oh they must have been about 3 feet high. They were filled with some sort of tropical plant, bush, tree, something. And uhm, I was sure I didn't want to go down to the **bottom** of the hill, because I knew I didn't have any strength in my hands, and I <u>couldn't turn the—the handle</u> [2:36:18] when I got to **the bottom** [2:37:18]; and y'really had to turn it quite hard to get **back to the top**.

G.

So she kept trying to talk me—to pester me and pester me and said, y'know, "Go try it; you'll have such a good time." So finally just to keep her quiet, I said, "I'll try it once and that's all."

H.

Okay, I got on, lay down on the Flexiflyer and I . . . I held on and she showed me on the top of the hill how to **turn the handle** [3:01:25]. And I **started down** the hill, and I was going faster and faster and I got to the bottom of the hill and she was saying "**<u>Turn it! TURN IT</u>**!" [3:07:03, 3:07:09] She's shouting to me "Turn it! Turn it!" I **<u>didn't</u>** [3:10:00] **turn it**

[3:10:18]. [*laughing*] I **ran** [3:11:29] **right into** [3:11:29] one of those big planter boxes at the bottom of the hill. **Banged** [3:16:00] **my eye** [3:16:13] [3:17:19] right above my eyebrow—**my left eye** [3:18:16].

[The remaining portion of the narrative details the injury, successful recovery, and speaker's return to school.]

IV

Linguistic Analysis
of Sign Language

12

More Than Just Handwaving: The Mutual Contributions of Sign Language and Linguistics

Susan D. Fischer
National Technical Institute for the Deaf
Rochester Institute of Technology

PREFACE

The academic year 1965/66 was a momentous one for me. I started protesting against the war in Vietnam, I got my first job as a linguist, I saw Noam Chomsky for the first time, and I was first introduced to the work of Ursula Bellugi. In an otherwise execrable psycholinguistics course, she gave a guest lecture about her work on language acquisition that truly excited and inspired me. *This* was what psycholinguistics should be about! Little did I imagine then as a lowly undergraduate that 5 years later I would have the opportunity to work with her as a fellow pioneer in the field of sign language studies. From the beginning of my 3 years in her laboratory (1970–1974), I was fascinated by such questions as the effects of channel on language structure, the commonalities between signed and spoken languages, and what sign language structure can tell us about language in general. The fact that that interest has persisted for the 25 years since I left serves as a tribute to the lasting influence Bellugi's (and Klima's) ways of thinking have had on me and on the field. I am therefore grateful to Ursula Bellugi for providing me with a chance to get in on the ground floor of an exciting new field of research and to Ed Klima for spurring me on to gain recognition for the field of sign language study as a legitimate area of linguistics.

INTRODUCTION, HISTORY, AND BACKGROUND

It is a universally acknowledged truth that a young person in possession of an intact mind must be in want of a language (with apologies to Jane Austen). If that person happens to be Deaf, the language is likely to be a language conveyed by gesture. Virtually any time Deaf people form a community, even a community of two, some kind of gestural system will develop. If the community has historical continuity, as in the case of a school or a Deaf family, that gestural system will evolve into a language, that is, a sign language. The persistence of sign languages in the world, even in the face of well-meaning but misguided attempts at repression and elimination, stands as a tribute to the robustness of the language faculty and the human need to communicate.

As I have come to know more about sign language, I have gained a great deal of respect for American Sign Language (ASL) in particular, and for sign languages in general. The past 25 years have seen a burgeoning of published research on the structure of an ever-increasing number of sign languages.[1] The study of these languages has much to teach linguists, just as the field of linguistics has much to teach students of sign languages. I am very happy that thanks to our efforts, fewer and fewer people hold the standard—often mutually contradictory—misconceptions about sign languages, such as the notion that sign languages are not languages and are degenerate forms of spoken languages, or that they are iconic and primitive.[2] Thanks to those years of research, we know that sign languages are able to express just as much and have grammars just as complicated (and in similar ways, although perhaps not always with similar means) and just as constrained as those of spoken languages.

---

[1] The first modern linguistic analyses of sign languages started out with the work of Stokoe (1961) and Tervoort (1975), about 40 years ago. But even earlier than that sign languages were recognized as distinct languages with their own grammar and richness of expression, by none other than Alexander Graham Bell—who wished to abolish their use in the mistaken belief that if Deaf people could be discouraged from intermarrying by not having a distinct language that isolated them from their hearing peers, Deafness could disappear. (Bell, 1892)

[2] There is an interesting historical discussion of this myth in a recent book by Douglas Baynton (1996).

The study of sign language first fascinated me because although it was (and is) communicated in a different channel, it was unmistakably language and therefore a worthy subject for a linguist to study. I continue to be fascinated with it for what it can tell us about language and the human mind. My main theme in this chapter is the mutual contributions of sign language and linguistic theory.

CONTRIBUTIONS OF LINGUISTIC THEORY
TO THE STUDY OF SIGN LANGUAGE

I would like to begin by discussing the ways in which linguistics has helped sign language studies. This has occurred on several fronts. First, linguistics has given us the tools to examine sign languages as languages. For example, Stokoe, who published some of the earliest linguistic research on ASL, studied phonology with Trager and Smith; he applied their methods of phonemic analysis to ASL (Stokoe, 1960) and was able to show that signs have analyzable parts, much as spoken words have analyzable segments. This was a major breakthrough, because previously, signs had been viewed as lacking internal structure. However, Stokoe treated the internal structure of signs as if all the phonemes (he used the word *cheremes*) in a word were simultaneous rather than linear. A generation after Stokoe first wrote about sign language, Liddell (1984) was able to apply newer theories of nonlinear phonology to ASL, thus achieving some important new insights, such as the deceptively simple notion that signs have beginnings, middles, and ends. The new tools of phonology enabled him for the first time to account for phenomena such as the coordination of facial expressions with signing, as well as the natural phonological changes that occur during fast or casual signing. Indeed, Liddell's work and that of his succesors and associates has continued to open up many new avenues of research on sign language phonology.

A second way that linguistics has helped the study of sign language has been the ability to find parallels between grammatical phenomena we find in sign languages and other spoken languages. When I first started studying sign language more than 25 years ago, we focused on differences between ASL and English, marveling at the apparently large degree of simultaneity compared to English. However, we soon realized that perhaps English was not the most appropriate language to compare to ASL: It shares some aspects of Japanese grammar, such as the extensive use of topicalizaton; some aspects of Navaho, such as the use of verbal classifiers; and some aspects of certain creole languages, such as the extensive use of intonation or its equivalent to express the scope of grammatical operators. In fact, virtually everything that we have found in sign language grammars has an equivalent in some spoken language. We have thus been able to use linguistics to provide evidence for the existence of sign languages as independent languages.

Finally, in addition to giving us tools to examine signed languages, linguistic theory gives us a lens with which to focus on important questions and issues. I firmly believe that it is difficult if not impossible to do linguistics from an atheoretical perspective. Thus, I use linguistic theories to decide where to look for interesting phenomena in sign languages. This is not to say that I ignore phenomena that do not fit the theories; rather, the theory and the study are in a synergistic relation.

WHAT SIGN LANGUAGE CAN TELL LINGUISTS

If we ask not what linguistics can do for sign language studies but what sign language studies can do for linguistics, we come up with some interesting answers: Sign language provides a new perspective on universals and design features; it lets us examine the effects of the modality in which language is communicated on the structure of the language itself; it may provide support for linguistic theories that may be unavailable in spoken languages; and it forces us to rethink our ideas of the constraints and possibilities of language.

What aspects of language are truly universal to *language* and which aspects of language universals are in fact specific to the channel of speech and audition? Language universals have been addressed in a variety of frameworks. Almost 40 years ago, the structuralist Charles Hockett (1963) elaborated a list of "design features," which he claimed only human language has *all* of, although some other communication systems such as bee dances may have some. His list included such familiar notions as displacement (the ability to talk about something that is not there), duality of patterning (the notion that there are different levels of analysis within a language and that some levels of analysis are meaningless), and the arbitrary relation between *signifiant* and *signifié*. In looking at Hockett's list, we see that whereas most of his design features are easily satisfied by sign languages, several are obviously not, most notably the one about being carried by the auditory channel. One must then ask if these features are all necessary criteria for language or if the list in fact requires revision in light of evidence from sign languages. In particular, the criterion of sound must, I think, be viewed in its historical context. At the time this was written, Hockett was mainly trying to exclude written or whistled language as an independent entity.[3] My guess is that he would not mind a "friendly amendment" to his list of criteria.

Coming at language universals from a different angle, Greenberg (1963) weighed in with important work on descriptive and implicational universals, based on many languages with disparate structures and family relationships. Thus, Greenberg noted for example that SOV languages such as Japanese are overwhelmingly postpositional. When one looks at sign languages from Greenberg's perspective, one sees that all the known sign languages fit his syntactic generalizations. Not all of his morphological generalizations apply to signed languages, but then more recently, counterexamples to those generalizations have been found in spoken languages as well.

At about the same time as Greenberg, Chomsky and his circle were looking at very different kinds of universals of grammar concerning the organization and content of grammar, including such things as the idea that all languages have several levels of syntactic analysis or obeyed certain syntactic constraints such as Ross's (1967) Coordinate Structure Constraint, and the idea that every language has nouns and verbs. Again, all full-fledged sign languages appear to obey these laws (see Fischer 1974; Lillo-Martin, 1985).

Indeed, if one looks carefully, one can see an unbroken thread between Greenberg's work and the work on principles and parameters within Chomskyian theory a generation later. Rather than specific universals, Chomsky's newer work (e.g., Chomsky, 1995; Chomsky & Lasnik 1993) concentrates on general innate principles that govern all language and a finite number of parameters on which they vary. Many of Greenberg's descriptive generalizations can be seen in current theoretical linguistics as refinements of parameters such as the head parameter. We return to this conception shortly.

I am fascinated as a linguist by signed languages because of the light

---

[3]Though there are indeed some notable cases of written languages, such as classical Arabic, that are quite far removed from their spoken counterparts. I believe that, because it permits rereading, the written medium also enables the structure of sentences to be more complex than the medium of spoken language. One needn't even go as far afield as non-Indo-European languages to find this; there is a gulf between spoken and written German in terms of syntactic complexity.

they can shed on the possible ways that the channel in which a language is communicated can help to shape the grammar of that language. We can easily see that written and spoken languages can differ as much as they do because of the different constraints (or lack thereof) imposed by visual versus auditory processing. One structure that occurs largely in written English only is the sentence-initial *that*-clause, as in, "That Irabu is a superstar is evidenced by his astronomical salary."

I am assuming that users of signed and spoken language have the same capacity for language. By this assumption, many differences between signed and spoken language grammars will be due to constraints on their respective channels of communication, that is, visual–gestural versus auditory–spoken. I am also assuming that any natural language will evolve to take advantage of the strengths and minimize the limitations of its channel of communication. For example, Bellugi and Fischer (1972) first noted that because they use much larger muscles, sign words take quite a bit longer to produce than spoken words. The simultaneous expression of information then becomes a necessity to keep up with the flow of thought,[4] and that simultaneity is in turn made possible by the ability of the visual–gestural channel to make use of such mechanisms as spatial grammar.

Because both signed and spoken languages have elements of linearity and simultaneity, this is only a tendency. However, one aspect of sign language that definitely takes advantage of the modality of communication is the simultaneous use of two articulators. In ASL, there are strictures against a monomorphemic sign that has two different handshapes where both hands move. However, in polymorphemic signs, this is permitted; consider the the NS (*Nihonsyuwa* = Japanese Sign Language) sentence DID-YOU-TELL-HER, shown in Fig 12.1.

This sign contains at least five morphemes: The root morpheme is TELL, whose citation form moves outward from the signer's mouth. However, this verb can agree with subject and indirect object, thus, "you tell me" is expressed with a different form of the verb than "I tell you." In this case, there is a third-person object, and the index for that object shows that it is not only a third person, but a female. The mouth shape "po" shows completive or realis mode, hence a past event in this context, and

---

[4]Some work I recently completed (Fischer, Delhorne, & Reed, in press) shows clearly that the bottleneck in sign communication is definitely at the production end rather than the perception end. We showed that at artificially produced higher speeds of production, native signers could understand and reproduce ASL sentences extremely well at two or more times the normal speeds.

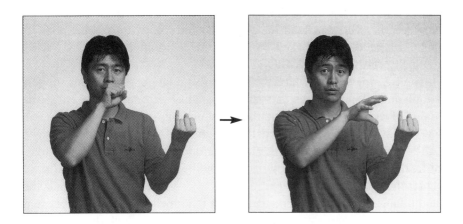

FIG 12.1.   NS sign for "Did you tell her?"

the raised eyebrows and tucked chin indicate a yes–no question.[5] The use of two different handshapes in a sign would be ungrammatical if it were monomorphemic, but it is possible in this case because one hand represents the verb TELL and the other hand represents the object HER.

As a theoretical linguist, I am very interested in the evidence that the study of sign languages can bring to bear on various aspects of linguistic theory. Let us first consider the domain of phonology. On the surface, this is one area where one would expect to find the most striking divergence between signed and spoken language, and indeed one does in the details but not in the generalities. Thus, it is easy to compare sign languages and show how there are different inventories of features in different sign languages, and that language-particular rules determine what things count as the same or different. So, for example, in NS, the spreading of fingers for many handshapes is noncontrastive, whereas in ASL, the spreading of fingers can differentiate between PROVE and JAIL. At the same time, it is clear that some sign elements are more marked than others and that there are physical as well as arbitrary linguistic constraints on combinations of those elements. An example of arbitrary constraints (arbitrary because they exist in one signed language but not another) would be that in Hong Kong Sign Language, an F handshape may contact parts of the body with the tips of the extended fingers; so, for example, the Hong Kong sign for

---

[5]Note that spoken Japanese has neither verb agreement nor grammatical gender marking.

"name" involves touching the tips of the fingers to the palm of the hand. However, in ASL, this handshape may touch the body only at the point or plane where the thumb and forefinger meet, as in HAVE-A-KNACK-FOR, SENTENCE, and IMPORTANT.

There is one way in which the study of sign language provides support for phonological theories that spoken languages cannot, namely, in the realm of autosegmental or nonlinear phonology and morphology (see, e.g., Goldsmith 1976). The main tenet of this theory is that what used to be called suprasegmental features can be autonomous, and different degrees of freedom in both morphology and phonology may have their own tier of representation, each associated to a template. Thus, for example, in some Bantu languages, tense is conveyed by a tone melody that is independent of any specific segments; indeed, if the segments to which they are originally attached disappear, the tone melody will often attach itself to some other segments instead (Goldsmith, 1976). But in spoken languages, to occur overtly, these tone melodies must be attached to some segment. Thus, arguments for the independence of segmental and suprasegmentals must be at least partially theory internal. However, with sign languages, the equivalent of suprasegmentals is facial expression, and unlike those in spoken languages, when the segment to which a facial expression is attached is omitted, the facial expression can stay. Here are two examples: First, there is a conjunction in ASL meaning something like "as a result." Although its usual gloss is SUCCEED, it is often referred to in Deaf culture as "pah" because it has a nonmanual component consisting of the mouthing of the syllable "pah." In an elicitation study a number of years ago (Fischer & Forman, 1980), Joan Forman and I asked 11 native signers to describe some pictures that showed someone unable to sleep, then taking a sleeping pill, and then falling asleep. Here is a typical response.

(1) MAN TOSS-AND-TURN, CAN'T SLEEP, DECIDE WALK-TO-BATHROOM, OPEN-CLOSET TAKE-MEDICINE, PAH! FALL-FAST-ASLEEP.

"A man, unable to sleep, decides to go to the bathroom and take a sleeping pill, enabling him to finally fall asleep."

This sentence, or something like it, was uttered by almost all of the 11 people we interviewed. However this is the full form of what was signed and often occurred if we asked people to repeat what they had just said. What they had just said looked like this:

(4) MAN TOSS-AND-TURN, CAN'T SLEEP, DECIDE WALK-
    TO-BATHROOM, OPEN-CLOSET TAKE-MEDICINE, "pah-
    face"! FALL-FAST-ASLEEP.

That is, everything was the same except that instead of the full sign PAH!,
only the facial expression "pah" remained. When we asked for a repetition, the full form emerged and clearly counted as a careful repetition.
Because "Pah-face" can occur by itself, without needing to be attached to
any segment, it provides extremely strong evidence in favor of the "auto"
in autosegmental phonology.[6]

Nonlinear morphology and even syntax are also supported by data from
sign languages. The second example deals with morphology. Supalla
(1982) analyzed verbs of motion and location in ASL as consisting of
complex paths overlaid by classifiers. In ASL, most classifiers are realized
as handshapes. Thus, there is an abstract verb "go uphill," which in ASL
can be realized only by putting in a dummy classifier (an unmarked handshape). If one substitutes this classifier with a real one, one gets the productive forms PERSON-GO-UPHILL or VEHICLE-GO-UPHILL, where
"person" is represented by the "1" handshape, and "vehicle" is represented by a "3" handshape. The handshape classifiers are also productive,
as they can occur with other path verbs, such as PASS-BY. This interleav-
ing of meanings is analogous to what McCarthy (1981) argued for Semitic
languages and was discussed at the phonological level by Sandler (1986).

As with research on less well-known languages, the study of sign languages can also contribute to our knowledge of how much languages can
vary. Most of the time, sign languages obey the principles and parameters
that have been discovered for other languages, such as the idea that heads
generally either precede or follow their complements. However, sometimes sign languages show the potential for human language in a different
light. I cite here important work by Lillo-Martin (1985), who investigated
null arguments in ASL; that is, items that may be missing from a sentence
but are inferred to be there underlyingly. One type is found in Italian,
which allows subject position to be empty because its person and number

---

[6]An anonymous reviewer suggested that "pah-face" is simply an alternative lexical item, and
therefore does not provide evidence for autosegmental phonology. I would maintain that it does, if one
admits the analogy of nonmanual markers in signed languages to intonation in spoken languages; in
spoken languages, there are no lexical items of which I am aware that consist only of an intonational
component, precisely because that intonational component must attach to a segment. There is no such
restriction in signed languages, thereby demonstrating the true independence of segmental and
suprasegmental components.

are identified by the verb; the other type occurs in Japanese, where subjects or objects can be missing if they are coreferential with discourse topics. Lillo-Martin found both kinds of null arguments in ASL, the first language to be found where the two coexist. At the same time that she was stretching the boundaries of what is possible in language, however, she also showed that the two types of null arguments nonetheless obeyed the different constraints on privilege of occurrence previously found in the Italian-type and Japanese-type languages.[7]

I can also give an example in my own work: I was looking at the head parameter in ASL and found that ASL is quite consistently head-initial but that this is somewhat obscured by extensive use of topicalization. I found that topicalization occurred not only at the sentence level but also within noun phrases and realized that such topicalization supports the DP hypothesis, which regularizes X-bar structure. Independently, Kuroda (1992) found similar structures in Japanese.

Ever since at least the time of the Prague school, linguists have been happy if they could divide things into two categories, whether it be the two values of a distinctive feature or two values of a parameter. It has been said that there are two kinds of language with regard to a certain category of movement. Specifically, Huang (1982) suggested that one type of language, including English, has overt movement of wh-words in both questions and relative clauses, whereas another type—including Japanese and Chinese—has no overt movement in the syntax but behaves in some respects as if movement has taken place. Huang suggested that in the case of Japanese and Chinese, movement occurs at the level of Logical Form, rather than in the overt syntax. Recently, Watanabe (1992) suggested that in both English-type and Japanese-type languages, there is syntactic movement, but that what moves in the syntax in Japanese is an invisible operator element.

According to work done by Lillo-Martin and myself (Lillo-Martin & Fischer, 1992), in ASL as in French, syntactic movement of wh-elements is optional in main clauses but obligatory in embedded clauses. Interestingly, ASL appears to provide some evidence in favor of Watanabe's ideas, because in ASL that invisible element is in fact visible if we consider the wh-operator in ASL to be a facial expression, which can move to the beginning of the sentence along with the wh-element, in which case it spreads autosegmentally over its c-command domain. However, if the wh-element

---

[7]Much of Lillo-Martin's work on this paper was done while she was working in the Bellugi-Klima lab.

remains in situ, the facial expression can still optionally move to the beginning of the sentence and then spread over its entire scope, as Watanabe (1992) suggested happens for spoken Japanese. Similar phenomena in NS that Osugi and I are currently investigating (Fischer & Osugi, 1998) suggest a modification of Watanabe's ideas, more consistent with Chomsky's (1995) Minimalist Program and more along the lines of Maki (1995), where only a feature rather than an operator need move.

One of the really exciting things about working on sign languages is the way in which sign language forces us to confront and rethink some messy issues that we have in the past preferred to sweep under the rug. Consider, for example, the role of discourse in grammar. Within the generative tradition, it has been commonplace to focus the study of syntax at the level of the sentence, because almost anything can theoretically be expressed within the boundaries of one sentence. But of course that is an oversimplification even for spoken language, and for sign language it is untenable. In spoken language, for example, the interpretation of pronouns is largely above the sentential level. A sentence like "She's gone home" does not occur in isolation; it is most natural as an answer to a question like "Where's Naomi?" or as a continuation of a sentence that starts "I wanted to talk to Naomi, but . . ."

In sign languages, there are certain grammatical forms that occur largely at the level beyond the sentence. The NS sentence depicted in Fig. 12.1 consists of a single complex sign. Verb agreement as well as anaphoric reference in all of the sign languages I have seen depends on a process called *localization*; in a discourse, a referent is often assigned a location in space, called a *locus*. Pronouns consist largely in pointing to those loci, and verb agreement, for those verbs that permit it, involves changing the orientation, direction, or both, of motion of the verb to show object (and possibly subject) or goal (and possibly source).[8] Whereas verb agreement may occur in a sentence without antecedent locus establishment, localization is used much more frequently in a discourse than in a sentence—the idea is that if the loci will not be referred to later, the signer does not bother to set them up. Although this kind of problem has arisen in spoken language, it has been easy to ignore because of the aforementioned theoretical assumption. With sign language, it cannot be ignored.

Another area in which sign language sheds new light on linguistics is

---

[8]Actually, NS is one language with an alternate form of verb agreement that is in fact shown in Fig. 12.1. A gender marker can take the place of a deictic locus. See Osugi and Fischer (in preparation) for discussion.

that of creoles. I showed (Fischer, 1978, 1996) that sign languages bear great resemblances, both grammatically and sociolinguistically, to creole or creolizing languages and suggested that there is a link between the grammatical structures of sign languages and their sociolinguistic provenance, namely, that most sign language users do not have parents who use the same language and that therefore sign language must be recreolized in every generation. The fact that the grammars of sign languages so closely resemble those of creoles argues against the monogenesis (i.e., Portuguese) theory of the origin of all creoles, because users of sign language would not likely have had contact with Portuguese traders. Sign languages are, however, unique among creolelike languages in terms of the source of the vocabulary. In fact, Pidgin Sign English is precisely the reverse of most pidgin situations; the vocabulary comes from the "colonized" language, ASL, whereas the grammar comes from the "colonizing" language, namely, English. When we look closely, we do find spoken language creoles that also contain vocabulary from the colonized language, such as Hawaiian Creole English, which has many Hawaiian words. It is interesting that many of the arguments about whether sign languages are languages in their own right are echoed in creole studies.

I already mentioned the problem of iconicity. Although by no means are all signs in a given sign language iconic, many have iconic origins (Frishberg, 1975). In any case, there appears to be a higher degree of iconicity in signed than in spoken language. I would claim that the reason is simple: because it can! A picture is indeed worth, if not a thousand words, then certainly a thousand grunts. It is much more difficult to show a relation between a sound and a meaning than between a moving hand and meaning. However, again this is not absolute: Languages like Japanese and Xhosa have many more sound-symbolic words than languages like English, and even English is not totally devoid of onomatopoeic words such as *thump*, *beep*, or *whoosh*. Whether we are talking about a difference in degree or in kind between signed and spoken languages remains to be determined.

Until very recently, even in schools for the Deaf that permitted the use of sign language, there were no sign language "language arts" courses available for children in these schools. Add to that the fact that even native signers differ in the nativeness of their parents and schoolmates, as well as different levels of education, and also the lack (until very recently) of a writing system, and the result is a large degree of variability in the grammar, although most signers will generally understand each other due to exposure, just as I might understand Valley Girl Talk even though I've never lived in Los Angeles. Many theoretical linguists ignore variation in spoken language structures, idealizing the notion that accounting for one idiolect (often one's own!) is just as valid as, or equivalent to, accounting for the language. Even if they recognize the concept of variation, they keep it "within bounds," as it were. They can maintain this illusion by talking to a restricted class of informants, often only themselves or, at best, other scholars. Because there are so relatively few native signers, a sign language linguist cannot pick and choose the way someone working on a mainstream language can. Once again, the issue of variation cannot be swept under the rug.

I mentioned earlier the fact that Deaf children do not learn about their language in school. The vast majority of Deaf schools in the United States conduct classes in English, although the channel might be signing. What is the effect of education and literacy on one's language? As before, this turns out to be an issue in spoken language as well as in sign language. In learners of English, there is a shift, documented in work by Read (1971) and Moskowitz (1973) among others, from a more surface representation of English vowels to a "deeper" one that reflects the regularities of English orthography. I would imagine that for Japanese, the acquisition of kanji has a profound effect on lexical representations; if two words are homonyms but have different kanji, it may be more difficult to see them even as rhyming. At another level, writing conventions often shape our perceptions of word and sentence boundaries. When we have sentence types that are never used in writing, our intuitions for what constitutes the end of a sentence may fail us. An example of such a case would be, for example, "I don't know, is the answer" (in response to the question "What is the answer?"). In the case of sign languages, the lack of a writing system leads to a lack of standardization and possibly even an acceleration of the process of language change.

This leads us to the issue of bilingualism and grammar. Can one's second language affect the structure of one's first? There is some evidence that it can. The kind of continuous (usually one-way) language contact that occurs with signers has no doubt influenced the fact mentioned earlier that ASL shares some properties with English as NS does with spoken Japanese. Also, the semantic range of some signs appears to be changing due to contact with English; for example, the sign GET means "obtain," but under the influence of English has come to be used for "become" as well, as in GET SICK. Sign language users are always translating, but as they usually are not specifically taught about appropriate translation between, say, English and ASL, those translations may be faulty. Furthermore, sometimes signers' knowledge of the matrix spoken language is imperfect, and this can be problematic for fieldworkers who rely on translation as an elicitation method, in addition to the problems caused by variability in informants and tendencies to codeswitch. My guess is that this problem exists as well for people working on spoken languages, especially stigmatized languages, and that some field results should be suspect.

In general, then, sign language studies forces us to face issues that as linguists we may not want to face, but we are the better for it.

CONTRIBUTIONS OF STUDIES OF SIGNED LANGUAGES TO THE HUMAN CAPACITY FOR LANGUAGE

In addition to the fields within core linguistics, the study of sign language can contribute a new perspective on other areas within the language sciences. More than 90% of Deaf people have hearing parents. This fact is nearly unique linguistically; it means that 90% of Deaf people learn their primary language (even if it is not the first language to which they are exposed) from persons other than their parents. The first exposure to language is often spoken language only. Because purely oral language teaching methods do not always "take," we thus have a gamut of ages at which Deaf people are exposed to a visually accessible language. This means that, at least as of now, close to 90% of Deaf persons begin to learn their primary language later than other children, often as late as adolescence. This situation has consequences not only for language acquisition but also for the kind of language that ends up being acquired. What we have in effect is an experiment of nature that lets us examine questions that for ethical reasons we might not otherwise be able to address, such as questions about critical periods for language acquisition. Such questions have indeed been asked (Mayberry, 1993; Newport, 1990), and in terms of both processing and the type of grammar acquired, the answers appear to confirm what we suspected all along, namely, that there are indeed critical periods for *language* and not just for *speech*. That is to say, a sign language must at least begin to be learned as a first language by the time of the critical period (around age 5 or so). Furthermore, even as a second language, early exposure is crucial (I have been studying ASL for more than 25 years, and I still sign with a "hearing" accent). We can also ask comparative questions about speed of acquisition, because there are many native signers, namely, hearing children of Deaf parents, who are effectively bilingual in signed and spoken languages. Studies of such children suggest that they develop grammar at about the same rate in both languages. The only difference is that the first sign recognizable to the parents appears earlier than the first recognizable spoken word. But that difference probably lies more in the perspicacity of the parents than in the precocity of the child. See, for example, the work of Scollon (1976) or Peters (1977), who showed that hearing children's first spoken words may occur much earlier than had previously been believed, because phonological variation makes it difficult for most parents to recognize semantic and contextual constancies. See also the work of Petitto (1988) who showed that Deaf parents often overattribute the use of signs by children who may not have even been exposed to any sign language.

Sign languages also permit us to consider the chicken-and-egg question of brain specialization for language. It is by now well established that spoken language is localized largely in areas of the left hemisphere near the motor and auditory cortexes. What about sign languages? Results are still preliminary and somewhat contradictory (neurolinguistics is notoriously messy), but thanks to work begun in Bellugi and Klima's laboratory, it is starting to look as though sign languages are localized on the left side of the brain, meaning that it is because it is language that it is localized on the left rather than because linear things are localized on the left. Furthermore, even though signed languages and spoken languages utilize different channels, and therefore one might presume different motor and perceptual areas, it is striking that not only the same side of the brain but the same perisylvian areas in the left hemisphere cause aphasias in both channels (Poizner, Bellugi, & Klima, 1987).

The area of language processing for sign language at both the psycholinguistic and neuropsychological levels is still very much in its infancy. But in the future, it is hoped that new technology will permit it to be addressed. However, once again, because we are talking about human language, those studies that have been done so far suggest that sign languages are processed in pretty much the same way as spoken languages, given of course accommodations for the difference in modality. For example, if processing is made more difficult (e.g., by making the stimulus difficult to see or by varying the linguistic competence of the participants), it occurs at a more superficial level. One study in which I have been involved (Fischer, Delhorne, & Reed, 1999) examines the processing of time-compressed signing and fingerspelling; results suggest that the processing limit is the same for time-compressed signing as it is for time-compressed speech, again suggesting that we are talking about modality-independent rather than peripheral constraints on language processing. See also Emmorey (1993) for more evidence of the parallels between the processing of signed versus spoken languages.

Another way of using sign language to address issues of language processing is to look at its success in the treatment of various language disorders. Mayberry (1976) successfully used sign language to treat speech disorders such as apraxia in children. These children had no problems with language comprehension, but with phonation. Her explanation was that giving children an alternative channel eased their stress level so that they were more willing to try to talk. Sign language has been used with varying degrees of success to treat spoken language aphasics. Again, the general result is that if the disorder is peripheral, giving the person another channel is helpful, but if the disorder is central, then sign language will not work. Finally, Abrahamsen, Lamb, Brown-Williams, & McCarthy (1991) used sign-augmented speech to work with Down syndrome children. What they found is that when retardation is relatively mild, children learn individual signs fairly well, but when the retardation is more severe, signing has no advantage over speech.

Language can be learned by any human of normal intelligence if he or she starts young enough and if the exposure is in the appropriate modality. But is it only humans who can do so? That is, is language a specifically human characteristic? Attempts have been made to teach language to non-human primates since at least the 1940s or 1950s. At first, attempts were limited to oral languages, but in the mid-to-late 1960s, three attempts were initiated using visually accessible communication: David Premack, using plastic chips; the Rumbaughs, using a limited context-free grammar with a computer interface; and the Gardners, and later Herbert Terrace, using signs from ASL. I will not comment on the first two media, which have been criticized elsewhere. The question is: Did the chimpanzees learn sign language, and if so, how did they do it?

My answer is that they did not. Indeed, they did learn quite a few names for things and some actions, but there is no evidence that they learned syntax—although they did indeed put two signs together, these were limited in a number of ways: First, most of the chimpanzees' two-sign combinations were what might be called fixed expressions, in that one of the two signs was a member of an extremely small set. Second, there is no evidence that the chimpanzees had any notion of grammaticality. In ASL, certain combinations of signs are rejected by native signers as ungrammatical. The chimpanzees do not reject anything.

The chimpanzees also do not really have any idea of what language is for. In what he hoped would be groundbreaking work, the behaviorist B. F. Skinner (1957) classified all language into what he called *mands* and *tacts*, that is, commands and names. Mands and tacts are all that the chimpanzees have. They do not comment, they do not predicate, and in fact they generally do not initiate conversations, in contrast to Deaf children, who do all of these things quite early. Furthermore, work by Petitto, Terrace, and others (see, e.g., Terrace, 1979) shows that generally chimpanzees do not—cannot?—learn in the way humans do; rather, they need to be explicitly taught, with many repetitions, not to mention the fact that they do not make eye contact.

I am not so doctrinaire as some who would exclude the possibility that language has evolved over time; indeed, I have suggested elsewhere (Fischer, 1994) that although chimpanzees clearly have the ability to name (which they share with lower primates), their internal language representation is less specified than for humans, which makes their learning less constrained and hence much more arduous for a chimpanzee than for a human, as a chimpanzee will not know what to ignore. It seems that after all, language is a uniquely human characteristic.

CONCLUSIONS

Thirty years ago, sign language was generally considered an oddity, a marginalized and messy system of communication with little or no autonomous grammar and little or nothing to teach linguists or linguistics. Over the last generation, thanks in no small part to the pioneering efforts of the honorees in this festschrift, sign languages all over the world have been recognized as full-fledged languages with much to teach us about the human capacity for language and the nature of language itself.

ACKNOWLEDGMENTS

Research for this chapter was supported by the Japan Foundation and the National Technical Institute for the Deaf, Rochester Institute of Technology, under an agreement with the U.S. Department of Education. A somewhat different version of this chapter was presented as the keynote of the 1997 spring meeting of the Linguistic Society of Japan. Parts have been published in different form in Fischer (1979, 1992, & 1994). I am grateful to S.-Y. Kuroda and Matayoshi Shibatani for comments on the earlier version, and to Yutaka Osugi for posing for the photographs, which were done by Mark Benjamin.

REFERENCES

Abrahamsen, A., Lamb, M., Brown-Williams, J., & McCarthy, S. (1991). Boundary conditions on language emergence: Contributions from atypical learners and input. In P. Siple & S. Fischer (Eds.), *Theoretical issues in sign language research, Vol. 2: Psychology* (pp. 231–254). Chicago: Chicago University Press.

Baynton, D. C. (1996). *Forbidden signs: American culture and the campaign against sign language.* Chicago: University of Chicago Press.

Bellugi, U., & Fischer, S. (1972). A comparison of sign language and spoken language: Rate and grammatical mechanisms. *Cognition, 1,* 173–200.

Chomsky, N. (1995). *The minimalist program.* Cambridge, MA: MIT Press.

Chomsky, N., & Lasnik, H. (1993). The theory of principles and parameters. In J. Jacobs, A. von Stechow, W. Sternefeld, & T. Vennemann (Eds.), *Syntax: An international handbook of contemporary research.* Berlin, Germany: de Gruyter.

Emmorey, K. (1993). Processing a dynamic visual-spatial language: Psycholinguistic studies of American Sign Language. *Journal of Psycholinguistic Research, 22,* 153–188.

Fischer, S. (1974). Sign language and linguistic universals. In C. Rohrer & N. Ruwet (Eds.), *Actes du colloque Franco-Allemand de grammaire transformationelle, Band II: Études de sémantique et autres* (pp. 187–204). Tübingen, Germany: Max Niemeyer Verlag.

Fischer, S. (1978). Sign languages and creoles. In P. Siple (Ed.), *Understanding language through sign language research* (pp. 309–331). New York: Academic Press.

Fischer, S. (1979). Many a slip 'twixt the hand and the lip: Applying linguistic theory to non-oral language. In R. Herbert (Ed.), *Metatheory III: Application of linguistics in the human sciences* (pp. 45–75). East Lansing: Michigan State University Press.

Fischer, S. D. (1992). Similarities and differences among sign languages: Some how's and why's. In *Proceedings of the World Federation of the Deaf* (pp. 733–739). Tokyo, Japan.

Fischer, S. D. (1994). The study of sign languages and linguistic theory. In C. Otero (Ed.), *Noam Chomsky: Critical assessments* (pp. 582–599). London: Routledge.

Fischer, S. D. (1996). By the numbers: Language-internal evidence for creolization. In W. Edmondson & R. Wilbur (Eds.), *International review of sign linguistics* (vol. 1, pp. 1–22). Mahwah, NJ: Lawrence Erlbaum Associates.

Fischer, S. D., Delhorne, L., & Reed, C. (1999). Effects of rate of presentation on the reception of American Sign Language. *Journal of Speech, Language, and Hearing Research, 42,* 568–582.

Fischer, S., & Forman, J. (1980,). *Causative constructions in ASL.* Paper presented at the annual meeting of the Linguistic Society of America.

Fischer, S., & Osugi, Y. (1998). *Feature movement in wh-questions: Evidence from ASL and NS.* Poster session, Theoretical Issues in Sign Language Research conference, Gallaudet University.

Frishberg, N. (1975). Arbitrariness and iconicity in sign language. *Language, 51,* 696–719.

Goldsmith, J. (1976). *Autosegmental phonology.* Unpublished doctoral dissertation, Masschusetts Institute of Technology.

Greenberg, J. (1963). Some universals of language. In J. Greenberg (Ed.), *Universals of Language* (pp. 58–90). Cambridge, MA: MIT Press.

Hockett, C. (1963). The problem of universals in language. In J. Greenberg (Ed.), *Universals of Language* (pp. 1–22). Cambridge, MA: MIT Press.

Huang, J. (1982). *Logical relations in Chinese and the theory of grammar.* Unpublished doctoral dissertation, Massachusetts Institute of Technology.

Kuroda, S.-Y. (1992). Judgment forms and sentence forms. In S.-Y. Kuroda (Ed.), *Japanese syntax and semantics: Collected papers* (pp. 13–77). Dordrecht, Netherlands: Kluwer.

Liddell, S. K. (1984). THINK and BELIEVE: Sequentiality in American Sign Language signs. *Language, 60,* 372–399.

Lillo-Martin, D. (1985). Two kinds of null arguments in ASL. *Natural Language & Linguistic Theory 4,* 415–444.

Lillo-Martin, D., & Fischer, S. (1992). *Overt and covert wh-structures in ASL.* Paper presented at the 4th International Symposium on sign language research, Salamanca, Spain, July, 1992.

Maki, H. (1995). *The syntax of particles.* Unpublished doctoral dissertation, University of Connecticut.

Mayberry, R. (1976). If a chimp can learn sign language, surely my nonverbal client can too. *Journal of Speech and Hearing Research, 118,* 223–228.

Mayberry, R. (1993). First-language acquisition after childhood differs from second-language acquisition: The case of American Sign Language. *Journal of Speech and Hearing Research, 36,* 1258–1270.

McCarthy, J. (1981). A prosodic theory of nonconcatenative morphology. *Linguistic Inquiry, 15,* 291–318.

Moskowitz, B. (1973). On the status of the vowel shift in English. In T. E. Moore (Ed.), *Cognitive development and the acquisition of language* (pp. 223–260). New York: Academic Press.

Newport, E. (1990). Maturational constraints on language learning. *Cognitive Science, 14,* 11–28.

Osugi, Y., & Fischer, S. (in prep.). *Gender marking in NS.* Unpublished manuscript.

Peters, A. M. (1977). Language learning strategies: Does the whole equal the sum of its parts? *Language 53,* 560–573.

Poizner, H., Bellugi, U., & Klima, E. (1987). *What the hands reveal about the brain.* Cambridge, MA: MIT Press.

Read, C. (1971). Preschool children's knowledge of English phonology. *Harvard Educational Review, 41,* 1–34.

Ross, J. R. (1967). Constraints on variables in syntax. Unpublished doctoral dissertation, Massachusetts Institute of Technology.

Sandler, W. (1986). The spreading hand autosegment of American Sign Language: A new approach to sequential segments and autosegments in ASL. *Sign Language Studies, 50,* 1–28.

Scollon, R. (1976). *Conversations with a one year old: A case study of the developmental foundation of syntax.* Honolulu: University of Hawaii Press.

Siple, L. (1995). *Uses of addition in sign language transliteration.* Unpublished doctoral dissertation, State University of New York at Buffalo.

Skinner, B. F. (1957). *Verbal behavior.* New York: Appleton-Century-Crofts.

Stokoe, W. (1960). *Sign language structure: An outline of the visual communication system of the American Deaf* (Studies in Linguistics Occasional Papers 8). Buffalo, NY: Dept. of Anthropology and Linguistics.

Supalla, T. (1982). *Verbs of motion and location in American Sign Language.* Unpublished doctoral dissertation, University of California, San Diego.

Terrace, H. (1979). *Nim: A chimpanzee who learned sign language.* New York: Knopf.

Tervoort, B. (1975). *Developmental features of visual communication: A psycholinguistic analysis of deaf children's growth in communicative competence.* Amsterdam: North-Holland.

Watanabe, A. (1992). Wh-in-situ, subjacency, and chain formation. In *MIT occasional papers in linguistics 2.*

13

Phonological and Prosodic Layering of Nonmanuals in American Sign Language

Ronnie B. Wilbur
Purdue University

One of the major issues that has intrigued linguists is the question of what effect the modality of perception/production has on the grammar of a language. If the grammar is viewed as composed of several components or modules, in which components would modality effects be observed? Is the modality difference between speech and sign reflected only in the nature of the phonetic features that map into production and perception? Or, given the substantial differences in the physics of speech and sign, might there not be higher level organizational differences between the two linguistic modalities, and if so, what and where? As a result of extensive discussion on this issue, Ed Klima, Ursula Bellugi, and I presented the concept of "layering" in an article that documented the phonological separation of sign components for morphological purposes (Wilbur, Klima, & Bellugi, 1983).

With respect to phonological separation, the observation is this: In both speech and sign, there is an inventory of phonological elements available as building blocks for word formation, whether monomorphemic or multimorphemic, but only in sign is a set of such elements reserved exclusively for use in the multimorphemic words, derived words, and inflected words. We know of no oral language in which a particular phoneme is reserved only for morphological purposes and never surfaces in a lexical item. Yet we clearly observe in American Sign Language (ASL) such restrictions: Neither the dynamic and rhythmic modifications used for aspectual inflections nor the spatial arrangements used for quantifying over nominal arguments are used for lexical formation.

With respect to layering, we noted that in ASL, each productive phonological element has the potential to contribute meaning to a larger grammatical unit (word, phrase, sentence) in a layered construction in such a way that cooccurring elements do not obscure or interfere with each other. For this to be possible, different morphological functions or semantic components have to be distributed to distinct phonological elements. For example, in a multimorphemic verb sign, the movement can carry the information regarding the transfer of a theme-object (e.g., GIVE), the starting location can carry the source-agent-subject, the ending location can carry the goal-recipient-indirect object, the handshape can carry the physical characteristics of the object itself (size and shape indicated by "handle" classifier), and each piece of information is phonologically distinct from the others. This phonological separation permits the handshape, starting location, and movement to be produced simultaneously yet clearly. It works similarly for handshape, ending location, and movement. But because starting and ending locations are both locations, they cannot be performed simultaneously (by one hand) and must be articulated sequentially. Layering is the separation of available phonological elements in such a way that particular functions are associated with productive phonological elements so that, when simultaneously performed, the phonological elements and their associated functions can be clearly identified. For example, handshapes are used to convey the theme (size and shape specifiers) or an agent handling the theme (HANDLE classifiers). Verbal aspect is carried by modifications of dynamic and rhythmic properties of movement. There are no productive uses of handshape in which it carries verbal aspect nor are there uses of dynamic and rhythmic properties of movement to convey information about the theme or an agent handling the theme.

In Wilbur et al. (1983), we wrote,

> The fact that ASL is a language with complex organizational properties implies that it will share certain principles of organization with other languages. The fact that it is a language in a different modality (visual/spatial rather than auditory/vocal) implies that there will be differences in its principles of organization. ASL exhibits formal structuring at the same two lev-

els as spoken languages (the internal structure of the lexical units and the grammatical structure underlying sentences). However, a fundamental difference between ASL and spoken languages is its surface organization: signed languages display a marked preference for co-occurring layered (as opposed to linear) organization. The inflectional and derivational devices of ASL make use of space and movement, nesting the basic sign stem in spatial patterns and complex dynamic contours of movement. In the lexical items, the morphological processes, the syntax, and even the discourse structure of ASL, the layering of linguistic elements is a pervasive structural characteristic (Bellugi, 1980; Wilbur & Petitto, 1983). There is, however, evidence for sequential affixation as well in ASL (Newkirk, 1979, 1980, 1981), which requires a linguistic analysis similar to those proposed for spoken languages. (p. 314)

We went on to suggest that this apparent difference, which we so readily attributed to a modality effect, might in fact be a matter of degree rather than of difference, with the extent of the required layering greater in ASL than in spoken languages but not unknown in spoken languages:

The currently emerging view of spoken languages similarly contains both simultaneous and sequential properties (McCarthy, 1979, 1981; Selkirk, 1982). Thus, the organization of the surface differences of ASL which seem most directly tied to the modality must nonetheless be included in universal grammar even when only spoken languages are considered. (p.314)

With the benefit of hindsight, it is now apparent that the high degree of layering in ASL is a linguistic adaptation to the modality serving prosodic and pragmatic purposes. It is the fact of adaptation that is critical, rather than merely the fact that ASL is produced in the manual–visual modality. Consider signed English, the coding of English into a manual–visual form. If layering is a pure modality effect, then it should exert itself on signed English and any other such signing system. But if layering is a reflection of evolutionary adaptation of a natural language to its modality, then layering should be absent from signed English, even in the most fluent signers. In this chapter, I first review the basic notion of layering and its importance for understanding sign language structure and then extend the notion to the nonmanuals that occur in ASL. Finally, I review data from adult fluent users of signed English to support the suggestion that layering is absent in that kind of signing due to the lack of historical adaptation to the modality.

LAYERING IN SIGN STRUCTURE

Selkirk's (1982) model of constituent structure for words provides a useful framework for discussing layering in signs. She noted that only three categories are needed for English word formation: Root, Word, and Affix. An English word may consist of only a Word, or of a Root plus Affix, or a Word plus Affix, or in the case of words that are compounds, Word plus Word. "Every monomorphemic nonaffix is redundantly a root, and in principle it may also be a word" (Selkirk, 1982, p. 98). Derivational affixes subdivide into two categories based on whether they affect the phonology of the form they attach to ("nonneutral") or not ("neutral"). Selkirk noted that nonneutral affixes can attach only to Roots, neutral affixes attach only to Words, and Root-level affixes may appear "inside" Word-level affixes but not the other way around. Thus, with Root-level *-ous* and Word-level *-ness*, *danger -ous -ness* is well-formed, but *danger -ness -ous* is not. Selkirk concluded that the two levels Root and Word are relevant to derivational processes but only one level—the Word—is relevant for inflectional processes. After Words have undergone derivational processes, inflectional processes can apply; these include plural, past tense, and other affixes that are limited to one per word and must always be on the "outside" edge.

In ASL, we found a similar split in the derivational processes, with some applying at the Root level and others applying at the Word level. This split requires recognition of a separation of sign movement into local movement and path movement. Path movement may be linear or arcing, with inflected forms that are circular, semicircular, or elliptical. Local movement refers to movement made at the wrist, knuckles, or fingers, including flicking of fingers, change in handshape, wrist rotation, wrist nodding, and finger wiggling.

One critical observation is that Root-level derivational processes affect only local movement (movements not involving path). For example, the pair DIRTY and FILTHY share the same formational characteristics except that DIRTY has finger wiggling and FILTHY has finger "spritz," The sign WRONG shares characteristics with SUDDENLY, with the latter having an additional wrist rotation. The signs QUIET and ACQUIESCE are similar, with the latter having an additional wrist pivot (see Klima & Bellugi, 1979, for discussion). Bellugi and Newkirk (1981, p. 22) referred to these as "idiomatic derivations" because they were unable to find consistent meaning associated with shifts in form. That is, these derivational changes make new Roots that have different but related meanings not predictable from either the base form or the change that is made.

In contrast, those derivational processes that apply at the Word level in ASL affect the Path movement and create predictable meaning changes, including changes in lexical category (noun, verb, adjective). Klima & Bellugi (1979) identified one movement change (movement made once, fast, and tense) with the meaning "to act like ____" or "to appear like ____." Applied to the old sign CHINA (made at the eye), the modified sign means "to seem Chinese," to CHURCH, "pious." The local movement of the Root is unaffected. Furthermore, in both CHURCH and CHINA, a path movement must actually be added so that it can be made once, fast, and tense for the derivational process.

For inflectional processes, Klima & Bellugi (1979, chap. 12) suggested at least eight types for ASL, and 11 phonological dimensions that can be used to mark these inflections. A critical observation here is that none of these phonological dimensions affect local movement. Furthermore, the inflectional processes divide into 2 groups: (a) those that affect the rhythmic and dynamic qualities of the movement, and (b) those that affect primarily the spatial arrangement of the movement (Wilbur et al., 1983). In the first group are Temporal Focus, Temporal Aspect, Onset–Offset Manner, and Degree, which use manner of movement changes, rate changes, tension differences, changes in evenness, size differences, differences in contouring, and cyclicity to modify the path movement to show inflection. The second group includes Indexical, Reciprocal, Number, and Distributional Aspect, which use planar focus, geometrical patterning, direction of movement, cyclicity, and doubling of the hands to modify the path movement to show inflection. Only cyclicity appears in both lists, reflecting the fact that in ASL, like other languages, reduplication is called on to serve a variety of functions (cf. discussion in Wilbur, 1973).

The phonological split of temporal characteristics for the first group and spatial characteristics for the second group is paralleled by a split in their morphosyntactic functions. The meaning modifications that result from the temporal modifications are interpreted with respect to the predicate itself (conveyed in English by adverbial phrases), whereas the spatial modifications contribute information about the arguments of the predicate (conveyed in English by pronouns, quantifiers, and prepositional phrases). This split makes it possible for different pieces of information about arguments and predicates to be conveyed in a single sign without obscuring each other or the basic lexical item. The required morphosyntactic information is layered on top of the lexical sign, conveying a bigger bundle of information in a complex sign in less time than would be required if each piece of information had to be signed in separate signs (as happens in signed English). The phonological component must cooperate with this information packaging conspiracy or the result would be unintelligibility, the signed equivalent of white noise.

Evidence of layering can also be seen in the further possibilities for embedding processes. Klima and Bellugi (1979) discussed combinations of "durational" and "exhaustive" on the sign GIVE. Durational alone on GIVE means "give continuously" (Fig. 13.1). Exhaustive means "to each" and when embedded in Durational means "give to each, that action recurring over time" (Fig. 13.2). However, Durational can be embedded in Exhaustive, to yield a form meaning "give continuously to each in turn" (Fig. 13.3). Finally, embedding Durational in Exhaustive and then the result into Durational yields "give continuously to each in turn, that action recurring over time" (Fig. 13.4), a form that might be used to describe the distribution of food at a soup kitchen over the course of a winter. A different form is created when the Exhaustive is embedded in the Iterative "occur again and again," creating "give to each, that act of giving occur-

GIVE[Durational]
'give continuously'

FIG. 13.1.   GIVE with Durational inflection (affects temporal characteristics).

GIVE[Exhaustive]
'give to each'

FIG. 13.2.   GIVE with Exhaustive inflection (affects spatial characteristics).

ring again and again" (Fig. 13.5), describing perhaps the distribution of food to individuals each major winter holiday. Using 4 temporal aspects (Iterative, Durational, Habitual, and Continuative) and 10 spatial aspects (Multiple/Plural, Exhaustive, Allocative Determinate, Allocative Indeterminate, Seriated Vertical, Seriated Horizontal, Apportionative Vertical, Apportionative Horizontal, Reciprocal, Dual), we constructed a matrix of combinations, which yielded the following possible embeddings: Embedding spatial in temporal 100%; embedding temporal in spatial 90%; embedding temporal in temporal 50%; and embedding spatial in spatial 35–67% (judgments differ; Wilbur et al., 1983).

Whereas all 10 spatial aspects can be embedded in all 4 temporal aspects, the reverse is not true. One spatially indicated inflection, the Multiple/Plural, does not allow any embeddings that would destroy its phonological shape, a smooth arcing sweep. Each of the four temporal aspects require repetitions that would break up the smooth sweep, rendering it

GIVE[[Exhaustive]Durational]
'give to each, that action
recurring over time'

FIG. 13.3. GIVE with Durational inflection embedded in Exhaustive inflection.

GIVE[[Durational]Exhaustive]
'give continuously to each in turn'

FIG. 13.4. GIVE with Exhaustive inflection embedded in Durational inflection.

GIVE[[[Durational]Exhaustive]Durational]
'give continuously to each in turn, that
action recurring over time'

FIG. 13.5.   GIVE with [Durational embedded in Exhaustive] embedded in
Durational.

unrecognizable and defeating the layering conspiracy (different phonological forms for different morphological functions). Embeddings of temporally indicated inflections in temporal inflections and spatially indicated
inflections in spatial inflections involve other factors in addition to
phonology (e.g., semantic conflict). For example, the Continuative could
be embedded in the Durational phonologically, but the form does not
occur, presumably due to their semantics (although a full analysis has not
to my knowledge been conducted).

Additional evidence of phonological separation for morphological purposes comes from a comparison of derived items and lexical items. Wilbur
et al. (1983) argued that these items can be separated in several ways: (a)
lexical entries do not make distinctive use of available modifications of
manner of movement (e.g., no minimal pairs differing in that one is tense
and the other lax; or reduplicated vs. single production); (b) lexical entries
do not make distinctive use of points in space (as opposed to points on the
body), thus APPLE and ONION are minimal pairs for locations on the
face, but there are no monomorphemic lexical pairs for distinct points in
space (starting point, ending point, or location of formation in space if distinctive are all provided by morphologically significant specifications);[1]
(c) similarly, direction of movement in space is not used without meaning,
thus we have pairs of opposites IN–OUT, UP–DOWN, IMPROVE–GET
WORSE that differ in the direction that the hand moves, but the opposite
direction always indicates opposite meaning; (d) root-level derivational
processes affect or add local movement; word-level derivational and

---

[1]However, Liddell (in press) suggests a possible counterexample pair, POINT and GOAL, which
he argues are monomorphemic signs distinguished by place of articulation in the signing space.

inflectional processes affect or add path movement and can modify rhythmic and spatial characteristics of movement, such as features of manner of movement, spatial location to orientation and arrangement, and direction (all of which are excluded from being distinctive in the lexicon). Hence, there is ample evidence of phonological separation in the ASL lexical signs, as well as in the derivational and inflectional morphology that applies to them. I turn now to a discussion of the evidence for layering in the nonmanual component of ASL.

LAYERING OF NONMANUALS

There are several ways in which layering is manifested in the nonmanual domain, the most obvious of which is the simultaneous production of nonmanual markings with manual signs. The nonmanuals provide additional information while the manual signs are being produced. Linguistic research has established the separation of grammatical nonmanual markings from purely affective facial expressions (Baker & Padden, 1978; Coulter, 1978, 1979; Liddell, 1978). Layering may also occur when affective facial expressions are used with grammatical nonmanual markings, although this is an area in need of considerably more research. The nonmanual markers include a number of independent channels: head position, body position, eyebrow and forehead position, eye gaze, nose position, and mouth, tongue, and cheek. In general, nonmanual cues provide morphemic information on lexical items or indicate the ends of phrases (boundary markers) or their extent (domain markers). It is the layering of these markers that is the focal point of my discussion. I talk about the phonological separation of nonmanuals for morphosyntactic purposes, a separation that in effect parallels that seen with spatial and temporal modifications for manual sign inflections.

Design Features for Layering of Nonmanuals

The concept of layering requires that phonological formation be distinct enough to permit simultaneous production of more than one morpheme without noise interference. Several features are available in the nonmanual domain to make this possible. One feature is the nonmanual onset and offset: gradual versus abrupt. Another feature is the number of productions: single versus repeated. A third feature is the scope: lexical item, edge marking, or domain marking. A fourth feature is the place of articulation:

head, eyes, nose, mouth, and shoulder or body. Nonmanuals can also be distinguished by articulator, for example, the eye area, the eyebrows, eyelids, and eyeballs (gaze) can each be recruited for specific functions. In the mouth area, the upper lip, lower lip, lip corners, tongue, and cheek are available for different uses.

Nonlinguistic versus Linguistic Nonmanuals. Consider the differences that distinguish linguistic uses of nonmanuals from the affective uses of similar-looking facial expressions. If several nonmanuals are to be produced simultaneously but over different domains, it has to be possible to easily determine whether each cue is present and for how long. The onset and offset of syntactic nonmanuals are abrupt and are coordinated with the constituents they modify, whereas the onset and offset of affective markers are gradual and not necessarily coordinated with syntactic boundaries (Baker-Shenk, 1983; Liddell, 1978, 1980). For example, the negative headshake is a grammatical marker in ASL; it has an abrupt onset and offset and is coordinated with the scope of the negative constituent. In contrast, negative headshakes used by nonsigning speakers of English have gradual onsets (sometimes barely perceptible) and offsets and occur in sentence positions seemingly unconnected with English syntactic structure (Veinberg & Wilbur, 1990). Research on the acquisition of nonmanuals indicates a very clear separation between early use of facial expressions for affective purposes and later use of facial expressions for linguistic functions (Anderson & Reilly, 1998; Reilly & Bellugi, 1996; Reilly, McIntire, & Bellugi, 1990). Regardless of place of articulation, articulator, or other specific features of the nonmanuals, the onset and offset provide a clear indicator of function: abrupt for syntactic functions, gradual otherwise. This distinction contributes to possible layering combinations.

Articulators and Scope Domains

Non-manuals are spatially distributed across the face, head, and shoulders, providing clear and separate information channels. In ASL, the nonmanual signals made on the face can be roughly divided into two groups, lower and upper. Recently, the nose has also received investigative attention.

Lower Face Possibilities. The lower portion of the face is used to provide adverbial and adjectival information. The mouth, tongue, and cheeks provide meaningful markers that associate with specific lexical items or phrases with those lexical items as heads (e.g., noun/NP, verb/VP). Liddell (1978, 1980) identified three lower facial positions with adverbial functions: (a) "mm," which is made with the lips pressed together; it indicates pleasure or enjoyment of an activity; (b) "th," which is made with a lax jaw, slightly separated lips, and critically, a protruding tongue tip; it indicates carelessness or incorrectness; (c) "cs," which is made with a slight head tilt and shoulder raise, tight lips, and clenched teeth; it indicates recency or closeness in time or space. As an example, in (1), the nonmanual marking "mm" is associated with the predicate but not with the subject:

_____mm_____

1. MAN FISH[I:continuous] "The man is fishing with relaxation and enjoyment."

Similar domains can be observed for adjectival uses of the lower face; for example, cheeks puffed for "big, fat" might occur with only a noun (TREE, TRUCK) or also with additional information in that NP (numbers, colors, other manual adjectives). These lower face markings are spatially separated from other nonmanuals by virtue of their place of articulation and they are functionally separated by virtue of their scope of occurrence. Several dozen other configurations of lips, teeth, tongue, cheeks, and tongue have been identified. Readers are referred to introductory textbooks on ASL, such as Baker and Cokely (1980) and Valli and Lucas (1992), for overviews. A detailed discussion of several types of meaningful tongue positions and flaps is given in Davies (1985).

Upper Face Possibilities. The nonmanuals supplied by the upper part of the face and the head (eyebrows, head position, head nods, eyegaze; Wilbur, 1991) occur with higher syntactic constituents (clauses, sentences), even if such constituents contain only a single sign (e.g., a topicalized noun). Indeed, traditional analyses of the upper face, head, and body positions refer to nonmanual markers for questions "q," relative clauses "rel cl," topics "t," conditionals "cond," wh-questions "whq," and rhetorical questions "rhq" as though each were associated uniquely with a syntactic structure (Baker & Padden, 1978; Baker-Shenk, 1983; Liddell, 1978, 1980). Coulter (1979) was among the first to sort through these conglomerates to identify the component pieces and their potential functions. Baker-Shenk (1983), Liddell (1986), Wilbur (1994a, 1994b, 1995a, 1995b), and Bahan (1996) subsequently identified functions for additional components. There are several recent reports documenting that nonmanuals spread across syntactic domains and are sanctioned by formal mechanisms (syntactic features, operators) rather than functional opportunities (pragmatics) (Aarons, 1994; Bahan, 1996; MacLaughlin, 1997; Neidle, Kegl, MacLaughlin, Lee, & Bahan, 1996; Petronio, 1993; Wilbur, 1995a; Wilbur & Patschke, 1999). Taken together, these studies support claims regarding Universal Grammar made by current formal theoretical frameworks. In particular, given the close association between these nonmanuals and their syntactic domains, it is clear that it is insufficient to say only that the nonmanuals have been "borrowed" from general facial and gestural indicators of conversational functions. Additional specifications to fully describe the role of each nonmanual in ASL syntax are required (much additional work is needed in this area). For example, although it is true that English-speaking hearing people use negative headshakes in negative situations, ASL does not have a rule that requires a negative headshake in a negative situation. There are a variety of ways that negation can be marked nonmanually, if at all (Veinberg & Wilbur, 1990; Wilbur & Patschke, 1998).

Liddell (1977, 1980) noted the larger scope of upper face and head nonmanuals when he discussed the nonmanual marking "q" for yes–no questions (lean forward, head forward, brows raised), as in (2):

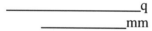

2. MAN FISH[I:continuous] "Is the man fishing with relaxation and enjoyment?"

This single example illustrates layering of inflectional modification on the predicate sign itself (continuous), lower mouth adverbial modification of that predicate ("mm"), and upper face, head, and body marking for the entire question ("q"), all on top of only two sequential lexical items. Compare the ASL to the English translation in terms of number of lexical items, and recall that the English is also layered, at least with respect to the use of pitch modifications for question intonation (as well as subject–auxiliary inversion). Information corresponding to a typical function of English intonation is provided throughout the ASL clause from beginning to end by the upper face and head.

Layers Within the Upper Face, Head, and Body: Edge and Scope.   Here I concentrate on layering within the upper head and body group and the prosodic functions that are served thereby, specifically blinks, eyebrows, eyegaze, head tilt, head nod, headshake, head thrust, body leans, and body shifting. These markers can be divided on one design feature: scope. They are either edge marking, meaning that the nonmanual comes at a constituent boundary, or domain marking, wherein the marker spreads across an entire syntactic domain (for discussion of the specific domains, either c-command or checking, see Wilbur, 1995a). The illustration of "q" in example (2) is of domain marking. Some nonmanuals may be used for either domain or edge marking; in such cases, they are distinguished by an additional design feature: number of occurrences. For example, a single head nod can be used as an edge marker whereas repeated head nodding can serve as a domain marker. Some nonmanuals can also cooccur with a single manual sign, for example, a slow blink may serve to emphasize a sign (Wilbur, 1994a), and a head thrust typically occurs on the last sign of the first clause in conditionals (Liddell, 1986). It is not clear if these uses belong in a separate category or if they are a form of edge marking, as they tend to occur on the last sign in a clause. Clear cases of edge marking occur after the last sign.

Layers Within the Upper Face, Head, and Body: Spatial Separation. Before proceeding, consider again the potential for layering given the spatial separation involved in these markers. Eyeblinks involve the eyes, specifically the eyelids, whereas eyegaze involves direction of eyeball looking. Many eyeblinks are accompanied by an eyegaze shift, that is, looking at a different location when the eyes reopen. Eyebrow position involves a different set of muscles than eyeblinks or eyegaze, thus all three can cooccur without interfering with each other. Head tilt involves the position of the head whereas headnod and headshake are movements; neck muscles are involved in all, but the absence or presence of movement differentiates tilt from nod and shake, whereas direction of movement differentiates nod (up or down) from shake (side to side). Head thrust takes advantage of the neck muscles that move the lower jaw or chin forward; nods (up and down) are differentiated by direction from thrust (forward). Body leans may be articulated in a variety of ways, including forward, backward, or sideways leaning of the head, head and shoulders, or upper body from the waist, or, if the signer is standing, taking a step forward (Wilbur & Patschke, 1998) or backward (Winston, 1989). Body shifting involves more of a twisting as compared to leans; we have not yet studied the interaction of the two to determine how each is articulated when layered.

Eyeblinks. Baker and Padden (1978) first brought eyeblinks to the attention of sign language researchers as one of four components contributing to the conditional nonmanual marker (the others were labionasal contraction, brow raise, and the initiation of head nodding). I recall my excitement when I brought this news to a sociologist colleague, Rich Frankel, who studies interpersonal communication. I thought sign language research had really come of age with this research on blinks, but this feeling did not last long. His first question was, "What kind of eyeblinks are they?" It took almost 15 years to answer that question and the answer turns out to be significant to the discussion of layering.

In their overview of the human ocular system, Stern and Dunham (1990) distinguished three main types of blinks: startle reflex blinks, involuntary periodic blinks (e.g., for wetting the eye), and voluntary blinks. Startle reflex blinks are not used linguistically in ASL, whereas both periodic blinks and voluntary blinks serve specific linguistic functions. Stern and Dunham noted that the frequency of periodic blinks is affected by perceptual and cognitive demands (e.g., 18.4 blinks per minute while talking and only 3.6 while watching video screens) and that blink location (when someone blinks) is also affected by task demands; for example, readers tend to place their blinks at semantically appropriate places in the text, such as the end of a sentence, paragraph, or page. These controlled blinks are referred to as *inhibited periodic blinks.*

The blinks identified by Baker and Padden (1978) are inhibited periodic blinks. As documented in Wilbur (1994a), they are a primary marker of the end (right edge) of Intonational Phrases in ASL, as determined by Selkirk's (1986, 1995) algorithm for spoken languages. Selkirk outlined a theoretical procedure for determining Intonational Phrases from syntactic structure (from ungoverned maximal projections). The utility of this algorithm received empirical support from Hale and Selkirk (1987) for Papago and Aissen (1992) for Mayan. When applied to ASL, where a signer might blink can be predicted with more than 90% accuracy (although it cannot be predicted that a signer *will* blink; Wilbur 1994a). Thus, eyeblink location provides information about constituent structure, both syntactic and prosodic.

There are also blinks that cooccur with lexical signs. These blinks are slower and longer than edge-marking blinks. Such lexical blinks are voluntary, not periodic, and they perform a semantic and/or prosodic function of emphasis, assertion, or stress, with a domain limited to the lexical item with which they occur. Voluntary blinks on lexical signs in final position in a clause can be followed (immediately) by periodic blinks at the end of the constituent, reflecting their different functions. Indeed, it was this pattern of blinking—long slow followed by short fast—that led us to investigate functions other than eyewetting for ASL blinks (Wilbur, 1994a)

Head Nods. Head nods perform a variety of functions. Liddell (1977, 1980) observed that head nods cooccurring with signs mark emphasis, assertions, and/or existence. Head nods have also been noted to correlate with syntactic locations where verbs are missing (Aarons 1994; Liddell 1977, 1980). Wilbur (1991) suggested that such head nods mark focus; that is, they may be the emphatic correlate of voluntary eyeblinks rather than the overt reflection of a missing verb. Liddell (1986) also mentioned the presence of small repeated head nods in a counterfactual conditional example. We also noted a repetitive head nod that has a higher frequency of repetition and smaller movement amplitude than other nods; it appears to signal "hedging" ("sort of," "kind of"). All of these head nods, whether single or repeated, mark a scope domain (lexical item, phrase, or clause).

Head nods not covered by these generalizations appear to serve as edge markers, much the same as inhibited periodic eyeblinks. One piece of evidence for this claim is that head nods that occur after the last sign of a phrase tend to be strongly associated with the occurrence of periodic blinking; that is, if there is a head nod, there is likely to be a periodic eyeblink. However, head nods do not *require* periodic eyeblinking (Wilbur, 1994a). It is not yet known if or how the function changes when a head nod occurs alone or with an eyeblink in these phrasal-edge environments.

Additional evidence that single head nods and inhibited blinking both perform a predominantly (although not entirely) prosodic function comes from research on the effects of signing rate on several variables associated with prosodic phrasing (e.g., narrative duration, sign duration, pause duration, number of signs, number of head nods, eyeblinks, and brow raises). Wilbur and Lynch (in preparation) report a study of signing rate in which signers were instructed to repeat a learned scripted story at different rates. As signing rate increased from slow (approximately 1.2 signs per sec.), to normal (1.5 signs per sec.), to fast (2.1 signs per sec.), there was no effect on the number of signs produced, confirming that with increased rate, signers made changes to prosodic variables rather than merely omitting signs from the scripts. In contrast, counts of prosodic events and measures of duration all decreased with increased signing rate. There were fewer blinks (from 12.3 blinks in slow to 7.8 in fast), fewer head nods (6.7 in slow to 4.2 in fast), and fewer brow raises (3.9 in slow to 3.3 in fast). Story duration decreased (19.4 sec. in slow to 11.1 sec. in fast), as did the duration of individual signs (0.7 sec. in slow to 0.4 sec. in fast) and the pauses between constituents (0.2 sec. in slow to 0.09 sec. in fast). The similar effect of signing rate on head nods and eyeblinks suggests a similarity in function.

The full range of functions and the exact phonological specifications (repetitions, speed of production, etc.) for each type of head nod is an area open to further research. From the existing research, it seems that there are three possible head nod functions corresponding to three different articulations: (a) single head nod as boundary marker, (b) slowed or deliberate head nod as a focus marker cooccurring with lexical signs, and (c) repetitive head nod covering constituent domains and conveying what semanticists refer to as the speaker's commitment to the truth of the assertion (large, slow nodding marking strong assertion; small, rapid nodding for hedging or counterfactuals).

Head Thrusts. Head thrusts, identified by Liddell (1986), present behavior that does not clearly pattern with edge-marking or domain-marking nonmanuals. A head thrust is articulated with the lower jaw thrust forward and cooccurs with the last sign of an "if" or "when" clause in ASL. The head thrust differs from other syntactically associated nonmanual markers, such as negative headshake or [+*wh*]-brow lowering, which spread across entire syntactic domains (discussed further later), in that the head thrust occurs only on the last sign of its clause. Head thrusts also differ from other edge-marking nonmanuals in that other edge markers may occur after the last sign of a clause, whereas head thrusts do not. To me, this suggests that the function of head thrust is neither prosodic nor syntactic but rather semantic: Head thrust could perform a semantic function similar to certain head nods discussed earlier, namely as an indication of the truth of or speaker's commitment to the assertion. Van Valin & Lapolla (1997) discussed the class of "evidentials," markers that languages use to reflect such distinctions as "eyewitness" versus "hearsay." They cited Derbyshire (1985), who suggested that the primary function of these markers is to "express the attitude or relationship of the speaker to what he is saying, including the degree of certainty and the authority for making the assertion" (p. 127). In the case of conditionals such as "if it is (or turns out to be) true that X, then Y," as in "If it rains tomorrow, the game will be postponed," a head thrust in the first clause might reflect the signer's certainty of the postponement of the game under the circumstances cited. It is clear that the head thrust cannot indicate the signer's commitment to the truth of the first clause, as the head thrust can occur in counterfactuals in which the first clause is known to be untrue, as in "If your parents knew about that, they wouldn't be happy" (in which the signer clearly thinks that the parents do not in fact know about something). The appearance of head thrust on the last sign in "when"-clauses is also consistent with this function: "When the announcement is made, everyone better be ready to get to work." If the head thrust does reflect evidential (or similar) marking, then only true conditionals should appear in ASL with head thrust. In English, there are pseudo-conditional structures with "if"-clauses, such as "If I may say so, you're not looking good." In such constructions, the truth of the "consequent" "you're not looking good" is in no way dependent on the content of the "if"-clause; in fact, the function of the "if"-clause is to comment on the relevance of the comment to the conversational partner. These expressions do not translate into ASL with conditional structures but rather with signs such as HONEST or BLUNT/DIRECT; for example, HONEST, YOU LOOK AWFUL. Head thrusts do not appear in such constructions.

Whatever the actual function of head thrust, the observation remains that head thrust is phonologically separated from the other nonmanual markers by virtue of its articulators and its unique domain (the last sign of "if" or "when" clauses). This separation allows it to cooccur with other nonmanuals without mutual interference.

Domain Marking

There is a group of nonmanual markers that are very clearly domain markers, in the sense that they begin in conjunction with the start of a syntactic constituent and end when the relevant constituent ends (Liddell, 1977). For each such marker, it would be nice if we could indicate what function it serves and what domain it marks. Such information is only now starting to become available. Here, I discuss what is known about eyebrow position, eyegaze and head tilt, negative headshake, body leans, and body shift.

Brows. There are three linguistically significant eyebrow positions: raised ("br"), lowered (furrowed "bf"), and neutral. Neutral brows occur on assertions. Furrowed brows occur uniquely and exclusively with *wh*-questions and embedded *wh*-complements. The lowering covers either the whole question (3) or just the *wh*-word or phrase (4), but only if the *wh*-word or phrase is in final position (5 is unacceptable; Aarons et al., 1992, 1994):

$$\overline{\hspace{3cm}\text{bf}\hspace{0.5cm}}$$

3. JOHN BUY t_i YESTERDAY WHAT$_i$
"What did John buy?"

$$\overline{\hspace{3.5cm}\text{bf}\hspace{0.3cm}}$$

4. JOHN BUY t_i YESTERDAY WHAT$_i$
"What did John buy?"

$$\overline{\hspace{1cm}\text{bf}\hspace{0.3cm}}$$

5. *JOHN BUY WHAT YESTERDAY

Raised brows are more difficult to explain, in that they occur on a large collection of seemingly unrelated structures: topics; topicalized constituents; left dislocations; conditionals; relative clauses; yes–no questions; *wh*-clauses of *wh*-cleft constructions; focus-preposed NPs associated with the signs SAME "even" and ONLY-ONE "only"; focus of THAT-clefts (the ASL equivalent of it-clefts; S. Fischer, personal communication, 1992); and everything that precedes (nondoubled) modals and negatives that have been moved to right-peripheral position. Early literature suggested that brow raising performs the pragmatic function of marking nonassertions (especially Coulter, 1978). However, I reported (Wilbur, 1994b, 1995a, 1999; Wilbur & Patschke, 1999) that there are two problems with this view: first, there are structures with "br" on new information, and second, nonasserted information frequently occurs without "br."[2] To use brow raise correctly in ASL, one must master a fairly sophisticated level of syntactic complexity: The commonality found in linguistic "br" usage is that all "br"-marked clauses are associated with [–wh]-operators (Wilbur, 1995a, 1996) and the "br" spreads only across the constituent associated with the operator restriction (specifically, the checking domain).[3]

---

[2]Also, raised brows do not occur on the NPs following focusers ("even," "only"), demonstratives (e.g., THAT), prepositions, quantifiers, numbers, or adjectives; they also do not occur on constructions with doubled negatives or modals or on negated assertions where the negative sign is unmoved (in situ; Wilbur & Patschke, 1999).

[3]In the minimalist linguistic framework, Chomsky (1995) argued that operators have morphological properties that differ across languages and that their syntactic properties are universal. In ASL, brow raise appears to be the overt morphological marker of [–wh]-operators, spanning the checking domain of the operator, but not the clause that follows (hence, not c-command). However, if Chomsky is correct, the syntactic properties that must be mastered are the same for all languages and only the morphology, in this case the use of "br," is different.

A simple example would be a topic with "br" followed by an assertion or a *wh*-question with brow lowering. Boster (1996) discussed such examples involving Quantifier Phrase splits, in which the noun is separated from its modifying quantifier or *wh*-word. The noun receives "br"-marking because it is topicalized, and the remaining clause is either unmarked if it is an assertion or marked with lowered brow as part of the *wh*-question face (Lillo-Martin & Fischer, 1992). The "br" from the topic does not extend over the whole question but only over the topic:[4]

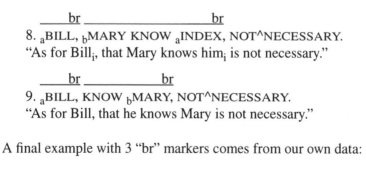

Each example has at least two such positions, reflecting the fact that brow position is separately indicated by operator type: Raised is associated with [*–wh*], furrowed is associated with [*+wh*], and neutral is associated with the absence of an operator. Because brow raise may be associated with different [*–wh*]-operators, there may be more than one in a sentence. Lillo-Martin (1986) cited the following examples, in which there is both a topic "br" and a second "br"-marked sentential subject associated with focused modal/negative NOT^NECESSARY:

    <u>   br   </u>   <u>   br   </u>

8. $_a$BILL, $_b$MARY KNOW $_a$INDEX, NOT^NECESSARY.
"As for Bill$_i$, that Mary knows him$_i$ is not necessary."

    <u>   br   </u>   <u> br   </u>

9. $_a$BILL, KNOW $_b$MARY, NOT^NECESSARY.
"As for Bill, that he knows Mary is not necessary."

A final example with 3 "br" markers comes from our own data:

    <u>   br   </u>   <u> br </u>   <u>   br   </u>

10. ELLEN$_a$, SEAFOOD, t_a t_b EAT SHRIMP REFUSE$_b$
"As for Ellen, as for seafood, she REFUSES to eat shrimp."

---

[4]In contrast, the brow lowering does cover the entire c-command domain of the [*+wh*]-operator, that is, the *wh*-question but not the topic.

In this example, the first "br" is on the left-dislocated ELLEN, the second is on the topic SEAFOOD, and the main verb REFUSE has been focused (moved to final position; cf. Wilbur, 1997, in press), which results in the third "br" on EAT SHRIMP as the associate of the focus operator (Wilbur, 1996). Some other operators that are associated with "br" include conditional, restrictive relative, yes–no question, the *wh*-clause on so-called rhetorical questions (the ASL *wh*-cleft; see further analysis of these and sentential subjects in Wilbur, 1994b, 1995a, 1995b, 1996), and the generic reading of bare plural subjects (Wilbur, 1998). Thus, "br"-marking is not like "bf"-marking for *wh*-clauses in a number of important respects: (a) the domain is limited to the scope position of the operator rather than larger syntactic (c-command) domains, and (b) there can be multiple "br"-marked phrases associated with different functions in the same sentence.

In the section on head nods, I reported the effects of increased signing rate as decreased counts of prosodic events, including blinks and brow raises. With respect to brow raises, what this decrease most likely reflects is the running together of brow raises due to the failure of signers to clearly return the brows to neutral position between individual brow raises in sequences such as that illustrated in (10). Such running together would affect the number of brow raises counted without actually changing the constituents that are properly marked by brow raise. In this sense, there is a modification of brow behavior prosodically but not syntactically.

Eyegaze and Head Tilt. Bahan (1996) and MacLaughlin (1997) discussed the use of eyegaze and head tilt to convey agreement information. Bahan (1996) noted that head tilt is used preferentially to indicate verb agreement with its subject and eyegaze to show agreement with the object. The major exception to this generalization occurs when the object is first person; given that signers cannot direct eyegaze at themselves, first person object agreement must be indicated instead by head tilt, which forces eyegaze to take the job of showing subject agreement. In intransitive constructions, where there is only one NP, head tilt, eyegaze, or both may be used to show agreement. MacLaughlin (1997) demonstrated that a parallel marking system is at work to show agreement with possessor and possessed NPs in determiner phrases. In both the verb and the noun cases, the eyegaze and head tilt span the syntactic (c-command) domain of the agreement feature source. Layering is possible, as eyegaze and head tilt can cooccur with each other and with different brow positions without interference.

Negative Headshake. Similarly, negative headshake can layer with different brow positions and eye positions. The interaction of negative headshake with different head positions (tilt, nod) requires further investigation, although on semantic grounds, we should expect headshake and head nod to be incompatible, as they reflect conflicting messages about the truth of the assertion.

Veinberg and Wilbur (1990) compared the headshakes used in negative contexts by signers and hearing nonsigners. They noted that the negative headshakes of signers begin and end abruptly with the syntactic constituent (within 15–19 msec.), consistent with Liddell's earlier observation and supporting the contention that they are grammatical rather than affective in nature. In contrast, the negative headshakes of hearing nonsigners while they are speaking English do not correlate with English syntactic structure, starting and stopping without apparent concern for syntactic constituency.

Body Leans. The earliest discussion of body leans identified forward lean as a component of the question nonmanual marker "q" (cf. Baker & Padden, 1978; Baker-Shenk, 1983). It was presumed to be there to indicate to the receiver that the signer expected an answer to the question. Penny Boyes-Braem (personal communication, 1994) first identified the rhythmic use of side-to-side body leans for prosodic purposes in her analysis of Swiss German Sign Language narrative structure. The leans she observed were left and right of a center vertical line; the leans crossed the center line when the signer narrated general information, but were restricted to either the left or the right side for specific narrative purposes, such as indicating other signers or different locative or temporal situations. In addition to this use of body leans in ASL, Wilbur and Patschke (1998) reported that leans can indicate (a) prosodic emphasis on particular lexical items, (b) semantic categories of inclusion "even" (lean forward) and exclusion "only" (lean back), (c) type of contrastive focus (e.g., Selecting [forward], Parallel [forward or back, right or left]), and (d) pragmatic affirmation (forward) or denial (backward) of a proposition or presupposition. We discuss an interesting case of layering, wherein an affirmation (forward) body lean is used on a negative construction (where a lean backward might be expected) to reaffirm the truth of the negative assertion:

11. A1: [context] Misha was invited to join the Communist Party
    but refused.

lean further forward

br

B1: MEAN PRO.3 MISHA **NOT** COMMUNIST NOT?
"You mean he's not a Communist?"

lean forward   lean forward

A2: RIGHT, PRO.3 **NOT** COMMUNIST, PRO.3 **NOT**.
"Right, he's *not* a Communist."

Body Shift. Movement of the body, usually from the waist but
sometimes just from the shoulders, has long been known to serve as
part of the pronoun system in ASL (Kegl, 1976a, 1976b, 1977, 1978).
Body shifting has been investigated as it interacts with the general use of
space in signed conversations for ASL (Emmorey, Corina, & Bellugi,
1995; Liddell, 1995; Winston, 1995) and most extensively, for Danish
Sign Language (Engberg-Pedersen, 1993). Initially, it appeared that the
body itself was serving as a pronominal referent to allow the signer to discuss the actions and thoughts of individuals who were not present in the
immediate discourse situation. Engberg-Pedersen (1995) and Lillo-Martin
(1995) argued for DSL and ASL that the purpose of body shifting is to
shift the reference system itself for purposes of changing the point of view
to someone else. That is, in shifted reference locations, when the signer
signs PRO.1 "I/me," the signer is indicating that "I" refers to someone
other than the signer. Lillo-Martin also provided additional arguments that
this perspective shift, which she called "point of view (POV) predicate,"
operates at the syntactic level, that is, as an overt verb that takes a complement clause. An interesting difference between the behavior of this predicate and nonmanuals such as leans is that POV is usually produced by
shifting the body after the signed subject and during the time when a verb
would ordinarily be signed. Even though the shift is held throughout the
duration of the complement clause (and perhaps subsequent utterances), it
does not start in conjunction with a manual sign the way that body leans,
brow raises, and other domain nonmanuals do. Instead, the shift itself
takes up its own phrasal timing slot with the body as the primary articulator and the new position is then held. In this regard, it could be considered
a left-edge marker, indicating the start of a new POV. It may be that on
closer examination, body leans and body shift will turn out not to be differentiated by articulation but by their prosodic behavior, with body leans

as markers limited to signs and body shifts as (combination of) left-edge marker with an as-yet-undetermined scope domain.

Nose.   One of the most overlooked areas of sign language research is the various contributions that are made by the nose. Nose wrinkling can take several forms, each with different meanings. The literature has already identified nose wrinkling as an affective marker for evaluative purposes; for example, to indicate speaker's attitude toward the topic under discussion or as a backchannel conversational reinforcer provided by the listener to the speaker (cf. review in Wilbur, 1987). Used by the signer to indicate attitude, the nose message can be easily differentiated from messages transmitted in the other nonmanual areas and can be layered (barring semantic conflict). However, Wood (1995, 1996) identified additional forms, two of which are single nose crinkle (NC) and multiple wrinkling (NW2-3). She demonstrated that neither of these nose markers performs evaluative or backchannel functions but that both serve contextual discourse functions. NC frequently cooccurs with lexical focus items SELF and THAT and may contribute a meaning of specificity (Coulter, 1978; Wood, 1995). NW2-3 is semantically a singular referring expression that can only refer to one specific, understood object at one specific time (Wood, 1997) and performs a pragmatic function "in that it is used by both speaker and addressee to indicate mutual understanding and agreement as to the context of the utterance" (p. 1) with roughly the meaning "yeah, I know who/what you mean and I agree with you." There are probably other nose forms and functions that remain to be uncovered, and the expectation is that when uncovered, layering of these forms will be a natural phonological possibility.

THE ABSENCE OF A LAYERING CONSPIRACY

ASL is a naturally evolved complex language that varies significantly from spoken English; it has a more flexible word order and does not allow stress shift (Wilbur, 1997). Nonmanual markers are integral components of the ASL intonation system, performing many of the same functions in the signed modality that pitch performs in the spoken modality (Baker & Padden, 1978; Battison, 1974; Frishberg, 1978; Siple, 1978; Wilbur, 1991, 1994a; Wilbur & Patschke, 1998, 1999). These differences in prosodic structure and intonational marking are the primary contributors to significant differences in syntactic structure between ASL and English. The prosodic, intonational, and syntactic structures evolved in concert to provide natural language capability in the signed modality (Wilbur, 1997). If, as I am contending, layering is not a modality effect but a feature of all natural languages resulting from diachronic adaptation to the production modality, then we should find no evidence of layering in signed English (SE). The sociolinguistic reasoning for this is as follows:

The various forms of SE are artificially created systems for communication in pedagogical situations. They are designed as a code to mimic the lexicon, morphology, and syntax of English. SE is produced in the manual–visual modality but is not a natural language. It is in essence recreated as it is learned by each learner, whether child or adult, and it is learned with the overriding constraint that it should follow English word order. Thus, syntactic structure is not available for adaptation for modality purposes; however, this fact by itself is not a problem, as there is no principled reason why a signed language could not have the word order of English if by syntax we mean merely the basic word order. More critically, SE is supposed to follow English morphology, which makes the morphological domain off-limits for modification for modality purposes. English morphology involves affixes that are added to the stems (plural, past tense, progressive, comparative, superlative, possessive) and free-standing grammatical words (future, prepositions, infinitival "to," and determiners). These are translated into SE as separate signs, each requiring independent articulation in sequence; the result is that SE sentences have substantially more signs per sentence than ASL. Therefore, SE takes at least 50% longer to produce the same set of propositions than either spoken English or ASL, which are roughly comparable (Bellugi & Fischer, 1972; Wilbur & Nolen, 1986). The constraint that SE should follow English morphology encourages sequentiality and prevents layering mechanisms from arising. Given the requirement that SE should match English, any child inventions for SE (such as those reported by Gee & Mounty, 1991; Supalla, 1991) involving the types of manual or nonmanual mechanisms that we discussed for ASL will be under pressure to normalize to the proper English sequence of signs. Under these circumstances, grammaticization of nonmanuals or manual sign modifications for functions like verb agreement cannot evolve. Furthermore, when adults (usually hearing) learn to sign English, they are already fluent in English and find it convenient to follow English principles, making innovations by this population less likely. In essence, then, the dominance of English sequentiality of words and morphemes in this communication situation suppresses layering adaptations of SE.

Wilbur and Petersen (1998) studied two groups of fluent SE users (minimum of 10 years daily use), those who also know ASL (adult children of Deaf adults, CODAs) and those who do not (SIMCOMs). The participant groups, stimuli, and tasks were chosen to permit investigation under the best possible circumstances by signers who could provide the best possible productions for analysis, thereby avoiding problems owing to lack of fluency or insufficient training. The study was also designed so that direct comparisons could be made between speech alone and speech with SE (SC), and between SE alone and SE in SC; the same stimuli were performed in all conditions. Both groups displayed the same general pattern across conditions: increased speech duration in SC compared to speech alone; longer signed sentence duration for SE alone than in SC; SE in SC produced with shorter sign durations, shorter gap durations, and more sign omissions than SE alone.

In this study, the signers who knew ASL were relatively diligent in using nonmanual markers to convey information while producing SE (with or without speech); that is, they extended layering from ASL to SE. Sometimes these nonmanual markers accompanied corresponding manual signs whereas other times the nonmanual marker was the sole carrier of the information. The signers who did not know ASL used minimal and occasionally incorrect nonmanual marking while signing SE. For example, for these signers, only 9 of 49 SE productions of yes–no questions had brow raise on them, and another 26 productions were inappropriately marked with brow lowering. Thus, fully 81% of the yes–no questions produced by these signers were not correctly marked by ASL standards. Other nonmanuals (blinks, negative headshakes) clearly differed between the two groups even though both groups were producing the same SE content. The signers who knew ASL were able to transfer nonmanuals to SE because SE has no specified linguistic nonmanuals of its own. The signers who did not know ASL but who are fluent users of SE did not have homogeneity of nonmanuals because none have developed for SE.

As discussed in this chapter, linguistic nonmanuals perform prosodic, syntactic, and semantic functions. Similarly, spatial arrangement can convey syntactic, semantic, and morphological information. If a verb is inflected for its arguments by showing starting and ending locations, then the nouns or pronouns do not need to be separately signed. Aspectual information carried in English by adverbs and prepositions phrases can be conveyed by modifying the verb's temporal and rhythmic characteristics. Information is layered, and thus ASL does not need separate signs for many of the concepts for which English has separate words. In this respect, the fact that ASL is a naturally evolved language in the visual–manual modality can be fully appreciated—more information is conveyed simultaneously than in comparable English renditions. SE lacks layering and must rely entirely on sequentiality.

In sum, the finding that there are systematic cues for intonation in signed languages provides insight into the universal structure of natural languages. One may infer that intonational information is a necessary component of the human linguistic and cognitive systems, and that at the prosodic level, the brain is indifferent to the modality in which such information is received, as long as it is present and appropriate. There are clear differences between naturally evolved languages prosodically suited to their modality by appropriate layering (ASL and English) and artificial systems like SE that take structure from one modality (spoken English) and attempt to convey it in another modality (signed) without regard to modifications that might be appropriate by the production modality.

ACKNOWLEDGMENTS

Funds were provided for this project by the National Institute of Deafness and Other Communicative Disorders R01-DC00935.

REFERENCES

Aarons, D. (1994). *Aspects of the syntax of ASL.* Unpublished doctoral dissertation, Boston University.

Aarons, D., Bahan, B., Kegl, J., & Neidle, C. (1992). Clausal structure and a tier for grammatical marking in ASL. *Nordic Journal of Linguistics 15,* 103–142.

Aarons, D., Bahan, B., Kegl, J., & Neidle, C. (1994). Subjects and agreement in ASL. In I. Ahlgren, B. Bergman, & M. Brennan (Eds.), *Perspectives on sign language structure: Papers from the Fifth International Symposium on Sign Language Research* (pp. 13–28). Durham, UK: International Sign Linguistics Association.

Aissen, J. (1992). Topic and focus in Mayan. *Language, 68,* 43–80.

Anderson, D. E., & Reilly, J. S. (1998). PAH! The acquisition of adverbials in ASL. *Sign Language & Linguistics, 1*(2), 3–28.

Bahan, B. J. (1996). *Non-manual realization of agreement in ASL.* Unpublished doctoral dissertation, Boston University.

Baker, C., & Cokely, D. (1980). *American Sign Language: A teacher's resource text on grammar and culture.* Silver Spring, MD: T. J. Publishers.

Baker, C., & Padden, C. (1978). Focusing on the non-manual components of ASL. In P. Siple (Ed.), *Understanding language through sign language research* (pp. 27–57). New York: Academic Press.

Baker-Shenk, C. (1983). *A microanalysis of the non-manual components of questions in American Sign Language.* Unpublished doctoral dissertation, University of California, Berkeley.

Battison, R. (1974). Phonological deletion in American Sign Language. *Sign Language Studies, 5*, 1–19.

Bellugi, U. (1980). The structuring of language: Clues from the similarities between signed and spoken language. In U. Bellugi & M. Studdert-Kennedy (Eds.), *Signed and spoken language: Biological constraints on linguistic form* (pp. 115–140). Deerfield Beach, FL: Verlag Chemie.

Bellugi, U., & Newkirk, D. (1981). Formal devices for creating new signs in American Sign Language. *Sign Language Studies, 30*, 1–35.

Bellugi, U., & Fischer, S. (1972). A comparison of sign language and spoken language: Rate and grammatical mechanisms. *Cognition, 1*, 173–200.

Boster, C. T. (1996). On the Quantifier–Noun Phrase split in American Sign Language and the Structure of Quantified Noun Phrases. In W. H. Edmondson & R. B. Wilbur (Eds.), *International Review of Sign Linguistics, Vol. 1* (pp. 159–208). Mahwah, NJ: Lawrence Erlbaum Associates.

Chomsky, N. (1995). *The minimalist program.* Cambridge, MA: MIT Press.

Coulter, G. (1978). Raised eyebrows and wrinkled noses: The grammatical function of facial expression in relative clauses and related constructions. In F. Caccamise & D. Hicks (Eds.), *ASL in a bilingual, bicultural context. Proceedings of the Second National Symposium on Sign Language Research and Teaching* (pp. 65–74). Coronado, CA: National Association of the Deaf.

Coulter, G. (1979). *American Sign Language typology.* Unpublished doctoral dissertation, University of California, San Diego.

Coulter, G. (1982). *On the nature of ASL as a monosyllabic language.* Paper presented to the Linguistic Society of America, San Diego, CA.

Davies, S. (1985). The tongue is quicker than the eye: Non-manual behaviors in ASL. In W. Stokoe & V. Volterra (Eds.), *SLR '83: Proceedings of the Third International Symposium on Sign Language Research* (pp. 185–193). Silver Spring, MD: Linstok.

Derbyshire, D. (1985). *Hixkaryana and universal grammar.* Arlington, TX: Summer Institue of Linguistics.

Emmorey, K., Corina, D., & Bellugi, U. (1995). Differential processing of topographic and referential functions of space. In K. Emmorey & J. S. Reilly (Eds.), *Language, gesture, and space* (pp. 43–62). Mahwah, NJ: Lawrence Erlbaum Associates.

Engberg-Pedersen, E. (1993). *Space in Danish Sign Language: The semantics and morphosyntax of the use of space in a visual language.* Hamburg, Germany: SIGNUM-Verlag.

Engberg-Pedersen, E. (1995). Point of view expressed through shifters. In K. Emmorey & J. S. Reilly (Eds.), *Language, gesture, and space* (pp. 133–154). Mahwah, NJ: Lawrence Erlbaum Associates.

Frishberg, N. (1978). The case of the missing length. *Communication and Cognition, 11*, 57–68.

Gee, J. P., & Mounty, J. (1991). Nativization, variability, and style shifting in the sign language development of deaf children of hearing parents. In P. Siple & S. Fischer (Eds.), *Theoretical issues in sign language research, Vol. 2: Psychology* (pp. 65–83). Chicago: University of Chicago Press.

Hale, K., & Selkirk, E. (1987). Government and tonal phrasing in Papago. *Phonology Yearbook, 4*, 151–183.

Kegl, J. (1976a). *Pronominalization in American Sign Language.* Unpublished manuscript, Massachusetts Institute of Technology.

Kegl, J. (1976b). Relational grammar and American Sign Language. Unpublished manuscript, Massachusetts Institute of Technology.

Kegl, J. (1977). ASL syntax: Research in progress and proposed research. Unpublished manuscript, Massachusetts Institute of Technology.

Kegl, J. (1978). Indexing and pronominalization in ASL. Unpublished manuscript, Massachusetts Institute of Technology.

Klima, E., & Bellugi, U. (1979). *The signs of language.* Cambridge, MA: Harvard University Press.

Liddell, S. K. (1977). *An investigation into the syntax of American Sign Language.* Unpublished doctoral dissertation, University of California, San Diego.

Liddell, S. K. (1978). Non-manual signals and relative clauses in American Sign Language. In P. Siple (Ed.), *Understanding language through sign language research* (pp. 59–90). New York: Academic Press.

Liddell, S. K. (1980). *American Sign Language syntax.* The Hague: Mouton.

Liddell, S. K. (1986). Head thrusts in ASL conditional marking. *Sign Language Studies, 52,* 243–262.

Liddell, S. K. (1995). Real, surrogate, and token space: Grammatical consequences in ASL. In K. Emmorey & J. S. Reilly (Eds.), *Language, gesture, and space* (pp. 19–41). Mahwah, NJ: Lawrence Erlbaum Associates.

Liddell, S. K. (In press). Blended spaces and deixis in sign language discourse. In D. McNeill (Ed.), *Language and gesture: Window into thought and action.*

Lillo-Martin, D. (1986). Two kinds of null arguments in American Sign Language. *Natural Language and Linguistic Theory, 4,* 415–444.

Lillo-Martin, D. (1995). The point of view predicate in American Sign Language. In K. Emmorey & J. S. Reilly (Eds.), *Language, gesture, and space* (pp. 155–170). Mahwah, NJ: Lawrence Erlbaum Associates.

Lillo-Martin, D., & Fischer, S. (1992, May). Overt and covert wh-questions in American Sign Language. Paper presented at the Fifth International Symposium on Sign Language Research, Salamanca, Spain.

MacLaughlin, D. (1997). *The structure of determiner phrases: Evidence from American Sign Language.* Unpublished doctoral dissertation, Boston University.

McCarthy, J. (1979). *Formal problems in Semitic phonology and morphology.* Unpublished doctoral dissertation, Massachusetts Institute of Techonology.

McCarthy, J. (1981). A prosodic theory of nonconcatenative morphology. *Linguistic Inquiry, 12,* 373–418.

Neidle, C., Kegl, J., MacLaughlin, D., Lee, R., & Bahan, B. (1996, September) *The distribution of non-manual correlates of syntactic features: Evidence for the hierarchical organization of ASL.* Paper presented at the Fifth International Conference on Theoretical Issues in Sign Language Research, Montreal.

Newkirk, D. (1979). *The form of the continuative aspect inflection on ASL verbs.* Unpublished manuscript, The Salk Institute for Biological Studies.

Newkirk, D. (1980). *Rhythmic features of inflections in American Sign Language.* Unpublished manuscript, The Salk Institute for Biological Studies.

Newkirk, D. (1981). *On the temporal segmentation of movement in ASL.* Unpublished manuscript, The Salk Institute for Biological Studies.

Petronio, K. (1993). *Clause structure in American Sign Language.* Unpublished doctoral dissertation, University of Washington, Seattle.

Reilly, J. S., & Bellugi, U. (1996). Competition on the face: Affect and language in ASL motherese. *Journal of Child Language, 23,* 219–239.

Reilly, J. S., McIntire, M., & Bellugi, U. (1990). The acquisition of conditionals in American Sign Language: Grammaticized facial expressions. *Applied Psycholinguistics, 11,* 369–392.

Selkirk, E. O. (1982). *The syntax of words. Linguistic Inquiry* Monograph No. 7.

Selkirk, E. O. (1986). *Phonology and syntax: The relation between sound and structure.* Cambridge, MA: MIT Press.

Selkirk, E. O. (1995). Sentence prosody: Intonation, stress, and phrasing. In J. Goldsmith (Ed.), *The handbook of phonological theory* (pp. 550–569). Cambridge, MA: Blackwell.

Siple, P. (1978). Visual constraints for sign language communication. *Sign Language Studies, 19,* 95–110.

Stern, J., & Dunham, D. (1990). The ocular system. In Cacioppo & Tassinary (Eds.), *Principles of psychophysiology: Physical, social, and inferential elements* (pp. 513–553). Cambridge: Cambridge University Press.

Supalla, S. J. (1991). Manually coded English: The modality question in signed language development. In P. Siple & S. Fischer (Eds.), *Theoretical issues in sign language research, Vol. 2: Psychology* (pp. 85–109). Chicago: University of Chicago Press.

Valli, C., & Lucas, C. (1992). Linguistics of American Sign Language: A resource text for ASL users. Washington, DC: Gallaudet.

Van Valin, R., & Lapolla, R. (1997). *Syntax: Structure, meaning, and function.* Cambridge: Cambridge University Press.

Veinberg, S., & Wilbur, R. B. (1990). A linguistic analysis of the negative headshake in American Sign Language. *Sign Language Studies, 68,* 217–244.

Wilbur, R. B. (1973). The phonology of reduplication. Unpublished doctoral dissertation, University of Illinois (Available from Indiana University Linguistics Club, Bloomington, IN).

Wilbur, R. B. (1987). *American Sign Language: Linguistic and applied dimensions.* Boston: College-Hill.

Wilbur, R. B. (1991). Intonation and focus in American Sign Language. In Y. No & M. Libucha (Eds.), *ESCOL '90: Proceedings of the Seventh Eastern States Conference on Linguistics* (pp. 320–331). Columbus: Ohio State University Press.

Wilbur, R. B. (1994a). Eyeblinks and ASL phrase structure. *Sign Language Studies, 84,* 221–240.

Wilbur, R. B. (1994b). Foregrounding structures in ASL. *Journal of Pragmatics, 22,* 647–672.

Wilbur, R. B. (1995a). What the morphology of operators looks like: A formal analysis of ASL brow-raise. In L. Gabriele, D. Hardison, & R. Westmoreland (Eds.), *FLSM VI: Proceedings of the Sixth Annual Meeting of the Formal Linguistics Society of Mid-America: Vol. 2. Syntax II & Semantics/Pragmatics* (pp. 67–78). Bloomington: Indiana University Linguistics Club.

Wilbur, R. B. (1995b). Why so-called 'rhetorical questions' (RHQs) are neither rhetorical nor questions. In H. Bos & T. Schermer (Eds.), *Sign language research 1994: Proceedings of the Fourth European Congress on Sign Language Research* (pp. 149–169). Hamburg, Germany: SIGNUM.

Wilbur, R. B. (1996). Evidence for the function and structure of wh-clefts in ASL. In W. H. Edmondson & R. B. Wilbur (Eds.), *International Review of Sign Linguistics* (Vol. 1, pp. 209–256). Mahwah, NJ: Lawrence Erlbaum Associates.

Wilbur, R. B. (1997). A prosodic/pragmatic explanation for word order variation in ASL with typological implications. In K. Lee, E. Sweetser, & M. Verspoor (Eds.), *Lexical and syntactic constructions and the construction of meaning* (pp. 89–104). Philadelphia: John Benjamins.

Wilbur, R. B. (1999). A functional journey with a formal ending: What do brow raises do in American Sign Language? In E. Moravcsik, F. Newmeyer, M. Noonan, & K. Wheatley (Eds.), *Functionalism and Formalism in linguistics, Vol. II: Case Studies* (pp. 295–313). Amsterdam: John Benjamins.

Wilbur, R. B. (1998). *Generic and habitual structures in ASL: What's brow raise got to do with it?* Sixth International Conference on Theoretical Issues In Sign Language Research, Gallaudet University.

Wilbur, R. B. (in press). Stress in ASL: Empirical evidence and linguistic issues. *Language and Speech.*

Wilbur, R. B., & Lynch, M. (in preparation). *The effects of signing rate on signs and non-manual events.*

Wilbur, R. B., & Nolen, S. (1986). The duration of syllables in American Sign Language. *Language and Speech, 29,* 263–280.

Wilbur, R. B., & Patschke, C. (1998). Body leans and marking contrast in ASL. *Journal of Pragmatics, 30,* 275–303.

Wilbur, R. B., & Patschke, C. (1999). Syntactic correlates of brow raise in ASL. *Sign Language & Linguistics, 2*(1), 3–40.

Wilbur, R. B., & Petersen, L. (1998). Modality interactions of speech and signing in simultaneous communication. *Journal of Speech, Language, & Hearing Research, 41,* 200–212.

Wilbur, R. B., & Petitto, L. (1983). Discourse structure of ASL conversations; or, how to know a conversation when you see one. *Discourse Processes, 6,* 225–241.

Wilbur, R. B., Klima, E., & Bellugi, U. (1983). Roots: On the search for the origins of signs in ASL. *Chicago Linguistic Society, 19,* 314–336.

Winston, E. A. (1989, July). *Timelines in ASL.* Paper presented at The Deaf Way, Washington, DC.

Winston, E. A. (1995). Spatial mapping in comparative discourse frames. In K. Emmorey & J. S. Reilly (Eds.), *Language, gesture, and space* (pp. 87–114). Mahwah, NJ: Lawrence Erlbaum Associates.

Wood, S. K. (1995). *Non-manuals and SELF in ASL.* Unpublished manuscript, Purdue University.

Wood, S. K. (1996, May). *Nose wrinkles in ASL: A discourse particle for co-construction.* Paper presented at the annual meeting of the American Association for Applied Linguistics.

Wood, S. K. (1997). *Semantic analysis of NW2-3 in ASL.* Unpublished manuscript, Purdue University.

14

A Two-Handed Manual Alphabet in the United States

Ruth C. Loew
Educational Testing Service
Princeton, NJ

C. Tane Akamatsu
Toronto District School Board
Ontario, Canada

Mary Lanaville
CSC Interpreters, Inc.
Hudson, NC

Our contribution to this festschrift has its origins in the grassroots of the Deaf community as well as in the hallowed halls of the ivory tower. The pioneering work of Edward Klima and Ursula Bellugi, from data collection to technical argumentation to acquiring funding for sign language research, has allowed a great number of scholars to benefit either directly or indirectly. Such benefit has also accrued to members of the Deaf community, who have always known that there existed a language and culture, but who are now empowered to study it from the inside. This piece, written by a linguist, a psychologist, and an interpreter married to a Deaf man, demonstrates the influence that Klima and Bellugi have had on many levels of scholarship and on the lives of Deaf people.

During a course on American Sign Language (ASL) structure, a sign meaning "no good" came to our attention. It was performed using what appeared to be the British two-handed alphabet letters N-G. This sign was described by Battison (1978), but according to our informant, it was not British. It was "from the old alphabet—the one all the older Deaf people know." This "old alphabet" is a two-handed American manual alphabet.

The most common form of American fingerspelling is single-handed. Two-handed fingerspelling is typically associated with British Sign Language (BSL; Deuchar, 1984) and with its documented descendants in Australia, New Zealand, Indonesia, and the former Yugoslavia (Carmel,1982). In Canada's Maritime Provinces, a few signers use (or at least know) the British manual alphabet (Simon Carmel, personal communication, January 30, 1990; Michael Rodda, personal communication, February 12, 1990), likely learned from British teachers at the Halifax school. There has been much manual communication research in the past 30 years, but with the exception of Battison's (1978) mention of the two-handed #N-G, there is no reference to any American alphabet other than the current single-handed one.

Yet there is a two-handed American alphabet that has been observed throughout the United States and with which many American signers are familiar. In many American residential schools for Deaf children, people apparently used this alphabet occasionally until about 1950, in the dormitories and on the playgrounds. Few people now use it productively, although some can demonstrate it by reciting it letter by letter, in order. Older Deaf people, and those who associate with them, take its existence for granted; younger Deaf people may not know it at all, and even fluent hearing signers may never have seen such an alphabet if they do not associate with older Deaf signers. This two-handed alphabet is obviously similar to the British manual alphabet, but it also shows some distinctive differences from the British, which are discussed later.

COMPARISON WITH BRITISH FINGERSPELLING

Overview

The American two-handed system is quite similar to the British system. Most of the consonants in the American two-handed alphabet are the same as, or cognate with, the consonants of the British manual alphabet. The most striking difference from the British is the vowels.

Vowels

The British manual alphabet uses fingertip vowels: The letter A is a point to the thumb; E, a point to the index finger; I, to the middle finger; O, to the ring finger; and U, to the little finger, as if the five vowels are being listed or counted off. The fingerspelled forms are not derived from the shapes of the written letters. These vowels have been in use for centuries, as evidenced by their appearance in Wilkins's 1641 document. Sutton-Spence (1995) called the vowels the most robust part of the British manual alphabet and a holdover from an arthrological system in which specific locations on the hand represented letters, to which the signer pointed in order to spell out words.

The American two-handed alphabet, however, has a totally different set of vowels, shown in Fig. 14.1. Four of the five vowels clearly look like their orthographic forms. The U has both a one-handed (illustrated in Fig. 14.1) and a two-handed variant (the same handshape laid on the palm of the nondominant hand). Oddly, the O, which is one of the few one-handed letters in this alphabet, is often made with the nondominant hand.[1] The letter I in this alphabet, a point to the eye, may be a pun on the English word *eye*, or a remnant from a corporal system (described by LaFin, 1692), in which the signer pointed to specific body parts to represent specific letters.

Consonants

Most of the consonants look very much like the British ones. The notable differences are presented in Figs. 14.2 and 14.3. The letters J and Z are completely different from their British counterparts.

Although the American Z does not look like its British counterpart, a Z very much like this one appears on early British manual alphabet charts (Smith, 1864). A British illustration from Defoe (1732) shows this Z. In fact, some members of Deaf British families remember seeing elderly relatives using this Z earlier in this century, even though it had vanished from the charts by then.

The other differences are less substantive. F is articulated symmetrically in the British alphabet but asymmetrically in the American one, in which the nondominant hand uses only an index finger extension. T

---

[1]After shooting the photographs for Figs. 14.1 through 14.3, we realized that our model is ambidextrous and switches hands frequently while signing. As a result, some of our claims regarding dominant versus nondominant hand may not be supported by the photographs. We have, however, also seen other nonambidextrous models switch dominance for C, L, O, and P.

FIG. 14.1.   American two-handed vowels.

involves a switch between dominant and nondominant hands. The L and C
are made by the dominant hand outlining an American one-handed L (or
C, respectively) on the nondominant hand.

If one relies on fingerspelling charts for information about the British
manual alphabet, there are a number of consonants that seem to be systematically different in the two alphabets. Several of the handshapes from
older British charts involve the extension of more fingers than do the
American versions. The finger extension seems to be conditioned to a
large extent by coarticulatory effects; British vowels are done on extended

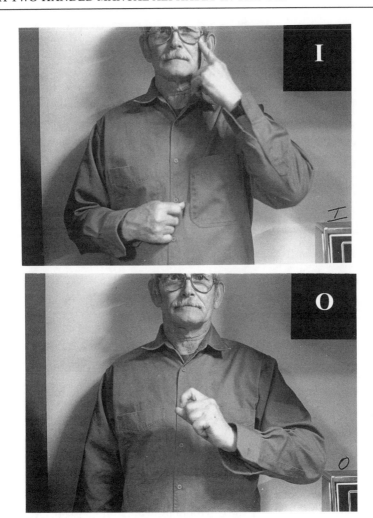

FIG. 14.1.   American two-handed vowels (continued).

fingers. However, Bencie Woll (personal communication, January 24 and February 22, 1990) noted that fingerspelling charts show, at best, citation forms and not necessarily what the letters look like in actual use. Especially in the case of older charts, we do not know if the charts are prescriptive or descriptive: that is, whether they show how someone thought the letters should look or how someone observed that they actually looked. Even the most modern British fingerspelling chart published in Sutton-Spence and Woll (1999) is also just of citation forms. It does not show the handshapes that occur in actual use as a result of coarticulatory

FIG. 14.1.   American two-handed vowels (continued).

effects. Moreover, charts do not show regional, contextual, or idiosyncratic variation. Because it is difficult to find Americans who still use the
two-handed alphabet, we often see what people remember about the
alphabet, rather than the alphabet in use, and we rarely see whole words.
Therefore, caution should be exercised in interpreting differences between
British and American letters.

WHO USED THIS ALPHABET?

So far, we have collected reports of the use of this alphabet from Michigan, Washington State, Idaho, Montana, Utah, Tennessee, North and
South Carolina, Kentucky, New York, Iowa, New Hampshire, Texas,
Kansas, West Virginia, Maryland, Louisiana, Pennsylvania, New Jersey,
Ohio, Massachusetts, and Wisconsin—all over the United States. There is
no obvious geographic pattern here. It seems likely that, as we collect
more data, we will find it in even more states. Usually people are glad to
be reminded of it. The only expressions of shock are that we, hearing people, know it or that they have not seen it for a long time. Typical comments
are: "I haven't seen that for 20 years." "Oh, I haven't seen that in years, but
if my parents didn't want the kids to understand them, they always used
it!" "My dad used to use that sometimes, for a joke. I thought he made it
up. You mean other people know it too? I had no idea!" We have recently

FIG. 14.2. American J and Z.

heard that in North Carolina, there are isolated mountain communities where people are still using the two-handed alphabet. One elderly Deaf informant there, who used it only with his family members, both Deaf and hearing, expressed surprise that "outsiders" knew it. Our subjective impression is that most American Deaf people who were in residential schools prior to World War II know this alphabet, and many younger Deaf people at least recognize it. A few people report having seen older people using the alphabet but not having learned it themselves.

FIG. 14.3.   American F, L, and T.

As far as we can determine, although many people can demonstrate this alphabet, it is rarely used. In general, only older signers can use it both receptively and expressively. Some of these people report that they still use it among themselves.

However, it must once have been used considerably more. Several phenomena point to this. One is the existence of at least one fingerspelled loan sign derived from this alphabet, the #N-G meaning "no good" cited earlier. Interestingly, although the N and the G of this alphabet are identical to the N and G of the British manual alphabet, the two-handed finger-

FIG. 14.3.   American F, L, and T (continued).

spelled loan sign #N-G is not used in Britain. Also, some signers who are far from fluent in this alphabet recognize certain words spelled in it. These words include #C-O-F-F-E-E and #T-O-D-A-Y. Presumably, these finger-spellings were once used commonly enough that younger Deaf people recall them, even if they cannot use the alphabet fully themselves. Third, some older Deaf people whose English names start with J have the J of this alphabet as their name sign, even though they may not be aware, without prodding, of the source of the name sign. Loan signs and name signs must have come from an alphabet that was in use at the time.

The alphabet seems to have been transmitted within families, from Deaf parents to their children, and within residential schools for Deaf children. Sometimes Deaf children who learned it at residential schools taught it to their families when they returned home. However, we have collected numerous anecdotal reports of hearing relatives of Deaf children learning it from other adults in the early 1900s. In each case, the relatives decided to learn some way to communicate with the Deaf child and, in a time before early intervention programs, found someone in the community, Deaf or hearing, who taught them this alphabet. Interpreters have reported going to hospitals to work with elderly Deaf people and finding the hearing family members struggling to communicate using the two-handed alphabet, which they had learned long before.

This alphabet is, however, clearly dying. There is in fact more variation in the forms of the letters than we have discussed here. In particular, some of the least frequently used letters (J and Z) have a number of variations, often apparently because signers cannot remember how to articulate them. Variability in the forms of rarely used items is common in a dying language, and the same may be true of a dying subsystem of a living language (Dorian, 1978).

HISTORY OF THE AMERICAN
TWO-HANDED ALPHABET

So far, the only printed historical evidence we have found of this alphabet is the Michaels (1923) chart (Fig. 14.4). This chart appears at the end of his book. Although the Z on this chart is like the modern British one, the J is clearly the American one described previously, and there are a few other letters that, although not quite like the most common American ones, are clearly a variation on the alphabet we are discussing. Many people have reported having seen the two-handed alphabet in print in the early 1900s (in a Boy Scout manual; in the *Little Blue Primer* or *Little Green Primer* in Tennessee; in a thick brown book of American Indian stories; and in a pamphlet like a comic book that a bookstore in Flint, Michigan, sold to students from the Michigan School for the Deaf). The only one of these sources that we were able to substantiate, and that one only very indirectly, is the Boy Scout manual. According to Sutton-Spence (1994), a sign language book by Benjamin Green, published in Ohio in 1916, includes a chart of the British two-handed alphabet. This book states that "this alphabet is used almost exclusively by the English Deaf, but it is used to some extent in this country and Canada. . . . This book is being sold to the Boy Scouts at 25 cents each." Because we do not know who Green was or how knowledgeable he was, it is not clear whether Americans were actually using the British manual alphabet at the time or whether current-day Americans are simply remembering that particular Boy Scout book.

The alphabet is so similar to the British that there is obviously a historical connection. Bencie Woll (personal communication, 1990) pointed out the absurdity of maintaining that the Deaf people of the United States were sitting meekly on the shore, hands at their sides, waiting for Clerc to arrive and teach them to sign. We can assume that the Deaf people of America were signing (and perhaps fingerspelling) something before Gallaudet and Clerc imported French Sign Language and French fingerspelling and founded the American School for the Deaf in 1817. Before

Clerc, American signing probably had elements of the sign languages of various European countries. British fingerspelling could readily have been brought to America with British Deaf immigrants, possibly as early as colonial times. Or perhaps some of the American children sent to study at the Braidwood schools in England (Lane, 1984) in the late 1700s or early 1800s brought it back with them. It is surprising that we know so little of BSL influence on ASL.

Similarities between a few of the American two-handed letters and early British forms (e.g., the Z described in Smith, 1864, and Defoe, 1732) suggest the possibility that this alphabet came to America in the 1700s or early 1800s. Because this Z is highly iconic, it is of course possible that it was invented twice. Nevertheless, even though the resemblance could be coincidental, we find it at least tantalizingly suggestive of a connection with earlier British fingerspelling. Interestingly, the two-handed alphabet of Indonesia has a Z like the American one. The Indonesian alphabet also came from the British one, but we do not know when it was brought to Indonesia.

Further evidence of such a connection, although admittedly even more tenuous, is that an asymmetrical F something like the American F also shows up on some British fingerspelling charts from the 1700s and early 1800s. However, the F's have varied so much that we are not sure how important this fact is. Another bit of evidence is that some British alphabets from between 1800 and 1850 have J's using the same (American one-handed) X handshape, but in neutral space, not on the face. This could again be coincidence, as the J in space looks like the written J, but it also suggests the possibility that the American J comes from an earlier British J. These similarities with the older British fingerspelling charts suggest the possibility that the American two-handed alphabet could have come from an early dialect of British fingerspelling that was brought to this country.

What about Canada? Some older Deaf people in the Maritime Provinces of Canada use the British alphabet, but we have so far found only one Canadian signer who knows the American two-handed alphabet. A school for the Deaf was established in Halifax, Nova Scotia, in the 1850s, using BSL. People used British fingerspelling there until about the 1920s. There are still Deaf people from the Maritimes who know the British alphabet because they or their parents learned it in school. However, so far there is no evidence that the American two-handed alphabet either developed in or was used in Canada.

What about Martha's Vineyard? This island off the Massachusetts coast had a high incidence of hereditary deafness, and it is reported that Deaf

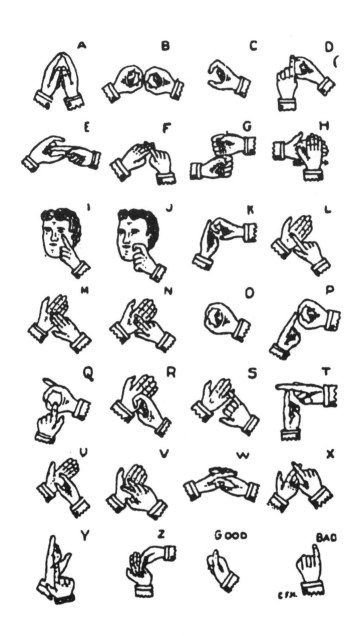

FIG. 14.4. Manual alphabet chart, from J. W. Michaels, 1923, Atlanta, GA:
Home Mission Board Southern Baptist Convention, p. 162.

256

and hearing alike used a sign language (Groce, 1985). The Islanders were descendants of immigrants from one small region of England, and these immigrants might have brought their own signing (and fingerspelling) with them. According to Groce, the fingerspelling that the Island Deaf used was standard American one-handed spelling, learned at the American School for the Deaf. However, Ronnie Wilbur (personal communication, 1994) reported that a two-handed X was used on the Vineyard. Moreover, Bahan and Nash (1998) reported that two-handed fingerspelling was in use there. So it is possible that Martha's Vineyard signing was a link in the development of this alphabet.

We do have one other small but interesting clue. A Deaf woman raised in India recognized the American two-handed alphabet because it is used in schools for the Deaf in some parts of India. She said that schools in other parts of India use the British alphabet. Another Deaf man, also from south Asia, demonstrated "his" fingerspelling to us, which included the American vowels. We do not know yet how this American two-handed alphabet was brought to this region; however, it is possible that in colonial times there were several dialects or variants of the British manual alphabet and that the same dialect was brought to south Asia and America; or that, as Richard Meier (personal communication, 1991) has suggested, Americans, perhaps missionaries, brought the American two-handed alphabet to Asia.

A likely hypothesis is that this alphabet was used among the Deaf of this country before 1817. Perhaps, after French sign and fingerspelling became well established, this alphabet went underground and became a private, "in-group" code rather than a public means of communication.

SUMMARY AND CONCLUSIONS

This study is significant for several reasons. First, it is a powerful demonstration of the reality of Deaf cultural history, namely, how little of the story of Deaf people has been told. This alphabet is tremendously widespread among American Deaf people and apparently was part of the culture of residential schools for the Deaf until comparatively recently; yet it was not documented.

Methodologically, it demonstrates the importance of collecting signed data from informants of various ages. Some studies have focused on younger, college-educated Deaf informants. Yet this alphabet is known mostly among older signers. A study of younger signers would miss it altogether. There are probably other aspects of manual communication that will die out along with their users unless information from older Deaf people is collected.

Historically, it at least hints at how Deaf people in America may have communicated prior to the importation and widespread use of French Sign Language (or at least, French signs and the French manual alphabet) in educational settings. Although it has long been recognized that Deaf Americans must have had a sign language before 1817 (Woodward, 1978), we know virtually nothing of what it was like. This alphabet provides a clue.

The American two-handed alphabet described here suggests origins that go back not to the French but to the British manual alphabet. Yet the vowels appear to be unique to former British colonies. If we assume that this alphabet is derived from the British, where did differences between the two alphabets—particularly the vowels—come from? Britain itself uses the fingertip vowels that were documented as early as 1641. Did the American vowels come earlier, say, with the Mayflower in 1620? Were the fingertip vowels discarded and a new set invented? Perhaps all two-handed alphabets (or at least those representing Roman characters) came from a pan-European manual alphabet, which the British adopted, replacing the vowels with their fingertip vowels (Sutton-Spence, personal communication, August 13–14, 1998). Unfortunately, we will probably never know, but we hope that this discovery will encourage other researchers to continue to explore other genetic and social relationships among the world's signed languages.

ACKNOWLEDGMENTS

This chapter grew out of papers originally presented at the Conference on Theoretical Issues in Sign Language Research, Boston, May 1990; and the Fourth New York Statewide Conference for Teachers of American Sign Language, New York, June 1994. We would like to express our appreciation to all Deaf people who demonstrated this alphabet and told us stories about it. We would also like to thank the following people who contributed their insights: Simon Carmel, Roger Carver, Tupper Dunbar, Nora Groce, Mildred Johnson, Judy Kegl, Harlan Lane, Rachel Mayberry, Richard Meier, Carol Padden, Michael Rodda, Rachel Sutton-Spence, Margaret Winzer, and Bencie Woll. All errors, of course, are our own.

REFERENCES

Bahan, B., & Nash, J. C. P. (1998). The formation of signing communities. In J. Mann (Ed.), *Deaf Studies IV Conference Proceedings.* Washington, DC: Gallaudet University Center for Continuing Education.

Battison, R. (1978). *Lexical borrowing in American Sign Language.* Silver Spring, MD: Linstok Press.

Carmel, S. J. (1982). *International hand alphabet charts* (Rev. ed.). Henrietta, NY: Author.

Defoe, D. (1732). *The life and adventures of Duncan Campbell.* London: E. Curll.

Deuchar, M. (1984). *British Sign Language.* London: Routledge & Kegan Paul.

Dorian, N. C. (1978). The fate of morphological complexity in language death. *Language, 54,* 590–609.

Green, B. (1916). *A handbook in the manual alphabets.* Toledo, OH: Author.

Groce, N. E. (1985). *Everyone here spoke sign language: Hereditary deafness on Martha's Vineyard.* Cambridge, MA: Harvard University Press.

LaFin. (1692). *Sermo mirabilis* (or the silent language).

Lane, H. (1984). *When the mind hears: A history of the Deaf.* New York: Random House.

Michaels, J. W. (1923). *A handbook of the sign language of the deaf.* Atlanta, GA: Home Mission Board Southern Baptist Convention.

Smith, S. (1864). *The deaf and dumb: Their deprivation and its consequences; the process of their education, with other interesting particulars.* London: William MacKintosh.

Sutton-Spence, R. (1994). *The role of the manual alphabet and fingerspelling in British Sign Language.* Unpublished doctoral dissertation, University of Bristol, UK.

Sutton-Spence, R. (1995). Very early manual alphabets. *Signpost, 8,* 32–35.

Sutton-Spence, R., & Woll, B. (1999). *The linguistics of British Sign Language: An introduction.* Cambridge, UK: Cambridge University Press.

Wilkins, J. (1641). *Mercury: Or the secret and swift messenger.* London: John Maynard and Timothy Wilkins.

Woodward, J. (1978). Historical bases of American Sign Language. In P. Siple (Ed.), *Understanding language through sign language research* (pp. 333–348). New York: Academic Press.

15

Iconicity and Transparency in Sign Languages: A Cross-Linguistic Cross-Cultural View

Elena Pizzuto
Virginia Volterra
Institute of Psychology,
National Research Council
Rome, Italy

ICONIC AND TRANSPARENT FEATURES OF SIGNS AND THEIR IMPORT FOR CROSS-LINGUISTIC CROSS-CULTURAL COMPARISONS

Since the beginning of research on sign languages, researchers have been intrigued by the fact that, in many cases, the forms of the signs resemble or bring to mind in some manner the forms of the object, action, or event they denote. There is thus an iconic relation of resemblance between the sign and its referent. One important consequence of iconicity in signs is that even naive, hearing observers who are not familiar with a particular sign language may more or less appropriately "guess" the meaning of a sign or at least see some connection between the sign and the object, event, or action it stands for.

As Bellugi and Klima (1976) and Klima and Bellugi (1979) remarked several years ago with respect to American Sign Language (ASL), these iconic features of signs (and the related transparency of sign meaning) are most apparent when individual signs are seen out of context, as when asking a signer "what's the sign for that?" and pointing for example to an object (such as a tree) or an action (such as walking). When, on the contrary, the signs are seen in context, within the flow of any sign language conversation among signers, a naive observer cannot easily guess the signs' meaning. In this condition in fact, Klima and Bellugi (1979) noted, "Without the help of an interpreter [a hearing naive observer] is very likely not able to guess even the topic of the conversation, much less the meaning of individual signs in the sign stream. Looking at an ongoing conversational signing [in ASL] is little different in this respect from listening to a conversation in a spoken language one doesn't know" (p. 10).

From a cross-linguistic standpoint, it is also important to stress that the iconic relation between a sign and its referent does not in any way determine the actual details of the form that individual signs have in different sign languages. This point was first made by Bellugi and Klima (1976) and Klima and Bellugi (1979), who showed how even signs for a very concrete object such as a "tree" can take fairly different forms in such different sign languages as ASL, Danish (DSL), and Chinese Sign Language (CSL). In all three sign languages, the signs for "tree" are iconic but differ one from one another in several or all formal details (e.g., in the hand configurations, locations, or movements used to produce the signs).

For example, the ASL sign TREE is made with the forearm upright, the hand spread wide, and a twisting of the wrist and forearm. In this sign form, the upright forearm appears to iconically represent the tree's trunk, while the outstreched hand represents the tree's branches and the twisting motion of the hand and forearm the branches moving in the wind. The DSL sign TREE, instead, is made with two symmetrical hands that outline in the air first the rounded shape of a tree's top and then move down to sketch the shape of the trunk. In the CSL sign TREE, two still different hands are used: The two hands symmetrically seem to encompass the shape of a tree's trunk and then, maintaining the same form, move upward.

One of the major objectives pursued by research on sign languages, and by comparative analyses of different sign and spoken languages, is to clarify which features of language structure are more directly linked to the specific visual–gestural or auditory–vocal modality of language production and perception, which features are related to a particular sign or spoken language, and which features instead appear to be modality and/or language independent, and can thus be characterized as universal features of language structure. In addition to providing more appropriate descriptions of specific signed and spoken languages, the ultimate goal of this line of investigation is to reach a more profound understanding of the human capacity for language.

In the tradition of research on spoken languages, iconic properties have been for the most disregarded or considered as marginal phenomena surfacing, for example, in a limited number of onomatopoeic words. More recently, there has been a growing interest for iconic features of speech, which have been identified at different structural levels including syntax, morphology, and phonology (see Haiman, 1985; Hinton, Nichols & O'Hala, 1994; Simone, 1995). A thorough comparison of the comparability of speech and sign along the dimension of iconicity is beyond the scope of this chapter (see Armstrong, Stokoe, & Wilcox, 1995; see also Pizzuto, Cameracanna, Corazza, & Volterra, 1995). The evidence available, to be reviewed here, however, indicates that the visual–gestural modality provides a richer source for iconic properties, leading in turn to a greater transparency of signs as compared to words. Iconic-transparent features seem thus to reflect, to an extent that remains to be ascertained, language-organizational principles proper of the visual–gestural modality that have no simple counterpart in the spoken modality. The nature of such features is, however, still poorly understood. In particular, very little is known about the culture- or language-dependent factors that may influence the perception of signs' iconicity, transparency, or both.

In this chapter, we describe a cross-linguistic and cross-cultural study we conducted to assess the comprehensibility of Italian Sign Language (LIS) signs by both hearing and Deaf participants in six different European countries. Before describing our study, it is useful to discuss in some detail the evidence provided by previous studies.

PREVIOUS STUDIES ON THE ICONICITY AND TRANSPARENCY OF SIGN LANGUAGES' LEXICAL ITEMS

Bellugi and Klima (1976) conducted three related studies to explore systematically whether iconicity could facilitate the comprehension of ASL signs by naive hearing participants. In the first of these studies, 10 American hearing participants who did not know any sign language and who had no Deaf acquaintances were shown a set of 90 ASL signs (signed on a videotape by a native signer) and were asked to write down their best guess for each sign. The signs used in this study corresponded to common concrete and abstract nouns of English (e.g., including signs such as

APPLE, BIRD, IDEA, and SCIENCE). Bellugi and Klima found that only 9% or 10% of the signs in this list were given the appropriate meaning by at least one participant. The remaining 81 ASL signs were not recognized by the participants, and all participants made very different guesses. This study thus indicated a very limited degree of transparency of the ASL signs examined.

In a second, less demanding study, Bellugi and Klima (1976) used the same set of 90 ASL signs to construct a multiple choice test in which they listed, for each sign, the correct English translation and four other possible meanings. Most of these alternative meanings were selected from the wrong responses given by the participants of the previous study and thus provided intuitively likely, although incorrect, meanings. A new group of 10 naive hearing participants was shown the 90 ASL signs, along with their alternative meanings, and was asked to mark the response that corresponded to what they thought the sign meant. The proportion of correct answers given by the participants (around 18%) was below chance level (20% on a test in which each item provided five choices). In addition, for only few signs (12 out of 90) a majority of participants selected the correct meaning, whereas for a large number of signs (36), not even a single participant selected the correct meaning. These results confirmed the conclusion reached by Bellugi and Klima in their first study, namely, that most of the ASL signs examined were not transparent but opaque.

In a third study, the same 90 ASL signs were shown to a new group of 10 naive hearing participants, but this time each sign was accompanied by its spoken English translation. Participants were instructed to describe what they considered to be the relation between the form of the sign and its corresponding English translation. For more than one half of the signs presented in this study, the participants' responses showed overall agreement and appeared to capture the form–meaning relation or, as Bellugi and Klima characterized it, the "translucency" of the signs (e.g., for the ASL sign WOOD, which somehow brings to mind the action of sawing a board, the answers given included "sawing a board," "sawing motion on a board," and "sawing a log"). As Klima and Bellugi (1979, pp. 24–26) remarked in reviewing these studies, the results of this latter study support the notion that many ASL signs have representational, iconic aspects. These iconic aspects, however, are often not sufficient to render the signs easily comprehensible by naive hearing speakers (as shown by the results of the two previous studies).

A somewhat different approach to the issues raised by the iconicity and transparency of signs was taken in a study done by Corazza and Volterra

(1988), who explored the comprehension of foreign sign languages not just in hearing participants, but also in Deaf signers. These authors used data from Woll's (1984) cross-linguistic project in which signers of several different nations of the world were shown a story book by Briggs (1978) and were then asked to retell the story in their national sign language. The book, entitled "The Snowman," consists only of colored images and tells a story about a child and a snowman. The events and actions portrayed in this story are particularly apt to elicit from signers not only easily classifiable lexical items and linguistic constructions but also linguistic elements and structures known as classifiers and classifier predicates: particular hand configurations and movements that may be used to represent classes of objects and actions. Although functionally equivalent to classifiers described in several spoken languages (Allan, 1977), the classifiers noted in sign languages appear to be used in a somewhat different manner and much more frequently or perhaps universally across several different sign languages (see Collins-Ahlgren, 1990; Corazza, 1990; Engberg-Pedersen, 1993; Pizzuto & Corazza, 1996; Supalla, 1986; Wallin, 1990; and the review by Brennan, 1990). The story also elicits other forms of expressions that have perhaps no equivalent in spoken languages and which are in part characterizable as complex forms of pantomime. Both classifier and pantomimic expressions may exhibit strong iconic features, and the story is thus particularly well suited to explore whether and how iconic features may facilitate the task of guessing meanings conveyed in an unknown sign language.

Corazza and Volterra (1988) showed the Briggs (1978) story in different sign languages to four groups of Italian Deaf signers (3 participants for each group) and to a group of 3 hearing participants who did not know any sign language. The signers, all from the northern city of Trieste, used a variety of LIS that differs in part from that found in other Italian cities. Each group of signers saw the story in only one of the following sign languages: (a) the Trieste and (b) the Roman variety of LIS; (c) DSL; (d) CSL. The hearing participants saw the story in CSL. The same questionnaire was then administered to the Deaf and hearing participants (in LIS and Italian, respectively) to assess their comprehension of key elements of the story.

Examining the proportion of correct answers provided by each group of participants to their questionnaire, Corazza and Volterra found that, as expected, Trieste signers had no difficulty in understanding the story in the Trieste and Roman sign languages (92% and 88% correct answers, respectively); the signers encountered some difficulties with the DSL version

(73% correct answers), and greater difficulties with the CSL version (47% correct answers). The hearing participants encountered remarkably greater difficulties with the CSL version of the story: They provided only 26% correct answers to the questionnaire. The minor or major difficulties Deaf participants encountered with the DSL and CSL versions of the story, respectively, thus appeared to reflect the minor (in the case of DSL) and major (in the case of CSL) geographical, cultural, and linguistic differences between LIS and these other two sign languages.

In addition, a more qualitative analysis of the Deaf and hearing participants' responses pointed out that their understanding was influenced by different degrees of iconicity, opacity, or both of the elements that were present in the signed stories. In particular, Corazza and Volterra (1988) noted that there were:

(a) Highly iconic, often pantomimic elements and signs (e.g., body postures and facial expressions used to express such meanings as "looking-outside-from-the-window") that were understood correctly by both Deaf signers and hearing participants.

(b) More linguistically encoded elements that were comprehensible for Deaf signers but not for hearing participants. These were mostly classifier-based elements (e.g., particular hand configurations and movements used to represent the "light falling of snow flakes on the ground"), which apparently obeyed similar organizational principles across different sign languages and could thus be understood by Italian Deaf signers even if they did not belong to LIS.

(c) Entirely language-specific elements that were understood only by Deaf signers, and only when they were encoded in their own sign language (e.g., specific lexical elements such as the signs for "mother" or "milk").

Corazza and Volterra (1988) observed that these results supported the hypotheses made by Boyes-Braem (1981, 1984). Boyes-Braem (1984) also analyzed data on the "snowman story" produced in several different signed languages and compared these signed texts with a pantomimed rendition of the same story performed by a very competent hearing mime. Boyes-Braem proposed that, within each sign language, it is possible to identify different types of expressive forms, distributed along a continuum. These include (a) a small core of pantomimic elements that appear to be common to both mime and sign, may be found in all sign languages, and are likely to be universally understood by both signers and hearing; (b) a set of more linguistically encoded classifier elements that may still be common across several or even all sign languages and are likely to be universally understood by signers but not by hearing speakers; (c) a third set of elements that differ from one sign language to the other; these comprise the particular formational parameters, classifiers, and lexical items specific to each sign language and can be comprehended only by signers of that specific sign language. In sum, the comprehensibility or incomprehensibility of lexical and textual elements of any specific sign language, for signers or hearing speakers of any other signed or spoken languages, appear to depend on the relative amount of more universally iconic, or more language-specific elements that are present in individual items or texts.

PREVIOUS STUDIES ON THE ICONICITY AND TRANSPARENCY OF LIS SIGNS

The pioneering studies conducted in the 1970s by Bellugi and Klima on ASL signs were recently replicated by Grosso (1993; 1997), who explored the comprehension of LIS signs by Italian hearing participants. The general design of Grosso's study was similar to that employed in Bellugi and Klima's original research on ASL and American participants, as described earlier. In this chapter, we discuss only one study in which hearing participants were asked to guess the meanings of the signs presented to them.

It must be noted that the Italian culture—in which both hearing speakers and Deaf LIS signers are immersed—can be characterized as a "gesture-prominent" culture (Kendon, 1995): one in which hearing adults frequently use, along with spoken words, a fairly large number of conventional, often iconic gestures. The significant and perhaps unique role that gestures play in the Italian culture is well attested and documented not only in De Jorio's (1832/1979) early work on Neapolitan gestures, but also in a new edition of Munari's (1963/1994) dictionary of Italian gestures and a volume by Diadori (1990) designed for learners of Italian as a foreign language. These two recent volumes describe about 100 gestures that are commonly used across the country and specify the linguistic and communicative contexts in which each gesture can be used. Due to this potentially enhanced "gestural culture," it is thus of particular interest to ascertain whether or to what extent Italian hearing nonsigners can understand the signs taken from the lexicon of a gestural natural language such as LIS, which has developed in the broader context of the same "gestural culture."

Grosso (1993) used a set of 92 LIS signs, selected according to the same major criterion employed by Klima and Bellugi (1979, p. 22): they had to be signs commonly known among Deaf LIS signers. Toward this end, Grosso (1993) first extracted from two basic LIS dictionaries compiled by Deaf authors a total of 159 signs that were represented and glossed in the same manner in both dictionaries (Angelini, Borgioli, Folchi, & Mastromatteo, 1991; Romeo, 1991) and which were also judged as signs of common usage by Italian Deaf native signers Grosso consulted for the preparation of her set of stimuli. The number of signs was subsequently reduced to 92 to facilitate both comparability with Bellugi and Klima's original studies employing 90 ASL signs and the participants' task. Note that, unlike in Bellugi and Klima's studies, which employed only signs corresponding to English nouns, the final set of 92 stimuli used by Grosso included signs that corresponded in meaning to Italian concrete and abstract nouns (47 signs), verbs (28 signs) adjectives (12 signs), adverbs (2 signs), and spatial relation terms (3 signs).

The signs were recorded on videotape by a native Deaf LIS signer, and were then presented to a group of 24 hearing participants (all middle-class, including 12 males and 12 females, age range 17–26 years, mean age 23 years). All participants had gone through compulsory education, most of them ($n = 20$) had a high school degree, and 8 of them were enrolled in university programs. None of the participants had any prior knowledge of LIS, and none had Deaf acquaintances.

Each participant was individually shown the signs and was requested to write down (on an answer sheet with numbers for each sign of the list) the meaning he or she felt could guess for each sign. There were no time restrictions, and all participants could see a particular sign more than once if they felt this was necessary before writing down their "best guess." Participants were encouraged to write down their best guess, but they were also told that if they encountered particular difficulties in guessing the meaning of particular signs they could put a question mark next to the number(s) corresponding to the specific difficult sign(s).

Grosso's (1993) scoring and subsequent analysis of the participants' answers was quite detailed, but for the purposes of this chapter, it will suffice to say that any given answer was considered broadly correct in two cases: (a) when the word the participants provided for a particular sign corresponded to the gloss Italian signers used for the same sign (e.g., "walk" for the LIS sign meaning "WALK"); and (b) when the word provided was close in meaning to the gloss (e.g., "run" for the sign "WALK"). Any given answer was considered wrong when the word given by the participants was unrelated to the sign gloss (e.g., "scissors" for the sign "WALK"). The degree of transparency or opacity of all the signs in the list, and of each individual sign presented, was assessed in terms of the number of participants providing correct or erroneous responses. Accordingly, any given sign was considered "transparent" when its meaning was correctly guessed by a large number of participants, and "nontransparent" or opaque when no participants or only very few (e.g., 1 or 2) correctly guessed its meaning.

The major results of this study showed that, based on the number of participants providing correct or incorrect guesses, the signs of the list could be distinguished in five different groups characterized by different degrees of transparency or opacity. In particular, one subset of 10 signs (or 11% of the list) appeared to be most transparent: They were guessed correctly by all or most participants (between 20 and 24 or 83%–100% of the participants providing correct answers). Another subset of 12 signs received a smaller but still significant number of correct answers: More than half of the participants guessed correctly the meaning of these signs (range: between 13 and 17 correct answers or 54%–71% of the participants). A third subset of 15 signs appeared to be less transparent: They were guessed correctly by a smaller and varying number of participants (from 6 to 12 or 25%–50% of the participants). The fourth group of signs (a total of 21) could be considered more opaque than transparent, as they received an even smaller number of correct answers (from 1 to 5, or 4%–21%). Finally, the fifth subset included 34 signs (or 37% of the 92 signs of the list) that appeared to be entirely nontransparent: They received zero correct answers.

In sum, this study showed that a significant proportion of the LIS signs appeared to be entirely opaque, or limitedly transparent: Grouping together the last three subsets of signs just described, there were a total of 70 signs (or 76% of the list) for which no participant provided correct answers or which were correctly guessed by at most 12 (50%) of the 24 participants tested. However, the remaining 22 signs of the list, included in the first two subsets specified earlier, constituted a sizeable proportion (24%) of entirely or partially transparent signs: They were guessed correctly by all, most, or in any case more than 50% of the participants.

Grosso's (1993) results also throw some light on the features that may contribute to determine the relative transparency or opacity of the LIS signs investigated. On the whole, the signs that were found to be most transparent exhibited one of the following two major, partially overlapping features:

1. Perceptual features whereby the signs stood in a well perceivable, more or less direct relation of physical resemblance to the action or object they represented. This was the case for two of the four signs that received 92% to 100% correct answers: (a) HEAR, in which the index finger pointing to the ear deictically directs attention toward a physical organ employed in hearing; and (b) BREAK, in which the two closed fists and a lateral twisting motion of the wrists resemble the action made when holding and breaking an object such as a stick or tree branch.

2. More culture-related (as well as perceptual) features: The signs were very similar to or even identical with conventional gestures that are commonly used, with the same meaning as the LIS signs, by Italian hearing people and which can be considered as "quotable gestures" or "emblems" in Kendon's (1995) terminology. This was the case, for example, of two other LIS signs that were correctly guessed by all or most participants, WELL/GOOD and HUNGER. Both signs were in fact described as typical Italian gestures by De Jorio (1832/1979) and Munari (1963/1994).

In contrast, the signs that were found to be nontransparent for hearing participants typically did not resemble gestures used within the hearing community. These included, for example, the signs AGE and LAWYER. Their "opacity" appeared to be determined chiefly by the language-specific, relatively arbitrary conventions and structural regularities that govern the formation of lexical items in LIS. Without a knowledge of the language lexicon, the meaning of these signs remained unaccessible to naive hearing participants.

PERCEPTUAL, CULTURAL, AND LINGUISTIC FACTORS THAT MAY INFLUENCE THE TRANSPARENCY AND OPACITY OF SIGNS

It is of interest to compare the major results of the Italian study with those obtained in Klima and Bellugi's similar study on the transparency of ASL signs. A precise cross-linguistic comparison certainly cannot be made due to differences in focus and methodology between the two studies. For example, the ASL and LIS signs examined in these studies obviously differed not only in form but also with respect to the meanings they covered and the classes of spoken words to which they corresponded (e.g., nouns only vs. nouns, verbs, and adjectives). The number of participants tested in the two studies also differed (10 in the American study, 24 in the Italian one). It is also very difficult to assess the comparability of the criteria used in the two studies for scoring the participants' answers as correct or wrong. Nonetheless, several observations can be made.

A common finding of the American and Italian studies is that, in spite of and beyond the presence of iconic features, the largest majority of the ASL and LIS signs presented (i.e. 90% and 76%, respectively) were not transparent for naive hearing participants. The results of the American and Italian studies differ, however, with respect to the following. First, it appears that at a global level, the Italian participants were able to guess the meaning of a larger number of LIS signs (24% of the signs in the list), compared to the American participants, who provided acceptable guesses for only 9 out of 90 (10%) of the signs they were presented. Second, Klima and Bellugi (1979) commenting on "the very few signs that were transparent to even one of the hearing subjects" remarked that "for each of these signs many responses were not acceptable translations," whereas "for the other 81 signs, the subjects made only incorrect and highly varied guesses" (p. 22). It would thus appear from this description that none of the ASL signs examined was transparent for all or most American hearing participants. This is unlike what was found in the Italian study, in which 10 (11%) of the signs were correctly guessed by most or all participants, and 12 other signs (an additional 13%) were correctly interpreted by more than 50% of the participants. The Italian study also pointed out varying degrees of transparency for individual LIS signs, whereas this phenomenon was not noted in the American study.

These observations raise several interrelated questions. First, one may ask whether the apparent "better performance" of the Italian hearing participants could be attributed to the richer gestural culture in which they are immersed—a culture that may have provided them with greater skills in interpreting gestural signals, even when these belong to the lexicon of a natural sign language. Alternatively, one may ask whether LIS signs may perhaps be globally more transparent than ASL signs. These questions point to the need for clarifying both the perceptual and the cultural factors that may be implicated in determining the greater or lesser transparency of signs.

From a broader perspective, we wish to restate a point we made earlier in this chapter: iconicity (and the related transparency of lexical items) appears to be a common, presumably universal cross-linguistic and cross-cultural feature of sign languages' lexicons. Insofar as this feature reflects structural differences in the organization of signed, as compared to spoken, languages, it is plausible to hypothesize that the perception or use of iconic features by Deaf signers may more or less significantly differ from that found in hearing speakers. In the same line of thinking, it is also plausible to hypothesize that the organizational principles underlying visual–gestural languages may more or less significantly influence Deaf signers' perception of those signs that are nontransparent for hearing speakers.

These observations suggest that cross-linguistic and cross-cultural evidence on Deaf signers, as well as on hearing speakers, may be crucial for clarifying the role of perceptual (modality-related), cultural, and linguistic factors in influencing the transparency (or opacity) of signs. Yet, to our knowledge, the evidence available thus far is very limited: Surprisingly little comparative, cross-linguistic, and cross-cultural research has been devoted to explore the comprehensibility of signs of a specific sign language across different cultures and language communities of both speakers and signers. To clarify these issues, we recently conducted a new cross-linguistic and cross-cultural study, described next.

A EUROPEAN CROSS-LINGUISTIC
AND CROSS-CULTURAL STUDY

The major aim of the study was to explore the comprehensibility of LIS lexical items by hearing and Deaf participants belonging to six different national cultures and 12 language communities (both signed and spoken) in the following countries: Denmark, The Netherlands, England, Switzerland, Spain, and Portugal. By providing new cross-linguistic and cross-cultural information on this topic, we also aimed to clarify the role that culture-specific, language-specific, or language-universal, presumably iconic and/or perceptual features, may play in determining the relative transparency, opacity, or both of a set of signs of a specific sign language.

Drawing on the indications provided by previous work, we addressed two major related questions:

1. Whether LIS signs that were found to be transparent for hearing Italian participants were also similarly transparent for hearing speakers and Deaf signers of other countries.
2. Whether LIS signs that were found to be nontransparent for hearing Italian participants were similarly opaque for hearing speakers and Deaf signers of other countries.

Of the hypotheses we formulated, our most general hypothesis was that the LIS signs that were found to be transparent for Italian hearing participants were likely also to be transparent for non-Italian participants. However, we also hypothesized that, within this set of signs, those that exhibited more culture-related transparent features were likely to be *nontransparent* for non-Italian participants. For example, we hypothesized that an LIS sign such as WELL/GOOD, which is identical to a conventional Italian gesture with the same meaning, and which was most transparent for Italian participants, would not be correctly guessed by non-Italian participants. With respect to the signs that were found to be nontransparent for hearing Italian participants, our major hypothesis was that insofar as their understanding appeared to require the knowledge of a specific sign language—LIS—they would be similarly nontransparent for non-Italian participants. Finally, we hypothesized that with respect to both transparent and nontransparent LIS signs, the patterns of responses of non-Italian Deaf participants would differ more or less significantly from those of hearing participants. The rationale underlying this hypothesis, supported by observations made on this topic by Boyes Braem (1986), was that Deaf signers' knowledge of a sign language could influence, to a degree to be ascertained, their perception and processing of the iconic and transparent or nontransparent features of the LIS signs.

Forty LIS Signs for Cross-Linguistic Comparisons

The materials for data collection consisted of a videotape with 40 Italian signs and an answer sheet with numbered lines corresponding to these signs. The signs were chosen from the list of 92 signs used in Grosso's (1993) earlier experiments with Italian hearing participants. The selection criteria were defined, along with the general methodology, during a preparatory workshop held for this purpose with our European Deaf and hearing colleagues involved in the study. After examining all the 92 signs previously used by Grosso, it was decided to focus the investigation on 20 signs defined as transparent and 20 signs defined as nontransparent according to the following criteria:

(a) The set of 20 signs defined transparent, illustrated in Fig. 15.1a,[1] were those that most—or in any case more than 50%—of the Italian hear-

---

[1]The sign drawings in Figs. 15.1a and 15.1b are taken from Angelini et al. (1991) and reproduced with permission of La Nuova Italia Editrice. We thank Barbara Pennacchi for her help in the preparation of these figures.

ing participants had guessed correctly in Grosso's (1993) study. This set comprised several signs that are likely to be very similar or identical across different sign languages, at least within western cultures, even in the absence of documented historical relationships among such languages. For example, signs very similar or even identical, in both form and meaning, to LIS signs such as BREAK, CAR, GLASS, EAT, HEAR, LISTEN, SAY, SHORT, and SKY (see Fig. 15.1a) can be found in dictionaries of ASL (Stokoe, Casterline, and Croneberg, 1976) and BSL (Brien, 1992), two languages that have no known historical relationship with LIS. The set of transparent signs also included five signs that exhibited more culture-related transparent features: ASTUTE, BEAUTIFUL, HUNGER, PAY, and WELL/GOOD (see Fig. 15.1a). We hypothesized that these five signs would be nontransparent for non-Italian participants.

(b) The set of 20 signs defined nontransparent, illustrated in Fig. 15.1b, were those for which no participants or at most 1 Italian hearing participant had provided correct guesses. To the extent that it was possible to evaluate before conducting the study, the signs in this set had no evident linguistic similarities with corresponding signs of the European sign languages involved in the study.

The signs were recorded on videotape in a randomized list, along with a "warm-up" example, by a Deaf native LIS signer (Corazza, Grosso, Pizzuto, Rossini, & Volterra, 1995). The same procedure was followed for showing the videotape to hearing and Deaf participants in the six countries involved in the study. The videotape was presented individually to each participant, whenever this was possible, or to small groups of no more than three participants. Before presenting the videotape, the experimenters explained to the participants that they would see a set of LIS signs and would be asked to play a "guessing game": they were requested to write down on an answer sheet, in their national written language, the meaning they could guess for each sign they were presented. There were no time restrictions, and participants could ask to see any given sign as many times as they wished if they felt this was necessary. Participants were asked to provide only one answer for each sign they saw and were told that if they could not guess the meaning of a particular sign, even after having seen it many times, they could put a question mark on the numbered line corresponding to that particular sign.

The same scoring criteria were used in each country. Participants' answers were analyzed and coded with the help of scoring sheets provid-

FIG. 15.1a. The 20 transparent LIS signs used in the cross-linguistic study.

ing English glosses for each LIS sign. The answers were considered correct if the words the participants wrote corresponded, or were reasonably close in meaning, to the English glosses for the LIS signs (e.g., "break" and "take apart" were both considered correct guesses for the LIS sign meaning BREAK). All the answers that significantly differed from the signs' glosses were considered wrong (e.g., "smell" for the LIS sign meaning BAD), but the words written by the participants were in all cases annotated for subsequent, more detailed analyses. Because the participants wrote their answers in their national language, in all the countries involved but England, the researchers administering the task were responsible for translating the participants' answers into English and for

FIG. 15.1b.   The 20 nontransparent LIS signs used in the cross-linguistic study.

assessing their appropriateness with respect to the English glosses. In addition, the researchers administering the experiment often made detailed observations on specific anwers provided by the participants, and these were very useful for an appropriate classification of the participants' answers. It must be noted, however, that, due to the time and resource limits of the study, possible sign interferences could not be accurately reported or evaluated. It must also be noted that, due to the many languages involved in the task, we were necessarily broad in our classification of what constituted a correct answer.

The Sample of European (Non-Italian) Deaf and Hearing Participants

In each country, the videotape was shown to two groups of participants; 6 hearing participants who did not know any sign language and had no Deaf acquaintances and 6 Deaf participants who knew their national sign language. A total of 72 European (non-Italian) participants were tested. Each national subgroup included an even number of female and male participants, except for the group of the Dutch Deaf signers, which was composed of 6 female participants. We also tried as much as possible to select hearing and Deaf participants who could be compared, in terms of age and educational background, not only to one another but also to the Italian hearing participants examined by Grosso (1993). We aimed to have middle-class participants aged between 18 and 28 years (mean age = 23 years), all of whom had at least completed compulsory education, and these conditions were on the whole satisfied. We also tried to include in each hearing and Deaf subgroup 3 participants with higher education (attending university or with a university degree), but this condition could not be met in three subgroups (Danish, Portuguese, and Swiss Deaf participants).

The selection of the Deaf participants was guided by the following additional criteria. We included in our sample both native and nonnative signers. In all countries, information on the age at which Deaf participants had learned to sign was collected, often along with additional information on the contexts in which this took place (generally in schools for the Deaf, except for native signers who learned it at home). On the whole, our entire sample of 36 Deaf participants included 7 native signers; of the remaining 29 Deaf participants, 19 had learned their national sign language between the ages of 3 and 6 years, 6 between 6 and 10 years of age, and 4 Portuguese signers learned to sign only around age 12.

We had also aimed to chose Deaf participants with little or no experience with foreign sign languages, but this condition could not always be met. Eleven of our 36 Deaf participants had at least some familiarity with, or had been exposed on some occasion, to one or more foreign sign languages (these included American, French, British, German, Finnish, Swedish, and Norwegian sign languages). None of the Deaf participants was familiar with LIS or, to the extent that this could be assessed, with Italian culture.

Seeing Through LIS Signs: The Deaf
and the Hearing View

All participants appeared to enjoy the task and were willing to provide their guesses. This was also apparent from the negligible number of "no answers" (signaled with a question mark on our answer sheets). Of the 2,880 possible guesses requested of the participants as a group (40 signs presented multiplied by 72 participants), only 126 or 4% were "no answers." Figs. 15.2a and 15.2b show the percentages of correct guesses provided by all European (non-Italian) participants, Deaf and hearing, to the transparent (including the culturally bound) and nontransparent LIS signs as previously defined.

These data support the major hypothesis we formulated. Most of the LIS signs we hypothesized to be transparent for non-Italian participants, namely 13 out 20, were guessed correctly by 50% or more of all participants. These were the signs BREAK, MOTORBIKE, EAT, LISTEN, DRINKING-GLASS, SKI, HUSBAND/WIFE, REMEMBER, SAY, CAR, HEAR, DRINK, and SPRING/AIR. In contrast, none of the nontransparent signs received 50% or more correct answers by the entire sample of hearing and Deaf non-Italian participants.

The data also support our second hypothesis, namely, that the five transparent signs exhibiting more culture-related features—ASTUTE, BEAUTIFUL, HUNGER, PAY, and WELL/GOOD—would not be transparent for non-Italian participants. In fact, these signs were guessed correctly by a remarkably smaller number of all participants (6% to 38%) and thus appeared to be scarcely or not at all transparent for non-Italian participants. There were two other signs that we found to be transparent for hearing Italian participants, namely, SHORT and SAD, which appeared to be scarcely transparent for non-Italian participants (guessed correctly by 25% and 38% of the participants, respectively).

Figs. 15.3a and 15.3b show the performance of the Deaf compared to the hearing European non-Italian participants. These data clearly support the third major hypothesis we made: The performance of our Deaf participants differed markedly from that of the hearing ones, with the Deaf providing a greater number of correct guesses compared to the hearing participants. A χ^2 test revealed that this difference was highly significant for both the transparent (p < 0.001) and the nontransparent signs (p < 0.001). Looking at Fig. 15.3b, it can be seen that several signs that we had hypothesized to be nontransparent, and which were indeed nontransparent for the non-Italian *hearing* participants, were correctly guessed by most or in any case by a significant number of *Deaf* participants. These

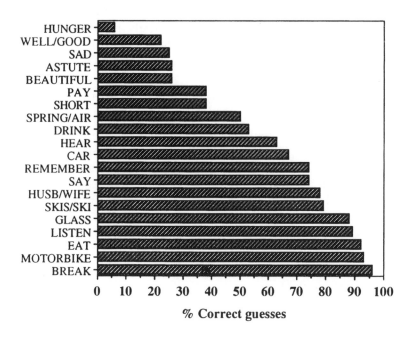

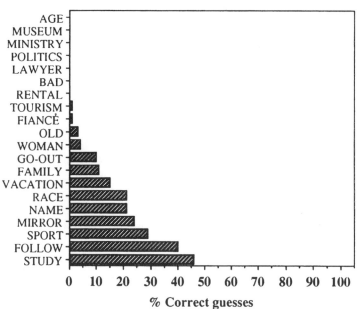

FIGS. 15.2a and 15.2b. Correct guesses for the transparent and nontransparent LIS signs provided by Deaf and hearing participants ($N = 72$) of six European countries.

included the signs SPORT, FOLLOW, and STUDY (correctly guessed by 58%–92% of the Deaf participants, thus entirely transparent for them according to our working definition) and also the signs FAMILY, VACATION, RACE, NAME, and MIRROR (correctly guessed by 22% to 47% of the Deaf participants).

Comparing the Deaf and the hearing participants' performance on the individual signs in the list, it can be observed that for 31 of the 40 signs presented (including 19 transparent and 12 nontransparent signs), the number of Deaf participants providing correct guesses was always greater—often much greater—than that of the hearing participants (e.g., compare the Deaf vs. hearing performance on the transparent signs SKI, HUSBAND/WIFE, REMEMBER, SAY, CAR, HEAR, and SAD). It is of interest to note that those transparent signs that are likely to be very similar across sign languages (e.g., BREAK, CAR, GLASS, EAT, LISTEN, SAY, and SKY) resulted most transparent not only, not surprisingly, for Deaf participants, but also for hearing participants. In addition, our Deaf participants, unlike the hearing ones, provided a considerable number of correct guesses for four of the five culture-related signs which we had hypothesized to be nontransparent outside of the Italian culture (see from top to bottom, in Fig. 15.3a, the values for WELL/GOOD, ASTUTE, BEAUTIFUL, and PAY).

There were only two signs (the transparent DRINK and the nontransparent GO-OUT), for which a slightly larger number of hearing participants provided correct guesses. The remaining seven signs of the list were entirely nontransparent for both the Deaf and hearing participants.

We also compared the performance of our European (non-Italian) participants with that exhibited, on the same set of 40 LIS signs, by the Italian hearing participants studied by Grosso (1993). A thorough comparison could not be done, due to the smaller number of participants in the Italian group ($n = 24$), and to the fact that the two non-Italian groups included Deaf or hearing participants from six different nations. Nonetheless, several observations could be made.

Comparing the European (non-Italian) Deaf with the Italian hearing participants we found that their performance was very similar on a subset of 16 signs: 12 of these signs were nontransparent for both groups, whereas 4 were equally transparent. However, another set of 14 signs were guessed correctly by more non-Italian Deaf than Italian hearing participants. Included in this subset were 6 transparent signs (EAT, GLASS, HUSBAND/WIFE, REMEMBER, SAY, and CAR), and 8 nontransparent signs (STUDY, FOLLOW, SPORT, MIRROR, NAME, RACE, VACATION,

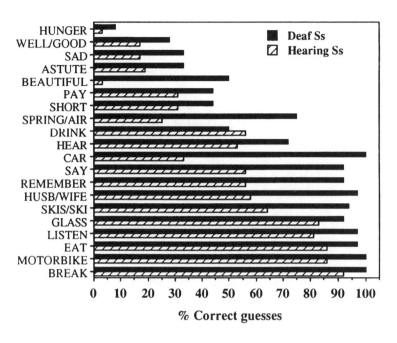

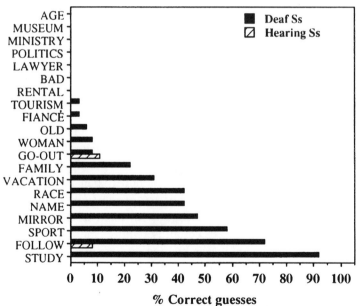

FIGS. 15.3a and 15.3b. Correct guesses for the transparent and nontransparent LIS signs provided by the Deaf (N = 36) as compared to the hearing (N = 36) participants of six European countries

and FAMILY). The non-Italian Deaf participants showed a lower performance, compared to the Italian hearing ones, only on the remaining 10, transparent signs of the list, which included the 5 culture-related signs. In sum, for 30 out of 40 signs in the list, that is, for the majority of signs, the group of non-Italian Deaf provided a number of correct answers that was equal to or greater than that given by the group of Italian hearing participants.

All of these data indicate that Deaf signers' perception of both the iconic–transparent and nontransparent features of the LIS signs differs from that of hearing participants. The data further suggest that Deaf signers' knowledge of their own visual-gestural language provides them with significantly greater skills in interpreting isolated lexical items of a foreign sign language. These greater skills were particularly evident in the correct guesses they provided for the signs that were opaque for all hearing participants, Italian as well as non-Italian. We must recall that in this study possible sign interferences could not be accurately evaluated. Our results must thus be considered preliminary, and further investigations are warranted to uncover to what extent these abilities are specifically linked to the visual–gestural modality of language perception and production or may also be related to as yet unexplored linguistic relations between LIS and the 6 different European sign languages used by the groups of signers we examined.

A different pattern emerged when comparing the group of non-Italian hearing with the Italian hearing participants. These two groups performed in a comparable manner on all nontransparent signs (equally nontransparent for both groups), and on the first two transparent signs of the list. But on the remaining 18 transparent signs of the list, the group of non-Italian hearing participants always provided a smaller number of correct answers compared to the Italian group. This "poorer" perfomance was noted not only, as expected, on the subset of five culturally rooted signs, which we had hypothesized to be nontransparent for non-Italian participants, but more generally on all the remaining transparent signs (with the two exceptions mentioned earlier). An appropriate assessment of the relevance of these apparent cultural differences certainly requires more detailed analyses of the responses provided by the hearing participants we examined in each country. However, at a global level, these results suggest that cultural factors may well play a role in facilitating (for the Italian hearing participants) or in rendering more difficult (for the non-Italian hearing participants) the task we proposed: The richer gestural culture in which Italian participants are immersed seems to give them greater skills in interpreting at least some signs of LIS.

CONCLUDING REMARKS

The results we obtained are consistent with the hypotheses we formulated and can be summarized as follows. First, we found that a subset of LIS signs hypothesized to be comprehensible across languages and cultures was comprehended by the majority of our European non-Italian participants, hearing and Deaf alike. These data confirm and extend the results of previous studies and indicate that there are some language- and culture-free, presumably universal iconic-transparent features of signs that may be perceived in the same manner by both speakers and signers. Second, we found that our European Deaf signers showed markedly greater skills in comprehending iconic and also putatively noniconic LIS signs, compared with both the non-Italian and Italian hearing participants. These data strongly suggest the existence of potential universals across sign languages. Additional research extended to signers of very different languages and cultures is needed to clarify the linguistic, cultural, perceptual, and cognitive grounds from which these putative universals may arise. Third, we found the performance of non-Italian hearing participants to be lower compared to that of Italian hearing participants, particularly for those signs that we hypothesized to be rooted in the Italian culture. These results indicate the relevance of culture-specific factors in the perception of signs' iconicity and further underscore the need for more in-depth studies on the topic.

More than 20 years ago, Ursula Bellugi and Ed Klima's insightful observations and ingenious experiments paved the way for meaningful explorations of the intricate interrelation between iconic and arbitrary features that is found not only in ASL but also in all sign languages investigated to date. Much sign language research conducted in the past 20 years has often tended to highlight the arbitrary features that render sign languages more readily comparable to spoken languages. The role of iconicity in sign language structure and processing, which appears to reflect relevant differences between sign and speech, has often been downplayed.

In our own research on LIS, also inspired by Penny Boyes Braem's work, we tried to pursue the exploration of both the many arbitrary features that render sign and speech more alike, and the many iconic features that undoubtely differentiate sign from speech. As we discuss more extensively elsewhere (Pizzuto et al., 1995), and in line with observations recently made by Armstrong et al. (1995), in our view a clearer understanding of the differences linked to the presence of iconicity in sign may ultimately lead to uncover iconic components of speech that are akin to those found in sign, and which appear to be derived from our perceptual-motor experience. On these grounds, we may be able to identify more profound similarities between sign and speech, even along the iconic dimension, and this may be another relevant contribution of sign language research to a more adequate description of human language systems.

ACKNOWLEDGMENTS

Part of the work reported in this chapter was developed within the European project "Intersign: Multi-Professional Study of Sign Language and the Deaf Community in Europe (Network)" and is described, in a different form, in Pizzuto and Volterra (1996). The financial support of the Commission of the European Comunities, Human Capital and Mobility Program (Contract N. ERBCHRXCT920023) is gratefully acknowledged. We wish to express a warm thank you to all the Deaf and European colleagues who made possible the realization of the European cross-linguistic study described in this chapter and greatly contributed to it not only with their substantial help in data collection and scoring but also with many thoughtful observations they shared with us: Karen Albertsen and Nanna Ebbesen (Doves Center for Total Communication, Copenhagen, Denmark); Heleen Boos and Wim Emmerick (Institute for General Linguistics, University of Amsterdam, The Netherlands); Linda Day and Rachel Sutton-Spence (Centre for Deaf Studies, University of Bristol, England); Penny Boyes Braem and Patty Herman-Shores (Center for Sign Language Research, Basel, Switzerland); Maria Augusta Amaral and Armando Coutinho (Casa Pia de Lisboa, Instituto Jacob Rodrigues Pereira, Lisbon, Portugal); and Lourdez Gomez and Cecilia Vicente (Centro Nacional de Recursos para la Educacion Especial, Madrid, Spain). We are particularly grateful to Penny Boyes Braem for her generous help in data coding and analysis. We also wish to thank Andrea Zingarini for technical assistance and Serena Corazza, Barbara Grosso, Enrico Jurato, Paolo Rossini and Vannina Vitale, all of whom greatly contributed in different ways to the planning and preparation of the project. Finally we thank all our Deaf and hearing participants across Europe, without whom the project simply could not have been done.

REFERENCES

Allan, K. (1977). Classifiers. *Language, 53,* 285–311.

Angelini, N., Borgioli, R., Folchi, A., & Mastromatteo, M. (1991). *I primi quattrocento segni* [The first 400 signs]. Florence, Italy: La Nuova Italia.

Armstrong, D.F, Stokoe, W.C., & Wilcox, S.E. (1995). *Gesture and the nature of language.* Cambridge, UK: Cambridge University Press.

Bellugi, U., & Klima, E.S. (1976). Two faces of sign: Iconic and abstract. In S. Harnad, D. Hoest, & I. Lancaster (Eds.), *Origins and evolution of language and speech* (pp. 514–538). New York: New York Academy of Sciences.

Boyes Braem, P. (1981). *Significant features of the handshape in American Sign Language.* Unpublished doctoral dissertation, University of California, Berkeley.

Boyes Braem, P. (1984, September). *Sign structure.* Paper presented at the International Sign Language Workshop, Bristol, UK.

Boyes Braem, P. (1986). Two aspects of psycholinguistic research: iconicity and temporal structure. In B. Tervoort (Ed.), *Signs of life—Proceedings of the Second European Congress on Sign Language Research* (No. 50, pp. 65–74). Amsterdam: University of Amsterdam, Publications of Institute of General Linguistics.

Brennan, M. (1990). *Word formation in BSL.* Stockholm: University of Stockholm.

Brien, D. (Ed.) (1992). *Dictionary of British Sign Language/English.* London: Faber & Faber.

Briggs, R. (1978). *The snowman.* London: Hamish Hamilton.

Collins-Ahlgren, M. (1990). Spatial-locative predicates in Thai Sign Language. In C. Lucas (Ed.), *Sign language research: Theoretical issues* (pp. 103–117). Washington, DC: Gallaudet University Press.

Corazza, S. (1990). The morphology of classifier handshapes in Italian Sign Language (LIS). In C. Lucas (Ed.), *Sign language research: Theoretical issues* (pp. 71–82). Washington, DC: Gallaudet University Press.

Corazza, S., Grosso, B., Pizzuto, E., Rossini, P., & Volterra, V. (1995). *Forty LIS signs for cross-linguistic and cross-cultural comparisons* [videotape]. Rome: Division of Neuropsychology of Language and Deafness, Institute of Psychology, National Research Council (CNR).

Corazza, S., & Volterra, V. (1988). La comprensione di lingue dei segni straniere [Comprehension of foreign sign language]. In T. De Mauro, T. Gensini, & M. E. Piemontese (Eds.), *Dalla parte del ricevente: Percezione, comprensione, interpretazione. Atti del XIX Congresso Internazionale SLI* (pp. 73–82). Rome: Bulzoni.

De Jorio, A. (1979). *La mimica degli antichi investigata nel gestire napoletano* [Mimicry in ancient times as seen in Neapolitan gestures]. Bologna, Italy: Arnaldo Forni. (Anastatic reprint of the original edition of 1832)

Diadori, P. (1990). *Senza parole: 100 gesti degli italiani* [Without words: 100 Italian gestures]. Rome: Bonacci.

Engberg-Pedersen, E. (1993). *Space in Danish Sign Language.* Hamburg, Germany: Signum Verlag.

Grosso, B. (1993). *Iconicità ed arbitrarietà nella lingua dei segni italiana. Uno studio sperimentale* [Iconicity and arbitrariness in Italian Sign Language: An experimental study]. Unpublished doctoral dissertation, Department of Psychology, University of Padua, Italy.

Grosso, B. (1997). Gli udenti capiscono i segni dei sordi? [Do hearing people understand the signs of the Deaf?] In M. C. Caselli & S. Corazza (Eds.), *Lis, Studi, esperienze e ricerche sulla Lingua dei Segni in Italia* (pp. 79–86). Pisa, Italy: Edizioni Del Cerro.

Haiman, J. (1985). *Iconicity in syntax.* Amsterdam: John Benjamins.

Hinton, L., Nichols, J., & O'Hala, J. (1994). *Sound symbolism.* Cambridge, UK: Cambridge University Press.

Kendon, A. (1995). Gestures as illocutionary and discourse markers in Southern Italian conversation. *Journal of Pragmatics, 23,* 247–279.

Klima, E. S., & Bellugi, U. (1979). *The signs of language.* Cambridge, MA: Harvard University Press.

Munari, B. (1994). *Dizionario dei gesti italiani* [Dictionary of Italian gestures]. Bergamo, Italy: Adnkronos. (Originally published as *Supplemento al dizionario italiano,* Milan: Muggiani, 1963)

Pizzuto, E., & Corazza, S. (1996). Noun morphology in Italian Sign Language (LIS). *Lingua, 98,* 169–196.

Pizzuto, E., & Volterra, V. (1996). *Sign language lexicon: Cross-linguistic and cross-cultural comparison.* Final Report delivered to the Commission of the European Communities, Project Inter-Sign (Network), Human Capital and Mobility Program 1993–1995.

Pizzuto, E., Cameracanna, E., Corazza, S., & Volterra, V. (1995). Terms for spatio-temporal relations in Italian Sign Language (LIS). In R. Simone (Ed.), *Iconicity in language* (pp. 238–256). New York: John Benjamins.

Romeo, O. (1991). *Dizionario dei segni* [Sign language dictionary]. Bologna, Italy: Zanichelli.

Simone, R. (Ed.) (1995). *Iconicity in language.* Amsterdam: John Benjamins.

Stokoe, W. C., Casterline, D. C., & Cronerberg, C. G. (1976). *A Dictionary of American Sign Language on Linguistics Principles* (new edition, first edition 1965). Silver Spring, MD: Linstok Press.

Supalla, T. (1986). The classifier system in American Sign Language. In C. Craig (Ed.), *Noun classes and categorization: Typological studies in language* (pp. 181–214). Amsterdam: John Benjamins.

Wallin, L. (1990). Polymorphemic predicates in Swedish Sign Language. In C. Lucas (Ed.), *Sign language research: Theoretical issues* (pp. 133–148). Washington, DC: Gallaudet University Press.

Woll, B. (1984). The comparative study of different sign languages: Preliminary analyses. In F. Loncke, P. Boyes Braem, & Y. Lebrun (Eds.), *Recent research in European sign languages* (pp. 79–92). Lisse, Netherlands: Swets & Zeitlinger.

16

Codeswitching in ASL and Written English Language Contact

Marlon Kuntze
Stanford University

I grew up without any clue that I was bilingual. The emphasis in schools had instilled the widespread belief that language meant English. The sign language that we used did not have a name. The prevailing myth was that Deaf people had a language problem. The assumption was that sign language was a lazy way of using English or that it constituted "broken English." Although Deaf people did not contest such a mistaken perception, they intuitively knew the importance of safeguarding the right to use sign language and the necessity of employing sign language in the education of Deaf children.

It was in college that a fortunate chain of events led me to find fascination in the study of literature. I was moved not only by the content but also by how the authors used language to convey their thoughts. Interestingly, it was through studying literary uses of English that I was led to reflect on the elegant ways sign language may be expressed and how it may be utilized to convey thoughts by authors I studied in English literature. In the back of my mind, I began to entertain the notion that there was something autonomous about sign language. This was during the early 1970s, the dawn of sign language research, and probably in indirect ways it somehow helped congeal the musings I had about sign language. Doubtless, the work spreadheaded by the likes of William Stokoe, Ursula Bellugi, and Ed Klima set the stage for viewing American Sign Language (ASL) in a whole new light. I was already becoming increasingly aware of the awesome beauty and potency of ASL when an opportunity surfaced for me to work as a research assistant for Ursula at The Salk Institute.

Ursula's zest for the study of language in general and her incessant questions about ASL provided the kind of intellectual environment conducive to drawing my interest into the study of linguistics and a formal study of ASL in particular. The initial view of myself as a monolingual person changed to that of a bilingual person once the linguistic difference between ASL and English became clear. I started to become intrigued with the notion of Deaf people as speakers of two languages. I began to think of the sociolinguistic characteristics of the Deaf community as a bilingual community. One aspect of the bilingual experience of Deaf people, to which I want to devote this chapter, concerns the nature of ASL–English interaction. Recognizing ASL as a bona fide language and making the recognition widespread were made possible largely due to the flurry of linguistic studies that in no small way were unleashed by the groundbreaking work of Ursula and Ed. Understanding that ASL is a language in itself and how it is grammatically structured was a necessary prerequisite for questions about how the interface between ASL and English played out in various discourse settings. The investigation of how two languages of different modalities interact with each other in signed discourse, especially among native speakers of ASL, would not have been conceivable if we were still in the dark ages in our notions about signed languages.

REVIEW OF THE LITERATURE

Over time, different investigators offered models to account for the ways ASL and English showed up in signed discourse. There is little, if any, indication of an attempt to draw on theories of codeswitching as a basis to construct a model of how English may be employed in ASL utterances. There are several probable reasons why that was the case. First of all, the field of research on codeswitching is still young and has been informed only by the studies on spoken languages. Furthermore, the question of codeswitching has only been examined within a limited number of bilingual situations worldwide. The claim that the interface between ASL and English results in codeswitching runs counter to the way codeswitching as a linguistic construct is presently understood, and it is largely due to the fact that ASL and English are languages of different modalities.

Codeswitching is conventionally thought of as the mixing of two languages in an utterance in which elements of each language retain the phonological and morphological structure of the mother language. It is a phenomenon that occurs only when a speaker "display[s] an awareness of the grammar of both languages and their relationship to one another and use[s] this knowledge to produce grammatical, albeit mixed, sentences" (Mahootian, 1993, p. 50). A distinction has been spelled out in the literature to differentiate the phenomenon of codeswitching from that of borrowing. Borrowing is defined as a phenomenon in which an element from one language becomes assimilated into the grammatical structure of the host language. For example, the Spanish word *burrito* is now a part of the English lexicon, and its use in an utterance neither reflects knowledge of Spanish nor is it said using Spanish phonology. A Spanish-English bilingual, on the other hand, in a discourse with another bilingual, after starting an utterance in English may choose to switch and say *un burrito* in the middle of the utterance. In effect, the speaker would be shifting from English phonology to using the Spanish pronunciation of *burrito*. The literature as it stands now says that when an element from another language shows up in a host language after undergoing phonological assimilation, it is a case of borrowing, not codeswitching. However, the distinction between borrowing and codeswitching is not always that clear-cut. For example, Sobin (1976, p. 42) said that for speakers of Spanish in Texas, some phonologically adapted items are switches rather than borrowings. Sankoff, Poplack, and Vanniarajan (1990) stated that morphology and syntax can serve as criteria to help disambiguate the borrowing and codeswitching distinction. If the morphology and syntax are consistent with only one of the languages, any nonnative lexical item must be borrowed. If not, then it is a case of codeswitching.

The discussion to date on the distinction between codeswitching and borrowing has not taken into account the contact situation of languages belonging to different modalities. The focus of interest in this chapter is the phenomenon of American Deaf bilingualism in which ASL and the written form of English constitute a language-contact situation. ASL and written English language contact results in a language phenomenon that bears many similarities with the codeswitching phenomenon. However, the uniqueness of how both languages interact lies in the fact that before elements of English may be inserted in ASL utterances, they have to be converted to manual form. It is a situation in which the interaction of both languages belonging to different modalities results in a one-modality product. In a way, it is akin to the process of relexification observed by Haugen (1977) who commented on how the Norweigan immigrants used English lexicon while maintaining the basic phonetic and grammatical structures of their native dialects. This supports the proposition that English elements may be inserted into ASL sentences once they have been relexified using one or other of ASL surface forms.

The situation with ASL and written English contact may be unique due not only to the typologies but also to the modalities of the languages involved. The question of how codeswitching is being currently defined should not be the deciding factor for considering whether or not ASL and written English contact should be analyzed within the framework of the literature on codeswitching. Myers-Scotton (1993) argued that borrowing and codeswitching are related processes, both of which can be accommodated within a model.

There are other kinds of language contact involving sign language. For example, in a situation involving two signed languages, it is possible to maintain the grammatical and phonological structure of the mother language at each switch because both languages share the same modality. In yet another kind of language contact, a hearing dyad fluent in both a signed language and a spoken language would be able to preserve the grammatical structure of the mother language by crossing modality at the beginning of each switch. The question this chapter tries to address is how the interaction of ASL and written English, which utilize different modalities, may be analyzed and explicated and whether present theories of codeswitching may provide an appropriate framework for analysis. The phenomenon of language contact in Deaf bilingualism, in which elements of English show up in a signed discourse, may be explained as a process whereby English is transformed from a written form to a manual form to conform to the modality of ASL. This is done so that elements of English may be embedded in ASL.

Stokoe (1969) was the first to go on record stating that English elements show up in signed discourse under certain circumstances. Drawing on Ferguson's (1959) introduction of diglossia as a linguistic phenomenon in which two varieties of a language assume functional specialization, Stokoe proposed Signed Language Diglossia as a model to account for the shift between what he observed to be ASL and a more English-based variety of signing that he labeled "Manual English." Apparently, Tervoort (1973) was the only one who attempted to follow up on Stokoe's idea of Manual English. He claimed that the bilingualism of American Deaf people pertains to a purely visual system on one hand and a creolization of English and ASL on the other hand. The idea of a creolized variety of ASL appears linguistically plausible. However, the proposal of either Manual English or creolized ASL never really gained currency. One probable reason is the difficulty in determining the boundary between ASL and Manual English. This may have led others such as Woodward and Markowicz (1975) to propose the existence of a continuum between ASL and English. Their data suggested that there are varieties of ASL that fall in different places along the continuum, according to the degree to which they approximate the syntactic properties of ASL and English. They called these signed varieties that are not pure ASL "Pidgin Signed English."

Woodward, in his 1973 dissertation, claimed that these varieties were like a pidgin because (a) there is a mixture of structures from two languages, (b) there are structures that do not belong to either language from which they are derived, (c) there is a reduction in structure, (d) they are not the native language of the user, (e) they are used in restricted social situations, and (f) there are negative attitudes toward them. Woodward did not, however, provide information on the sociolinguistic context of the utterances. It is not known if any utterances of this type were made between bilingual Deaf individuals. The utterances with reduced structure that Woodward noted probably came from a contact-language situation such as one between a Deaf person and a hearing person who does not have nativelike competency in ASL. Lucas and Valli (1991) likewise argued that Woodward's (1973) claims came from limited data and were not research based. They collapsed all the varieties on the continuum into an entity that they called "Contact Signing" (CS). They defined it as a "kind of signing that results from the contact between ASL and English" (Valli & Lucas, 1992, p. 201) and exhibits features of both languages. They proposed that the lexical forms in CS are a combination of ASL signs and English lexicon expressed through either mouthing or fingerspelling. The morphological structure of CS consists of reduced ASL and English morphology. The syntactic structure is a "combination of English and idiosyncratic constructions."

There is an important distinction in how the contact between ASL and English is manifested depending on the linguistic background of the individuals involved in the discourse. The observations Woodward (1973) made appear characteristic of discourse between a Deaf native and a hearing nonnative speaker of ASL. The structure and vocabulary that a Deaf person uses reflects an attempt to accommodate the hearing signer. The hearing signer may be at the interlanguage stage as a learner of ASL as his or her second language or may have fossilized at some point in the process of acquiring ASL. The Deaf native signer, in response to the limited knowledge that the hearing interlocutor has about ASL, would naturally make accomodations by resorting to a simplified version akin to "foreigner talk" (Cokely, 1983). Foreigner talk is a form of controlled use of the target language. The native speaker of ASL would make utterances utilizing a more Englishlike word order that is syntactically and propositionally less complex, thus avoiding the more marked aspects of ASL. Lucas and Valli (1991) maintained that CS is a phenomenon typical of a hearing–Deaf interaction. Although they acknowledged that it also occurs in a Deaf–Deaf interaction, they have not done much to distinguish these two types of contact language situations.

In the situation between Deaf bilinguals, there is no need to accommodate the addressee. I doubt whether anyone has adequately investigated how bilingually competent Deaf people communicate among themselves. Codeswitching is probably a more accurate descriptor of the language behavior they exhibit in certain contexts. It is intriguing that Deaf dyads fluent in ASL would embed English structure in their sentences. Given the observation that codeswitching seems to be a universal characteristic of bilinguals who share knowledge of the same set of languages, it should not come as a surprise that the more skills a Deaf person has in written English, the greater the likelihood he or she may codeswitch. One challenge to the claim that codeswitching occurs in the signing of bilingual Deaf individuals is the need to explicate what the term "English" means given the lack of a clear linguistic description of the entity hitherto labeled as either Manual English or a creolized variety of ASL.

A solution to the theoretical problem of considering an ASL–English interaction in signed discourse as one of codeswitching may come from looking at a sample interaction beyond its surface level of representation. For the sake of analogy, written English may be perceived on the surface level as completely different from spoken English. However, we still call it English. The elements of English are changed on the surface level when they are represented manually, although underlying the surface form they remain English. The most direct means of manually representing elements of English is through fingerspelling. Fingerspelling is patterned on the orthographic representation of English. Other instances of manually representing English elements without using fingerspelling would occur when they are relexified using ASL lexicon. It is on the semantic level that the evidence of English presence may be detected. A signed phrase "EAT LIKE HORSE" means the same as the English idiom "eat like a horse." On the surface, the phrase is stripped of its English phonology and orthography, and the English grammar is modified in a limited way, namely, dropping the article. However, all of the necessary English semantics are maintained and the phrase, although converted to a manual form, is readily interpreted in semantically the same way as its written or spoken version.

The level of the interlocutor's familiarity with English is one of the crucial factors influencing the speaker's decision about whether codeswitching is appropriate and how to do it. The likelihood of codeswitching in a signed discourse is also a function of the context of the discourse. For example, in the context of a lecture there may be a preponderance of codeswitching. This may be due to where some of the content in the lecture came from. Certain information may have been drawn from text read previously about the subject. In a classroom situation where both the teacher and the students are bilingual, codeswitching may be more prevalent. My data were drawn from a classroom setting during the first part of a lesson when the teacher was giving a lecture. More frequent occurrences of codeswitching took place during the lecture part of the class. After the teacher completed his lecture and opened the class up for discussion, he codeswitched considerably less. This should not be surprising given the types of discourse expected in a lecture as opposed to a discussion. Blom and Gumperz (1972) found that in Norway, teachers deliver formal lectures in the official standard form of Norweigan but shift to regional dialect to encourage discussion among the students. In the Deaf bilingualism, the use of English switches in a lecture has the effect of making the discourse more objectivized, whereas more straight ASL in a discussion has the effect of making the discourse more personalized.

METHOD

The paucity of discourse data in ASL may be due to the difficulty inherent in recording ASL conversations in a naturalistic setting. It cannot be recorded with a single piece of equipment in the way a spoken conversation is done. It is not possible to shift a camcorder from one person to the next at each turn of the conversation. Moreover, back-channeling and some of the variables influencing how an interlocutor responds to the speaker will be missed. For this reason, I had to use elaborate techniques to record the entire discourse of the class. The system that I set up involved four camcorders. I used a special piece of equipment to synthesize all four images in a way that each can be viewed in its respective quadrant of the screen. When playing the tape, all four images are shown simultaneously, and it is thereby possible to follow the whole discourse of the lesson.

The site of the data collection was a residential school for Deaf students. The uniqueness of a residential school is that it serves a large population of Deaf students providing the needed critical mass to ensure the presence and viability of ASL schoolwide. The school espouses a philosophy that promotes the use of ASL as the language of instruction. The class I videotaped was a seventh-grade social studies class. The teacher was a native speaker of ASL, and most of the students were offspring of Deaf parents.

The codeswitched utterances used in the present analysis were only those made by the teacher during the lecture part of the lesson, even though the teacher posed questions to elicit student participation. The focus of the lecture was the dilemma the emperor faced when making the decision to build the Great Wall of China. The construction of the Great Wall was deemed necessary to shield China from the constant attacks from the Mongols, but it was an expensive project that would inflict a high toll on human lives and the economy.

ANALYSIS

There is a methodological issue to deal with in order to do an analysis of codeswitching in ASL sentences. Sometimes fingerspelled English words, especially those that already have signed counterparts, are good places to look for evidence of codeswitching. If the ASL lexicon rather than fingerspelling is used to manually represent the English lexicon, it is no longer possible to look at the lexicon itself for possible markers of codeswitching. Instead, the sentences have to be analyzed on the syntactic or semantic level. One methodological strategy is to identify sentences that appear to contain switched English elements and reconstruct them by replacing the switches with ASL equivalents. The resulting hypothetical ASL sentences are then compared with their codeswitched counterparts. This will help highlight the suspected sites of codeswitching. Sentence 1a is an actual sentence pulled from the data. The glosses in bold are the parts of the sentence identified as English switches. Sentence 1b is a hypothetical sentence constructed by replacing the switches identified in 1a with their ASL equivalents.

1a. CS: fs-MONGOLIANS[1] **KEEP ON** ENTER+[2] **FROM NORTH.**

1b. ASL: fs-MONGOLIANS SAME-THING++ ENTER+ NORTH IX-to-south.

In English, the utterance means "Mongolians kept on entering from the north." The English idiom "keep on" is relexified using ASL lexicon in a way that the sign-for-word correspondence with English is retained. In straight ASL, the meaning for KEEP ON would be conveyed using different lexicon, namely, SAME-THING++. The ASL "ON" has a more restricted semantic range than the English "on." In ASL, it is mostly used to designate spatial relations such as that in "NOT ON #TV, IX-loc TABLE" ("It is not on TV; it is over there on the table"). When the use of the ASL "ON" extends beyond its usual semantic range and assumes semantics similar to that of English, it would become a candidate for evaluation as to whether it is actually an English switch.

A somewhat different procedure was used to reach the decision that FROM NORTH (same sentence) is also an English switch. The ASL "NORTH" is similar in meaning to the English "north." The semantics of the sign "FROM" as it is intended in the sentence falls within the semantics of both ASL and English. This is an example of why even the semantic approach to analysis may at times be inadequate, and why a hypothetical ASL sentence may provide further insight to help evaluate where switches take place. While making the utterance, the teacher was making use of the world map as a visual medium. It is hypothesized that if straight ASL is desired, a different way of using the phrase would be utilized. One would sign NORTH and point on the map to where the entrance into China would be and track downward toward the south to capture the semantic intent of "entering from the north." So with that in mind and the data showing that the phrase "FROM NORTH" was used, it seems reasonable to mark it as a probable switch. Yet, it may not be a clear case of switching because the phrase still differs from the grammatical English version, which would have required the teacher to include the article "the." It is possible that in the process of converting the English switch into a manual form, assimilation was inevitable. This may have resulted in the article being stripped.

---

[1] "Fs" as in "fs-MONGOLIANS" means that the lexical item is fingerspelled.
[2] The symbol "+" as in "ENTER+" means that the sign is inflected to convey iterated action.

One form of codeswitching that is easy to detect is when English words are fingerspelled. Whereas it is true that fingerspelling is also used in ASL, fingerspelled words are good sites to check for the presence of switches. There are various categories of fingerspelling usage in ASL. Fingerspelling is chiefly used as a device to access English lexicon either for borrowing or codeswitching. There are some clear ways to identify a fingerspelled word as being an English switch, distinct from a fingerspelled word more properly considered as being borrowed. Sometimes English words may be borrowed through the process of fingerspelling in characteristic ways such as fingerspelling them in phonologically salient ways reflective of the ASL phonology (Battison, 1978). "#JOB" is an example of an English word that has become ASL lexicalized. Fingerspelled English words such as proper nouns (e.g., fs-MONGOLIANS) for which there are no ASL signs may arguably be considered borrowed. However, when fingerspelling is used in lieu of ASL signs such as (fs-WHEN) in Sentence 2a, it is arguable as being an English switch.

2a. CS: $_T$GREAT fs-WALL$_T$[3], **fs-WHEN fs-WAS fs-IT** FIRST BUILD fs-WHEN?

2b. ASL: $_T$GREAT fs-WALL$_T$, WHEN FIRST BUILD WHEN?

2c. Eng: When was the Great Wall first built?

Fs-WALL, on the other hand, may be more properly considered borrowed even though there is an ASL sign WALL, because according to the conventions of ASL, "wall" in the proper noun "Great Wall" is to be fingerspelled rather than signed. Other fingerspelled words like "was" or "it" are considered English switches because ASL grammar does not call for their use.

Of interest for a different reason was the switch to insert "fs-WAS fs-IT." ASL does not utilize passive voice construction as the hypothetical sentence (2b) indicates. The judgment that the sign BUILD is not a part of the English switch comes from the reasoning that if the extent of the English switch is to include BUILD, the fingerspelled "built" would either be used instead or inserted following the sign BUILD. The sign BUILD by itself does not convey the participle form of the English verb.

---

[3]"T," short for "topicalized," is a nonmanual signal used during the topic part of a sentence in which the topic–comment structure is used.

Another way to look for possible sites of switches is to observe how an adjective is modified. The fact that a modifier fs-SO (in Sentence 3a) is used instead of the ASL morphology for modifying the degree of thickness, such as knitting the brows and pursing the lips, which the gloss SO-THICK (in 3b) represents, is an indication that fs-SO is an English switch. Another switch in Sentence 3a, fs-DENSE, is curious because it does not add more information to the sentence. A meaning in ASL similar to the English word "dense" in the context of the utterance can be achieved by inflecting the sign THICK to create SO-THICK. The reason for including the fingerspelled "dense" may be pedagogical. Perhaps the word "dense" was in the textbook, and in the flow of the conversation it just surfaced as a switch in the teacher's utterance. The teacher might have anticipated its use in his sentence and interjected THICK just before fs-DENSE as a hedge against the chance that a student may not grasp the meaning or probably as an opportunity to illuminate what the English word *dense* means. The teacher might also employ the practice of exposing students to the English lexicon through discourse in ASL, thus preparing them to face it when reading about the subject in their textbook.

3a. CS: FOREST **fs-SO** THICK **fs-DENSE THAT** DIFFICULT
     FOR SOLDIER **TO** GO-THROUGH.

3b. ASL: $_T$FOREST$_T$ $_{KB}$SO-THICK$_{KB}$,[4] $_{RB}$DIFFICULT
     SOLDIER GO-THROUGH$_{RB}$.[5]

3c. Eng: The forest is so thick and dense that it would be difficult
     for soldiers to go through it.

The scope of switches in a given sentence could be debated. Sentence 3a is a good example because the English switch THAT seems to have a repercussion on the rest of the sentence construction. ASL grammar does not require a complementizer. The complementizer in Sentence 3a may have induced another switch and as a result, the English element FOR was inserted. The grammar of ASL does not require the sign FOR. It may be argued that the switch is actually phrasal, "DIFFICULT FOR SOLDIER," rather than morphemic, "FOR." English grammar would call for the

---

[4]"KB," short for "knitted brow," is a kind of nonmanual signal that accompanies an inflection in which the movement of THICK is modified to indicate that the degree of thickness is great.

[5]"RB," short for "raised brows," is a nonmanual signal that accompanies and marks the rest of the sentence as a resultant of the condition specified in the earlier part of the sentence.

phrase "DIFFICULT FOR SOLDIERS" whereas ASL grammar would call for the phrase "DIFFICULT SOLDIER." However, I am inclined to think that it is a morphemic switch. Because there is a complementizer present, for DIFFICULT and SOLDIERS to be considered English elements, a phrasal switch incorporating the verbal construction "would be" would have been required.

Furthermore, the complementizer "THAT" in Sentence 3a seems to be what also induced the insertion of TO, another switch that occurred later, probably due to a syntactic intent to incorporate an English infinitive. In ASL, "TO" is used only as a preposition but not as a function word as in English's infinitive construction. It is possible to consider that the scope of the switch starting with "TO" includes the verb GO-THROUGH. However, this may be debatable because semantically, GO-THROUGH is a verbal derivation of the preposition THROUGH. So an alternative would be to consider "TO" as a free morpheme switch.

There is another example in the data in which a switch is involved in an infinitivelike construction (Sentence 4a). The phrase "TRY ENTER," which is expected in a straight ASL sentence, is equivalent to the English phrase "try to enter." Sentence 4a has fs-TO inserted between both verbs. Sentences 3a and 4a are examples of how the English word *to* can be converted into two possible manual forms. In the earlier example, a prepositional ASL sign TO is used, but it assumes an English semantic value. In the latter, fingerspelling is used as a manual means of representing the orthographical form of the English word *to*.

4a. CS: **fs-SO** BATTLE **ON WATER**, TRY **fs-TO** ENTER-
(China) **FROM WATER** DIFFICULT (WATER is
contextualized as sea based on the content before this sentence.
"China" is also already implied.)

4b. ASL: _TIF SHIP WATER BATTLE, SHIP-MOVE-IN TRY
ENTER (China)_T DIFFICULT.

4c. Eng: Trying to enter China through waging battles on the sea
would be difficult.

The literature on the structure of ASL is not clear on whether ASL vocabulary for prepositions like *from*, *on*, and *to* is a part of the language. They may be examples of borrowings from English that have become grammaticized into ASL. However, as in the hypothetical Sentence 4b, from the perspective that ASL grammar is basically spatial, it is entirely possible to create a sentence without using any prepositions. From that perspective, ON WATER and FROM WATER could be argued as legitimate English switches.

DISCUSSION

Using codeswitching as a framework for analyzing ASL sentences that have English elements embedded in them provides a useful strategy for delving into the question of how ASL and written English interact. The position I have adopted is that it is through examining sentences on the semantic and syntactic levels, in addition to the lexical level, that different sites of switches may be detected. It is through fingerspelling only that the lexical level of analysis may be utilized. In addition to using the English translation, the methodological strategy of creating hypothetical ASL sentences free of English elements helps concretize the process of analysis by providing a visual means to cross-examine suspected sites of codeswitching. The nature of utterances in the discourse of Deaf bilinguals has been puzzling at times, and it has clouded efforts to understand the more complex syntax of ASL.

Furthermore, the literature on the ASL–English contact situation shows that previous investigations have not been adequately developed in this area. It is important to differentiate language-contact utterances made by Deaf bilinguals with each other from those that occurred in other contact contexts. The foreign-talk register used by Deaf people to accommodate nonnative speakers of ASL contain some Englishlike structures and semantics; however, the syntax is elementary. Both languages do not interface with each other in ways as interesting as those in a codeswitching situation. Furthermore, the English-influenced utterances made by nonnative speakers of ASL should be contextualized as a product of various circumstances. The speakers may try to compensate for the gaps in their linguistic knowledge of ASL by drawing on the structures of English in a complementary way. They may have reached a plateau in their acquisition of ASL as a second language and their knowledge of ASL may have fossilized at a point. For others, it may be due to the manner in which they learned ASL as a second language. They may have relexified English lexicon into ASL and used it with English syntax.

The field of ASL research has yet to enter fully into the area of discourse analysis. Utterances created in a naturalistic context, although understandably difficult to record, will provide rich material that will help advance the study of ASL structure. It behooves us to start thinking about how we may begin to accurately study data and what framework we should use to operationalize the procedure of analysis. This discourse data will more than likely come from individuals who are bilingual. Recognizing that utterances with English elements embedded in them coming from the discourse between Deaf bilingual dyads are different from those coming from other language-contact situations involving ASL and English is an important step in creating a more differentiated data set.

Operationalizing the phenomenon of ASL discourse in which English elements are present as one of codeswitching resulting from an ASL–written English language-contact situation may point the investigation in a direction leading to the construction of a model to account for how ASL and written English may interface with each other. Understanding how both languages interact with each other may provide a new approach to investigate ASL syntax. Because analyzing codeswitched ASL sentences forces the investigator to look past the lexicon and into the syntax and semantics of both languages, it affords a methodological means for examining both languages beyond their surface representations. Codeswitched sentence samples provide an opportunity to construct hypothetical, straight ASL sentences. The analysis of how the sentences in each pair compare with each other may yield interesting insight not only into the syntax of ASL but into how the two grammars interact with each other at a deeper level. Furthermore, such an analysis will also contribute to a better understanding of the characteristics of a naturally occurring system by which elements of written English are manually represented. It will also help explicate the process in which parts of written English are transformed to create manual English switches.

Studying how Deaf bilinguals construct utterances with other Deaf bilinguals is an opportunity to study how speakers who have more than one language, more than one way of saying something, may construct sentences with other speakers who share the same linguistic background. The ability to account for the different utterances they make is a necessary step toward understanding the various social and psycholinguistic motivations for codeswitching.

IN CLOSING

A study of how ASL and written English language contact plays out in discourse among bilingual Deaf people will be an opportunity to investigate how the grammars of the languages belonging to two completely different modalities may interact with each other. From a linguistic point of view, such a study may yield a useful angle from which to investigate the syntax of ASL. The investigation of codeswitching in ASL may also be interesting from a sociolinguistic perspective. The fact that this is a common linguistic phenomenon in the Deaf community may account for the reason why Deaf people in the past were uncertain about how to contest the mistaken perception that sign language was broken English. Paradoxically, it was not a case of semilingualism as originally thought, but evidence of Deaf people's bilingual competency. The ability to combine two grammars to produce a discourse that flows pleasantly is a testimony to the linguistic prowess of bilingual Deaf people.

The complete turnabout in the assessment of Deaf people's linguistic capabilities is due in large part to the past three decades of linguistic investigation of ASL. For that turnabout, Deaf people are grateful. The work of Ursula and Ed produced findings that contributed to the excitement in the linguistics world and in the field of ASL research, inspiring many others to follow suit.

REFERENCES

Battison, R. M. (1978). *Lexical borrowing in American Sign Language.* Silver Spring, MD: Linstok Press.

Blom, J.-P., & Gumperz, J. J. (1972). Social meaning in linguistic structures: Codeswitching in Norway. In , J. J. Gumperz & D. Hymes (Eds.), *Directions in sociolinguistics* (pp. 407–434). New York: Holt, Rinehart & Winston.

Cokely, D. (1983). When is a pidgin not a pidgin? An alternate analysis of the ASL–English contact situation. *Sign Language Studies, 38,* 1–24.

Ferguson, C. (1959). Diglossia. *Word, 15,* 325–340.

Haugen, E. (1977). Norm and deviation in bilingual communities. In P. Hornby (Ed.), *Bilingualism: Psychological, social and educational implications* (pp. 91–102). New York: Academic Press.

Lucas, C., & Valli, C. (1989). Language contact in the American Deaf community. In C. Lucas (Ed.), *The sociolinguistics of the American Deaf community* (pp. 11–40). San Diego, CA: Academic Press.

Mahootian, S. (1993). *A null theory of codeswitching.* Unpublished doctoral dissertation, Northwestern University, Evanston, IL.

Myers-Scotton, C. (1993). *Duelling languages: Grammatical structure in code-switching.* Oxford, UK: Oxford University Press.

Sankoff, D., Poplack, S., & Vanniarajan, S. (1990). The case of the nonce loan in Tamil. *Language Variation and Language Change, 2,* 71–101.

Sobin, N. (1976). Texas Spanish and lexical borrowing. *Papers in Linguistics, 9,* 15–47.

Stokoe, W. (1969). Sign language diglossia. *Studies in Linguistics, 21,* 27–41.

Tervoort, B. (1973). Could there be a human sign language? *Semiotica, 9*(4), 347–382.

Valli, C., & Lucas, C. (1992). *Linguistics of American Sign Language.* Washington, DC: Gallaudet University Press.

Woodward, J. (1973). Some characteristics of Pidgin Sign English. *Sign Language Studies, 3,* 39–46.

Woodward, J., & Markowicz, H. (1975). *Some handy new ideas on pidgins and creoles: Pidgin sign languages.* Paper presented at the International Conference on Pidgins and Creole, Honolulu, HI.

17

Indicating Verbs and Pronouns: Pointing Away From Agreement

Scott K. Liddell
Gallaudet University

During the mid-1970s, while I was a research assistant working with Ed Klima and Ursula Bellugi in their lab at The Salk Institute, it was common for linguists and nonlinguists alike to ask whether American Sign Language (ASL) had a grammar and whether it "qualified" as a real language. Now, more than two decades later, such questions are no longer asked, because the status of ASL as a real language is taken for granted. Some researchers, however, are still reluctant to consider the possibility that ASL discourse might include a significant amount of nonphonologically controlled gestures. This appears to be based on the concern that prior to being recognized as a language, ASL was regarded as merely a collection of gestures—not a language. Talking about gestures in ASL strikes some as a step in the wrong direction.

One of the unique aspects of ASL discourse is the ability of signs to be directed or placed in space. This soon became analyzed as part of what was described as a spatial grammar. This chapter takes issue with the general claim that space is part of the grammatical structure of ASL sentences. I outline an analysis in which the spatial use of signs depends on directing and placing signs with respect to mental representations that are

distinct from grammatical representations. It follows from this that directing verbs and pronouns toward elements of such mental representations is
not controlled by phonological features but by the ability to point. This
does not amount to a claim that ASL is no longer a language or has no
grammar. Rather, it is a claim that some of the aspects of ASL discourse
that were thought to be morphemes marking grammatical functions are
playing a different role.

From the beginnings of research into the structure of ASL, the space
surrounding the signer has been treated as articulatory space. In particular,
when the hands move through space to produce signs, this movement has
been treated as simply the movements of articulators carrying out phonologically definable articulatory instructions. For example, to produce the
sign THINK, the index finger moves to the forehead. To produce the sign
MILK, the hand moves to the space several inches ahead of the shoulder
as the hand articulates the sign. In producing THINK, the hand reaches a
location on the body. In producing MILK, the hand reaches a location in
space. There is no theoretical distinction drawn between locations on the
body and in space. It is assumed that either type of location is describable
in phonological terms. The only difference between the two locations is
that one of them is on the body and the other is in space.

But there are other types of signs in ASL. Some signs, such as SEE,
appear to point directly at things in the environment. For example, directing the sign SEE toward a dog would be understood to mean, "see the
dog." What makes SEE different from THINK and MILK is the fact that
the direction the hand takes in producing the sign is not lexically determined. The directionality of the hand depends on the whereabouts of the
dog. If the dog is lying down on the signer's right, the sign will point
downward and to the right—toward the dog. Regardless of where around
the signer the dog happens to be, the sign will point in that direction. This
type of pointing behavior has been treated no differently from the articulatory behavior of the hands in producing signs such as THINK and MILK.
Analysts simply propose that, somehow, the grammar extracts the correct
phonologically defined location in the space ahead of the signer toward
which the hand will move, then the hand moves toward that location just
as it would in producing THINK or MILK. In the most recent treatments,
the directionality of signs like SEE, whose direction is determined by the
locations of actual entities, is considered to be the realization of a grammatical agreement process.

GRAMMATICAL TREATMENTS OF SPACE

In this section, I briefly review proposals in which points in space (spatial loci) are treated as grammatical elements. Each proposal about the grammatical functioning of directional signs is intimately connected with a set of assumptions about the nature of space. I have, where possible, separated claims about the grammatical roles of directional signs from assumptions about the nature of space.

The Nature of Spatial Loci

Table 17.1 summarizes the major claims made about the nature of spatial representations from the beginning of this line of research until the present. Initially, spatial loci were claimed to be pronouns (Woodward, 1970). This was followed by the claim that spatial loci were points in space corresponding to indexes of logical structure (Lacy, 1974). Later, Klima and Bellugi (1979) proposed that loci are points on a horizontal plane ahead of the signer at about the level of the abdomen. Padden (1988) treated spatial loci as affixes consisting of complexes of articulatory features. Liddell and Johnson (1989) proposed a phonological representation system that treats spatial loci as complexes of phonological features. Bahan (1996) treated spatial loci as points in space that correspond to bundles of "phi features."

TABLE 17.1
Representative Claims about Spatial Loci

Source	Claim About the Nature of Spatial Loci
Woodward (1970); Fischer (1975)	Loci are pronouns.
Lacy (1974); Kegl (1985); Lillo-Martin and Klima (1990)	Loci are points in space that correspond to indexes of logical structure.
Klima and Bellugi (1979)	Loci are points on a horizontal plane that come to be associated with referents.
Padden (1988)	Loci are affixes consisting of complexes of phonological features.
Liddell and Johnson (1989)	Loci are phonologically describable points in the signing space that serve as places of articulation for signs.
Janis (1995)	Loci are either locative or non-locative agreement controllers.
Bahan (1996)	Loci are points in space that correspond to complexes of phi features.

We often tend to assume that newer things are better than older ones. This is evident, for example, in software "upgrades" as well as newer model cars. We have the same expectations when it comes to scientific proposals. We expect newer proposals to identify and fix problems with older proposals. If the problems cannot be solved using the older conception, that conception would be discarded in favor of a newer conception capable of solving the problems. In such a scientific tradition, there is some reason to believe that the newer ideas handle the data better than the older ideas. But the history of proposals about space in ASL has not been of this type. In general, new proposals were made almost without regard to the existence of earlier ones. Earlier proposals were not discarded based on scientific merit but were simply ignored. Because earlier proposals have, in general, not been subjected to scrutiny in the literature, there is no real basis for deciding whether one proposal is superior to any other.[1]

The Nature of the Grammatical Process

Claims about the nature of the grammatical processes involved have been as varied as the claims about the nature of space itself. Table 17.2 shows that the claims include affixation, cliticization, deictic verb inflection, indexical inflection, and verb agreement. The claims about the nature of the grammatical processes involved, like claims about the nature of the spatial loci, have not been subjected to scrutiny in the sign language literature. As with claims about the nature of space, what we have is a set of relatively independent claims about the type of grammatical processes that might be involved.

Phonological implementation

One very interesting aspect of these various proposals about space in ASL has been the lack of serious attention given to their phonological implementation. That spatial features need to have phonological substance in a grammatical analysis was recognized very early in the history of this issue: "When I refer to 'distinct phonological forms' [of pronouns] above I am referring to formational distinctness in terms of categorial phonological features at the systematic phonemic level" (Lacy, 1974, p. 15). Lacy

---

[1]There are occasional exceptions to this generalization. Meier (1990), for example, argued against the three-person agreement system proposed by Padden (1988).

TABLE 17.2
Representative Claims about the Grammatical Process

Source	Claim About the Nature of the Grammatical Process
Woodward (1970)	Pronouns affixed to verbs
Fischer (1975)	Pronouns cliticized to verbs
Lacy (1974); Lillo-Martin and Klima (1990)	Indexical inflection
Klima & Bellugi (1979)	Deictic verb inflection
Padden (1988)	Person agreement on verbs (first, second, and third person)
Liddell and Johnson (1989)	Subject and object agreement on verbs
Janis (1995)	Locative or nonlocative agreement on verbs
Bahan (1996)	Subject and object agreement on verbs (agreement is with phi features—unspecified)

recognized that a grammatical analysis of space will need a phonological system of representation capable of giving phonological substance to proposed grammatical units. In the early part of this history, the only system of representation available was that originally proposed by Stokoe (1960) and Stokoe, Casterline, and Croneberg (1965). In this representation system, the space ahead of the signer is undifferentiated. Within this system, any sign made in space would be considered to have the same location, transcribed with the symbol Ø. Stokoe et al. (1965, p. x) described this location as "zero, the neutral place where the hands move [in space], in contrast with all places below."[2] Regardless of the spatial direction of the sign, it would still be considered to have the same location. So obviously, a lot of work remained to be done in order to implement various types of grammatical proposals concerning space. But in the early days of this research, there was reason to assume that it was simply a matter of time before an appropriate system would be developed. As a result, analysts felt free to propose grammatical analyses without the (customary) need to describe the phonological implementation of the proposal.[3] This is apparent in Table 17.3.

---

[2]I have been involved in many discussions where people have talked about "neutral space." This term evidently developed from Stokoe et al.'s (1965) original description of "the neutral place."

[3]Clearly, in the analysis of spoken languages, no one would seriously consider analyses of affixes, clitics, agreement morphemes, and so forth, unless those proposing the analysis were able to phonologically describe the grammatical element.

TABLE 17.3
Representative Claims about Phonological Implementation

Source	Phonological Implementation of the Grammatical Process
Woodward (1970)	Not described
Fischer (1975)	Not described
Lacy (1974)	Not described
Kegl (1985)	Not described
Lillo-Martin and Klima (1990)	Not described
Klima and Bellugi (1979)	Not described
Padden (1988)	first person = near signer's body second person = in direction of addressee third person = at a locus point i assigned to 3rd person nominal
Liddell and Johnson (1989)	Complex set of phonological features indicating vector, height and distance from the signer
Janis (1995)	Not described
Bahan (1996)	Not described

In Padden (1988), the directionality of indicating verbs is claimed to reflect subject and object agreement.[4] The proposed basis for the agreement is the person of the subject or object of the verb. She proposes that ASL has a set of agreement affixes that attach to the verbs, providing them with their directionality. The first-person affix places the sign near signer's body. The second-person affix places the sign in direction of addressee, and the third-person affix places the sign at a locus point i assigned to third-person nominal. Although Padden's descriptions attempt to give substance to the proposed affixes, they are not part of a phonological system. This means that these descriptions need to be thought of as narrative descriptions of form rather than as phonological features. Additionally, note that descriptions like "in direction of addressee" could be realized in an unlimited number of ways, depending on the location of the addressee. Thus, even if this description was to be thought of in phonological terms, it doesn't really provide directionality to the hand in linguistic terms, because the location of the addressee is variable.

---

[4]This category of verbs has been called "inflecting verbs" (Padden 1988) and "agreement verbs"(Liddell & Johnson, 1989). I now use the term "indicating verbs" for reasons that will become apparent.

Liddell and Johnson (1989) developed a phonological representation system for ASL. This system includes a means for segmenting signs into sequences of movements and holds, features for describing hand configurations, as well as the location and orientation of the hands. Within that system, hands move toward locations on the body or in space. For indicating verbs (e.g., SEE, GIVE), the location in space is identified by means of a vector radiating away from the signer, a distance away from the signer on that vector, and a height feature. The system has seven vectors, four distances away from the signer and potentially, several possible height features. The combinations of vector, distance, and height features result in a very large number of possible locations (loci) in the signing space ahead of the signer. Here is how this system was supposed to work. The signer would select the locus that was closest to being "in the direction of" the person or thing present. The sign would then be made at that phonologically definable spatial location. The problem with this system of representation is that signers do not select from a predetermined number of vectors or heights if the person or thing is present. Suppose, for example, that the addressee is not in line with any of the predefined vectors but is closer to one than another. If signers really selected the vector that was nearest to being correct, then we ought to see signers directing signs along those predetermined vectors, even if that meant that the sign is not exactly directed toward the appropriate person or thing. Similarly, the signer would somehow select the height that most closely matched the direction of the entity. But this is not what happens. The system of directing signs is based on directing signs at physically present entities, regardless of where the entity is with respect to the signer.[5]

Summary

Over the past three decades, there have been numerous, relatively independent proposals about signs that use space. The proposals concern the nature of space and the type of grammatical processes exemplified by that use of space. Each proposal carries with it a certain set of assumptions. Although not all are explicit on this issue, they all share the assumption that some sort of spatial morpheme is somehow attached to the verb. Second, all these proposals assume that such a spatial morpheme can be

---

[5]The system of heights ranged from the top of the head to the waist. This range is not adequate to deal with the much greater number of possible heights at which such signs can be produced.

described by a set of phonological features. No adequate means of giving phonological substance to those proposals currently exists. A third assumption shared by all these proposals is that the space ahead of the signer is part of the grammatical representation of sentences. This is especially apparent when a spatial locus is described as a clitic, a morpheme, or an affix.

AGREEMENT

There is not only disagreement about the nature of agreement as a grammatical process, but there is also disagreement concerning exactly which kind of linguistic phenomena count as examples of agreement (Ferguson & Barlow, 1988). To examine claims that the ASL indicating verbs exemplify a grammatical agreement process, we first need a working definition of agreement. Not everyone will accept the following definition, but it will, nevertheless, provide a basis for discussion. If other analysts disagree with this definition, then they can at least be explicit about the definition that guides their analysis.

Lehmann (1988, p. 55) proposed the following definition of agreement:

Constituent B agrees with constituent A (in category C) if and only if the following three conditions hold true:

There is a syntactic or anaphoric relationship between A and B.

A belongs to a subcategory c of a grammatical category C, and A's belonging to C is independent of the presence or the nature of B.

C is expressed on B and forms a constituent with it.

English does not have much in the way of agreement phenomena. However, it is widely accepted that in (1) the verb agrees with the subject of the sentence. The agreement is marked by the suffix -s attached to the verb. In (1) the verb (B) agrees with its subject (A) in person and number. The agreement suffix -s appears only with a third-person singular subject.

(1) The earth revolves around the sun.

All three conditions described in Lehmann's (1988) definition are met. First, there is a syntactic relation between the subject and the verb. Second, the subject is third-person singular (two subcategories of the person and number categories). These properties of the subject are independent of the presence and nature of the verb. Finally, third-person singular is expressed on the verb by the suffix -*s* and forms a constituent with it.

ASL "Agreement"

Most recently, authors who have ascribed grammatical functions to indicating verbs in ASL seem to have settled on the idea that indicating verbs reflect grammatical agreement. The most explicit description of the basis for agreement appears in Padden (1988), where the directionality is claimed to be governed by the category "person." Padden claimed that the agreement categories are first-person, second-person, and third-person. Meier (1990) argued that ASL does not distinguish first-, second-, and third-person forms. Rather, ASL only distinguishes between first-person and non-first-person forms. If person were the basis for agreement, then there should be a first-person form and a non-first-person form.[6] Instead of two directions corresponding to first- and non-first-person forms, respectively, there is an open-ended number of possible non-first-person forms. This open-ended number of distinctive directional forms is inconsistent with a two-person grammatical system. Other agreement proposals have generally been fairly inexplicit about the basis for agreement.

In (2), agreement analyses would claim that the verb TELL agrees with its object. For purposes of discussion, I will assume that the actual mother is present. In that case, the sign TELL would begin its movement at the chin and then move outward toward the actual mother.

(2) PRO-1 TELL MOTHER.
"I told mother"

As with the previous English example, to determine whether this is agreement, Lehmann's (1988) three criteria will be tested. There is no problem with the first criterion because there is a syntactic relation between the verb and its object, MOTHER. The second and third criteria require finding a grammatical property of the object MOTHER being encoded onto the verb. Four common controllers of agreement across languages are person, gender, number, and case (Pullum, 1985). Meier (1990) showed that person is not the basis for the directionality of indicat-

---

[6] In a three-person system like that proposed by Padden (1988) there would be (not counting allomorphy) three forms. We do not find this either.

ing verbs. Gender does not seem to be an issue in ASL nouns. Even if gender were a property of nouns in ASL, it is clear that ASL does not have an unlimited number of genders corresponding to the unlimited number of possible directions of the verb. Similarly, number is also not controlling the directionality of the verb. Case is unmarked in ASL nouns and could also not account for the directionality of the verb. Any possible agreement analysis will have to identify the property of the object being encoded onto the verb.

It is uncontroversial that the sign TELL points toward the location of the physical mother. But the physical mother is not a constituent of the sentence. In fact, there is no sense in which the actual mother is a part of (2). If sentences contained the actual things being discussed, then (3) would contain a lot of salt water. The point, of course, is that although (2) mentions the mother, she is not part of the sentence.

(3) I love the Atlantic Ocean.

Recall that Lehmann's (1988) definition restricts agreement to two constituents of a sentence. In (2), the two constituents are the verb TELL and the object MOTHER. There are no properties of the sign MOTHER being marked on the verb TELL. Thus, there is no basis for saying that the verb agrees with its object. The directionality of the verb, however, is highly significant because the hand is directed toward the actual mother being talked about. Because the actual mother is not part of the sentence, it does not make sense to say that the verb "agrees" with the actual mother. In addition, as discussed earlier, no one has been able to successfully propose a phonological system capable of describing the unlimited directionality of indicating verbs. Thus, there is no grammatical basis for an agreement analysis and no existing phonological system capable of implementing an agreement analysis.

INDICATING VERBS, PRONOUNS, AND PRESENT REFERENTS

Indicating Verbs

In (2) [PRO-1 TELL MOTHER], the sign TELL begins with the index finger in contact with the chin. The hand then moves outward toward the actual mother and ends with the index finger pointing at the mother. The directionality of the sign TELL in this example is crucial. Without it, signers would judge the signing to be incorrect.[7] Clearly, then, the directionality of indicating verbs is highly significant. The question remains, however, as to the role of this directionality.

In human languages, sentences mention things. For example, (4) uses the meaningful phrase, *the turquoise ring* to talk about a ring. Any English speaker could use the same phrase to talk about a different ring. That is, the phrase *the turquoise ring* encodes a description of an entity, but does not encode the actual entity in the world being talked about. The actual entity being talked about is dependent on who uses the phrase and under what conditions. This point is central to the development of mental space theory (Fauconnier, 1985, 1997).

(4) I just bought the turquoise ring.

Of all the possible turquoise rings in the world, how is the addressee to know which ring the speaker has in mind? The definite article *the* helps narrow down the possibilities. The definite article is used when the entity being talked about is known to both the speaker and addressee. This greatly simplifies the addressee's task because now the addressee needs only to consider turquoise rings that are known to both participants in the discourse. If the addressee recalls a shopping trip the day before in which both looked at a turquoise ring, then the addressee now has a basis for deciding which ring is being discussed.

An addressee is constantly faced with the task of making connections between the meanings encoded by words, phrases, and clauses and the real or hypothetical entities described or mentioned in the grammatical representation. If the entity is physically present, speakers typically assist the addressee in making the connection by producing a deictic gesture toward the entity. While producing (5) through (7), for example, the speaker would be expected to either produce a deictic gesture or to show, in some other way, the addressee which entity is being talked about.

---

[7] I purposely avoided using the term *ungrammatical* here, because that term is generally reserved for improperly constructed combinations of grammatical units. Here, I am claiming that the syntax is fine but that a required deictic gesture is missing. The lack of a required gesture would make this example incorrect. It is not difficult to find parallel examples from spoken language. Without a gesture, and while maintaining eye contact with the addressee, it would be equally incorrect for a man to talk about the shoes he is wearing by saying, "These shoes are very expensive." This would be true even if the shoes being worn by the speaker were the only shoes in sight.

(5) Sign your name right here.

(6) I'll take one of those.

(7) This is my favorite pen.

While uttering (5), the speaker would typically make a pointing gesture toward the place where the signature is expected. It is also frequent to see the speaker write a mark on the piece of paper where the signature is expected while uttering a statement like (5). Similarly, while uttering (6), the speaker would be expected to produce a pointing gesture toward the desired entity. The types of gestures that could accompany (7) might be more varied. In addition to a pointing gesture, the speaker could also, for example, simply lift the pen into the air. Lifting the pen into the air is not a pointing gesture, but it accomplishes the same end by making the pen prominent. In other words, it identifies the pen as the entity in the world that corresponds to the spoken description.

I assume that giving prominence to a physically present entity being talked about is a general characteristic of human discourse. This can be done in a number of ways, but the most typical is a deictic gesture of some sort. Making the entity prominent appears to be a signal to the addressee that the entity corresponds to something in the verbal description. I assume further that the purpose of giving that prominence is to allow the addressee to make a connection between the semantic structure of the utterance and the present entity. The addressee is constantly faced with making connections between semantic representations and real or hypothetical entities (Fauconnier 1985, 1997). Giving prominence to physically present entities simplifies the addressee's ongoing task. Given this set of assumptions, we can now return to the previous example of an indicating verb, repeated here for convenience.

(2) PRO-1 TELL MOTHER.
   "I told mother"

Langacker (1987, 1991) provided a means of talking about semantic structures within the theory of cognitive grammar. The semantic structure of the verb TELL includes not only a representation of the act of telling but in addition, two schematically represented participants. That is, a prototypical act of telling involves an entity to do the telling and an entity toward which the telling is directed. For this verb, the entity within the semantic representation conceived of as performing the action would be called the *trajector* and the entity within the semantic representation conceived of as receiving the information would be called the *landmark*. In the semantic representation of the verb TELL, both the trajector and landmark are unelaborated entities.

By grammatically combining the verb TELL with its object MOTHER, the signer overtly encodes that the landmark has the semantic property "mother." In Langacker's terms, the object MOTHER elaborates the landmark of the verb TELL. As a result of the grammatical combination of TELL and MOTHER, the landmark has gone from an unelaborated entity to an entity with the property "mother." There are billions of people and animals on earth with the property "mother." Thus, even though the landmark has been elaborated with the semantic property "mother," the addressee still has the task of associating the landmark with some real or hypothetical entity. In the analysis proposed here, I claim that the directionality of the sign TELL indicates the entity to be correlated with the verb's landmark. By observing the directionality of the sign TELL, the addressee can see who was told. It is simply a matter of observing the entity toward which the sign points.

Recall that the landmark is a semantic entity that is part of the semantic structure of the verb. In the case of TELL, the landmark is the recipient of the information being conveyed in the act of telling. In (2), the addressee comes to know two things about the landmark of the verb TELL. As a result of the grammatical encoding accomplished by the verb–object construction, the addressee learns that the landmark has the property "mother." As a result of the indicating nature of the verb (e.g., it points at the actual mother), the addressee comes to know the entity in the real world that corresponds to the landmark. Mapping the concept "mother" onto the landmark is grammatically encoded, whereas mapping the actual mother onto the landmark is indicated by means of a deictic gesture.[8]

Pronouns

For the purposes of this discussion, I look only at the singular, non-first-person pronoun, which I call PRO. It is made with a "1" handshape, with the palm facing to the side. The hand typically makes a small outward

---

[8]I am using the term *mapping* in the sense developed in Fauconnier (1997).

movement followed by a hold. Semantically, the pronoun encodes a single entity, unspecified for animateness, gender, or case.

Regardless of the language used, addressees are faced with associating pronouns with real or hypothetical entities. If the entity is present, English speakers could identify it by producing a deictic gesture toward it. In (8), for example, the speaker would have several options for identifying the person corresponding to the pronoun *he*, including pointing with the index finger, a tilt of the head, facing and gazing at the person, and so forth. Regardless of the form of the deictic gesture, if the gesture points toward the referent, the identity of the referent will be apparent to the addressee.

(8) He did it.

In ASL discourse, addressees also have the ongoing task of associating pronouns with real or hypothetical entities. They are greatly assisted in this task by the requirement that PRO point at its referent, if present. Note that the directionality of PRO performs the same discourse function as the directionality of indicating verbs. In both cases, the pointing helps the addressee make a connection between an entity within a semantic representation and an entity in the immediate environment of the signer.

I know of no viable alternative to this analysis when the entities being talked about are present. That is, all the analyses discussed previously involve associating an entity with a locus in space. For example, Lillo-Martin and Klima (1990) proposed that when the entity is present, the signer selects a "referential locus" between the signer and the entity and directs signs toward that locus. The basic problem with the claim that signs are directed toward a locus when the entity is present is that when signs are directed toward a physically present person, each sign has a body part toward which it is directed. The body parts include the forehead, nose, chin or neck, chest, and abdomen. A sign like GET-SAME-IDEA-SAME-TIME is directed toward the forehead. SAY-NO is directed toward the nose, or slightly below. GIVE is directed toward the chest, and INVITE is directed toward the abdomen. These facts about signing are simply inconsistent with the notion that signs are directed toward a referential locus. That is, a locus that might be right for GET-SAME-IDEA-SAME-TIME would be wrong for SAY-NO, GIVE, and INVITE. As a result, it appears to me that even supporters of a grammatical analysis of space will have to grant that when the actual entity is present, signs simply point at the entity.

INDICATING VERBS, PRONOUNS,
AND ABSENT REFERENTS

When the entities being discussed are not physically present, both indicating verbs and pronouns still point. In fact, most of the claims about spatial loci in Table 17.1 concern missing referents. The idea is that a point in space, generally referred to as a locus, becomes associated with the missing referent. The claims, in general, have been that signs are then directed toward these loci. I have argued that this type of association is not necessarily with a point in space but with a three-dimensional volume of space. I referred to such spatial entities as "tokens" (Liddell, 1994). Tokens can range in size from essentially a point to something greater than a foot tall. The distinction between locus and token arises because once a spatial association is made with an entity, signs are not, as a rule, directed toward a point in space (Liddell, 1994). Rather, if the token represents a standing human, some signs will be produced at the height of the abdomen, others at the level of the chest, and so on, up to about the level of the nose.[9] I cannot conceive of a way that the claim that a sign is directed toward a single locus when the entity being talked about is not present can accommodate these facts about signing.

In addition, signers can also conceive of nonpresent entities (people or things) as if the actual entity were present. Such a conceptually present entity is called a surrogate (Liddell, 1995). For example, if a person is conceived of as present, then the signer can direct signs toward that conceptually present person just as if that person were really present. In contrast to a token, a surrogate has the form expected of the actual entity. That is, a surrogate person would have the appropriate size and shape of the actual person. Signers direct signs toward surrogates and interact with surrogates, just as if they were physically present.

I claimed earlier that if the actual entity being talked about is physically present, indicating verbs and pronouns will be directed toward the actual entity. When the actual entity is not present, tokens and surrogates function as conceptually present referents.[10] Understanding that tokens and

---

[9] If the token represents a human lying down, then the token will not have the same height described in the text. See Liddell (1994) for a more complete discussion of this issue.

[10] This chapter does not address the nature of the spatial representations. I have claimed elsewhere that spatial representations in ASL are examples of mental spaces. Signers either direct signs toward entities in Real Space or to entities in blends with Real Space (Liddell, 1998, in press; Liddell & Metzger, 1998).

surrogates are conceptually present entities allows the behavior of indicating verbs and pronouns to be described in a unified way. Indicating verbs and pronouns both point at things. The things they point at are meant to be connected with entities within semantic representations. In the case of the indicating verb TELL, the pointing identifies the thing to be connected with the verb's landmark. In the case of the pronoun PRO, the pointing identifies the entity to be associated with the pronoun's semantic representation.[11]

If the thing is physically present, then the verb or pronoun points at it. If the thing is conceived of as present, either in the form of a token or surrogate, then an indicating verb or pronoun will be directed toward that conceptually present entity. The function of the pointing is the same regardless of whether the entity being talked about is physically or conceptually present. In both cases, the pointing identifies a thing to be associated with a part of the semantic representation.

CONCLUSION

I claimed that when the entities being talked about are present, indicating verbs and pronouns are simply directed toward them. If the entity is a person, signs are directed toward specific body parts. This strongly argues against spatial loci being the targets of the movement when the actual entity is present. Suppose the entity in question is not present. Proposals claiming that spatial loci have grammatical status and that directing signs toward such spatial loci reflects a grammatical process suffer from a number of shortcomings. First, they assume without argument that spatial loci have grammatical status. Second, in general, they claim that a grammatical process is involved without being explicit about the nature of the process. Where the basis for agreement is made explicit (Padden, 1988), it has been shown to be inadequate. Third, even assuming that the assumptions about space were correct and that a grammatical process could really be demonstrated, these proposals lack a phonological means of implementing the proposals. Finally, supporters of a grammatical analysis would apparently have to claim that indicating verbs and pronouns behave

---

[11] This entity is typically called the "referent" of the pronoun. The concept of a referent is clearer when the entity is present. If the physical entity is absent, but there is a conceptually present entity associated with the physical entity, then it is no longer as clear which of the two is the pronoun's referent.

in two completely different ways. If the entity is present, the sign is directed toward the entity through nonphonological means. If the entity is not present, the sign points at a spatial locus by means of phonological features—even though no such features exist.

My proposal is that indicating verbs and pronouns simply point at entities. The purpose of the pointing is to allow the addressee to make an association between the entity and the semantic representation of the verb or pronoun. The means by which the sign points is not phonological. Rather, the sign points because the signer knows where the entity is and knows how to point. This analysis applies to both physically and conceptually present entities.

REFERENCES

Bahan, B. (1996). *Non-manual realization of agreement in American Sign Language.* Unpublished doctoral dissertation, Boston University.

Fauconnier, G. (1985). *Mental spaces.* Cambridge, MA: MIT Press. Rev. ed. New York: Cambridge University Press, 1994.

Fauconnier, G. (1997). *Mappings in thought and language.* Cambridge, UK: Cambridge University Press.

Ferguson, C. A., & Barlow, M. (1988). Introduction. In M. Barlow and C. A. Ferguson (Eds.), *Agreement in natural language: Approaches, theories, descriptions* (pp. 1–22). Stanford, CA: Center for the Study of Language and Information.

Fischer, S. (1975). Influences on word order change in American Sign Language. In Li, C. (Ed.), *Word order and word order change* (pp. 1–25). Austin, TX: University of Texas Press.

Janis, W. D. (1995). A crosslinguistic perspective on ASL verb agreement. In K. Emmorey and J. Reilly, (Eds.), *Language, gesture, and space* (pp. 195–223). Mahwah, NJ: Lawrence Erlbaum Associates.

Kegl, J. (1985). *Locative relations in American Sign Language word formation, syntax, and discourse.* Unpublished doctoral dissertation, Massachusetts Institute of Technology.

Klima, E. S., & Bellugi, U. (1979). *The signs of language.* Cambridge, MA: Harvard University Press.

Lacy, R. (1974, December). *Putting some of the syntax back into semantics.* Paper presented at the Linguistic Society of America Annual Meeting, New York.

Langacker, R. W. (1987). *Foundations of cognitive grammar, Volume I: Theoretical prerequisites.* Stanford, CA: Stanford University Press.

Langacker, R. W. (1991). *Foundations of cognitive grammar, Volume II: Descriptive application.* Stanford, CA: Stanford University Press.

Lehmann, C. (1988). On the function of agreement. In M. Barlow and C. A. Ferguson (Eds.), *Agreement in natural language: Approaches, theories, descriptions* (pp. 55–65). Stanford: Center for the Study of Language and Information.

Liddell, S. K. (1994). Tokens and surrogates. In I. Ahlgren, B. Bergman, & M. Brennan (Eds.), *Perspectives on sign language structure: Papers from the Fifth International Symposium on Sign Language Research* (vol. 1, pp. 105–119). University of Durham, UK: The International Sign Linguistics Association.

Liddell, S. K. (1995). Real, surrogate, and token space: Grammatical consequences in ASL. In K. Emmorey & J. Reilly (Eds.), *Language, gesture, and space* (pp. 19–41). Mahwah, NJ: Lawrence Erlbaum Associates.

Liddell, S. K. (1998). Grounded blends, gestures, and conceptual shifts. *Cognitive Linguistics, 9*(3), 283–314.

Liddell, S. K. (in press). Blended spaces and deixis in sign language discourse. In D. McNeill (Ed.), *Language and gesture: Window into thought and action.* Cambridge, UK: Cambridge University Press.

Liddell, S., & Johnson, R. (1989). American Sign Language: The phonological base. *Sign Language Studies, 64,* 195–277.

Liddell, S. K., & Metzger, M. (1998). Gesture in sign language discourse. *Journal of Pragmatics, 30*(6), 657–698.

Lillo-Martin, D., & Klima, E. (1990). Pointing out differences: ASL pronouns in syntactic theory. In S. Fischer & P. Siple (Eds.), *Theoretical issues in sign language research I: Linguistics* (pp. 191–210). Chicago: University of Chicago Press.

Meier, R. (1990). Person deixis in American Sign Language. In S. Fischer & P. Siple (Eds.), *Theoretical issues in sign language research I: Linguistics* (pp. 175–190). Chicago: University of Chicago Press.

Padden, C. (1988). Interaction of morphology and syntax in ASL (Garland outstanding dissertations in linguistics, Series 4). New York: Garland.

Pullum, G. K. (1985). How complex could an agreement system be? In Alvarez et al. (Eds.), *ESCOL '84: Proceedings of the first Eastern States Conference on Linguistics* (pp. 79–103). Ithaca, NY: DMLL Publications.

Stokoe, W. C. (1960). *Sign language structure: An outline of the visual communication system of the American deaf* (Studies in Linguistics, Occasional Papers 8). Buffalo, NY: University of Buffalo Press.

Stokoe, W. C., Casterline, D., & Croneberg, C. (1965). *A dictionary of American Sign Language on linguistic principles.* Washington, DC: Gallaudet University Press.

Woodward, J. (1970). *Personal pronominalization in American Sign Language.* Unpublished manuscript, Georgetown University.

V
Language Acquisition

18

Viewing Deaf Children in a New Way: Implications of Bellugi and Klima's Research for Education

Jeffrey G. Bettger
San Francisco State University

Consider two scenarios. In the first scenario, a child frolics contentedly in a crib. Nevertheless, anxious parents eagerly look for any indication that their child can hear them. Louder and louder the parents call the child's name. The child does not respond. Seeing a toy horse in the crib, the child gleefully points to it. Without noticing, the parents look at each other somberly. The doctor was right. Their child cannot hear.

In the second scenario, a child frolics contentedly in a crib. The happy parents eagerly look for any indication that their child is trying to communicate. Seeing a toy horse in the crib, the child smiles and points to it. The parents joyfully recount to each other what has just happened, not with spoken words, but with manual signs. Quickly and naturally, the parents pick up the toy, make sure the child is still watching, and then display the manual sign "horse." The parents then proudly position the child's tiny hands into the same shape. Their child can sign!

The two scenarios differ in many ways. For example, only in the second scenario do we see evidence of joint attention, recognized intentions, language training, and social bonding. From this information alone, what might researchers and educators predict about the cognitive development and language acquisition of the two children? Notice that I did not say *English* acquisition. I said *language* acquisition.

In the early 1970s, Ursula Bellugi and Ed Klima were awarded a grant to study the acquisition of American Sign Language (ASL) by Deaf children. This chapter is a tribute to their 30 years of sign language research and its many implications for Deaf education. Consequently, I review past trends in Deaf education, point out the key elements of the Bellugi and Klima acquisition research, and then discuss the impact of their research on current Deaf education.

Before continuing, two clarifications must be made. First, it needs to be said that no one or two people can make a truly important contribution alone. Therefore, in the remainder of this chapter, all references to "the research of Bellugi and Klima," should be interpreted as, "the research of Bellugi and Klima, along with their numerous outstanding Deaf and hearing colleagues, postdoctoral researchers, graduate students, consultants, technicians, and staff." Perhaps the true genius of their legacy has been Bellugi's and Klima's ability to motivate and guide bright young minds and experts in other fields to join in the study of ASL.

The second clarification is that all references to Deaf children in this chapter do not include children who have become deafened postlingually or who have hearing losses so mild so as not to significantly impair their ability to hear English. A common problem in Deaf-related research and education is that the term *deafness* is used to cover a wide range of hearing losses and onsets. Clearly, a child who loses some hearing at age 8 does not follow the same language acquisition path as does a child born with complete hearing loss. Unfortunately, many educational policies must cover such a broad range of children.

A MATTER OF PERSPECTIVE

When you have been influenced by the Bellugi and Klima research being celebrated in this book, you take for granted that ASL is a language equal to any spoken language, that hearing people should communicate with Deaf persons in sign or through a signing interpreter, that spoken languages and educational signing systems (e.g., SEE) cannot be a Deaf child's first language, and that much is left to learn about Deaf cultures and sign languages around the world. In general, Deaf persons are seen as different, not necessarily disabled. In the education world, this general attitude has been traditionally adopted only by the residential schools for the Deaf.

More commonly, professionals associated with hearing impairment (educators, speech therapists, audiologists) have felt that Deafness is a medical condition needing a cure and have traditionally valued Oralism (the use of speech and lipreading) or systems of English-based signing over ASL, contending that natural sign languages (such as ASL) do not help produce literacy skills or the production of speech (such as English). These opinions have led to an abundance of research based on the following questions: How can auditory input be increased for hearing-impaired children? How can these children become members of the hearing world? What is causing low English literacy skills in Deaf children?

This philosophy, commonly referred to as the "Medical Model," has led to the following: the development of cochlear implants; "inclusion" of Deaf children in classrooms in which they may be the only nonhearing child; laws that label the Deaf community as a singular, homogeneous, disabled group; standards for teaching credentials that do not include mandatory proficiency in ASL or Deaf culture; and Deaf children who are frequently not proficient in ASL or English. In fact, much of the education research pertaining to Deaf children's language acquisition does not contain any assessment of their ASL skills. For audiologists, speech pathologists, and many educators of the Deaf, the message is clear: Language equals English.

HISTORY OF DEAF EDUCATION

Prior to 1880, sign language was commonly the language of instruction for Deaf children, and approximately 50% of all teachers of the deaf were Deaf themselves (Lane, 1984). However, in 1880, the International Congress of Educators of the Deaf met in Milan, Italy, and decided that the availability of a sign language hindered a Deaf child from learning how to speak. Therefore, it was decided that signing should be discouraged and that Deaf children should be encouraged to develop lipreading and speaking skills (i.e., Oralism). This philosophy inevitably led to a decline in the percentage of Deaf teachers. No longer were their experience, insight, culture, and sign language valued.

In the 1970s, educators observed that English literacy scores for deaf children were still low and that the children were using sign language on the playground. This led to the idea that perhaps combining ASL signs and the grammar of English would lead to improved literacy scores. Thus was born various systems of signing English. Using this system, hearing

teachers try to speak English while simultaneously producing corresponding sign forms. Neither this signing English philosophy nor the Oral
method has been the desired cure-all for Deaf literacy woes.

TO BRAVELY GO

Given this history and the two scenarios presented at the beginning of this
chapter, one can see the polarized and emotional arena in which Bellugi
and Klima have conducted their sign language research over the years.
Their first major obstacle, however, came not from emotional parents or
dogmatic educators but rather from uninterested academics.

After choosing to study ASL, Bellugi and Klima soon discovered that
the study of language acquisition cannot proceed until journal editors and
granting agencies believe you are studying a "real" language. With his
experience studying the syntax of spoken languages and a keen understanding of the required elements of a natural language, Klima brought the
tools of linguists to the study of ASL. As can be seen in other chapters in
this book, this linguistic work continues today and promises many yet
undiscovered treasures for the future.

Moreover, it was Bellugi's training with Roger Brown at Harvard and
her passion for issues related to language acquisition that kept her focused
on signing children. By observing the apparent rule-based errors children
made while acquiring ASL, she was able to show that ASL was not pantomime. Furthermore, she was able to convince other developmentalists
that the study of ASL could provide important new insights into age-old
questions. This was no small feat.

With Bellugi's lead, ASL acquisition research has been guided by
themes well-known to developmentalists: acquisition milestones and
timetables, motherese, turn-taking, first word or sign, and so forth. Early
questions about Mean Length of Utterance (MLU) in ASL in turn pointed
out the need for a better understanding of ASL morphology, which in turn
allowed for better study of acquisition. Such interdisciplinary dependency
and gain has existed throughout their research over the years.

It is paramount to recognize an additional benefit of having their
research programs guided by the questions of established fields such as
developmental psychology and linguistics. First, as experiments were
completed, their research was quickly accepted at a wide range of academic conferences, not just sign language or Deaf education conferences.
This far-reaching exposure is responsible for bringing many experts of

diverse fields to collaborate on sign language projects. Second, having their research guided by developmental and linguistic theories, rather than by traditional educational issues, helped to expand the types of data available regarding Deaf children.

DEAF CHILDREN OF DEAF PARENTS

To me, the underlying truth discovered, studied, and scientifically explained by Bellugi and Klima's study of ASL acquisition is that Deaf children born to Deaf parents (DD) are similar to hearing children born to hearing parents (HH) in a way that most Deaf children born to hearing parents (DH) are not. That is, if you are exposed to a language (signed or spoken) from birth that you can comprehend and produce, and if you can interact socially with your parents in an easy and natural manner, then normal development occurs. The early exposure of sign language available to Deaf children born to Deaf parents provides them with the tools necessary to play pretend games, tell creative stories, label objects in the world, question, and make themselves understood (refer back to the second scenario presented at the beginning of this chapter). Unfortunately, only about 10% of Deaf children have Deaf parents.

What of the 90% of Deaf children who have hearing parents? Their world is often one of delayed and impoverished language input and limited interaction with nonsigning parents and peers. In these children, one can see clearly the symbiotic relation between language, social, and cognitive development disrupted. Therefore, within a random group of Deaf children, there may exist children who are fluent in ASL with various levels of English skill, children with limited ASL and limited English skills, and children with only limited English skills. Therefore it is insufficient to say that "a group of Deaf children was tested."

While at The Salk Institute, Jeff Bettger, Karen Emmorey, Stephen McCullough, Margaret Wilson, and others completed several studies exploring the effects of sign language exposure on cognitive development (see Emmorey, 1998, for a review). Within nonlinguistic cognitive domains, differentiating groups of children and adults by parental signing ability suggests that signers (Deaf and hearing) who have Deaf parents actually show enhanced or unique performance, relative to nonsigning peers, on tasks such as mental rotation (Emmorey, Kosslyn, & Bellugi, 1993), face discrimination (Bettger, Emmorey, McCullough, & Bellugi, 1997), and short-term memory (Wilson, Bettger, Niculae, & Klima,

1997). More recently, Remmel, Bettger, and Weinberg (1998) found a positive correlation between signing ability and performance on Theory of Mind tasks. When combined, these studies suggest that early knowledge of a visual–gestural language has a positive influence on cognitive development and may be a more important factor than is auditory deprivation per se (see Parasnis, Samar, Sathe, & Bettger, 1996 for relevant cross-cultural evidence).

It is interesting that subscribers of the "Medical Model" seem to ignore these data and focus on data collected by hearing researchers that suggest that Deaf children of hearing parents in oral or English-based signing classrooms are "impulsive and distractible" (Quittner, Smith, Osberger, Mitchell, & Katz, 1994) and show performance patterns similar to those of autistic children on Theory of Mind tasks (Peterson & Siegal, 1998). Their argument is that because most Deaf children do not have Deaf parents, whatever is learned about Deaf children of Deaf parents is not relevant. In essence, because society as a whole is hearing and uses spoken language, the appropriate goal, according to the Medical Model, is to make Deaf children of hearing parents join the hearing world as fully as possible. Those Deaf adults who eventually choose to self-identify with the Deaf world and use sign language as their primary language are seen as failures.

Please note that the logic of the Medical model makes Hearing adults, not Deaf adults, the proper role models for Deaf children. Partial English skills are considered more important than are fluent ASL skills. This logic also places the burden of effort on the child. That is, it is the Deaf child's job to become literate in English, rather than the hearing parent's job to learn sign language. This attitude is perplexing given recent studies showing that the Deaf children with the best signing skills also have the best English literacy skills (Hoffmeister, 1996; Padden, 1996; Strong & Prinz, 1997).

CURRENT DEAF EDUCATION

Deaf education is extremely heterogeneous around the world. Many countries have adopted an exclusive Oral approach, whereas other countries, such as Holland, provide early signing intervention for hearing parents of Deaf children. Within the United States, one can find the full range of possible pedagogical philosophies—Oral, Cued Speech, English-based signing, Total Communication, and ASL.

A current trend in the United States is to include in normal classrooms those children who have been historically put into special education classrooms. A common justification for this idea is that special education children need to be around normal peers in order to learn appropriate social skills. For children with behavioral problems, such an argument makes a great deal of sense.

Because Deaf Education falls under the Special Education umbrella, many Deaf children are also being included in typical classrooms. Obviously, this is better than being placed in a special education classroom with children who have emotional or behavioral difficulties. However, the issue is whether a Deaf child can ever be fully included in a classroom with a nonsigning teacher and classmates? A common solution to this problem is to provide an adult who tries to interpret for the Deaf child, using whatever means the child best understands (voicing, gesturing, signing). Is this the least restrictive environment for the child? Does the Deaf child have equal access to all information, activities, and peer relationships? Who are the appropriate role models for a Deaf child—nonsigning classmates and teachers or signing classmates and teachers?

When asked what Bellugi and Klima's research has done for deaf education, Dr. Henry Klopping, Superintendent of the California School for the Deaf at Fremont stated (1998, personal communication), "It made the study of ASL legitimate. It made it palatable to teach ASL in the classroom. In fact, the current Bilingual–Bicultural movement in Deaf education owes a debt to their research." The Bilingual–Bicultural movement suggests that all Deaf children should be given ASL skills first and then be taught English as a second language, while appreciating equally the Deaf and hearing worlds.

Another way to assess the impact of Bellugi and Klima's work on Deaf education is to look at the number of Deaf people who have received training in their lab. Early in their research, Bellugi and Klima realized that it was critical to have Deaf native signers involved in all stages of experimentation, from stimuli development to data coding. For example, Deaf native signers collect the data to ensure that the child is not signing down to the often inferior signing skills of nonfluent hearing experimenters. In Bellugi and Klima's research, the Deaf person is the expert of sign language and Deaf culture, not a victim of hearing impairment. It is important to recognize that a number of the Deaf researchers who have worked in the lab have gone on to earn graduate degrees, including doctorate degrees. Therefore, Bellugi and Klima have directly contributed to the education of many of today's top Deaf researchers.

SUMMARY

At its core, Deaf education is not about theories and experiments. It is about funding structures, pedagogical techniques, standardized test scores, traditions, and goals determined by the majority hearing culture. I believe that the research of Bellugi and Klima has (a) shown the benefits of applying developmental theories and techniques to Deaf-related research and (b) has inspired an increasing number of researchers to analyze other sign languages (British Sign Language, Dutch Sign Language, etc.). As we learn more about how sign languages and spoken languages around the world are the same and different, we learn more about the comprehension and production of visual information in general. The result of such knowledge should lead us to better ways of providing content information to deaf children via signed and written modes. In this way, English literacy once again becomes a mean, not the end, of Deaf education.

The first step in the improvement of Deaf education is the more complete understanding of the Deaf child's linguistic, cognitive, and social development. Although much is left to be discovered, the research program started by Bellugi and Klima discovered many of the big pieces of this puzzle. These pieces are visual and manual, for all to see.

IN MEMORY

"Hope lies in dreams, in imagination, and in the courage of those who dare to make dreams into reality." —Dr. Jonas Salk

I cannot end this tribute without remembering the support and courage to dream offered by Dr. Jonas Salk. It is hard to separate the Bellugi and Klima lab from The Salk Institute. Having worked there, one feels that the interdisciplinary spirit of the Institute has energized the lab (especially Ursula) over the years. By all accounts, Dr. Salk was happy to have sign language research conducted at his institute. In the beautiful vision he had for the world, how appropriate that he included a beautiful language!

REFERENCES

Bettger, J., Emmorey, K., McCullough, S., & Bellugi, U. (1997). Facial processing: The influence of American Sign Language experience. *Journal of Deaf Studies and Deaf Education, 2,* 223–233.

Emmorey, K. (1998). The impact of sign language use on visual-spatial cognition. In M. Marschark & D. Clark (Eds.), *Psychological perspectives on Deafness* (Vol. 2, pp. 19–52). Mahwah, NJ: Lawrence Erlbaum Associates.

Emmorey, K., Kosslyn, S. M., & Bellugi, U. (1993). Visual imagery and visual-spatial language: Enhanced imagery abilities in deaf and hearing ASL signers. *Cognition, 46,* 139–181.

Hoffmeister, R. J. (Sept., 1996). *A piece of the puzzle: ASL and reading comprehension in deaf children.* Paper presented at the Fifth International Conference on Theoretical Issues in Sign Language Research, Montreal, Quebec, Canada.

Lane, H. (1984). *When the mind hears: A history of the deaf.* New York: Random House.

Padden, C. (Sept., 1996). *ASL and reading ability in deaf children.* Paper presented at the Fifth International Conference on Theoretical Issues in Sign Language Research, Montreal, Quebec, Canada.

Parasnis, I., Samar, V., Sathe, K., & Bettger, J. (1996). Does deafness lead to enhancement of visual spatial cognition in children? Negative evidence from deaf nonsigners. *Journal of Deaf Studies and Deaf Education, 1,* 145–152.

Peterson, C. C., & Siegal, M. (1998). Changing focus on the representational mind: Deaf, autistic and normal children's concepts of false photos, false drawings and false beliefs. *British Journal of Developmental Psychology, 16,* 1–19.

Quittner, A. L., Smith, L. B., Osberger, M. J., Mitchell, T. V., & Katz, D. B. (1994). The impact of audition on the development of visual attention. *Psychological Science, 5,* 347–353.

Remmel, E., Bettger, J., & Weinberg, A. (Nov., 1998). *The impact of ASL on theory of mind development.* Paper presented at the Sixth International Conference on Theoretical Issues in Sign Language Research, Gallaudet University, Washington, DC.

Strong, M., & Prinz, P. (1997). A Study of the relationship between American Sign Language and English literacy. *Journal of Deaf Studies and Deaf Education, 2,* 37–46.

Wilson, M., Bettger, J., Niculae, I., & Klima, E. S. (1997). Differing strengths in the deaf and the hearing: Implications for models of short term memory. *Journal of Deaf Studies and Deaf Education, 2,* 150–160.

19

Shared Motoric Factors in the Acquisition of Sign and Speech

Richard P. Meier
University of Texas at Austin

Twenty years ago, when I was lucky to be a research assistant in Ursula Bellugi's lab at The Salk Institute, I noticed certain errors that young children made in sign formation. I particularly remember watching one old reel-to-reel videotape that showed a Deaf child producing a rendition of the sign GUM. The child's hand made appropriate contact at the cheek, but the movement was driven entirely from the shoulder. In contrast, the adult H-hand sign (first and second fingers extended) is articulated with a bending movement at the second knuckle of the extended fingers. A little library research even let me put errors like this one in context: In the development of motor skills, children show a tendency to proximalize movement. In other words, they tend—in movements of the legs and arms—to use articulators that are closer to the torso than an adult would use. I noted a few examples of early signs that seemed to fit this pattern, and then stored the mental and physical 3 x 5 cards away. The mental note stuck with me. The actual 3 x 5 card seems to have been lost in some move.

In the intervening years, I worried about other things: whether iconicity affects acquisition in signed languages, how verb agreement is acquired in American Sign Language (ASL), and whether first signs are produced earlier than first words. Where the acquisition of sign matched speech, I attributed this fact to properties of language and cognition that are not specific to a particular language modality (cf. Meier, 1982, 1987). Where sign and speech seemed to diverge, I, like others, invoked modality-specific factors of perception and production. For example, when Elissa Newport and I argued that the onset of first words in language acquisition is delayed vis-à-vis the onset of first signs (Meier & Newport, 1990), we cited motoric factors as one possible cause.

There are indeed impressive differences between the articulatory systems in speech and sign. In speech, the sound source is internal to the speaker, whereas in sign, the light source is external to the signer. Supraglottal articulation in speech may alter the size of resonance chambers, add an additional chamber (through lowering of the velum), or create audible turbulence. In sign, the movements and postures of the manual articulators modify patterns in the reflected light that falls on the addressee's retina. There are other differences: the oral articulators are largely hidden from view (hence, the inefficacy of lipreading), whereas the manual articulators must be largely visible to the addressee if communication is to take place. Moreover, the oral articulators are considerably less massive than the manual articulators. Not surprisingly, the comparatively massive manual articulators move more slowly than the oral articulators. This fact appears to have consequences for the rate at which individual signs are produced and may promote the relatively simultaneous organization of morphology in signed language, as Ed Klima and Ursula Bellugi suggested in *The Signs of Language* (1979). Last, the manual articulators are paired, although the facts of hemispheric specialization mean that the nondominant hand is by no means independent of the dominant hand.

These are readily apparent differences between the articulatory systems in the two major language modalities. It is tempting, therefore, not to seek motoric explanations for commonalities in linguistic structure or in language development. Instead, a demonstration that the properties of signed and spoken languages are similar tempts us to conclude that the source of that similarity must lie in a linguistic or cognitive capacity that is common to all language modalities. This conclusion is going to be correct in many, if not most, instances: for example, no motoric or sensory explanation is likely to be available for commonalities in what kinds of grammatical notions are encoded by inflectional morphology. But as I suggest here, motoric factors can also be used to explain certain similarities between sign and speech. In some instances, similar structures and similar developmental patterns may arise from commonalities in how the motor systems of speech and sign are organized.

I consider three topics in this chapter: (a) the oscillatory movements that occur in babbling, (b) the movement of articulators in the production of first signs and words, and (c) place of articulation in sign and speech.

OSCILLATORY MOVEMENTS IN MANUAL AND VOCAL BABBLING

Oscillatory movements underlie much of human action, whether walking, chewing, breathing, talking, or signing. Although there are several relatively independent oral articulators (e.g., the lips, tongue tip, tongue dorsum, velum, and mandible), it is the mandible that appears to be the single predominant oscillator in speech (MacNeilage & Davis, 1993). Repeated cycles of raising and lowering the mandible yield a regular alternation between a relatively closed and relatively open vocal tract. This articulatory cycle is perceived as an alternation between consonants and vowels.

It is harder to identify a single, predominant oscillator in sign. Production of a sign such as DAY entails the rotation at the shoulder of the arm. The arm rotates toward the midline along its longitudinal axis. Signs such as MEMBER involve primarily the abduction and adduction of the shoulder. GOOD is articulated through the extension of the arm at the elbow, whereas TREE involves the rotation of the forearm at the radioulnar joint. YES involves the repeated flexion and extension of the wrist. The movement of still other signs is localized at particular articulators within the hand (e.g., TURTLE: repeated internal bending of the thumb; COLOR: repeated extension and flexion of the fingers at the first knuckle; BUG: repeated bending at the second knuckle). Still other signs involve articulation at more than one joint; for example, one form of GRANDMOTHER overlays repeated rotation of the forearm on top of an outward movement excursion executed by extension of the arm at the elbow.

Although the oscillators recruited for speech and sign are quite different, commonalities between prelinguistic gestures and vocalizations could arise from properties of motor organization that are shared by the separate systems controlling the manual and oral articulators. One way to compare the acquisition of sign and speech is to ask when regular oscillatory movements of the oral and manual articulators emerge in infant behavior. MacNeilage and Davis (1993) argued that the reduplicative babbling of 7- to 8-month olds is fundamentally a mandibular oscillation, with the onset of such babbling associated with the maturation of the Supplementary Motor Area (SMA). The SMA is one candidate for a neural substrate that may underlie repetitive movements in both sign and speech: Electrical stimulation of the SMA yields repetitive movements of the hand and arm, as well as syllabic vocalizations (Penfield & Welch, 1951). Thelen (1979) reported longitudinal data from hearing children on rhythmic stereotypies (i.e., simple, repetitive movement patterns such as repeated kicking, foot rubbing, wrist flexion, and wrist rotation) that appear during the first year. Frequencies of rhythmic stereotypies peak at different ages depending on the articulator involved. Stereotypies involving the hand are rare before 24 weeks, then increase rapidly in frequency, peak between 28 and 36 weeks (7–9 months), and subsequently decline. Crucially, manual stereotypies peak at the same age at which canonical babbling emerges in hearing children. The term *canonical babbling* refers to the production of adultlike consonant–vowel syllables (Oller & Eilers, 1988); such syllables are often reduplicated (e.g., [baba] or [dædædæ]). The onset of canonical babbling in a sample of 21 hearing children examined by Oller and Eilers ranged from 6 to 10 months.

The coincidence in timing between peak production of manual stereotypies and the emergence of canonical babbling could be just that—coincidence. But we took the seeming convergence between prelinguistic vocalization and gesture seriously. In 1991, Petitto and Marentette reported that Deaf, sign-exposed children produce manual babbles at roughly the same time that hearing children produce vocal babbles. We reasoned that their finding might be explained not only by the emergence of a linguistic ability that detected syllabic patterns in the parental language, as they suggested, but might also have an explanation in Thelen's earlier finding that stereotypies of the arms and hands are most frequent in 7- to 9-month-old infants. Specifically, we reasoned that both manual and vocal babbling might be understood as recruiting stereotyped actions of their respective articulators. Neither was likely to be just a set of stereotypies, but at least early in development both might depend on such stereotypies. We were also led, by two facts, to hypothesize that meaningless prelinguistic gestures might be relatively common in Deaf and hearing children, irrespective of sign exposure: (a) Thelen (1979) demonstrated that stereotypies of the arms and hands are frequent even in hearing children, and (b) Hearing children without sign exposure do not stand in a position comparable to profoundly deaf children who have limited auditory experience. The delayed onset of canonical vocal babbling in deaf children can be attributed to one or both of two factors: lack of auditory experience with the speech of others (i.e., deaf children are largely deprived of speech input) and lack of auditory feedback from their own vocalizations (i.e., a profoundly deaf child cannot hear his or her own vocalizations well). By contrast, hearing children receive visual feedback from their own gestures and may also view the nonlinguistic gestures produced by the adults around them. Consequently, we reasoned that hearing, sighted children might produce babble-like gestures even in a modality in which they had no linguistic experience. Our reasoning here therefore differs from Petitto and Marentette's (1991): They emphasized the importance of linguistic experience, arguing on the basis of their results that, without experience in a given linguistic modality, children will not babble in that modality.

With this background in mind, we began a longitudinal study of prelinguistic gesture in Deaf and hearing children.

Manual Babbling

To date, we have collected videotaped samples of the prelinguistic development of 8 Deaf and 7 hearing children. Results from 5 of these children (3 Deaf children of Deaf parents and 2 hearing children) are reported in Meier and Willerman (1995). As in the results of Petitto and Marentette (1991), we identified rhythmic, signlike gestures that may reasonably be called manual babbles. These manual babbles were meaningless, nonreferential gestures; although they might be produced in a communicative context of parent–child interaction, no meaning or reference could be assigned to the gesture itself. We also coded "communicative" gestures that referred to objects or locations in the environment (e.g., points, communicative reaching gestures, gimme gestures) or that were otherwise meaningful (e.g., symbolic gestures whose forms were representational, as in a gesture at the face for telephone). To analyze our data, we tracked for each child the proportion of manual babbles (out of the total set of communicative gestures and manual babbles, ignoring signs so as to make the data from Deaf and hearing children comparable). We identified a high proportion of manual babbles in both groups at 7 to 10 months of age. Even when considering the rate at which manual babbles were produced (i.e., normalized rate of production of manual babbles per hour), the two participant groups overlapped. This proportion declined with age in Deaf and hearing children, mirroring an increasing proportion of communicative gestures in both groups. These results differ from those reported by Petitto and Marentette (1991), who found that Deaf and hearing children were sharply differentiated in their production of manual babbles, with only the Deaf children who were exposed to ASL or Quebec Sign Language showing a high proportion of manual babbles. They also found the proportion of manual babbles increased from 10 to 14 months in their Deaf participants.

We were able to replicate the fundamental results of Meier and Willerman (1995) in a follow-up study. In that study, my research group (Cormier, Mauk, & Repp, 1998) reported data from a new group of subjects: 5 Deaf children of Deaf parents (3 girls & 2 boys) and 5 hearing children of hearing parents (4 girls & 1 boy). We analyzed data from videotaped samples recorded at 7, 10, and 13 months: 543 gestures were identified, of which 280 were babbles. As in Meier and Willerman, the hearing and Deaf subjects did not differ in the proportion of their gestures that was constituted by babbles. Nonetheless, two possible effects of the linguistic environment were identified in our studies: in Meier and Willerman, the Deaf subjects showed a significantly greater proportion of multi-cyclic gestures than did the hearing infants. Multicyclic signs (i.e., signs with repeated movement) are a prominent part of the linguistic environment of signing children. In Cormier et al., the Deaf subjects used significantly more pointing gestures than did their hearing counterparts. Pointing signs, which we coded as communicative gestures, are integral to the grammar of ASL in that much of the pronominal system consists of pointing signs.

Overall, the results of our qualitative coding revealed a broad pattern of similarity in the prelinguistic gesture of Deaf and hearing infants. We would not be surprised, however, if future work uncovers more robust effects of sign input on prelinguistic gesture, especially in older infants. A well-defined notion of canonical manual babbling might better reveal such differences and may help reconcile our results and those reported by Petitto and Marentette (1991). However, in the meantime, we (Meier & Willerman, 1995) have advanced the interpretation that the similarity we found between Deaf and hearing infants arises from the fact that manual babbles are rooted in stereotypic motor patterns that are typical of all normally developing children, Deaf or hearing. Effects of linguistic experience are, we expect, likely to be identified against a background constructed of the motoric and developmental factors that are shared by Deaf and hearing infants.

Is vocal babbling similarly rooted in motor stereotypies of the oral articulators? MacNeilage and Davis (1993) argued that the reduplicative babbling of 7- to 8-month-olds is fundamentally a mandibular oscillation. Note that it would be simplistic to view babbling as being just a motor stereotypy or even just a set of stereotypies. For example, reduplicative vocal babbling demands the coordination of oral articulation with respiration and phonation. Nonetheless, we wondered whether we could identify developmental evidence that would directly implicate stereotypic movements of the mandible in the development of vocal babbling. Here, our work on the acquisition of sign pushed us to ask new questions with regard to the acquisition of speech.

Silent Mandibular Oscillations in Vocal Babbling

In the light of Thelen's work on motor stereotypies in infant development and of MacNeilage and Davis's hypothesis that vocal babbling is fundamentally a mandibular oscillation, we wondered whether infants might produce silent mandibular oscillations, a behavior that we refer to as a "jaw wag." The production of such oscillations would demonstrate the existence of a mandibular stereotypy produced without the respiratory and phonatory activity required of normal speech production. We also wondered whether such a behavior, if identified, could be shown to be related to speech development. In Meier, McGarvin, Zakia, and Willerman (1997), we reported a longitudinal study of 14 infants, whose ages ranged from as early as 5 months to as late as 15 months over the course of the study and who were videotaped at biweekly or monthly intervals. We defined a jaw wag as an event of opening and then, without pause, closing the mandible. (Note that an open, then close, sequence was not criterial; events of closing and then opening the mandible were also coded as jaw wags.) An event of jaw wagging may include just one open–close cycle of the mandible, or it may be multicyclic, including two or more open–close cycles. Our definition further specified that a jaw wag could not be accompanied by phonation. Any motion of the mandible that seemed, on the basis of appearance or contextual cues, to be involved in chewing or other ingestive activity was excluded from the category of jaw wags. A total of 213 jaw wags were identified in the longitudinal study. Eleven of 14 children produced jaw wags; among these 11 children were 4 with hearing losses, including 2 children who each had a severe hearing loss. The preponderance of jaw wags recorded on videotape were multicyclic. Across all participants, the median number of cycles—that is, the median number of mandibular oscillations—per token was two. The maximum number of cycles in a recorded instance of jaw wagging was 23. Clear evidence that jaw wags are related to the development of phonated speech comes from examples in which phonated and nonphonated babbling alternate without pause within a single utterance, as shown in Table 19.1.

The jaw-wagging behavior that we documented in this study is a motor stereotypy similar to those that Thelen (1979) identified in many arenas of infant motor development. We demonstrated that, in many children, jaw wags are produced during the babbling stage and are part and parcel of speech development. For those infants who produce silent babbles, the babbled syllable is not an unstructured complex of respiration, phonation, and supraglottal articulation. Instead, the production of jaw wags demonstrates that supraglottal articulation is sometimes disassociated from phonation and, presumably, from respiration. The production of jaw wags by 4 children with hearing losses, including 3 Deaf children of Deaf parents, suggests that speechlike mandibular oscillation is relatively resilient in the face of limited speech input, as well as limited auditory feedback from one's own vocalizations.

The Transition Between Manual Babbling and First Signs

The data in Table 19.1 demonstrate that silent mandibular oscillations are very much a part of vocal babbling. We further know that the properties of vocal babbling predict important aspects of children's productions of first words; for example, when speaking children fail to produce a consonant

TABLE 19.1

Examples of Babbling Sequences That Incorporate Mandibular Oscillation
With and Without Phonation

Alison (a hearing child of hearing parents)
(0;10,0) 1) ma.ma.JW.JW.JW.JW.JW
         2) JW.JW.JW.JW.JW.a.ma.ma.ma
         3) ba.ba.JW.JW.JW.JW.JW.JW.JW.ma.ma.JW.JW.JW

Janey (a hearing-impaired child of hearing parents)
(0;11,1) 4) ba.ba.ba.ba.ba.JW.JW.JW.JW.JW
         5) ma.ma.JW.JW.ma.ma.ma
(0;11,27) 6) ha.βa.βa.JW
         7) a.ya.ba.ba.ba.JW.JW.JW.ba.ba.ba.ba.ba

Katie (a Deaf child of Deaf parents)
(0;9,2)   8) a.JW.JW.a.va

Note: The notation "JW" indicates one cycle of nonphonated mandibular oscillation (i.e., one cycle of jaw wagging).

expected in the adult model, they are likely to have substituted a consonant drawn from the repertoire of frequently babbled consonants (Locke, 1983). Petitto and Marentette (1991) reported data indicating that there is a similarly smooth transition between manual babbles and true signing. In our data (Cheek, Cormier, & Meier, 1998), the articulatory preferences shown in the manual babbling of 5 Deaf and 5 hearing children were generally consistent with the kinds of errors that 4 Deaf children of Deaf parents made in early signing. For example, for both Deaf and hearing infants, a handshape with spread fingers (either the 5-hand with fully extended fingers or a lax variant of the 5) was overwhelmingly the favored handshape in manual babbles; in early signs, the 5-hand was, much more than any other handshape, frequently substituted into children's productions that showed the wrong handshape. Similarly, the downward palm orientation was most frequent for Deaf and hearing in manual babbling and was likewise the most frequent palm orientation in children's signs productions that were incorrect with respect to palm orientation. Results such as these suggest that the articulatory patterns apparent in the gestures that we identified as manual babbles carry over into children's sign productions.

I turn now to a more detailed discussion of children's early production of signs and words.

COORDINATING MOVEMENT IN THE PRODUCTION OF SIGNS AND WORDS

A hallmark of increasing skill in the child is the release of degrees of freedom, as indicated by a reduction of stiffness (a product of co-contraction of agonist and antagonist muscle groups), by the involvement of additional joints in the construction of movement, or by both. Since the work of Gesell and Thompson (1934), a proximal-to-distal trend in infant motor development has been observed, such that children appear to show relatively better early control of proximal segments of the arms and legs than of distal segments (see discussion in Newell & McDonald, 1994).[1] By freezing distal articulators, children reduce the degrees of freedom that must be controlled. Jensen, Ulrich, Thelen, Schneider, and Zernicke (1995) tracked the increasing independence of knee and hip joint actions.

---

[1]Obviously, infants have functional movements of the distal articulators, for example, the neonate's grasping reflex.

All infants kick a lot, but very young infants drive those kicks at the hip joint. By 7 months, they gain greater control over the distal segments and more independent action takes place at the knee and ankle. Similarly, in the development of drawing, the young child primarily uses the shoulder and arm to move a pencil across the page (e.g., Saida & Miyashita, 1979). Only by age 5 do children exhibit the small finger and hand movements characteristic of adults.

The articulation of signs entails the coordination of the shoulder, elbow, forearm, wrist, and fingers within each arm, as well as the coordination of the two arms for those signs that require both. Leaving aside articulation internal to the hand, the child must learn to control at least seven degrees of freedom: three at the shoulder, one at the elbow, one associated with the radioulnar joint of the forearm, and two at the wrist. Articulation at joints that are relatively proximal to the torso (e.g., the shoulder and the elbow) is controlled by projections from both the ipsilateral and contralateral hemispheres, whereas distal articulators (e.g., the wrist and fingers) are controlled by the contralateral hemisphere (Wiesendanger, Wicki, & Rouiller, 1994). The bilateral control over proximal segments may promote the proximal-to-distal trend in motor development that was observed by Gesell and Thompson (1934).

This same proximal-to-distal trend has often been observed in adults who are learning or relearning new motor skills. By proximalizing movement, adults—like children—can reduce the number of degrees of freedom that must be controlled. For example, Newell and McDonald (1994) analyzed handwriting in adults who were asked to use their nondominant arm. They found that participants tended to freeze the wrist and elbow joints. Even with extensive practice, more distal control of the limb segments did not appear in adult writing with the nondominant arm. However, other experiments examining adult acquisition of new motor skills (e.g., a skiing task reported in Vereijken, van Emmerik, Whiting, & Newell, 1992) identified alternative strategies by which adults can manage the problem of controlling a large number of degrees of freedom. Proximalization of movement can also arise as a consequence of neurological damage in adults, specifically in hearing adults with ideomotor apraxia (Poizner, Mack, Verfaellie, Gonzalez Rothi, & Heilman, 1990). Note, however, that proximalization is not an inevitable result of impaired motor control: Brentari and Poizner (1994) reported a tendency to distalize sign movement in a Deaf Parkinsonian signer.

We (Meier, Mauk, Mirus, & Conlin, 1998) examined longitudinal data from 3 Deaf children of Deaf parents, beginning as early as 7 months and continuing until as late as 17 months; each of these children has at least one Deaf grandparent and thus each has at least one parent who is a native signer of ASL. Videotaped gestures were coded as signs only if recognizably related to an adult sign in form and if used in an appropriate context for that adult sign. All signs thus identified were coded on various communicative and articulatory dimensions, including specification of which joints were involved in the execution of the sign. Our coding of the videotaped data yielded 372 tokens of 79 signs.

Because we coded the particular articulators that children used in producing early signs, we were able to test the notion that the development of mature motor skills typically proceeds from proximal to distal articulators. We tested two hypotheses: (a) if an adult sign requires the use of two or more articulators (e.g., the sign GRANDMOTHER), children will more frequently omit the more distal articulator; and (b) if a child uses a joint that would not be anticipated in the adult citation-form sign, that joint will likely be proximal to the most proximal of the expected joints.[2] Both of these hypothesized tendencies proved to be reliable in our data. As an example, consider one girl's production of the sign KITE: In Noel's production of this sign at age 15 months, 2 weeks, she substituted a twisting movement of the torso for the twisting movement of the forearm that characterizes the adult sign. In another instance from the same videotape, Noel signed FINISH by raising the arms at the shoulder; as in the previous example, the expected form of the adult sign would have a rotation of the forearm.

Proximalization of sign movement is not just a developmental fact: In some instances, Deaf mothers enlarge signs that lack path movement by adding a path movement driven by a proximal articulator (Holzrichter & Meier, 2000). Enlarged, proximalized signs may occur in certain sign registers, just as distalized signs may characterize sign whispering; see Brentari (1998) for discussion. Proximalization of sign movement may also occur in the productions of adult learners of signed languages. In a preliminary study (Mirus, Rathmann, & Meier, 1998), we examined how hearing individuals with no knowledge of a sign language imitate videotaped signs drawn from the vocabularies of ASL and German Sign Lan-

---

[2]Again, note that I am not saying that the infant is incapable of any distal articulation: In tokens that we have seen, the sign MILK is articulated by some kind of hand-internal movement, usually a simple opening and closing movement of the hand. In many instances, however, very young children omit hand-internal movement from adult signs that combine a more gross movement of the arm with hand-internal movement.

guage. These naive adults frequently produced more proximalized movements than were present in the videotaped stimuli; this was particularly true in their imitations of signs that require articulation at more than one joint. Our results suggest that a tendency in learners to proximalize sign movement may be an aspect of the acquisition of new motor skills and is not just a product of the immature motor systems of infants.

Do the motoric constraints that I just sketched for the development of sign also characterize speech development? The mature, fluent speaker controls a system in which there are a large number of degrees of freedom associated with the various oral articulators: Within a single syllable, the lips may be first rounded and then spread (as in the word *wean*), the tongue tip and the tongue body may each block airflow (as in *tagged*), the velum may be lowered then raised (as in *snore*), and so on. But the infant may be much more constrained: MacNeilage and Davis (1993) argued that the young babbler has very limited possibilities for independently controlling the tongue within the single mandibular oscillation of a syllable. On this account, the tongue is coupled to the mandible within two available syllable frames: a so-called "pure frame" that yields syllables such as [ba] and a "fronted frame" that yields syllables such as [di]. Further variegation within babbling is due to the varying amplitude of mandibular oscillation; therefore MacNeilage and Davis expected to find babbled sequences such as [dedi] or [dædi] but did not expect [babi] or [bada]. In contrast to the mature system, the infant speech motor control system—as described by MacNeilage and Davis—functions with very few degrees of freedom.

The idea that infants—whether in walking, talking, or signing—are more constrained than adults (in this instance, that they control fewer degrees of freedom than adults) is hardly news. I'd like to suggest a more specific comparison between the problems of controlling complex actions in sign and speech. This comparison suggests that some children confronted by the task of producing words with place contrasts may reduce the number of degrees of freedom that they must control by adopting a speech analog of the proximal-to-distal trend we have seen in sign development.

In the acquisition of phonology literature, there is a well-known phenomenon called place harmony. Children as old as age 3 who are producing true words—in particular, disyllabic words or words containing closed syllables—frequently eliminate place contrasts across consonants; the result is a production that shows place harmony. An analysis of data from 51 children reported in Stemberger and Stoel-Gammon (1991) indicates that coronals are the prime targets of place harmony. In Table 19.2, I listed examples of place harmony drawn from a diary that I'm keeping on my daughter Erica's language development. At the time that I was revising this chapter, Erica was 2;9.

In Erica's speech, as in the data in Stemberger and Stoel-Gammon (1991) and as in the extensive diary data on 2 children reported in Pater (1997), coronals are the prime targets of harmony. Neither bilabials nor

TABLE 19.2

Examples of Consonant Harmony in Erica's Speech. After 2;5, Coronal Stops
No Longer Harmonized to Preceding Velars. The Age at Which Erica
Produced Each Token Is Expressed in "Years; Months, Days."

Coronal stop/Velar stop

1;11,5	[gak]	dog
1;11,14	[gʌk]	duck
1;11,15	[gʌgi]	duckie
1;11,20	[gagi]	doggy
1;11,27	[gak]	dark
2;0,15	[gɪk]	stick
2;1,5	[gʌk]	stuck
2;1,13	[gagiz]	doggies
2;4,1	[kɪkʌ]	tickle
2;4,6	[krʌk]	truck
ca. 2;5,13	[gakr]	doctor
2;5,19	[gark]	dark
2;6,12	[kɪkɪt]	ticket
2;8,21	[stap kakɪŋ]	Stop talking!
2;9,0	[skakiŋ]	stocking
2;9,5	[skɪk]	stick (Compare 2;9,6 [stim] 'steam')

Coronal fricative/Velar stop

1;8,28	[saks]	socks [Correctly pronounced]
1;10,14	[gak]	socks
2;0,8	[gɪk]	music
2;4,7	[kæŋkʸuʷ]	thank you
2;6,15	[gɪk]	music

Velar stop/Coronal stop

2;2,19	[gok]	goat
2;2,19	[kak]	caught
2;2,26	[yoᵘgʊk]	yogurt
2;4,4	[kak]	count
2;5,13	[kʌt]	cut
ca. 2;5,13	[gɪt]	get
ca. 2;5,13	[bʌkɪt]	bucket
2;6,4	[kæts]	cats
2;6,4	[gʊd]	good
2;6,5	[kikæt]	kitty cat
2;6,12	[kɪkɪt]	ticket

velars were ever harmonized; I heard no errors in place of articulation in words such as *buggy, book, bag,* or *milk.*[3] Erica had no trouble articulating coronals in words not containing a place contrast: for example, [dædæ] "Daddy." With a single exception (specifically, one early token of *diaper* in which the /d/ harmonized to [b]), words containing both a coronal stop and a bilabial stop (e.g., *bed, diaper,* and *tubbies,* as in *Teletubbies*) were never subject to harmony, nor were words (e.g., *bus*) containing a bilabial stop and coronal fricative subject to harmony. In just a few words, a labial stop or a labiodental fricative triggered harmony; in those words, the harmonized segment was either an alveolar flap (as in *bottle* [babu]) or a lateral (as in *leaf* [fif]).[4] In contrast, velars consistently triggered the harmonization of coronals: Coronals, including stops, fricatives, affricates, glides, and possibly nasals, were generally subject to harmony in the environment of a velar. Also as reported by Pater, coronals were more likely to harmonize when preceding a velar than when following one. There is a developmental trend in Erica's speech such that perseverative harmony disappeared by 2;6, whereas anticipatory harmony continued well beyond that age (again, see Table 19.2).

An effect of harmony is to reduce the number of distinct articulatory gestures that must be recruited in the production of a single word. The child's production system appears to favor repetitive use of a given articulatory gesture, even at the cost of neutralizing phonological contrasts. Thus, the oscillatory tendencies that characterize the infant's production of jaw wags, of reduplicative vocal babbling, and of much of manual babbling may persist well into children's production of true words. Repetition appears to be a stable attractor state (in the terminology of dynamic systems theory) for neuromuscular systems generally, irrespective of whether or not those neuromuscular systems are responsible for the production of language (Thelen, 1991).

In our analyses of early sign development (Meier et al., 1998), we likewise noted that signing children favor repetition. If an adult sign has repeated movement (e.g., the signs CAT and DOG), that repetition is reli-

---

[3]The 2 participants reported in Pater (1997) showed some instances of bilabials assimilating to velars, but this phenomenon disappears earlier in development than does the harmonization of coronals to velars and is always less consistent. Erica has never, to my knowledge, harmonized bilabials to velars.

[4]Of the participants reported by Stemberger and Stoel-Gammon (1991), equal numbers of children demonstrated the harmonization of coronals to bilabials (18 children) as compared to the harmonization of coronals to velars (19 children); the relative frequency of bilabial versus velar harmony in the speech of any given child was not reported. Stemberger and Stoel-Gammon explained the tendency to harmonize coronals in terms of underspecification theory.

ably preserved in children's output. In contrast, if the adult sign has a single, nonrepeated movement, then children frequently add repetition. For example, 2 of our participants produced versions of the sign BLACK with repeated movement. In the adult language, the citation form of this sign has a single movement across the forehead.

But, returning to the specific issue of place harmony: Given that velars are not the most favored consonants in babbling, why should some children apparently favor velars over coronals in their production of adult words that have a place contrast? There are four points of comparison between the tendency toward proximalization of movement that we noted in our sign data and some children's tendencies to harmonize place contrasts in favor of velars: (1) Even though it is unjointed, the tongue, like the arm, can be thought of as containing linked segments; the tongue tip is distal to the tongue root, whereas the tongue body is proximal. It is of course the tongue tip that obstructs the airflow in coronals, whereas the tongue body does so in velars. As in the arm, the cumulative number of degrees of freedom that must be controlled in the mature movement of a segment increases as one moves from proximal to distal segments; see Poizner, Bellugi, and Lutes-Driscoll (1981) for pertinent discussion in the context of work on the perception of signs. (2) The muscles that raise the tongue body (e.g., the styloglossus) are extrinsic to the tongue, whereas the muscles that raise the tongue tip are intrinsic to it. Similarly, much of the musculature responsible for raising the entire arm (e.g., the deltoid) or rotating it at the shoulder is extrinsic to the arm, whereas the musculature responsible for rotating the forearm (the pronator and supinator muscles) is intrinsic to it. (3) The muscles that raise the tongue tip are relatively small (i.e., fine), whereas the muscles that control the tongue body are relatively large (i.e., gross), just as the shoulder muscles are much larger than the comparatively small muscles that move the fingers. Finally, (4) the anatomical relations between hand and shoulder and between tongue tip and tongue body are such that there is an asymmetrical relation between the control of the distal segment and its proximal counterpart. Mature control of the hand and tongue tip are dependent on mature control of the shoulder and tongue body, respectively. The converse is not true. All these factors may favor velars, when the child attempts an adult word that requires coordinated movement of the tongue tip and tongue body within a single syllable or adjacent syllables.[5]

---

[5]See Cruttenden (1978) for a suggestion regarding the disfavoring of coronals in harmony that is similar to the ones I have made.

The comparisons just made do not by any means constitute a full analysis of place harmony in speech; they hardly rise above the level of speculation. I only hope to have suggested that–despite the very different looking articulators in sign and speech–it may nonetheless be possible to develop interesting, testable hypotheses that suggest common factors underlying motor control in sign and speech. Moreover those motor factors might, in some instances, form the basis of accounts for how development proceeds in the two language modalities.

ACQUIRING THE PLACE FEATURES
OF SIGN AND SPEECH

Thus far, I compared sign and speech movements, specifically the oscillatory movements of certain articulators and the coordination (or inhibition) of the movement of different segments of a single articulator (the tongue or the arm). These kinds of movements are generally not directly specified in the lexical representations of spoken words (i.e., neither mandibular oscillation nor the transition movement between /t /and /k / is phonologically specified) and may only be partially specified in the representations of signs (cf. Brentari, 1998). Can we directly compare children's acquisition of the articulatory specifications of signs and words?

Place of Articulation

Place of articulation is a plausible point of comparison between sign and speech. We (Conlin, Mirus, Mauk, & Meier, 2000; Meier et al., 1998) examined longitudinal data on early sign production in 3 third-generation Deaf children whose ages ranged, as noted earlier, from 7 to 17 months over the course of the study. We considered overall error rate on the three major parameters of sign formation: place of articulation, handshape, and path movements (see Fig. 19.1). The key result here is the very low error rate on place of articulation, especially by comparison to the high rate of error on handshape. This low rate of error on place was also reported in a diary study of 9 children (Siedlecki & Bonvillian, 1993) and in a case study using videotaped data (Marentette & Mayberry, 2000). We interpreted this pattern by reference to the developmental functions for gross and fine motor development: Young children may lack the fine motor control necessary to produce the array of distinct handshapes that occur in ASL, whereas the gross motor control required to reach a location, whether a toy or a place on the child's own body, is well developed before the first year. In essence, achieving correct place of articulation requires the child to reach to a location on his or her upper body.

In contrast to the converging data on the acquisition of place in ASL, the place harmony data discussed earlier raise the possibility that there may be a more prolonged period over which place is mastered in speech (where mastery is defined in terms of accuracy). Grunwell (1982; reviewed in Vihman, 1996) reported that speaking children aged 1;6–2;0 typically have a stable contrast only between bilabials and alveolars. A stable three-way contrast that includes velars reportedly emerges between 2;0 and 2;6 or later.

Most spoken languages have at least a three-way contrast in place of articulation: Typically spoken languages have a bilabial series (e.g., /p b m/), a dental or alveolar series (e.g., /t d n s z/), and a velar series (e.g., /k g ŋ/). Many spoken languages exploit just this three-way contrast. But in addition to these distinctive places of articulation, there are a relatively small number of additional distinctive place specifications that are recruited in other spoken languages: for example, dental, palatal, uvular, and pharyngeal. No spoken language exploits the entire set of available place contrasts. The result is that English, for instance, has six contrastive places of articulation (seven if glottal /h/ is included): bilabial, labiodental, interdental alveolar, alveopalatal, and velar. In contrast, signed languages generally seem to have a large number of contrastive places of articulation. The very early analysis developed in Stokoe, Casterline, and Croneberg

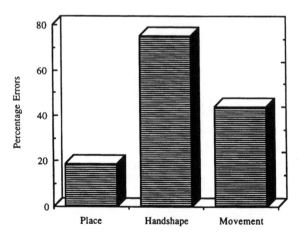

FIG. 19.1. Average error rate on three major parameters of sign formation (from Meier et al., 1998, reprinted with permission from CSLI Publications, copyright 1998).

(1965) proposed 12 contrastive places of articulation for ASL; this is likely an underestimate. Liddell and Johnson (1989) listed 18 "major" locations on the body for ASL. Apparently the size of the contrast set available in ASL for place of articulation does not delay the acquisition of place vis-à-vis the acquisition of place contrasts in spoken languages.

Aside from the sheer number of place contrasts available in signed languages, there is a more interesting difference between signed and spoken languages. At least two independent articulators can commonly obstruct the airflow in speech: The two lips together or the lower lip alone obstruct the air stream in bilabials and labiodentals, respectively. Other place contrasts require occlusion by different regions of the tongue: for example, the tongue tip is generally responsible for the obstruction of airflow in interdentals, dentals, and alveolars; the tongue blade creates the obstruction in palatals; and the tongue body creates the occlusion in velar and uvular consonants. Another independent supraglottal articulator, the epiglottis, is recruited in Arabic and some other languages in the pronunciation of pharyngeal consonants. Use of a particular articulator, whether the lips, a specific region of the tongue, or the epiglottis, is largely, but not wholly, confounded with place of articulation; a clear exception is the contrast between retroflex and nonretroflexed alveopalatals, which differ not in place but in which region of the tongue serves as the articulator. The labiodental and interdental fricatives of English might constitute another exception: At least for some speakers (see Ladefoged, 1982), these two sets may differ not in place but in articulator (i.e., the lower lip vs. the tongue tip).

In ASL, the contacting articulator is, with one small class of exceptions, always the hand, although various regions of the hand may make contact with the specified place of articulation.[6] The small class of exceptions are signs made in neutral space in which the elbow of the dominant arm (or a location somewhat distal to the elbow) contacts the nondominant hand; examples of such signs are TREE, DAY, MORNING, and AFTERNOON.

---

[6]The various contacting regions of the hand in ASL might seem comparable to the different regions of the tongue that obstruct airflow in a spoken language. However, the linguistic status of hand contacting region is not comparable to that of tongue region. Use of the tongue tip versus the tongue dorsum as an articulator is confounded, for obvious physiological reasons, with the production of alveolar versus velar consonants; the tongue tip cannot obstruct the airstream at the velum. In contrast, the choice of contacting region is independent of place of articulation in ASL but is instead partially determined by handshape. Certain handshapes admit only a very limited number of contacting regions. Interestingly, the relation between handshape and contacting region varies across signed languages; for discussion, see Chapters 2 and 6 of Klima and Bellugi (1979).

However, in general, parts of the arm other than the hand (e.g., the forearm or the elbow) are not possible contactors; to my knowledge, there are no ASL signs in which the elbow makes contact with the torso or in which the forearm contacts the chin, forehead, or some other region of the face. Such gestures are possible to produce, although some may seem awkward. In sum, unlike in speech, a single articulator bears the burden of attaining the targeted place of articulation.

Other factors may also facilitate the child's production of correct place values in ASL. As noted earlier, moving the hand toward contact with a phonologically specified region on the face, torso, or nondominant arm largely requires gross motor control of the muscles in the shoulder and upper arm; fine motor control over muscles within the hand is crucial to the production of the correct handshape but is much less important to the production of the appropriate place value. Finally, monomorphemic signs in ASL exhibit very few place contrasts within a given sign.

Acquiring Phonological Contrasts

Tracking the acquisition of particular aspects of sign formation is important and necessary, but direct connections to the speech literature may be few; even the comparison made here between place in speech and sign is not straightforward. Obviously, voicing has no direct counterpart in sign. Similarly, the many handshape postures of ASL and other signed languages have no obvious counterparts in speech. So it is clear that analyses that contrast sign and speech development cannot be limited to the kinds of motor control factors on which I focused in this chapter.

One way of enabling effective comparisons between the development of how children articulate early signs and words may lie in the contrastive function of phonology. Phonological representations in sign and speech specify discrete units of form that allow signs and words with distinct meanings to be distinguished. What factors could affect the number of contrasts controlled at any point in development? (a) Linguistic and cognitive maturation: The child may have the capacity to represent only a limited number of contrasts. (b) Vocabulary size: The number of contrasts represented by the child may in part be a function of the size of the child's vocabulary and the problems in storing a growing vocabulary (cf. Lindblom, 1992). (c) Articulatory skill: The number of contrasts produced by a child might be limited by that child's effective articulatory ability. The first two factors would not lead us to expect differences between sign and speech development. In contrast, the development of the requisite articulatory skills may differ across the two domains and may lead to differing predictions as to the number of contrasts that signing and speaking children can accurately produce at any given point in development.

In analyzing our data from signing children, we are currently examining the number of place contrasts that children control. In very preliminary analyses of longitudinally collected videotaped data from 3 third-generation Deaf children, Heather Knapp and I adopted the criterion that, if a child's production of a given place of articulation is 70% accurate and if the child has correctly produced at least five sign tokens that require that place value, the child is credited with controlling that place of articulation. The children were followed through 15 months in the case of 1 participant and through 17 months in the other two cases.[7] On this criterion, participants were credited with control of either five or six contrasts, depending on the child in question.[8] This finding is consistent with the results of two other studies: Marentette (1995) reported a longitudinal case study of a single signing child whose age ranged from 1;0 and 2;1 over the course of data collection; Marentette concluded that this child controlled eight place contrasts. Based on an analysis of diary data from 9 signing children, Siedlecki and Bonvillian (1993) concluded that 16-month-olds typically use nine places of articulation correctly.

The large number of place contrasts in adult ASL raises the possibility that, by and large, each contrastive place of articulation is associated with a relatively small cohort of signs. This possibility, combined with evidence of children's early mastery of a sizable number of contrastive places of articulation, suggests a possible interpretation of reports of somewhat precocious early vocabulary development in signing children (see Meier & Newport 1990; Abrahamsen, chap. 20, this volume; but also Petitto, 1988, and Volterra & Iverson, 1995, for questions about the reliability of these reports). Newport and I (Newport & Meier, 1985) suggested that such reports might in fact be due to earlier recognition of signs than words by parents and experimenters alike. Early proficiency in the production of place of articulation in sign, when combined with the possibility that a given place of articulation in ASL may have a relatively small cohort of signs associated with it (in particular, a relatively small cohort likely to be

---

[7]Data from 2 of these participants are reported in Fig. 19.1.

[8]A somewhat more conservative criterion would require that, to be credited with contol of a given place of articulation, a child must have correctly produced at least two sign types that require that place. On this criterion, one of these 3 participants would be credited with only three places, even though she had produced 11 correct tokens at each of two other places of articulation.

produced by a young child), may enable parents to recognize their signing children's productions at an early age. On this account, signing children are not attempting signs any earlier than their speaking counterparts; they are just more likely to get through to their parents.

CONCLUSION

Ursula Bellugi and Ed Klima have devoted 30 enormously productive years to the task of identifying what the commonalities between signed and spoken language are and what the sources of those commonalities might be. Those commonalities may be attributable in many instances to the constraints of the human language capacity or to the localization of much of that capacity in the left hemisphere. In this chapter, I suggested that certain commonalities in how signed and spoken languages develop in the child might be attributable to aspects of the child's developing motor capacities that are fundamental to the production of oral and manual gestures. For example, prelinguistic gesture and vocalization may both be built on a foundation of rather stereotyped, oscillatory movements.

Ursula and Ed have also paid continuing attention to modality effects in language; one difference between sign and speech lies in the spatialized syntax of signed languages (Klima & Bellugi, 1979). The visual–gestural modality allows the use of spatial distinctions; the human language capacity does not preclude the syntax of ASL and other signed languages from making crucial use of such distinctions. I have had little to say about modality differences here, although I've noted in passing that, for instance, there may not be a single predominant oscillator in signing as there is in speech; there is no obvious counterpart in sign to mandibular oscillation.

Some differences between sign and speech may be quantitative and not qualitative. For example, the relatively high frequency of iconic signs in adult sign languages has allowed researchers working on the acquisition of ASL to determine that children are largely inattentive to iconicity in acquisition; children may be biased toward treating signs and words as arbitrary, whether or not the adult form truly is arbitrary (cf. Meier, 1991; Newport & Meier, 1985, for reviews). But when they have no alternative, children can exploit iconicity. The invented home signs of deaf children of hearing parents are highly iconic almost by necessity; otherwise they would not be understood by their parents (Goldin-Meadow & Mylander, 1990). Another area of possible quantitative differences lies in the demands that the output systems place on the child and on the adult. We have little reason to think that the demands imposed by articulating words and signs are equivalent at all points in development. If we can understand the differing demands of articulating words versus signs, we may be able to understand whether and how motoric factors interact with other capacities that we would properly ascribe to grammar, for example, the capacity to represent linguistic contrasts or the capacity to combine words or signs within simple sentences.

ACKNOWLEDGMENTS

This work has been supported by a grant (RO1 DC01691) from the National Institute on Deafness and Other Communication Disorders to RPM. I thank Peter MacNeilage, Barbara Davis, Harvey Sussman, and Randy Diehl for discussion of some of the issues raised here. I particularly thank Adrianne Cheek and Heather Knapp for their great assistance in the writing of this chapter.

REFERENCES

Brentari, D. (1998). *A prosodic model of sign language phonology.* Cambridge, MA: MIT Press.

Brentari, D., & Poizner, H. (1994). A phonological analysis of a deaf Parkinsonian signer. *Language and Cognitive Studies, 9,* 69–99.

Cheek, A., Cormier, K., & Meier, R. P. (1998, November). *Continuities and discontinuities between manual babbling and early signing.* Paper presented at the Sixth International Conference on Theoretical Issues in Sign Language Research, Gallaudet University, Washington, DC.

Conlin, K. E., Mirus, G., Mauk, C., & Meier, R. P. (2000). Acquisition of first signs: Place, handshape, and movement. In C. Chamberlain, J. P. Morford, & R. Mayberry (Eds.), *Language acquisition by eye* (pp. 51–69). Mahwah, NJ: Lawrence Erlbaum Associates.

Cormier, K., Mauk, C., & Repp, A. (1998). Manual babbling in deaf and hearing infants: A longitudinal study. In E. Clark (Ed.), *Proceedings of the Child Language Research Forum* (Vol. 29, pp. 55–61). Stanford, CA: CSLI Press.

Cruttenden, A. (1978). Assimilation in child language and elsewhere. *Journal of Child Language, 5,* 373–378.

Gesell, A., & Thompson, H. (1934). *Infant behavior.* New York: McGraw-Hill

Goldin-Meadow, S., & Mylander, C. (1990). Beyond the input given: The child's role in the acquisition of language. *Language, 66,* 323–355.

Grunwell, P. (1982). *Clinical phonology.* London: Crom Helm.

Holzrichter, A. S., & Meier, R. P. (2000). Child-directed signing in ASL. In C. Chamberlain, J. P. Morford, & R. Mayberry (Eds.), *The acquisition of linguistic representation by eye* (pp. 25–40). Mahwah, NJ: Lawrence Erlbaum Associates.

Jensen, J. L., Ulrich, B., Thelen, E., Schneider, K., & Zernicke, R. (1995). Adaptive dynamics in the leg movement pattern of human infants: III. Age-related differences in limb control. *Journal of Motor Behavior, 27,* 366–374.

Klima, E. S., & Bellugi, U. (1979). *The signs of language.* Cambridge, MA: Harvard.

Ladefoged, P. (1982). *A course in phonetics* (2nd ed.). San Diego, CA: Harcourt Brace Jovanovich.

Liddell, S. K., & Johnson, R. (1989). American Sign Language: The phonological base. *Sign Language Studies, 64,* 195–271.

Lindblom, B. (1992). Phonological units as adaptive emergents in lexical development. In C. A. Ferguson, L. Menn, & C. Stoel-Gammon (Eds.), *Phonological development: Models, research, implications* (pp. 131–163). Timonium, MD: York.

Locke, J. L. (1983). *Phonological acquisition and change.* New York: Academic Press.

MacNeilage, P. F., & Davis, B. L. (1993). Motor explanations of babbling and early speech patterns. In B. de Boysson-Bardies, S. de Schonen, P. Jusczyk, P. F. MacNeilage, & J. Morton (Eds.), *Developmental neurocognition: Speech and face processing in the first year of life* (pp. 341–352). Dordrecht, Netherlands: Kluwer.

Marentette, P. F. (1995). *It's in her hands: A case study of the emergence of phonology in American Sign Language.* Unpublished doctoral dissertation, McGill University.

Marentette, P. F., & Mayberry, R. (2000). Principles for an emerging phonological system: A case study of acquisition of early ASL. In C. Chamberlain, J. P. Morford, & R. Mayberry (Eds.), *Language acquisition by eye* (pp. 71–90). Mahwah, NJ: Lawrence Erlbaum Associates.

Meier, R. P. (1982). *Icons, analogues, and morphemes: The acquisition of verb agreement in American Sign Language.* Unpublished doctoral dissertation, University of California, San Diego.

Meier, R. P. (1987). Elicited imitation of verb agreement in American Sign Language: Iconically or morphologically determined? *Journal of Memory and Language, 26,* 362–376.

Meier, R. P. (1991). Language acquisition by deaf children. *American Scientist, 79,* 60–70.

Meier, R. P., Mauk, C., Mirus, G. R., & Conlin, K. E. (1998). Motoric constraints on early sign acquisition. In E. Clark (Ed.), *Proceedings of the Child Language Research Forum* (Vol. 29, pp. 63–72). Stanford, CA: CSLI Press.

Meier, R. P., McGarvin, L., Zakia, R. A. E., & Willerman, R. (1997). Silent mandibular oscillations in vocal babbling. *Phonetica, 54,* 153–171.

Meier, R. P., & Newport, E. L. (1990). Out of the hands of babes: On a possible sign advantage in language acquisition. *Language, 66,* 1–23.

Meier, R. P., & Willerman, R. (1995). Prelinguistic gesture in deaf and hearing children. In K. G. Emmorey & J. Reilly (Eds.), *Language, gesture, and space* (pp. 391–409). Mahwah, NJ: Lawrence Erlbaum Associates.

Mirus, G. R., Rathmann, C., & Meier, R. P. (1998, November). *Proximalization of sign movement by second language learners.* Paper presented at the Sixth International Conference on Theoretical Issues in Sign Language Research, Gallaudet University, Washington, DC.

Newell, K. M., & McDonald, P. V. (1994). Learning to coordinate redundant biomechanical degrees of freedom. In S. Swinnen, H. Heuer, J. Massion, & P. Casaer (Eds.), *Interlimb coordination: Neural, dynamical, and cognitive constraints* (pp. 515–536). San Diego, CA: Academic Press.

Newport, E. L., & Meier, R. P. (1985). The acquisition of American Sign Language. In D. I. Slobin (Ed.), *The crosslinguistic study of language acquisition. Volume 1: The data* (pp. 881–938). Mahwah, NJ: Lawrence Erlbaum Associates.

Oller, D. K., & Eilers, R. E. (1988). The role of audition in infant babbling. *Child Development, 59,* 441–466.

Pater, J. (1997). Minimal violation and phonological development. *Language Acquisition, 6,* 201–253.

Penfield, W., & Welch, K. (1951). The supplementary motor area of the cerebral cortex. *A.M.A. Archives of Neurology and Psychiatry, 66,* 289–317.

Petitto, L. A. (1988). "Language" in the pre-linguistic child. In F. S. Kessel (Ed.), *The development of language and language researchers* (pp. 187–221). Mahwah, NJ: Lawrence Erlbaum Associates.

Petitto, L. A., & Marentette, P. (1991). Babbling in the manual mode: Evidence from the ontogeny of language. *Science, 251,* 1493–1496.

Poizner, H., Bellugi, U., & Lutes-Driscoll, V. (1981). Perception of American Sign Language in dynamic point-light displays. *Journal of Experimental Psychology: Human Perception and Performance, 7,* 430–440.

Poizner, H., Mack, L., Verfaellie, M., Gonzalez Rothi, L. J., & Heilman, K. M. (1990). Three-dimensional computergraphic analysis of apraxia. *Brain, 113*, 85–101.

Saida, Y., & Miyashita, M. (1979). Development of fine motor skill in children: Manipulation of a pencil in children aged 2 to 6 years old. *Journal of Human Movement Studies, 5*, 104–113.

Siedlecki, T., Jr., & Bonvillian, J. D. (1993). Location, handshape, and movement: Young children's acquisition of the formational aspects of American Sign Language. *Sign Language Studies, 78*, 31–52.

Stemberger, J. P., & Stoel-Gammon, C. (1991). The underspecification of coronals: Evidence from language acquisition and performance errors. In C. Paradis & C.-F. Prunet (Eds.), *The special status of coronals* (pp. 181–199). San Diego, CA: Academic Press.

Stokoe, W. C., Casterline, D. C., & Croneberg, C. G. (1965). *A dictionary of American Sign Language on linguistic principles.* Washington, DC: Gallaudet University Press.

Thelen, E. (1979). Rhythmical stereotypies in normal hearing infants. *Animal Behaviour, 27*, 699–715.

Thelen, E. (1991). Motor aspects of emergent speech: A dynamic approach. In N. A. Krasnegor, D. M. Rumbaugh, R. L. Schiefelbusch, & M. Studdert-Kennedy (Eds.), *Biological and behavioral determinants of language development* (pp. 339–362). Mahwah, NJ: Lawrence Erlbaum Associates.

Vereijken, B., van Emmerik, R. E. A., Whiting, H. T. A., & Newell, K. M. (1992). Free(z)ing degrees of freedom in skill acquisition. *Journal of Motor Behavior, 24*, 133–142.

Vihman, M. M. (1996). *Phonological development: The origins of language in the child.* Cambridge, MA: Blackwell.

Volterra, V., & Iverson, J. M. (1995). When do modality factors affect the course of language acquisition? In K. G. Emmorey & J. Reilly (Eds.), *Language, gesture, and space* (pp. 371–390). Mahwah, NJ: Lawrence Erlbaum Associates.

Wiesendanger, M., Wicki, U., & Rouiller, E. (1994). Are there unifying structures in the brain responsible for interlimb coordination? In S. Swinnen, H. Heuer, J. Massion, & P. Casaer (Eds.), *Interlimb coordination: Neural, dynamical, and cognitive constraints* (pp. 179–207). San Diego, CA: Academic Press.

20

Explorations of Enhanced Gestural Input to Children in the Bimodal Period

Adele Abrahamsen
Washington University

When Ursula Bellugi began her studies of American Sign Language (ASL) in 1970, she gathered around her a congenial cohort of graduate students from UCSD's departments of linguistics and psychology plus talented collaborators: Bonnie Gough translated the English sentences we pitched at her into ASL, Susan Fischer added analysis, and Ed Klima raised problems. Ursie, then as now, did everything and ran everything. I have one sharp snapshot in my mind's eye of the earliest days of the weekly research meeting: In a not-yet-furnished suite of rooms in The Salk Institute, several of us sat at a round table on brightly colored little plastic stools shaped like angular hourglasses. On the table were pads of paper that we filled with our puzzlements and in the center were shards of Hershey's Special Dark chocolate that we communally munched. My colleagues who study false memory have made me cautious. After visiting Ursie's new lab last spring and discovering her mental album did not contain the same snapshot of the old lab, I was inspired to check with a couple of other members of the group. The chocolate was confirmed immediately, and the stools eventually (by a member of the next cohort).

There is a different snapshot that everyone recalls and everyone except me finds amusing: Asked to form a "D" while trying to learn fingerspelling,

I formed an "F" instead and replied to the group's protests by repeatedly insisting "It *is* a D!!" This error illustrates one of the group's early findings: Formationally similar handshapes can be confused in sign, just as formationally similar sounds can be confused in speech (Siple, Fischer, & Bellugi, 1977). Although with practice I became less confused, regrettably I never became proficient in fingerspelling or ASL. Instead, I put most of my efforts into my dissertation on memory for verbs (aided by Ed and Ursie, who both served on my committee). Then I took a position at Rutgers and there my interest in language and cognition took a developmental turn. The desire to understand change and then origins pulled me eventually all the way back to the second year of life, and I couldn't help bumping into the manual modality again—now in a different role than it plays in sign language, an earlier role that is transitional toward any language.

In this chapter I discuss a few pieces of my own and others' research comparing the vocal and manual/bodily modalities.[1] I owe to Ursie and Ed my interest in examining more than one kind of language input, especially involving the manual modality, and I share their more recent interest in examining more than one kind of language learner. I also have a particular interest in considering variability in addition to average values in examining outcomes for particular kinds of input and learner. My data points are in a sparse region of the research space that only slightly overlaps Ursie and Ed's galaxy of findings, but I hope to be convincing that this region is part of the foundation for the whole story of language.

My region of the research space is defined in part by its focus on the single-word period of development (typically in full bloom at 12 to 19 months of age, although it begins as early as 9 or 10 months for some children and continues until 26 months or later for others). When children move beyond this period by beginning to combine words into structured sequences, usually they carry forward a starter vocabulary that betokens the influence that adult culture has already imposed. But the single-word period is distinctive in a number of ways that have more to do with the concerns and competencies of 1-year-olds than with the form of parental language. One characteristic is that early words are connected to nonlinguistic contexts, not to other words. Another is that they develop slowly

---

[1]Although manual movements are the most noticeable forms involved in gesturing or signing, other bodily movements are important as well. For example, children learn early that a headshake can convey refusal, and in ASL a variety of grammatical (and even lexical) roles are performed by head postures and facial expressions (see Reilly, chap. 22, this volume). I generally use *manual modality* as an abbreviated term of reference for *manual/bodily modality*.

and not always linearly. For example, at 13 months, a child might start saying *kuh* whenever she wants her cup; the word may then fade away until it reappears at 20 months—less bound to context and more adultlike in pronunciation.

A third characteristic of the so-called single-word period prompts me to call it the *bimodal period* instead: During these intriguing months, gestures can play a role as important as that of words. Our illustrative child might reach for the cup while saying *kuh* or might even put her hand to her lips instead of saying *kuh*.

A number of investigators compared the manual and vocal modalities as vehicles for early communication and symbolization. In brief (some details follow), they found that the two modalities are approximately *equipotential*, with three caveats: (a) by at least one indicator (early, spontaneous production of words and signs), manual forms have an advantage over vocal forms; (b) by another indicator (elicited production of words and signs for children whose exposure to sign begins after 12 months), it is vocal forms that have the advantage; but (c) more important than isolated differences in mean performance is the fact that individual children vary dramatically in their spontaneous production in each modality, often for no discernable reason. Data distributions stretch as wide in the manual modality as in the vocal modality when carefully defined (contrary to my initial expectation), and under some circumstances, all possible individual patterns are well-represented (manual and vocal vocabulary both high or both low; manual leading vocal; and vocal leading manual). Although striking, this variability is transitory: As children exit the bimodal period, they typically acquire the language of their parents, whether it is signed or spoken. Acquiring such a language requires, among many other capabilities, procedures for rapid acquisition of the physical form of numerous lexical items. At the end of this chapter, I present data suggestive that such procedures can be equally powerful in both modalities—one of several incarnations of human bimodality that lie beyond the bimodal period.

Our understanding of the bimodal period comes primarily from studies of children growing up in naturally occurring input situations, in which parents make some use of gesture but primarily communicate via a structured language. When this is a spoken language, such as English, researchers generally compare children's words to their manual gestures. This is informative about the most typical course of events, but any differences between words and gestures could be due to differences in the qualities and quantity of parental input rather than something about the modalities as such.

Although gestures are forms that are used intentionally to express meanings, like the vocabulary of a language, parental gesturing lacks syntactic structure and other kinds of systematicity that permeate parental language. Gestures also have a restricted range of functions: For both parents and children, gestures tend to be deictic, performative, interactive, social, and/or routinized (e.g., pointing, reaching to request an object, nodding yes, waving bye-bye). Words can perform these functions, but more notably, they can be disembedded from actions and interactions in order to convey information. For example, common nouns can be used to descriptively refer to a class of animate or inanimate objects or to a member of a class; proper nouns can be used to nondescriptively refer to a particular individual; and verbs and adjectives can be used (in part) to specify actions and attributes. The earliest such uses collectively can be called *labeling* (or *naming*). When words are combined syntactically, reference gets more complex and predication becomes a separate function (see McNamara, 1982). Hence, it is important to observe children acquiring a signed language such as ASL, for whom input in the manual modality exhibits systematicity and a full range of functions, and to compare acquisition of signed and spoken languages.

In naturalistic studies of this kind, input in the manual modality has been treated essentially as a binary subject variable: A child has been exposed either to ordinary gesturing (along with spoken language) or to a signed language (along with gesturing and varying degrees of exposure to spoken language). My own research originated in the following question: What if gestural input is enhanced within an otherwise ordinary spoken-language environment so as to include a number of gestures for animate and inanimate objects, actions, and attributes? Deliberately manipulating the manual-input variable in this way opens up a previously empty region of the research space. As it turns out, most 1-year-olds take to *enhanced gestural input* like ducks to water, and this motivates adults to engage in an increasing flow of gestural interaction.

To enhance input in the manual modality, an adult learns or invents new gestures (sometimes by adapting existing forms) and uses them simultaneously with selected nouns, verbs, and adjectives in the speech stream. These gestures inherit the meanings of the words they accompany and thereby gain the potential to function not only as requests but also as labels and later in more advanced ways. With some hesitation at proliferating terminology, I use *object-related* as a relatively neutral term for gestures (or words) that specify animate and inanimate objects and their actions and attributes; then such terms as *request*, *label*, *reference*, and *predication* can be added to convey their emerging functions.

Like words, such object-related gestures should not be bound to particular contexts, but sometimes they start out this way for children in the early bimodal period. For Linda Acredolo and Susan Goodwyn, who have done the most extensive research on what I call enhanced gestural input, such gestures qualify as *symbolic gestures* once they satisfy certain criteria (Goodwyn & Acredolo, 1993; Acredolo, Goodwyn, Horobin, & Emmons, 1999; based in part on Snyder, Bates, & Bretherton, 1981): (a) multiple uses (e.g., a word must be reported in at least three biweekly parent interviews); (b) spontaneous use (vs. imitated or elicited); (c) noninstrumental use; (d) context-flexible use, as evidenced by more than one exemplar of the same class (possibly including an absent referent), the same exemplar in more than one situation, or the same exemplar in more than one function (usually requesting and labeling). Two additional criteria have the effect of excluding symbolic play schemes, such as briefly putting a toy cup to the lips: (e) the gesture must be communicative in intent; and (f) it must be empty-handed. Some investigators use the term *referential* equivalently to *symbolic*; others use it equivalently to *object-related* (encompassing both symbolic and nonsymbolic usage); and some restrict it to nominals.

In the remainder of this chapter, I sketch some of the most salient results on the bimodal period obtained from naturally occurring input situations and then show how research on enhanced gestural input produces a more complete picture. Just 11 of the participants in my own study of enhanced gestural input were typical bimodal-period children at onset (and 3 others were older). Hence, any persuasive power of this picture relies heavily on the work of others—especially the unparalleled contributions of Acredolo and Goodwyn.

NATURALISTIC STUDIES OF THE BIMODAL PERIOD

Children Acquiring a Spoken Language

At first glance, the two modalities seem to play quite different, complementary roles in the bimodal period and to develop by different timetables for children acquiring a spoken language. A deeper look uncovers the potential for greater parity.

Milestones. The initial milestone events are the emergence of the first few gestures in the few months preceding the first birthday, followed by the appearance of the first word close to the first birthday (on average). The inventory of gestures and words increases across the next half-year (slowly and steadily for most children), but then gestures level off as words burgeon. (This transition was already underway for most of the 20-month-olds studied by Capirci, Iverson, Pizzuto, & Volterra, 1996.)

Forms and Functions. The earliest gestures are nonsymbolic and context bound. They also are remarkably similar across children and include ritual requests, showing, giving, and communicative pointing (Bates, Benigni, Bretherton, Camaioni, & Volterra, 1979). Later gestures are more diverse, but still most are deictic, performative, social, and/or embedded in routinized actions or interactions. Often these are imitative (e.g., finally waving bye-bye in response to a parent who has been enthusiastically waving and saying "bye-bye!"), but some gestures are invented and initiated by the child (usually by adapting them from a song or other routine involving gestures or from an action schema, e.g., raising both arms as a request to be picked up). In form, the prototypical gesture is manual (a handshape or movement of one or both hands and arms, for example, an extended arm and clenched-unclenched hand as a ritual request), but as already noted, some gestures involve other bodily movements. What all gestures have in common is that a reasonably consistent form in the manual/bodily modality is used intentionally to express a reasonably consistent meaning or function and that their primary connections are to contexts and vocal forms, not to other gestures. (Limited kinds of gesture combinations make an occasional appearance, as described later; they reflect an important transitional capacity to combine elements but do not rise to a level I would credit as truly syntactic.)

Words also are meaning-bearing forms, but they occupy a particular, intermediate level (between morphemes and phrases) in the sentences of a culturally transmitted language. Hence, by definition they *can* and must be combined syntactically and *cannot* be wholly invented by the child—two characteristics, beyond modality, by which they apparently differ from ordinary gestures. Also, as noted earlier, words seem to exhibit a broader range of functions than do gestures and in particular are used symbolically (e.g., as context-flexible labels for a class). Generally, at least some of the first 10 words qualify as symbolic (about half for "referential" children and about two for "expressive" children according to Harris, Barrett, Jones, & Brookes, 1988).

More on Forms and Functions. That is the rough sketch. Digging a little deeper reveals that most of the differences are not absolute. First, *words are not as distinct from gestures as they first appear.* Children in the bimodal period use a variety of vocal forms meaningfully. As shown by Halliday (1975) for one child in detail, some are clearly idiosyncratic and transitory and others apparently have their origins in the adult words they resemble. Including all of these in the inventory of vocal forms studied (i.e., not limiting the count to those that approximate adult words) should reduce both the age of emergence and the percentage that are object-related, increase the number that are context bound, and add some that are invented—making the vocal modality more similar in these respects to the manual modality. In fact, investigators such as Bates et al. (1979) and Lock (1980) used the term *vocal gestures* for certain early vocal forms, thereby emphasizing how they functioned rather than whether their forms resembled words. For arguments that the earliest signs and words may have little if any real distinction from idiosyncratic manual and vocal gestures used at the same age, see Abrahamsen, Cavallo, and McCluer (1985), Caselli and Volterra (1990), and Volterra and Caselli (1985).

Despite their resemblance to adult forms, it is not until signs or words become incorporated into a structured linguistic system that they complete the process of differentiation from gestures and forever leave behind the bimodal period. The insufficiency of form alone as the child exits the bimodal period struck Bellugi and Klima (1982) when they noticed that children's mastery of gestural pointing did not ease the transition to use of the same forms within the pronominal system of ASL. The hard part was developing the underlying system, a process traced by Pettito (e.g., 1988).

Just as important to this deeper look, *gestures are not as distinct from words as they first appear.* Children can and do use a small number of gestural labels, even without enhanced gestural input. The most impressive demonstration is in the doctoral dissertations of Susan Goldin-Meadow and Heidi Feldman (see Feldman, Goldin-Meadow, & Gleitman, 1978). Observing children who were receiving spoken language input (but Deaf and therefore not in a position to encode much of it), they found that these children invented numerous "characterizing gestures." Defined similarly to object-related gestures, these clearly attained symbolic status. Eventually they entered into combinations with each other and with deictic gestures (pointing or showing); importantly, many of these expressed relational meanings between two symbols (e.g., Agent + Action). This research provided a formal description of the *homesign* manifestation of linguistic capacity.

A skeptic might respond that necessity was the mother of invention for these children, but Goldin-Meadow and Morford (1985) and others have demonstrated that even ordinary hearing children in an ordinary spoken-language environment invent or pick up a few object-related gestures. Caselli (1983) observed the following developmental sequence (reexpressed in our current terminology): context-bound deictic gestures, context-bound object-related gestures, and finally (around the same time as early words), context-flexible object-related gestures. Volterra (1983) replicated this decontextualization of gestures, and she ascribed symbolic status only to those that were fully context flexible (rather than those that had reached an initial level of context flexibility as in Acredolo and Goodwyn).

The first studies of object-related gestures that involved more than a handful of children were by Acredolo and Goodwyn (1988). In their longitudinal study, 16 mothers kept weekly records of their children's gestures and contexts of use from age 11 months to 20 months. Counting only those gestures that met symbolic criteria, the number per child ranged from 1 to 17 (mean 5.06). The average child had two or three object gestures (usually based on an action performed *on* an object, e.g., sniffing to name FLOWER, or an action performed *by* an agentive object, e.g., panting to name DOG), one or two request gestures (e.g., making a knob-turning movement to request going OUT or moving the hands up and down to request playing the PIANO), and one attribute gesture (e.g., blowing with the mouth for HOT or raising the arms for BIG). Similar results were obtained in a cross-sectional study in which 38 mothers of 16- to 18-month-olds were interviewed (range 0–16 and a mean of 3.9 symbolic gestures—a slightly smaller mean because there is one less gesture in the object category, on average).

More recently, Volterra and her colleagues have expanded their investigations to examine the number and kinds of gestures used by children acquiring Italian (see Volterra & Iverson, 1995). Based on a parental questionnaire for 23 children at 12 months (and not applying symbolic criteria), they found the average child had 11 gestures and 5.5 words. These and other findings indicated to them that presymbolic communicative development is bimodal but may exhibit a gestural advantage for at least some children.

Later they videotaped 12 of the children at 16 and 20 months of age interacting with the mother. One of the most valuable aspects of this project is their decision to code every conceivable kind of gesture (Iverson, Capirci, & Caselli, 1994). In the vocal modality, their word counts included nonword forms with fixed reference (e.g., *baba* for bottle) but not such forms as the urgent *uh uh uh* that may accompany a reaching gesture. (Inclusiveness must be considered when comparing manual and vocal counts.)

Iverson et al. (1994) found that variations on the usual four deictic gestures were prominent, yielding 82% of the tokens at 20 months. There were just 58 additional gesture types across the 12 children at 20 months; they called this mixed bag of nondeictic gestures "representational gestures." Among them, 26 (about 2 per child) were labels: 8 were empty-handed object gestures (usually based on a related action) and 18 specified predicates (actions like DRIVING or attributes like TALL). Another 23 were conventional (social and routinized gestures, such as waving BYE-BYE, shaking the head NO, or putting a finger to the lips for QUIET), 4 were predicates for which an object was in hand (e.g., SQUEEZE a lemon), and 5 were object gestures for which an object was in hand (e.g., briefly "drinking" from a cup as an enactive name, CUP; these are usually regarded as playing a transitional role into symbolic play and have been studied extensively by Bates and her colleagues). In the earlier session (age 16 months), there were 39 different representational gestures with a somewhat different distribution across these subcategories (e.g., fewer predicates, more gestures with an object in hand).

Volterra (1983), Goldin-Meadow and Morford (1985), and Capirci et al. (1996) all found as well that gestures play a transitional role toward syntax by providing a vehicle for simple two-item combinations. Gesture + Gesture combinations usually emerge first (around 15 months). However, in contrast to the findings on Deaf children, one or both of the combined gestures is always deictic (e.g., POINT [at cookie] + GIVE). Within 1 to 3 months, Word + Gesture combinations arise and quickly dominate—especially semantically redundant (and usually simultaneous) combinations like POINT [at cookie] + *cookie* or BIG + *big*, but joined within another 1 to 3 months by more informative combinations like SHOW [torn page] + *broken*. After yet another 1 to 3 months (about 6 months after the first two-gesture combinations), Word + Word combinations make their appearance, and this is finally the means by which two object-related symbols get combined (e.g., *little + kitty*). (There is only one example across the three studies of a combination that included two object-related or other representational gestures.) Soon thereafter, truly syntactic utterances sprout in the vocal modality. Individual object-related gestures show little further elaboration, but a flow of gesturing that is temporally coupled to speech eventually develops (David McNeill called this "gesticulation" and published a landmark book exploring it in 1992).

Children Acquiring a Signed Language

What happens when the referential potential of the manual modality is given the same kind of encouragement as is typically available in the vocal modality? Some preliminary answers are available from studies of children whose parents use a signed language such as ASL as the primary language in the home.

Folven and Bonvillian (1991) provided the most extensive data on the developmental sequence by which various functions emerge in the manual modality for children whose primary language environment is ASL. They combined diary and videotaped data in a longitudinal study of 9 children (8 hearing, 1 Deaf) with at least one Deaf parent. When a child formed a recognizable ASL sign in an appropriate context, it was classified as non-referential if it imitated an immediate model, was part of a routine, anticipated a familiar routine, or named a familiar action. A sign was classified as referential if it was used for "naming new things," such as DOGGIE for an unfamiliar dog or CRY when a baby is crying in a store . Because they based this criterion on Bates et al. (1979), it is likely that varied but not completely unfamiliar exemplars were sufficient. To maintain a consistent terminology within this chapter, I call their referential forms *symbolic signs*. However, it should be noted that for Folven and Bonvillian (1991), this class did not include forms used only to request familiar items, whereas Acredolo and Goodwyn would credit them if multiple exemplars or situations were involved.

Consistent with earlier work by Folven and Bonvillian, signs appeared at earlier ages than are usually cited for words: the first sign occurred by a mean age of 8.2 months and the first 10 signs by a mean age of 13.6 months ($n = 9$). Several investigators had criticized the original claim of early signs on the grounds that inadequate functional or linguistic criteria had been applied (e.g., Pettito, 1988). Indeed, when Folven and Bonvillian limited their analysis to signs qualifying as symbolic ($n = 8$ because contextual information was not available for one child), the first sign was not credited until a mean age of 12.6 months—4 months later than the first nonsymbolic sign and about the same time that most children produce their first symbolic word. In the interim, the four usual deictic/performative gestures appeared, a sequence consistent with other studies in which pointing precedes the first symbolic word. Finally, the children in this study had varying amounts of exposure to spoken language despite the predominance of ASL in their homes. Their first words (both symbolic and nonsymbolic) were observed at an average age very close to that of their first symbolic signs.

With smaller numbers of children involved, Caselli (1983) and Volterra (1983) both found that their own characterizations of gestural development applied equally to children acquiring a spoken or a signed language. For example, Volterra studied 3 children learning Italian and 1 learning Italian Sign Language (LIS) and found developments in the manual modality to be the same until the point at which the child learning LIS produced combinations of two representational items in the manual modality. Those learning Italian produced combinations of representational items only in the vocal modality. Most important here, though, is that all of the children in both studies—whether their primary linguistic input was signed or spoken—did attain a small inventory of object-related (and other representational) gestures.

Taken together, the research results on children acquiring a signed language and those acquiring a spoken language suggest that the earliest signs may not really differ from gestures during the bimodal period of development. In addition to inventing their own gestures, which eventually meet symbolic criteria, both sets of children pick up some of their parents' gestures. Those whose parents use a signed language also pick up some of their parents' signs, using the same process of approximating a parental model. The difference comes at the end of the bimodal period, when only those children who are acquiring a signed language start combining object-related forms in the manual modality. As Volterra has argued, only then are the child's signs actually signs (vs. symbolic gestures that resemble parental signs).

The most obvious way to move more deliberately toward a within-subjects strategy would be to study hearing children with one Deaf and one hearing parent who get lots of exposure to both a signed language and a spoken language (usually not simultaneously). Data do exist on this kind of situation, but generally limited to individual cases (e.g., one is briefly discussed by Meier & Newport, 1990). A good way to get much larger amounts of quantitative data on the consequences of bimodal input is to make enhanced gestural input available to children. A bonus to such a strategy is that the results can then be compared to those on ASL acquisition to get some idea of how much difference the considerable reduction in manual input makes. Hence, we turn now to the question raised earlier: What if gestural input is enhanced within an otherwise ordinary spoken-language environment so as to include an unusually large number of object-related gestures?

ENHANCED GESTURAL INPUT DURING
THE BIMODAL PERIOD

Studies of enhanced gestural input occupy a previously almost-empty region of the research space on language acquisition. Figure 20.1 is a sketch of the part of this space that is formed by two dimensions for the nature of *input to the learner* and one dimension for different *types of learners*. Some salient research areas and researchers are located within the space. Not shown are dimensions involving the *age of the learner*, such as the age at which input begins and the age at which language is being assessed; these ages lie somewhere within the bimodal period for most of the research areas shown.

The first thing to notice is the positioning of enhanced gestural input on the manual input dimension. That dimension is anchored by two naturally occurring types of input—ordinary gesturing and ASL—and between these lie a variety of systems deliberately designed to accompany speech. Many borrow signs from ASL, but in construction and purpose they break into two distinct groups: Enhanced gesturing can be viewed as an extension or enhancement of ordinary gesturing, whereas Manually Coded English (MCE) systems are sign–speech hybrids that manually encode aspects of English grammar and morphology and obtain a large open-class vocabulary from ASL citation forms and, often, fingerspelled English words.

Enhanced gesturing has ordinary gesturing as its base but adds some 10 to 100 open-class vocabulary items (usually signs borrowed from ASL or gestures that are adapted from action schemes or invented; for the learner, they inherit the meanings of the English nouns, verbs, and adjectives that they accompany). The resulting inventory of gestures is much more heavily loaded in the object-related category than is ordinary gesturing, and may feature some additional social gestures as well (e.g., HELLO, I-LOVE-YOU). Although more than one word in a sentence may be accompanied by such gestures, there is no explicit encoding of syntax or grammatical morphology in the manual modality—not that of English or ASL or any invented system.

The systems themselves are not so much a continuum as a binary dimension that has sprouted variants engineered to be more Englishlike. However, they are ordered left-to-right to represent increasing frequency with which a child is likely to be exposed to object-related gestures or signs.[2] The second dimension comes closer to being a continuum; it cap-

---

[2]Note that this differs in a number of respects from Adam Kendon's continuum (see McNeill, 1992, pp. 37–40). Kendon's goal was to isolate and define different types of gestures, whereas the manual input dimension distinguishes different input situations (each a particular mix of different types of gestures).

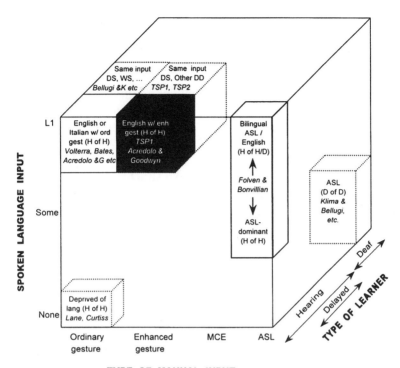

TYPE OF MANUAL INPUT

FIG. 20.1. Part of the research space for language emergence in two modalities. Research areas (labeled interior cubes) are each situated at the intersection of a particular manual and vocal input situation and a particular type of learner. Comparisons across research areas enable a better understanding of bimodal development. For example, the current chapter examines studies along the top front edge of the research space (cubes with solid borders), in which typical children provided with enhanced gestural input (black cube) are compared with similar children exposed to ordinary gesture or to ASL. Note that the original compelling comparison by Bellugi and Klima that inspired others to search and research this space involves naturally occurring input situations at two far corners: findings on Deaf individuals acquiring and using signed languages considered against the body of knowledge about hearing individuals acquiring and using spoken languages. More recently, they pioneered comparisons of Williams syndrome (WS) to Down syndrome (DS); this region, and others not discussed in the current chapter, have dotted borders.

---

[2] Note that this differs in a number of respects from Adam Kendon's continuum (see McNeill, 1992, pp. 37–40). Kendon's goal was to isolate and define different types of gestures, whereas the manual input dimension distinguishes different input situations (each a particular mix of different types of gestures).

tures the fact that exposure to spoken language may range from none through the level typical of a first language.

It turns out that enhanced gesturing along with speech is a highly appropriate environment for children in the bimodal period. It appears to be even better suited than ordinary gesture to the mixing of modalities that characterizes this phase of development. However, enhanced gesturing had its origins in attempts beginning in the 1970s to adapt simultaneous communication to the needs of older hearing children with delayed speech due to such conditions as autism, cerebral palsy, and Down syndrome. Usually the original intention was to make structured language available in the manual modality, and it was not uncommon for the earliest papers to identify that language as ASL. However, the actual input (and output) tended to be closer to enhanced gesturing than to any natural or designed sign language. In any event, these signs qua gestures did prove to be more easily learned than words for many of the participating children.

It occurred to me that there would be considerable benefit in filling a then-empty region of the research space by making enhanced gestural input available to a different population of learners: normally developing hearing children who were in or near the bimodal period of development. First, the results could be inserted into the gap between those on ordinary gesture (at one extreme) and early ASL vocabulary (at the other extreme) to get a more complete picture of each modality's potential during the bimodal period. This newly occupied part of the research space is shaded in Fig. 20.1 (black cube), and the comparison areas have solid borders. Second, if delayed children (older, but developmentally in the bimodal period) were provided with the same enhanced gestural input, we might begin to uncover the developmental roots of later modality assymmetries in particular subgroups of children. This region is directly behind the black cube (with dotted borders).

In the remainder of this section, I focus on the first goal: understanding the typical range of achievements in the two modalities during the bimodal period. I begin with a very brief overview of Toddler Sign Program 1 (TSP1), which I developed in order to study the consequences of using enhanced gestural input along with spoken English for a variety of children (see Abrahamsen et al., 1985, for more details). Then I turn to newer studies from Acredolo and Goodwyn, who followed up their naturalistic research by designing a very user-friendly variety of enhanced gestural input and obtaining extensive data on a large number of children. To my knowledge, these two sets of studies are the primary sources of information on typical development when enhanced gestural input accompanies adults' child-directed speech.[3]

Toddler Sign Program: Overview and a Prediction

Design of enhanced gestural input. In the 1980s, my collaborators and I provided enhanced gestural input to several groups of children. When originally designing our bimodal input, a convergence of considerations led to the decision to use signs borrowed from ASL simultaneously with corresponding target words of English. ASL signs were not the only possible manual forms (Acredolo and Goodwyn used invented, iconic forms), but they were familiar and convenient. Omitting any independent syntax or morphology from the manual modality was also not the only possible decision, but I viewed it as the only reasonable one for two reasons. First, I knew it would be difficult to bring any appropriate sign grammar into alignment with the grammar of English for use in bimodal utterances. Second, the input had to be within the grasp of adults with little or no previous experience with sign language—teachers, parents, and research assistants.

Because my interest was in vocabulary acquisition prior to syntax, I decided to make explicit that only a small target vocabulary would be bimodally expressed; I called this *unbalanced bimodal input* because grammar and many words were instantiated only in the vocal modality, and because input was simultaneous in the two modalities. I also suggested that, properly speaking, the children's signs should be referred to as *sign-gestures* if nonsymbolic, *sign-symbols* if symbolic (symbolic signs or gestures in the terminology of the current chapter), and *signs* if linguistically structured (Abrahamsen et al., 1985, pp. 183–184; cf. the terminology proposed by Erting & Volterra, 1990, and an earlier 1986 version reproduced there). Then, as now, I usually left these distinctions implicit, using the term *sign* in a second, superordinate sense for convenience in referring to our target vocabulary. Most often, these items would have qualified as sign-symbols (but not as linguistic signs) when used by the

---

[3]Holmes and Holmes (1980) contributed a pioneering case study in which they exposed their hearing child to manually coded English along with spoken English; it is often compared to Prinz & Prinz's (1979) study of a hearing child acquiring ASL as well as spoken English. Of the two studies, Holmes and Holmes comes closest to enhanced gesturing.

adults who were learning them for this project, and as sign-gestures or sign-symbols when picked up by the children. My focus in this chapter is on object-related signs, sometimes with symbolic criteria applied and sometimes not; one set of social signs was also used in the program.

Participants. The first wave of participants were 25 hearing children in an infant stimulation program for ages 0 to 3 years, for whom both chronological ages (CA) and developmental ages (DA) were available.[4] Twelve were developmentally delayed, 4 with Down syndrome and 8 with other biologically-based disorders (including 4 with hydrocephalus— 3 treated by shunts and 1 treated medically). Of the 13 normally develop- ing children, 9 were in an age range approximating the bimodal period (CA 13–25 months; DA 12–25 months) at the beginning of the 9-month study and 3 were older (CA 31–32 months; DA 29–33 months). Addition- ally, data were obtained from 2 children whose participation had already begun before or near the onset of the bimodal period (rather than after it was already underway): The remaining child in the infant program (pseu- donym Shawn; CA 12 months, DA 11 months at onset) and 1 child who received the same kind of enhanced gestural input but only at home (inconsistently beginning at CA 5 months and almost daily by late in her first year; her pseudonym is Natasha, and a single developmental assess- ment at 10 months placed her at DA 9–10 months). Their outcomes dif- fered from those of the other children and are presented separately.

Procedure. I and my research assistants conducted two to four half- hour structured sessions of bimodal input per week, and bimodal input was also provided to some extent by teachers during other activities and by parents using specially designed picture books with illustrations of the targeted signs. Approximately every 6 weeks, the same picture books were used to assess the current set of target sign–word pairs and to pretest the next set: "What's that?" to elicit production and a model to elicit imitation plus follow-ups such as "Can you sign it?" Two measures were calculated for signs and words separately: the percentage that were produced (called

---

[4]A child's DA is determined by developmental assessments for which norms are available. A 15- month-old (CA) with a DA of 13 months is developmentally at the level of an average 13-month-old. Children within the same DA range (e.g., 16–19 months) should perform more homogeneously than children selected because they fall within the corresponding CA range. Another advantage of group- ing children by DA range is that delayed children can be compared to normally developing children who are at the same level of development.

production in the 1985 paper and *elicited production* here) and the percentage that were produced and/or imitated (called *production/imitation* in the 1985 paper and *elicited imitation* here). These measures yielded a good range of quantitative data for comparing groups, ages, and modalities.

Instances of spontaneous production were also recorded based on researchers' direct observations and reports from teachers and parents. For the current chapter, these records were combined with the elicitation results to obtain cumulative measures of sign types and word types at two levels of evidence. Cumulative signs and cumulative words included any item produced at least once (whether elicited or spontaneous). Cumulative symbolic signs and cumulative symbolic words were based on stronger criteria similar to those of Acredolo and Goodwyn: An item was credited if it was produced at least three times involving at least two contexts (e.g., picture book, mealtime, infant room, home, zoo) or functions (e.g., labeling, requesting), and at least one use had to be spontaneous rather than elicited. Contrary to Acredolo and Goodwyn's nonsymbolic measures, imitations did not count (given the amount of eliciting we did, it seemed advisable to err on the side of conservatism).

A Within-Group Prediction From a Between-Groups Result. Abrahamsen et al. (1985) provided a number of results for elicited imitation and production on this first wave of children, including both individual and group data (note, however, that a printer's error resulted in mislabeling of the two subparts of Table 2; the correct DA ranges are in the table title). In what follows, I summarize those results for subsets of the 12 normally developing children who were older than 12 months when they began receiving enhanced gestural input. I also provide individual results for the 2 children whose input began earlier than 12 months, as well as new data on cumulative vocabulary. First, though, I must briefly convey the major finding from the entire group of 25 normally developing and developmentally delayed children, because it was the impetus for closely attending to measures of variability in the present analyses.

We found that our three groups of participants, when equated for overall developmental level (DA 12–19 months or 20–26 months), all performed *similarly on signs* but differed dramatically in acquisition of words First, children with Down syndrome produced and imitated significantly *fewer words* than the normally developing group (i.e., below expectation based on their overall developmental level). Conversely, our particular sample of children with hydrocephalus or other conditions causing delayed development imitated significantly *more words* than the normally developing group (i.e., above what would be expected based on their overall developmental level). This was an island of strength; their elicited production of words was only at the level expected for their developmental level. Yet, we viewed it as a possible precurser to a characteristic of some older children and adults with hydrocephalus: speaking verbosely but with minimal meaning in production ("cocktail chatter" syndrome) or imitation (echolalia).

Hence, the answer to the question in the title of Abrahamsen et al. (1985)—"Is the Sign Advantage a Robust Phenomenon?"—was *no*. Depending on biological status of the learner and the measure examined, one could find (a) no difference, (b) a sign advantage, or (c) a word advantage. What was robust was the *timetable* by which signs themselves emerged, in contrast to the differing timetables for words in biologically different groups. Because the direction of advantage is due entirely to whether words are behind or ahead of schedule, it is more accurate to speak of a word disadvantage than a sign advantage (as pointed out by Meier and Newport, 1990, in arguing that peripheral factors delay the emergence of early words relative to early signs). In retrospect, our choice of title for the 1985 article was somewhat misleading. It is sometimes cited as claiming that there is a sign advantage (which is correct only if one is careful to specify elicited imitation and production for children with Down syndrome below DA 27 months or early-onset children below DA 20 months.) Others have taken our claim of a robust timetable for signs to mean that signs are early in general, when it actually means that biologically different groups share the same DA-entrained timetable on a given measure, whether that is early or late. One cannot even talk about robustness within a single group; it is a characterization of how biologically different groups compare. (See Abrahamsen, Lamb, Brown-Williams, & McCarthy, 1991, for additional discussion as well as results from Toddler Sign Program 2 [TSP2] on additional children with Down syndrome.)

I am not aware of any other studies in which enhanced gesturing has been made available to both normally developing and delayed children; this design can ascertain the expected timetable in both modalities and determine which groups depart from which timetable in which direction. Nonetheless, there is a wealth of evidence on an important part of this story: the typical timetable for spoken language and data on departures from it. It has long been known that substantial delays in speech are common in a wide range of disorders. More recently, due to landmark work emanating from The Salk Institute (e.g., Bellugi, Klima, & Wang, 1997;

Reilly, Klima, & Bellugi, 1990), it has been learned that a rare genetic disorder—Williams syndrome—is characterized by the opposite pattern, particular strength in spoken language. Although slow to get started (Harris, Bellugi, Bates, Jones, & Rossen, 1997), the speech of older children and adults with Williams syndrome is not only fluent but also meaningful and exhibits grammatical and discourse structure beyond expectation—a more impressive speech advantage than the relatively meaningless but verbose language that sometimes arises from hydrocephalus.

Hence, there is convincing evidence beyond the small number of children and disorders studied in the Toddler Sign Program [TSP] that the timetable for spoken language is not robust. Depending on the particular biological disorder and on details such as DA range and what is measured, speech can be somewhat decoupled from overall development in either direction (much better or worse than expected). Given this variability *across* groups, I wondered whether speech would be especially variable *within* groups as well. Perhaps the two extremes of performance on words in children with different biological disorders in TSP1 were an amplification, in some sense, of greater variability in the vocal modality when all systems are intact. If so, distributions of scores (or acquisition ages) for words should be more spread out, with more extreme scores, than those for gestures or signs. This seemed to be supported in a few existing data sets (e.g., Iverson et al., 1994, reported larger standard deviations for gestures than for words), but for reasons indicated later, none were decisive.

The results that follow include some answers to the usual question of whether (or when) both modalities have similar average performance. The question of primary interest here, though, is whether they are equally variable. Contrary to my hypothesis, *variability was the same for signs and words*. Statistical tests of the differences between variances reported later were all nonsignificant ($p > .15$ except one that is reported individually); however, these were limited to late-onset children and were low in statistical power due to low N. Fortunately, the data from Acredolo and Goodwyn that follow the TSP1 results are a goldmine in permitting this question to be more adequately addressed—and yield the same answer.

Toddler Sign Program: Within-Group Results

Mean percentages for both elicited imitation and elicited production are shown in Table 20.1 separately for four DA ranges (13–15 months, 16–19 months, 21–25 months, and 30–39 months). To ensure that each child would contribute data to just one DA category, these percentages were calculated on the two target sets (17 word–sign pairs) that were made available to almost all of the children at the beginning of the program. (Data from 2 children who joined the program late are not included in Table 20.1.) Although truncating the longitudinal data in this manner puts just 2 to 3 children in each DA range, these cross-sectional results are quite orderly.

Elicited Imitation Is Similar for Words and Signs. The elicited imitation measure primarily reflects the ability to imitate a model on request, but it is calculated as a hybrid measure because children who had just produced both the word and sign were not asked to imitate them as well. The means grew from less than 15% for the youngest children to more than 90% for the oldest children. Imitation is often regarded as an uninteresting measure, but here it is clearly developmentally progressive. As children move through and even beyond the bimodal period, they master the physical forms of an increasing number of familiar manual and vocal vocabulary and (as revealed by pretests) eventually become more capable of immediately imitating unfamiliar vocabulary.

The sizable improvement with age also reflects the fact that responding to elicitations is itself a challenge at the lower end of the bimodal age range and still a bit wobbly as late as 21 to 25 months. This is even more apparent in the results for the elicited production measure. Table 20.1 indicates that elicited production, like elicited imitation, is developmentally progressive. Unlike both elicited imitation and spontaneous production, however, it is not a very useful measure early in the bimodal period: elicited production percentages were near zero at DA 13 to 15 months.

The data on each elicitation measure can be combined across DA 13 to 25 months to statistically address this question: How bimodal is the bimodal period? For the 7 children in this range, the mean percentage of

TABLE 20.1
Mean Percentage Correct on the First Two Target Sets
for Children Receiving Enhanced Gestural Input

Age Range (Months)			Elicited Imitation		Elicited Production	
CA	DA	N	Signs	Words	Signs	Words
15–16	13–15	3	13.9	8.6	0.0	2.0
16–18	16–19	2	76.3	67.9	27.7	25.4
22–26	21–25	2	84.1	74.1	46.5	61.2
32–36	30–39	3	90.2	98.0	56.7	85.5

Note: Adapted from Abrahamsen et al., 1985.

target vocabulary that were at least imitated was 51.8 (*SD* 37.2) for signs and 44.3 (*SD* 39.5) for words. The first thing to notice is that ability to approximate forms is similar for signs and words (often but not necessarily with the support of a model). The small difference of 8% in favor of signs does not approach statistical significance (neither does the 8% difference in favor of words at DA 30–39 months). The equipotentiality of modalities is clearly reflected in this measure, regardless of whether the hint of a slight shift with age might later be confirmed. The more important thing to notice is that variability across participants is almost identical for signs and words. The equivalence of signs and words is even more apparent in the fuller, longitudinal data set. Nine children (the 7 just mentioned plus the 2 who joined the program late) had one or more elicitation sessions within DA 13 to 26 months. Combined across sessions, their mean percentages were 54.4 (*SD*=24.7) for signs and 53.0 (*SD*=27.2) for words. The similarity in both means and standard deviations adds to the evidence that the bimodal period is impressively bimodal, even for children in a generally speech-dominant environment.

Elicited Production Is Better for Words Than Signs. Mean production percentages from Table 20.1 for DA 13 to 25 months (*N*=7) are 21.2 (*SD*=22.9) for signs and 25.6 (*SD*=129.3) for words. In the longitudinal data set for the same period (DA 13–26 months, *N*=9), means were 16.7 (*SD*=18.6) for signs and 30.5 (*SD*=24.1) for words. In this latter comparison, words outperformed signs, $t(8)=2.78$, $p=.02$. The small differences in variability are nonsignificant and probably artifactual (variability can be expected to rise with the mean in this range of percentages).

Individuals Differ in Degree, Not Direction, of Effects. Although the spread in scores is about equal for the two modalities, it is equally *high*. The most obvious source is developmental progression across the wide range of ages involved, rather than large individual differences on each measure within each narrower age range. Examination of the data for individuals underlying Table 20.1 reveals that there are only four cases in which a data point from one age group overlaps into those of another age group. Three involve the same child, Michael, whose performance was "too high" on each measure except word production.

The more important question is the extent to which there are individual differences in acquisition of words versus signs. There were enough elicitation trials in the longitudinal data to carry out significance tests within individuals, and this was done in the 1985 article using McNemar tests for correlated proportions on data through DA 35 months. For production, similarity across children in modality preference would certainly be supported if difference scores were positive and statistically significant. In fact, 7 of the 9 children produced more words than signs, a difference that was significant for 4 children (d=22.5% to 41.2%, $p<.05$ for each) and nonsignificant for 3 (d=8.8% to 11.8%, $p>.15$ for each); the remaining 2 children had essentially no difference (d=0.0% and –2.5%). The 3 oldest children (DA 30–49 months for the entire study) also produced more words than signs, and this difference was significant for 2 of them. Given this consistency across children in producing more words than signs, the apparent lack of a modality difference at 13 to 19 months in the cross-sectional production data (Table 20.1) was either temporary or a fluke; 4 of the 5 children went on to perform better on words in the longitudinal data.

For the elicited imitation measure, which yielded similar average scores for signs and words, it is a lack of significant McNemar tests that would suggest that the group result also is characteristic of individuals. In fact, the difference scores were within 0%–6% for 7 of the 12 children. The largest difference, and the only one with p less than .10, was a word advantage of 18.2% ($p < .05$) for Michael. This is not to say there are no interesting individual differences at all; particular children on particular assessments do have more extreme scores. There is no satisfactory way to judge to what extent this reflects simple error variance, unstable effects such as mood on the day of the assessment, or genuine changes in how a particular child is relating to each modality. Whatever fine-grained effects might be lurking in the data, the main conclusions are clear: Means and standard deviations are very similar, except that words are favored in elicited production, and the large size of the standard deviations within each modality is due primarily to the wide range of ages.

Does Age of Onset Matter? This brings us back to the importance of considering the age dimensions that are not shown in Fig. 20.1. Most of the findings just summarized apply to children who were assessed in the DA range 13 to 26 months and did not begin getting enhanced gestural input until DA 12 months or later—after the bimodal period had already been underway for 2 to 6 months or longer. Recall that for 2 additional children, exposure began by DA 11 months. Their elicitation results were so different from those of the later-onset children that age of exposure had to be suspected as a factor.

First, Shaun's exposure to enhanced gesturing began in earnest at 11 months (although he had incidental exposure earlier due to the presence of older participants in different rooms of the same center). Consider his outcomes on two assessments of the first target set (10 mealtime items) at DA 14 to 15 months. (An earlier assessment was essentially a pretest, and he was uncooperative on a fourth assessment.) Shaun showed a remarkably strong sign advantage (more accurately, a word disadvantage). On elicited imitation his sign performance (85% correct) was at the level attained by other children at 21 to 25 months, whereas his word percentage (25%) was a little high for his age but well below the 16 to 19 month level (see Table 20.1). On elicited production (60% of signs vs. 15% of words correct), his sign performance was even more disportionate to his age: Only 1 child (DA 31 months) produced a higher percentage of the same 10 signs. If diary records of spontaneous use through DA 15 months are added to all elicitation results, he produced (not just imitated) every one of the first set of 10 signs at least twice. Of the corresponding words, only the 3 words successfully elicited using pictures met this criterion (but for 4 additional words, one spontaneous use each was observed). Symbolic criteria were satisfied by 7 of the 10 signs and 3 words. Diary records on other signs and words (which were less complete) add at least 4 signs and 11 words, bringing the total symbolic items to at least 11 signs and 14 words.

Natasha was exposed at home to enhanced gesturing inconsistently at 5 months and almost daily by late in her first year; during her second year, the number of sign–word targets increased. At CA 13 to 15 months Natasha used a number of signs at home; for example, at 13 months she could produce nine signs but only two words. However, she hardly responded to elicitation attempts in the laboratory. At 16 to 19 months, she too showed a strong sign advantage (word disadvantage) both on elicited imitation (40.5% on signs vs. 12.7% on words across 79 trials in two assessments) and elicited production (19.0% vs. 7.6%). Her signs then remained stable while words overtook them at 20 to 26 months. (Across 71 trials in three assessments, elicited imitation was 40.8% for signs vs. 67.6% for words; elicited production was 18.3% vs. 42.2%.) In a later assessment of the original two target sets (17 items) at 30 months, she produced 58.8% of the signs and 47.1% of the words. At 47 months, according to her mother, she still occasionally used signs (e.g., signing IN and UNDER while looking at a book by herself).

The outcomes for Shaun and Natasha were tantalizingly different from those of the other participants but raised more questions than they answered. Would all children provided with early exposure to enhanced gesturing show a substantial sign advantage for several months? Is "early" best defined by CA, DA, or by specific milestones such as whether a child has begun talking? I did not obtain answers to these questions myself, but Acredolo picked up the trail when she became intrigued by her own daughter's proclivity for object-related gesturing. In a long-term collaboration using more naturalistic input and assessment methods than ours, Acredolo and Goodwyn have obtained a wealth of data on children getting ordinary gestural input (summarized earlier) and, in a later training study, on children getting enhanced gestural input beginning at 11 months. They have published several important academic papers on this work but also captured the attention of numerous nursery schools in the area of Davis, California, and wrote a parent-friendly how-to book, *Baby Signs* (Acredolo & Goodwyn, 1996).

In the next section, I highlight some of the key findings of Acredolo and Goodwyn's training study in comparison to Folven and Bonvillian's results on children acquiring ASL. Thereafter, I look at "the big picture" by examining selected results from the entire top front edge of the research space in Fig. 20.1, including more of my own counts of symbolic and nonsymbolic cumulative vocabulary.

Acredolo and Goodwyn's Symbolic Gesture Training Studies

A New Way to Enhance Gestural Input and Its Effect on Spontaneous Production. As noted earlier, Acredolo and Goodwyn (1988) found that under ordinary input conditions, children develop a few symbolic gestures—5 on average but as many as 17. They had the idea of training parents to provide enhanced gestural input to their children, thereby encouraging greater use of this special kind of gesturing ("symbolic gesturing" or "baby signs" in their terms). To make it as easy as possible, they showed parents how to invent gestures rather than asking them to learn signs borrowed from ASL. One motivation was their hypothesis that such gestures could, by giving added "practice" to an emerging symbolic function, actually *accelerate* the development of object-related words. This clearly contrasted with a common expectation that too much emphasis on gestures might *interfere* with the development of spoken words.

To get parents of the 32 11-month-olds in their "Sign Training" group started, Acredolo and Goodwyn constructed an initial target set of eight easily formed gestures with salient meanings (FISH, FLOWER, BIRD, FROG, AIRPLANE, WHERE-IS-IT?, MORE, and ALLGONE).

Arguably, all eight are object-related gestures, which potentially could be used either to make a request or to label an object or the existential state of an object. (It is unclear under what circumstances Iverson et al., 1994, would classify the last three gestures as conventional rather than predicative. It is, however, clear that the deictic gesture category was excluded from consideration.) Parents were encouraged to use the eight gestures simultaneously with the corresponding English words at appropriate moments and to come up with additional gestures of interest to their child.[5]

Every 2 weeks, a researcher conducted a detailed telephone interview to obtain information about which gestures and words the child had used since the last call and also about the contexts in which they were used. Information was gathered on all of the child's object-related gestures and words, not just those targeted by the parent. From the interview records, Acredolo and Goodwyn were able to make a monthly tabulation of the cumulative number of forms produced and to determine how many of these had been produced spontaneously and met the other criteria for symbolic status that had been originally developed for their naturalistic studies. The interviews ended after a child acquired 100 words or reached 24 months of age. They also included laboratory sessions to obtain additional measures of progress in spoken English and general development.

Can Outcomes Be Similar When Input Is Not? A wealth of findings can be extracted from this extensive body of data, and Acredolo, and Goodwyn, Horobin, & Emmons (1999) and Goodwyn & Acredolo (1993, 1998) have already offered a variety of new insights about bimodal development. Here I wish to further pursue just one of the questions they have addressed: How does acquisition of symbolic gestures under enhanced gestural input compare to acquisition of symbols (signs or words) under full linguistic input? Is the huge difference in amount and quality of input reflected in the learners' output? Within the manual modality, a between-subjects comparison can be made between the gestures of children getting enhanced gestural input (the "Sign Training" group) and the signs of children getting ASL input. Across modalities, a within-subjects comparison can be made between the gestures and words of children getting enhanced gestural input. The unusually large N permits close quantitative comparisons of means and variability for children, like Shaun and Natasha,

---

[5]There was also a target set of eight words with no gestures for a separate "Verbal Training" group that I do not discuss; the two groups were compared to successfully confirm the prediction that adding gestures would accelerate word acquisition.

whose exposure to enhanced gestural input begins early—analyses that could be conducted in the TSP1 only for children whose exposure began later.

Comparing gestures to words presents a challenge, however: Some children gallop ahead in acquiring words so rapidly that there aren't enough gestures in the input (or in children's own inventions) to give gestures a chance at parity. Hence, if one compares total number of symbols at a particular age, the outlier scores alone can make not only the means, but the standard deviations as well, higher for words (or signs) than gestures; this was the case for Iverson et al.'s (1994) comparison of gestures to words.

Longitudinal studies provide a way to bypass this difficulty: comparing the ages at which children attain certain early milestones rather than total vocabulary. Folven and Bonvillian (1991) provided data on age at first sign, first symbolic sign, first symbolic word, and tenth sign. Goodwyn and Acredolo (1993) examined age at first symbol and fifth symbol for a subset of children from their final sample and from a pilot study who had not yet produced any symbolic words at the onset of their participation (a restriction that permitted them to show that beginning enhanced gestural input at 11 months results in a gestural advantage, although only a small one, for children who were not yet committed to a modality).

There are many pitfalls in determining the ages at which milestones are achieved and especially in comparing these ages across different studies. Meier and Newport (1990) identified a number of these pitfalls and sought to reach the best possible conclusions about milestones in sign and speech given the available data (which included an earlier report of Folven and Bonvillian's 1991 findings). In brief, they found the evidence persuasive that the earliest words are delayed relative to the earliest signs, and that some disparity in vocabulary size may continue at least through the first 50 items. In contrast, milestones involving relations between cognition and language, such as first symbol, appeared to be achieved at comparable ages for signs and words. They found the evidence on a difference in onset of early combinations unpersuasive but incomplete; they noted that a delay in word combinations, if supported in later research, might be due to difficulties involving form rather than deeper cognitive-linguistic factors.

Acredolo and Goodwyn's use of enhanced gesturing has yielded new evidence against which to examine children's ages at milestones. Although enhanced gesturing is just one of several relevant input situations, it provides an important opportunity to carry out within-subjects comparisons in addition to the more problematic between-subjects comparisons. It also can be compared to other input situations—those with different degrees of imbalance between modalities—to assess the importance of amount of input. Finally, Acredolo and Goodwyn's complete sample of 32 children (vs. the subsample that excluded early talkers) provided an especially valuable opportunity to examine standard deviations in a relatively large sample. To enable me to test my hypothesis that variability would be greater for words than gestures within a group of normally developing children, Linda Acredolo generously made available each child's monthly cumulative totals for gestures and words. In addition to incorporating these in Figs. 20.2 and 20.3, I calculated means, standard deviations, and ranges, which are shown in Table 20.2 along with comparable statistics from Folven and Bonvillian's (1991) findings on ASL signs. (The statistics on tenth ASL sign in Table 20.2 and on total signs in Fig. 20.3 were calculated for this chapter from individuals' data supplied to me by John Bonvillian.) In what follows, AG refers to Acredolo and Goodwyn and FB refers to Folven and Bonvillian.

Comparisons Within and Between Enhanced Gesturing and ASL

Age of Attainment of Milestones: Differences in Means? (Mostly No). Table 20.2 indicates that mean ages at each milestone for both modalities and both studies (when available) are within a month of each other, with the important exception that the first sign is 3 to 4 months earlier than the first word. Comparisons between studies require caution, however, due to a number of methodological differences; the footnotes to Table 20.2 identify some of these differences and describe adjustments that were made to some of the investigators' original numbers (e.g., most of AG's ages reflect my adjustment of −0.5 months). There is also the question of consistency with previous studies; for example, AG's ages for 10th word are a month or two younger than usual. The within-study comparisons are therefore most secure, but any net impact on the between-studies comparisons of more closely aligning the studies is unlikely to change the overall findings.

The modality difference for first form (milestone 1) replicates previous results from Bonvillian's laboratory. Although not obvious in Table 20.2, the relative delay for word forms may continue throughout the bimodal period (see Meier & Newport's 1990 review in which Bonvillian's current and previous ages for 10th sign and 50th sign were judged $1^1/_2$ to 2 months earlier than norms for words). When symbolic criteria are added,

TABLE 20.2

Age (in Months) at Attainment of Milestones for Words Versus Symbolic Gestures (Acredolo & Goodwyn) and Words Versus ASL Signs and Deictic/Performative Gestures (Folven & Bonvillian)

Six Milestones[a]	N (n_g, n_w)[b]	Mean[c]		Standard Deviation		Range	
		Gestures/Signs	Words	Gestures/Signs	Words	Gestures/Signs	Words
1. First Form[d]							
ASL signs versus words[e]	6 (9, 8)	8.3	11.5	1.80	1.42	6–11	10–15
2. Deictic/performative gestures							
Ritual request	5 (7)	9.2	–	0.84	–	7–11	–
Show, give	5 (7)	10.0	–	1.00	–	9–11	–
Communicative point	5 (7)	10.8	–	0.45	–	10–13	–
3. First symbolic form							
ASL signs versus words[f]	6 (8, 6)	12.5	12.2	2.13	1.42	10–16	10–14
Gestures versus words	31 (32, 32)	11.8	11.9	0.65	0.71	12–15	12–15
4. 10th form							
ASL signs	6 (9)	13.5	–	2.02	–	10–16	–
Gestures versus words	31 (31, 32)	14.1	13.3	1.71	1.63	12–19	12–19
5. 10th symbolic form							
Gestures versus words	31 (31, 32)	14.8	13.8	2.11	1.60	12–19	12–21
6. First combination[g]							
ASL signs	9	16.1	–	–	–	13–19	–
G + W or G + G	24	15.5	–	–	–	–	–
W + W	24	17.9	–	–	–	–	–

[a] Folven and Bonvillian (1991) presented evidence that the milestones are almost always attained in the order shown, except that milestone 1 splits according to modality: The first ASL sign precedes all other developments, but the first word comes between milestones 2 and 3.

[b] Children who lack data on any of the vocabulary milestones (1, 3, 4, or 5) are excluded from the means and standard deviations for milestones 1–5. Ranges include these children on the milestones for which they have data (as indicated by the ns in parentheses for gestures/signs and words, respectively). If the means had been based on these larger ns, only the age at first word form would differ by more than 0.2 months (see footnote e).

c Some of the means have been adjusted from the original data to better align the two studies, because AG and FB obtained their data at different intervals and calculated their ages differently. For example, AG's "17 months" refers to attainments on or before the 17th monthly birthday; the last data included would be those reported in a telephone interview conducted as close as possible to the exact monthly birthday and therefore would cover (approximately) the 16th month. In Fig. 20.3, this is written as 17.0 months. FB's mean ages were calculated from exact dates (of diary entries and videotapes) that were rounded to the nearest tenth of a month; hence, their means in Table 20.2 do not require adjustment. (However, each child's age for each deictic/performative gesture was reported with no decimal places; these were simply averaged here without adjustment because FB did not specify what range of exact ages were included. Also, child 7 was preterm, and in later publications his age was adjusted by 6 weeks; if adjusted here, the upper end of the range would be reduced by 1 to 2 months for first word, communicative point, and first combination.) AG's mean ages were calculated from cumulative monthly totals, counting each item in the first month at which it was reported as being imitated or produced (milestone 4) or as being used flexibly (milestones 3 and 5). AG's ages were made more comparable to FB's ages by subtracting subtracting 0.5 months (the approximate average discrepancy) from each mean. For 10th form or symbolic form further compensation was needed (because many children went well beyond their 10th item in the month they first reached 10 items); an approximation was achieved by using age at 9th rather than 10th item in addition to subtracting 0.5 months for milestones 4 and 5. For combinations, ages were calculated to the nearest half month and therefore were adjusted by subtracting only 0.25 months (rounded to 0.2) from the reported ages. Descriptions of their underlying calculations of age were obtained from Linda Acredolo and John Bonvillian (personal communications, February 1999).

d AG's ages for first form (milestone 1) are not included because all except two children had already achieved this milestone in their first monthly total at 12.0 months. If AG's families had begun enhanced gesturing and data collection several months earlier, age of attainment would probably have been close to FB's ages for milestone 1 and may have have been lowered a bit for some later milestones.

e For all 8 hearing children, the mean ages were 12.3 for first word (and 8.5 for first sign). Note that a recent large-N norm cited by Meier and Newport (1990) was 11.3 months for first word; this difference of 1 month may be due in part to less than usual exposure to English for some of FB's participants.

f FB did not count requests for familiar objects as evidence for symbolic status. This probably made their ages for milestone 3 a few weeks later than they would have been using AG's criteria (which did count such requests if observed for more than one object or context). Moreover, there were several minor differences between FB and AG in what types of items were excluded; these may have partly canceled each other out.

g Only 2 of the children acquiring ASL combined words before the study ended; in both cases, this was later than they combined signs. The data on combinations of gestures (G) and/or words (W) are from Acredolo, Goodwyn, Horobin, and Emmons (1999), and exclude 8 children who never combined gestures. For all 32 children, the age for W + W is 18.1 months (see footnote c concerning an age adjustment of 0.2 months).

however, the ages for first form (milestone 3) are quite close, not only within studies but also between studies. This similar timing for the first linkage of an available form to a context-flexible meaning is especially noteworthy when you consider that the input to AG's participants strongly favored words, whereas the input to most of FB's participants strongly favored signs. By milestones 4 and 5, these input imbalances apparently were starting to have some impact; FB did not report data for 10th sign, and AG's modality difference had grown from essentially none to about a month in favor of words. In fact, of the 31 children in Goodwyn's and Acredolo study who attained 10 gestures (one stopped at 8), 14 never attained more than 14 gestures (13 symbolic gestures). Hence, many children are slowing down already by the time of the 10th-gesture milestone, making the 5th-gesture milestone used by Goodwyn and Acredolo (1993) preferable. The difference between modalities was only 0.4 months on this measure: The 5th symbolic word was attained at 13.4 months ($SD = 1.36$) and the 5th symbolic gesture at 13.8 months ($SD = 1.28$). For means, then, the bottom line is that *grossly unequal input can coexist with essentially equal output*. Neither modality nor quantity of input nor linguistic status of input has much effect, if any, on the average age at which the earliest vocabulary milestones are met.

Age of Attainment of Milestones: Differences in Variability? (No).

The outcomes just described are important, but our particular interest in this chapter is in the measures of variability rather than means. Recall the prediction that standard deviations (and equivalently, variances) would be larger for words than signs. This was based on the idea that the two extremes of performance on words in children with different biological disorders might be a kind of amplification of greater variability in the vocal modality when all systems were intact. Contrary to this prediction, however, standard deviations were similar in the two modalities in data from children in TSP1. Would this be the case as well for the studies in Table 20.2? Acredolo and Goodwyn's study provides a larger sample with earlier onset of enhanced gesturing. Folven and Bonvillian's sample is about as small as mine but is of interest because his participants received even earlier and more elaborate input in the manual modality.

The outcome is easily summarized. First, simply inspecting the table suggests that age of milestone attainments are no more spread out for words than for gestures or signs. To confirm this, I performed a test of the significance of the difference between correlated variances for the variances computed from each pair of standard deviations in Table 20.2, and also for the results on age at 5th symbol reported earlier. Not a single pair of variances differed significantly. The only one that even approached marginal significance was for AG's data at milestone 5—where variability was a little higher in the manual modality rather than in the vocal modality, $t(29) = 1.71$, $p = .11$. The two tests on FB's data were statistically weak, but there too the small differences between sample variances were in the opposite direction of that predicted.

This is not to say that data sets will never be found in which variability does differ, for any of a number of possible reasons. However, Acredolo and Goodwyn's data set is the best currently available for addressing the question; the only better ones would be (a) word and sign data from two dozen or so children acquiring a spoken language from one parent and a signed language from the other parent (or both languages from both parents), or (b) between-subjects comparisons involving even larger numbers of comparable children acquiring such languages monolingually and followed using similar methods.

Until either of these ships comes in, *I must tentatively conclude that the equipotentiality of modalities is reflected not only in means but especially in measures of variability. The fact that biologically different groups of children vary so dramatically in word acquisition apparently is an outcome of how different kinds of damage impact development and has no deeper cause in a disproportionate variability in speech within our species.* The acquisition of early words does seem to be more vulnerable to damage than early gestures, as evidenced by the large number of children with biologically-based developmental disorders who are delayed in speech beyond their overall delay but can benefit from enhanced gesturing. However, as the group at Salk has shown both behaviorally and neurobiologically (see Bellugi et al., 1997, for a review), Williams syndrome's distinctive effects on the brain have the atypical consequence that spoken language is well-preserved relative to many nonlinguistic abilities. This gives additional force to my revised claim that speech outcomes have to do with type of damage rather than a preexisting disposition to variability in speech (see especially Jernigan & Bellugi's 1994 examination of relative sizes of brain areas for individuals with Williams syndrome vs. Down syndrome).

Number of Symbols: Individual Differences in Modality Asymmetries. Returning to the ordinary children studied by Acredolo and Goodwyn, our main point about variability was that it is the same for both modalities when measured using milestone ages. Two additional points are true of the milestone data but are most clearly displayed in a

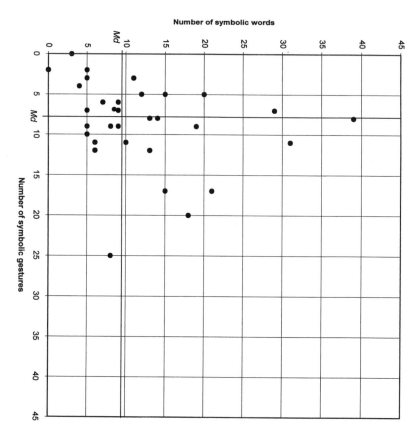

FIG. 20.2. Cumulative number of symbolic gestures and symbolic words through age 14.0 months for each child provided with enhanced gestural input. This scatterplot display is based on data provided to the author by L. Acredolo. Note that the actual age varies slightly across children; the last telephone interview included was made as close as possible to each child's 14th monthly birthday (see Footnote 6).

scatterplot (Fig. 20.2), in which each of 32 data points represents the total number of symbolic gestures and symbolic words for 1 child at age 14.0 months. First, variability is quite high in both modalities. Second, all possible patterns of relation between the two modalities are about equally represented.

A median-split procedure adapted from that of Goodwyn and Acredolo (1998) illustrates this second point. Within the four boxes created by drawing medians for each modality, there are 7 children in each of the two boxes representing a modality asymmetry (word-dominant and gesture-dominant), and 9 children in each of the two boxes representing a balance between modalities (both-low and both-high).[6]

This outcome is far from inevitable. One reasonable hypothesis is that children would tend to have a dominant modality at 14 months (e.g., words if the child is an early talker and gestures otherwise). If true, this would have placed the data points in just the word-dominant and gesture-dominant boxes. Alternatively, if performance is driven by some centralized capacity that is shared by both modalities, one would expect the opposite pattern (equivalent to data points in the both-low and both-high boxes).[7] Perhaps the patterns in Fig. 20.2 result from modality-specific factors overlaid on a developing centralized capacity. If so, and extrapolating from results on ASL, very early onset of enhanced gesturing (e.g., 8 or 9 months) might push the modality-specific factors in a direction favoring gestures and therefore toward a less equal distribution of points. However, variances could remain equal even as the means got pushed apart.

Due largely, although not wholly, to the verbal outliers (children with more than 20 words), summary statistics for words ($M = 12.0$, $SD = 8.68$) are higher than for gestures ($M = 8.6$, $SD = 5.36$) when calculated on the data points in Fig. 20.2. However, if only the children who are actually early in the process are examined (those with 10 or fewer items in each modality), the statistics are very close for words ($M = 5.9$, $SD = 2.70$) and gestures ($M = 5.8$, $SD = 3.12$). This illustrates that the distribution of total number of items for all children at a given *age* includes a mixture of outcomes from different levels of development and therefore is not the best measure for comparing means or standard deviations at a given *level of development* (e.g., the developmental period during which the earliest symbolic words and gestures emerge, as captured by the subset of data for

---

[6]These numbers are not identical to the distribution of points as drawn; they incorporate a correction for ties at each median that is equivalent to moving one point from the both-low box into the both-high box and one from the word-dominant box into the both-high box. Also note that age 14 months was was chosen for Fig. 20.2 because it is the last age at which the medians for number of symbolic gestures (7.83) and words (9.25) are fairly close. They then diverge as increasing numbers of children are launched onto a rapid trajectory of word acquisition, at which time effects of the input disparities finally are evident and a fair comparison between modalities is no longer possible.

[7]In fact, that pattern was found on a different measure (elicited imitation) for children in TSP1 who were older at both onset and assessment. On yet another measure (elicited production), scores from the same TSP1 children were equivalent to the both-low and word-dominant boxes. Hence, although it is important to know that all patterns are about equally represented for spontaneous production with early onset, variations with age and measure underscore once again what a complicated set of developments is unfolding.

10 or fewer items.) This is especially the case when the comparison involves two modalities and just one of them will ultimately dominate, and this is one of the reasons I prefer to report results within DA ranges rather than by CA.

The Big Picture: Additional Comparisons Across Studies

The Onset of Symbolic Gesturing. We saw in Table 20.2 that with respect to age at the first symbolic form, there is apparently little or no advantage in being exposed to a full language from birth (e.g., ASL or English) compared to the much reduced input provided in the manual modality by enhanced gesturing. Although this conclusion is somewhat tentative due to differences in methodology and samples, it is unlikely to be altered to an interesting degree by future research. The earliest symbolic signs of a child acquiring ASL apparently are equivalent in many if not all respects to the earliest symbolic gestures of children acquiring English and (revisiting our earlier discussion of terminology) probably should be called *gestures* or *sign-gestures* rather than *signs*.

But this comparison involves enhanced gesturing. What of children with ordinary gestural input? I have not succeeded in locating an explicit age of first symbolic gesture from a large sample of children, but some plausible inferences from AG's own earlier work suggest that enhancing versus not enhancing parental gesturing makes little difference in the age at which this particular milestone is reached.[8] Any differences in development brought by enhanced gestural input should show up later in the bimodal period, when children are increasing their inventories of words and gestures rather than getting them started. Hence, despite the difficulties with total number of items as a measure, it is worth using it to make one final set of comparisons across studies.

Total Symbolic Gestures at the Peak of the Bimodal Period. How many gestures have children attained when the bimodal period is at

---

[8]First, half of the 16 children in the naturalistic longitudinal study (Acredolo & Goodwyn, 1988, Table 4) attained their first symbolic gesture before their first (nonsymbolic) word; AG do not report that age, but all except 2 of the children in the data set used for Table 20.2 had attained their first word by 12.0 months. Making plausible interpolations, an approximate median age for first symbolic gesture with ordinary input would be very close to the 11.8 months listed in Table 20.2 for children receiving enhanced gesturing.

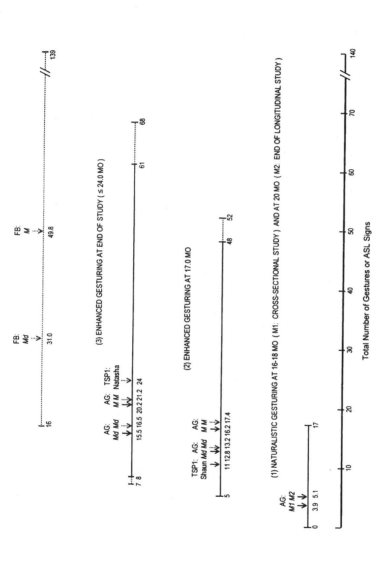

FB:
Md
↓
31.0

FB:
M
↓
49.8

FB:
Md
↓
16

(3) ENHANCED GESTURING AT END OF STUDY (≤ 24.0 MO)

|—·······—·······—//——|
7 8   139

AG: AG: TSP1:
Md Md   M M   Natasha
↓ ↓   ↓ ↓   ↓
15.5 16.5   20.2 21.2 24

(2) ENHANCED GESTURING AT 17.0 MO

TSP1: AG: AG:
Shaun Md Md   M M
  ↓ ↓ ↓   ↓ ↓
11 12.8 13.2 16.2 17.4

|—————————————|
5   48 52

(1) NATURALISTIC GESTURING AT 16-18 MO (M1: CROSS-SECTIONAL STUDY) AND AT 20 MO (M2: END OF LONGITUDINAL STUDY)

AG:
M1 M2
↓ ↓
3.9 5.1

|————————|
0   17

|———//————|
0   10   20   30   40   50   60   70   140

Total Number of Gestures or Signs

FIG. 20.3. Cumulative number of gestures or signs obtained by several investigators: Acredolo and Goodwyn (AG), Folven and Bonvillian (EB), and Abrahamsen et al. (TSP1). Arrows indicate means and medians and bars indicate ranges. Solid lines indicate results for items meeting symbolic criteria; broken lines add items that did not meet symbolic criteria but were produced spontaneously, elicited, or imitated at least once. Data points representing the 2 early-onset participants in TSP1 are displayed with results at comparable ages from AG: Shaun's cumulative symbolic signs through 17.0 months (on bar 2) and Natasha's cumulative signs (at least one elicited production) through 23.0 months (bar 3).

391

its peak? Figure 20.3 displays means, medians, and ranges for cumulative vocabulary at the time data collection ended for several of the studies we discussed (plus additional results at 17.0 months for one study). This gives us a somewhat later window than the one provided in Table 20.2 for looking at the impact of quantity and quality of input. At the bottom is the overall yardstick (number of gestures or signs) for assessing the extent to which children are using the manual modality as a vehicle for object-related symbols. (A few social gestures may also be included in some data sets, but deictic gestures are excluded.)

Bar 1 displays data we already noted: the total number of symbolic gestures attained by children acquiring a spoken language under ordinary circumstances (Acredolo & Goodwyn, 1988). Above that are two bars representing the increase obtained by providing an environment of enhanced gesturing (the 32 families in AG's "Sign Training" group for whom milestones are indicated in Table 20.2). Bar 2 (total gestures at 17.0 months) provides the closest comparison to Bar 1 (16–18 months). Bar 3 incorporates whatever additional learning occurred by the end of the study (before 20.0 months for almost half the children but as late as the cutoff age of 24.0 months for 2 children who never attained 100 words). Although there is considerable variability, the increase brought by enhanced gestural input (vs. ordinary gestural input) can be substantial.

Finally, at the top is a bar representing the further increase obtained by providing constant exposure to full linguistic input in the manual modality—the 9 children followed by Folven and Bonvillian (1991) for whom the language of one or both parents was ASL. Their study ended at a mean age that can be estimated as 17.4 months (by using the ages in their 1997 Table 2 to calculate a mean and adding .5). The cumulative sign vocabularies compiled at this time did not consider symbolic criteria, but they can be compared to Acredolo and Goodwyn's total number of object-related gestures at 17.0 months (dotted arrows and ranges). The most prolific signers at 17 months have almost three times as many items as the most prolific gesturers at 17 months, and the mean is almost double. Nonetheless, there is a substantial region of overlap: Almost half of the gesturers (15 of 32) and 7 of the 9 signers have cumulative vocabularies between 16 and 52.

Figure 20.3 also contains data points from the 2 participants in TSP1 whose exposure to enhanced gesturing had begun by 11 months. Recall that Shaun had a cumulative total of 11 symbolic signs at DA 15 months (CA 16.0 months), near the end of the program. This places him slightly below the median of 12.8 symbolic gestures for Acredolo and Goodwyn's children at 17.0 months (as well as their similar median of 12.5 at 16.0 months). At the same age, Shaun had at least 14 symbolic words, many of which had been gained within the most recent month (cf. a median of 28.5 symbolic words for Acredolo and Goodwyn's children at 16.0 months). For Natasha, there was insufficient information to apply symbolic criteria. However, at 23 months the cumulative number of object-related signs she had produced to a picture referent at least once was 24—a bit above AG's comparable mean (broken arrow on Bar 3). Her comparable total for words was 13.

All in all, it appears that bimodal-period children are so ready to lap up whatever meaningful forms are offered to them that even modest enhancements in gestural input can have a disproportionate impact. There are two important limitations to this conclusion, however, that we will explore briefly. First, despite a number of methodological differences between studies, all of the children in Fig. 20.3 began getting enhanced gesturing or ASL input by age 11 months. This suggests that early onset may be a key factor in producing substantial spontaneous and elicited production at 12 to 17 months. However, the only data on later onset children are from TSP1, and the only measures on which they have been compared to the early-onset children are elicited production and imitation (on which they do not show Shaun and Natasha's sign advantage). Might age at onset matter less when spontaneous signs are added to elicited signs? Second, Fig. 20.3 indicates that there is limited growth from 17 months to the end of the study. Has bimodality run its course by 17 months or so? In the next two sections, we show that (a) incorporating records of spontaneous signing does not change the conclusion that early onset matters; and (b) when spontaneous production in the manual modality begins to lag, other measures pick up the pace.

Age of Onset Revisited

First, I carried out the same kind of compilation of diary and other records as described earlier for Shaun, but now through the first 5 months of the program for 5 TSP1 children whose exposure began at CA 13 to 16 months (DA 12–14 months). I limited myself to the first set of 10 target words and signs, because these had the most complete records, and applied the same 10-item limitation to Shaun for comparison (cf. his data point in Fig. 20.3 without this limitation).

For Shaun at DA 13 or 14 months, all 10 signs and 6 of the 10 words were produced at least once; of these, 7 signs and 1 word met the symbolic criteria. None of the children with a slightly later onset came close to this: The two most prolific children produced (in some context) 5 or 6 of the 10 signs (1–2 symbolic) and 7 or 8 of the 10 words (2–3 symbolic). The other 3 children ranged from 0 or 2 signs and 0 or 1 words (all symbolic). Even allowing for the possibility that we missed a few signs that had been mastered but produced infrequently, there is essentially no overlap between these later onset TSP1 participants and the early-onset children for whom symbolic gesture data are available (Shaun in TSP1 and AG's 32 participants).

Another way of comparing the early and late onset children is to tabulate cumulative vocabularies late in the project (at DA 20–26 months) for the same children plus 2 others. By then, 27 target word–sign pairs had been assessed. Even without applying symbolic criteria, cumulative production averaged only 6 signs and 11 words per child; compare AG's mean of 21.1 gestures at their comparable age (24.0 months or less). Hence, by both analyses, *late-onset children lost much of the advantage that enhanced gesturing might otherwise have brought.*

Bimodality Beyond 17 Months: The Importance of What Gets Measured

As noted previously, even early-onset children seem to level off in the manual modality by 17 months or so. One interpretation is that once children have made the transition to speech dominance (as had the majority of their participants by 17.0 months), gesture plays a modified role in which new object-related gestures are of limited salience. But *if outcomes other than spontaneous use of individual vocabulary items are examined, it can be seen that the effects of enhanced input in fact do not level off at 17 months.* First, Table 20.2 shows that although the number of gestures may not be increasing very much, AG's children are using them in transitional combinations of two items (a gesture plus another gesture or a word) more than 2 months before they combine two words. Most interesting, these include combinations in which both items are symbolic gestures—a type of combination that children receiving ordinary gestural input virtually never produce. Again we see that what might seem to be a modest enhancement (adding perhaps not much more than 10 or 20 object-related gestures to ordinary communication) has considerable impact. Furthermore, this provides better evidence than previously available that combinations of two referential manual symbols precedes combinations of two referential vocal symbols.

Another example of continued development is the increasing tendency for children in TSP1 to use signs and words simultaneously, contrary to an earlier tendency (in imitation at DA 12–15 months) to have words for some referents and signs for different referents (Abrahamsen & Lamb, 1987).

A third example can be found in the performance of children at 30 months or beyond. TSP1 offers relevant data from 4 of the 5 oldest children in Table 20.1 (one 31-month-old had left the program after the first target set). These children were learning so quickly that beginning in the 4th month of the program (at 30 months or older), they were provided with a real challenge: 42 signs to learn (38 objects and 4 attributes). In an elicitation 6 to 8 weeks later, each child could at least imitate 97.4% to 100% of the signs and could produce most of them (26–37 signs). Elicited production percentages were 68.4% and 88.1% for 2 children (DA about 30 months by this time) and 71.4% for each of the other 2 children (DA 36–40 months). On a more difficult set of 46 signs for actions and attributes that 3 of these children received next, production percentages were considerably lower (17.4–30.4%, compared to 43.5–65.2% for the corresponding words). On elicited imitation, signs were just a bit lower than words (the sign percentages were 63.0% for one child and 93.5% for two others). Combined with earlier target sets, these results produce cumulative production vocabularies of considerably more than 50 signs per child (and an even higher number of words).

To adapt a term from Susan Carey, these older children were not just "word magnets"; given an opportunity, they were "sign magnets" as well. But why? They were far beyond the age at which children are drawn to signs as a vehicle for spontaneous production and begin to use them symbolically. Indeed, my records of spontaneous use in natural contexts are rather sparse for these children. However, they often were enthusiastic learners during the times set aside to focus on signing and often took pleasure in demonstrating their knowledge.

I would suggest two factors. The less interesting one is that there was a good deal of social support for signing in the program; seeing other children sign (including younger children and speech-delayed children) made this a relevant, if circumscribed, activity. The more interesting factor is that the ability to rapidly master new forms is just as important to acquiring the large vocabulary of a 3- or 4-year-old as is the ability to form meanings and link them to those forms. Elicited imitation is a measure that focuses especially on this ability to approximate adult forms and is useful for assessing it separately. Elicited production assesses which forms and meanings have already been acquired and linked such that the form can be quickly accessed when appropriate. *The procedures for mastering forms apparently can continue to operate bimodally beyond the bimodal period and are modularized enough that they can and will be exercised even in the absence of desire to use the forms to communicate.*

In this connection, note that Acredolo and Goodwyn (1988) gathered data on ability to imitate gestures in the laboratory at 17.0 months; they found no correlation with any of their symbolic gesturing measures and pointed to both the lack of communicative function and to the unfamiliarity of the laboratory situation as explanations. I would suggest, however, that performance on that task might correlate with how quickly or successfully children become "sign magnets" in the ensuing months. To the extent that shared capabilities are involved in the procedures for each modality, the gesture imitation task might also predict children's success as "word magnets."

Concluding Remarks

The desire to communicate, the ability to approximate adult forms, and the ability to use forms symbolically have a complex, intertwined history in the development of each child. These milestones are achieved gradually in that order beginning at 8 or 9 months, and a rather slow process involving not many forms and meanings characterizes the bimodal period until vocabulary speeds up around 20 months and syntax begins to emerge. Very efficient procedures for rapidly acquiring words apparently develop during the transitional period of 20 to 26 months and are quite powerful by 27 or 30 months and beyond. If these older children are provided with enhanced gestural input, procedures for acquiring object-related signs or gestures are almost as powerful and can be measured in elicitation sessions. Finally, well beyond the bimodal period and its immediate successors, gesticulation develops in coordination with speech and becomes the dominant form of bimodal expression through the rest of the lifespan.

Questions to be resolved in the future include (a) Although early exposure to enhanced gesturing or sign language is not necessary for a child of age 30 to 40 months to rapidly master manual forms, would a child with early exposure develop the underlying procedures a bit earlier? (b) For children given either early or later exposure to both words and enhanced gesturing or sign language, would the age at which procedures for rapid acquisition of forms emerge be later or more variable for words than for manual forms? If the answer to either of these questions is yes, some revisions would be in order for the tentative conclusion reached earlier: that high variability in speech across children with different biologically based disorders is *not* rooted in high variability even when all systems are intact. No evidence currently available points to the need for any revision, however.

ACKNOWLEDGMENTS

Toddler Sign Program 1 was conducted with the support of Social and Behavioral Sciences Research Grant 12–47 from the March of Dimes Birth Defects Foundation to the New School for Social Research. Data analysis was also supported in part by Washington University in St. Louis and by Grant HD–06016 from the National Institute of Child Health and Human Development to Georgia State University. I especially wish to thank Kathryn LeLaurin, Marie M. Cavallo, and J. Allison McCluer for their many contributions to this research. Portions of the data have been included in previous publications, in which methodological details and more complete acknowledgments are provided. I thank Linda Acredolo, Karen Emmorey, and Patricia Siple for commenting on an earlier draft, and am very grateful to Linda Acredolo and John Bonvillian for providing unpublished data and other information about their respective research projects.

Correspondence concerning this chapter should be addressed to Adele Abrahamsen, Department of Psychology, Campus Box 1125, Washington University, One Brookings Drive, St. Louis, Missouri 63130-4899; e-mail: abrahamsen@twinearth.wustl.edu.

REFERENCES

Abrahamsen, A. A., Cavallo, M. M., & McCluer, J. A. (1985). Is the sign advantage a robust phenomenon? From gesture to language in two modalities. *Merrill-Palmer Quarterly, 31,* 17–209.

Abrahamsen, A. A., & Lamb, M. (1987, July). *Modality relations in toddlers with and without Down syndrome.* Paper presented at the Fourth International Symposium on Sign Language Research, Lappeenranta, Finland.

Abrahamsen, A. A., Lamb, M., Brown-Williams, J., & McCarthy, S. (1991). Boundary conditions on language emergence: Contributions from atypical learners and input. In P. Siple & S. Fischer (Eds.), *Theoretical issues in sign language research, Vol. 2: Psychology* (pp. 231–252). Chicago: University of Chicago Press.

Acredolo, L., & Goodwyn, S. (1988). Symbolic gesturing in normal infants. *Child Development, 59,* 450–456.

Acredolo, L. P., & Goodwyn, S. W. (1996). *Baby signs: How to talk with your baby before your baby can talk.* Chicago: NTB/Contemporary Publishers.

Acredolo, L. P., Goodwyn, S. W., Horobin, K. D., & Emmons, Y. D. (1999). The signs and sounds of early language development. In L. Balter & C. Tamis-LeMonda (Eds.), *Child psychology: A handbook of contemporary issues.* Philadelphia, PA: Psychology Press.

Bates, E., Benigni, L., Bretherton, I., Camaioni, L., & Volterra, V. (1979). *The emergence of symbols: Cognition and communication in infancy.* New York: Academic Press.

Bellugi, U., & Klima, E. S. (1982). From gesture to sign: Deixis in a visual-gestural language. In R. J. Jarvella & W. Klein (Eds.), *Speech, place, and action: Studies of indeixis and related topics* (pp. 297–313). New York: Wiley.

Bellugi, U., Klima, E. S., & Wang, P. P. (1997). Cognitive and neural development: Clues from genetically based syndromes. In D. Magnusson (Ed.), *The lifespan development of individuals: Behavioral, neurobiological, and psychosocial perspectives: A synthesis* (pp. 223–243). New York: Cambridge University Press.

Capirci, O., Iverson, J. M., Pizzuto, E., & Volterra, V. (1996). Gestures and words during the transition to two-word speech. *Journal of Child Language, 23,* 645–673.

Caselli, M. C. (1983). Communication to language: Deaf children's and hearing children's development compared. *Sign Language Studies, 39,* 113–143.

Caselli, M. C., & Volterra, V. (1990). From communication to language in hearing and Deaf children. In V. Volterra & C. J. Erting (Eds.), *From gesture to language in hearing and deaf children* (pp. 263–277). Berlin: Springer-Verlag.

Erting, C. J., & Volterra, V. (1990). Conclusion. In V. Volterra & C. J. Erting (Eds.), *From gesture to language in hearing and deaf children* (pp. 299–303). Berlin: Springer-Verlag.

Feldman, H., Goldin-Meadow, S., & Gleitman, L. (1978). Beyond Herodotus: The creation of language by linguistically deprived deaf children. In A. Lock (Ed.), *Action, gesture and symbol* (pp. 351–414). New York: Academic Press.

Folven, R. J., & Bonvillian, J. D. (1991). The transition from nonreferential to referential language in children acquiring American Sign Language. *Developmental Psychology, 27,* 806–816.

Goldin-Meadow, S., & Morford, M. (1985). Gesture in early child language: Studies of deaf and hearing children. *Merrill-Palmer Quarterly, 31,* 145–176.

Goodwyn, S. W., & Acredolo, L. P. (1993). Symbolic gesture versus word: Is there a modality advantage for onset of symbol use? *Child Development, 64,* 688–701.

Goodwyn, S. W., & Acredolo, L. P. (1998). Encouraging symbolic gestures: A new perspective on the relationship between gesture and speech. In J. M. Iverson & S. Goldin-Meadow (Eds.), *The nature and functions of gesture in children's communication. New Directions for Child Development, No. 79* (pp. 61–73). San Francisco: Jossey-Bass.

Halliday, M. A. K. (1975). *Learning how to mean: Explorations in the development of language.* London: Edward Arnold.

Harris, M., Barrett, M., Jones, D., & Brookes, S. (1988). Linguistic input and early word meaning. *Journal of Child Language, 15,* 77–94.

Harris, N. G. S., Bellugi, U., Bates, E., Jones, W., & Rossen, M. (1997). Contrasting profiles of language development in children with Williams and Down syndromes. *Developmental Neuropsychology, 13,* 345–370.

Holmes, K. M., & Holmes, D. W. (1980). Signed and spoken language development in a hearing child of hearing parents. *Sign Language Studies, 28,* 239–254.

Iverson, J. M., Capirci, O., & Caselli, M. C. (1994). From communication to language in two modalities. *Cognitive Development, 9,* 23–43.

Jernigan, T. L., & Bellugi, U. (1994). Neuroanatomical distinctions between Williams and Down syndromes. In S. Broman & J. Grafman (Eds.), *Atypical cognitive deficits in developmental disorders: Implications for brain function* (pp. 57–66). Mahwah, NJ: Lawrence Erlbaum Associates.

Klima, E., & Bellugi, U. (1979). *The signs of language.* Cambridge, MA: Harvard University Press.

Lock, A. (1980). *The guided reinvention of language.* New York: Academic Press.

MacNamara, J. (1982). *Names for things: A study of human learning.* Cambridge, MA: MIT Press.

McNeill, D. (1992). *Hand and mind: What gestures reveal about thought.* Chicago: University of Chicago Press.

Meier, R. P., & Newport, E. L. (1990). Out of the hands of babes: On a possible sign advantage in language acquisition. *Language, 66,* 1–23.

Petitto, L. A. (1988). "Language" in the prelinguistic child. In F. S. Kessel (Ed.), *The development of language and language researchers: Essays in honor of Roger Brown* (pp. 187– 221). Mahwah, NJ: Lawrence Erlbaum Associates.

Prinz, P. M., & Prinz, E. A. (1979). Simultaneous acquisition of ASL and spoken English in a hearing child of a deaf mother and hearing father. Phase I: Early lexical development. *Sign Language Studies, 25,* 283–296.

Reilly, J. S., Klima, E. S., & Bellugi, U. (1990). Once more with feeling: Affect and language in atypical populations. *Developmental Psychopathology, 2,* 367–391.

Siple, P., Fischer, S. D., & Bellugi, U. (1977). Memory for nonsemantic attributes of American Sign Language signs and English words. *Journal of Verbal Learning and Verbal Behavior, 16,* 561–574.

Snyder, L. S., Bates, E., & Bretherton, I. (1981). Content and context in early lexical development. *Journal of Child Language, 8,* 565–582.

Volterra, V. (1983). Gestures, signs, and words at two years. In J. G. Kyle & B. Woll (Eds.), *Language in sign: An international perspective on sign language* (pp. 109–115). London: Croom Helm.

Volterra, V., & Caselli, M. C. (1985). From gestures and vocalizations to signs and words. In W. Stokoe & V. Volterra (Eds.), *SLR '83: Proceedings of the III International Symposium on Sign Language Research* (pp. 1–9). Silver Spring, MD: Linstok.

Volterra, V., & Iverson, J. M. (1995). When do modality factors affect the course of language acquisition? In K. Emmorey & J. S. Reilly (Eds.), *Language, gesture, and space.* Mahwah, NJ: Lawrence Erlbaum Associates.

21

Early and Late in Language Acquisition: Aspects of the Syntax and Acquisition of *Wh*-Questions in American Sign Language

Diane Lillo-Martin
*University of Connecticut
and Haskins Laboratories*

In 1980, Ursula Bellugi and a group of researchers from The Salk Institute came to California State University Northridge for a week-long workshop on the research activities of the Laboratory for Language and Cognitive Studies (LLCS). As an undergraduate majoring in Linguistics with an interest in American Sign Language (ASL) and not a clear understanding of how those two interests were related to each other, I attended the workshop and came away a changed person. I remember how exciting and stimulating the workshop was, and I remember thinking how lucky those researchers were to be able to devote their time to understanding the linguistics (and psycholinguistics and neurolinguistics) of a language in another modality. I applied to graduate school at the University of California San Diego (UCSD), and nowhere else, confident that what I wanted to do was learn at the feet of the masters.

My years at UCSD and LLCS, studying and working under the guidance of Ed Klima and Ursula Bellugi, proved to me that I had made the right choice. Nowhere else could I receive the experience and education that prepared me and allowed me to follow a career like those "lucky" researchers. Under Ed and Ursie, I learned much about syntactic argumentation and psycholinguistic research, lessons that have proved invaluable to me to this day. This is not to say that my time there was all sun and roses! It was tough work (as it should have been), and Ed and Ursie were taskmasters, requiring hard work and dedication. They showed me that the career I dreamed of would mean long hours and many uncertainties—though an appreciation for classical music would be tolerated.

While I was working at Salk, Ursula had the opportunity to write a chapter for a Festschrift in honor of her mentor, Roger Brown (Bellugi, 1988). I learned then that this is not an easy thing to do, because one wants to convey the depth of appreciation for the person as well as the education, in a way not too technical but not too personal. I decided to use this chapter to discuss some of the results of a research project I have been involved in (with collaborators Carole Tenny Boster, Kazumi Matsuoka, Michiko Nohara, Deborah Chen Pichler, and Doreen Simons-Marques), investigating the acquisition of *wh*-questions in ASL. The project (still in progress) involves issues I studied under Ed and Ursie, including both syntactic analysis and studies of language acquisition. It is a topic I will continue to study, as it is a good example of how syntactic studies and acquisition studies can contribute to each other. And it relates to specific interests of Ursie's and Ed's, harking back as it does to one of their first articles together, on the acquisition of *wh*-questions in English (Klima & Bellugi-Klima, 1966).

BACKGROUND

The formation of *wh*-questions in ASL allows for a greater variety of surface forms than that found in English. This means that Deaf children learning ASL would seem to have a relatively difficult job, needing to sort out which options are possible and which are not. Furthermore, ASL *wh*-questions employ a specific nonmanual marker with well-defined restrictions, which children also must pick up. We are investigating the development of *wh*-questions in young children learning ASL as a native language to see whether or not they obey the grammatical rules concerning *wh*-questions in ASL and whether they use the full variety of forms available. Data from children may also contribute toward our understanding of the mechanisms involved in the adult grammar that allow these various forms.

For example, in ASL (an underlying SVO language) the *wh*-element can often be found sentence initially, sentence finally, or "doubled," in both initial and final position. Examples of such *wh*-questions are given in Examples (1) to (3). These different orders might well be used in different contexts, but we do not focus on this aspect of them here.

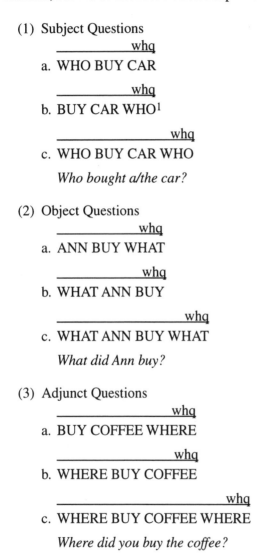

(1) Subject Questions

                      whq

  a. WHO BUY CAR

                      whq

  b. BUY CAR WHO[1]

                            whq

  c. WHO BUY CAR WHO

    Who bought a/the car?

(2) Object Questions

                      whq

  a. ANN BUY WHAT

                      whq

  b. WHAT ANN BUY

                            whq

  c. WHAT ANN BUY WHAT

    What did Ann buy?

(3) Adjunct Questions

                        whq

  a. BUY COFFEE WHERE

                        whq

  b. WHERE BUY COFFEE

                            whq

  c. WHERE BUY COFFEE WHERE

    Where did you buy the coffee?

---

[1]The grammaticality status of subject questions with only a sentence-final *wh*-phrase—such as (1b)—and object questions with only a sentence-initial *wh*-phrase—such as (2b)—is a matter of some debate in the literature. For both of these sentence types, there is variation in acceptability judgments given by adults, with differences often relating to different discourse contexts. For extensive discussion, see Neidle, Kegl, Bahan, Aarons and MacLaughlin (1997) and Petronio & Lillo-Martin (1997).

In the "a" examples, the *wh*-element in initial or final position could be considered not to have moved from its underlying position; that is, it might be in situ. However, in the "b" examples, the *wh*-element appears to have been displaced from its deep structure position to the sentence-initial or sentence-final position. In the "c" examples, a *wh*-element is found in both initial and final positions.

In part because of the variety of surface forms found, two competing analyses of *wh*-questions in ASL have been proposed. Both proposals conclude that *wh*-elements may either move or be left in situ. Neidle and her colleagues (Neidle et al., 1997, and other works cited there) proposed that the syntactic operation of *wh*-movement in ASL is rightward, to a rightward position called spec CP. Petronio and Lillo-Martin (1997; also Lillo-Martin & Fischer, 1992; and other works cited in these works), on the other hand, proposed that this movement operation moves *wh*-elements leftward, to a leftward spec CP. Each analysis can account for the appearance of *wh*-elements in other positions by appealing to independent processes: under Neidle et al.'s (1997) account, a leftward *wh*-element in doubled questions can be a base-generated topic; whereas under Petronio and Lillo-Martin's (1997) account, a rightward *wh*-element is analyzed as a base-generated focused element in double questions as well as some other cases. The two accounts have similar (though not identical) empirical coverage, differing largely in theoretical concerns, and in judgments of grammaticality for some examples.

An additional component of ASL *wh*-questions is a nonmanual marker (studied in detail by Baker-Shenk, 1983). Simultaneously with the manual signs, the signer articulates a specific facial gesture, which includes squinted eyebrows, a head tilt, possible slightly forward body position, and possible raised shoulders. This nonmanual marker serves a syntactic function (Liddell, 1980) and is a required component of ASL interrogatives. As examples (4) to (5) show, the extent of the nonmanual marker is syntactically constrained.

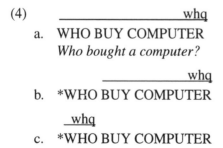

(4)   _____whq
    a.   WHO BUY COMPUTER
       Who bought a computer?

                      _____whq
    b.   *WHO BUY COMPUTER

            _whq
    c.   *WHO BUY COMPUTER

(5) _____ hn ___whq
    JOHN BUY WHAT
    John bought something. What?

In general, the nonmanual marker indicates the scope of the *wh*-question and cooccurs with all of the signs of the question. In some cases, a *wh*-question consists of just the *wh*-phrase, which follows a separate sentence not marked by the *wh*-question nonmanual marking, as in (5). The leftward and rightward analyses differ in the details of their treatment of the nonmanual *wh*-question marker. However, both emphasize its syntactic role, obligatoriness, and scope.

The syntactic evidence for the leftward analysis is strong but is not discussed further here (see Neidle et al., 1997; Petronio & Lillo-Martin, 1997). Whichever analysis is correct, the child learning ASL must be able to make sense of the input to determine the basic structure of ASL *wh*-questions, the options for other possible word orders, and the concomitant use of the non-manual *wh*-question marker. We investigated the development of *wh*-questions in young children learning ASL as a native language to see how they dealt with this difficult situation.

METHOD

The data reported here come from an ongoing study of Deaf children learning ASL with different types of exposure to it. In this chapter, we report only on a subset of the results analyzed so far from Deaf children of Deaf, signing parents. These children receive input in ASL from birth and are known to acquire it in general along the same time course found for the acquisition of spoken languages (for summaries of research on the acquisition of ASL, see Lillo-Martin, 1999; Newport & Meier, 1985). The data from 17 children, ages 4;1 to 6;9 (five 4-year olds and 6 each of 5-year-olds and 6-year-olds) are reported here.[2]

We used an elicited production task to gather a relatively large number of *wh*-questions from each child. As illustrated in Figure 21.1, two Deaf native signers interacted with each child individually. The experimenters knew the children, who were usually tested in a recreation room at their

---

[2]The full study, to include children at other ages and children with hearing parents, will be reported in greater detail in a separate paper.

FIG. 21.1.   Experimental situation.

school. All sessions were recorded on videotape for later analysis. One experimenter, whom we call the storyteller, acted out stories with toys and props. The other experimenter was dressed as a cat and acted the part of a knowledgeable but shy individual, who liked to interact with children but not with adults. After making sure that the child knew names for all the props, the storyteller would tell in ASL a story such as the one in (6).

(6) Here is a lion, an elephant, a sandwich, some potato chips, and a pie. The lion and the elephant just arrived at the zoo after a long trip. They're both very hungry. Hmm, let's see now, about the lion. He wants to eat something, but I don't know what. The cat knows a lot about lions. Ask him what.

With such prompting, the child could respond with a *wh*-question like one of those in (7).

(7)   _____whq

   a. WHAT LION EAT

           _____whq

   b. LION EAT WHAT

                _____whq

   c. WHAT LION EAT WHAT
     What does the lion eat?

Using this methodology, we created target sentences for one- and two-clause subject, object, and adjunct questions. There were 14 target *wh*-questions.

The videotapes were transcribed verbatim by a Deaf native signer. Then, using the transcripts and reexamining the videos, we coded every *wh*-question produced by the children in intersecting categories according to question type and position of the *wh*-element. We also coded the use of the nonmanual *wh*-question marker.

RESULTS AND DISCUSSION

Position of the *Wh*-Element

We elicited 209 codable one-clause *wh*-questions from the 17 children. There were also numerous "long-distance" questions, and although indirect questions were not elicitation targets, they were also produced by most of the participants. Here, we present only the one-clause ("matrix") question results.

For the current analysis, we determined the position of the *wh*-phrase as initial, final, or double. We then calculated the proportion of each of these positions for each question type. Figures 21.2 to 21.4 show these proportions for matrix questions. It is clear that the children used all of the possible *wh*-positions but not in the same way across sentence types. Initial is the overall most preferred position, especially for subject and adjunct questions. Note that for subject questions, initial *wh*-phrases might be in situ; similarly, final, the most preferred position for object questions, is indistinguishable from in situ in most of our examples. However, the initial position is presumably not the in situ position for adjunct questions.

Now let us consider the proportions of use of the different *wh*-positions across the age groups. Figure 21.2 shows the *wh*-positions for matrix subject questions. Clearly, for all age groups, initial is the preferred position. Double is the next most commonly used construction, especially for the older children. Relatively few *wh*-subjects in final position were found. Examples of children's matrix subject questions are given in (8).

(8)   whq
      a. Initial   (age 4;1)   WHO SHOULD BATHE
                                   Who should bathe?

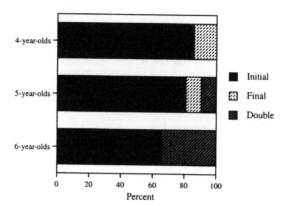

FIG. 21.2. Matrix subject *Wh*-question production

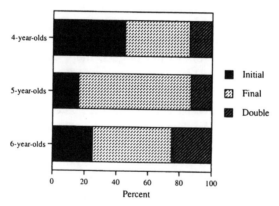

FIG. 21.3. Matrix object *Wh*-question production

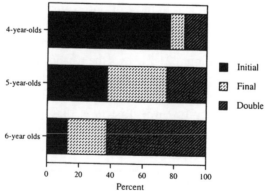

FIG. 21.4.368 Matrix adjunct *Wh*-question production

			whq

b. Final   (age 5;5)   IT(box) INSIDE IT(b) WHAT
What's inside it(b)?

c. Double (age 6;0)   WHO DRIVE TRACTOR WHO
Who drives the tractor?

On the other hand, Fig. 21.3 shows that the preferred *wh*-positions for matrix object questions are quite different. Although the 4-year-olds continue to use a large number of initial *wh*-elements (clearly not in situ), the 5-year-olds strongly prefer final (plausibly in situ) *wh*-elements. Examples of children's matrix object questions are given in (9).

(9)   _____ whq

a. Initial   (age 5;5)   WHAT YOU FEEL
What do you think?

b. Final   (age 5;9)   TURTLE EAT WHAT
What does the turtle eat?

                                        _____ whq
c. Double (age 5;5)   WHAT YOU FEEL YOU WHAT
What do you think?

Finally, Fig. 21.4 shows the distribution of positions for matrix adjunct questions. In these examples, the preference for the younger children again returns to sentence-initial position. The older children use a large number of double structures. Examples of children's matrix adjunct questions are given in (10).

(10) a. Initial   (age 5;10)   WHY MONSTER COOK CAKE
Why did cookie monster make a cake?

b. Final   (age 5;10)   LION SLEEP WHERE
Were does the lion sleep?

c. Double[3] (age 6;0)   LION WHERE SLEEP BED WHERE
Where does the lion sleep?

---

[3]The example in (10c) is counted as a double even though the sign LION occurs before the first *wh*-element. We assume that LION is a topic and that the *wh*-sign WHERE is in the usual position for initial *wh*-elements (including the initial *wh*-sign in a double construction). This kind of example, which is also accepted by adults, is most consistent with the leftward movement analysis, and the fact that children used such structures supports this analysis. This point was also made by S. Fischer in her comments on an earlier version of this chapter.

Overall, then, we find that especially for the youngest children, there was a strong preference for the sentence-initial *wh*-element. For subject questions, this could be an in situ *wh*-phrase, consistent with the preference for in situ (final) object questions. However, there was also a clear preference for sentence-initial *wh*-elements in adjunct questions for the youngest children.

Our results are most compatible with the proposal that spec CP is on the left in ASL. Using this syntactic analysis, our results indicate that children readily use movement to (the leftward) spec CP, as well as in situ *wh*-questions, which are permitted by the adult grammar. This is consistent with findings from the acquisition of languages such as English (in which children consistently use correct leftward moved *wh*-questions) and Japanese (in which children consistently use correct in situ *wh*-questions). Question forms utilizing additional syntactic structures (e.g., the double form) are much less frequently used by the younger children. On the other hand, under the rightward spec CP analysis of ASL *wh*-questions, it would seem that the youngest children use *wh*-topics more frequently than movement to spec CP—a curious sequence.

We would like to point out that even the youngest children for whom we have data here use a variety of *wh*-question types (with differing frequency). In addition to initial, final, and double *wh*-elements, these children produced a few examples of other types of ASL *wh*-questions. For example, even some of the youngest children (4;3, 4;10) produced null *wh*-elements and split *wh*-questions, illustrated in (11); Lillo-Martin and Fischer (1992) discussed these types of ASL *wh*-questions.

(11)   _____whq

    a. Null   LION EAT INDEX(food)
             (Which food) does the lion eat?

    b. Split WHICH YOU GUESS HE(seal) EAT INDEX(food)
             Which food do you guess he(s) eats?

Use of the Non-Manual *Wh*-Question Marker

Despite the children's use of several different *wh*-constructions, there is one aspect of their *wh*-questions that is far from accurate. This is the use of the nonmanual *wh*-question marker. Of the children analyzed, many did not use it at all. Of those who did use it, none used it completely consistently.

Let us consider the nonmanual markers used by one child, whom we call Lisa (tested at ages 5;5 and 5;7), in some detail. Lisa used the nonmanual *wh*-question marker most consistently. Almost all of her matrix questions were correctly marked. On the other hand, none of her direct questions on an embedded constituent were marked.

As a generalization, for Lisa (and for the other children), when a nonmanual *wh*-question marker was used, it was used correctly. The main error is one of omission. Correct use involves spreading of the nonmanual marker over all the manual signs in the sentence. There are very few exceptions to this generalization, two of which are given in (12).

(12) <u> whq </u>

    a. WHO CAN DRIVE
    Who can drive?

                           <u> whq </u>

    b. (ME YOU ASK) WHO WILL DRIVE WHO
    (I'm asking you), Who will drive?

The two examples in (12) are the only examples we found for Lisa in which the nonmanual marker appears not to have spread. In (12b), it is possible that the final *wh*-element constitutes a separate sentence—and the example is grammatical on this analysis (cf. Petronio & Lillo-Martin, 1997). (12a) is ungrammatical.

The observation that the nonmanual *wh*-question marker is delayed relative to the manual markers was earlier made by Reilly and McIntire (1991), who found that Deaf children younger than 3 did not use the nonmanual *wh*-question marker productively, and even children older than 3 frequently used a nonstandard nonmanual marker (e.g., a head tilt but no brow furrow). This finding is consistent with other work by Reilly and McIntire, in which they found a delayed use of nonmanual markers for constructions in which a manual marker can also signal a grammatical function (e.g., conditionals; see Reilly, chap. 22 in this volume, for a summary of much of this work.) However, the finding of both these studies that even 6-year-old Deaf children do not consistently appropriately use nonmanual grammatical markers is quite surprising and puzzling and is the subject of our continued further study.

SUMMARY

We found that 4-year-old Deaf children use a variety of surface structures in their productions of *wh*-questions in ASL. However, they showed a strong preference for sentence-initial *wh*-elements. Older children used a larger number of structures other than initial, particularly in situ *wh*-elements, and they also more frequently used *wh*-doubles. Even the oldest children did not use the nonmanual *wh*-question marker consistently when required, but when it was used, it was almost always used correctly. This pattern of results is most consistent with the proposal that overt *wh*-movement in ASL is to a leftward spec CP. The observation that universally, languages seem to have spec CP on the left (despite variation in the position of other specifiers) is thus supported by the ASL data.

ACKNOWLEDGMENTS

This research was supported in part by NIH-NIDCD grant #DC-00183 and by the University of Connecticut Research Foundation. I would like to thank Carole Tenny Boster, Kazumi Matsuoka, Michiko Nohara, Deborah Chen Pichler, and Doreen Simons-Marques, for valuable help with data analysis; Karen Emmorey, Susan Fischer, and two anonymous UConn WPL reviewers for editorial comments; the faculty and staff at the California School for the Deaf in Fremont, and the Maryland School for the Deaf in Frederick, and our testers at these two locations, for their assistance in conducting the study; and especially the students who participated in the study. Some of the research reported in this paper was presented at the LSA Annual Meeting; San Diego, California, January 1996; and published in the University of Connecticut Working Papers in Linguistics (Lillo-Martin, Boster, Matsuoka, & Nohara, 1996).

REFERENCES

Baker-Shenk, C. (1983). *A micro-analysis of the nonmanual components of questions in American Sign Language.* Unpublished doctoral dissertation, University of California, Berkeley.

Bellugi, U. (1988). The Acquisition of a Spatial Language. In F. Kessel (Ed.), *The development of language and language researchers: Essays in honor of Roger Brown* (pp. 153–185). Mahwah, NJ: Lawrence Erlbaum Associates.

Klima, E., & Bellugi-Klima, U. (1966). Syntactic regularities in the speech of children. In J. Lyons & R. Wales (Eds.), *Psycholinguistic papers* (pp. 183–208). Edinburgh: University of Edinburgh Press.

Liddell, S. (1980). *American Sign Language syntax*. The Hague, Netherlands: Mouton.

Lillo-Martin, D. (1999). Modality Effects and Modularity in Language Acquisition: The Acquisition of American Sign Language. In W. Ritchie & T. Bhatia (Eds.), *Handbook of language acquisition* (pp. 531–567). San Diego, CA: Academic Press.

Lillo-Martin, D., & Fischer, S. D. (1992, May). *Overt and covert wh-questions in American Sign Language*. Talk presented at the Fifth International Symposium on Sign Language Research, Salamanca, Spain.

Lillo-Martin, D., Boster, C. T., Matsuoka, K., & Nohara, M. (1996). *Early and late in language acquisition: Aspects of wh-questions in American Sign Language*. University of Connecticut Working Papers in Linguistics.

Neidle, C., Kegl, J., Bahan, B., Aarons, D., & MacLaughlin, D. (1997). Rightward wh-movement in American Sign Language. In D. Beerman, D. LeBlanc, & H. vanRiemsdijk, (Eds.), *Rightward movement* (pp. 247–278). Amsterdam: John Benjamins.

Newport, E., & Meier, R. (1985). The acquisition of American Sign Language. In D. Slobin (Ed.), *The crosslinguistic study of language acquisition; Volume 1: The data* (pp. 881–938). Mahwah, NJ: Lawrence Erlbaum Associates.

Petronio, K., & Lillo-Martin. D. (1997). Wh-movement and the position of spec CP: Evidence from American Sign Language. *Language 73*, 18–57.

Reilly, J., & McIntire, M. (1991). Where shoe? The acquisition of wh-questions in American Sign Language. *Papers and Reports on Child Language Development, 30*, 104–111.

22

Bringing Affective Expression Into the Service of Language: Acquiring Perspective Marking in Narratives

Judy Reilly
San Diego State University

It gives me immense pleasure to contribute to this volume for Ursie and Ed. For almost 15 years now, we have shared coffee and cookies, numerous hours chatting and discussing, laughing and writing. When I first came to the lab as a postdoc, I was interested in how Deaf infants make the transition from first using facial expression to convey and interpret emotion (similar to hearing infants) to acquiring American Sign Language (ASL) and also using facial expression as part of the nonmanual grammar. The multifunctionality of facial expression in ASL, that is, that it serves both grammatical and affective roles, appeared to be a unique opportunity to explore the relations between these two communicative systems, affect or emotion and language. This journey has been profitable and the question has broadened to include numerous intersections of language and the expression of emotion. Ursie, Ed, and I have continued to work on some of these together, for example, affective expression and evaluative language in narratives of children with Williams syndrome (Bellugi, Losh, Reilly, & Anderson, 1998; Reilly, Klima, & Bellugi, 1990). But in this chapter, I would like to focus on the original question and our first domain of collaboration: the acquisition of grammatical facial behaviors in ASL and its relation to emotional expression. Specifically, in this chapter, we examine how children integrate language and emotion to signal perspective changes in narratives. Before we begin, however, a brief overview of grammatical facial expression in ASL might be helpful.

FACIAL MORPHOLOGY IN ASL

Similar to other signed languages, in the ASL nonmanual grammar, specific constellations of facial behaviors serve as the obligatory morphological marking for a variety of linguistic structures, and these facial behaviors cooccur with the manual string over which they have scope. Facial signals in ASL play three different roles:

(1) Lexical:

$$\overline{\hspace{2.5cm}\text{th}}$$
LATE   NOT YET

(2) Adverbial:

(2a) BOY WRITE LETTER

"The boy is writing/wrote a letter"

$$\overline{\hspace{3.5cm}\text{mm}}$$
(2b) BOY WRITE LETTER

"The boy writes/wrote letters regularly or easily"

$$\overline{\hspace{3.5cm}\text{th}}$$
(2c) BOY WRITE LETTER

"The boy writes/wrote letters carelessly"

(3) Syntactic

$$\overline{\hspace{1.5cm}\text{cond.}}$$
EAT BUG, SICK YOU

"If you eat a bug, you get sick"

(With respect to transcription conventions, the nonmanual signal is denoted by a line over the manually signed utterance [in CAPS]; the length of the line depicts the scope and duration of the nonmanual behavior;

these signals are labeled at the end of the line. Additional information on transcription is in the Appendix.)

Grammatical facial behaviors in ASL often constitute the sole morphological signal for a particular linguistic structure, as in conditionals. If the utterance in Example (3) is produced without the conditional nonmanual marker, rather than being interpreted as the antecedent and consequent clauses of a conditional sentence, the utterance is two simple declarative statements. Thus, in this instance, the nonmanual signal is the conditional marker.

Although the facial morphology uses the same muscles as those that are recruited for affective expression, their timing, scope, and context often differ. Whereas affective facial expression can be used independently of language, for example, we might smile in response to a toddler's first steps, grammatical facial behaviors invariably cooccur with a manually signed utterance. Secondly, the timing of grammatical facial expression is linguistically constrained. It begins milliseconds before the initiation of the manual string over which it has scope and immediately attains apex intensity that is maintained until the termination of the manual string. In contrast, emotional facial expression is variable in intensity, and its timing is inconsistent and inconstant. These patterns are graphically contrasted in Examples (4) and (5):

(4) Grammatical facial expression

BOY WRITE LETTER

(5) Affective facial expression

MY CAT BORN[+] BABY {excitedly} "My cat had kittens!"

BABYFACE: THE EARLY STUDIES

In our studies chronicling the acquisition of grammatical facial expression, we began with the smallest of pieces, single sign productions of Deaf toddlers (Reilly, McIntire, & Bellugi, 1990). Focusing on early multichannel productions, namely, constructions that included both a manual sign and a cooccurring facial behavior, we found that initially, before the age of 2 years, these single-sign productions appeared to be acquired as chunks or gestalts, much as hearing children early on acquire whole unanalyzed phrases (e.g., MacWhinney, 1978). For example, when toddlers signed HAPPY or SAD, the manual sign was accompanied by the appropriate emotional facial expression; when they asked "WHAT," they generally furrowed their brows in puzzlement. At about 2- to $2^1/2$ years of age, as children begin producing sentences, however, we found that the facial behaviors that we had previously witnessed were often missing from these same signs or structures. The same children were fluently using manual signs and manually signed grammatical constructions that required grammatical facial expressions, for example, wh-questions, however, their faces were often blank (Reilly & McIntire 1991).

For example, if we look at this developmental profile for wh-questions, we know that in the adult model, wh-sign questions in ASL include a wh-sign (e.g., WHAT, HOW, WHERE, etc.) as well as a furrowed brow and head tilt; these nonmanual behaviors begin immediately before the manually signed string and have scope over the entire wh-question (Baker & Cokely 1980; Baker-Schenk, 1983). The questions produced by the very youngest children (before age 2 or so) often included aspects of the adult nonmanual behavior, but the timing and components of the facial expression did not necessarily match the adult model as in the two following examples:

(6) Corinne (1;6)

    _____ 4 [brow furrow]

    "WHAT"

(7) Corinne (1;9)

    _____ 51<>52_ [headshake]

    WHERE MELON

    "Where's the melon?"

(On the nonmanual line, numbers reflect specific muscle contractions, called *Action Units* (from Facial Action Coding System [FACS], Ekman & Friesen, 1978).

In contrast, by about 2- to $2^1/2$ years of age, children were producing many questions, but they often omitted the required furrowed brow; their faces were neutral:

(8) Kate (2;3) WHERE   "WHAT"

"Where is it?"

Interestingly, we found this same pattern of acquisition of facial morphology for linguistic structures that had formally and functionally similar communicative counterparts, for example, negation, which is signaled nonlinguistically, as well as linguistically, with a headshake. The same pattern was also apparent in structures that are unique to ASL, for example, adverbials such as *mm* or *th*. That is, similar to *wh*-questions, for both very early adverbials and negation, we have examples of toddlers producing single manual signs with what appeared to be an appropriate nonmanual facial behavior, as in the following early productions:

(9)   Kate: (1;8) _____neg headshake

STINKY

"[It's] not stinky."

(10)   Kate (2;3)   _____18+44 (puckered lips pucker+squint)

SCADS

Soon thereafter, these same types of constructions were signaled uniquely in the manual channel. Whether the structure had a comparable communicative counterpart, such as the headshake for negation, or was exclusively a linguistic structure of ASL, did not appear to influence the developmental pattern. From this behavioral profile, we inferred that during the early period of single signed utterances, children were using facial behaviors that expressed an affective–communicative function. Once the child began producing multisigned utterances and had analyzed facial behaviors into linguistic components, she no longer recruited these earlier affective abilities. It appears that once children were producing sentences, they were not able to directly generalize their affective and communicative abilities to the appropriate linguistic context.

We have now looked at a range of grammatical structures varying in complexity from single lexical items such as emotion signs (Reilly et al., 1991) and negation (Anderson & Reilly, 1997) to adverbials (Anderson & Reilly, in press) and clausal structures, such as conditionals (Reilly, McIntire, & Bellugi, 1990) and *wh*-questions (Reilly and McIntire, 1991), In each of our developmental investigations, after about age 2, we found the identical developmental pattern: Children invariably begin producing the linguistic structure using only the manual sign and omitting the required nonmanuals. Only after the structure is fluently conveyed in the manual channel do children begin to add the non-manual components, and these are often acquired gradually and componentially rather than as a whole (for a discussion and more examples, see Reilly, McIntire, & Bellugi, 1991). We are nearing the end of this journey and are now ready to look at the acquisition of even larger nonmanual components, those that signal discourse units and potentially span multiple clauses. The current study focuses on the development of perspective marking or what has been commonly known in the literature as *role shift*. (e.g., Padden, 1986; Smith, Lentz, & Mikos, 1988). Role shift recruits emotional facial expression (which can function to reflect the character's emotion) to linguistically delineate the scope of direct quote or reported action. As such, the acquisition of role or referential shift provides an additional perspective on how emotional expression comes to serve language.

REFERENTIAL SHIFT

In spoken English narratives, speakers can identify point of view through labeling and pronominal shifts, and sometimes by a distinctive voice quality. In ASL, in addition to manual lexical means, such as naming characters or pointing at an established spatial locus, point of view is also signaled through changes in eye gaze, body shifts, and the use of affective facial expressions. Engberg-Pedersen (1993, 1995) proposed a thoughtful analysis of features involved in role shift from Danish Sign Language. She identified several types of "shifters": *shifted reference, shifted attribution of expressive elements*, and *shifted locus* which appear independently or in concert. For our purposes, only the first two are pertinent.

Shifted reference is limited to direct quotes or reported speech. The narrator uses pronouns from another person's perspective; for example, when the narrator is talking as if she were the character, the first-person pronoun may refer to the character or person being quoted, rather than to the speaker or signer herself. In shifted attribution of expressive elements, the attitude or emotion expressed is attributed to another person besides the speaker. This strategy is often used to indicate changes between two participants in a (reported) dialogue and may indicate characteristic features of the quoted sender or his affect. In addition to occurring with a person or character's quoted utterance, it may also coincide with his actions or thoughts, but here we are concerned with direct discourse and both spoken and signed languages can use this mechanism for direct quotation. As Engberg-Pedersen (1995) stated, "shifted attribution of expressive elements contributes to the impression that the events of the narrative are presented through the psyche of one of the characters" (p. 145).

When a signer's own locus is "taken over" by one of the referents, this is the phenomenon, we believe, that is most frequently intended when signers talk about role shift. One context of role shift or referential shift, and the one we are concerned with here, is that of direct quotation. In direct quotation, the affective facial behaviors are attributed to the character who is being quoted and the manual signs are the content of the discourse, that is, the "speech" (sign) of the character. In addition to facial expressions, role shift is also signaled by other nonmanual behaviors, such as change in eye gaze, head movement, and body shifts.

In an earlier study comparing the acquisition of direct quote to reported action in 15 Deaf children acquiring ASL as their native language (Emmorey & Reilly, 1998), we found that the children used direct quotes and appeared to have mastered the necessary linguistic conventions to do so significantly earlier than they fluently used reported action in narratives. Now we are ready to consider in more detail how children acquire the devices to signal direct quotes in ASL narratives, and specifically the role emotional expression plays in this process.

In related work on narratives in preschoolers, both Deaf and hearing, we saw how their extensive use of affective expression, especially prosody, is effectively used by these youngest storytellers to maintain the floor, increase addressee involvement and broadly signal that the child is in the midst of performing a narrative (Reilly 1992, in press). In these early stories, affective expression appears to be a reflection of the child's own current emotion and enthusiasm in telling the story. In this chapter, we focus on the transition from using affective expression reflecting the child's own involvement in the storytelling process to its codification in the service of language to signal change of perspective and to demonstrate the emotion of a character in a story. Their challenge is now to convey that they are representing a character rather than themselves as narrator or themselves as children, in such a way that it conforms to linguistically defined specifications.

As our past studies on the acquisition of facial morphology showed, Deaf children do not generalize their earlier acquired proficiency with emotional facial expression to the appropriate linguistic context. Rather, the acquisition of grammatical facial expression invariably follows a slow patterned development common in the acquisition of bound morphology

(Brown, 1973, Slobin, 1973). However, because the facial expression in direct quotes actually reflects the character's emotion, we might predict that these facial behaviors would demonstrate a different acquisition profile. In fact, we might hypothesize that because the child just has to "pretend" to be the character, she would immediately recruit her affective abilities and quickly master the nonmanual signaling of direct quotes.

THE STORIES: CONVEYING PERSPECTIVE

To understand how children acquire the system for signaling character point of view, we collected and analyzed stories from 28 Deaf children of Deaf parents who are acquiring ASL as their first language, and five adult native signers. The children range in age from 3;0 to 7;5 and are evenly distributed across the age range. We chose the story of "The Three Bears" because it is familiar even to the youngest age group, and it includes four different characters: Goldilocks and the three Bears. Moreover, in this story, Deaf adults include numerous shifts of point of view, and it is especially rich in direct quotes (Emmorey & Reilly, 1998). Using a version illustrated by Galdone (1972) in which all words were concealed, the child first looked through the book and then told the story. To decrease memory load, the picture book was available to the children throughout the storytelling. All stories were videotaped and transcribed using a combination of modified Baker and Cokely (1980) transcription and FACS (Ekman & Friesen, 1978). After the stories were transcribed, our analyses focused on the seven episodes in the story that traditionally include direct quotes: from the Bears' initial conversation regarding cereal to Goldilocks' comments on the qualities of the Bears' porridge ("too hot," "too cold," and "just right") and the Bears' chairs and beds ("too hard," "too soft," and "just right") and to the later episodes including all three Bears as they discover that someone has been in their house and tampered with their porridge, chairs, and beds. We coded and analyzed each of these episodes for the following linguistic features:

Manual Aspects

(1) The manually signed utterances
(2) Labels, that is, the names of the characters, and pointing to the book or a locus in space to signal the source of the quote, that is, who they were talking for

Pertinent Nonmanual Behaviors

(3) Eye gaze: plus or minus eye contact with the addressee; gaze direction and shifts in direction
(4) Facial expression: the individual components (according to FACS); and their timing, that is, onset and offset with reference to the manually signed utterance
(5) Head and body shifts.

DIRECT QUOTES IN THE ADULT STORIES

As expected, the five adult stories are replete with direct quotes that are signaled both manually and nonmanually. Manually, adults introduce the quote by naming the character, for example, FATHER. They also use affective facial expression to reflect the character's emotional state or response. Eye-gaze behaviors play a critical role as both morphological and discourse markers. Gaze may be directed: (a) to the addressee, in which case the signer is either the narrator or himself; (b) toward a linguistically or discourse-driven point, for example, toward an assigned locus in the signing space; or (c) gaze may also be "nondirected," or looking in the direction that the character would look, indicating that the narrator has assumed the character's point of view (see also Bahan & Supalla, 1995).

When viewed in real time, the nonmanual behaviors signaling direct quote appear to emerge as a whole; however, frame-by-frame viewing reveals a pattern of sequential events: To produce a direct quote, and to signal that they are "taking on the perspective" of that character (referential shift), adults frequently label the character first, for example, MOTHER. Accompanying this sign, the signer maintains eye contact with the addressee (in the role as narrator) and often raises brows to signal topic; he may also point to the already established locus in the signing space. Then, to signal that the quote is beginning, as the signer lowers his brows, he breaks eye gaze with the addressee, shifts head and often body position (taking on the stance of the character in contrast with that of the narrator), and assumes the facial expression of that character's emotional response to the current situation. Finally, the character's utterance is signed manually; this manual string, which may span multiple clauses, dictates the scope of the accompanying nonmanual behaviors (gaze, head position, and facial expression). For example,

(11)

```
_____topic _____surprise
_____+K  _____-K
```

BABY BEAR LOOK-AT LETS-SEE MY Cl: C

Baby Bear looked at his soup, "Let's see my bowl.

```
_____pouting
_____distress
_____-K
```

HEY GONE SOUP Cl:1 SOMEONE FINISH EAT ALL

Hey my soup's gone! Someone ate it all up!"

(+K = eye contact with addressee; -K = signals a gaze shift averting gaze from addressee.)

Across the adult instances of perspective shift, eye gaze and head behaviors are consistent with respect to timing and quality. As such, we infer that they constitute the required grammatical markers to signal a change in perspective or role shift. The occurrence of body shifts is less consistent and appears to be a supplementary device. With respect to the accompanying facial expression, they are clearly affective in nature, differing from signer to signer. Specifically, individual signers use appropriate but different affective expressions (different configurations of facial muscles) for the same character in the same episode in the story. For example, when the baby bear discovers his cereal is gone, some signers convey surprise and others sadness or distress, or both, as in 11. Also, although this pattern or sequence of nonmanual behaviors typified the vast majority of direct quotes in the adult stories, in some cases, the character's emotional facial expression emerges slightly earlier, as the signer labels the character. Nonetheless, the scope of the facial behaviors remains relatively constant and is clearly constrained by the quoted utterance of the character. In these instances, affect is truly working in the service of language.

We should also note that the frequent labeling of the character in these stories may reflect the number of characters in the discourse and the switches in perspective from narrator to one of the characters. In recounting a multiturn dialogue between two characters, after initially establishing the loci of the two characters, the narrator may exclusively use non-manual behaviors—changes in head position, gaze, and facial expression—to signal change of perspective (Rossini, Reilly, Fabretti, & Volterra, 1998).

THE CHILDREN'S STORIES: THE ACQUISITION OF DIRECT QUOTE

To be certain that the children indeed used direct quotes, we first tallied the number of direct quotes in the seven target episodes of the 28 Three Bears stories. Altogether, there were 19 potential situations for direct quotes. We found that although their stories were short and not terribly coherent, a subset of even the youngest children (aged 3 years) included some direct quotes. Therefore, we were able to use the coding categories mentioned previously. Overall, it appears that by age 6, children have mastered the manual and nonmanual signals for direct quote, with the exception of body shift, which occurred infrequently in our developmental data.

When we look at the acquisition and integration of these manual and nonmanual behaviors, initially we find that some of the 3-year-olds use gaze shifts and affective facial expression and that they sometimes label the character. However, all of these behaviors are used erratically, by only some of the children some of the time.

Nonmanual Features

Let us first consider shifts in gaze. As noted earlier, in narratives, when the signer makes eye contact with the addressee, he is functioning as narrator. To "become" a character, he shifts gaze to focus at an "undirected" location or where the character would be looking. As depicted in Fig. 22.1, these gaze shifts are used by two thirds of 3-year-olds and all 4-year-olds as well as the older children. Thus, gaze shifts appear to be the first marking of direct quote to be mastered.

With respect to emotional facial expression when signing for a character, it is frequently employed by children in all age groups. Fig. 22.2 shows that even the youngest children recruit some type of affective facial expression for direct quotes some of the time.

However, even though the 3- and 4-years-olds use facial expression frequently, Fig. 22.3 shows that it is not until ages 6 and 7 that they use it consistently and differentially for individual quotes, in the adult manner.

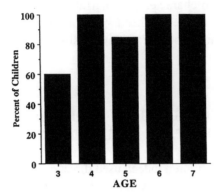

Fig. 22.1.   Gaze shifts.

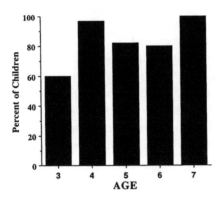

Fig. 22.2.   Use of facial expression in direct quotes.

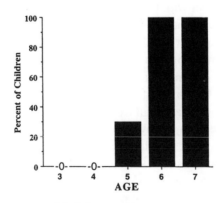

Fig. 22.3.   Consistent use of facial expression.

Preschoolers' use of facial expressions for characters differs from the adult model in three ways: (a) they are not precisely timed to the manual utterances of the character, (b) the same facial expression may be used continuously for utterances from different characters, and (c) its occurrence is erratic. For example, in Example (12), the child has eye contact (+K) with the addressee as she establishes the character by pointing at the book (PTBK). She then averts her gaze (-K) as she signs for the mother bear. She renews eye contact to establish the perspective of the baby bear and again averts her gaze as she signs for him. Thus, character point of view is indicated by appropriate gaze shifts and manual points to establish the character. However, the facial expression has inappropriate scope: The onset of the expression of surprise begins with the initial establishment of the mother as referent and continues on to terminate with the baby bear's utterance.

12) _____+K _____-K _____+K

_____surprise

PTBK(mother bear)   WHO EAT MY FOOD   PTBK (baby bear)

_____-K

_____surprise

WHAT HAPPEN MINE ALL WHO EAT MINE ALL

Mother bear said "Who ate my food?" Baby bear said "What happened to my food? Who ate up all my food?"

Manual Features

With respect to the manual channel, some of the youngest children use labels for the characters, but it is not until age 6 that all children are labeling who they are signing for 80% of the time, whereas adults use labels in this story 95% of the time (Fig. 22.4).

Unlike adults, we found that some children use another manual strategy, the verb SAY, to introduce direct quotes. Fig. 22.5 shows when and how often children use this strategy to introduce a quote.

Interestingly, 5 year olds use the manual sign SAY more frequently than any other age group to introduce a direct quote. They continue to use facial expression and gaze shifts but also add this manual sign, as in the following example in which character point of view is indicated by gaze shift, manual label, facial expression, and the manual sign SAY.

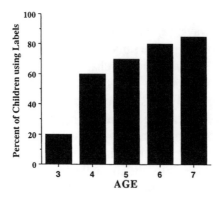

Fig. 22.4:   Use of labels to introduce direct quote.

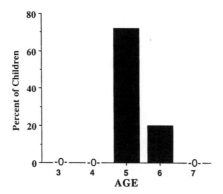

Fig. 22.5:   Use of SAY to introduce direct quote.

13)   disgust   disgust   disgust
_____K+ __K- _____K+ ___K- ___K+ _____K-
FATHER SAY   HOT   MOTHER SAY   WARM   BABY   SAY COLD
"Father Bear said '(this is too) hot!' Mother Bear said '(mine is) warm.' Baby Bear said '(mine is too) cold!'"

Because this lexical marker does not occur in the adult stories and rarely at the other ages, we infer that the use of SAY indicates some degree of linguistic reorganization on the part of the child. This over-marking is reminiscent of the overuse and reorganization of definite articles by young French-speaking children (Karmiloff-Smith, 1979). In our case, direct quotes are introduced lexically before the nonmanual behaviors are linguistically integrated with the manually signed utterance. Specifically, younger children (3- and 4-year-olds) have considerable difficulty with the timing and use of character facial expression; they use emotional facial expression frequently, but indiscriminately. SAY is an alternative means to signal a direct quote. Its appearance signals a significant development in the process of reanalyzing early affective and communicative behaviors for new linguistic purposes.

CONCLUSIONS

Deaf adults recruit a variety of facial expressions (and a constellation of additional required nonmanual behaviors, e.g., eye-gaze shifts) to signal that they are expressing a specific point of view (Engberg-Pedersen 1995). These behaviors are precisely timed to the manual utterance(s) and have scope over the entire discourse of that character. In contrast, younger children often use the same facial expression for multiple characters and the timing and scope of the facial expressions and gaze shifts are not appropriately coordinated with the accompanying utterance(s). From this global and undifferentiated use of affective facial expression, we infer that the deaf children are employing facial expression in much the same way that both signing and speaking preschoolers use affective prosody (Reilly, 1992, in press). At age 5, when the children consistently use SAY to indicate direct quotes, we infer that even though in direct quote, facial expression conveys emotional information, its timing and scope are constrained by the linguistic system; as such, children use the same basic strategy to master direct quote as we have seen in the acquisition of all other nonmanual signals. Even when facial expression is used to convey affective information, if it is in a linguistically dictated structure, children persist in using the same developmental strategy: The lexical manual sign(s) precedes the acquisition of the non-manual behaviors. Once again, ASL demonstrates the enormous flexibility of language: Whereas 99.9% of the world's people use facial expression to convey emotion, signed languages have recruited this signaling system for linguistic purposes. However, these acquisition data also demonstrate the constraints and rigidity of the language acquisition process. Even when linguistic facial expression is used to convey emotion, children cannot just generalize their prelinguistic affective knowledge to the appropriate linguistic context. Rather, similar to other complex bound morphology, linguistic facial expression is acquired gradually in a linguistically driven manner. Regardless of the structure, from single sign adverbials to multiclausal chunks of discourse, if the structure is conveyed with both manual and nonmanual signals, the acquisition pattern is the same. Before children can smoothly integrate the nonmanual behaviors, the structure is signaled manually, and as we saw with the verb SAY, even to the point of inventing strategies that do not occur in the adult model.

Now we are at the end of this journey, and if we look back over our studies as a chronicle of the relations of language and affect, our data suggest that initially, during the very early stages of language acquisition, both language and emotional expression have access to an underlying symbolic function. Children at the one sign stage draw on early affective and communicative abilities collaboratively with their first signs. However, as language emerges, especially as syntax develops and the child begins to combine signs, there is a reorganization and language unfolds as an independently organized system following its own rather constrained developmental path.

ACKNOWLEDGMENTS

This chapter was partially supported by NIDCD 00539, and aspects of these data were presented at the Boston University Child Language Conference. I would like to thank Karen Emmorey and Rachel Mayberry for their helpful comments, and Cindy Batch for her careful transcription. Finally, my thanks go to California School for the Deaf at Fremont and the many children and families who have participated in these studies over the years.

REFERENCES

Anderson, D. S., & Reilly, J. S. (1997). The puzzle of negation: How children move from communicative to grammatical negation in ASL. *Applied Psycholinguistics, 18*, 411–429.

Anderson, D., & Reilly, J. S. (in press). PAH! The acquisition of non-manual adverbials in ASL. *International Journal of Sign Linguistics*.

Bahan, B., & Supalla, S. (1995). In K. Emmorey, & J. Reilly (Eds.) *Language, gesture, and space* (pp. 171–191). Mahwah, NJ: Lawrence Erlbaum Associates.

Baker, C., & Cokely, D. (1980). *American Sign Language: A teacher's resource text on grammar and culture*. Silver Spring, MD: TJ Publishers.

Baker-Shenk, C. (1983). *A microanalysis of the non-manual components of questions in American Sign Language*. Unpublished doctoral dissertation, University of California, Berkeley.

Bellugi, U., Losh, M., Reilly, J., & Anderson, D. (1998). *Excessive use of linguistically encoded affect: Stories from young children with Williams syndrome* (Tech. Rep. No. CND-9509). La Jolla: University of California, San Diego, Center for Research in Language, Project in Cognitive and Neural Development.

Brown, R. (1973). *A first language: The early stages.* Cambridge, MA: Harvard University Press.

Ekman, P., & Friesen, W. (1978). *Facial action coding system.* Palo Alto, CA: Consulting Psychologists Press.

Emmorey, K., & Reilly, J. (Eds.). (1995). *Language, gesture and space.* Mahwah, NJ: Lawrence Erlbaum Associates

Emmorey, K., & Reilly, J. (1998). The development of quotation and reported action: Conveying perspective in ASL. In E. Clark (Ed.), *Proceedings of the Stanford Child Language Forum.* Stanford, CA: Stanford Linguistics Association and Center for the Study of Language and Information.

Engberg-Pedersen, E. (1993). *Space in Danish Sign Language.* Hamburg, Germany: SIGNUM-Verlag.

Engberg-Pedersen, E. (1995). Point of view expressed through shifters. In K. Emmorey & J. Reilly (Eds.), *Language, gesture and space.* Mahwah, NJ: Lawrence Erlbaum Associates.

Galdone, P. (1972). *The Three Bears.* New York: Clarion Books.

Karmiloff-Smith, A. (1979). *A functional approach to child language: A study of determiners and reference.* Cambridge: Cambridge University Press.

MacWhinney, B. (1978). Processing a first language: The acquisition of morphophonology. *Monographs of the Society for Research in Child Development, 43* (1–2, Serial No. 174).

Padden, C. 1986. Verbs and role-shifting in ASL. In C. Padden (Ed.), *Proceedings of the Fourth National Symposium on Sign Language Research and Teaching.* Silver Spring, MD: National Association of the Deaf.

Reilly, J. S. (1992). How to tell a good story: The intersection of language and affect in children's narratives. *Journal of Narrative and Life History, 2*(4), 355–377.

Reilly, J. S. (in press). From affect to language: A cross-linguistic study of narratives. In L. Verhoeven & S. Stromqvist (Eds.), *Narratives in a multi-lingual context.*

Reilly, J. S., & McIntire, M. L. (1991). WHERE SHOE: The acquisition of wh-questions in ASL. *Papers and Reports in Child Language Development* (pp. 104–111). Stanford, CA: Stanford University, Department of Linguistics.

Reilly, J., McIntire, M., & Bellugi, U. (1991). BABYFACE: A new perspective on universals in language acquisition. In P. Siple (Ed.), *Theoretical issues in sign language research: Psycholinguistics* (pp. 9–23). Chicago: University of Chicago Press.

Reilly, J., Klima, E. S., & Bellugi, U. (1990). Once more with feeling: Affect and language in children from atypical populations. *Development and Psychopathology, 2, 4,* 367–392

Reilly, J., McIntire, M., & Bellugi, U. (1990). FACES: The relationship between language and affect. In V. Volterra & C. Erting (Eds.), *From gesture to language in hearing and deaf children.* New York: Springer-Verlag.

Reilly, J., McIntire, M., & Bellugi, U. (1990). Conditionals in American Sign Language: Grammaticized facial expressions. *Applied Psycholinguistics, 11, 4,* 369–392.

Rossini, P., Reilly, J. Fabretti, D,. & Volterra, V. (1998, Sept.). *Non-manual behaviors in Italian Sign Language.* Paper presented at the Italian Sign Language Conference, Genoa, Italy.

Slobin, D. I. (1973). Cognitive prerequisites for the development of grammar. In C. A. Ferguson & D. I. Slobin (Eds.). *Studies in child language development* (pp. 175–208). Mahwah, NJ: Lawrence Erlbaum Associates.

Smith,C., Lentz, E., & Mikos, K. (1988). *Signing naturally: Teacher's curriculum guide.* Berkeley, CA: Dawn Sign Press.

APPENDIX: TRANSCRIPTION
CONVENTIONS

Manual Signs

SIGN: Words in capital letters represent English glosses for ASL signs.

SIGN-SIGN: Multiword glosses connected by hyphens are used where more than one English word is required to translate a single sign.

#W-O-R-D: Fingerspelled words

SIGN^SIGN: Sign glosses conjoined by a circumflex denote a compound sign.

SIGN [+++]   Sign glosses accompanied by a plus indicate that the citation form of the sign has been modified and the meaning modulated.

_____x
SIGN: A line over a sign or string of signs indicates a particular nonmanual signal occurring simultaneously with the sign, adding some grammatical meaning.

Nonmanual Morphology

+K: Eye contact with addressee.

-K: Gaze away from addressee.

mm: Lips pressed together; the bottom lip may protrude in a slight pout; indicates performing an activity with regularity or normally. (FACS AU 15 + 22)

th: Produced by relaxing the jaw, parting the lips slightly and showing the tongue; it conveys something done carelessly. (FACS AU 19 + 26)

Pertinent Facial Action Units

(From Ekman & Friesens, 1978, FACS)

AU 1:   Inner Brow Raise
AU 2:   Outer Brow Raise
AU 4:   Furrowed Brows
AU 5:   Widened Eyes
AU 6:   Cheek Raise
AU 7:   Lids Tight
AU 18: Lip Pucker
AU 19: Tongue Show
AU 44: Squint
AU 45: Blink

AU 51: Head Turn Left
AU 52: Head Turn Right
AU 55: Head Tilt Left
AU 56: Head Tilt Right
AU 57: Head Forward
AU 58: Head Back

23

Search for the Missing Link: The Development of Skilled Reading in Deaf Children

Carol A. Padden
University of California, San Diego

Vicki L. Hanson
IBM Research Division

Since 1970, reading research with Deaf children has been occupied with the problem of how to describe the reading process in this population. Most generally accepted models of reading development in hearing children recognize the important role of phonological coding in the development of skillful reading (Perfetti, 1991; Stanovich 1991; see Committee for the Prevention of Reading Difficulties in Young Children, 1998). Perfetti (1991) argued that phonology is involved in beginning reading and later develops into an abstract awareness when the child becomes more familiar with the alphabetic representation and has a growing vocabulary of words in print. He portrayed phonological awareness as a reflective skill, in which the child analyzes words in print as being made up of phonemes and syllables and productively uses this knowledge to analyze less common and less regular words. Later, the child comes to appreciate orthographic systematicities and can blend phonological awareness and visual or orthographic awareness into an effective and efficient reading process.

Landmark research on Deaf readers was carried out by Conrad (1979), using a population of orally trained British high school students. He found that among the small number of Deaf individuals in his population who were reading well, they exhibited an ability to engage in phonological coding as evidenced by their performance on a test of serial recall for printed letters. Specifically, these good readers recalled fewer items from rhyming than nonrhyming lists, the pattern exhibited by hearing children who are good readers. He contrasted these Deaf good readers' performance with that of Deaf poorer readers. These poorer readers showed no rhyme effect but, instead, recalled fewer items from visually similar than visually dissimilar lists, suggesting that they were using a visual code for letter recall.

Conrad's (1979) conclusion about the reason for reading difficulties among Deaf students is well-known: Deafness inhibits the development of a phonological code. He hypothesized that this phonological code is essential to successful reading. However, is it? Is a phonological code as optimal for Deaf readers as it appears to be for hearing readers? How can a phonological code develop in Deaf readers? Are there alternatives to phonological coding that might also serve the development of skilled reading for Deaf children?

The work of Ursula Bellugi and Edward Klima on sign language illuminated a rich and complex interaction of language and cognition that has challenged previous conceptions of language processing. Their research program changed our perspective on the question of phonological coding in Deaf readers. In homage to their work and the impact it has had on a wide range of fields, from linguistics to reading, we outline here some of these newly emerging issues.

We begin first with a short review of the literature on reading processes in Deaf readers as background to new work. We aim to show that there has been a slight but perceptible shift in the types of questions that are now asked in reading research with Deaf populations. Rather than focusing on the issue of deafness, per se, the focus is now on questions related to language and how language structure influences the reading process for Deaf children.

PHONOLOGICAL CODING IN READING

It seems clear that for hearing children, phonological codes play an important role in the development of skillful reading. From a wide assortment of measures, and from many longitudinal studies, hearing children who can demonstrate early phonological knowledge are much more likely to develop good reading skills than those who do not show these skills early or prominently (Bryant, MacLean, Bradley, & Crossland, 1990; Chaney, 1992; Liberman & Shankweiler, 1991).

Stanovich (1991) explained that phonological processing of words in print is necessary because it provides the tools for associating spoken words they know with their analogs in print. Visual processing, such as analyzing the visual shape of letters in print, is not rich or detailed enough. Instead readers need to establish and sustain associative mechanisms with spoken words. This association is thought to be an intimate one, developing as part of a discovery of reading at the early stages, and later as sustaining development into skillful reading. Accordingly, Perfetti and Zhang (1995) proposed a "universal phonological principle" in which they argue phonological processing is instrumentally involved in print word recognition in any writing system, not only alphabetic systems but Chinese ideographs as well. They did not rule out semantic or graphemic processing, because they did find evidence of semantic mediation under certain task demands. Their argument was that all reading, whatever the writing system, involves phonological processing at some level.

In the presence of deafness, how would it be possible for Deaf children to develop skillful reading at all, if they cannot hear sounds? The first answer is that it is very difficult to develop skillful reading in such circumstances, as attested to by surveys of reading achievement in Deaf populations. Moreover, studies measuring reading achievement by hearing loss show that as hearing loss increases, reading difficulty increases as well (see, e.g., Conrad, 1979; Karchmer, Milone, & Wolk, 1979).

However, focus on group averages for Deaf readers obscures the fact that there are profoundly Deaf persons who do become skillful readers (see, e.g., Conrad, 1979; Reynolds, 1975), demonstrating grade-level and college-level reading skill. In a series of studies, Hanson and her colleagues explored the nature of reading ability in these skilled Deaf readers. In a first study with Deaf adults, Hanson (1982) used a task of short-term serial recall of printed words. As a group, the Deaf participants, like Conrad's participants, recalled fewer rhyming than nonrhyming items. Similarly, Lichtenstein (1985; see also Hanson & Lichtenstein, 1991), in a large-scale study of students at National Technical Institute for the Deaf (NTID), found that Deaf good readers demonstrated rhyme effects in the serial recall of printed words. While no influence to visual similarity of words was in evidence for Hanson's subjects, several of Lichtenstein's college students were influenced by the visual similarity of words. Careful analysis by Lichtenstein, however, showed that the visual coding used these students was not effective in supporting serial recall.

Specifically, students who used this code recalled fewer items in Lichtenstein's study than did students who used phonological coding.

Hanson, Liberman & Shankweiler (1984) asked Deaf beginning readers to remember lists of printed letters. As with Conrad, the children who were good readers recalled fewer letters from lists that rhymed than from lists that did not rhyme. The children experiencing difficulty in learning to read displayed no rhyme effect.

Hanson & Fowler (1987) asked Deaf and hearing participants to respond to pairs of letter strings and determine whether they were words or nonwords. Of interest were two conditions: (a) words that were spelled alike and rhymed (e.g., bribe–tribe); and (b) words that were spelled alike but did not rhyme (e.g., have–cave). Responses to these were pairs were compared to responses on matched control words. Deaf college students, like hearing college students, demonstrated evidence of phonological processing in this task involving a short-term memory component. Compared with the control pairs, both Deaf and hearing students, as a group, responded faster to the rhyming than the nonrhyming pairs. When individual differences were examined, Hanson and Fowler found some participants, both hearing and Deaf, who did not respond differently to the rhyming and nonrhyming words. More Deaf than hearing participants fit this nonphonological pattern.

Waters & Doehring (1990) suggest that the phonology used by Deaf readers is post-lexical, not pre-lexical. Deaf readers appear to not to "sound out" a word as a way to access and recognize a word, but rather analyze its sound elements after they have recognized the word. In their research on the use of spelling-sound information in reading, Waters & Doehring find no use of spelling-sound information in a group of orally-trained students, ages 7 to 20, in word recognition.

Whereas these studies suggested that Deaf readers can use phonological information in short-term memory tasks, they do not indicate whether or not they use this information in actual reading. To address this question, Hanson, Goodell, and Perfetti (1991) asked 16 Deaf college students to evaluate the semantic acceptability of sentences containing tongue twisters (e.g., "The talented teenager took the trophy in the tournament") while also retaining memory of a sequence of numbers with initial sounds similar to those in the tongue-twister sentences. Both hearing and Deaf participants had difficulty judging acceptability of tongue-twister sentences if they were also asked to remember like-sounding numbers. This specific interference related to phonological similarity indicates the use of phonological information when reading connected text.

We propose that the search for phonological mediation, and when it appears in the development of skillful reading, must distinguish between different reading processes and the demands they place on readers. The studies reviewed so far suggest (a) that prelingual and profound deafness does not preclude the ability to access phonological information, and (b) that Deaf skillful readers, both children and adults, display the ability to use phonological information in processing text when short-term memory is involved. That phonological coding is found to be used by Deaf skilled readers is intriguing in how it points to its role in skilled reading. This role may derive from its unique ability to retain serial order, a necessary component of syntactic processing (Hanson & Lichtenstein, 1990; Mattingly, 1975). That is, as words in a sentence are read, they are put in a short-term memory store while syntactic parsing of the sentence occurs. Given the presence of serial information in English syntax, it may be necessary to use this short-term memory store to retain order information.

Do these findings, however, rule out a role for sign or visual processes in the reading acquisition of Deaf children? Absolutely not. In the case of Deaf children, early reading may not use phonological mediation at all. It may only be when the reader passes a critical level of difficulty, perhaps above the fourth- or fifth-grade reading level, that evidence for use of phonological information can be found. It would be in the case of reading complex material that the Deaf reader might need to learn to use phonological information. In addition to exploring at what level of reading development phonological coding might be used by Deaf readers, several researchers have called for more investigation of the use of alternatives to phonological coding by Deaf readers, particularly in the beginning reading of Deaf children (Grushkin, 1998; Marschark, 1996; Padden & Ramsey, 2000; Waters & Doehring, 1990).

Interrelations Between Language Abilities and Reading Skill in Signing Deaf Children

In large part because of the work of Ursula Bellugi and Ed Klima in identifying the language and cognitive abilities of young native signers, a number of reading researchers began to identify and examine reading skills in native signers. Conrad (1979) found 3 Deaf students in his study who were reading at grade level. Of these, 2 had Deaf parents. However, Conrad did not speculate about the nature of reading in those children with good sign language ability. Hanson and her colleagues studied native signers in several studies (Hanson, 1982; Hanson et al., 1991; Krakow &

Hanson, 1985) and found many of them to be skilled readers. Other studies show an association between native ability in American Sign Language (ASL) and reading achievement (Mayberry, 1989; Moores & Sweet, 1990; Singleton, Supalla, Litchfield, & Schley, 1998; Prinz & Strong, 1998). In a longitudinal study of 24 young Deaf readers, Harris and Beech (1998) observe that among the 4 best readers in their sample, 2 had Deaf parents and were native signers. (Their participant pool had a total of 4 native signers.)

On its face, it is not clear why a relation should exist between skill in ASL and the ability to develop reading skill in another language, in this case, English. The two languages share neither phonological features, nor a grammar. Chamberlain and Mayberry (2000) suggest the relation is largely due to early acquisition of a natural language, which allows for timely development of other cognitive skills, including memory for verbal and nonverbal material. The development of good working memory skills is an important component of reading development (Adams, 1990).

Padden & Ramsey (2000) review several additional possible accounts for generally better performance of native signers. Possibly, Deaf children of Deaf parents perform better because as a group they comprise a well-defined participant population with similar demographics, in contrast to the population of Deaf children of hearing parents whose backgrounds are more variable. Not only are Deaf children of hearing parents more likely to learn sign language later in childhood, but more come from non-white families or have immigrated from countries with poorer education for Deaf children. Thus, better performance in the group of Deaf children of Deaf parents is observable only because the remaining population performs so variably. Moores and Sweet (1990) made a similar observation.

Another possible account follows from the observation that while many native signers develop good reading ability, not all of them do. Some skilled native signers experience difficulty learning to read. Although Harris and Beech (1998) found in their longitudinal study that 2 of the 4 best readers had Deaf parents, they also had 2 native signers who did not perform at this level.

Padden and Ramsey (1998, 2000) proposed a refinement of the early language exposure account, arguing that while early language experience is crucial, it is not sufficient. Reading ability needs to be cultivated by parents and other adults in the form of prereading and reading activities. Because these reading interactions are only recently being described, there is not a great deal of detail about where researchers might look for opportunities to "cultivate" reading skill in Deaf children. Padden and

Ramsey suggested that among Deaf signing adults who teach Deaf children to read, there may exist "associative elements" in ASL that serve as a "platform" from which reading development can be launched. In other words, Deaf parents and adults may be designating relations between specific elements of ASL and counterparts in English print as associations to begin reading development. As an example, they examine whether fingerspelling could be such a platform, among some other possibilities.

In a study of 27 fourth- and eighth-grade Deaf children attending a residential school and a public school program for Deaf children, Padden and Ramsey (1998) reported correlations between several measures of ASL ability and performance on the reading comprehension subtest of the Stanford Achievement Test. These correlations held for native signers as well as skilled, but non-native signers who attended these schools. Each measure involved a different level of ASL grammar: one test measured the ability of the subject to repeat accurately ASL sentences recently viewed on videotape; another measured the ability to provide a correct verb inflection when shown the verb stem; and the third measured the ability to produce a sentence with correct subject and object order in response to pictures of actions. Across all levels of ASL grammar, these measures correlated with reading performance.

Padden and Ramsey (1998) also administered a test developed with their associates in which participants were shown a list of ASL sentences containing a single fingerspelled word. On a question prompt, the students were asked to write the fingerspelled word's counterpart in English print. As with ASL measures, performance on this test correlated with reading performance ($n = 22$; $r = .43$, $p < .05$) as well as with the ASL measures themselves. Thus, students who were better readers were also those who were good signers and could write fingerspelled words in English print.

Whereas the correlations suggest a relation between different language skills and reading, they do not account for the nature of this relationship. Is fingerspelling used as an internal code for processing words in print? It is unlikely that it is. Several studies have found no evidence that fingerspelled similarities influence memory for words in print (Hanson & Lichtenstein, 1990; Mayberry, 1989; Treiman & Hirsch-Pasek, 1983). Harris and Beech (1998) asked young Deaf British children to fingerspell the alphabet, their own name, and eight individual letters. They did not find a relation between ability to perform this task and reading ability. However, they noted that almost none of the children in their group were fluent in fingerspelling at the time of the study. In contrast, Padden and Ramsey's (1998) skilled readers in their studies were also skilled fingerspellers.

The argument we propose here is a different one: Fingerspelling is a mediating tool that provides a platform for the development of rudimentary phonological coding.[1] Skilled fingerspelling involves an awareness that words in print are made up of segments. When skilled fingerspelling is achieved, signers may also develop a "speech surrogate" that maps onto fingerspelled forms. It is common to watch fingerspellers mouth out companion sounds as they fingerspell words. Hanson (1991) suggested that phonological awareness in her skilled adult readers developed from a combination of knowledge gleaned from fingerspelling, lipreading, and general knowledge about speech. Possibly, fingerspelling interacts with lipreading and mouthing, reflecting awareness about sound segments. It is often observed that Deaf adults mouth words while fingerspelling toward the orthographic form, for example, pronouncing "quiche" as [kwich] instead of [kich] or "debt" as [debt] instead of [det]. In such cases, the mouthing reflects a phonemic version of the orthographic form being fingerspelled.

In a follow-up study, Padden and her associates administered a different fingerspelling test to 56 Deaf children ages 8 to 14. Approximately half were native signers. The students attended a signing residential school with a strong commitment to use of ASL in the classroom. In this test, the fingerspelled words were controlled for print frequency with half of the words high frequency in print and the other half low frequency. As in the earlier test (Padden & Ramsey, 1998), students watched a list of sentences in ASL, each containing exactly one fingerspelled word, followed by a question prompt. The students were given the same test twice but under two different response conditions. Under the first administration, they responded by circling the picture associated with the fingerspelled word, from a choice of four pictures per sentence. One of the four choices is a picture of a semantically compatible but incorrect object. The second time they saw the test (with sentences in different order), they were asked to write the words in print. Performance on the picture and written versions were compared with each other as well as with performance on a reading measure, the vocabulary and grammar portions of the Gates–MacGinitie Test of Reading.

Correlations were found between performance on both versions of the fingerspelled tests and the reading measures (picture version: $r = .50$,

---

[1]We thank Mark Marschark and colleagues attending a reading conference at the Rochester Institute of Technology/National Technical Institute for the Deaf (NTID) for suggesting this possibility to us.

$p < .01$; written version: $r = .71$, $p < .01$) On the picture version, all subjects performed at a low error rate, averaging only 2.6 errors out of a possible 30. The youngest children, ages 8 to 9 years, were significantly more likely to make errors writing responses to fingerspelled words than older children. These children were also sensitive to word frequency in the written version, making more errors with low-frequency print words than those of high frequency.

Several conclusions may be drawn from these tests. First, the low error rate shows that the signing children in this group are skilled at understanding fingerspelling. They are able to correctly select the object named by the fingerspelled word nearly 95% of the time. This is a population of not only skilled signers but also skilled fingerspellers. They can comprehend words fingerspelled to them. But the youngest children had more difficulty writing these same words in print. For these children, they had better success if the words, were those they see often in their print materials at school. Although they could understand fingerspelled words that appeared less frequently in their print materials, they had difficulty writing them correctly. This indicates to us that the ability to write words in English from fingerspelled form involves experience with reading, which is not yet attained in these young Deaf children.

It is possible that fingerspelling recognition may be more logographic at early ages, developing into a different level of awareness at the time Deaf signing children begin to read. At this point, Deaf children start to develop an awareness of the segmental possibilities of fingerspelled words at the same time they start to write letters and combine them to make words. From studies with preschoolers (Padden, 1991; Padden & LeMaster, 1985), young signers tend to fingerspell words with simpler movement units, capturing the general movement envelope of the word, and do not begin letter-by-letter fingerspelling until a later time. They may be able to fingerspell a small store of words by memorizing a series of handshapes, but productive fingerspelling, or being able to produce any series of handshapes to constitute a fingerspelled word, typically does not appear until they develop more knowledge of words in print, that is, begin to read.

This particular course of development of fingerspelling in young skilled signers, including native signers, would not be found in another population of Deaf children, for example, those reared orally, or those reared in other environments with little involvement of fingerspelling. Dodd (1987) studied children reared orally and proposed some involvement of lipread segments in memory for words in print. Harris and Beech (1998) found a number of their British Deaf children not highly skilled in fingerspelling. We expect that for the very broad population of Deaf and hard-of-hearing children, there may be constellations of skills interacting in different ways with reading development. Before there can be any global assessment of "Deaf reading," there must be detailed descriptions of processes, skills, and strategies among well-defined populations of Deaf readers, that is, those who share similar language backgrounds and similar social experiences. Furthermore, the search for processes must take into consideration that there is not a single process involved in reading, but instead several operating interactively. Reading research cannot simply track a single process but must study its interaction with other processes over time, as skill unfolds.

CONCLUDING REMARKS

We began this chapter paying homage to Ursula Bellugi and Edward Klima and we end on a similar note. Although our work concerns reading, an area not directly related to sign-language analysis, it would not have been possible without the intellectual groundwork laid by the two of them. Using knowledge from sign-language analysis, we were able to speculate about what role fingerspelling might play in reading development. Their abiding interest in space and movement in sign languages brought us to the study of similar elements in fingerspelling. Perhaps one of the more interesting discoveries about early fingerspelling use by Deaf children is the fact that they are sensitive to movements in fingerspelled words before they are aware of the association of such words to print (Akamatsu, 1982; Padden, 1991; Padden & LeMaster, 1985; Wilcox, 1992). This allowed us to consider how language skills might interact with reading skills. Also, from their studies of early sign language acquisition, we were made aware of the importance of early language exposure on development of working memory, an important component of reading skill (Mayberry & Fischer, 1989).

The problem of reading difficulty among Deaf children has been a long-standing one. There has been a revival of sorts in reading research, bringing us once more to a thorny problem, one with deep social implications. Where reading research once seemed centered on the role of deafness and reading, it has now turned to a multifaceted approach to the problem, including questions about language as well. Ursula and Ed began their long career with a series of questions about how sign languages work and how they influence the brain. Here we ask, how do signers learn to read and how does reading take place in such readers? The questions are slightly different, but the new tradition of sign language study that they have inspired has made them possible.

ACKNOWLEDGMENTS

Research carried out by Padden and her colleagues was supported by a grant to Carol A. Padden and Claire Ramsey from the U.S. Department of Education, #HO23T30006 and a grant to Carol A. Padden from the National Science Foundation, #SBR9601542.

REFERENCES

Adams, M. (1990). *Beginning to read.* Cambridge, MA: MIT Press.

Akamatsu, C. (1982). *The acquisition of fingerspelling in pre-school children.* Unpublished doctoral dissertation, University of Rochester, NY.

Bryant, P., MacLean, M., Bradley, L., & Crossland, J. (1990). Rhyme and alliteration, phoneme detection and learning to read. *Developmental Psychology, 26,* 429–438.

Chamberlain, C., & Mayberry, R. (2000). Theorizing about the relationship between ASL and reading. In C. Chamberlain, J. Morford, & R. Mayberry (Eds.), *Language acquisition by eye* (pp. 221–259), Mahwah, NJ: Lawrence Erlbaum Associates.

Chaney, C. (1992). Language development, metalinguistic skills and print awareness in 3-year-old children. *Applied Psycholinguistics, 13,* 485–514.

Committee for the Prevention of Reading Difficulties in Young Children. (1998). *Preventing reading difficulties in young children.* Washington, DC: National Academy Press.

Conrad, R. (1979). *The deaf schoolchild.* London: Harper & Row.

Dodd, B. (1980). The spelling abilities of profoundly pre-lingually deaf children. In U. Frith (Ed.), *Cognitive processes in spelling* (pp. 423–440). London: Academic Press.

Dodd, B. (1987). Lipreading, phonological coding and deafness. In B. Dodd & R. Campbell (Eds.), *Hearing by eye: The psychology of lipreading* (pp. 177–189). London: Lawrence Erlbaum Associates.

Grushkin, D. (1998). Why shouldn't Sam read? Toward a new paradigm for literacy and the deaf. *Journal of Deaf Studies and Deaf Education, 3,* 179–204.

Hanson, V. (1982). Short-term recall by deaf signers of American Sign Language: Implications for order recall. *Journal of Experimental Psychology: Learning, Memory, and Cognition, 8,* 572–583.

Hanson, V. (1989). Phonology and reading: Evidence from profoundly deaf readers. In D. Shankweiler & I. Liberman (Eds.), *Phonology and reading disability: Solving the reading puzzle* (pp. 69–89). Ann Arbor: University of Michigan Press.

Hanson, V. (1991). Phonological processing without sound. In S. Brady & D. Shankweiler (Eds.), *Phonological processes in literacy: A tribute to Isabelle Y. Liberman* (pp. 153–161). Mahwah, NJ: Lawrence Erlbaum Associates.

Hanson, V., & Fowler, C. (1987). Phonological coding in word reading: Evidence from hearing and deaf readers. *Memory & Cognition, 15,* 199–207.

Hanson, V., & Lichtenstein, E. (1990). Short-term memory coding by deaf signers: The primary language coding hypothesis reconsidered. *Cognitive Psychology, 22,* 211–224.

Hanson, V., Goodell, E., & Perfetti, C. (1991). Tongue-twister effects in the silent reading of hearing and deaf college students. *Journal of Memory and Language, 30,* 319–330.

Hanson, V., Liberman, I., & Shankweiler, D. (1984). Linguistic coding by deaf children in relation to beginning reading success. *Journal of Experimental Child Psychology, 37,* 378–393.

Harris, M., & Beech, J. (1995). Reading development in prelingually deaf children. In K. Nelson, & Z. Reger (Eds.), *Children's language* (pp. 181–202). Mahwah, NJ: Lawrence Erlbaum Associates.

Harris, M., & Beech, J. (1998). Implicit phonological awareness and early reading development in prelingually deaf children. *Journal of Deaf Studies and Deaf Education, 3,* 205–216.

Karchmer, M., Milone, A., & Wolk, S. (1979). Educational significance of hearing loss at three levels of severity. *American Annals of the Deaf, 124,* 97–109.

Krakow, R., & Hanson, V. (1985). Deaf signers and serial recall in the visual modality: Memory for signs, fingerspelling and print. *Memory & Cognition, 13,* 265–272.

Liberman, I., & Shankweiler, D. (1991). Phonology and beginning reading: A tutorial. In L. Reiben & C. Perfetti (Eds.), *Learning to read: Basic research and its implications* (pp. 3–17). Mahwah, NJ: Lawrence Erlbaum Associates.

Lichtenstein, E. H. (1985). Deaf working memory processes and English language skills. In D. S. Martin (Ed.), *Cognition, education, and deafness: Directions for research and instruction* (pp. 111–114). Washington, DC: Gallaudet College Press.

Marschark, M. (1996). Success and failure in learning to read: The special case of deaf children. In C. Cornoldi & J. Oakhill (Eds.), *Reading comprehension difficulties: Processes and intervention* (pp. 279–300). London: Lawrence Erlbaum Associates.

Mayberry, R. (1989, April). *Deaf children's reading comprehension in relation to sign language structure and input.* Paper presented at the Society for Research in Child Development, Kansas City, Kansas.

Mayberry, R., & Fischer, S. (1989). Looking through phonological shape to sentence meaning: The bottleneck of non-native sign language processing. *Memory & Cognition, 17,* 740–754.

Moores, D., & Sweet, C. (1990). Factors predictive of school achievement. In D. Moores & K. Meadow-Orlans (Eds.), *Education and developmental aspects of deafness* (pp. 154–201). Washington, DC: Gallaudet University Press.

Padden, C. (1991). The acquisition of fingerspelling by deaf children. In P. Siple & S. Fischer (Eds.), *Theoretical issues in sign language research. Vol. 2: Psychology* (pp. 191–210). Chicago: University of Chicago Press.

Padden, C. & LeMaster, B. (1985). An alphabet on hand: The acquisition of fingerspelling in deaf children. *Sign Language Studies, 47,* 161–172.

Padden, C., & Ramsey, C. (1998). Reading ability in signing deaf children. *Topics in Language Disorders, 18,* 30–46.

Padden, C., & Ramsey, C. (2000). American Sign Language and reading ability in deaf children. In C. Chamberlain, J. Morford, & R. Mayberry (Eds.), *Language acquisition by eye.* Mahwah, NJ: Lawrence Erlbaum Associates.

Perfetti, C. (1991). Representations and awareness in the acquisition of reading competence. In L. Rieben & C. Perfetti (Eds.), *Learning to read: Basic research and its implications* (pp. 33–44). Mahwah, NJ: Lawrence Erlbaum Associates.

Perfetti, C., & Zhang, S. (1995). Very early phonological activation in Chinese reading. *Journal of Experimental Psychology: Learning, Memory, & Cognition, 21,* 24–33.

Prinz, P., & Strong, M. (1998). ASL proficiency and English literacy within a bilingual deaf education model of instruction. *Topics in Language Disorders, 18,* 47–60.

Ramsey, C., & Padden, C. (1998). Natives & newcomers: Literacy education for deaf children. *Anthropology and Education Quarterly, 29*(1), 5–24.

Reynolds, H. (1986). Performance of deaf college students on a criterion-referenced modified cloze test of reading comprehension. *American Annals of the Deaf, 131,* 361–364.

Singleton, J., Supalla, S., Litchfield, S., & Schley, S. (1998). From sign to word: Considering modality constraints in ASL/English bilingual education. *Topics in Language Disorders, 18,* 16–29.

Stanovich, K. (1991). Changing models of reading and reading acquisition. In L. Rieben, & C. Perfetti

(Eds.), *Learning to read: Basic research and its implications* (pp. 19–32). Mahwah, NJ: Lawrence Erlbaum Associates.

Treiman, R., & Hirsh-Pasek, K. (1983). Silent reading: Insights from second-generation deaf readers. *Cognitive Psychology, 15,* 39–65.

Waters, G., & Doehring, D. (1990). Reading acquisition in congenitally deaf children who communicate orally: Insights from an analysis of component reading, language and memory skills. In T. Carr & B. Levy (Eds.), *Reading and its development: Component skills approaches* (pp. 323–373). New York: Academic Press.

Wilcox, S. (1992). *The Phonetics of fingerspelling.* Philadelphia: John Benjamins.

24

On the Biological Foundations of Human Language

Laura Ann Petitto
McGill University

INTRODUCTION: WITH THANKS TO URSULA AND EDWARD

Fall in New York City never looked so beautiful to me as it did on that second day of September 1976 the day that I had to leave it for Kennedy Airport's last flight to San Diego. That evening, I left for graduate study in Theoretical Linguistics at the University of California San Diego and to meet the woman who was to be my graduate advisor and research director, Ursula Bellugi. She had a lab down the road at The Salk Institute for Biological Studies. But earlier that day, I did not want to go. Nim Chimpsky did not want me to go either, and he showed me so by subjecting me to the single most ferocious attack that I had experienced in my many years of living and working with him.

Nim Chimpsky, the West African male chimpanzee who had been my charge since infancy, was part of a grand experiment at Columbia University, called "Project Nim," led by Herbert Terrace and Tom Bever. Although only a college undergraduate, I moved into a large mansion on the Hudson Palisades in New York City with this wild animal and attempted to raise him like a child while exposing him to American Sign

Language (ASL). Our question concerned whether aspects of human language were species specific, or whether human language was wholly learnable from environmental input. As I left Project Nim for Ursula Bellugi's California laboratory, Nim's successes and failures with this marvel that we call "Language" had already given me insight into where the answer to this profound question would lie.

Although there is still much controversy surrounding the ape language studies, one enduring finding has remained surprisingly uncontroversial. All chimpanzees fail to master key aspects of human language structure, even when you give them a way to bypass their inability to speak—for example, by exposing them to other types of linguistic input such as natural signed languages. This fact raised the hypothesis to me that humans possessed something at birth in addition to the mechanisms for producing and perceiving speech sounds that aided them in acquiring natural language. Indeed, whatever this elusive "something" was, I knew that attempts to understand it first required a solid grasp of the biological foundations of human language. This, in turn, I thought would provide the key basis from which to discover the essential features that distinguished human language from the communication of all other animals. And, from all that I had heard from Terrace and Bever about "Ursie" and her "brilliant research," there was no other place in the world to study the biological foundations of language than in her laboratory at The Salk Institute.

What a world it was! I was right to feel initial butterflies about going to the place and about Ursula. With Nim's teeth marks still pressed into my torn skin, I walked into her laboratory to find, at once, the most thrilling and intimidating intellectual climate that I had ever known. I had never met anyone like Ursula. At breakneck speed, language streamed from her mouth and hands. Ideas. She had so many. She exuded them, most times whole and, at times, in tantalizing parts. Like the ring at the carousel, we would grasp at those parts, because we knew that when Ursula said something it was important. She had little patience for people who couldn't get to the point. We lived for those moments when she looked at us with clear, open eyes (meaning that she approved of an idea) and wanted to jump off the Torrey Pines cliffs when she gazed at us with the dreaded squinted eyes (the sure sign that she was bored, or, worse, thought what was being said was off the mark).

Both then and now, Ursula was masterful at listening and at pulling out "the question." She was equally masterful at knowing just what types of ingredients would ultimately constitute "the answer," just what paths to take. Then, after assessing our strengths and weaknesses, she would plonk us down on a path and make us go. Ursula also had a unique gift for knowing how to bring the right people together, how to create the right chemistry within which the intellectual explosion would occur—something that has remained one of the hallmarks of her laboratory to this day.

It was in this context that I first met Edward Klima and was fortunate to come to know his brilliance. Ed had an uncanny ability to surmise exactly what one wanted to say no matter how garbled it came out. He especially knew what one was trying to say in writing. He had (and still has) a stunning command of the word, which he demonstrated repeatedly by dragging our fragments of sentences up from the ditches and turning them into elegant prose. But more than this, I learned from Ed how to hold an idea in the palm of my hand, how to examine it, turn it about, and, how to use it like bricks to build the strongest possible logical structure.

No doubt, Ursie and Ed have given all of us who have been lucky enough to meet and know them some of the same things and a little something different. For me, in addition to everything else, they gave me the gift that comes from sharing one's intellectual passions with others. They propelled forward my passion for sign language, for language, for child language and, most of all, my passion for the magnificent universe within the human body that runs the show, the human brain.

In this chapter, I want to honor Ursula Bellugi and Edward Klima by outlining the nature of the discoveries that I have made in my own laboratory over the past 15 years since completing my doctoral dissertation under both Ursie's guidance at Salk and Roger Bown's at Harvard University (where life's twists and turns eventually settled me). But it is I who am honored to have worked with Ursie and Ed and, through them, to have been fortunate enough to know and work with the other extraordinary scientists who grace the pages of this book. My science and my life have been touched by Ursie, by Ed, and by them all.[1]

---

[1] I am indeed grateful to Ursie and Ed for all of the remarkable people that I came to know through them. On the afternoon that I arrived in Ursie's lab, she put me in an office with a desk jutting out between Ted Supalla on one side and Ella Mae Lentz and Carlene Pederson on the other, "because," she said, "you know sign language." These three extraordinary individuals promptly took me apart and, over the course my time there, were kind enough to put me back together, being stronger and wiser! I also am especially fortunate that I came to know Benjamin Bahan and Richard Meier, as well as Carol Padden and Sam Supalla. My discussions with many others in and around Ursie's laboratory greatly influenced me, including the many scientists who visited it: Tane Akamatsu, Elizabeth Bates, Robbin Battison, Collin Blakemore, Penny Boyes-Braem, Bernard Bragg, Benedicte de Boysson-Bardies, David Corina, Francis Crick, Karen Emmorey, Lou Fant, Susan Fischer, Angela Fok, Nancy Frishberg, Victoria Fromkin, Vicki Hanson, Judy Kegl, Harlan Lane, Scott Liddell, Diane Lillo-Martin, Ruth Loew, Marina McIntyre, Madeline Maxwell, Helen Neville, Don Newkirk, Elissa Newport, Lucinda O'Grady, Frank Paul, Elena Pizzuto, Howard Poizner, Judy Reilly, Patricia Siple, Ovid Tzeng, Virginia Volterra, and Ronnie Wilbur. What an amazing group of scientists and friends!

RESEARCH ON BIOLOGICAL
FOUNDATIONS OF HUMAN LANGUAGE

Over the past 15 years, my research program at McGill University has been directed at understanding the specific biological and environmental factors that together permit early language acquisition to begin in our species. Prevailing views about the biological foundations of language assume that very early language acquisition is tied to speech. Universal regularities in the maturational timing and structure of infants' vocal babbling and first words have been taken as evidence that the brain must be attuned to perceiving and producing spoken language in early life. Without a doubt, a frequent answer to the question "How does early human language acquisition begin?" is that it is the result of the development of the neuroanatomical and neurophysiological mechanisms involved in the perception and the production of speech. An assumption that also underlies this view is that spoken languages are better suited to the brain's maturational needs in development. Put another way, the view of human biology at work here is that evolution has rendered the human brain neurologically "hardwired" for speech (Liberman & Mattingly, 1985, 1989; Lieberman, 1984).

My work with Nim Chimpsky first caused me to be suspicious of this view. As noted earlier, Nim did not fail to acquire human language merely because he could not speak. But my studies of very early signed language acquisition offered me the clearest window by far into why the previous account was wholly incomplete. If, as has been argued, very early human language acquisition is under the exclusive control of the maturation of the mechanisms for speech production and speech perception (Locke, 1983; Van der Stelt & Koopmans-van Bienum, 1986), then spoken and signed languages should be acquired in very different ways. At the very least, fundamental differences in the timing and structure of early spoken versus signed language acquisition may be observed, presumably due to their use of different neural substrates in the human brain.

To investigate these issues, I conducted many comparative studies of children acquiring two spoken languages—English and French—and children acquiring two autonomous signed languages—ASL and Langue des Signes Québécoise (LSQ)—from ages birth through 48 months. The empirical findings from these cross-linguistic and cross-modal studies are clear, involving surprising similarities in the overall timing and structure of early signed and spoken language acquisition.

SIMILAR TIMING MILESTONES IN SIGNING
AND SPEAKING INFANTS

Deaf children exposed to signed languages from birth acquire these languages on an identical maturational time table as hearing children acquire spoken languages. Deaf children acquiring signed languages do so without any modification, loss, or delay to the timing, content, and maturational course associated with reaching all linguistic milestones observed in spoken language (e.g., Charron & Petitto, 1987, 1991; Petitto, 1984, 1985, 1987a, 1988; Petitto & Charron, 1988; Petitto & Marentette, 1990, 1991); this finding has also been corroborated by the important discoveries of other researchers (e.g., Bellugi & Klima, 1982; Meier, 1991; Newport & Meier, 1985). Beginning at birth and continuing through age 3 and beyond, speaking and signing children exhibit the identical stages of language acquisition. These include the (a) *syllabic babbling stage* (7–11 months) as well as other developments in babbling, including *variegated babbling*, ages 10 to 12 months, and *jargon babbling*, ages 12 months and beyond; (b) *first-word stage* (11–14 months); (c) *first two-word stage* (16–22 months); and the grammatical and semantic developments beyond.

Surprising similarities are also observed in Deaf and hearing children's timing onset and use of gestures as well (Petitto, 1992; see also the important work by Abrahamsen, Volterra, and others, in this volume). Signing and speaking children produce strikingly similar prelinguistic (9–12 months) and postlinguistic (12–48 months) communicative gestures. They do not produce more gestures, even though linguistic "signs" (identical to the "word") and communicative gestures reside in the same modality, and even though some signs and gestures are formationally and referentially similar. Instead, Deaf children consistently differentiate linguistic signs from communicative gestures throughout development, using each in the same ways observed in hearing children.

Throughout development, signing and speaking children also exhibit remarkably similar complexity in their utterances. For example, analyses of young ASL and LSQ children's social and conversational patterns of language use over time, as well as the types of things that they "talk" about over time (its semantic and conceptual content, categories, and referential scope), demonstrated that their language acquisition follows the same path seen in age-matched hearing children acquiring spoken language (Charron & Petitto, 1987, 1991; Petitto, 1992; Petitto & Charron, 1988). As many others in this volume first discovered, signing infants also exhibit the classic grammatical errors that are universally seen in speaking children, despite the iconic nature of some signs. To name just a few, these include phonological substitutions, "overregularizations," principled question-formation and negation errors, anaphoric referencing confusions, and even systematic pronoun reversal errors. Here, for example, an 18-month-old child will treat an indexical point directed at a person in the second-person addressee role ("YOU") as if it signified a first-person pronoun ("ME"), a surprising error for at least two reasons: The linguistic symbol to convey this information is the nonarbitrary point, and during this same period, children continue to use the point as a communicative gesture in rich ways (e.g., pointing to an adult's blouse to indicate a missing button; e.g., Meier, 1991; Petitto, 1984, 1987a).

Recent research in my laboratory focuses on two very unusual populations. One population involves *hearing* infants in bilingual-"bimodal" homes (e.g., one parent signs and the other speaks). The second population involves hearing infants who are being exposed only to signed languages from birth, with no systematic exposure to spoken language whatsoever. In the first group of hearing bimodal babies, we found that they demonstrate no preference for speech even though they can hear. If speech were neurologically privileged at birth, these babies might be expected to glean any morsel of sound and speech that they encounter, perhaps even turning away from the signed input; the prediction here is that these babies might achieve the early linguistic milestones in each modality on a different maturational time course. Instead, they acquire both the signed and the spoken languages to which they are being exposed on an identical maturational timetable (Petitto & Herscovitch, in preparation; Petitto & Katerelos, 1999). That is, the onset of all early linguistic milestones in both the signed and the spoken modalities occurs at the time. For example, the hearing bilingual-bimodal babies acquiring LSQ and French, as well as those acquiring ASL and English, begin babbling in each modality in a time-locked manner and exhibit parallel stages of babbling over time in each modality. One intriguing observation here that is presently under intensive study is that these babies' manual and vocal babbling appear to be produced simultaneously more frequently than not. So, for example, an 11-month-old baby who is producing canonical vocal babbling in his crib is highly likely also to be observed producing canonical manual babbling, even though the phonetic and syllabic formational properties of each type of babbling is produced quite differently. In babies acquiring two spoken languages from birth, such as Italian and French, this particular situation would not be possible given the obvious constraint of having only one mouth. Moreover, these hearing bimodal babies produce their first sign in LSQ or ASL and their first word in French or English within hours of each other, respectively. We have also found that these babies' early lexicons in each modality can be "mutually exclusive" (e.g., a baby's first ASL sign is DOG and first English word is "more") or overlapping (e.g., a baby's first LSQ sign is CHAPEAU [hat] and first French word is "chapeau"); some babies exhibit both mutually exclusive and overlapping lexical items in each modality at the same time. Crucially, this is precisely what we have found in our hearing bilingual controls, those babies acquiring French and English from birth (Petitto & Herscovitch, in preparation; Petitto et al., 1999; Petitto, Costopoulos, & Stevens, in preperation). To be sure, the findings from our studies found that hearing babies acquiring signed and spoken languages from birth do so in the same manner observed in other babies acquiring two different spoken languages from birth in bilingual homes.

The findings from the hearing babies with no systematic spoken language input are especially compelling. These babies can hear, but they are receiving no systematic speech stimulation from the moment of birth through around 30 months. Instead, they receive only signed language input from their profoundly Deaf parents as well as their extended Deaf families living in distinct communities outside of Montreal. Two types of families were studied, monolingual and bilingual. In the monolingual families, one group of hearing infants was being exposed only to LSQ from their LSQ Deaf parents and relatives, and another group of hearing infants was being exposed only to ASL from their ASL Deaf parents and relatives. In the bilingual families, one of the parents (originally from the United States) signed only ASL to their babies and the other parent (originally from Quebec) signed only LSQ to their babies; hence, the hearing babies being raised by these sets of parents received bilingual language exposure, but only in signed language!

All of these particular families were further unique in the following way: By choice, all of these parents had made the decision to expose their infants exclusively to their native signed languages, and, thus, these hearing infants received no systematic spoken language input in early life; note that a firm commitment to one's native language is entirely commensurate with the accepted practices in contemporary Quebec society.[2] The con-

---

[2]The primary reason that these parents' commitment to their children's exclusive exposure to a native sign language was eventually abandoned by around 30 months is because, in all cases, the parent at home wanted to return to work. Thus, for pragmatic reasons only, the children were placed in either state-run day care centers or with neighbors (hearing or deaf) who took in other children (typically hearing).

struct of "systematic input" is key here. Whereas it is likely that these infants may have occasionally overheard the speech of others in the supermarket and the like, children in such contexts generally do not acquire knowledge of a language from such unsystematic fragments of overheard (non-child-directed) speech. As further corroboration of this fact, the babies' productive and receptive vocabulary skills in both spoken French and English were tested at regular intervals and, crucially, prior to their entry into systematic spoken language exposure, and it was demonstrated to be either nonexistent (i.e., they had no spoken words in production and comprehension) or restricted to knowledge of one or two highly ritualized social greeting words such as "bye-bye" when leaving a room.

Our intensive study of these hearing babies acquiring only signed languages in early life surprised us. These babies achieve all linguistic milestones on a normal maturational time table. If early human language acquisition were wholly determined neurologically by the mechanisms for speech production and reception, then these hearing babies raised without systematic spoken language stimulation should show atypical patterns of language acquisition. Instead, all of these groups of hearing babies produced manual babbling, first signs, first two-signs, and other milestones, at the same time as is seen in all other children, be they hearing acquiring speech or Deaf acquiring sign. Further, the bilingual group here (those hearing babies receiving early exposure to both ASL and LSQ, but not speech) demonstrated highly similar patterns of bilingual language acquisition observed in our hearing controls acquiring French and English, and the bilingual-bimodal hearing infants acquiring one signed and one spoken language (Petitto & Herscovitch, in preparation; Petitto et al., 1999; Petitto, Costopoulos, & Stevens, in preparation). Thus, entirely normal language acquisition occurs in these hearing babies—albeit, signed—without the use of auditory and speech perception mechanisms, and without the use of the motoric mechanisms for the production of speech.

Having established that the overall time courses of signed and spoken language acquisition are highly similar, questions remain about just how deep the similarities are in acquisition at the specific, structural level. I now review studies that address this issue in an attempt to shed new light on the mechanisms that may underlie early language acquisition.

STRUCTURAL HOMOLOGIES IN SIGNING
AND SPEAKING INFANTS: THE DISCOVERY
OF MANUAL BABBLING

In trying to understand the biological roots of human language, researchers have naturally tried to find its "beginning." The regular onset timing and structure of vocal babbling—the "bababa" and other repetitive, syllabic sounds that babies produce—led researchers to conclude that babbling represents the beginning of human language acquisition, albeit, language production. Babbling—and thus early language acquisition in our species —is said to be determined by the development of the anatomy of the vocal tract and the mechanisms subserving the motor control of speech production (Locke, 1983; Thelen, 1991; Van der Stelt & Koopmans-van Bienum, 1986). The behavior has been further used to argue that the human language capacity must be uniquely linked to innate mechanisms for producing speech in ontogeny (Liberman & Mattingly, 1985, 1989). It has also been used to argue that human language has been shaped by properties of speech in evolution (Lieberman, 1984).

In the course of conducting research on Deaf infants' transition from prelinguistic gesturing to first signs, I noticed a class of hand activity containing linguistically relevant units that was different from all other hand activity during the Transition Period (9–12 months; Petitto, 1984, 1987a, 1987b). Deaf babies appeared to be "babbling," albeit with their hands (see Petitto, 1987a, page 18, section 4.1.2). An additional study was undertaken to understand the basis of this extraordinary behavior. This time, however, a key control group was added: hearing babies who were acquiring spoken language with no exposure to signed language. In Petitto and Marentette (1991), we analyzed all of the hand activity produced in our sample of Deaf and hearing babies. Once again, the findings revealed unambiguously a discrete class of hand activity in Deaf babies only that was virtually identical to characterizations of vocal babbling observed in hearing babies. Further, critical analyses of the structure and use of manual babbling revealed that it was fundamentally distinct from all babies' communicative gestures. It was distinct from Deaf babies' attempts to produce real first signs (including immature phonetic approximations to adult signs, baby signs, and the like). It was further distinct from what I have called "excitatory motor hand activity" that all Deaf and hearing babies make during this developmental period: For example, the excitatory opening and closing hand and arm movements that infants produce on being presented with a new object (or some abrupt change in the external stimulation); such excitatory motor hand activity would constitute instances of the class of rhythmic "motor stereotypies" that Thelen (1979) and other scientists have observed in all young babies. Indeed, only one class of hand activity exhibited all of the key defining features of human infant babbling, and it was only observed in sign-exposed Deaf babies as opposed to the hearing controls; hence, the discovery of "manual babbling" in profoundly Deaf babies exposed to natural signed languages.

In studies of hearing babies' vocalizations, a composite of several key defining features is used to distinguish vocal babbling from all other vocal activity. At least five general features have been used by scientists to help in the identification of genuine instances of vocal babbling, with the first three being most widely accepted for several decades based on a vocalization's (a) phonetic and syllabic structure, (b) manner of use, and (c) stages of development throughout early language acquisition. Vihman and others further identified that there is (d) a continuity of phonetic form and syllable type within an individual baby's vocal babbling and first words (Vihman et al., 1985). An additional feature that helps to pin down one particularly crucial babbling stage was offered by Oller and Eilers (1988) and others, and is called the (e) syllabic ratio. Beginning roughly around ages 7 to 11 months, babies begin producing what Oller first coined syllabic or "canonical" babbling. This involves the production of well-formed consonant–vowel (CV) clusters produced with repetitive, multicycle reduplications (e.g., "bababa") and in a rhythmic manner that reflects the prosody (timing, stress) of natural language. Oller and Eilers found that once babies begin producing such well-formed CV babbling syllables, they generally comprise about 20% or more of the infants' total vocal activity; hence, the 20% ratio (percentage of syllabic to total vocal utterances) was offered as a yardstick to aid in the classification of infants' vocal activity as being in the syllabic (canonical) vocal babbling stage of language acquisition. More recently, other researchers have added to the previous list of criteria by analyzing the specific physical properties of babbling, especially manual babbling, as a way to identify and harness this fascinating phenomenon in all children (e.g., involving analyses of the behavior's temporal duration, velocity, path trajectories, and movement cycles-per-second that are discussed later in this chapter; see also Meier, Chap. 19, this volume).

Remarkably, the manual babbling that Petitto and Marentette found in sign-exposed Deaf babies was fundamentally similar to hearing babies' vocal babbling in precisely the ways noted earlier.

Phonetic and Syllabic Structure. Like vocal babbling, by 10 months, the Deaf babies began producing a restricted set of sign phonetic units in sign syllables (more later) with distinct repetitive, multicycle hand and arm movements, which were temporally constrained. This particular behavior constituted an especially important finding, and I later returned to study its specific properties (discussed subsequently).

Manner of Use. Like vocal babbling, the Deaf babies used manual babbling as if the forms had no meaning, with no apparent intent to signify or represent external objects in the world or internal states and intentions. Like hearing babies, they instead used communicative gestures during this developmental period for such purposes, such as the point. Crucially, however, there was a decidedly deliberate manner in which the Deaf babies used manual babbling that was fundamentally unlike the way that they used all other hand activity, especially other excitatory motor hand activity during this period (more later). Like hearing babies, the Deaf babies appeared to understand that this specific activity was something that adults valued and something that is used between one person to another. Without wanting to attribute too much to children, it was almost as if they understood that this activity had some role in "communication." For example, one enduring finding from my lab has been that all babies (be they hearing or Deaf) will produce rich babbling protocol if they are in the presence of two adults having a conversation, but one where they (the babies) are personally excluded; that is, one where the two adults do not address any of their conversation to the baby. Under such circumstances, most babies will begin producing a surprisingly high degree of babbling. For the Deaf baby, this is quite dramatic, as they will actually raise their hands(s) and arm(s) into the mother's "sight-line" and begin producing meaningless babbling units, often giggling out loud in apparent delight when mother finally turns her head to acknowledge this behavior.

Interestingly, our analyses of Deaf mothers' (and Deaf adults') "motherese" during this developmental period demonstrated that adults consistently respond differently to their babies' manual babbling as compared to all other hand activity, even the excitatory motor hand activity that occurs during this period whose rhythmic, multicycle form shares some resemblance with manual babbling (Petitto, Ostry, Sergio, & Levy, in press). Deaf adults respond to a baby's manual babbling with language, pure and simple. Here, adults either expand on the baby's fragmentary syllabic units and turn them into real signs that they then sign back to the baby, or they simply "play with" the infant's linguistic morsels by producing the very fragments back to the child; frequently, they query the infant, asking the equivalent of "What are you trying to say to mommy?" Conversely, adults respond both to an infant's manual gestures and to an infant's excitatory motor hand activity during this period with actions. Alas, this appears to be yet another of those behaviors in child language that scientists have excitedly "discovered" in the laboratory, yet mothers (in this case Deaf mothers and adults) appear to have tacitly known about this phenomenon for a long time.

To be sure, we have consistently observed that the way in which Deaf babies use their manual babbling is fundamentally different from the way that they use other hand activity, especially other excitatory motor hand activity that occurs during this period. Finally, Deaf babies often look at their own hands when manually babbling in the same way that hearing babies appear to be attending to the sounds in their own vocal babbles, for example, as has been observed in their solitary "crib speech." Deaf babies do not look at their own hands when producing other excitatory motor hand activity. Such fundamental differences in the manner of use between Deaf babies' manual babbling versus their other excitatory motor hand activity during this period is important and has significance for the additional studies of manual babbling discussed later.

Stages of Development Throughout Early Language Acquisition. Manual babbling emerged on the same maturational time table as vocal babbling and exhibited the identical "stages" of babbling. For example, hearing babies begin CV productions at around 4 to 6 months, but sometime between 7 to 11 months most babies enter the syllabic or canonical babbling stage that was discussed earlier. By around 10 to 12 months "variegated babbling" is produced, whereby different CV units are strung together, as in "gabada" (Oller, 1980). Beginning around 12 months and continuing well into children's production of early words and sentences, "jargon babbling" is produced; here, children produce strings of wordlike CV units that exhibit the prosodic organization of a simple sentence, albeit meaningless. The Deaf babies in our study exhibited structurally similar stages in manual babbling and did so on the same timetable as hearing babies' vocal babbling.

Continuity in Structure With First Words and the Syllabic Ratio. As in vocal babbling, the sign phonetic units that were most predominant in the Deaf babies' manual babbling were later observed to be those units that were most predominant in their first signs (Petitto &

Marentette, 1991). Moreover, the Deaf babies met and surpassed Oller and Eilers's (1988) syllabic ratio in their manual babbling. Manual babbling constituted 32% to 71% of the manual activity in Deaf infants. Whereas, instances of what Petitto and Marentette (1991) also called "manual babbling" in the hearing controls constituted a mere 4% to 15% of their manual activity—a nonetheless intriguing phenomenon that I now examine.

What further interested me about the findings first reported in Petitto and Marentette (1991) is that the hearing babies also produced a behavior that superficially looked like manual babbling. Like the Deaf babies in this study, the hearing babies with no exposure to signed languages produced repetitive, multicycle hand and arm movements from around ages 7 to 12 months. Recall that the attribution of true babbling, be it vocal or manual, is not made based on the presence of one or two features but involves a composite of key defining features that we found to be absent in the hearing infants' manual productions. The physical form of the hearing babies' manual babbling—or, the extent to which it could be said to possess sign phonetic and sign syllabic structure—was less complex than the manual babbling of Deaf babies; it contained far fewer hand shapes, movements, orientations, and locations. For example, hearing babies' manual babbling contained only 3 handshapes that resembled sign-phonetic units, as compared with the Deaf babies' 13, and they produced only 1 movement as compared with Deaf babies' 13. The hearing babies' handshapes were also organized into far fewer syllable types. They produced only one unit that resembled a sign syllable as compared to the Deaf babies' four. The manner of use differed in the important ways discussed earlier, including the fact that the hearing babies did not produce their manual babbling in an apparently deliberate (yet meaningless) and communicatively appropriate manner. They also did not look at their own hands when they produced these forms and the like. There were no stages of development evidenced, as the forms did not increase in complexity over time. For obvious reasons, there was no continuity between these hand forms and first signs (recall that these hearing babies were acquiring only spoken languages). Finally, as noted previously, the hearing infants' manual babbling violated Oller and Eilers's (1988) "syllabic ratio." Thus, we concluded that the hearing babies' manual babbling was really fundamentally similar to the excitatory motor hand activity observed in all young babies, especially to the motor-stereotypies described by Thelen (1979) and others (Petitto & Marentette, 1991).

Our initial finding of manual babbling in the hearing babies nonetheless compelled our attention. How could this rather remarkable hand activity in hearing babies be possible? Why was similar excitatory motor hand activity also present in the Deaf babies at the same time as their manual babbling? Might the occurrence and developmental timing of this behavior in all infants suggest something about the "ready-state" nature of the human body to express language from multiple pathways? In Petitto and Marentette, I argued just that: The presence of so-called manual babbling in the hearing babies who had no sign input suggested that there is a biological "equipotentiality" of the spoken and signed modalities to receive and produce natural language. My earlier studies had already taught me that both the signed and the spoken modalities were recruited with equal ease in development depending on the modality of the input language (and, of course, hearing status). The remaining puzzle was this: How could such seemingly effortless and instantaneous transfer from one modality to the next exist if all of acquisition was exclusively determined by the maturation of the mechanisms for producing and receiving speech? I therefore reasoned that an additional mechanism had to be contributing to the human language acquisition process—one that existed in addition to important motor and perceptual constraints. I hypothesized that accidental evolutionary processes must have provided humans with a mechanism that is sensitive to elementary aspects of the temporal and distributional patterning of natural language structure independent of modality; I thought of this as the sort of biologically plausible mechanism that later "grammatical knowledge" could build itself up from. I further argued that this mechanism must be neurologically yoked to motor production and perceptual constraints, but it must be nonetheless engaged in discrete processing of low-level aspects of natural language patterning. Although at the time, I was not sure about the specific temporal properties of this mechanism, the fact that units of about the same size and duration were being pushed out onto the hands and tongue in very early signed and spoken language acquisition led me to conclude that some sort of dedicated temporal sensitivity was contributing to the human acquisition process and was very the mechanism that apes lacked! Based on the manual babbling findings, I hypothesized that babies may be born with a mechanism that is first sensitive to a brief temporal window and especially to units with rapid alternations (hence, the infants' ability to attend to, perceive, and ultimately produce, maximally contrasting phonetic units within a basic syllable); I was to return to this idea in the next study. What seemed clear at the time, however, was that this mechanism could develop equally well in ontogeny with either the hands or tongue, thereby explaining why all infants could attend to and, crucially, produce units of about the same size and organization, and on the same maturational time table, across such radically different modalities. This was the biological mechanism that was driving the identical timing milestones and this was the mechanism that explained the clear equipotentiality of signed and spoken languages in acquisition. One very surprising implication of this view is that the human language modality is neurologically set after birth depending upon the modality of language input, which, in the end, I believe will be found to be correct (Petitto, 1994; Petitto & Marentette, 1991; for a more detailed discussion of the properties of this hypothesized mechanism, see also Petitto, 1997).

Because we have a mechanism that is going to become neurologically wed to a modality in the first year of life, and because, I hypothesized, both the tongue and hands at birth are equipotential language articulators, the prediction is that we will see languagelike articulations spill out into the "unused" modality, albeit in unsystematic ways. Having received no systematic signed language input, a hearing baby's hands will nonetheless approximate syllabiclike manual units, although in unsystematic ways. Further, they will occasionally hit on real handshapes and movements that happen to exist in natural signed languages due to specific physical affordances of the human body (in this case, the hands) that all natural language phonologies exploit to a greater or lesser extent. In order for the equipotentiality argument to hold, the identical phenomenon should also be seen in profoundly Deaf infants—and it is. Having received no systematic spoken language input, this Deaf infant will occasionally produce a well-formed CV vocal syllable in unsystematic ways. Here, aspects of the human oral-facial cavity make possible this profoundly Deaf infant's ability to hit on a real CV vocal unit (such as "ba"), albeit unsystematically, even though they have never heard this syllable.[3]

The hearing infants' ostensible manual babbling and Deaf infants' ostensible vocal babbling can be further witnessed within this developmental period (6–12 months) due to another developmental factor: Development of the primary and secondary motor cortices is occurring during this time and is evidenced by characteristic changes in infant motor behavior, whose movements change from rhythmically oscillating bursts (e.g., rhythmic flexing of the hands and feet when excited) to more coordinated

---

[3]Contrary to Lenneberg's (1967) provocative claims, both my own research and the research of others (e.g., Oller, 1980) have demonstrated clearly that a profoundly Deaf infant with no auditory augmentation and no auditory training does not spontaneously produce systematic canonical CV babbling on the same time course and with the same complexity as is observed in hearing infants.

body and limb control. The proclivity toward rhythmic body movements during this period, in combination with particular affordances provided by the human body's hands and oral-facial cavity, can further account for the appearance of the accidental manual babbling forms in hearing babies and vocal babbling forms in Deaf babies. However, the significantly reduced frequency and complexity of these ostensible babbling forms in the hearing and Deaf babies, as compared with the frequency and complexity of the babbling forms in each group's respective primary language modality, again, caused me to argue that the former constituted a class of fundamentally nonlinguistic motor hand activity, whereas the latter was fundamentally linguistic (Petitto & Marentette, 1991).

As is often the case, the discovery of babbling in another modality answered some questions but raised many more. The discovery of manual babbling confirmed the hypothesis that babbling represents a distinct and critical stage in the ontogeny of human language. However, it disconfirmed existing hypotheses about why babbling occurs: It disconfirmed the view that babbling is exclusively determined by the neurological maturation of the speech-production mechanisms. For example, it has been rigorously argued that the "baba" CV alternation that infants produce results from the rhythmic opening and closing of the jaw (MacNeilage & Davis, 1990). But the study raised important questions about the phenomenon as well. The Deaf babies' syllabic (or canonical) manual babbling (ages 7–11 months) was especially compelling because it was produced with distinct, repetitive, multicycle hand and arm movements; it further appeared to possess strikingly different temporal organization as compared with other hand activity, although the physical properties of its temporal organization were not fully understood. But other hand activity in the Deaf babies, as well as in the hearing babies, contained repetitive, multicycle movements. Was this important behavior that we identified as being "syllabic manual babbling," a fundamentally linguistic or motor activity? (How similar were its physical properties to hearing infants' vocal babbling at this time?) Were the manual babbles observed in Deaf infants and the manual babbles in hearing infants fundamentally similar or different? Crucially, was the manual babbling observed in Deaf and hearing babies fundamentally similar or dissimilar to the rhythmic excitatory motor hand activity that all infants make? Said another way, was all infants' manual babbling fundamentally similar to the motor stereotypies seen in young infants by Thelen (1979) and others (e.g., Meier, Mauk, Mirus, & Conlin, 1998)? Answers to these questions would prove to be essential in understanding whether the human brain possesses a discrete mechanism dedicated to aspects of natural language patterning that aids language acquisition, or whether the early seemingly linguistic activity in babies is fundamentally determined by general motor constraints.

It struck me that the key to answering these questions would entail a deeper understanding of the physical properties that constrain a baby's production of the basic manual babbling unit, with an understanding of its temporal oscillations being crucial. The Petittto and Marentette (1991) study had already reported that the basic manual babbling unit contained "syllabic organization." Drawing from existing linguistic descriptions of the sign syllable, Petitto and Marentette identified the syllable in signed languages to consist of a restricted set of sign phonetic units whose structural nucleus contained movement: described in physical terms as a rhythmic opening and closing (or the rhythmic hold–movement alternations) of the hands and arms (e.g., Liddell & Johnson, 1989; Perlmutter, 1992). Although healthy controversy has continued to thrive among theoretical linguists concerning the definition of the sign syllable (Brentari, 1999; Liddell & Johnson, 1989; Perlmutter, 1992), this working definition succeeded in differentiating classes of manual activity across all of our young Deaf and hearing babies. To test this further, we applied all existing linguistic definitions of the sign syllable to our data, and all existing definitions resulted in a differentiation of the classes of manual activity that we had identified. In particular, none failed to identify Deaf babies' manual babbling as being a distinct class of manual activity. Note that similar lively debates about the definition of the syllable in spoken languages have gone on for decades. Nonetheless, an equally long history of psychological research—and now cognitive neuroscience studies of language processing and cerebral activation—has established that the syllable is a "real" perceptual and production unit in natural language processing. Thus, my goal (both then and now) has been to discover the systematic physical properties of infant hand activity, irrespective of contemporary controversy over its abstract formalization.

Although syllabic organization was indeed observed in the Petitto and Marentette study, nothing was understood about its temporal organization, which I found distinctive. When Deaf babies manually babbled, I noticed that the reduplicated temporal patterning of these opening and closing (hold-movement) hand and arm movements appeared to be different from the temporal patterning of their gestures, attempts to sign, or simply the movements of their hands when excited. In other words, it is not just the presence or absence of syllabic organization that distinguishes among the classes of infant manual activity, but the presence of this organization in conjunction with a highly specific temporal patterning that appears to be key. However, it is simply not possible to measure such temporal oscillations through mere videotape inspection (qualitative analyses) and can only be studied with methods that permit precise quantification. But how was I to do this?

To study the temporal patterning of infant hand activity, I conducted a series of studies with my colleague, David Ostry, and students Lauren Sergio and Bronna Levy, using our "OPTOTRAK Visual-Graphic Analysis System" (see Petitto, 1993, 1997; Petitto, Ostry, et al., in preparation). Both sign-exposed and speech-exposed infants were studied at ages 6, 10, & 12 months (cross-sectional and longitudinal design) while participating in a series of tasks that were designed to elicit manual activity, including manual babbling. The precise physical properties of all manual activity produced by all infants were measured by placing tiny Infrared-Emitting Diodes (IREDs) on their hands, arms, shoulders, and feet. The IREDs transmitted light impulses to cameras that, in turn, fed signals into computer software that extracted information analogous to the spectrographic representation of speech but adapted for the spectrographic representation of sign. Specifically, we were able to record the timing, rate, path movement, velocity, and "f_o" (fundamental frequency) for all infant hand activity and to obtain 3-D graphic displays.

We were first interested in whether distinct classes of manual activity would "fall out" of the OPTOTRAK data based exclusively on their quantitative physical properties. In this case, we could not see the actual manual form the baby produced, we only had access to its physical features, such as its temporal duration, velocity, trajectory path through space, number of movement cycles per second, and the like. We were then interested in whether manual activity specifically identified as "syllabic (or canonical) manual babbling" (ages 7–11 months, based on all existing qualitative criteria) was physically distinct from or similar to other classes of manual activity, such as the (a) rhythmic excitatory motor hand and leg activity that all young infants make to novel objects (e.g., Thelen, 1979), (b) communicative gestures, (c) attempts to sign, and the like. Many analyses were conducted, but several key ones included a comparison of the physical properties of sign-exposed babies' syllabic manual babbling with their own excitatory motor hand and leg movements; then we compared the sign-exposed babies' excitatory motor hand and leg movements with this same class in speech-exposed babies. We also examined the physical properties of the speech-exposed infants' instances of "manual babbling" with all of the mentioned activity, and so forth.

Briefly, we found that distinct classes of manual activity fell out of the data based on their physical properties. Systematic differences existed between the rhythmic timing, velocity, and spectral frequencies of sign-exposed infants' syllabic manual babbling versus all infants' rhythmic excitatory motor hand activity, communicative gestures, and so forth, during this identical time period (7–11 months). Speech-exposed infants' "manual babbling" possessed physical features more closely related to all infants' class of excitatory motor hand activity. Syllabic manual babbling units in sign-exposed infants alone were produced in a tightly constrained space and were typically produced exclusively with hand and upper arm movements, with no accompanying leg movements. Crucially, syllabic manual babbling in sign-exposed babies only was produced with a slower velocity and rate as compared with all other hand activity. Here, an average of one to two manual babbling movement units were completed within repetitive temporal bursts of approximately 1.2 seconds. By contrast, other rhythmic excitatory motor hand activity was faster in both the sign-exposed and speech-exposed infants; here, an average of three to four completed movement units were produced within 1.2 seconds, and, crucially, such hand activity was always accompanied by leg movements. This whole-body involvement when infants produced excitatory motor manual activity was very striking. When sign-exposed babies were manually babbling, only the top half of their body was involved. By contrast, when all children produced other rhythmic motor hand activity, the lower part of their body became involved as well. Further analyses reveal that the temporal patterning of syllabic manual babbling in sign-exposed babies is similar to the temporal patterning of early vocal babbling in speech-exposed babies, range 6 to 10 months, and present analyses are exploring how close this relation is and how it changes over time.

Once again, the findings suggest some answers and raise more questions. Manual babbling is a robust phenomenon in sign-exposed babies. Moving away from videotape analyses, innovative technology informs us that manual babbling is physically distinct from other types of other rhythmic excitatory motor hand activity (motor-stereotypies) in principled ways, and it is distinct from speech-exposed babies' less frequent and less complex instances of ostensible manual babbling. Remarkably, a common temporal constraint may be operating, even though the neural substrates for sign and speech are distinct. How is this possible?

TESTING HYPOTHESES ABOUT THE
BIOLOGICAL FOUNDATIONS OF LANGUAGE:
INSIGHTS FROM PET STUDIES OF ADULT
SIGNING AND SPEAKING ADULTS

In Petitto (1997), I proposed a hypothesis as to how it is possible for signed and spoken languages to be acquired so similarly. The hypothesis has several components, some of which I summarized earlier. In addition to suggesting that the same dedicated brain mechanism underlies both signed and spoken language acquisition, I went one step further and hypothesized that the same brain tissue is subserving the acquisition of both. I further specified that this brain tissue constitutes a mechanism that has peaked sensitivity to maximally contrasting, temporally oscillating bundles of about 1.2 seconds that initially permits all infants to discover sublexical and prosodic patterning in the input (be it signed or spoken) and soon after to produce them. If correct, this theory further predicts that adult signed and spoken languages should utilize the same sites in the human brain. Ursula, Ed, and colleagues including Howard Poizner and others had already conducted their pioneering studies of brain-damaged Deaf adults showing that Deaf signers suffer the classic Broca's and Wernicke's aphasias in sign language following left-hemisphere lesions as has been observed in speech (see also others in this volume, such as Corina, Damasio, Damasio, Emmorey, and Kegl). Yet, I wondered just how specific this was: Was the identical brain tissue involved in the processing of indentical linguistic functions across sign and speech?

Recently, I, Robert Zatorre, and our colleagues conducted a series of studies of cerebral blood flow (rCBF) in profoundly Deaf signing adults and hearing people with no knowledge of signed language using Positron Emission Tomography (PET) technology in combination with Magnetic Resonance Imaging (MRI) (Petitto et al., 1997, 1998, 1999). Many intriguing findings were observed, but one of particular relevance here involves activation that we observed within one highly specialized brain site, the Planum Temporale, a major site within the Wernicke's receptive language area that receives auditory projections from the auditory afferent system (e.g., Binder, Frost, Hammeke, Rao, & Cox, 1996; Galaburda & Sanides, 1980) and that is widely considered to have a unimodal auditory processing function. We observed the expected activation in the Planum Temporale when hearing people processed highly specific phonetic-syllabic units auditorially. Remarkably, however, we observed entirely unexpected activation in the Planum Temporale of Deaf people when they processed the identical level of language organization visually—that is, phonetic-syllabic units on the hands. The discovery of common brain activation sites in languages with and without sound provides powerful corroborating evidence with the acquisition findings that the brain may possess mechanisms dedicated to processing specific patterns unique to natural language—and not sound or speech.

Taken together, both the acquisition and the adult processing findings have intriguing implications regarding the evolution of the linguistic capacity in our species, as they support the idea that aspects of the abstract grammatical patterning of natural language may be a product of evolutionary processes (e.g., Donald, 1993; Pinker & Bloom, 1990; see also Woll, 1996, for a discussion of the evolutionary implications of signed languages and language evolution). A by-product of the existence of evolved mechanisms that are sensitive to the abstract patterning of human language, per se, would be that humans could generate multiple pathways for perceiving and producing language. Quite powerfully, this is precisely what the very existence of natural signed languages has taught us.

ON THE BIOLOGICAL FOUNDATIONS
OF HUMAN LANGUAGE

The key issue for students of early brain development is not the fact that signed and spoken languages are acquired similarly but to determine why this is so. Given the different neural substrates, where does the capacity to produce common linguistic structures come? How is it possible that the modality of language transmission and reception can be changed at birth—from speech to sign, or vice versa—without any delay or alteration to the time course and nature of human language acquisition? How can the brain tolerate this radical change in the morphology of its expressive and receptive mechanisms for language, and what is the genetic basis for such stunning equipotentiality?

The present findings suggest that the brain at birth cannot be working under rigid genetic instruction to produce and receive language via the auditory-speech modality. If this were the case, then both the maturational time course and the nature of signed and spoken language acquisition should be different. By contrast, using a wide variety of techniques and participants populations, I and others have discovered that the acquisition of signed and spoken language is fundamentally similar.

What the present findings do suggest is that the neural substrates that support the brain's capacity for language can be potentiated in multiple ways in the face of varying environmental pressures. The fact that the brain can tolerate variation in language transmission and reception, depending on different environmental inputs, and still achieve the target behavior, provides support for there being a strong genetic component underlying language acquisition, possibly involving the type of mechanisms that I suggested here: specifically, those sensitive to aspects of the abstract patterning of natural language structure. At the same time, the language acquisition process is biologically flexible (neurologically plastic) in that language can be perceived and expressed via the hands or tongue.

In conclusion, the present findings have led me to propose a new way to construe human language ontogeny. Rather than being exclusively hardwired for *speech* or sound, the young of our species are initially hardwired to detect aspects of the patterning of *language*. I suggested here that this initial sensitivity is to aspects of its temporal and distributional regularities initially corresponding to the syllabic and prosodic levels of natural language organization. If the environmental input contains the requisite patterns unique to natural language, human infants will attempt to produce and acquire those patterns, irrespective of whether the input is on the hands or the tongue.

As always, the studies discussed here answer some questions and raise many others—especially regarding the specific nature of the "temporal and distributional sensitivities" that I and others have hypothesized to exist in the newborn brain (e.g., Marcus, Vijayan, Bandi Rao, & Vishton, 1999; Newport & Suppala, chap. 7, this volume; Saffran, Aslin, & Newport, 1996). Of course, I will continue to pursue these questions. Because like Ursula and Ed, I cannot stop myself. Because when I passed through Ursula's laboratory many years ago, this is one of the enduring gifts that they gave me: the courage, strength, and sheer stamina to follow one's passion to know.

ACKNOWLEDGMENTS

I thank the Deaf and hearing families who gave me their time and trust over the years, thereby enabling this work to continue. I thank the students and research assistants who worked on these studies with me. I thank Kevin N. Dunbar and Karen Emmorey for their important comments on this chapter, and Karen Emmorey for her helpful editorial suggestions.

I am grateful to Harlan Lane for his encouragement. I thank the agencies who helped fund this research, including the National Sciences and Engineering Research Council of Canada, Medical Research Council of Canada, Social Sciences and Health Research Council of Canada, and the MacDonald Pew Centre for Cognitive Neuroscience Research Grant. I thank The Guggenheim Foundation for appointing me a 1998 Fellow, thereby giving me precious time to write this and other works. I am also especially grateful to Professor Massimo Piattelli-Palmerini for inviting me to the Università Vita-Salute San Raffaele, in Milan, Italy, where I am currently writing and conducting research.

REFERENCES

Bellugi, U., & Klima, E. (1982). The acquisition of three morphological systems in American Sign Language. *Papers and Reports on Child Language Development, 21,* 1–35.

Binder, J. R., Frost, J. A., Hammeke, T. A., Rao, S. M., & Cox, R.W. (1996). Function of the left planum temporale in auditory and linguistic processing. *Brain, 119,* 1239–1247.

Brentari, D. (1999). *A prosodic model of sign language phonology.* Cambridge, MA: MIT Press.

Charron, F., & Petitto, L.A. (1987). Semantic categories in the acquisition of Langue des Signes Québécoise (LSQ) and American Sign Language (ASL). Published *Abstracts of the Twelfth Annual Boston University Conference on Language Development.* Boston, MA, p. 28.

Charron, F., & Petitto, L. A. (1991). Les premiers signes acquis par des enfants sourds en langue des signes québécoise (LSQ): Comparaison avec les premiers mots. *Revue Québécoise de Linguistique Théorique et Appliquée, 10*(1), 71–122.

Donald, M. (1993). Precis of origins of the modern mind. *Brain and Behavioral Sciences, 16,* 737–791.

Galaburda, A., & Sanides, F. (1980). Cytoarchitectonic organization of the human auditory cortex. The *Journal of Comparative Neurology, 190,* 597–610.

Lenneberg, E. (1967). *The biological foundations of language.* New York: Wiley.

Liberman, A. M., & Mattingly, I. G. (1985). The motor theory of speech perception. *Cognition, 21*(1), 1–36.

Liberman, A. M., & Mattingly, I. G. (1989). A specialization for speech perception. *Science, 243* (4890), 489–494.

Liddell, S., & Johnson, R. (1989). *Sign Language Studies, 64,* 195–278.

Lieberman, P. (1984). *The biology and evolution of language.* Cambridge, MA: Harvard University Press.

Locke, J. L. (1983). *Phonological acquisition and change.* New York: Academic Press.

MacNeilage, P. F., & Davis, B. (1990). Acquisition of speech production: Frames, then content. In M. Jeannerod (Ed.), *Attention and performance XIII: Motor representation and control* (pp. 453–476). Mahwah, NJ: Lawrence Erlbaum Associates.

Marcus, G., Vijayan, S., Bandi Rao, S., & Vishton, P. M. (1999). Rule learning by seven-month old infants. *Science, 283,* 77–80.

Meier, R. P. (1991) Language acquisition by Deaf children. *American Scientist, 79,* 60–70.

Meier, R. P., Mauk C., Mirus, G. R., & Conlin, K. E. (1998). Motoric constraints on early sign acquisition. In E. Clark (Ed.), *Proceedings of the 29th Annual Child Language Research Forum* (pp. 63–72).

Newport, E. L., & Meier, R. P. (1985). The acquisition of American Sign Language. In D. Slobin (Ed.), *The crosslinguistic study of language acquisition* (Vol. 1, pp. 881–938). Mahwah, NJ: Lawrence Erlbaum Associates.

Oller, D. K. (1980). The emergence of the sounds of speech in infancy. In G. H. Yeni-Komshian, J. F. Kavanagh, & C. A. Ferguson (Eds.), *Production, Volume 1 of child phonology* (pp. 93–112). New York: Academic Press.

Oller, D. K., & Eilers, R. E. (1988). The role of audition in infant babbling. *Child Development, 59,* 441.

Perlmutter, D. (1992). Sonority and syllable structure in American Sign Language. *Linguistic Inquiry, 23*(3), 407–442

Petitto, L. A. (1984). *From gesture to symbol: The relationship between form and meaning in the acquisition of personal pronouns in American Sign Language.* Unpublished doctoral dissertation, Harvard University, Cambridge, MA.

Petitto, L. A. (1985). Are signed languages acquired earlier than spoken languages? Published *Abstracts of The Society for Research in Child Development.* Volume 5. Toronto, Ontario, p. 269.

Petitto, L. A. (1987a). On the autonomy of language and gesture: Evidence from the acquisition of personal pronouns in American Sign language. *Cognition, 27*(1), 1–52.

Petitto, L. A. (1987b, July). *Theoretical and methodological issues in the study of sign language babbling: Preliminary evidence from American Sign Language (ASL) and Langue des Signes Québécoise (LSQ).* Paper presented at the Fourth International Symposium on Sign Language Research, Lappeenranta, Finland.

Petitto, L. A. (1988). "Language" in the pre-linguistic child. In F. Kessel (Ed.), *Development of language and language researchers: Essays in honor of Roger Brown* (pp. 187–221). Mahwah, NJ: Lawrence Erlbaum Associates.

Petitto, L. A. (1992). Modularity and constraints in early lexical acquisition: Evidence from children's first words/signs and gestures. In M. Gunnar & M. Maratsos (Eds.), *Modularity and constraints in language and cognition: The Minnesota Symposia on child psychology* (pp. 25–58). Mahwah, NJ: Lawrence Erlbaum Associates.

Petitto, L. A. (1993). On manual babbling: New analyses yield new insights into the essence of early language acquisition. Published *Abstracts of The Society for Research in Child Development.* Volume 9. New Orleans, Louisiana, p. 540.

Petitto, L. A. (1994). On the equipotentiality of signed and spoken language in early language ontgeny. In B. Snider (Ed.), *Post-Milan ASL and English literacy: Issues, trends, and research* (pp. 195–223). Washington, DC: Gallaudet University Press.

Petitto, L. A. (1997). In the beginning: On the genetic and environmental factors that make early language acquisition possible. In M. Gopnik (Ed.), *The inheritance and innateness of grammars* (pp. 46–71). Mahwah, NJ: Lawrence Erlbaum Associates.

Petitto, L. A., & Charron, F. (1988, May). *The acquisition of semantic categories two sign languages.* Paper presented at Theoretical Issues in Sign Language Research, Washington, DC.

Petitto, L. A., & Herscovitch, L. (in preparation). *Are bilingual infants "delayed" and "confused"? Evidence from the timing of the first-word milestone in young infants exposed to two languages from birth.*

Petitto, L. A., & Marentette, P. (1990). The timing of linguistic milestones in sign language acquisition: Are first signs acquired earlier than first words? Published *Abstracts of the 15th Annual Boston University Conference on Language Development,* Boston, MA, p. 34.

Petitto, L. A., & Marentette, P. (1991). Babbling in the manual mode: Evidence for the ontogeny of language. *Science, 251,* 1483–1496.

Petitto, L. A., Katerlos, M., Levy, B. G., Guana, K., Tétreault, K., & Ferraro, V. (1999, submitted). *Bilingual signed and spoken language acquisition from birth: Implications for the mechanisms underlying early bilingual language acquisition.*

Petitto, L. A., Costopoulos, N., & Stevens, L. (in preparation). *The identity of linguistic milestones in signed and spoken languages: Evidence for a unitary timing mechanism in the ontogeny of language.*

Petitto, L. A., Zatorre, R. J., Nikelski, E. J., Gauna, K., Dostie, D., & Evans, A. C. (1997). Cerebral organization for language in the absence of sound: A PET study of Deaf signers processing signed languages. In *Abstracts of the 27th Annual Meeting Society for Neuroscience, Vol. 23, Part 2,* p. 2228 (no. 867.8).

Petitto, L. A., Zatorre, R. J., Nikelski, E. J., Gauna, K., Dostie, D., & Evans, A. C. (1998). By hand or by tongue: Common cerebral blood flow activation during language processing in signed and spoken languages. *NeuroImage, 7,* 4, S193.

Petitto, L. A., Zatorre, R. J., Nikelski, E. J., Gauna, K., Dostie, D., & Evans, A. C. (Submitted 1999). *Speech-like cerebral blood flow pet activation in deaf natural signed languages.*

Petitto, L. A., Ostry, D., Sergio, L., & Levy, B. G. (in preparation). *Linguistic versus non-linguistic manual activity in signing and non-signing infants under one year: The motoric underpinnings.*

Pinker, S., & Bloom, P. (1990). Natural language and natural selection. *Brain and Behavioral Sciences, 13,* 707–784.

Saffran, J., Aslin, R., & Newport, E. (1996). Statistical learning by 8-month-old infants. *Science, 274,* 1926–1930.

Thelen, E. (1979). Rhythmical stereotypies in normal human infants. *Animal Behaviour, 27,* 699–715.

Thelen, E. (1991). Motor aspects of emergent speech: A dynamic approach. In N. A. Krasnegor, D. M. Rumbaugh, R. L. Schiefelbusch, & M. Studdert-Kennedy (Eds.), *Biological and behavioral determinants of language development* (pp. 339–362). Mahwah, NJ: Lawrence Erlbaum Associates.

Van der Stelt, J. M., & Koopmans-van Bienum, F. J. (1986). The onset of babbling related to gross motor development. In B. Lindblom & R. Zetterstrom (Eds.), *Precursors of early speech* (pp. 163–173). New York: Stockton Press.

Vihman, M. M., Macken, M. A., Miller, R., Simmons, H., & Miller, J. (1985). From babbling to speech: A re-assessment of the continuity issue. *Language, 61,* 397–445.

Woll, B. (1996, April). *Do sign languages tell us anything about the origins of human language?* Paper presented at the Evolution of Human Language Conference, University of Edinburgh.

VI

The Neural Organization
of Sign Language

25

Language and the Brain

Antonio R. Damasio
Hanna Damasio
University of Iowa College of Medicine

What do we neuroscientists talk about when we talk about language? Mostly we talk about the ability to use words—or signs, if our language is one of the sign languages of the Deaf—and to combine them in sentences so that concepts in our minds can be transmitted to other people. We also talk about the opposite, that is, how we apprehend words spoken by others and turn them into concepts in our own minds.

Language arose and persisted because it serves as a supremely efficient means of communication, especially for abstract concepts. But language also helps categorize the world and reduce the complexity of conceptual structures to a manageable scale.

The word "screwdriver," for example, stands for many representations of such an instrument, including visual descriptions of its operation and purpose, specific instances of its use, the feel of the tool, or the hand movement that pertains to it. "Democracy" denotes an immense variety of

---

This text is an updated version of an article published in *Scientific American*, 1992. Permission to reprint parts of the text has been granted by *Scientific American*.

conceptual representations. The cognitive economies of language, its ability to pull together many concepts under one symbol, make it possible for people to establish ever more complex concepts and think at levels that would otherwise be impossible.

In the beginning, however, there were no words. Language seems to have appeared in evolution only after humans, and species before them, had become adept at generating and categorizing actions and at creating and categorizing mental representations of objects, events, and relations. Similarly, infants' brains are busy representing and evoking concepts and generating myriad actions long before they utter their first well-selected word and even longer before they form sentences and truly use language. However, the maturation of language processes may not always depend on the maturation of conceptual processes, because some children with defective conceptual systems have nonetheless acquired grammar. The neural machinery necessary for some syntactic operations may be capable of developing autonomously.

Language exists both as an artifact in the external world—a collection of symbols in admissible combinations—and as the embodiment in the brain of those symbols and of the principles that determine their combinations. The brain uses the same machinery to represent language that it uses to represent any other entity. As we come to understand the neural basis for the brain's representations of external objects, events, and their relations, we simultaneously gain insight into the brain's representation of language and into the mechanisms that connect the two.

We believe the brain processes language by means of three interacting sets of structures. First, a large collection of neural systems in both the right and left cerebral hemispheres represents nonlanguage interactions between the body and its environment, as mediated by varied sensory and motor systems—that is to say, anything that a person does, perceives, thinks, or feels while acting in the world.

The brain not only categorizes these nonlanguage representations, along lines such as shape, color, sequence or emotional state, it also creates another level of representation for the results of its classification. In this way, people organize objects, events, and relations. Successive layers of categories and symbolic representations form the basis for abstraction and metaphor (see Fig. 25.1, Panel A).

Second, a smaller number of neural systems, largely located in the left cerebral hemisphere, represent phonemes, phoneme combinations, and syntactic rules for combining words. When activated from within the brain, these systems assemble word forms and generate sentences to be spoken or written. When stimulated externally by speech or text, they perform the initial processing of auditory or visual language signals.

A third set of structures, also located largely in the left hemisphere, mediates between the first two. It can take a concept and stimulate the production of word forms, or it can receive words and cause the brain to evoke the corresponding concepts (see Fig. 25.1, Panel B).

Such mediation structures have also been hypothesized from a purely psycholinguistic perspective. Levelt (1992) suggested that word forms and sentences are generated from concepts by means of a process component he calls "lemma," and Garret (1992) held a similar view.

The concepts and words for colors serve as a particularly good example of this tripartite organization. Even those affected by congenital color blindness know that certain ranges of hue (chroma) band together and are different from other ranges, independent of their brightness and saturation. As Berlin and Rosch showed, these color concepts are fairly universal and develop whether or not a given culture actually has names to denote them. The retina and the lateral geniculate nucleus perform the initial processing of color signals, but the primary visual cortex and at least two other cortical regions (known as V2 and V4) also participate in color processing; they fabricate what we know as the experience of color.

We have found that damage to the occipital and subcalcarine portions of the left and right lingual gyri, the region of the brain believed to contain the V2 and V4 cortices, causes a condition called *achromatopsia*. Patients who previously had normal vision lose their perception of color. Furthermore, they even lose the ability to imagine colors. Achromatopsics usually see the world in shades of gray. When they conjure up a typically colored image in their minds, they see the shapes, movement, and texture but not the color. When they think about a field of grass, no green is available, and red or yellow will also not be part of their otherwise normal evocation of blood or banana. No lesion elsewhere in the brain can cause a similar defect. In some sense, then, the concept of colors depends on this region (Damasio, Yamada, Damasio, Corbett, & McKee, 1980; Rizzo, Smith, Pokorny, & Damasio, 1993; Zeki, 1993).

Patients with lesions in the left posterior temporal and inferior parietal cortex do not lose access to their concepts, but they have a sweeping impairment of their ability to produce proper word morphology regardless of the category to which a word belongs. Even when they are properly experiencing a given color and attempting to retrieve the corresponding word form, they produce phonemically distorted color names—they may say "buh" for "blue," for example.

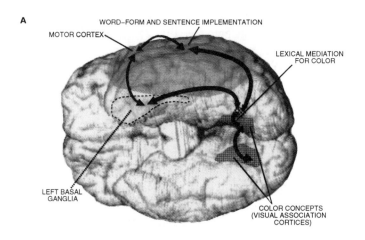

A

WORD–FORM AND SENTENCE IMPLEMENTATION

MOTOR CORTEX

LEXICAL MEDIATION
FOR COLOR

LEFT BASAL
GANGLIA

COLOR CONCEPTS
(VISUAL ASSOCIATION
CORTICES)

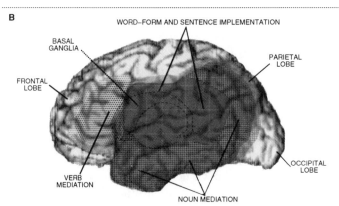

B

WORD–FORM AND SENTENCE IMPLEMENTATION

BASAL
GANGLIA

PARIETAL
LOBE

FRONTAL
LOBE

OCCIPITAL
LOBE

VERB
MEDIATION

NOUN MEDIATION

FIG. 25.1   Panel A: Brain systems involved in the retrieval of words denoting color.

Panel B: Brain systems for language in the left hemisphere include areas involved in the implementation of word forms and sentences as well as areas concerned with mediation between concept retrieval (to some extent dependent on right-hemisphere structures) and word implementation.

480

Other patients, who sustain damage in the temporal segment of the left lingual gyrus, suffer from a peculiar defect called *color anomia*, which affects neither color concepts nor the utterance of color words. These patients continue to *experience* color normally: they can match different hues, correctly rank hues of different saturation, and easily put the correct colored paint chip next to objects in a black-and-white photograph. But their ability to put names to color is dismally impaired. Given the limited set of color names available to those of us who are not interior decorators, it is surprising to see patients use the word "blue" or "red" when shown green or yellow and yet be capable of neatly placing a green chip next to a picture of grass or a yellow chip next to a picture of a banana. The defect goes both ways: Given a color name, the patient will point to the wrong color.

At the same time, however, all the wrong color names the patient uses are well formed, phonologically speaking, and the patient has no other language impairment. The color-concept system is intact, and so is the word-form implementation system. The problem seems to reside with the neural system that mediates between the two.

The same three-part organization that explains how people manage to talk about color applies to other concepts as well. But how are such concepts physically represented in the brain? We believe there are no permanently held "pictorial" representations of objects or persons as was traditionally thought. Instead, the brain holds, in effect, records of the neural activity that takes place in the sensory and motor cortices during interaction with a given object. The records are patterns of synaptic connections that can recreate the separate sets of activity that define an object or event; each record can also stimulate related ones. For example, as a person picks up a coffee cup, her visual cortices will respond to the colors of the cup and of its contents as well as to its shape and position. The somatosensory cortices will register the shape the hand assumes as it holds the cup, the movement of the hand and the arm as they bring the cup to the lips, the warmth of the coffee, and the body change some people call pleasure when they drink the stuff (Damasio, Damasio, Tranel, & Brandt, 1990). The brain does not merely represent aspects of external reality; it also records how the body explores the world and reacts to it. The neural processes that describe the interaction between the individual and the object constitute a rapid sequence of microperceptions and microactions, almost simultaneous as far as consciousness is concerned. They occur in separate functional regions, and each region contains additional subdivisions: The visual aspect of perception, for example, is segregated within smaller systems specialized for color, shape, and movement.

Where can the records be found that bind together all these fragmented activities? We believe they are embodied in ensembles of neurons within the brain's many "convergence" regions (Damasio & Damasio, 1994). At these sites, the axons of forward-projecting neurons from one part of the brain converge and join with reciprocally diverging backward projections from other regions. When reactivation within convergence regions stimulates the backward projections, many anatomically separate and widely distributed neuron ensembles fire simultaneously and reconstruct previous neural patterns.

In addition to storing information about experiences with objects, the brain also categorizes the information so that related events and concepts—shapes, colors, trajectories in space and time, and pertinent body movements and reactions—can be reactivated together. Such categorizations are denoted by yet other records in other convergence regions. The essential properties of the entities and processes in any interaction are thus "recorded" in an interwoven fashion. The collected knowledge that can be so "represented" includes the fact that a coffee cup has dimensions and a boundary; that it, is made of something and has parts; that if it is divided, it no longer is a cup, unlike water, which retains its identity no matter how it is divided; that it moved along a particular path, starting at one point in space and ending at another; that arrival at its destination produced a specific outcome. These aspects of neural representation bear some resemblance to the primitives of conceptual structure (Jackendoff, 1994) and the cognitive semantic schemas hypothesized by linguists (Lakoff, 1987).

Activity in such a network, then, can serve both understanding and expression. The activity in the network can reconstruct knowledge so that a person experiences it consciously, or it can activate a system that mediates between concept and language, causing appropriately correlated word forms and syntactical structures to be generated. Because the brain categorizes perceptions and actions simultaneously along many different dimensions, symbolic reworkings such as metaphor can emerge from this architecture.

Damage to parts of the brain that participate in these neural patterns should produce cognitive defects that clearly delineate the categories according to which concepts are stored and retrieved (the damage that results in achromatopsia is but one example of many). Warrington studied category-related recognition defects and found patients who lose cognizance of certain classes of object. Similarly, we showed that access to concepts in a number of domains depends on particular neural systems (Damasio & Tranel, 1993; Damasio, Grabowski, Tranel, Hichwa, &

Damasio, 1996; Goodglass, Wingfield, Hyde & Theurkauf, 1986; Tranel, Damasio, & Damasio, 1997; Warrington & McCarthy, 1983; Warrington & Shallice, 1984; Warrington & McCarthy, 1987).

For example, one of our patients no longer retrieves concepts for any unique entity (a specific person, place, or event) with which he was previously familiar. He has also lost concepts for nonunique entities of particular classes. Many animals, for instance, are completely strange to him even though he retains the concept level that lets him know that they are living and animate. Faced with a picture of a raccoon, he says, "It is an animal," but he has no idea of its size, habitat, or typical behavior.

Curiously, when it comes to other classes of nonunique entities, his cognition is apparently unimpaired. He can recognize and name objects, such as a wrench, that are manipulable and have a specific action attached to them. He can retrieve concepts for attributes of entities: He knows what it means for an object to be beautiful or ugly. He can grasp the idea of states or activities such as being in love, jumping, or swimming. And he can understand abstract relations among entities or events such as "above," "under," "into," "from," "before," "after," or "during." In brief, he has an impairment of concepts for many entities, all of which are denoted by common and proper nouns. He has no problem whatsoever with concepts for attributes, states, activities, and relations that are linguistically signified by adjectives, verbs, functors (prepositions, conjunctions, and other verbal connective tissue), and syntax. Indeed, the syntax of his sentences is impeccable.

Lesions such as this patient's, in the anterior and middle regions of both temporal lobes, impair the brain's conceptual system. Injuries to the left hemisphere in the vicinity of the sylvian fissure, in contrast, interfere with the proper formation of words and sentences. This brain system is the most thoroughly investigated of those involved in language. More than a century and a half ago, Paul Broca and Carl Wernicke determined the rough location of these basic language centers and discovered the phenomenon known as cerebral dominance—in most humans language structures lie in the left hemisphere rather than the right. This disposition holds for roughly 99% of right-handed people and two thirds of left-handers.

Studies of aphasic patients from different language backgrounds highlight the constancy of these structures. Indeed, Edward Klima and Ursula Bellugi discovered that damage to the brain's word-formation systems is implicated in sign-language aphasia as well (Bellugi, Poizner, & Klima, 1989). Deaf individuals who suffer focal brain damage in the left hemisphere can lose the ability to sign or to understand sign language. Because the damage in question is not to the visual cortex, the ability to see signs is not in question, just the ability to interpret them (Klima & Bellugi, 1979).

By contrast, Deaf people whose lesions are in the right hemisphere, far from the regions responsible for word and sentence formation, may lose awareness of objects on the left side of their visual field, or they may be unable to correctly perceive spatial relations among objects, but they do not lose the ability to sign or understand sign language. Thus, regardless of the sensory channel through which linguistic information passes, the left hemisphere seems to be the base for linguistic implementation and language to concept mediation systems.

Investigators have mapped the neural systems most directly involved in word and sentence formation by studying the location of lesions in aphasic patients. In addition, other investigators have stimulated the exposed cerebral cortex of patients undergoing surgery for epilepsy and also made direct electrophysiological recordings of the response. (Lesser & Gordon, 1994; Hart & Gordon, 1992; Howard et al., 1996; Ojemann, 1983)

Damage in the posterior perisylvian sector, for example, disrupts the assembly of phonemes into words and the selection of entire word forms. Patients with such damage may fail to speak certain words, or they may form words improperly. They may, in addition, substitute a pronoun or a word at a more general taxonomic level for a missing one or use a word semantically related to the concept they intend to express. Fromkin (1998) elucidated many of the linguistic mechanisms underlying such errors.

Damage to this region, however, does not disrupt patients' speech rhythms or the rate at which they speak. The syntactic structure of sentences is undisturbed even when there are errors in the use of functor words such as pronouns and conjunctions.

Damage to this region also impairs processing of speech sounds, and so patients have difficulty understanding spoken words and sentences. Auditory comprehension fails not because, as has been traditionally believed, the posterior perisylvian sector is a center to store "meanings" of words but rather because the normal acoustic analyses of the word forms the patient hears are aborted at an early stage.

The systems in this sector hold auditory and kinesthetic records of phonemes and the phoneme sequences that make up words. Reciprocal projections of neurons between the areas holding these records allow for cross-activation of those areas.

These regions connect to the motor and premotor cortices, both directly and by means of a subcortical path that includes the left basal ganglia and nuclei in the forward portion of the left thalamus. This dual motor route is especially important: The actual production of speech sounds can take place under the control of either a cortical or a subcortical circuit, or both. The subcortical circuit corresponds to "habit learning," whereas the cortical route implies higher level, more conscious control and "associative learning."

For instance, when a child learns the word form "yellow," activations would pass through the word-formation and motor-control systems via both the cortical and subcortical routes, and activity in these areas would be correlated with the activity of the brain regions responsible for color concepts and mediation between concept and language. In time, we suspect, the concept-mediation system develops a direct route to the basal ganglia, and so the posterior perisylvian sector does not have to be strongly activated to produce the word "yellow." Subsequent learning of the word form for yellow in another language would again require participation of the perisylvian region to establish auditory, kinesthetic, and motor correspondences of phonemes. It is likely that both cortical "associative" and subcortical "habit" systems operate in parallel during language processing. One system or the other predominates, depending on the history of language acquisition and the nature of the item.

The anterior perisylvian sector, on the front side of the rolandic fissure, appears to contain structures that are responsible for speech rhythms and grammar. The left basal ganglia are part and parcel of this sector, as they are of the posterior perisylvian one. The entire sector appears to be strongly associated with the cerebellum; both the basal ganglia and the cerebellum receive projections from a wide variety of sensor regions in the cortex and return projections to motor-related areas. The role of the cerebellum in language and cognition, however, remains to be elucidated.

Patients with damage in the anterior perisylvian sector speak in flat tones, with long pauses between words, and have defective grammar. They tend to leave conjunctions and pronouns out of their utterances, and grammatical order is often compromised. Words for nouns come easier to patients with these lesions than words for verbs, suggesting that separate regions are largely responsible for their respective production.

Patients with damage in this sector have difficulty understanding meaning that is conveyed by syntactic structures. Zurif, Saffran, and Schwartz have shown that these patients do not always grasp reversible passive sentences such as "The boy was kissed by the girl," in which boy and girl are equally likely to be the recipient of the action. Nevertheless, they can still assign the correct meaning to a nonreversible passive sentence such as "The apple was eaten by the boy," or the active sentence "The boy kissed the girl" (Schwartz, Saffran, & Marin, 1980; Saffran, Schwartz, & Marin, 1980; Zurif, Swinney, Prather, Solomon, & Brushells, 1993).

The fact that damage to this sector impairs grammatical processing in both speech and understanding suggests that its neural systems supply the mechanics of component assembly at sentence level. The basal ganglia serve to assemble the components of complex motions into a smooth whole, and it seems reasonable that they might perform an analogous function in assembling word forms into sentences. We also believe, based on experimental evidence of similar, although less extensive structures in monkeys, that these neural structures are closely interconnected with syntactic mediation units in the frontoparietal cortices of both hemispheres.

Between the brain's concept-processing systems and those that generate words and sentences lie the mediation systems we are proposing. Evidence for this neural brokerage is beginning to emerge from the study of neurological patients. Mediation systems not only help select the correct words to express a particular concept, but they also direct the generation of sentence structures that express relations among concepts.

When a person speaks, these systems govern those other systems responsible for word formation and syntax; when a person understands speech, the word-formation systems drive the mediation systems. Thus far, we have begun to map the systems that mediate words for proper nouns and common nouns that denote entities of a particular class.

Consider the patients whom we will call A.N. and L.R., who had sustained damage to the anterior and midtemporal cortices. Both can retrieve concepts normally: When shown pictures of entities or substances from virtually any conceptual category—human faces, body parts, animals and botanical specimens, vehicles and buildings, tools and utensils—A.N. and L.R. know unequivocally what they are looking at. They can define an entity's functions, habitats, and value. If they are given sounds corresponding to those entities or substances, whenever a sound happens to be associated with them, A.N. and L.R. can recognize the item in question. They can perform this task even when they are blindfolded and asked to recognize an object placed in their hands.

Despite their obvious knowledge, however, they have difficulty in retrieving the names for many of the objects they know so well. Shown a picture of a raccoon, A.N. will say, "Oh! I know what it is—it is a nasty animal. It will come and rummage in your backyard and get into the garbage. The eyes and the rings in the tail give it away. I know it, but I cannot say the name." On the average, they come up with less than half of the names they ought to retrieve. Their conceptual systems work well, but

A.N. and L.R. cannot reliably access the word forms that denote the objects they know.

The deficit in word-form retrieval depends on the conceptual category of the item that the patients are attempting to name. A.N. and L.R. make fewer errors for nouns that denote tools and utensils than for those naming animals, fruits, and vegetables. This phenomenon was reported in similar form by Warrington and McCarthy, and by Caramazza (Caramazza & Hillis, 1991; McCarthy & Warrington, 1988; Warrington & McCarthy, 1983, 1987; Warrington & Shallice, 1984). The patients' ability to find names, however, does not split neatly at the boundary of natural and man-made entities. A.N. and L.R. can produce the words for such natural stimuli as body parts, whereas they cannot do the same for musical instruments, which are as artificial and as manipulable as garden tools.

In brief, A.N. and L.R. have a problem with the retrieval of words for common nouns denoting certain entities, regardless of their membership in particular conceptual categories. There are many reasons why some entities might be more or less vulnerable to lesions than others. Of necessity, the brain uses different neural systems to represent entities that differ in structure or behavior or entities that a person relates to in different ways.

A.N. and L.R. also have trouble with words for proper nouns. With few exceptions, they cannot name friends, relatives, celebrities, or places. Shown a picture of Marilyn Monroe, A.N. said, "Don't know her name but I know who she is; I saw her movies; she had an affair with the president; she committed suicide; or maybe somebody killed her; the police, maybe?" These patients do not have face agnosia or prosopagnosia—they can recognize a face without hesitation—but they simply cannot retrieve the word form that goes with the person they recognize.

Curiously, these patients have no difficulty producing words for verbs. These patients perform just as well as matched control participants on tasks requiring them to generate a verb in response to more than 200 stimuli depicting diverse states and actions. They are also adept at the production of prepositions, conjunctions, and pronouns, and their sentences are well formed and grammatical. As they speak or write, they produce a narrative in which, instead of the missing noun, they will substitute words like "thing" or "stuff" or pronouns such as "it," "she," or "they." But the verbs that animate the arguments of those sentences are properly selected and produced and properly marked with respect to tense and person. Their pronunciation and prosody are similarly unexceptionable.

The evidence that lexical mediation systems are confined to specific regions is convincing. Indeed, the neural structures that mediate between concepts and word forms appear to be graded from back to front along the occipitotemporal axis of the brain. Mediation for many general concepts seems to occur at the rear, in the more posterior left temporal regions; mediation for the most specific concepts takes place at the front, near the left temporal pole. We have now seen many patients who have "lost proper nouns" but "retain all or most common nouns." Their lesions are restricted to the left temporal pole and medial temporal surface of the brain, sparing the lateral and inferior temporal lobes. The last two, in contrast, are always damaged in the patients with common noun-retrieval defect. (Damasio et al., 1996, 1997).

Patients such as A.N. and L.R., whose damage extends to the anterior and midtemporal cortices, miss many common nouns but still name colors quickly and correctly. These correlations between lesions and linguistic defects indicate that the temporal segment of the left lingual gyrus supports mediation between color concepts and color names, whereas mediation between concepts for unique persons and their corresponding names requires neural structures at the opposite end of the network, in the left anterior temporal lobe. One of our more recent patients, G.J., has extensive damage that encompasses all of these left occipitotemporal regions from front to back. He has lost access to a sweeping universe of noun word forms and is equally unable to name colors or unique persons. And yet his concepts are preserved. The results in these patients support Ojemann's (1983) finding of impaired language processing after electrical stimulation of cortices outside the classic language areas.

It appears that we have begun to understand fairly well where nouns are mediated, but where are the verbs? Clearly, if patients such as A.N. and L.R. can retrieve verbs and functor words normally, the regions required for those parts of speech cannot be in the left temporal region. Preliminary evidence points to frontal and parietal sites. Aphasia studies performed by our group (Damasio & Tranel, 1993) and by Miceli, Silveri, Villa, and Caramazza (1984) and Berndt and Caramazza (1980) show that patients with left frontal damage have far more trouble with verb retrieval than with noun retrieval.

Additional indirect evidence comes from positron emission tomography (PET) studies conducted by Petersen, Fox, Posner, Montun, and Raichle (1988), Posner and Petersen (1990), and Raichle et al. (1994). They asked research participants to generate a verb corresponding to the picture of an object—for example, a picture of an apple might generate "eat." These participants activated a region of the lateral and inferior dorsal frontal cortex that corresponds roughly to the areas delineated in our studies. Damage to these regions not only compromises access to verbs and functors, it also disturbs the grammatical structure of the sentences that patients produce. We have been able to replicate these studies (Grabowski et al., 1996; Grabowski, Damasio, & Damsio, 1998).

Although this phenomenon may seem surprising at first, verbs and functors constitute the core of syntactic structure, and so it makes sense that the mediation systems for syntax would overlap with them. Further investigations, either of aphasic patients or of normal participants, whose brain activity can be mapped by PET scans, may clarify the precise arrangement of these systems and yield maps like those that we have produced to show the differing locations of common and proper nouns.

During the past two decades, progress in understanding the brain structures responsible for language has accelerated significantly. Tools such as magnetic resonance imaging (MRI) have made it possible to locate brain lesions accurately in patients suffering from aphasia and to correlate specific language deficits with damage to particular regions of the brain. And both PET and fMRI offer the opportunity to study the brain activity of normal participants engaged in linguistic tasks (Damasio & Damasio, 1989).

Considering the profound complexity of language phenomena, some may wonder whether the neural machinery that allows it all to happen will ever be understood. Many questions remain to be answered about how the brain stores concepts. Mediation systems for parts of speech other than nouns, verbs, and functors have been only partially explored. Even the structures that form words and sentences, which have been under study since the middle of the 19th century, are only sketchily understood. Nonetheless, given the recent strides that have been made, we believe that these structures will eventually be mapped and understood. The question is not if but when.

REFERENCES

Bellugi, U., Poizner, H., & Klima, E. S. (1989). Language, modality and the brain. *Trends in Neurosciences, 10*, 380–388.

Berndt R., & Caramazza A. (1980). A redefinition of the syndrome of Broca's aphasia: Implications for a neuropsychological model of language. *Applied Psycholinguistics, 1*, 225–278.

Caramazza A., & Hillis A. E. (1991). Lexical organization of nouns and verbs in the brain. *Nature, 349*, 788–790.

Damasio, A. R. (1992, February 20). Aphasia. *New England Journal of Medicine 326*, 531–539.

Damasio, A. R., & Damasio, H. (1994). Cortical systems for retrieval of concrete knowledge: the convergence zone framework. In C. Koch (Ed.), *Large-scale neuronal theories of the brain* (pp. 61–74). Cambridge, MA: MIT Press.

Damasio, A. R., & Tranel, D. (1993). Nouns and verbs are retrieved with differently distributed neural systems. *Proceedings of the National Academy of Sciences, 90,* 4957–4960.

Damasio, A. R., Damasio, H., Tranel, D., Brandt, J.P. (1990). Neural regionalization of knowledge access: Preliminary evidence. In *Cold Spring Harbour Symposia on Quantitative Biology, Vol. 55: The brain.* Cold Spring Harbor Laboratory Press.

Damasio, A. R., Yamada, T., Damasio, H., Corbett, J., & McKee, J. (1980). Central achromatopsia: Behavioral, anatomic and physiologic aspects. *Neurology, 30,* 1064–1071.

Damasio, H., & Damasio, A. R. (1989). *Lesion analysis in neuropsychology.* New York: Oxford University Press.

Damasio, H., Grabowski, T. J., Tranel, D., Hichwa, R., & Damasio, A. R. (1996). A neural basis for lexical retrieval. *Nature, 380,* 499–50.

Fromkin, V. (1998). *An introduction to language* (6th ed). New York: Holt, Rinehart & Winston.

Garret, M. (1992). Disorders of lexical selection. *Cognition, 42,* 143–180.

Goodglass, H., Wingfield, A., Hyde, M. R., & Theurkauf, J. C. (1986). Category specific dissociations in naming and recognition by aphasic patients. *Cortex, 22,* 87–102.

Grabowski, T. J., Damasio, H., Damasio, A.R. (1998). Premotor and prefrontal correlates of category-related lexical retrieval. *NeuroImage, 7,* 232–243.

Grabowski, T. J., Frank, R. J., Brown, C. K., Damasio, H., Boles-Ponto, L. L., Watkins, G. L., Hichwa R. D. (1996). Reliability of PET activation across statistical methods, subject groups, and sample sizes. *Human Brain Mapping, 4,* 23–46.

Hart, J., & Gordon, B. (1992). Neural subsystems for object knowledge. *Nature, 359,* 60–64.

Howard, M. A., Volkov, I. O., Ollendieck, M., Damasio, H., Abbas, P., & Gantz, B. (1996). Electrical stimulation of human auditory cortex. *Society for Neuroscience, 22,* 1624.

Jackendoff, P. (1994). *Patterns in the mind. Language and human nature.* New York: Basic Books.

Klima, E. S., & Bellugi, U. (1979). *The signs of language.* Cambridge, MA: Harvard University Press.

Lakoff, G. (1987). *Women, fire, and dangerous things. What categories reveal about the mind.* Chicago: University of Chicago Press.

Lesser, R., & Gordon, B. (1994). Electrical stimulation and language. *Journal of Clinical Neurophysiology, 11,* 191–204.

Levelt, W. J. M. (1992). Accessing words in speech production: Stages, processes and representations. *Cognition, 42,* 1–22.

McCarthy, R. A., Warrington, E. K. (1988). Evidence for modality-specific meaning systems in the brain. *Nature, 334,* 428–30.

Micelli, G., Silveri, M. C., Villa, G., & Caramazza, A. (1984). On the basis for the agrammatic's difficulty in producing main verbs. *Cortex, 20,* 217–220.

Ojemann, G. A. (1983). Brain organization for language from the perspective of electrical stimulation mapping. *Behavioral and Brain Sciences, 2,* 189–230.

Petersen, S. E., Fox, P. T., Posner, M. I., Mintun, M., & Raichle, M. E. (1988). Positron emission tomographic studies of the cortical anatomy of single-word processing. *Nature, 331,* 585–589.

Posner, M. I., & Petersen, S, E. (1990). The attention system of the human brain. *Annual Review Neuroscience 13,* 25–42.

Raichle, M. E., Fiez, J. A., Videen, T.O., MacLeod, A. M. K., Pardo, J. V., Fox, P. T., & Petersen, S. E. (1994). Practice-related changes in human brain functional anatomy during nonmotor learning. *Cerebral Cortex, 4,* 8–26.

Rizzo, M., Smith, V., Pokorny, J., & Damasio, A. R. (1993). Color perception profiles in central achromatopsia. *Neurology, 43,* 995–1001.

Saffran, E. M., Schwartz, M. F., & Marin, O. S. M. (1980a). Evidence from aphasia: Isolating the components of a production model. In B. Butterworth (Ed.), *Language production.* London: Academic Press.

Saffran, E. M., Schwartz, M. F., & Marin, O. S. M. (1980b). The word order problem in agrammatism II. Production. *Brain and Language, 10,* 263–280.

Schwartz, M. F., Saffran, E. M., & Marin, O. S. M. (1980). The word order problem in agrammatism.

I. Comprehension. *Brain and Language 10,* 249–262.

Tranel, D., Damasio, H., & Damasio, A. R. (1997). A neural basis for the retrieval of conceptual knowledge. *Neuropsychologia, 35,* 1319–1327.

Warrington, E. K., & McCarthy, R. (1983). Category specific access dysphasia. *Brain 106,* 859–878.

Warrington, E. K., & McCarthy, R. A. (1987). Categories of knowledge: Further fractionations and an attempted integration. *Brain, 110,* 1273–1296.

Warrington, E. K., & Shallice, T. (1984). Category specific semantic impairments. *Brain, 107,* 829–854.

Zeki, S. (1993). *A vision of the brain.* Cambridge, MA: Blackwell Scientific Publications.

Zurif, E., Swinney, D., Prather, P., Solomon, J., & Brushells, C. (1993). An on-line analysis of syntactic processing in Broca's and Wernicke's aphasia. *Brain and Language, 45,* 448–464.

26

Some Observations Regarding Paraphasia in American Sign Language

David P. Corina
University of Washington

One avenue for understanding the neural systems that underlie language has been to provide a description of language behaviors that emerge from compromised language systems. Through this process, we may uncover subsystems of language by distinguishing those language properties that appear resistant to disruption from those properties that are more fragile following specific types of brain damage. The linguistic analysis of language errors, or paraphasias, observed in aphasics illustrates this approach. Two critical assumptions underlie this approach: First, the clinical phenomenon of aphasia does in fact represent an ordered dissolution of the language system rather than some random collection of deficits; second, linguistic theory provides a reliable classification of extant language properties. Of course, whereas one may hope that the classifications proposed by a linguistic theory map dutifully onto the structural levels exposed during dissolution, this is not a necessary condition for making progress in the inventory of behavioral disturbance.

This chapter explores the nature of paraphasic errors in sign language. It is not meant to be an in-depth analysis of all phonemic errors in American Sign Language (ASL), but rather a status report of types of errors that have been observed and some that might be expected to occur but are, as of yet, unattested. The chapter provides a possible explanation for the underrepresentation of location and movement errors in sign paraphasia and calls attention to the fact that a more comprehensive and detailed assessment of phonemic versus phonetic disruption in sign paraphasia is needed.

SPOKEN LANGUAGE PARAPHASIA

Speech errors evidenced in aphasia are often collectively referred to as *paraphasia*. This general label is applied to any unintended error of word or sound choice. Theoretically, paraphasias exclude sound distortions arising from phonetic impairment; however, in practice, it is quite difficult to distinguish true paraphasic errors from phonetic-based sound distortions.

Verbal paraphasia refers to the substitution of an unexpected word for an intended target. Most verbal paraphasias have a clear meaning relation to the desired word and represent the same part of speech; hence, they are referred to as *semantic paraphasias* (Goodglass, 1993). In contrast, phonemic or "literal" paraphasia refers to the production of unintended sounds or syllables in the utterance of a partially recognizable word (Blumstein, 1973; Goodglass, 1993). It is often the case that a phonemic sound substitution results in another real word, related in sound but not meaning (e.g., *telephone* becomes *television*). Also attested are cases in which the erroneous word shares both sound characteristics and meaning with the target (*broom* becomes *brush*; Goodglass, 1993).

Nearly all aphasics, regardless of clinical classification, manifest some phonological difficulties in speech output. Generally speaking, studies of spoken languages reveal that both Broca's and Wernicke's aphasics demonstrate phonological planning errors. In addition, Broca's aphasics have well-described phonetic implementation problems, especially in the coordination of two independent articulators. However, there is growing evidence that Wernicke's aphasics may have subtle phonetic implementation problems as well (Baum, Blumstein, Naeser, & Palumbo, 1989; Ryals, 1986).

SIGN LANGUAGE PARAPHASIA

In the sign aphasia literature, there are numerous reports of signing paraphasia. Early reports of "neologistic" signing are found in Leischner (1943), which described a Deaf subject with left-hemisphere damage who produced "fluent but nonsensical signing," although little description of these errors was provided. Chiarello, Knight, and Mandel (1982) provided some of the first descriptions of paraphasic signing in participant L.K. Further reports followed in the seminal work of Poizner, Klima, and Bellugi (1987) titled *What the Hands Reveal About the Brain*, which documented both semantic and phonemic sign language paraphasia. Additional references to signing errors were made in several individual case studies, and differences between aphasic sign paraphasia and phonetic sign disturbances resulting from extrapyramidal damage were described by Brentari and Poizner (1994) and Corina (1999). Regrettably, most of these descriptions tend to be for illustrative purposes, and at this time, a comprehensive corpora of error types has not been published. Nevertheless, based on the few examples provided, we may begin to identify specific types of sign paraphasia and focus on some initial patterns in these errors.

Semantic Paraphasia

Several well-documented examples of semantic paraphasias have been reported. Participant P.D. (Poizner et al., 1987) produced clear lexical substitutions: BED for CHAIR; DAUGHTER for SON; QUIT for DEPART, and so forth. Participant N.S., reported by Brentari, Poizner, and Kegl (1995), also appeared to make semantic paraphasic errors. This participant substituted the sign FOX for WOLF, and IN-TWO-YEARS for EVERY-TWO-YEARS. The semantic errors of P.D. and N.S. generally overlap in meaning and lexical class with their intended targets, a pattern that has been routinely observed in spoken language semantic paraphasia. Participant W.L. (Corina, Poizner, Feinberg, Dowd, & O'Grady, 1992) evidenced interesting semantic blends in signing, errors conditioned, in part, by perseverations from earlier items. For example, in the context of a picture-naming task, when shown a picture of a tree, W.L. signed TREE with the G handshape. Previously, W.L. had been asked to name the color green. Both the lexical signs GREEN and TREE share a twisting motion of the wrist and share very similar articulatory postures. In another instance, when asked to name a picture of a book, W.L. made the movement and location of the sign OPEN-PAGES but with the handshape appropriate for the sign SEE (i.e., the "V" handshape).

These ASL semantic paraphasias suggest an organizational principle of lexical structure along semantic dimensions, whereby similar semantic items share representational proximity. In this view, coactivation of closely related representations or an absence of appropriate inhibition from competing entries may lead to substitutions and blends. Finally, it is important to note that all three participants had relatively fluent aphasia and posterior perisylvian lesion foci.

Posterior perisylvian lesions often lead to semantic paraphasia in users of spoken language. Taken together, these data suggest similar functional-anatomical organization for semantic properties of spoken and signed language.

Phonemic Paraphasia

Formational paraphasias are one of the most striking characteristics of aphasic signing. ASL formational errors have often been termed phonological or phonemic paraphasia. Whereas this terminology may serve descriptive purposes, careful linguistic analysis is required to substantiate the structural level of impairment in these errors. As with spoken languages, ASL formational errors include both phonological and phonetic levels of impairment. However, to date the distinction between these two types of errors has not been carefully evaluated. An initial attempt to separate out these structural levels by examining closely errors produced by aphasic participant W.L. is presented next. This case study, investigated while I was a research assistant working with Ursula Bellugi and Ed Klima, was originally described in Corina et al. (1992). In revisiting these data, I am attempting to futher specify the neural representation of human language, an endeavor pioneered by the insightful research of Bellugi and Klima.

A priori, we may expect to find true phonological errors affecting the four major formational parameters of ASL phonology: handshape, movement, location, and orientation. However, it is becoming clear that these error types are not uniformly represented. In other words, not all parameters are equally vulnerable to disruption. A closer examination of errors along the parameters may shed light on the structural principles underlying sign formation.

ERRORS IN HANDSHAPE

The most common formational errors observed in aphasic signing involve the parameter of handshape. Specifically, these errors most often affect handshape configurations (as opposed to handshape movements or orientations). Participants L.K. (Chiarello et al., 1982; Poizner et al., 1987), W.L (Corina et al., 1992), and E.N. (Brentari et al., 1995) all have well documented errors in hand configurations.

Data from the globally aphasic signer W.L. serve as a rich source of handshape errors. Table 26.1 presents data from W.L. cast within the phonological model proposed by Corina (1989) and Corina and Sagey (1989) and developed further in Corina (1996).[1] This model, originally developed for description of phonological patterns found in normal ASL signing, argues for an underspecified representation of ASL handshapes, in which redundant feature information is removed. In this framework, a handshape consists of monovalent distinctive features that code for the presence or absence of specified fingers. These features, [T, I, M, R, P] (thumb, index, middle, ring, pinky), function as major nodes within a hierarchical feature arrangement or feature hierarchy (Clements, 1985). Position features, proposed by Brentari (1990), encode the "shape" of finger specifications in ASL handshapes. Specifically, the position features encode the relative joint angles of the individual specified fingers in an ASL handshape. Following are Brentari's definitions of these features, [+/– peripheral] and [+/– open]:

[open]	+: proximal joints of the specified finger are bent to greater than 90° angle (abducted) with respect to the palm.
	–: proximal joints of the specified fingers are bent to less than or equal to a 90° angle (adducted) with respect to the palm.
[peripheral]	+: the fully abducted and fully adducted handshapes with respect to the specified fingers.
	–: handshapes that are partially adducted or abducted.

By using the four possible combinations of these two features, we are able to describe the major hand configurations found in ASL: open, closed, bent, and hooked (or curved).

	+ peripheral	– peripheral
+ open	open	hooked
– open	closed	bent

---

[1]The model adopted to describe these errors is but one of many possible models.

Additional features needed to describe ASL handshapes are [+/– spread] and [+/– closing]. The feature [spread] refers to whether the specified fingers are fanned or parallel. The feature [closing] is a contour feature, which spells out a lexical monomorphemic handshape change in ASL. This dynamic feature is in some ways analogous to the SPE feature [delayed release] used to describe some spoken-language segments.

An additional property of this model concerns the fate of finger nodes that are "unspecified" in underlying representation. According to the model, the final configuration of these unspecified fingers is assigned by default redundancy rules; that is, it is predictable on the basis of the configuration of the underlying specified fingers. Briefly, the redundancy rules state that if specified fingers are closed, unspecified fingers are open, and otherwise unspecified fingers are closed. The model proposes that the application of redundancy rules occurs relatively late in a phonological derivation.

Table 26.1 lists errors produced by W.L. The left column indicates the target sign, the next two columns indicate the handshape and feature specifications of the intended target handshape, and the two rightmost columns specify the observed handshape errors and the feature specifications of these errors. The errors are grouped into five categories: errors in which configuration features change but specified fingers remain largely unchanged; errors in which specified fingers are added and configuration features remain largely unchanged; errors in which specified fingers are deleted; errors in contour features; and complex multifeatured errors. The multiple listing of "toothbrush" indicates three successive approximations.

Several interesting patterns emerge from these data. First, it is striking that out of the 20 errors listed in Table 26.1, 17 involve a change in one or two distinctive features. Thus, there is a great deal of similarity between the error and the intended target. Second, in errors where specified fingers are added, the originally specified finger is always present. This is not a necessary outcome; for example, it is possible that an 'I' handshape would substitute for a '1' handshape. Under the present analysis, this would be considered a change in a single feature specification. However, this type of error is not seen. Instead it is much more likely that specified fingers remain. The similarity between the intended and observed handshapes suggests a further organizational principle of the ASL lexicon. Specifically, these data suggest that the organization of handshape information in the mental lexicon consists of neighborhoods of configurally related handshapes.

Another pattern of interest relates to theories of markedness in ASL handshapes. Two analyses of markedness in ASL handshape are relevant

TABLE 26.1
Formational Paraphasic Errors From Left-Hemisphere-Damaged Signer W.L.

Target Sign		Intended Handshape	Position Feature Specification	Observed Handshape	Position Feature Specification
			Changes in Configuration Features		
1	FINE	5	[+p, +o]	O	[+p, −o]
2	COOKIE	5~	[−p, +o]	5	[+p, +o]
3	BALL	5~	[−p, +o]	5	[+p, +o]
4	MEDICINE	o8	[−p, −o]	8	[+p, −o]
5	SNOW	5	[+spd]	5	[−spd]
6	MATCHES	X	[−p, +o]	F	[+p, −o], [T]
7	SISTER	L	[+p, +o]	F	[+p, −o]
			Addition of Specified Fingers		
8	TOOTHBRUSH	1	[I]	H	[I,M]
9	TOOTHBRUSH	1	[I]	Y	[I,M,R], [−o]
10	TOOTHBRUSH	1	[I]	I-P	[I,P]
11	AGREE	1	[I]	H	[I,M]
			Deletion of Specified Fingers		
12	FINE	5	[T,I,M,R,P]	Y	[I,M,R], [−o]
13	NO	H>	[T,I,M], [−p, −o]	L	[T,I] [+p, +o]
14	DOCTOR	M	[I,M,R]	N	[I,M]
15	SISTER	L	[T,I]	1	[I]
16	FLOWER	fO	[T,I,M,R,P]	W	[I,M,R], [−o]
			Changes in Contour Features		
17	WHITE		5 —> O [−closing]		O—>5 [+closing]
18	MILK		5 —> O [−closing]		O —>5 [−closing]
			Complex Feature Changes		
19	UGLY		1 —> X [I] [[−p, +o] [−closing]		1 [I] [+p, +o] {no contour}
20	DRY		1 —> X [I] [[−p, +o] [−closing]		1 [I] [+p, +o] {no contour}

to this discussion. One, proposed by Battison (1978), concerns the overall form of the handshape. Battison proposed that the "unmarked" handshapes in ASL are 1, 5, C, A/S, B & O, and the bent and laxed variations of these handshapes. In contrast, Brentari (1990) proposed an interpretation of markedness stated at the featural level. Under Brentari's proposal, handshapes marked [+peripherial] are unmarked in ASL. Thus, according to Brentari's proposal, the "bent and laxed" variants of 1, 5, C, A/S, B & O handshapes, which are specified as [–peripheral], are considered marked, whereas handshapes like Y and H will be considered "unmarked," as these handshapes with their fully open configurations will be specified as [+peripheral].

The present data are curious in light of these theoretical differences in the statement of handshape markedness. It is interesting that all substitutions yield [+peripheral] forms. Furthermore, the seven paraphasic examples where the target handshapes are specified [–peripheral] are realized with handshapes specified as [+peripheral]. Thus, using a feature-based definition of markedness, we may state that W.L.'s errors favor unmarked forms. However, if we adopt Battison's (1978) definition of markedness, we observe frequent violations of markedness. For example, note that errors 8, 9, 10, 11 and 12 in Table 26.1 have intended targets with "unmarked" errors in Battison's sense, and yet the substituted errors contain "marked" handshapes. The handshape data presented from left-hemisphere-damaged signers E.N. (Brentari et al., 1995) and L.K. (Poizner et al., 1987), when analyzed with respect to a feature-based assessment of markedness, are also similar to W.L. in that they tend to err in the direction of unmarked (+peripheral) handshapes.[2]

In spoken languages, phonological paraphasic substitutions tend to become less marked. As discussed earlier, adopting the feature-based analysis of markedness proposed by Brentari (1990) would place these handshape errors more in line with facts of markedness observed in spoken-language paraphasia.

An important question concerns whether the errors of W.L. are phonemic paraphasias or phonetic distortions. Several facts suggest that many of these errors are phonemic in nature. First, consider errors 6 and 7 in Table 26.1. In each case, we have handshape errors that differ only in configuration features. In 6, [–p, +o] goes to [+p, –o] and in 7, [+p, +o] goes to [+p, –o]. What makes these errors particularly informative is that these new configurations have implications for redundancy rules in unspecified representations. Recall that redundancy rules serve to spell out the configurations of the unspecified fingers. Moreover, these rules are traditionally considered to operate late in the derivation of a form. In the case of W.L.'s errors, what we observe is that the unspecified fingers have surfaced in

---

[2] Somewhat surprisingly, Brentari, Poizner, and Kegl (1995) made a different claim with respect to E.N. They remarked on the "violations" of markedness in some of E.N.'s handshape substitutions. Apparently, they adopted Battison's treatment of markedness in their analysis.

accordance with the *incorrect* configuration of specified fingers in underlying representation. For example, in the normal case, the underlying handshape for the sign SISTER has specified fingers (index and thumb) configured as open, and this specification triggers the redundancy rules to configure the remaining fingers (middle, ring, and pinky) closed. In W.L.'s paraphasia, it would appear that the specified thumb and index fingers incorrectly receive a closed configuration. The application of redundancy rules to this incorrect thumb and index configuration results in the middle, ring, and pinky fingers being specified as open, and the resulting surface substitution yields an "F" handshape. Note that it is entirely reasonable that this handshape error could have surfaced with a handshape in which the thumb and index are closed and the middle, ring, and pinky fingers are also closed (perhaps as a fist or baby "O" handshape). These facts suggest that the incorrect selection of the position features of the specified index and middle finger occurred prior to the implementation of the redundancy rule. This would suggest that W.L.'s handshape errors were occurring early in the phonological specification and that they do not appear to be phonetic distortions of an already fully specified handshape.

Additional evidence that these errors are due to phonemic impairment comes from the contour feature errors. The representation of handshapes with contours remains controversial. In the model proposed in Corina (1996), the interpretation of a contour feature in which the underlying handshape surfaces as an ordered sequence of two handshapes is considered a late process, dependent on syllabification. Thus an error occurring in the initial selection of a contour feature will have a different outcome than a phonetic error that operates on the surface of the contour output. In the former, we may predict that a feature substitution of a contour feature would result in an incorrect direction of contour. In contrast, a phonetic implementation problem influencing a contour may result in either a distortion of the surface handshape(s) or perhaps an absence of the contour altogether. In fact, both of these error types are observed in the W.L. corpora. The errors in 17 and 18 show a reversal in the sequence of the two handshapes involved in the contour, rather than a problem in the transition from one to the other. In contrast, in 19 and 20 we expect to find a handshape contour, but instead observe none. These data comprise a strong argument in favor of errors occurring both at the phonemic and phonetic levels.

Other possible impairments at the phonological level, errors involving orientation, location, and movement, are in fact clearly underrepresented in the published observations. Next we consider some of these errors and discuss the paucity of these paraphasic forms.

ERRORS OF ORIENTATION

Only two documented errors of hand orientation are contained in the Chiarello et al. (1982) description of participant L.K. They reported that in a repetition task, L.K. produced the signs MORON and BIRD with the fingertips pointing sideways rather than facing toward the signer as in the sign MORON or away from the signer as in the sign BIRD. It is difficult to assess from these limited data whether these constitute phonetic distortions or are true phonemic substitutions of orientation specifications.

Changes in orientation have been reported in cases of signers with motor execution problems. For example, in Parkinsonian signing (Brentari & Poizner, 1994), hand orientations have been shown to migrate toward less-marked orientations about the sagittal plane, and reductions in the magnitude of orientation changes required by some signs have been documented. The prevailing interpretation of this signing pattern is that it reflects an ease of articulation. The findings from Parkinsonian signing are consistent with a general disruption of motor control that leads to phonetic disruptions in signing, rather than higher level phonemic disruptions that are apparent in aphasic signing.

ERRORS OF LOCATION

One of the least-reported classes of errors are errors affecting the location, or place of articulation, of signs. Once again, it is participant L.K. who is cited as producing this type of error; the only published example shows the sign SEE as being signed on the chin rather near the cheek. However, most would agree that using the chin as a place of articulation for the sign SEE is well within the range of normal phonetic variation observed for this sign.

ERRORS IN MOVEMENT

One of the most potentially interesting categories of error is impairment in movement. Errors affecting sign movements have been described in cases of anterior aphasic signer G.D. (Poizner, Klima, & Bellugi, 1987) as well as posterior aphasic signer L.K.[3] The most common movement error exhibited by G.D. is one that I refer to as a "groping" error. This is where

---

[3] Chiarello et al. refer to this subject as L.K., while Poizner, Klima and Bellugi refer to this subject as K.L.

Correct form   Gail D's form

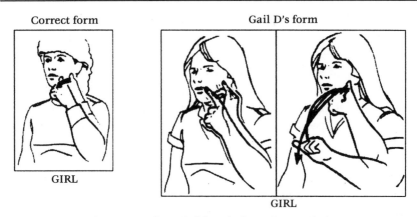

GIRL

GIRL

FIG. 26.1. "Groping" error from left-hemisphere-damaged signer G.D. (Copyright Dr. Ursula Bellugi, The Salk Institute, La Jolla, CA.

the participant makes repeated and often increasingly more accurate attempts to articulate the sign. This is clearly illustrated in Figure 26.1, which shows G.D.'s groping attempt to sign GIRL.

Four examples of substitution in movement categories are reported for L.K. These include the sign ENJOY (which was articulated with an up-and-down movement rather than a circular movement), the sign GIRL (which was articulated with a contact rather than a downward brush), and finally the sign NAME (which was articulated with a back-and-forth movement rather than a downward movement). Finally, Chiarello et al. (1982) reported that L.K. incorrectly used a downward movement (rather than an upward movement) when copying the sign OVERSLEEP. Unfortunately, no illustration of this error is provided. It is curious that the compound OVERSLEEP has both a downward and upward component, as this error may also have been due to a deletion of the final upward movement.

DISCUSSION

Several interesting patterns emerge from these data. Most apparent is the finding that there appears to be a highly unequal distribution of paraphasic errors among the four parameters of sign formation. The most widely reported errors are those that affect handshape configuration. Not only have these errors been observed in many different aphasic signers, but the frequency of occurrence in individuals who exhibit this disruption is quite high. In contrast, there are few reports of paraphasias affecting movement, location, and orientation. Indeed, most of the reports concern signer L.K. The constellation of "paraphasic" errors attributed to signer

L.K., particularly those involving orientation, location, and perhaps movement, raises questions as to whether this signer's signing style following her stroke reflects not only aphasic elements but articulatory implementation problems as well. Her particularly fluent and loquacious signing style leads one to question whether errors observed in these reports of "paraphasia" may, in part, be due to coarticulatory effects arising from hyperfluent signing, especially in the context of nondominant hand signing.

Even if L.K.'s errors are examples of paraphasia, the unequal distribution of paraphasic errors among the four parameters of sign formation requires explanation. One possible explanation is that errors affecting movement, location, and orientation parameters are difficult to assess systematically or are simply underreported. However, the distribution may reflect a more fundamental difference in the status of phonological parameters, with the handshape parameter being more vulnerable to disruption. Two properties of ASL handshapes are relevant to this observation.

First, in many phonological models of ASL, handshape is considered to be a separate autosegment (Brentari, 1990; Corina, 1989; Sandler, 1989). In general, autosegmental representations attempt to capture the independence observed among certain aspects of phonological structure and have been extremely useful in describing linguistic phenomena in which there does not appear to be a direct mapping of a linguistic element to a segment. The overrepresentation of handshape errors may reflect this relative independence of configural handshape information from the rest of the sign form. Second, in spoken-language phonemic paraphasia, consonant sounds are particularly susceptible to phonological paraphasia (Shankweiler & Harris, 1966). This is particularly interesting given the fact that linguistic analyses of ASL have suggested that handshape specifications may be more consonantal in nature, whereas movement components of ASL may be analogous to vowels (see Corina & Sandler, 1993, for discussion). Thus, the overrepresentation of handshape errors may be a reflection of this category difference. It is noteworthy that ASL phonemic errors appear to honor these linguistically motivated distinctions.

The lack of orientation-specific errors remains a mystery. Some phonological models (Brentari, 1990; Sandler, 1989) have proposed separate orientation features that are constituents of hand configuration representations. A priori we might expect vulnerability of these features, just as we observed with hand configuration features describing finger positions. In contrast, Wilbur (1993) made use of an articulatory node position that dominates an orientation node and a handshape node. This structural arrangement of features at least permits selective disruption of hand configuration independent from disruptions of orientation specifiations.

Regardless of which feature arrangement one adopts, this lack of orientation disruption remains unexplained; either analysis would require an explicit statement referring to the integrity of orientation features. One possibility to be explored is that orientation specifications are in fact not present in underlying representations and thus are immune to disruption at the phonological level. Instead, orientation may be predictable and thus subject to default redundancy rules that are realized at the phonetic level. This would help explain why orientation disruptions are observed in Parkinsonian signing, which results in a general disruption of motor control but not in aphasic errors, which stem from phonological disruption.

The need for overt specification of movement elements in sign structure has been widely questioned (Hayes, 1993; Stack, 1988; Uyechi, 1996). In an analysis of ASL syllable structure (Corina, 1996), I proposed that dynamic elements of ASL phonology have a prosodic status in underlying representations. In this analysis, I argued that path movement could be treated as an underlying moraic location element. For example, a location which in underlying representation is moraic will manifest as a movement toward or away from that specific location in surface representation (for details, see Corina, 1996). This treatment eliminates the need for specification of a large class of ASL movements (specifically, straight path movements with contact to physical or zero space locations). Bearing this in mind, it is interesting that one enduring quality of spoken-language paraphasic errors is that these errors adhere to the structural integrity of higher order prosodic units such as the syllable. In spoken languages, word-initial singleton consonants are most susceptible, and rarely do errors result in violations of phonotactic or morpheme structure constraints of the language. Although there is some tendency to replace marked syllable structures (i.e., V, VC) with less-marked structures (i.e., CV, CVC), violations of syllable structure are not attested. These data suggest that prosodic units may have special status within phonological representations and thus may be protected from disruption in aphasia. These observations lead me to speculate that the lack of location and movement errors reflects the unitary status of these surface elements in underlying representations. In addition, the resistance of these elements to disruption may be a further reflection of the prosodic specification of this class of structural elements.

However, it is clear that this is not an absolute prohibition against disruption of prosodic elements. Indeed, as I argued in Corina (1996), in underlying representations, contour handshape sequences, like movements to or away from a location, are represented as a unitary specification of a handshape with moraic status. Syllabification serves to spell out the surface handshape sequence. Consistent with this treatment is the observation that when phonemic paraphasic errors do involve contour handshapes (see previous discussion of errors 17 & 18 in Table 26.1), the surface form results in a misapplication of the direction of the contour but not an omission of the handshape change. A similar explanation may be considered in the case of L.K., whereby the precise direction of the movement path may be disrupted (up-and-down movement substituting for circular movement), but movement (and in this case, repeated movement) is preserved.

CONCLUSION

In summary, the analysis of errors observed in aphasic signing provides insights into the subsystems of language that underlie the organization of ASL. Through an examination of errors, we provided evidence for principles of lexical organization along semantic and phonological dimensions and elucidated distinctions between phonemic and phonetic levels of disruption. The patterns of formational errors provide evidence for structural differences in the representation of signs. Patterns of disruption in which handshape appears particularly vulnerable are in accord with linguistic analyses that argue for a special status of handshape information in ASL. In addition, the relative underrepresentation of movement and location errors in sign paraphasia highlights the need to acknowledge prosodic and nonprosodic elements of sign formation. Finally, the cross-language and cross-modality similarities of paraphasic errors evidenced in left-hemisphere-damaged individuals strongly suggests invariant principles of organization of the neural systems underlying human language.

ACKNOWLEDGMENTS

This work was supported by NIDCD grant R29 DC03099 awarded to the author. I thank Susan McBurney for insightful discussion and editorial assistance.

REFERENCES

Battison, R. (1978). *Lexical borrowing in American Sign Language.* Silver Spring, MD: Linstok Press.
Baum, S., Blumstein, S. E., Naeser, M. A., & Palumbo, C. (1989). Temporal dimensions of consonant and vowel production: An acoustic and CT scan analysis of aphasic speech. *Brain and Language, 39*(1), 33–56.

Blumstein, S. E. (1973). *A phonological investigation of aphasic speech.* The Hague: Mouton.

Brentari, D. (1990). *Theoretical foundations of American Sign Language phonology.* Unpublished doctoral dissertation, University of Chicago.

Brentari, D., & Poizner, H. (1994). A phonological analysis of a deaf Parkinsonian signer. *Language and Cognitive Processes, 9,* 69–99.

Brentari, D., Poizner, H., & Kegl, J. (1995). Aphasic and Parkinsonian signing: Differences in phonological disruption. *Brain and Language, 48*(1), 69–105.

Chiarello, C., Knight, R., & Mandel, M. (1982). Aphasia in a prelingually deaf woman. *Brain, 105,* 29–51.

Clements, G. N. (1985). The geometry of phonological features. *Phonology Yearbook 2,* 225–252.

Corina, D. (1999). Neural disorders of language and movement: Evidence from American Sign Language. In L. Messing & R. Campbell (Eds.), *Gesture, speech, and sign.* New York: Oxford University Press.

Corina, D. P. (1989). Handshape assimilation in hierarchical phonological representations. In C. Lucas (Ed.), *Sign language research: Theoretical issues* (pp. 27–50). Washington, DC: Gallaudet University Press.

Corina, D. P. (1993). To branch or not to branch: underspecification in ASL handshape contours. In G. R. Coulter (Ed.), *Phonetics and phonology: Current issues in ASL phonology* (pp. 63–95). San Diego, CA: Academic Press.

Corina, D. P. (1996). ASL syllables and prosodic constraints. *Lingua, 98,* 73–102.

Corina, D. P., & Sandler, W. (1993). On the nature of phonological structure in sign language. *Phonology, 10*(2), 165–207.

Corina, D. P., & Sagey, E. (1989) Are phonological hierarchies universal? Evidence from American Sign Language. In K. de Jong & Y. No (Eds.), *ESCOL 1989* (pp. 73–83). Columbus, OH: Ohio State University Press.

Corina, D. P., Poizner, H. P., Feinberg, T., Dowd, D., & O'Grady, L. (1992). Dissociation between linguistic and non-linguistic gestural systems: A case for compositionality. *Brain and Language, 43,* 414–447.

Goodglass, H. (1993). *Understanding aphasia.* San Diego, CA: Academic Press.

Hayes, B. (1993). Against movement: Comments on Liddell's article. In G. R. Coulter (Ed.), *Phonetics and phonology: Current issues in ASL phonology* (pp. 213–225). San Diego, CA: Academic Press.

Leischner, A. (1943). Die "Aphasie" der Taubstummen. *Archiv für Psychiatrie und Nervenkrankheiten, 115,* 469–548.

Poizner, H., Klima, E. S., & Bellugi, U. (1987). *What the hands reveal about the brain.* Cambridge, MA: MIT Press.

Ryals, J. H. (1986). A study of vowel production in aphasia. *Brain and Language, 29,* 49–67.

Sandler, W. (1989). *Phonological representation of the sign: Linearity and nonlinearity in American Sign Language.* Dordrecht, Netherlands: Foris Publications.

Shankweiler, D., & Harris, K. (1966). An experimental approach to the problem of articulation in aphasia. *Cortex, 2*(3), 277–92.

Stack, K. (1988). *Tiers and syllable structure in American Sign Language: Evidence from phonotactics.* Unpublished master's thesis, University of California, Los Angeles.

Uyechi, L. (1996). *The geometry of visual phonology.* Stanford, CA: Center for the Study of Language and Information.

Wilbur, R. (1993). Syllables and segments: Hold the movement move the holds! In G. R. Coulter (Ed.), *Phonetics and phonology: Current issues in ASL phonology* (pp. 135–168). San Diego, CA: Academic Press.

27

The Structure of Language as Motor Behavior: Clues From Signers With Parkinson's Disease

Howard Poizner
Rutgers University

Diane Brentari
Purdue University

Martha E. Tyrone
Rutgers University and City University London

Judy Kegl
*Rutgers University and
University of Southern Maine*

Ursula Bellugi and Edward Klima pioneered investigations into areas central to the relation of language, mind, and brain. They have an infectious fascination and delight with ASL as a three-dimensional language that sculpts the air with sweeps of the hand and twists of the wrists, all the while punctuated by a myriad of facial expressions complexly coupled to sequences of body positionings and gestures of the limbs. Ursula Bellugi and Ed Klima didn't stop with simply a linguistic description of American Sign Language (ASL). For them, language in space provided a natural segue to bigger questions of how language in all its varied modalities of expression is organized and how it is represented in the brain. They demonstrated unequivocally that language is not restricted to the auditory–vocal modality and that the left cerebral hemisphere in humans has an innate predisposition for language independent of language modality (Corina, Vaid, & Bellugi, 1992; Hickok, Bellugi, & Klima, 1996; Poizner, Klima, & Bellugi, 1987). Their studies generated a fertile testing ground for competing explanations of the brain's organization for language, how the brain comes to be so organized, and how it can or cannot be modified. Our own research has benefitted greatly from their insightful thinking and clear focus on the biological foundations of language. The work presented here on what is to be learned from the study of errors produced by signers with Parkinson's disease follows in the footsteps of Bellugi and Klima's groundbreaking research that brought language in another modality to the forefront of research in both theoretical linguistics and cognitive neuroscience. We hope to add one more piece to the puzzle of how language and movement are represented in the human brain.

Studies on hearing patients with Parkinson's disease have reported a number of abnormalities in their movements in comparison with control participants. These abnormalities include a decrease in the accuracy of movement, especially in the absence of vision (Adamovich, Berkinblit, Feldman, Hening, & Poizner, 1997; Flash, Ingelberg, Schechtman, & Korcgyn, 1992; Flowers, 1976; Klockgether & Dichgans 1994); absence of the normal nearly linear scaling of movement velocity to movement distance (Berardelli, Dick, Rothwell, Day, & Marsden, 1986; Flowers, 1976); reduced movement velocity and increased movement duration; fragmented movement trajectories with multiple velocity peaks rather than a bell-shaped velocity profile (Flash et al., 1992; Poizner et al., 1998); increased trial-to-trial variability in movements produced (Sheridan & Flowers, 1990); and an inability to automatically execute multiple motor tasks either sequentially or simultaneously (Beneke, Rothwell, Dick, Day, & Marsden, 1987; Marsden, 1982; Poizner et al., 1997).

The speech of hearing individuals with Parkinson's disease is also disturbed, and has been characterized as "hypokinetic dysarthria" (Darley, Aronson, & Brown, 1975). This disturbance can be exhibited in a variety of ways, which include a reduction in the range of movement due to rigidity of the articulators (jaw and lips) and instability of the tongue (Abbs, Hunker, & Barlow, 1983). Errors include the frication of plosive sounds (/t,d,p,b/ pronounced as /s,z,f,v/), deletion of word-final plosive sounds, and "aprosodic" speech, exhibited by abnormalities of pitch, duration, and intensity (Canter, 1963, 1965a, 1965b).

The analysis of deficits in Parkinsonian signing provides an important new vehicle for understanding Parkinson's disease and the role of the basal ganglia in language processing. First, movements of the articulators in sign language are directly observable rather than hidden from view. Thus, by analyzing the nature of movement breakdown in Parkinsonian signing, we can provide a fresh view of how linguistic movements are impaired in Parkinson's disease. This should help inform us about the general nature of Parkinson's disease. Because spoken language articulators are not directly visible in most cases, it is often difficult to pinpoint the place of physiological breakdown that causes a particular acoustic effect. For example, some Parkinsonian speakers exhibit overlap in Voice Onset Time in their productions of voiced and voiceless obstruents—for example /b/ and /p/ (Lieberman, 1991). This acoustic effect might be caused by any number of possible articulatory breakdowns. To name a few: Breath support may not be sufficient to achieve adequate intraoral pressure for /p/, muscle tone of the lips may be insufficient, or there may be lack of coordination of the articulatory movements. Such inferences are not necessary with Parkinsonian signing; in sign, we can directly observe and measure disruptions in articulators that consist of rigid, jointed links, namely, the limbs. Also, because ASL involves—among other body parts—the limbs, we can gather information about how heavier articulators that involve the joints of the arm are affected by Parkinson's disease. However, unlike the analyses of gross motor movements or gestures, the phonological system of ASL gives us highly specific, fine motor targets against which to compare productions.

The results reported here come from our work with six Parkinsonian signers over the past 7 years, given in (1). All of our participants identified themselves culturally with the Deaf community, attended schools for the Deaf, considered ASL their primary language, and were prelingually Deaf. The classification of our participants' severity is based on observed behavioral symptoms at the time of testing. One participant exhibited mild-to-moderate symptoms (LN), three moderate-to-severe symptoms (AC, RH, and JH), and two exhibited severe symptoms (XM and JW).[1] All participants were on anti-Parkinsonian medication. Only participant LN withheld medication and only in his initial testing session.[2]

---

[1] A more detailed account of LN is given in Loew, Kegl, and Poizner (1995); of RH in Brentari and Poizner (1994); of RH and XM in Brentari, Poizner, and Kegl (1995); of JH in Poizner and Kegl (1993); of LN, JH, and JW in Kegl and Poizner (1998); and of JH and LN in Tyrone, Kegl, and Poizner (in preparation).

[2] Unfortunately, uniform information was not available for all of the participants. Cerebrovascular accident subsequent to initial testing, difficulties with mobility, the variation of prescribed medication, and participants' willingness to abstain from taking their medication for the purposes of our testing add to the heterogeneity of this group.

(1) Our participant pool

Participant	Age	Sex	Severity
JW	79	male	severe
XM	79	male	severe
JH	79	male	moderate-to-severe
AC	65	male	moderate-to-severe
RH	64	male	moderate-to-severe
LN	72	male	mild-to-moderate

In language, there is a constant interplay between ease of production and ease of perception with the maintenance of relevant distinctions remaining a primary goal. The analysis of motor deficits in Parkinsonian signing provides a new vehicle for understanding this interplay. We find that Parkinsonian signers of varying degrees of severity appear to exhibit spared linguistic abilities at all levels of linguistic organization, despite the presence of significant motor and memory deficits that serve to restrict articulation and hinder the retention of input. The phonetic and morphosyntactic structure of our participants' signing are each examined next, and the insights gained for phonological representation of ASL are presented.

PHONETIC EFFECTS

Signers with Parkinson's disease exhibit the full range of sentence types, derivational and inflectional morphology, and classifier forms that are seen in control signers (Kegl, Poizner, & Fuller, 1993; Loew et al., 1995); however the surface production of these grammatical features is phonetically simplified with respect to its complexity and temporal properties. Taken together, these phonetic effects show that signers with Parkinson's disease have particular difficulty in executing properly timed and coordinated independent motor subsystems. Although the relative topography of the signing space is maintained and target phonological parameters preserved, the surface sign productions contain systematic reductions and simplifications in the expression of articulatory substructures and distinctive features, as well as in the timing properties of the signed utterance. A list of these is given in (2), and described in detail subsequently. Nowhere in ASL are coarticulation and timing effects more prominent than in fingerspelled words, and we found that words fingerspelled by participants with Parkinson's disease provide a particularly useful testing ground for timing and coordination phenomena (Tyrone et al., in preparation).

(2) Simplifications in the sign productions of Parkinsonian signers

    a.   Simplifications in the expression of articulatory substructures of ASL

        i.   facial masking

        ii.   distalization of movement

        iii.   deletion of contact

        iv.   reduction of the signing space

        v.   blending of selected finger features of handshapes (i.e., coalescence)

        vi.   shadowing (i. e., H1 → H2 assimilation)

        vii.   handshape and orientation laxing (i.e., neutralization)

    b.   Simplifications in the timing properties of the signed utterance

        i.   flattening of prosodic contrasts in pause durations

        ii.   oversynchronization of substructures of handshape-internal movement and path movement

        iii.   feature unraveling

        iv.   segmentation of letters of the manual alphabet in fingerspelled words

        v.   atypical assimilation effects across signs

To emphasize an important point at the outset, the set of errors was not uniformly exhibited by all participants. Simplification in motor output is achieved in a variety of ways. For example, one participant breaks apart pieces of a hand-internal movement of a fingerspelled word, another blends the handshapes to avoid making the transitional movement between letters, and yet another exhibits hypersegmentation of the letters. Even though the surface form is different in each case, all are strategies that reduce the complexity of the motor plan.

Simplifications in the Expression of Articulatory Substructures

In each of the following distortions found in the Parkinsonian sign productions, there is simplification or reduction of the complexity of the articulatory substructures of ASL. In the case of handshape, place of articulation, and orientation, we see simplification; in the case of movement and facial expression, we see reduction.

Facial Masking

Facial expression, conveying both linguistic and affective information is muted, and facial masking increases with the severity of the disease (Abbs et al., 1983; Brooks, 1986). Facial expressions are damped in mild Parkinsonian LN's signing, and affect facial expressions are barely detectable in moderate-to-severe Parkinsonian JH and RH; in severe Parkinsonians XM and JW, aside from eye movements, facial expression does not change.

Distalization of Movement

The first and probably the most robust type of movement error is distalization of movement. It involves maintaining the shape of a path movement, but the movement is transferred to a relatively more distal joint, rather than being articulated at a more proximal one. The effect is a reduction in amplitude of the movement. Examples of this occurred in the set of signs given in (3), taken from Parkinsonian RH. Importantly, in both RH's and the control signer's productions, the shape (the feature [tracing]) or direction of the movement is the same.

(3) Distalization of movement in the signing of Parkinsonian RH[3]

---

[3] The notational conventions used in this chapter are as follows: A word in capital letters is a gloss for a sign (e.g., HARD); single fingerspelled letters and grammatical aspect categories are indicated by single quotation marks (e.g., 'G', 'exhaustive'); English translations are indicated by double quotation marks ("perform a handstand"); distinctive features are indicated in square brackets (e.g., [direction]); person agreement is indicated by the corresponding numeral and assumed singular unless otherwise indicated (e.g., 1-GIVE-3); loan signs are indicted with a "#" (e.g., #ASL).

Sign	Control Joint	→	Parkinsonian RH Joint	Feature Path
LOOK 'exhaustive'	wrist		knuckles	[direction]
LOOK 'continuative'	elbow		wrist/elbow	[direction]
CHILDREN	wrist		knuckles	[direction]
POOR	elbow		wrist	[direction]
BETTER	elbow		knuckles/wrist	[tracing]
HARD	elbow		wrist	[tracing]

Loss of Contact With a Place of Articulation or Nondominant Hand

The moderate-to-severe and the severe Parkinsonian signers (RH, JH, XM, and JW) systematically omitted contact in signs—either contact of the dominant hand with a place of articulation or contact between the two hands. For example, JH deleted contact between the two hands in the sign NEW; RH deleted contact between the two hands in WRITE and HARD; XM deleted contact between the hand and the cheek in DEAF; and JW deleted contact with the forehead in the signs KNOW and REMEMBER. The severe Parkinsonian signers rarely articulated two-handed signs at all and almost never raised a hand above waist level to contact a body part on the head or trunk.

Displacement and Reduction of the Signing Space

For some Parkinsonian signers, not only are sign movement amplitudes reduced and distalized, but there is a spatial shift of the signing space that seems to vary based on the severity of the disease (Kegl, Cohen, & Poizner, 1999). Mild Parkinsonian LN, whose sign movements are reduced, still maintains contact with target locations on the head; as a consequence, his signing space is raised overall. At later stages of the disease, when sign intensity is even weaker and fighting gravity becomes more of a strain, the signing space systematically lowers, and contact with the face is lost. In Parkinsonian JH's signing, THINK and REMEMBER, typically executed at the forehead, are lowered to the cheek; LOOK-AT and SEE, typically made at eye-level, are lowered to the chin level, and DRINK and GRANDMOTHER, normally articulated at the chin, are lowered to mid-chest level. More severely involved RH lowers more signs into the torso area, and in Parkinsonian XM and JW, all signs are produced at low-to-mid chest level.

Blending of Selected Finger Features of Handshapes (i.e., Coalescence)

Sequential blending is the simultaneous production of two (or more) different letters in a fingerspelled word, such that the letters completely overlap in time. This is accomplished by modifying the selected finger constellation (i.e., the group of fingers selected for a given handshape) so that it resembles the combination of the selected finger constellations of two letters, or by combining the selected finger constellation from one letter with another feature (usually thumb position) from another letter. What distinguishes sequential blending from normal coarticulation is that in the former case, the letters both begin and end simultaneously rather than overlapping only partially. Parkinsonian signers LN and RH both made this type of error, but Parkinsonian LN made it slightly more frequently. For example, in P-I-L-L-S, LN produces the first two letters of the word completely synchronously, by forming one handshape that is a coalescence of the P and I handshapes. Sequential blending employs a strategy of simplifying coarticulation by combining two articulatory gestures into one, thereby reducing the number of necessary transitions between letters and the motor demands of the task (Tyrone et al., 1998).

Sequential blends also occur in Parkinsonian signing across signed words. An example of a portmanteau sequential blend occurs in Parkinsonian RH's two-sign sequence WHERE FROM, in which the 'X' handshape of FROM is articulated with the place of articulation, orientation, and movement of WHERE.

Shadowing (i.e., H1 → H2 Assimilation)

Shadowing is the assimilation of movement or handshape from the dominant hand, H1 (used for one-handed signs and fingerspelling) to the non-dominant hand, H2. There are three types of two-handed signs: those whose H1 and H2 handshapes are the same and the movement occurs on both hands (type 1; e.g., SUNDAY, BICYCLE); those whose H1 and H2 handshapes are the same and movement occurs only on H1 (type 2; e.g., REMEMBER, WORK); and those whose H1 and H2 handshapes are different (type 3; e.g., WRITE, READ; Battison, 1978). For example, in WRITE [Continuative] ("write for a long time"), the citation form of the sign is executed with 3 to 4 repetitions of a circle path by H1; at one point during each repetition, the dominant hand touches the palm of H2, which remains stationary. In Parkinsonian RH's production, both hands execute the circle repetitions in WRITE [Continuative]. Movement shadowing also occurs in Parkinsonian JH's form of NEW, where H2, which is normally static, copies the movement of H1.

Shadowing of handshape occurred frequently in mildly Parkinsonian LN in one-handed signs. In SELF and BIRD, normally articulated only by H1, he articulated the handshape on both hands, and in the case of BIRD, the hand-internal movement was copied by H2 as well.

Handshape and Orientation Laxing (i.e., Neutralization)

The "default" or "rest position" settings were often substituted for both the handshape and orientation specifications of Parkinsonian LN, JH, RH, and XM's productions. The rest position of the hand is with fingers slightly spread and relatively open (i.e., a nonflexed metacarpal joint connecting the fingers with the hand), with each finger's joints progressively more closed from index to pinkie (Brentari 1998; Luttgens, Deutsch, & Hamilton, 1992). For example, LN produces most signs with approximations to a single default handshape. A total of 86% of the signs in one narrative use this single default handshape as a substitute for seven distinct target handshapes; however, slight differences in articulation still preserved distinctions between independent phonemes (Loew et al., 1995). The handshapes for 'G' and 'V', although greatly laxed and less contrastive than the same handshapes produced by controls, still preserved distinctions signaled by the selected fingers, being articulated in the same plane of articulation, as shown in Fig. 27.1.

The fundamental standing position is with the palms facing the midsagittal plane (Luttgens et al., 1992); deviations from this "rest orientation" are supination or pronation of the palm. JH and RH show laxing, not only in handshape but also in orientation. This means that the orientation of signs that have a horizontal plane of articulation with the palm facing upward (i.e., supination) or downward (i.e., pronation) is displaced toward the midline. We see this in the signs in (4); in the sign OH-I-SEE, for example, the palm is normally oriented downward; in Parkinsonian RH's production, the palm was oriented toward the midsagittal plane. JH systematically laxes the orientation of the basehand in signs such as SCHOOL and STUDY, when the two hands are not opposed in orientation

/G/ handshape   /V/ handshape

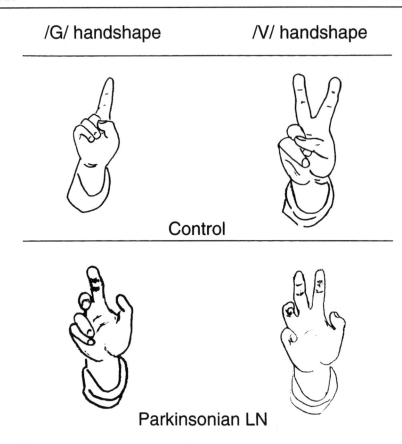

Control

Parkinsonian LN

FIG. 27.1. Laxed handshape production in Parkinsonian LN. From "Flattening of Distinctions in a Parkinsonian Signer," by R. Loew, J. Kegl, and H. Poizner, 1995, *Aphasiology, 9*(4), pp. 381–396. Reprinted with permission.

but parallel as in NEW. He laxes the dominant hand as well. In READ, he actually reverses the orientation of H1 to make the two hands parallel and laxed in orientation. Even the orientation of his fingerspelling is laxed toward the midsagitta plane.

(4) Orientation neutralization (i.e., change from x-plane (horizontal plane) to z-plane (midsagittal plane)).

Parkinsonian	
signer	*Sign*
RH	OH-I-SEE, PAPER, WRITE[continuative], READ, etc.
JH	YES, NEW, READ, ENGLISH, NEXT, GOOD, etc.

Simplifications in the Timing Properties of the Signed Utterance

The following disruptions seen in the productions of Parkinsonian signing involve the timing characteristics of signed utterances. Prosodic units, such as words and phrases, are signaled not only by pause duration between signs but also by the way that the features of handshape and movement are timed with respect to one another.

Flattened Prosodic Cues: Disrupted Pause Durations

Data on pause duration for utterances excerpted from a control signer's and Parkinsonian LN's renditions of the nonverbal cartoon, "Mr. Koumal Flies Like a Bird," reveal an excessive pause at initiation of the utterance in the LN's production (Loew et al., 1995); such excessive pauses were also observed in Parkinsonian XM. The frequent occurrence of these excessively long pauses perturbs the pattern of rhythmic variations that signal the hierarchical organization of linguistic units at the discourse level. These differences can be seen in Figure 27.2a. In addition, we see a highly regular, almost mechanical stepwise acceleration or deceleration in the pauses between signs across an utterance (Fig. 27.2b and c). These extrinsic timing patterns imposed by the general motor deficit resulting from Parkinson's disease obscure the natural variations in pausing that signal constituent information. The differences between word-final, phrase-final, and utterance-final pauses in Parkinsonian RH are reduced compared with those of the controls.

Oversynchronization of Handshape-Internal and Path Movement

The handshape change duration/movement duration ratio (abbreviated HSΔ/Mov ratio) is the amount of time a participant took to execute a given handshape change simultaneously with a given movement. Consider the example in Fig. 27.3a. In the ASL sentence WORD BLOW-PAST-EYES MISS SORRY ("The word went by too quickly. I missed it, sorry."), the handshape remains the same throughout the signs WORD and SORRY; that is, there is no word-internal handshape change . There is a word-internal handshape change in the signs BLOW-PAST-EYES and MISS. Between WORD and BLOW-PAST-EYES and between BLOW-PAST-

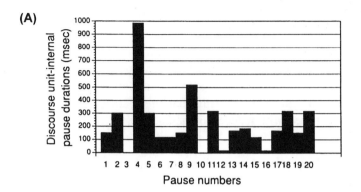

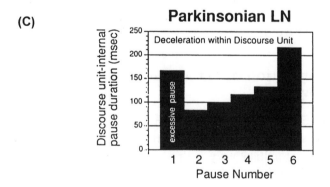

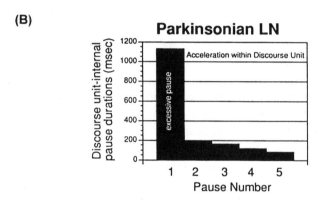

FIG. 27.2. Pause durations from a sample narrative from the story "Mr. Koumal flies like a bird" for a control signer (a) and for Parkinsonian LN (b) as he accelerates (b) and decelerates (c) production within a discourse. Adapted from "Flattening of Distinctions in a Parkinsonian Signer," by R. Loew, J. Kegl, and H. Poizner, 1995, *Aphasiology 9*(4), pp. 381–396.

EYES and MISS there is also a handshape change, but it is a transitional one between signs.

Brentari and Poizner (1994) and Brentari et al. (1995) examined the degree of coupling in changes between handshapes and movement within the lexical domain of a sign and in the nonlexical transitions between signs and found a difference in control signers. They measured the HSΔ/Mov ratio, and within lexical signs, control signers couple handshape change and movement such that the length of time used to complete the handshape change is linked to the duration of the lexical movement of the sign. In the nonlexical transitions between signs these two aspects of articulation are decoupled. In other words, the HSΔ/Mov ratio is very high word-internally and very low between words. In Parkinsonian RH, however, the HSΔ/Mov ratio was uniformly high (i.e., monotonously coupled) within and across signs in an utterance.

We see typical coupling and decoupling of the two articulatory subsystems of movement (i.e., hand-internal movement and path movement) if we examine the first and second handshape changes by the control signer. Between WORD and BLOW-PAST-EYES, the handshape change takes only a small portion of the movement and is not temporally linked to the beginning and end of the movement (i.e., a low HSD/Mov ratio—approximately 40%), whereas the word-internal handshape change in BLOW-PAST-EYES is temporally linked with the beginning and end of the movement (i.e., a high HSΔ/Mov ratio—approximately 100%—Fig. 27.3b and c). Parkinsonian RH reduced the complexity of the motor plan by keeping the same coarticulatory pattern to the greatest extent possible.

Unraveling of Hand-Internal Movement Features

Feature unraveling is the decoupling of one feature from the other features of a fingerspelled letter, such that it is produced either before or after all of the other features. It is a way of taking parts of a hand-internal movement involving the finger joints, thumb, and wrist, and executing them one at a time, rather than together, as typically executed. Tyrone et al. (in press) reported that while making the transition from 'S' to 'L' in the loan word #ASL, mild Parkinsonian LN does not begin the finger movement of 'L' until the thumb extension is almost fully completed; as a result, it almost looks like an A has been inserted between the 'S' and the 'L', whereas the control signer executed the thumb and index finger's movements together (see Fig. 27.4). Whereas blending of fingerspelled letters and the oversyn-

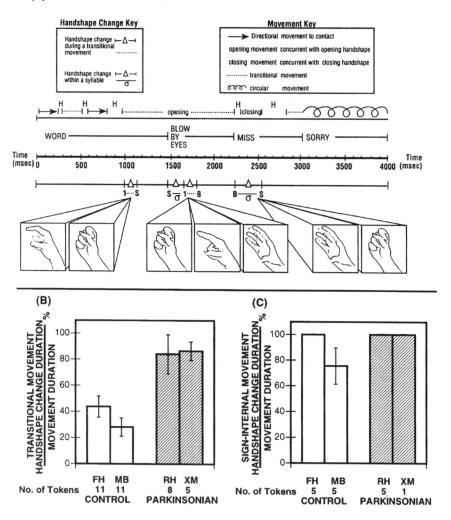

FIG. 27.3. The absolute values for HSΔ and Movement Duration for the utterance BLOW-PAST-EYES MISS SORRY by a control signer (a). The average HSΔ/Movement Duration ratios for 2 control signers and for Parkinsonian signers RH and XM for transitional movements (b) and for sign-internal movements (c). Adapted from "Aphasic and Parkinsonian Signing: Differences in Phonological Disruption," by D. Brentari, H. Poizner, and J. Kegl, 1995, *Brain and Language, 48,* pp. 69–105.

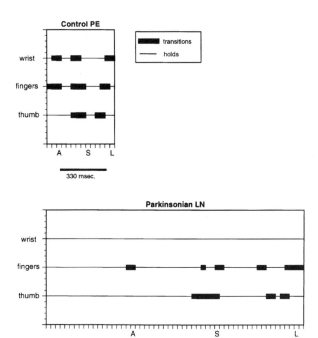

FIG. 27.4.   Timing properties and composition of finger, thumb, and wrist movement during the production of the abbreviated loan sign #ASL by a control signer PE (a) and by Parkinsonian LN (b). Articulator transitions are marked the horizontal bars, and articulator holds are marked by horizontal lines.

chonization of hand-internal and path movements have the effect of simplifying the motor plan by overregulatization, feature unraveling simplifies the motor plan by handling movements executed by different joints one at a time.

The movements of independent articulators in the Parkinsonian signers were also markedly further apart and more variable than those of the control signer (see Fig. 27.1). In the control data, finger and thumb transitions into a given letter of the manual alphabet always began within 67 msec of the previous letter. In Parkinsonian signers LN and JH, the intervals between the thumb and finger transitions for a given letter were as long as 133 msec in some cases (Tyrone et al., in preparation).

Segmentation of Letters of the Manual Alphabet in Fingerspelled Words

Segmentation can be seen as an attempt to bypass requirements of coarticulation by separating articulatory gestures temporally so that they can be produced more independently from one another. Segmentation pulls apart articulatory gestures in time so that they overlap only minimally, but unlike feature unraveling, this separation keeps all of the subparts of the letter of the manual alphabet together. It is the simultaneous lengthening of holds in the finger, thumb, and wrist movements in a fingerspelled word, such that the fingerspelling has a halting, deliberate quality. Individual letters in the fingerspelled word are stretched out in time and transitions between letters are proportionally shorter. Segmentation errors were produced often by moderate-to-severe Parkinsonian JH. For example, when he produced the fingerspelled word B-L-O-O-D-C-L-O-T, Parkinsonian JH held some of the letters for an extremely long time, despite the fact that the transitions between the letters were relatively normal in duration. Moreover, the entire word was not produced uniformly slowly; the last four letters were produced fairly swiftly, which suggests that segmentation is not merely a manifestation of slowed movement frequently exhibited in PD (Tyrone et al., in preparation).

Atypical Assimilation Effects Across Signs

The crisp distinctions between lexical sign and transitional movement are further blurred in Parkinsonian signers by anticipatory articulations, in which certain components (most often the handshape) are produced prematurely or by sequential blends that merge two signs into a single portmanteau form containing components of each of the signs. An example of an anticipatory articulation with premature handshape and hand-internal movement articulation was reported in (Loew et al., 1995). In Parkinsonian LN's articulation of BIRD, the handshape is fully formed and the handshape-internal movement begins during the prelexical transitional movement. Loew et al. (1995) also presented the hyperassimilated phrase *WOMAN WALK* produced by LN as an example of a more complete sequential blend. In this misarticulated phrase, the handshape and hand-internal movement of WALK is coupled with the initial location of WOMAN and continued throughout the phrase.

INTACT MORPHOLOGICAL
AND SYNTACTIC STRUCTURE

None of our participants exhibited grammatical disruptions of morphology or syntax (Brentari et al., 1995; Kegl & Poizner, 1993; Poizner & Kegl, 1993). Detailed analyses of Parkinsonian JH (Kegl et al., 1999; Loew et al., 1995) showed that he uses space to establish agreement of verbs with locations and person referents, even in so-called backwards verbs such as 3-INVITE-1 that require movement from the signer (object) to third person (subject), a reversal of the typical pattern for other verb classes. Although his movements are very small and executed with the wrist rather than the whole arm (distalized), his movement trajectory and orientation still serve to correctly mark morphological agreement with subject and object, and when orientation is used morphologically to signal verb agreement, it is systematically retained, unlike nonmorphologically distinctive orientation (as seen in the sign NEW). With respect to classifier predicates and locative agreement, in a long monologue recounting his days as a daredevil motorcycle acrobat, in which he would move to a headstand position while operating his motorcycle and would perform various acrobatic tricks, Parkinsonian JH used every conceivable form of locative agreement possible. These included various verbs of motion with embedded verbs of location inside of them, including one meaning "to-move-forward-while-moving-to-a-headstand-position-on-the-handlebars-of-a-motorcycle." In addition, JH described in detail a number of complicated diving maneuvers he used to be able to perform, where each description demonstrated complex use of classifier choice, agreement with complex locations (agreeing with a spatial locus established for the edge of a high diving board), and complex embeddings of motion–location verbs within other motion–location verbs (e.g., twisting orientation from front to back while diving off and downward).

USE OF PARKINSONIAN ERRORS
TO PROVIDE INSIGHT INTO
REPRESENTATIONS AND PROCESSING

The errors seen in Parkinsonian signing provide us with points of contrast with typical sign productions, and by doing so, highlight aspects of structure important in the typical production that are missing or altered in the Parkinsonian productions. Three areas of phonological structure illuminated by the Parkinsonian participants' productions are the representation of movement, the segmental structure of signs, and "default" values of distinctive features. Example (5) presents the way that features are organized in the prosodic model of sign language phonology (Brentari, 1998).

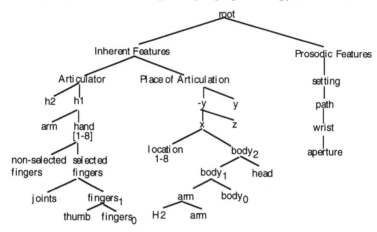

We refer to this structure when discussing Parkinsonian results. All movement features are dominated by the prosodic features branch, including path movements of the shoulder and elbow, orientation changes, and hand-internal movements (i.e., handshape changes).

(5) Feature tree in the prosodic model of sign phonology (Brentari, 1998)

Representing Movement

The modifications that signers with Parkinson's disease make to sign movements involve the distalization of joints, and in some cases, the failure to add a movement that control signers typically do. When Parkinsonian signers distalize a movement, it is displaced from a higher to a lower joint in the feature structure, but the actual shape or direction feature of the movement is still intact.

Features of sign movements are realized by the joints that will typically execute them. Handshape changes are executed by the finger joints, orientation changes by the wrist, path features by the elbow, and setting changes by the shoulder. Signs are often executed by more than the one set of joints specified by its underlying prosodic features, however, or by a set of joints other than those that execute the movement in the default case. The theory of phonetic enhancement (Stevens & Keyser, 1989; Stevens,

Keyser, & Kawasaki, 1986) is helpful in explaining this phenomenon. In spoken languages, three features are primary—[sonorant], [continuant], and [coronal]. Secondary features, such as [voice], [strident], and [nasal] may enhance the primary features in specific ways to increase perceptual salience.

If the prosodic feature nodes of ASL are arranged according to physiological adjacency, placing shoulders at one end of a range of possible joints used to articulate a movement and finger joints at the other end, as shown in (5), we can understand how movement migration works, generally, and, specifically, how distalization in Parkinsonian signers works. *Movement migration* is the group of phenomena involving changes in the joints by which sign movements are executed. There are contexts in which a movement specified in the input by a feature or set of features that would otherwise be executed by the default joints may migrate proximally (i.e., toward a larger joint). This is called phonetic enhancement or *proximalization*, and it is seen in the control signer's fingerspelled production of #ASL, which has hand-internal movements in the input.[4] However, it is realized with accompanying wrist movements (see Fig. 27.4) to increase the salience of the movements. There is also evidence suggesting that in young children sign movements are often proximalized (Conlin, Mirus, Mauk, & Meier, 1998). As we saw in the section "Distalization of Movement," distalization in Parkinsonian signers' productions displaces the movement to a more distal joint, thereby making the movement of the sign less perceptually salient; however, the path features are maintained.

In neither case of movement migration—proximalization or distalization—are the distinctive features of the input changed, but the outputs are different. We want to be able to represent these operations because they are relevant to steps in language development and language breakdown. The important advantage for the proposed representation is that a local movement (i.e., a hand-internal movement or orientation change) can spread easily to a path movement (i.e., a setting change or path feature) or vice versa. Using the structure in (5), this type of spreading can be straightforwardly handled by the addition of an association line to the adjacent prosodic feature node (6). Moreover, movement migration makes clear that there is an internal, hierarchical structure to the representation of movement on the basis of the joints typically used to articulate signs.

---

[4] We used the loan sign symbol (#) here for the targets of both the control and the Parkinsonian productions of ASL, but they may be different. The target for our control is clearly a loan sign form, which obeys more of the phonotactics of the native vocabulary. An acronym form, which obeys less of these phonotactics, also exists, and this may be the Parkinsonian signer's target structure. See Battison (1978), Padden (in press), and Brentari and Padden (in press) for discussions of the different types of words containing letters of the manual alphabet and their phonological properties.

(6) Distalization of the sign HARD by Parkinsonian RH

a. HARD (control signer) b. HARD (Parkinsonian RH)

Segmentation

The systematic coupling within signs and decoupling between signs of handshape changes and movements as shown in Fig. 27.3 has an important theoretical implication. It is evidence that there are timing units in the representation because we know that, in purposeful nonlinguistic gesture, the joints are systematically coordinated but not necessarily cotemporal (Poizner, Mack, Verfaillie, Rothi, & Heilman, 1990; Poizner et al., 1995).[5] Because ASL is a system of purposeful gestures, we would expect coordination between local and path movements similar to purposeful gestures of normal participants, but not necessarily cotemporal linking. All of the features grouped together as prosodic features in the model are temporally linked in the same manner with units on the timing tier. This is support for grouping these features together in the phonological representation, and it is an important step in establishing the fact that changing features are alike with respect to their behavior toward timing units. The timing units are constructed on the basis of the type and number of prosodic features (Brentari, 1998).

Feature Structures and Feature Values

In the displacement and reduction of the signing space, we see that either the head region or the torso region can assume the range of place of articulation contrasts typically seen in the head and torso regions together. The

---

[5] Three-dimensional computer graphic analysis of normal and apraxic participants' production of gestures, such as slicing bread or unlocking a door, reveal that, in controls, these gestures are executed with systematic coordination of joint rotation involved in the gestures, whereas apraxic participants exhibited a lack of this coordination.

head and the torso are given separate substructures in the phonological representation in (5), which allows the whole signing space to be localized, simplified, or moved without changing the eight internal oppositions within each region. The articulatory planes are the x-plane (i.e., ventral or

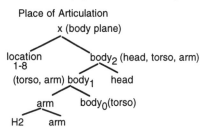

body plane), the y-plane (i.e., the horizontal plane), and the z-plane (i.e., the midsagital plane). Whereas the z- and y-planes have only ipsilateral, contralateral, proximal, or distal settings, the x-plane has eight distinctive oppositions. Descending from the highest to the lowest nodes, the articulatory subsystems of place of articulation are the head, torso, arm, and H2. The x-plane branches into the $body_2$, $body_1$, and $body_0$ nodes; each one can combine with a location (1–8) within that area. $Body_2$ (torso, arms, head) branches to $body_1$ (torso and arms) and head, which in turn branches to $body_0$ (torso) and arm.

(7) Hierarchical organization of the planes and places of articulation.

CONCLUSION

Parkinson's disease so taxes the motor planning and articulation system in Deaf signers that every linguistic act is measured and deliberate, leaving no room for excess effort or redundant distinctions. We are left with the essence of what is central to the production of ASL. The breakdown of signed language production as a result of the motor execution and planning impairments of Parkinson's disease not only sheds further light on the consequences of the disease process itself, but allows us to glean from the spared linguistic abilities in these remarkable signers clearer insight into what constitute the core distinctions and indispensable components of signed language phonology. Ursula Bellugi and Ed Klima always showed a powerful fascination and delight in ASL as a language. They were also enthralled by errors in sign language, errors such as slips of the hand, short-term memory errors, and errors produced by aphasic signers. They used such errors to provide insights into sign language structure, representation, and brain organization. Our work on the errors of signers with Parkinson's disease continues this tradition, and we hope brings them additional fascination and delight.

ACKNOWLEDGMENTS

Supported in part by research grant 5 R01 NS36449 from the National Institute of Neurological Disorders and Stroke, National Institutes of Health, research grant DC 01664 from the National Institute on Deafness and Other Communication Disorders, National Institutes of Health, and SBR-9513762 from the National Science Foundation to Rutgers, The State University of New Jersey. We would like to thank Patricia Trowbridge, Joanne Lauser, Drucilla Ronchen, Vicki Joy Sullivan, Toni Fuller, Jimmy Challis Gore, Ruth Loew, and The George Neville Home for their contributions to this research.

REFERENCES

Abbs, J. H., Hunker, C. J. , & Barlow, S. M. (1983). Differential speech motor subsystem impairments with suprabulbar lesions: Neurophysiological framework and supporting data. In W. Berry (Ed.), *Clinical dysarthria*. San Diego, CA: College Hill Press.

Adamovich, S. V., Berkinblit, M. B., Feldman, G., Hening, W., & Poizner, H. (1997). Deficits in sensorimotor transformations in Parkinson's disease. *Society for Neuroscience Abstracts, 23,* 1989.

Battison, R. (1978). *Lexical borrowing in American Sign Language.* Silver Spring, MD: Linstok Press.

Benecke, R., Rothwell, J. C., Dick, J. P. R., Day, B. L., & Marsden, C. D. (1987). Disturbance of sequential movements in patients with Parkinson's disease. *Brain, 110,* 361–379.

Berardelli, A., Dick, J. P. R., Rothwell, J. C., Day, B., & Marsden, C. D. (1986). Scaling of the size of the first agonist EMG burst during rapid wrist movements in patients with Parkinson's disease. *Journal of Neurology, Neurosurgery, and Psychiatry 49,* 1273–1279.

Brentari, D. (1998). *A prosodic model of sign language phonology.* Cambridge, MA: MIT Press.

Brentari, D., & Padden, C. (in press). A language with multiple origins: Native and foreign vocabulary in ASL. In D. Brentari (Ed.), *Foreign vocabulary in sign language: Grammatical constraints and social contexts.* Mahwah, NJ: Lawrence Erlbaum Associates.

Brentari, D., & Poizner, H. (1994). A phonological analysis of a deaf parkinsonian signer. *Language and Cognitive Processes, 9,* 69–99.

Brentari, D., Poizner, H., & Kegl, J. (1995) Aphasic and Parkinsonian signing: Differences in phonological disruption. *Brain and Language, 48,* 69–105.

Brooks, V. B. (1986). *The neural basis of motor control.* New York: Oxford University Press.

Canter, G. J. (1963). Speech characteristics of patients with Parkinson's disease I. Intensity, pitch and duration. *Journal of Speech and Hearing Disorders, 28,* 221–229.

Canter, G. J. (1965a). Speech characteristics of patients with Parkinson's disease II. Physiological support for speech. *Journal of Speech and Hearing Disorders, 30,* 44–49.

Canter, G. J. (1965b). Speech characteristics of patients with Parkinson's disease III. Articulation, diadochokinesis, and overall speech adequacy. *Journal of Speech and Hearing Disorders, 30,* 217–224.

Conlin, K. E., Mirus, G. R., Mauk, C., & Meier, R. (1998). Acquisition of first signs: Place, handshape, and movement. In C. Chamberlain, J. P. Morford, & R. I. Mayberry (Eds.), *Language acquisition by eye.* Mahwah, NJ: Lawrence Erlbaum Associates.

Corina, D., Vaid, J., & Bellugi, U. (1992). The linguistic basis of left hemisphere Specialization. *Science, 255,* 1258–1260.

Darley, F. L., Aronson, A. A., & Brown, J. R. (1975). *Motor speech disorders.* Philadelphia: W. B. Saunders.

Flash, T., Inzelberg, R., Schechtman, E., & Korczyn, A. (1992). Kinematic analysis of upper limb trajectories in Parkinson's disease. *Experimental Neurology, 118,* 215–226.

Flowers, K. (1976). Visual "closed-loop" and "open-loop" characteristics of voluntary movement in patients with parkinsonism and intention tremor. *Brain, 99,* 269–310.

Hickok, G., Bellugi, U., & Klima, E. S. (1996). The neurobiology of sign language and its implications for the neural basis of language. *Nature, 381,* 699–702.

Kegl, J., Cohen, H., & Poizner, H. (1999). Articulatory consequences of Parkinson's disease: Perspectives from two modalities. *Brain and Cognition, 40,* 355–386.

Kegl, J., & Poizner, H. (1998). Shifting the burden to the interlocutor: Compensation for pragmatic deficits in signers with Parkinson's disease. *Journal of Neurolinguistics, 11,* 137–152.

Kegl, J., Poizner, H., & Fuller, T. (1993). What interpreters should know about signers with brain damage. *NJRID Mediator: The Newsletter of the New Jersey Registry of Interpreters for the Deaf* (Spring issue). Trenton, NJ: New Jersey Registry of Interpreters for the Deaf.

Klockgether, T., & Dichgans, J. (1994). Visual control of arm movements in Parkinson's disease. *Movement Disorders, 9,* 48–56.

Lieberman, P. (1991). *Uniquely human.* Cambridge, MA: Harvard University Press.

Loew, R., Kegl, J., & Poizner, H. (1995). Flattening of distinctions in a Parkinsonian signer. *Aphasiology, 9,* 381–396.

Luttgens, K., Deutsch, H., & Hamilton, N. (1992). Kinesiology: Scientific basis of human motion (8th edition). Dubuque, IA: Brown and Benchmark.

Marsden, C. D. (1982). The mysterious motor function of the basal ganglia. *Neurology, 32,* 514–539.

Padden, C. (in press). The ASL lexicon. *Sign Language and Linguistics 1.*

Poizner, H., Klima, E.S., & Bellugi, U. (1987). What the hands reveal about the brain. Cambridge, MA: MIT Press/Bradford Books.

Poizner, H., Mack, L., Verfaillie, M., Rothi, L., & Heilman, K. M. (1990) Three-dimensional computergraphic analysis of apraxia: Neural representations of learned movements. *Brain, 111,* 282–307.

Poizner, H., & Kegl, J. (1993). Neural disorders of the linguistic use of space and movement. In P. Tallal, A. Galaburda, R. Llinas, & C. von Euler (Eds.), *Annals of the New York Academy of Science, Temporal Information Processing in the Nervous System* (Vol. 682, 192–213). New York: New York Academy of Sciences Press.

Poizner, H., Clark, M., Merians, A. S., Macauley, B., Rothi, L., & Heilman, K. M. (1995). Joint coordination deficits in limb apraxia. *Brain, 118,* 227–242.

Poizner, H., Levin, Adamovich, A., Hening, W., Patel, A., Feldman, G., Berkinblit, M., & Feldman, A. (1997). Timing deficits in arm-trunk coordination in Parkinson's disease. Paper presented at the *National Parkinson's Foundation, Inc. International Symposium on Parkinson's Disease,* New Orleans, November.

Poizner, H., Fookson, O., Berkinblit, M. B., Hening, W., Adamovich, S. V., & Feldman, G. (1998). Pointing to remembered targets in 3D space in Parkinson's disease. *Motor Control, 2,* 251–277.

Sheridan, M. R., & Flowers, K. A. (1990). Movement variability and bradykinesia in Parkinson's disease. *Brain, 113,* 1149–1161.

Stevens, K., Keyser, S. J., & Kawasaki, H. (1986). Toward a phonetic and phonological theory of redundant features. In J. Perkell & D. Klatt (Eds.), *Invariance and variability in speech processes* (pp. 426–449). Mahwah, NJ: Lawrence Erlbaum Associates.

Stevens, K., & Keyser, S. J. (1989). Primary features and their enhancement in consonants, *Language, 65,* 81–106,

Tyrone, M., E., Kegl, J., & Poizner, H. (in preparation). Deficits in coordination in Deaf signers with Parkinson's disease. *Neuropsychologia.*

28

On the Uniqueness of Language

Victoria A. Fromkin
University of California, Los Angeles

I cannot remember when I first met Ursula Bellugi or Ed Klima. They were there, as leading figures in the field of linguistics and psycholinguistics, when I first entered the field. This was before either of them became interested in sign language. But already each had contributed to our understanding of three major questions that have been the center of research in the field of linguistics (Chomsky, 1986). What constitutes knowledge of language? How is knowledge of language acquired? How is knowledge of language put to use? Their work on both spoken and sign language throughout these years has provided insightful answers to these questions on the acquisition, mental representation, structure, and processing of languages and thus to an understanding of the nature of human language in general. Much of this evidence comes from sign language research in support of Descartes's "revolutionary" statement in his *Discours de la méthode* of 1637:

> It is not the want of organs that [prevents animals from making] known their thoughts . . . for it is evident that magpies and parrots are able to utter words just like ourselves, and yet they cannot speak as we do, that is, so as

to give evidence that they think of what they say. On the other hand, men who, being born deaf and mute . . . and lack the organs which serve the others for talking, are in the habit of themselves inventing certain signs by which they make themselves understood.

Descartes' concerns were in keeping with those philosophers and scientists who, for thousands of years, have attempted to understand the nature of human language, motivated by the historic assumption that language is a "mirror of the mind." But despite the deep insights of Descartes and the centuries of scientific study, the genetically determined human ability to acquire and use language was still misunderstood even among linguists. In 1887, Fournie referred to "Speech (as) the only window through which the physiologist can view the cerebral life," reflecting the views of his time and the persistent mythology that the modality of a human language must be sounds heard by the ear and produced by the vocal tract. But speech (production and perception) is behavior, the use or performance of those who know a spoken language. Speech, as was understood by Bellugi and Klima, is not language, the abstract mental cognitive system that permits one to speak, or to sign and comprehend what is being spoken or signed. Bellugi and Klima were among the first to point out that to equate speech with language is to obscure the nature of the linguistic systems that form the bases for all spoken languages and all signed languages throughout the world. As long as researchers concerned themselves only with spoken languages, there was no way to separate what, on the one hand, is essential to the linguistic cognitive system from, on the other hand, the constraints imposed, productively and perceptually, by the auditory–vocal modality —no way to discover, that is, the genetically and biologically determined, linguistic ability of the human brain.

The human brain seems to be uniquely suited for the acquisition and use of language. We now know, through the work of scholars like Bellugi and Klima conducting research on sign languages (Bellugi, Poizner, & Klima, 1983; Klima & Bellugi, 1979; Klima, Bellugi, & Poizner, 1985; Poizner, Klima, & Bellugi, 1987), initiated by Stokoe's seminal work in 1960, that signed and spoken languages are more similar than they are different, that they are subject to the same constraints on their structures, and that they relate forms and meanings by the same kinds of computations and rules. This therefore suggests that the human brain is organically equipped for language in any modality, and that the kinds of languages that can be acquired are not determined by the motor or perceptual systems but by higher order brain mechanisms.

If this is so, then one can seek and find language universals that pertain to all human languages signed and spoken—a view accepted by Roger Bacon in the 13th century when he wrote the following:

> He that understands grammar in one language, understands it in another as far as the essential properties of Grammar are concerned. The fact that he can't speak, nor comprehend, another language is due to . . . the accidental properties of grammar.

Whereas these accidental properties may prevent a speaker of English from understanding a speaker of Arabic, or a user of American Sign Language (ASL) from understanding a signer of Chinese Sign Language or of spoken English, there is growing evidence from the cross-linguistic studies of spoken and signed languages, from studies of language disorders following brain injury, from the investigation of normal and abnormal language use using new technologies such as PET, CT, fMRI, and ERPs, from an analysis of performance errors such as slips of the tongue and hand, that all human languages—spoken or signed—appear to be governed by the same universal principles and constraints, thereby supporting the view that the human brain seems to be uniquely suited for the acquisition and use of any language the child is exposed to.

In 1980, Ed Klima and I presented a paper in Berlin at the Dahlem Conference on Signed and Spoken Language: Biological Constraints on Linguistic Form (Fromkin & Klima, 1980). The main question we addressed in that paper of almost two decades ago concerned the issue of whether there are certain properties of human language that are unique to language or whether they are derivative of more general cognitive capacities. It is interesting that this continues to be a question today, one that is being debated by linguists, psychologists, and neuroscientists. In that paper, Klima and I supported the view that there are specific and unique aspects of language, although recognizing that there were also substantive constraints on language that are derivative of general intellectual abilities.

With some small changes in Fodor's definition of modularity (Fodor, 1983), this issue relates to whether the language system is domain specific, informationally encapsulated, subserved by specific neural architecture, and subject to idiosyncratic pathological breakdown.

EVIDENCE FOR THE SPECIFICITY AND UNIQUENESS OF THE LANGUAGE MODULE

Savants and Asymmetry of Abilities

The psychological literature documents many cases of individuals known as savants who, despite severe general cognitive disabilities, nevertheless show remarkable talents. Among these individuals will be found some who, without the required ability to take care of themselves, are superb musicians, or artists, or draftsmen, or human calculators, who can perform complex arithmetic processes at phenomenal speed, or date calculators who are able to calculate the day of the week of a given date several millennia into the future.

Until recently, most of the savants were reported to be linguistically handicapped. Whereas such cases strongly argue for domain-specific abilities and suggest that certain talents do not require general intelligence, if such individuals show little linguistic knowledge, they do not decisively respond to the suggestion that language is one ability that is derivative of general cognitive abilities.

A more telling case can be made if there are individuals who *have* acquired the highly complex system that we call grammar, without parallel abilities of equal complexity. There are now a number of such studies of children and adults who have few cognitive skills and virtually no ability to utilize language in sustained meaningful communication and yet have extensive mastery of linguistic structure.

Yamada (1990) reported on one severely retarded young woman named Laura, with a nonverbal IQ of 41 to 44, lacking almost all number concepts including basic counting principles, drawing at a preschool level, and possessing an auditory memory span limited to three units, who, at the age of 16, produced syntactically complex sentences like "She does paintings, this really good friend of the kids who I went to school with last year and really loved."

Although Laura produces sentences with multiple embeddings, can conjoin verb phrases, produce passives, inflect verbs for number and person to agree with the grammatical subject, and forms past tenses when the time adverbial structurally refers to a previous time, she can neither add $2 + 2$, nor read nor write nor tell time. She does not know who the president of the United States is or what country she lives in and does not know her own age. Her drawings of humans resemble potatoes with stick arms and legs. In a sentence-imitation task, she both detected and corrected surface syntactic and morphological errors, but she is unable to tie her shoes.

A similar and perhaps even more dramatic case was reported on by Smith and Tsimpli (1995); it concerned Christopher, a 37-year-old man, who is institutionalized because he is unable to take care of himself. As Smith and Tsimpli reported, he finds the tasks of buttoning a shirt, cutting his fingernails, or vacuuming the carpet too difficult. Yet, when given written texts in some 15 or 16 languages, he translates them immediately into English. The languages include Germanic languages like Danish, Dutch, and German; Romance languages like French, Italian, Portuguese, Spanish; as well as Polish, Finnish, Greek, Hindi, Turkish, and Welsh. He has a low nonverbal performance IQ (75 or 76, as compared to the average of 100, on the Raven's Matrices tests) and 42, 67, and 52 on the performance part of the Wechsler test as opposed to 89, 102, and 98 on the verbal part of the same test.

Christopher's conversation is quite laconic, repetitive, and filled with parts that appear to have been memorized from textbooks. Smith and Tsimpli (1995) therefore conducted controlled experiments to test his command of English syntax and pragmatics and the syntax of other languages.

They concluded, after a meticulous investigation of Christopher's knowledge of English, that his

> linguistic competence in his first language is as rich and as sophisticated as that of any native speaker. Moreover, despite his intellectual deficit, this linguistic knowledge is integrated into his general cognitive function sufficiently to allow him to pass some tests of his pragmatic (inferential) ability successfully. Nonetheless, it is clear that some linguistic phenomena lie outside his capabilities [and] that these are *not* due to a deficit in his grammar, but rather that they arise from processing difficulties which involve the interaction of his modular, linguistic faculty with central system operations.

Finally, Smith and Tsimpli concluded that "Christopher's linguistic ability (is) independent of his general cognition," supporting the notion of encapsulation of the language module.

Laura and Christopher are but two of many examples of children who display well-developed phonological, morphological and syntactic linguistic abilities, seemingly less developed lexical, semantic, or referential aspects of language, and deficits in nonlinguistic cognitive development. A number of such cases, studied at UCLA by Curtiss and Yamada (1981) and others have been reported. One of their cases, Anthony, at the age of 5 years 2 months is reported to have had a Leiter IQ of 50 and a mental age of 2 years 9 months. His scores on nonlinguistic cognitive tests were below all the norms, or below the 2-year-old level, or both, contrasting sharply with his high scores on language tests and his spontaneous speech, in which he used 61 of the 68 different elements and structures analyzed, including infinitival and sentential complements, relative clauses, and other subordinate clauses. They concluded that: "his ability to use a wide range of syntactic devices . . . to encode his limited and confused thoughts, illustrates the discrepancy between Anthony's grammatical knowledge and his conceptual/cognitive knowledge."

These cases demonstrating that syntax can be acquired even with severely impaired or limited conceptual and cognitive development are further supported by the studies of children with internal hydrocephaly whom Cromer (1991) referred to as having the "chatterbox syndrome"— they talk excessively but their speech lacks content. One case studied extensively by Cromer, referred to in the literature as D.H, whose "speech is fluent, appropriate and not bizarre, is filled with complex syntactic forms, shows the correct use of semantic constraints, an extensive vocabulary, and incorporates the use of normal pragmatic devices. But on a large variety of standardized tests she performs at the severely retarded level and functions in everyday life at the retarded level. She has been unable to learn to read and write in her late teenage years and cannot add or handle money, yet D.H. performs almost without error on grammaticality judgments." Cromer's conclusion was that "language acquisition proceeds on a different course, basically independent of general cognitive development" and suggests that such cases "seem to show that general cognitive mechanisms are neither necessary nor sufficient for the growth of language."

Any notion that linguistic ability results simply from communicative abilities or develops to serve communication functions is also negated by studies of Blank, Gessner, and Esposito (1979) which concerned a child with fully developed structural linguistic knowledge but with almost no communicative skills, and by Cromer (1991), who showed a dissociation between pragmatic and syntactic abilities. Similar cases of schizophrenic and autistic children are also reported. It thus seems clear that the ability to communicate in a social setting depends on different cognitive skills than the acquisition of language.

Interesting studies of genetic disorders such as Turners syndrome and William's syndrome also reveal domain specificity. Five out of six children with Turner's syndrome (a chromosomal anomaly) studied by Curtiss and Yamada (1981) and Curtiss, Kempler, and Yamada (1981) revealed normal or advanced language simultaneous with serious nonlinguistic cognitive deficits. Similarly, the studies by Bellugi, Marks, Bihrle, and Sabo (1988) of language development in William's syndrome children reveal a unique behavioral profile in which there appears to be a selective preservation of specific cognitive abilities and loss of others.

There is also ongoing research looking for the specific genetic basis of human language ability. Gopnik (1992) and Gopnik and Crago (1991) reported on a study of a family in which, of 30 members across three generations, 16 suffered from the inability to acquire morphosyntactic rules. Otherwise, the 16 were normal, as were the unaffected family members. They suggested that this reflects a genetic-based syntactic ability, which some linguists would refer to as Universal Grammar: "There is now empirical evidence that shows that a single dominant gene is associated with the ability to construct symbolic rules in the grammar." They added, "Converging evidence from our study and several other recent studies has established that this genetic disorder affects the normal development of language, but does not affect other cognitive functions."

The actual dominant gene(s) are yet to be discovered biologically, however, and there are many questions that have been raised about these conclusions. Nonetheless, there are numerous other studies suggesting that Specific Language Impairments (SLI) are hereditary, showing up as they do in members of the same family, although this in itself does not mean that the deficit is hereditary.

But, whether one looks at the selective impairment or preservation of language abilities in child development or in the mature brain, one can find little to support the view of language as derivative of some general intellectual capacity.

Aphasia Evidence for Modularity

Evidence for the separation of linguistic and other cognitive abilities is also provided by research on aphasia. Focal injuries to different parts of the brain not only lead to selective cognitive disorders but may also lead to damage of distinct components of language or of specific linguistic processing mechanisms. Aphasia, the disruption of the linguistic system, can often occur with no loss of other cognitive functions. Furthermore, following damage to different parts of the left hemisphere, syntax may be impaired with phonology retained, for example, or vice versa—as is the case of jargon aphasics who produce many neologisms but properly inflect them as shown in the following examples from Buckingham (1981):

1.   The leg vilt**ed** from here down.

2.   This is the krebekack**s** where the frej**es** get out after the chew.

The aphasic disorder referred to as agrammatism—a term first used by Pick in 1913—has been of particular interest in the attempts to understand the nature of abnormal as well as normal language. Pick observed that the sentences produced by some Broca's aphasics were ungrammatical although the patients seemed to be aware of their "intended preverbal meaning." Pick also showed linguistic sophistication when he distinguished between lexical and grammatical formatives. This distinction was revealed in certain patients after brain damage, as shown in the different reading responses to lexical and grammatical words of an acquired dyslexic patient of Newcombe and Marshall (1981, 1984). GR, as he is referred to in the literature, makes numerous errors in reading lexical content words, substituting words that are in the same semantic class. Thus, for example, he read *bean* as "soup," *hour* as "time," and *hymn* as "bible." He was, however, totally unable to read any of the grammatical formatives that are homonymous with the lexical content words, for example, *been* ([bin] in British English), *our*, or *him*. When shown a printed word of a grammatical morpheme, he would either answer "no" or would respond "I hate those little words," as he did when shown the word *would*, although previously he had read *wood* correctly, a "littler" word than *would*. It appears that GR had a tacit knowledge of the distinction between the two classes of words as well as an inability to access that part of the lexicon that includes the grammatical morphemes.

Agrammatism was originally considered to be a disorder of speech production in which some Broca's aphasic patients delete such grammatical formatives as auxiliaries, pronouns, determiners and some prepositions, and inflectional affixes. Until the 1970s, it was believed that the comprehension of these patients was intact, thus suggesting that the disorder was due to a problem in processing grammatical formatives during speech production. However, controlled experimental studies showed that where comprehension depends on the syntactic structure of sentences, syntactic comprehension deficits (also referred to as asyntactic comprehension) also arise in these patients (Caramazza & Zurif, 1976; Heilman & Scholes, 1976; Kean, 1977, 1985).

The observation that asyntactic comprehension occurs with agrammatical production led to the view that agrammatism is a central deficit of the syntactic component of the grammar (Linebarger 1990; Linebarger, Schwartz, & Saffran, 1983; Luketela, Crain, & Schankweiler, 1988). More recently, less global theories of the deficit were proposed, which focus on some particular aspect of syntactic processing as the locus of failure (Cornell, Fromkin, & Mauner, 1993; Grodzinsky, 1984, 1986, 1990; Hickok, 1992; Mauner, Fromkin, & Cornell, 1993).

The fact that specific lesion sites produce different aphasic symptoms while leaving other cognitive functions intact argue for language as a distinct module as well as for the modularity of the linguistic grammar itself. The neural architecture that is correlated with the processing of different types of aphasia and cognitive disorders is revealed by Magnetic Resonant Imaging techniques (MRI), functional MRI (fMRI), and Positron Emission Tomography (PET).

ERP Evidence

The study of event-related potentials or ERP is another method being used for investigating brain mechanisms involved in linguistic and nonlinguistic processing. Such experiments present various stimuli to participants and study the evoked electrical activity, recorded from electrodes placed on the scalp in a conventional set of locations. One study by Neville, Nicol, Barss, Forstern, and Garrett (1991) was concerned with whether language comprehension processes are decomposable into separate subsystems or modules, including distinct systems for semantic and syntactic processing. They found that ERPs

> to syntactically well-formed but semantically anomalous sentences revealed a pattern of brain activity that is distinct in timing and distribution from the patterns elicited by syntactically deviant sentences, and further, that different types of syntactic deviance produced distinct ERP patterns.

As in prior research, the semantically anomalous sentences, such as Example (3), produced a negative potential, N400, that was bilaterally distributed and was largest over posterior regions. The phrase structure violations, as in (4) and (5), enhanced the N125 response over anterior regions of the left hemisphere and elicited a negative response (300–500 msec) over temporal and parietal regions of the left hemisphere. The specific types of syntactic violations, such as specificity constraints and subjacency constraints, elicited distinct timing and distribution responses.

3. #The man admired Don's headache of the landscape.

4. *The man admired Don's of sketch the landscape.

5.   *What$_i$ was [^{NP} a sketch of t$_i$] admired by the man?

The investigators concluded that "the distinct timing and distribution of these effects provide biological support for theories that distinguish between these types of grammatical rules and constraints and more generally for the proposal that semantic and grammatical processes are distinct subsystems within the language faculty."

Evidence From Sign Language

Perhaps the most telling findings on the brain–language–cognition relation, which supports the conception of the brain and mind as consisting of neurological and cognitive interactions but autonomous modules, is revealed by the exciting research on sign language conducted by Bellugi and Klima and their colleagues (Bellugi et al., 1988; Poizner, Klima, & Bellugi, 1987). The linguistic study of sign language over the past 30 or more years has already revealed, as mentioned earlier, that these languages of the deaf have all the crucial properties common to all spoken languages, including highly abstract underlying grammatical and formal principles.

Because the same abstract linguistic principles underlie all human languages—spoken or signed—regardless of the motor and perceptual mechanisms that are used in their expression, it is not surprising that deaf patients show aphasia for sign language similar to the language breakdown in hearing aphasics following damage to the left hemisphere. Furthermore, although these patients show marked sign language deficits, they can correctly process nonlanguage visual–spatial relations. The left cerebral hemisphere is thus not dominant for speech, as had been suggested, but for language, the cognitive system underlying both speech and sign. Hearing and speech are not necessary for the development of left-hemispheric specialization for language.

This has been a crucial point in determining that the left-hemisphere specialization in language acquisition is not due to its capacity for fine auditory analysis but for language analysis per se.

Given the universal principles common to all human languages signed and spoken, referred to as Universal Grammar, it is not surprising that deaf children of deaf signing parents acquire language in the same way as hearing children and parallel the stages of spoken language acquisition in their signing development. In the early months, they "babble" manually, then begin to produce single signs similar to the single words in the earliest stage of spoken language acquisition and then begin to combine signs. There is also a telegraphic stage in which the "grammatical" signs—function words—are omitted. Grammatical or function signs appear at around the same age for deaf children as function words in spoken languages.

In 1979, Bellugi and Klima pointed out that deaf children's acquisition of negation in ASL shows very much the same pattern as in spoken language. NO and NEG (a headshake) are frequently used signs in adult ASL, with different restrictions on their use. The children acquiring ASL used them interchangeably in initial position of a signed sentence, like hearing children starting negative sentences with *no* but unlike the ways in which negative signs are used in adult ASL. Thus, the acquisition of ASL cannot be simple imitation any more than spoken language is acquired simply by imitation.

Studies of hearing and deaf infants babbling also contribute to our understanding of the biologically determined language faculty, which is independent of the modality in which it is expressed. Recent studies of the vocal babbling of hearing children and manual babbling of deaf children suggest that babbling is a specifically linguistic ability related to the kind of language input the child receives. These studies by Petitto and Marentette are summarized in an article in *Science* (1991; see also Petitto, chap. 24, this volume). The similarities between manual and vocal babbling suggest that babbling is a specifically linguistic ability related to the kinds of language input the child receives. Contrary to prevailing accounts of the neurological basis of babbling in language ontogeny, the speech modality is not critical in babbling. Rather, "babbling is tied to the abstract linguistic structure of language and to an expressive capacity capable of processing different types of signals (signed or spoken)."

Other sign language studies concerned with acquisition further contribute to our understanding of the biological basis of language and relate to the question of language specificity. The critical age hypothesis in relation to language first proposed in Lenneberg's (1967) seminal work refers to the period during which language acquisition occurs apparently without effort, at a relatively fast pace, and without external intervention or teaching, following which the ability to acquire language weakens considerably. Lenneberg had little direct evidence to support his hypothesis because, except for pathology, hearing children are exposed to a language immediately after birth and although some seem to produce their first words and sentences a little earlier than others, by the time they are 8 or 10, most of the grammar has been acquired by all the children.

There have been a few "experiments in nature" testing the critical age hypothesis, including the case of Genie, studied and extensively documented by Curtiss (1977). When Genie, isolated from social contact and from language until puberty, began to receive linguistic input, she was able to learn certain parts of the grammar and not others—words and correct word order, lexical semantics, but little of the complex morphology or syntax. This was also true of Chelsea, a deaf woman who heard no language until she was 32, at which time she was provided with auditory amplification and thus was able to hear spoken English. These cases suggest that there is a critical period for the acquisition of syntax (and its related inflectional morphology), which further suggests that these are the components of language that constitute Universal Grammar, the innate initial state of the language faculty.

It is extremely difficult, if not impossible, to conduct the kind of controlled studies testing the critical age hypotheses with normal hearing individuals. Deaf individuals, however, present a unique opportunity for those interested in the neural basis of language and in testing Lenneberg's (1967) hypothesis, because one can study a large number of deaf individuals, matched for general cognitive abilities, normal in all other respects except that they receive linguistic input at different times in their development.

Newport (1981, 1990) and Newport and Meier (1985), conducted a number of important insightful and highly controlled studies with a sizeable number of deaf participants who acquired sign language at different chronological ages. The results of these studies support—I believe unequivocally—the hypothesis that there is a critical age for the acquisition of signed languages. We do not have equally compelling evidence for a critical age for spoken languages, but based on the sign language studies and what evidence we do have for spoken languages, we can conclude that Lenneberg (1967) was essentially correct if we recognize that all components of language are not created equally or equally innate. The findings of Curtiss (1977) in her study of Genie and Chelsea are paralleled by those from the study of sign language acquisition in this way: Whereas all the deaf participants did acquire much of the grammar of sign, the major difference between those exposed to sign input before puberty and those exposed after concerns the acquisition of syntactic and morphological complexities.

Once more, we have strong evidence for the basic universality of all languages, signed and spoken, and evidence that leads to an understanding of the neural basis for language that could not have been achieved through the sole study of spoken languages.

CONCLUSION

The more we look—whether at studies of neonates, or development, or lesions; whether at studies of cognitive processes using measures such as blood flow or ERP or fMRI; whether at spoken languages or signed—the more we find that knowledge and processing of language is separate from the ability to acquire and process other kinds of knowledge; the more we realize that the asymmetry between general knowledge and linguistic knowledge shows language to be independent of general intellectual ability; and the more we appreciate that language itself, as well as other cognitive systems, is distinct both anatomically and functionally. We also have, through studies such as those conducted by Bellugi and Klima, conclusive evidence that the human animal is biologically endowed with the capacity for language—whether spoken or signed.

AUTHOR'S NOTE

Parts of this chapter are taken from Fromkin, 1991, 1997.

REFERENCES

Bellugi, U., Marks, S., Bihrle, A., & Sabo, H. (1988). Dissociations between language and cognitive functions. In K. Mogford & D. Bishop (Eds.), *Language development in exceptional circumstances* (pp. 177–189). London: Churchill Livingston.

Bellugi, U., Poizner, H., & Klima, E. S. (1983). Brain organization: Clues from sign aphasia. *Human Neurobiology, 2,* 155–170.

Blank, M., Gessner, M., & Esposito, A. (1979). Language without communication: A case study. *Journal of Child Language, 6,* 329–352.

Buckingham, H. W., Jr. (1981). Lexical and semantic aspects of aphasia. In M. T. Sarno (Ed.), *Acquired aphasia* (pp. 183–210). New York: Academic Press.

Caramazza, A., & Zurif, E. (1976). Dissociation of algorithmic and heuristic processes in language comprehension: Evidence from aphasia. *Brain and Language, 3,* 5.

Chomsky, N. (1986). *Barriers.* Cambridge, MA: MIT Press.

Cornell, T. L., Fromkin, V. A., & Mauner, G. (1993). A linguistic approach to language processing in Broca's aphasia: A paradox resolve. *Current Directions in Psychological Science, 2*(3), 47–52.

Cromer, R. F. (1991). *Language and thought in normal and handicapped children.* Oxford, UK: Basil Blackwell.

Curtiss, S. (1977). *Genie: A psycholinguistic study of a modern-day "wild-child."* New York: Academic Press.

Curtiss, S. (1982). Developmental dissociations of language and cognition. In L. K. Obler & L. Menn (Eds.), *Exceptional language and linguistics* (pp. 285–312). New York: Academic Press.

Curtiss, S., Kempler, D., & Yamada, J. (1981). The relationship between language and cognition in development: Theoretical framework and research design. *UCLA Working Papers in Cognitive Linguistics, 3,* 161–175.

Curtiss, S., & Yamada, J. E. (1981). Selectively intact grammatical development in a retarded child. *UCLA Working Papers in Cognitive Linguistics, 3,* 61–91.

Fodor, J. A. (1983). *The modularity of mind.* Cambridge MA: MIT Press.

Fromkin, V. A. (1991). Redefining the goals and methodology of linguistics. In A. Kasher (Ed.), *On the Chomskyan turn: Early generative linguistics, philosophy and mathematics* (pp. 78–103). Oxford, UK: Basil Blackwell.

Fromkin, V. A. (1997). Some thoughts about the brain/mind/language interface. *Lingua, 100,* 3–27.

Fromkin, V. A., & Klima, E. S. (1980). General and special properties of language. In U. Bellugi & M. Studdert-Kennedy (Eds.), *Signed and spoken language: Biological constraints on linguistic form* (pp. 13–28). Deerfield Beach, FL: Verlag Chemie.

Gopnik M. (1992, Feb.). *Linguistic properties of genetic language impairment.* Paper presented at The American Association for the Advancement of Science.

Gopnik, M., & Crago, M. B. (1991). Familial aggregation of a developmental language disorder. *Cognition, 39,* 1–50.

Grodzinsky, Y. (1984). The syntactic characterization of agrammatism. *Cognition, 16,* 99–120.

Grodzinsky, Y. (1986). Language deficits and the theory of syntax. *Brain and Language, 27,* 135–159.

Grodzinsky, Y. (1990). *Theoretical perspectives on language deficits.* Cambridge, MA: MIT Press.

Heilman, K. M., & Scholes, R. J. (1976). The nature of comprehension errors in Broca's, conduction, and Wernicke's aphasics. *Cortex, 12,* 258–265.

Hickok, G. (1992). *Agrammatic comprehension and the trace-deletion hypothesis* (Occasional Paper No. 45, MIT Center for Cognitive Science). Cambridge, MA: MIT Press.

Kean, M. L. (1977). The linguistic interpretation of aphasic syndromes: Agrammatism in Broca's aphasia, an example. *Cognition, 5,* 9–46.

Kean, M. L. (Ed.). (1985). *Agrammatism.* New York: Academic Press.

Klima, E. S., & Bellugi, U. (1979). *The signs of language.* Cambridge, MA: Harvard University Press.

Klima, E. S., Bellugi, U., & Poizner, H. (1985). Sign language and brain organization. In V. Volterra & W. C. Stokoe (Eds.), *Proceedings of the Third International Symposium on Sign Language Research* (pp. 71–78). Springfield, MD: Linstok Press.

Lenneberg, E. H. (1967). *Biological foundations of language.* New York: Wiley Liss.

Linebarger, M. C. (1990). Neuropsychology of sentence parsing. In A. Caramazza (Ed.), *Cognitive neuropsychology and neurolinguistics* (pp. 55–122). Mahwah, NJ: Lawrence Erlbaum Associates.

Linebarger, M., Schwartz, M. F., & Saffran, E. M. (1983). Sensitivity to grammatical structure in so-called agrammatic aphasics. *Cognition, 13,* 361–392.

Lukatela, K., Crain, S., & Shankweiler, D. (1988). Sensitivity to inflectional morphology in agram-matism: Investigation of a highly inflected language. *Brain and Language, 33,* 1–15.

Mauner, G., Fromkin, V. A., & Cornell, T. L. (1993). Comprehension and acceptability judgments in agrammatism: Disruptions in the syntax of referential dependency and the two-chain hypothesis. *Brain and Language, 45,* 340–370.

Neville, H., Nicol, J. L., Barss, A., Forster, K. I., & Garrett, M. F. (1991). Syntactically based sentence processing classes: Evidence from event-related brain potentials. *Journal of Cognitive Neuroscience, 3*(2), 151–165.

Newcombe, F., & Marshall, J. C. (1981). Lexical access: A perspective from pathology. *Cognition, 10,* 209–214.

Newcombe, F., & Marshall, J. C. (1984). Varieties of acquired dyslexia: A linguistic approach. *Seminars in Neurology, 4*(2), 181–195.

Newport, E. L. (1981). Constraints on structure: Evidence from American Sign Language and language learning. In W. A. Collins (Ed.), *Aspects of the development of competence. Minnesota Symposium on Child Psychology* (Vol. 14). Mahwah, NJ: Lawrence Erlbaum Associates.

Newport, E. L. (1990). Maturational constraints on language learning. *Cognitive Science, 14,* 11–28.

Newport, E. L., & Meier, R. (1985). The acquisition of American Sign Language. In D. Slobin (Ed.), *The cross-linguistic study of language acquisition* (Vol. 1, pp. 881–938). Mahwah, NJ: Lawrence Erlbaum Associates.

Petitto, L. A., & Marantette, P. F. (1991). Babbling in the manual mode: Evidence for the ontogeny of language. *Science, 251,* 1493–1496.

Pick, A. (1913). *Die agrammatischen Sprachstörungen* [Agrammatical speech disturbance]. Berlin: Springer-Verlag.

Poizner, H., Klima, E. S., & Bellugi, U. (1987). *What the hands reveal about the brain.* Cambridge, MA: MIT Press.

Smith, N., & Tsimpli, I. M. (1995). *The mind of a savant: Language learning and modularity.* Oxford, UK: Basil Blackwell.

Stokoe, W. C., Jr. (1960). Sign language structure. In G. L. Trager (Series Ed.), *Studies in linguistics, Occasional Paper 8.* Buffalo, NY: University of Buffalo Press.

Yamada, J. E. (1990). *Laura: A case for modularity of language.* Cambridge, MA: MIT Press.

Author Index

Y

Z

Subject Index